A LIBRARY OF LITERARY CRITICISM

LEONARD S. KLEIN
General Editor

A Library
of Literary Criticism

VOLUME IV

SUPPLEMENT
TO THE FOURTH EDITION

 Frederick Ungar Publishing Co., New York

MODERN AMERICAN LITERATURE

Compiled and edited by

DOROTHY NYREN

MAURICE KRAMER

ELAINE FIALKA KRAMER

Library of Congress Cataloging in Publication Data   (Revised)

Curley, Dorothy Nyren, comp.
  Modern American literature.

  (A Library of literary criticism)
  Includes bibliographies.
  Vol. 4: Supplement.
  1. American literature—20th century—History and
criticism. 2. Criticism—U. S. I. Kramer, Maurice,
joint comp. II. Kramer, Elaine Fialka, joint comp.
III. Title. IV. Series.
PS221.C8   1969   810.9'005   76-76599

FOREWORD TO THE SUPPLEMENT

The three-volume fourth edition of *Modern American Literature* presented the critical response to some three hundred authors through 1967. This supplement aims to bring the criticism up to date on many of those authors (approximately half, or 145, are updated) and to present criticism on 49 additional writers. This volume follows the same basic principles of selection and presentation set forth in the first edition of *Modern American Literature* in 1960 and developed through subsequent editions. The goal has been to balance evaluative comments with those that explain and illuminate.

The new authors (chosen and compiled by Dorothy Nyren) range from a few older writers who have been rediscovered or whose reputations have continued to grow in recent years (these include Caroline Gordon, James Weldon Johnson, and Jean Toomer) to some very interesting young writers who had just begun to publish when the fourth edition was being compiled (among them Rosalyn Drexler and Ishmael Reed). Three new authors of major importance have emerged: the inexhaustibly productive Joyce Carol Oates, the gentleman-scholar narrator John Gardner, and the tragic poet Sylvia Plath. Another significant writer, Kurt Vonnegut, Jr., has been writing over a long period of time, turning out his best work during the years of the earlier editions of *Modern American Literature*. These ironic masterpieces were not recognized then; indeed, they were dismissed as science fiction and therefore not worthy of critical attention.

The updating (by Maurice and Elaine Kramer) of authors from the three-volume fourth edition was done selectively, with the idea of including those writers who continue to attract considerable critical and popular interest. Some important writers—Thomas Wolfe and John Steinbeck, for example—are not in this supplement because it was felt that there has been no significant reassessment since the fourth edition appeared. Writers like Eliot, Hemingway, and Faulkner, however, are constantly being reexamined from different perspectives. Among writers who are still adding to their oeuvre, it seemed undesirable to present criticism on each book that has appeared since 1967. Rather, an effort has been made to cull comments that provide revaluations or substantial reinforcement of earlier opinions. Of course, there are many statements—both reviews and retrospective assessments—about individual books of unquestionable importance, including some very recently published works.

In choosing sources, there has been continuing stress on book reviews, but to these has been added more material from a broad spectrum of scholarly journals and from books. There is also more criticism from England, reflecting the increasing prestige of and interest in American literature among English critics and readers.

The bibliographies at the end of this book have been updated for all authors in the three-volume fourth edition (even if their criticism has not been) and are complete for the 49 added writers.

The editors are grateful to the many copyright holders who have granted permission to reproduce the selections in this book. Only in a very few instances was it necessary to omit an excerpt because a copyright holder either withheld permission or made unreasonable demands. The Kramers wish to thank the staffs of the Humanities Division of the Brooklyn College Library and of the Literature section of the main branch of the Brooklyn Public Library for their unfailing helpfulness and good will. Finally, Miss Nyren, the publisher, and the series editor all thank Dr. Rita Stein for research and suggestions on the new authors.

D.N.

M.K.

E.F.K.

AUTHORS INCLUDED

Authors added in this volume are preceded by a bullet.

Adams, Henry
Agee, James
Aiken, Conrad
Albee, Edward
Algren, Nelson
● Ammons, A. R.
Anderson, Sherwood
● Ashbery, John
Auchincloss, Louis
Auden, W. H.
Baldwin, James
Barnes, Djuna
Barth, John
● Barthelme, Donald
Bellow, Saul
● Berger, Thomas
Berryman, John
Bierce, Ambrose
Bishop, Elizabeth
Blackmur, Richard
● Bly, Robert
Bogan, Louise
Bowles, Paul
● Brautigan, Richard
Brooks, Gwendolyn
Buechner, Frederick
● Bukowski, Charles
● Bullins, Ed
Burke, Kenneth
Burroughs, William
Caldwell, Erskine
● Calisher, Hortense
Capote, Truman
Cather, Willa
Chandler, Raymond
Cheever, John
Chopin, Kate

Condon, Richard
● Connell, Evan S., Jr.
● Coover, Robert
Cowley, Malcolm
Crane, Hart
Creeley, Robert
Cullen, Countee
Cummings, E. E.
Dahlberg, Edward
De Vries, Peter
Dickey, James
Dickinson, Emily
● Didion, Joan
● Doctorow, E. L.
Doolittle, Hilda
Dos Passos, John
Dreiser, Theodore
● Drexler, Rosalyn
Dugan, Alan
Duncan, Robert
● Eastlake, William
Eberhart, Richard
Eliot, T. S.
Elliott, George P.
Ellison, Ralph
Faulkner, William
Fiedler, Leslie
Fitzgerald, F. Scott
Frederic, Harold
Friedman, Bruce Jay
Frost, Robert
Fuchs, Daniel
● Fuller, R. Buckminster
● Gaddis, William
● Gardner, John
Garrigue, Jean
● Gass, William H.

Ginsberg, Allen
- Goodman, Paul
- Gordon, Caroline
Hammett, Dashiell
- Hansberry, Lorraine
Hawkes, John
Heller, Joseph
Hellman, Lillian
Hemingway, Ernest
Himes, Chester
- Horovitz, Israel
- Howard, Richard
Howells, William Dean
Hughes, Langston
James, Henry
James, William
Jarrell, Randall
Jeffers, Robinson
- Johnson, James Weldon
Jones, James
Jones, LeRoi
Kerouac, Jack
- Kesey, Ken
- Kinnell, Galway
- Kosinski, Jerzy
Kunitz, Stanley
Lardner, Ring
Lattimore, Richmond
Levertov, Denise
Lewis, Sinclair
London, Jack
Lowell, Robert
McCarthy, Mary
McCullers, Carson
Macdonald, Ross
- McGuane, Thomas
MacLeish, Archibald
Mailer, Norman
Malamud, Bernard
Mencken, H. L.
- Meredith, William
Merrill, James
Merwin, W. S.
Miller, Arthur
Miller, Henry
Moore, Marianne
Morris, Wright

Mumford, Lewis
Nabokov, Vladimir
Nemerov, Howard
Nin, Anais
- Oates, Joyce Carol
O'Connor, Flannery
- O'Hara, Frank
O'Hara, John
- Olson, Charles
O'Neill, Eugene
- Ozick, Cynthia
Percy, Walker
- Plath, Sylvia
Porter, Katherine Anne
Pound, Ezra
- Purdy, James
Pynchon, Thomas
- Rabe, David
Rahv, Philip
Ransom, John Crowe
- Reed, Ishmael
Rexroth, Kenneth
Rich, Adrienne
Robinson, Edward Arlington
Roethke, Theodore
Roth, Philip
Rukeyser, Muriel
Salinger, J. D.
Sandburg, Carl
Santayana, George
Saroyan, William
Sarton, May
Schwartz, Delmore
Scott, Winfield Townley
- Selby, Hubert
Sexton, Anne
Shapiro, Karl
- Sheed, Wilfrid
- Shepard, Sam
Simpson, Louis
- Singer, Isaac Bashevis
Snodgrass, W. D.
- Snyder, Gary
- Stafford, William
Stein, Gertrude
Stevens, Wallace
Stickney, Trumbull

Styron, William
Tate, Allen
Taylor, Peter
● Toomer, Jean
Twain, Mark
Updike, John
Van Doren, Mark
Viereck, Peter
● Vonnegut, Kurt, Jr.
● Wakoski, Diane
Warren, Robert Penn
Welty, Eudora
West, Nathanael

Wharton, Edith
Wheelwright, John Brooks
Wilbur, Richard
Wilder, Thornton
Williams, Tennessee
Williams, William Carlos
Wilson, Edmund
Winters, Yvor
Wright, James
Wright, Richard
Wylie, Elinor
● Yurick, Sol
● Zukofsky, Louis

PERIODICALS USED

Where no abbreviation is indicated, the periodical references are listed in full.

Am	America (New York)
ABC	The American Book Collector (Arlington Heights, Ill.)
ALib	American Libraries (Chicago)
AL	American Literature (Durham, N.C.)
APR	American Poetry Review (Philadelphia)
AS	The American Scholar (Washington, D.C.)
	Américas (Washington, D.C.)
	Art and Literature (Paris)
	Art in America (New York)
	Art News (New York)
At	The Atlantic Monthly (Boston)
BW	Book Week (New York)
	Book World (Chicago)
Bkm	The Bookman (New York)
BuR	Bucknell Review (Lewisburg, Pa.)
	The Carleton Miscellany (Northfield, Minn.)
CW	Catholic World (New York)
CentR	The Centennial Review (East Lansing, Mich.)
CR	Chicago Review (Chicago)
CST	Chicago Sunday Tribune Book Section (Chicago)
CC	The Christian Century (Chicago)
CSM	The Christian Science Monitor (Boston)
CLAJ	CLA Journal (Baltimore)
Cmty	Commentary (New York)
Com	Commonweal (New York)
CP	Concerning Poetry (Bellingham, Wash.)
CL	Contemporary Literature (Madison, Wisc.)
ContR	Contemporary Review (London)
Crisis	The Crisis (New York)
CQ	The Critical Quarterly (Manchester)
	Criticism (Detroit)
	Critique (Atlanta)
	Cue (New York)
DalR	The Dalhousie Review (Halifax, N.S.)
	Denver Quarterly (Denver)
	Diacritics (Ithaca, N.Y.)

ETJ	Educational Theatre Journal (Washington, D.C.)
	Encounter (London)
EJ	English Journal (Urbana, Ill.)
	English Studies (Lisse, Netherlands)
	Epoch (Ithaca, N.Y.)
	Esquire (New York)
FPt	The Far Point (later Northern Light; Winnipeg, Man.)
Harper	Harper's Magazine (New York)
HC	The Hollins Critic (Hollins College, Va.)
HdR	The Hudson Review (New York)
IowaR	The Iowa Review (Iowa City, Ia.)
JML	Journal of Modern Literature (Philadelphia)
KanQ	Kansas Quarterly (Manhattan, Kan.)
LJ	Library Journal (New York)
	Life (New York)
List	The Listener (London)
LW	Living Wilderness (Washington, D.C.)
Lon	London Magazine (London)
MarkhamR	The Markham Review (Staten Island, N.Y.)
MR	The Massachusetts Review (Amherst, Mass.)
MedR	The Mediterranean Review (Orient, N.Y.)
MQR	The Michigan Quarterly Review (Ann Arbor, Mich.)
	Midstream (New York)
MissQ	The Mississippi Quarterly (Mississippi State, Miss.)
MD	Modern Drama (Toronto)
MPS	Modern Poetry Studies (Buffalo, N.Y.)
	Mosaic (Winnipeg, Man.)
Nation	The Nation (New York)
	National Review (New York)
NewAR	New American Review (New York)
NL	The New Leader (New York)
NMQ	New Mexico Quarterly (Albuquerque, N.M.)
NR	The New Republic (Washington, D.C.)
NS	New Statesman (London)
NYHT	New York Herald Tribune Book Section (New York)
NYM	New York Magazine (New York)
NYR	The New York Review of Books (New York)
NYT	The New York Times Book Review (New York)
NYTd	The New York Times, daily (New York)
NYTmag	The New York Times, Sunday Magazine (New York)
NYTts	The New York Times, Sunday theater section (New York)
NY	The New Yorker (New York)
Nwk	Newsweek (New York)
	Opportunity (New York)
	Parnassus (New York)
PR	Partisan Review (New Brunswick, N.J.)
	Performance (New York)

	Phylon (Atlanta)
	Players (DeKalb, Ill.)
PMLA	PMLA: Publications of the Modern Language Association of America (New York)
	Poetry (Chicago)
PoetryR	Poetry Review (London)
PrS	Prairie Schooner (Lincoln, Neb.)
PULC	The Princeton University Library Chronicle (Princeton, N.J.)
Ren	Renascence (Milwaukee)
Reporter	The Reporter (New York)
	Salmagundi (Saratoga Springs, N.Y.)
SR	Saturday Review (New York)
SwR	The Sewanee Review (Sewanee, Tenn.)
	Shenandoah (Lexington, Va.)
SAQ	South Atlantic Quarterly (Durham, N.C.)
SHR	Southern Humanities Review (Auburn, Ala.)
SoR	The Southern Review (Baton Rouge, La.)
SWR	Southwest Review (Dallas, Tex.)
Spec	The Spectator (London)
	Spirit (South Orange, N.J.)
SpR	Springfield Republican (Springfield, Mass.)
SLitI	Studies in the Literary Imagination (Atlanta)
SN	Studies in the Novel (Denton, Tex.)
	The Survey (New York)
	Synergy (San Francisco)
TSLL	Texas Studies in Literature and Language (Austin, Tex.)
	Time (New York)
TLS	TLS: The Times Literary Supplement (London)
TCL	Twentieth Century Literature (Los Angeles, later Hempstead, N.Y.)
VV	The Village Voice (New York)
VQR	The Virginia Quarterly Review (Charlottesville, Va.)
WAL	Western American Literature (Logan, Utah)
WHR	The Western Humanities Review (Salt Lake City, Utah)
WR	Western Review (Silver City, N.M.)
WSCL	Wisconsin Studies in Contemporary Literature (later Contemporary Literature; Madison, Wisc.)
YR	The Yale Review (New Haven, Conn.)
	Yale/Theatre (New Haven, Conn.)

ADAMS, HENRY (1838–1918)

[Adams's] experience as a novelist contributed to the development of his later, more imposing literary presence. The example of his work is one of unresolved tension between a mind drawn toward a new "way of seeing" the possibilities in certain materials and a method restrained by the inertial force of the uses conventionally made of those materials. More than ordinarily familiar with advanced intellectual currents of the day, more than ordinarily gifted as a writer of language, he was also more than ordinarily dependent on available instead of invented fictive techniques.

For this very reason, however, Adams conveys through his fiction (the product of an unsustained "moment" in his literary life as a whole) an arrested image, static yet charged, of the late-nineteenth-century American novelist: drawn by personal conviction and cultural persuasion toward new assumptions about the purposes and responsibilities of his art, but constrained as well by the contrary tug of established attitudes and practices. Adams the novelist failed to solve this dilemma, although in *The Education of Henry Adams* he succeeded as well as any writer of the age in expressing a comprehension of the larger cultural dilemma to which it belonged.

Gordon O. Taylor in *The Interpretation of Narrative*, edited by Morton W. Bloomfield (Harvard). 1970. p. 173

I believe that Adams always misconceived his principal talent. He wanted the recognition of scientists for his theories in a field where he was not equipped to make any serious contribution. The picture of Adams, the descendant of presidents, a kind of early American "Everyman," a survival from the Civil War in the day of the automobile, traveling from one end of the globe to the other in quest of the absolute, pausing before Buddhas and dynamos, has so caught the imagination of the academic community that his biography, which he wrote as well as lived, has become, so to speak, one of his works, and his most fantastic speculations the subjects of serious theses. Yet to me his primary contributions to our literature were aesthetic. He is far closer to Whitman and Melville than to Bancroft or Prescott, and he is not at all close to Einstein.

Louis Auchincloss. *Henry Adams* (Minnesota). 1971. p. 39

AGEE, JAMES (1909–1955)

In the two novels [*A Morning Watch* and *A Death in the Family*] we
see the essential quality of Agee's art. The novels are lyric—like the
camera he understood so well, they focus on static scenes to portray
universal reactions to human sorrow: guilt, courage, awakening, love.
Such scenes work well. But the saddest thing about them, and about
Agee's fiction in general, is his inability to believe in the present reality
of his celebrations. They are of a certain time and place, protected,
nurtured, and embalmed by memory. Agee's ideal world is a lost world,
out of touch with present living. Even stylistically, none of Agee's
abundant personal charm and vitality enters these books. In large measure, Agee's penchant for innocence is a death wish.

Richard H. Rupp. *Celebration in Postwar
American Fiction* (Miami). 1970. p. 110

An intense desire to know himself marked Agee's work in the three
great pieces of sustained prose that lie at the heart of his achievement.
In *Let Us Now Praise Famous Men* Agee describes the process by which
he came to a new and deep understanding of himself and his world. In
The Morning Watch he looked back at himself as at the age of twelve he
had come to an earlier appreciation of his own identity and importance.
In *A Death in the Family* he looks even farther back and exposes the
roots from which that twelve-year-old character had grown. And of the
three works perhaps the frankest and most revealing is *A Death in the
Family*. The young boy who is the central character in this novel is
named Rufus, Agee's middle name which was the name he used almost
exclusively in signing the letters to Father Flye.

Erling Larsen. *James Agee* (Minnesota).
1971. pp. 36–7

AIKEN, CONRAD (1889–1973)

A poet unconcerned with changing fashions, at the beginning playing
vast iambic symphonies, and at the end, suites of lyrics, rarely varying
the tone, [Aiken] isn't easy to take in a great dose like this one [*Col-*

lected Poems]. . . . The mind sometimes wanders away, or it is mesmerized by the music, of star, water, leaf, web, tree, sleep, hill, needing more meat than beautiful sound or lovely repetition for its teeth to chew on.

He moves me most and keeps me riveted when he inserts characters in dramatic situations into his poems. . . . But sometimes the poetry is like a tone poem, or program music; we only get hints from the notes of what it is all about; themes recur, words and images do; but the composer himself has finished suffering elsewhere. The cry is evoked but we don't touch the man. This tendency to the abstract, when poetry was becoming more and more concrete and specific, put Aiken out of the running for popularity. He wrote for the ear (and many of these poems might benefit by reading aloud) when the eye had become the organ of the poem.

Harold Witt. PrS. Fall, 1971. p. 267

It is in *Time in the Rock* that the concept of God as a projection of the many facets of the self is most fully developed. Here Aiken is even more explicit than in *Preludes for Memnon* in demanding that man give up what he regards as the delusions and false comforts of fantasy and live with a continual awareness of the beauty and power of the ephemeral in nature and man; he asks, moreover, that man recognize the symbolic nature of the "angels" and "churches" that have for so long served to distract him from the reality of chaos and death, and he demands a way of life that reflects man's consciousness of his own symbolic constructions. . . . Aiken expresses neither despair nor anger at this revelation of essential human narcissism; in fact, he seems to exult in his increasing awareness of the unconscious feelings expressed in traditional myths and to expose their nature and meaning with a kind of ruthless love for man, his "mad order," and the very symbols he uses to disguise its terrors. . . .

Recognizing that it is fundamentally man's "hunger" for security and grandeur that "shapes itself as gods and rainbows" (*Time in the Rock*, XVIII), Aiken creates a new mythical concept: God is finally the symbolic expression of man's capacity for full consciousness of the anxieties, conflicts, and longings, the terror of his own limitations, and especially of death, which he has for so long repressed or acknowledged only in distorted and misleading forms; God is at the same time man's consciousness of all that he can achieve and enjoy in the face of the monstrous within himself and nature. The god in man functions in the poet when he employs the chaos of the unconscious mind as the material of creation, imposing order and beauty on its apparent formlessness.

Lillian Feder. Ancient Myth in Modern Poetry
(Princeton). 1971. pp. 391–2

Ushant is the artistic reflexion of a life truly and fully and with difficulty lived, of a mind and conscience examined. Even its working out at 365 pages has a mythological appropriateness in this writer whose pious awareness of the cosmos is present even in domestic and daily doings; the Great Circle which he chose as the title of one of his novels being not only the path followed by Atlantic liners but also the circle of the year.

One more thing, a somewhat surprising result of reading *Ushant* again. For several days since, I've found that most any narrative I've picked up, by anyone at all, began to get itself woven into the fabric and symbolism of this one—an unexpected result of the echoing, musical method of composition, whereby Aiken may yet become the hidden author of a large part of our literature. All authors try to write the world, but only a very few succeed in teaching us how to read it.

Howard Nemerov. Reflexions on Poetry &
Poetics (Rutgers). 1972. p. 96

As a prose poem—for in fact "essay" often *means* poem within this lightly encoded account of Aiken's life, just as "play" means novel and "novel" means this reflexive writing—*Ushant* joins the company of modernist works-in-progress, descendants of Wordsworth's *Prelude*, in which precariously narcissist voices move toward epic comprehensiveness as they try to name their own vocations. But unlike *The Cantos* or *Paterson*, *The Anathemata* or *The Maximus Poems*, this poem presents its "exfoliation" or "passacaglia" or "onomasticon" of metaphors through a lucid narrative and discursive style, focuses its evolutionary whirl in a long meditative moment (suspending more than five decades of a full life within a 365-page Joycean day of swirling shipboard introspection), and includes not only the matrix of experience from which it seems in the act of emerging but also its own critical explication. Rendering in public terms Aiken's private drama of "language extending consciousness and then consciousness extending language," *Ushant* aims to share in what D. [the protagonist] calls "the great becoming *fiat* in the poetic of the great poem of life." And surely no other modern American writing gives us with greater sympathy and wit the iridescent texture of that process. . . .

When Aiken allows cosmic rhyme to inform the particulars of his personal experience, the result is a serio-comic richness of tone, an intellectual complexity, and a vividness of detail that had never entered his verse.

Thomas R. Whitaker. Parnassus. Fall–Winter,
1972. pp. 60, 65

ALBEE, EDWARD (1928–   )

In his one-act plays Albee often reaches into the vitals of American attitudes to strike at what he thinks sham and superficiality. In *The Zoo Story* he reveals the complacent businessman to be a vegetable incapable of experiencing any kind of real feeling; in *The American Dream* he presents our idealization of physical beauty and sexual power in all its vacuity. The validity of the satire in these plays rests on the exposure of the veneer that disguises fear, ruthlessness, savagery and self-interest without any attempt to solve the problems. There is always an implicit recognition of the depth of the problem. It cannot be solved by any quick panacea. . . . The conclusion of *Who's Afraid of Virginia Woolf?*, however, advocates a simple standard: no salvation from without, a reliance on "truth" and the resources of the personality. Though Albee sounds the "maybe" of caution with regard to the final situation of George and Martha, he also holds out a "romantic" hope that "it will be better." But the ironist of the first two-and-a-half acts has left his imprint on the play. There seems no reason why the old cycle of games should not begin again.

Thomas E. Porter. Myth and Modern American
Drama (Wayne State). 1969. pp. 246–7

There are such strong surface dissimilarities among the Albee plays that it is easier and in some ways more rewarding to think of *The Zoo Story* in relation to Samuel Beckett and Harold Pinter and *A Delicate Balance* in terms of T. S. Eliot and Enid Bagnold than it is to compare the two plays, even though both start from the same dramatic situation: the invasion . . . of private territory. . . . Yet the comparison is obvious once it is made. Each new Albee play seems to be an experiment in form, in style (even if it is someone else's style), and yet there is unity in his work as a whole. . . .

Separateness is the operative word for Albee characters, for, even though his zoo provides suites for two people (*Who's Afraid of Virginia Woolf?*) or for more (*A Delicate Balance*), they are furnished with separate cages.

Gerald Weales. The Jumping-Off Place
(Macmillan—N.Y.). 1969. pp. 28–30

Suspicion is born of Albee's very brilliance. His plays are too well crafted, his characters too modishly ambiguous, his dialogue too carefully cadenced. This is not to say that he writes perfect plays—whatever that may be—but his surface polish seems to deny subsurface search, much less risk. . . . Albee's plays are not devoid of suffering, and in any case one cannot measure the quality of a play by some putative pain of the playwright. Nevertheless, Albee's craftsmanship recalls the meditation of the disembodied voice of *Box*: "arts which have gone down to craft." And it is particularly ungrateful to turn his own finely modulated words against Albee. But just because his verbal craft *is* so fine, one longs for the clumsy upward groping toward art.

Ruby Cohn. Dialogue in American Drama
(Indiana). 1971. pp. 168–9

All Over provides reason for being rather more sanguine about Albee's future than we have had the right to be for some years. His only two previous attempts at a fusion between his off-Broadway experimentalism and his Broadway naturalism were *Tiny Alice* and *A Delicate Balance*: the new play is a more honest piece of writing than the former and more original than the latter. He is still one of the most powerful influences in the American theatre, although he has not yet equalled the success of *Who's Afraid of Virginia Woolf?* and his three adaptations seriously damaged his reputation. The rival pulls of Beckett and Broadway have brought his talent dangerously near to disintegrating but there is still hope that it will recover.

Ronald Hayman. Edward Albee (Ungar).
1973. p. 138

Edward Albee's play *Seascape* . . . is fundamentally a play about life and resolution. It is that currently rare thing, a comedy rather than a farce, and it is a curiously compelling exploration into the basic tenets of life. It is asking in a light-hearted but heavy-minded fashion whether life is worth living. It decides that there is no alternative.

As Mr. Albee has matured as a playwright, his work has become leaner, sparer and simpler. He depends on strong theatrical strokes to attract the attention of the audience, but the tone of the writing is always thoughtful, even careful, even philosophic. . . . Mr. Albee is suggesting that one of the purposes of an individual human existence is quite simply evolution—that we all play a part in this oddly questionable historic process. So that the purpose of life is life itself—it is a self-fulfilling destiny. We have to come out of the water and get onto the beach, we have to live and we have to die, simply because life is about life.

Clive Barnes. NYTd. Jan. 27, 1975. p. 20

Unlike some other eminent playwrights, Mr. Albee has never been content merely to rework his old successes in new guises and present them as new plays. He has sometimes been accused of rewriting the old successes of others—*All Over*, for instance, sounded uncannily like a newly-unearthed late play by T. S. Eliot—but with *Seascape* he is certainly free of that accusation. The new play is short (less than two hours, with intermission), bizarre, and curious, and its strange premise is fraught with all sorts of implications and possibilities. But it seems unfinished, as if Albee had not quite known how to work out his intriguing premise.

Like *All Over*, his play, and *Box* and *Quotations from Chairman Mao Tse-tung*, the double bill before that, *Seascape* is very spare, very cerebral, very distanced, very uninvolved in the immediate intensities of experience. This is not necessarily a bad way to write plays, but none of these recent works of Mr. Albee have really been very satisfactory; perhaps he needs to get back into closer touch with himself.

Julius Novick. VV. Feb. 3, 1975. p. 84

ALGREN, NELSON (1909–   )

There is no place in this or any other society for a man who is made of W. C. Fields and François Villon; there would seem to have been no choice for Algren but to become a novelist, the inventor of a world that is, if not reasonable, at least possible, not to say beautiful. By the same unhappy logic, it follows that Algren would become a most misunderstood novelist, a hero to hack reporters and jejune sociologists, an inventor who is seldom credited for his inventions, a dreamer of words who is presumed never to close his eyes. So his time is thought to have passed, when in reality the time of a true fictionist is always beginning.

Earl Shorris. Harper. Aug., 1972. p. 107

No writer has been more relentlessly faithful to his scene and cast of characters than Nelson Algren. His scene is the "wild side," the "neon wilderness," the seamier sprawls of Chicago and its spiritual extensions across this broad land—America as Chicago. And his characters are the drifters and grifters, clowns and carnies, pimps and pushers, hustlers and hookers, gamblers and touts, junkies and lushes, marks and victims, conmen and shills, freaks and grotesques—the born losers who constitute a half-world, an anti-society to the society that never appears, not even as a sensed or felt presence, in Algren's work. Over the four decades of his life as a writer, scene and characters have never changed. Atmosphere, obsessions, talk, ways of putting in the time—all are fixed, held in suspension, dreamed and long after hazily recalled, caught not as they once were but as they are remembered, just as they are about to dissolve and become ballads. The mythical time, whatever the calendar reads, is always the '30s, somewhere around the longest year of 1935.

Saul Maloff. *NR.* Jan. 19, 1974. p. 23

Nelson Algren hasn't written any novels for going on 20 years now— which is sad in a way. But it's not like he's been exactly idle in the years between: *The Last Carousel* is the third collection of short pieces he has published since his last novel. Unlike the other two (*Who Lost an American?* and *Notes from a Sea Diary*), this one contains a lot of short fiction. . . .

Algren's journalism is a little hard to tell from his fiction. They look a lot alike. Algren puts himself right in the middle of his non-fiction, too, sets scenes beautifully, and tells it all with dialogue and colorful details interwoven through the narrative. In other words, to give it a recently-stylish label, it's New Journalism—and Nelson Algren was writing it this way when Tom Wolfe was still at Yale working on his PhD in American Studies. This being the case and with journalism being exalted today in some quarters high above fiction as a mode of serious expression. I can't for the life of me figure out why he hasn't retained greater eminence.

Bruce Cook. *Com.* Feb. 8, 1974. p. 469

• AMMONS, A. R. (1926–   )

These poems [in *Expression of Sea Level*] take place on the frontier between what the poet knows and what he doesn't; perhaps that explains their peculiar life and sensitivity. They open to accommodate surprises and accidents. The poet's interest is extended generously toward what he didn't expect, and his poems move by their nature in that direction.

The poems are worked out, not by the application of set forms to their materials, but in an effort to achieve form—in accordance with a constant attentiveness to, a hope for, the possibility of form—the need of anything, once begun, to complete itself, meaningfully.

Wendell Berry. *Nation.* March 23, 1964. p. 304

Now, in the 1960s, poets are beginning to work towards an expansion of subject matter and a synthesis of style between the traditional forms and the open forms fostered by William Carlos Williams and others. The talented young poet A. R. Ammons . . . reveals some interesting aspects of that search. Ammons uses a variety of cadenced open forms to concentrate the kind of knowledge out of which he makes his images. He extends the subject of the poem by using a range of interesting facts, often scientific in character. At first some of his poems seem too prosaic, but reading them carefully one perceives that his facts build to a startling perception. . . . His rhythms do not sing; they separate and define. His tone is essentially philosophic, not dramatic, yet there is a distinctly individual quality to his diction.

James Schevill. *SR.* July 4, 1964. pp. 30–1

There is a constant playing off of the interior world of mind and cells against the exterior world of things where self lies dispersed and in need of the gathering force of the poem. . . . Intellectuality is a prime trait of Ammons' work. . . . Occasionally the poems seem to lack vigor. . . . Yet, a careful look at the whole body of Ammons' work . . . will show that we are dealing with a major talent, one who has the courage and the heuristic power to discover new form, as well as the eye and the ear and the mind to hold us and to give us what [Dylan] Thomas called "the momentary peace of the poem."

John Logan. *Nation.* April 24, 1967. p. 542

The publication of A. R. Ammons' *Selected Poems* should bring him wider recognition than has come on the basis of his three previously published volumes. At forty-two Ammons is one of the most accomplished writers of his generation in America. His work, both in subject matter and execution, has certainty and assurance, and he possesses a creative intelligence perfectly aware of what it can do and what it ought not to try, and happily at ease within its recognized and accepted boundaries. Within those boundaries Ammons' poems speak with settled authority, and are not afraid of repeating themselves, which they often do with conviction and without monotony. In this respect he resembles Wallace Stevens a little, although in most other ways the minds of the two poets come through very differently. But as with Stevens, so with Ammons: when one begins to read him, the best way to understand one poem is to read a great many. This is usual with poets obsessed with one or two central themes in their work to which they return on every creative occasion. Once the clue to Ammons' master pattern is seized (and it is not at all difficult) his poems are unusually easy to read. Nevertheless, a reader wholly unacquainted with Ammons' poetry and coming across one or two of his poems for the first time—especially if they were from his earlier work—might understandably be a little puzzled.

Marius Bewley. HdR. Winter, 1968–9. p. 713

[Ammons] is decidedly his own man and possesses his own vision, his own accents, and even his own solicitude about the sheer sculptured *appearance* of each poem against its whitenesses and silences (once having examined a late and characteristic Ammons poem, you could never confuse his patterns with the patterns of anybody else).... Mr. Ammons just might be our finest contemporary "nature poet," always excepting the incomparable case of James Dickey. Sometimes he employs nature—landscapes and waterscapes, the being and grave motions of creatures—as a source for metaphors by which to trace out subtle generalizations about crucial human experiences, about the perplexities and mysteries of consciousness. On other occasions, he deliberately halts short after displaying for us—no negligible feat—the bright and resonant *thing*ness of things. . . .

Mr. Ammons's best poetry will not heal us perfectly, of course. What could? Yet now and then it can return to us significant parts of our world and of ourselves, parts that we had always gazed at but had never before studied with loving closeness.

Robert Stilwell. MQR. Fall, 1969. p. 278

I am writing of Ammons as though he had rounded his first circle in the eye of his readers, and there is no other way to write about him, even if my essay actually introduces him to some of its readers. The fundamental postulates for reading Ammons have been set down well before me, by Richard Howard and Marius Bewley in particular, but every critic of a still emergent poet has his own obsessions to work through, and makes his own confession of the radiance. Ammons's poetry does for me what Stevens's did earlier, and the High Romantics before that: it helps me to live my life. If Ammons is, as I think, the central poet of my generation, because he alone has made a heterocosm, a second nature in his poetry, I deprecate no other poet by this naming. It is, surprisingly, a rich generation, with ten or a dozen poets who seem at least capable of making a major canon, granting fortune and persistence. Ammons, much more than the others, has made such a canon already. A solitary artist, nurtured by the strength available for him only in extreme isolation, carrying on the Emersonian tradition with a quietness directly contrary to nearly all its other current avatars, he has emerged in his most recent poems as an extraordinary master, comparable to the Stevens of *Ideas of Order* and *The Man with the Blue Guitar*. To track him persistently, from his origins in *Ommateum* through his maturing in *Corson's Inlet* and its companion volumes on to his new phase in *Uplands* and *Briefings* is to be found by not only a complete possibility of imaginative experience, but by a renewed sense of the whole line of Emerson, the vitalizing and much maligned tradition that has accounted for most that matters in American poetry. [1970]

Harold Bloom. *The Ringers in the Tower:*
Studies in Romantic Tradition (Chicago).
1971. p. 261

Corson's Inlet . . . opens with a poem that nicely illustrates the perfected diction Ammons has now achieved, a rhythmical certainty which does not depend on syllable-counting or even accentual measure, but on the speed and retard of words as they move together in the mind, on the shape of the stanzas as they follow the intention of the discourse, and on the *rests* which not so much imitate as create the soft action of speech itself. There is a formality in these gentle lines which is new to American poetry, as we say that there is a draughtsmanship in the "drip-drawings" of Pollack which is new to American painting: each must be approached with a modulated set of expectations if we are to realize what the poet, the painter is about. . . . It is characteristic that so many of these poems . . . take up their burden from the shore, the place where it is most clearly seen that "every living thing is in siege: the demand is life, to keep life." . . . Ammons rehearses a marginal, a transitional experience, he is a littoralist of the imagination because the shore, the beach, or the coastal creek is not a *place* but an *event*, a transaction where land and water create and destroy each other, where life and death are exchanged, where shape and chaos are won or lost. It is here . . . that Ammons finds his rhythms.

Richard Howard. *Alone with America*
(Atheneum). 1971. pp. 11–4

The latest volume of A. R. Ammons, *Uplands*, is a better book than Stafford's [*Allegiances*], partly perhaps because it is slim. As usual, Ammons has treated himself with great critical rigor. These poems, like his earlier works, are primarily about the nature of human perception. Some readers might be tempted to say of him what is sometimes said of his mentor, Wallace Stevens, that his subject is poetry. This is true but only in the largest possible meaning of the word "poetry," for to both writers "poetry" is a way of describing the essence of human perception. In the poetry of Ammons one is constantly finding passages in which nature itself seems to be writing poems, that is, making creations that we see as having the kind of fluent form that Ammons seeks in poetry. . . .

Nature itself falls into forms as the rockslide reveals "streaks and scores of knowledge." Thus the rocks, the streams, the mountains, the pines, move through lines that only the human imagination can express. . . . In its discipline and toughness of mind this volume would provide a good antidote for the loose and flimsy writing being done today by poets who feel that Whitman is now a license for any kind of verbal meandering.

Louis L. Martz. YR. Spring, 1971. pp. 413–4

At first sight A. R. Ammons seems a nature poet, and perhaps, with a difference, this is what he really is. He has the essential characteristic of the nature poet, which is to use observed pieces of nature as the reality of an organic order defending him against the reality of human disorder. . . .

But, like Robert Frost, he is aware too of the evil within the natural order. . . .

He passes the test of nature poets by doing very precise and beautiful things and by occasionally producing a line which has the effect of an explosion on the page. . . . The new note in his observation is his sense of the impermanence of the permanent-seeming things. At their best, his poems give the feeling of the opaque being rayed through to make it transparent, the most solid being hollowed with tunnels through which winds blow, time undermining timelessness.

Stephen Spender. NYR. July 22, 1971. p. 4

Many of Ammons' poems are metaphysically framed sketches from nature. Some are realistic, some a kind of animated cubism, and some abstractly patterned. The "metaphysical" aspect is rather like that in Wallace Stevens: the same issue of reality and illusion. It almost seems obvious that Ammons' opening poem, "Snow Log," is a conscious allusion to Stevens' "The Snow Man," as a starting point from which <i>Uplands</i> goes on to explore possible directions of form and phrasing on a wider range than Stevens engaged himself with. Ammons does have certain advantages over Stevens: his knowledge of geological phenomena (an <i>experienced</i> knowledge) and his ability to use language informally and to create open rhythms. Everything he writes has the authority of his intelligence, of his humor, and of his plastic control of materials. What he lacks, as compared to Stevens, is a certain passionate confrontation of the implicit issues such as makes Stevens' music a richer, deeper force. There <i>is</i> a great deal of feeling in Ammons; but in the interest of ironic self-control he seems afraid of letting the feeling have its way, in the sense that Stevens lets his bitterness flood through "The Emperor of Ice-Cream." Stevens was certainly self-ironic, and hardly an emotional screamer, yet he <i>hated</i> the illusoriness of human ideals and understanding that the fact of death forced him to face. What

Ammons presents is a certain delight or dismay at the imponderable, while at the same time he refuses to strike for effects of power we yearn for in a poet with such a mind and such an ear.

M. L. Rosenthal. *Shenandoah*. Fall, 1972. p. 88

In . . . extravagant and beautiful poems—verse essays really—Ammons maintains a virtuoso current of phrasing that embraces all types of vocabulary, all motions of thought, and leads us back now to Whitman and now to the accumulative (if hopefully cumulative) strain of Pound's *Cantos* or Williams's *Paterson*. Building on a non-narrative base, that is, on a will-to-words almost sexual in persistence, he changes all "flesh-body" to "wordbody" and dazzles us with what he calls "interpenetration"—a massively playful nature-thinking, a poetic incarnation of smallest as well as largest thoughts. . . .

No one in his generation has put "earth's materials" to better use, or done more to raise pastoral to the status of major art.

Geoffrey H. Hartman. *NYT*.
Nov. 19, 1972. pp. 39–40

Ammons' poetry is a poetry which is profoundly American, without being in any way limited by this characteristic. His use of language, his vocabulary and phrasing are utterly and flexibly American. The universal terms of science emerge accurately and naturally from the poems' roots.

The poetry can now be read in its bulk and ripeness. It is science-minded, passionately absorbed with the processes around the poet, the constant, complex, fascinating processes of water, wind, season and genus. But if Ammons' poetry is in the tradition of "nature poets," its essence is far different from the lyric, limpid joy of John Clare, or the *paysage moralisé* of Wordsworth, or the somber farmer-wisdom of Robert Frost, or the myth-ridden marvels of D. H. Lawrence's tortoises, serpents and gentians. Ammons sees the datum of nature as *evidence*; intricate, interlocking fragments of a whole which cannot be totally understood, but which draws him deeper and deeper into its identity. No poet now writing in English has so thoroughly created on the page the huge suggestion of the whole through its most minute components.

Josephine Jacobsen. *Diacritics*.
Winter, 1973. p. 34

The fascination of [Ammons's] poetry is not the transcendental but his struggle with it, which tends to turn each poem into a battleground strewn with scattered testimony to the history of its making in the teeth of its creator's reluctance and distrust of "all this fiddle."

Reading the poems in sequence one soon absorbs the rhythm of

making-unmaking, of speech facing up to the improbability of speech.
. . . The movement is the same, from the visible if only half-real flotsam
of daily living to the uncertainties beyond, but one forgets this from one
poem to the next; each is as different as a wave is from the one that
follows and obliterates it. . . .

Much has been written about the relation of the so-called "New
York School" of poets to the painting of men like Pollack, but in a
curious way Ammons's poetry seems a much closer and more successful
approximation of "Action Painting" or art as process. ("The problem
is/how to keep shape and flow.")

John Ashbery. NYR. Feb. 22, 1973. p. 4

What [Ammons] does is remarkable both in its sparseness and in its
variety. One can't say "richness" because there is no sensual "give" in
this poetry—but it does attempt an imitative re-creation, no less, of the
whole variety of the natural world, if not, regrettably, of what Stevens
calls its "affluence." But if, as Ammons seems to think, affluence is
brought rather by the perceiving and receptive mind, as a quality, rather
than inhering in nature itself (nature, who perceives herself singly, we
may say, as an acorn here, a brook there, rather than corporately con-
gratulating herself on all her brooks), then a poem attempting this
ascetic unattributiveness must refrain from celebrating the multiplicity
of the world in human terms. Why it should be so wrong to let in human
gestalt-making is another question; Ammons permits himself entry when
the poem is about himself, but he won't have any of those interfering
adjectival subjectivities when he's occupied with morning-glories or
caterpillars or redwoods. This discipline of perfect notation is almost
monklike, and, monklike, it takes what comes each day as the day's
revelation of, so to speak, the will of God.

Helen Vendler. YR. Spring, 1973. p. 420

Ammons is a visionary poet in the Neoplatonic tradition introduced and
best represented in our (American) poetry by Emerson. I would guess
that he has read a good deal of Emerson and pondered much on what he
has read. Maybe not. Maybe he has read only a little and gotten all his
Emersonianism from that little, working out for himself, as Emerson
did, the consequences of a few major ideas about the relations of the
Many and the One. Or maybe it has come to him at second and third
hand, through Pound and Williams, Whitman and Frost, all of whom
make their appearance in his poetry. . . .

Ammons has a *mind*, too good a mind to be content with the kinds
of superficial Romanticism that are becoming fashionable in contemporary poetry. I would like to call him a philosophical poet—except that

description might turn away some of those who should read him, and except also that the phrase is in part intrinsically misleading in its suggestion that he deals principally in abstractions. He deals with the perfectly concrete felt motions and emotions of the particular self he is and, like Emerson again, looks for and often sees "Correspondences" between these motions and those of animate and inanimate nature, both nature-as-observed (winds, tides, seeds, birds) and nature-as-known-about (the chemistry of digestion, entropy).

Hyatt H. Waggoner. *Salmagundi.*
Spring–Summer, 1973. pp. 286–7

Having sacrificed the dramatic, having dieted and professored his Romanticism, having drained off all but a wetting of the implicit, Ammons has left almost everything to his intelligence, the crispness of his language, the geniality of his tone, and the greatness of his subject, his *reasonable* approach to Romantic "spirituality." If the result is the "open" American counterpart of the closed Augustan verse essay— equally an *essay*—still in this reader's palm, at first weighing, it feels major. Though it has nothing of the feat about it it has scope, is original and blandly imposing. And to his linear discourse Ammons gives just enough "jangling dance" to shock "us to attend the moods of lips." Although almost nothing in the poem [*Sphere*] moves or ravishes, almost everything interests and holds—holds not least because it tests, and finds thin, the spiritual satisfactions available in being a conscious part of a universe afloat in nothingness. The talk is not desperate but, by and large, is just talk. The subject is not really in Ammons as the kind of happiness that threatens to swell into a yelp or surf onto silence. But Romanticism has always been in trouble; dissatisfaction is its nature; Ammons is doing what he can.

Calvin Bedient. *NYT.* Dec. 22, 1974. pp. 2–3

ANDERSON, SHERWOOD (1876–1941)

As for the writing itself in *Sherwood Anderson's Memoirs*—I refer to the whole work, not just the somewhat difficult-to-identify new writing —there is much that is strong and free and good and that helps to extend one's view of Anderson's originality or to see better his relationship to some of his contemporaries (for example, William Carlos Williams and Dreiser) as well as to Whitman and Twain. There is added evidence here for the range of Anderson as a comic writer. His affinity with

Twain in the "high and delicate art of how to tell a story" comes out more strongly when one can see in the narrative of the soldier boys in Cuba the same quiet, subversive humor of Twain's "The Private History of a Campaign that Failed"; and the new version of the story of Jacques Copeau's shirts touches the wild hilarity of Faulkner's humor. The narrative of Stella, the sister who took on the family after the mother's death, shows something in Anderson that has not, I think, been sufficiently remarked upon, an insight into human experience that goes far deeper than any cliché of buried lives.

Susan J. Turner. AS. Winter, 1969–70. p. 158

To a younger generation of readers and writers, Anderson's sentiment seems curiously old-fashioned. Even a fellow worker in the vineyard of the grotesque, Flannery O'Connor, has expressed her disappointment at the bittersweet taste of his "twisted apples." . . .

Still, for better or for worse, Anderson established in modern American literature the use of the grotesque as a metaphor for the inner failure of the contemporary man. Indeed, *Winesburg, Ohio* is startlingly modern in the way in which it gives a sense of the defects of society through the deformity of its citizens.

Paul Levine in Minor American Novelists,
edited by Charles Alva Hoyt (Southern
Illinois). 1970. p. 96

Anderson's novelty lay in his appropriating to ordinary and sub-ordinary Americans a sensibility conventionally attributed to gorgeous young aesthetes or to Stephen Daedalus-like intellectuals. But the gestures of Anderson's passionate young woman stripping off her clothes and running out onto the street in the rain ("Adventure"), of his race track swipe who sees in the barroom mirror not his own face but a girl's, and of the same swipe becoming entangled in a horse's skeleton in the moonlight as he is pursued by Negroes intending rape ("The Man Who Became a Woman") are the gestures of Oscar Wilde, or more ludicrously, of Lautréaumont rather than of Mark Twain. Anderson took from Twain a character and a tone. His boys and men are first Sherwood Anderson, and second Huck Finn. The tone, however, is violated by the persistent brooding, the search for the pastoral past, and the foggy, half-baked philosophizing that characterizes Anderson's indifferent average in fiction.

John McCormick. The Middle Distance
(Free). 1971. pp. 22–3

• ASHBERY, JOHN (1927–   )

Some Trees is made up of poems which display a great deal of irresponsible yet often engaging imagination. With one half of the mind feeling like a mystified but somehow willing accomplice, and the other half becoming more and more skeptical, one follows the bright, faddish jargon Ashbery talks with considerable obscure brightness, trying patiently, with some engagement, to decide which of several possible meanings each poem intends. The poems have over them a kind of idling arbitrariness, offering their elements as a profound conjunction of secrecies one can't quite define or evaluate. One doesn't feel, however, that Mr. Ashbery has been at great pains to fabricate these puzzles; on the contrary, this manner of writing seems perfectly natural to him, which must, I suppose, qualify him as an original of some sort. . . .

Though Mr. Ashbery enjoys a real facility with language, and is able to handle difficult forms, like the pantoum and the sestina, with remarkable ease, his poems amount to nothing more than rather cute and momentarily interesting games, like those of a gifted and very childish child who, during "creative play period," wrote a book of poems instead of making finger paintings. [1957]

James Dickey. *Babel to Byzantium*
(Grosset). 1971. pp. 58–60

Let me admit first off that I am not the reader for Mr. Ashbery. . . . If a state of continuous exasperation, a continuous frustration of expectation, a continuous titillation of the imagination are sufficient response to a series of thirty-one poems, then these have been successful. But to be satisfied with such a response I must change my notion of poetry, my reading of it, my source of pleasure in it. . . . Isolated lines . . . and exciting juxtapositions . . . tell me of the strength and integrity of this poet's imagination. Affection for his definition of poetry I must leave to others.

Mona Van Duyn. *Poetry*. Sept., 1962. p. 393

John Ashbery is one of the most original of contemporary poets. His four books of poems . . . are full of startling metaphors and fresh juxtapositions of words and perceptions. He keeps pushing the limits of language; he lives on the most thinly held, the most dangerous, frontiers. His impatience with the merely remembered phrase is evident in every line, though he occasionally uses a cliché to evoke a standard response which he then swamps with irony. He is not without antecedents and influences, however. He has gone to school to Wallace Stevens, from whom he gets both elegance and a furious concentration; to the French Surrealist poets, who have taught him to find fresh images in immersions in the subconscious; and to the "action" painters of the New York School of the 1950's, who have taught him to work with abandon at his canvas and to pray for happy accidents. But his voice is unmistakably his own; it is a voice that does not falter in a world of discontinuities.

Stephen Stepanchev. *American Poetry since 1945* (Harper). 1965. pp. 188–9

I assume that Mr. Ashbery's concern is to give the process of the mind as it moves through reflections, not merely the results of reflection. It is an extreme version of the common distinction between "a mind speaking" and "what is being said." But it is a dangerous aesthetic, an inescapable temptation to bad work. When the dark is light enough, Mr. Ashbery writes with remarkable delicacy and ease, the meditation a lovely "wooing both ways" between landscape and mind. . . But the price is high, the subjective mode exorbitant.

Denis Donoghue. *NYR*. April 14, 1966. p. 19

Mr. Ashbery has often chosen to publish the records of his experiments as if they were finished works of art, has led a number of responsible and perceptive critics to question his seriousness and to express serious reservations about his work. . . . Many who have held such reservations will now cheerfully set them aside. . . . Consciously or not, he has realized that work of the complexity to which he has aspired demands placement against a background fully documenting his wrestlings with problems of scale, syntactical limitations, dislocation, and organization. . . . [In "The Skaters"] the man has found his scale and hit his stride. He knows it and can do almost nothing wrong. . . . The chances are very good that he will come to dominate the last third of the century as Yeats, also afflicted with "this madness to explain," dominated the first.

Howard Wamsley. *Poetry*. Dec., 1966. p. 185

[Ashbery] is among a group of artists—it includes Raymond Roussel and Ronald Firbank—who never quite seem fully serious about their plainly serious art. Like them, hiding things is one of his themes; like them, he loves the convoluted, the cryptic and the frivolous. He builds his toy crystal palaces with enormous care, but at any moment they are likely to come tinkling down, poked in by an attack of his quaint petuance. . . .

His effects are cumulative; it is sometimes amazing what forceful "moments" he is able to generate from the webby substance of the poems. The sudden "drench" of feeling that makes his work so strong is slowly prepared, and it is especially strong for being so underplayed.

Stephen Koch. *Nation.* Dec. 12, 1966. p. 650

John Ashbery is the Sphinx of the generation [of 1962]. Not only are all of his poems enigmas or simply impossible to understand but they appear to promise esoteric wisdom one finds nowhere else in American poetry. Fellow poets, critics and students admit to despair at ever discovering the key (if one exists) to the riddle of the poems in *The Tennis Court Oath* (1962) and *Rivers and Mountains* (1966). . . .

One quality most of Ashbery's poems share, on the other hand, is something like the peculiar excitement one feels when stepping with Alice behind the Looking Glass into a reality bizarre yet familiar in which the "marvelous" is as near as one's breakfast coffee cup or one's shoes being shined by an angel in the barbershop. In an Ashbery poem the marvelous is, in fact, the cup and the shoes—and the angel. His gift is to release everyday objects, experiences and fragments of dream or hallucination from stereotypes imposed on them by habit or preconception or belief: he presents the world as if seen for the first time. But the problem is: each poem is the first time in its own way unlike any past or future Ashbery poem. One way to read an Ashbery poem, it seems to me, might be to remember all one has felt or learned about poetry, including his poems—and then forget it and let the poem at hand do its own work.

Paul Carroll. *The Poem in Its Skin*
(Follett). 1968. pp. 207–8

Like many folk tales, the idylls of Theocritus, the "Alice" books, *The Importance of Being Earnest*, the novels of Firbank and P. G. Wodehouse, *A Nest of Ninnies* is a pastoral; the world it depicts is an imaginary Garden of Eden, a place of innocence from which all serious needs and desires have been excluded.

It is possible, I think, that in our time pastoral is the genre best suited to pure fiction. . . .

A young novelist who is attracted by the pastoral should be warned, however, that it is extremely difficult to do well. I am not surprised to learn that, though *A Nest of Ninnies* is only 191 pages long, it took Messrs. Ashbery and Schuyler several years to write. Their patience and artistry has been well rewarded. I am convinced that their book is destined to become a minor classic.

W. H. Auden. *NYT.* May 4, 1969. p. 20

The shifting of conventional emphasis in *A Nest of Ninnies* consists of no emphasis at all. It is a weightless, pointless, and delightful book. The characters suffer, at most, passing irritations. They are solaced by many things and interested in everything—music, cars, parties, trips, movies, poems. They spend all the time ordering, cooking, serving, and eating food that, in fact, we do spend ordering, cooking, serving, and eating food. . . .

Why such luck? What do these ninnies do to deserve it? They talk. The real subject is expression, varieties of expression in English, and so it is impossible to punish, severely, anyone who can open his mouth. . . .

What the writers share with the readers is a fondness for every fixed form or phrase in English. It is not mockery, but a delight in the basic inanity of these forms—in the delicious fact that life can be conducted pleasantly and even competently by linking words like sausages, let bygones be bygones.

Mary Ellmann. YR. Oct., 1969. p. 116

Ashbery's impressive talents, serving so brilliant and skeptical a mind, make for a difficult poetry; and it would be condescending to his accomplishment, as well as disingenuous, to ignore the difficulty. In his intense explorations into the fictions not only of an essential self but also of an essential art, Ashbery's discontinuous meditations often become intensely private, and at times inaccessible. As with earlier "visionary" poets like Blake and of course the later Stevens, with whom Ashbery is often linked and from whom he happily steals in a poem like "Chateau Hardware," it sometimes happens that the world of familiar objects and relations recedes. "You" designates a somewhat solipsistic "I," and everyone and everything else becomes a dimly-perceived "them" and "it." On these occasions, Ashbery's poetry runs the risk of vanishing into the imagined world of its own favorite dream, the risk of consulting only with its own motions, as its ideas and tones constantly dissolve into and out of one another like a beautiful drift of clouds. It's as if, sometimes, the poetry were so private and self-sufficient that it could dispense with the irksome necessity of an audience. . . .

It's exhilarating to watch Mr. Ashbery maintain his precarious balance on an "esthetic ideal" which seems to be raised higher with each new book. The latest, *Three Poems* (three extended meditations in prose), will excite aficionados of his work, but it probably won't, as an introduction, win him new converts.

Alan Helms. PR. Fall, 1972. pp. 624–5

Of the American poets now in mid-career, those born in the decade 1925–1935, John Ashbery and A. R. Ammons seem to me the strongest. . . . Ashbery goes back through Stevens to Whitman, even as Ammons is a more direct descendant of American Romanticism in its major formulation, which remains Emerson's. Otherwise, these two superb poets have nothing in common except their authentic difficulty. Ammons belongs to no school, while Ashbery can be regarded either as the best poet by far of the "New York School" or—as I would argue—so unique a figure that only confusion is engendered by associating him with Koch, O'Hara, Schuyler and their friends and disciples. . . .

The Coda of "The Recital" [in *Three Poems*] is a wholly personal apologia, with many Whitmanian and Stevensian echoes, some of them involuntary. . . . Against the enemy, who is an amalgam of time and selfishness, Ashbery struggles to get beyond his own solipsism, and the limits of his art. On the final page, an Emersonian-Stevensian image of saving transparence serves to amalgamate the new changes Ashbery meets and welcomes. This transparence movingly is provided by a Whitmanian vision of an audience for Ashbery's art: "There were new people watching and waiting, conjugating in this way the distance and emptiness, transforming the scarcely noticeable bleakness into something both intimate and noble." So they have and will, judging by the response of my students and other friends, with whom I've discussed Ashbery's work. By more than 15 years of high vision and persistence he has clarified the initial prophecy of his work, until peering into it we can say: "We see us as we truly behave" and, as we can see, we can think: "These accents seem their own defense."

Harold Bloom. *Salmagundi*. Spring–Summer,
1973. pp. 103, 131

AUCHINCLOSS, LOUIS (1917–   )

The strong underlying unity of this collection [*Second Chance*] results from a remarkable similarity in theme, character, and setting in each of the seventeen stories. For in the short fiction brought together in this volume Mr. Auchincloss is largely concerned with the crises in the lives of sophisticated middle-aged or elderly people who live in New York or adjacent suburbia. . . . What must surely win the admiration of many readers is the skill with which Mr. Auchincloss tells each story. For whether writing of lawyers, publishers, curators of museums, or society matrons, whether choosing as narrative method first person or omniscient author he is always easy, fluent, and civilized.

VQR. Winter, 1971. p. xiv

Auchincloss is a writer of moral and ethical issues as well as manners, and his fiction works on both levels. *I Come as a Thief* is concerned not only with how much freedom a person has in his society but also with how much freedom he has been granted by God. The answer, to which Auchincloss returns in novel after novel, is that if he has the freedom to sin he also has the obligation of expiation; Auchincloss is, for all his wit and sophistication, a stern Christian who demands that the people in his world pay for their transgressions.

In many respects he is indeed an anachronism. His themes—crime and punishment, faithlessness and faith, freedom and obligation—are old-fashioned, and so are the form and language of his novels. But his is a refreshing conservatism; there is still something to be said for a firm religious vision, a lucid prose style, and a clear understanding of one's world—even if it is the world of the rich.

Jonathan Yardley. NR. Sept. 16, 1972. p. 30

A proper question to raise before entering any new Auchincloss novel is whether, after 22 books, Auchincloss has anything to say that he hasn't said before. When does a writer write himself out? John O'Hara never quite did it. Louis Auchincloss hasn't either. The reason is partly because Auchincloss writes about others instead of himself. The practicing attorney feeds facts, feelings, insights to the moonlighting writer like a kindly literary patron. Auchincloss continues to have more to tell us because his other life keeps him mining a vein of upper middle-class hopes, conflicts, failures, survivals. Of course talent and effort serve him. Auchincloss observes like a cat. He makes judgments with subtlety and sophistication, usually about human character under the strain of slowly compressing environment. In Auchincloss's fiction there is no escape from the self because the enveloping environment also consists of the personality operating within it. . . .

Auchincloss does a few new things in *The Partners*. He gets closer to sex, which hasn't been one of his larger enthusiasms. He wrestles with the possibility that while the institutional foundations of our society are changing, what men and women may want is changing faster. Freedom. Belief. Sensation. But he does best what he has always done. He is the gentlest of moralists. He takes us inside human beings. He makes us believe they are worthy of our interest and concern. For a while we are caught up in the narrowness of other lives and are reminded that we may expand our own. Auchincloss is a good man to have writing.

Webster Schott. NYT. Feb. 24, 1974. p. 2

In a society where matters of importance are invariably euphemized (how can an antipersonnel weapon actually kill?) a writer like Louis

Auchincloss who writes about the way money is made and spent is going to have a very hard time being taken seriously. For one thing, it is now generally believed in bookchat land that the old rich families haven't existed since the time of Edith Wharton while the new-rich are better suited for journalistic exposés than for a treatment in the serious . . . novel. It is true that an indiscriminate reading public enjoys reading Auchincloss because, unlike the well-educated, they suspect that the rich are always with us and probably up to no good. But since the much-heralded death of the Wasp establishment, the matter of Auchincloss's fiction simply cannot be considered important.

This is too bad. After all, he is a good novelist, and a superb short-story writer. More important, he has made a brave effort to create his own literary tradition—a private oasis in the cactus land of American letters. He has written about Shakespeare's penchant for motiveless malignity (a peculiarly American theme), about Henry James, about our women writers as the custodians and caretakers of the values of that dour European tribe which originally killed the Indians and settled the continent.

Gore Vidal. NYR. July 18, 1974. p. 11

AUDEN, W. H. (1907–1973)

The integrity of Auden's work is too large a subject to be undertaken here. Perhaps, though, even this inadequate postscript on his post-war writings may suggest that he has not reversed direction. His understanding of his early beliefs brought him to the point where they were no longer serviceable. At that point he could make the new assumptions that led him to a journey's end satisfactory for him. . . . Our concern is with the brilliantly composed looking-glass world in which he has re-enacted his journey. He has continued to meet Geoffrey Grigson's criterion for *New Verse* that a poem should take notice "for ends not purely individual, of the universe of objects and events." The ends have changed. But the later poems still create from their objects and events a dramatic myth that extends their bearings beyond local and immediate relevancy. So it was with his "marxism." Of all the thirties poets he was most at home in the poetic fable he constructed from it. A knowledge of Marx enlightens many of Auden's poems; Auden's poems create their own luminous after-image of marxism.

D. E. S. Maxwell. Poets of the Thirties
(Routledge). 1969. p. 172

The persona of [Auden's] early poems was an intense and interesting man. Central to his character was the need to know and, once he felt he had gained knowledge, the need to teach. The resultant effect of this "needing to" is a feeling of movement in the poems. We hear the voice of the persona admonishing us, as he moves from uncertainty to certainty and back to uncertainty, to look on ourselves and our world with hard, questioning eyes, accepting nothing as final, except death. . . .

If one were to give the above description of Auden's persona and verse to a prospective reader and then were to have him read the poems in *About the House* without telling him they were Auden's, his response would probably be, "What do these poems have to do with W. H. Auden?" The answer would be "Nothing," for although there are technical similarities between the work of the early Auden and that of the Auden of the sixties, the poems are written by what amounts to two different men and they show it; comparing them is like comparing the poems of Byron and Tennyson, or those of Pope and Blake.

The most important fact about the poetry of the "new" Auden, which one encounters for the first time in *Nones*, is the lack of tension between the poet and his experience. Both man and world simply are; no more, no less. The only problem, a nonmetaphysical one, is recognizing, accepting, and praising the existence of both.

> Gerald Nelson. *Changes of Heart: A Study of the Poetry of W. H. Auden* (California). 1969. pp. 144–5

Auden's writing offers us a vision of the nature of personal being and becoming which is fully consistent with and an important contribution to an intellectual position underlying a significant body of twentieth-century literature. At the center of his thought and art in the later period is a vision of the nature of individual action which is related to a dilemma central to the contemporary world, the fragmentation in belief of a whole civilization. If he is committed to one solution of that dilemma, it is not without an awareness of the difficulties and responsibilities of that commitment, nor is it without sympathy for those who do not wish to or cannot take upon themselves the problems of what Kierkegaard has called "the religious sphere." In man's weakness Auden sees his potentialities, and his art continues to be didactic in the best sense: it directed man toward knowledge of himself.

> George W. Bahlke. *The Later Auden* (Rutgers). 1970. pp. 83–4

So many, so various, so handsome and so insinuating are the by-products of Auden's career among us that our indolence as well as our thirsty media risk persuading us that it is all one: one utterance altered, merely, according to the various circumstances of its occasion. This is not so. There is the poet Auden, who in this newest book [*City without Walls*] has added another dozen to the great poems in his canon, as well as a number of "pieces he has nothing against except their lack of importance"; and there is the witty, generous, rather bromidic public man we must not condescend to by allowing his good humor and his eccentricities . . . to obscure his greatness. Which is abundantly here and clear in this latest book so much under the sign of a consented-to mortality; from the title poem to the "Ode to Terminus," the book is concerned with boundaries, limitations, precarious identifications which make our life possible: that naming which was Adam's first task and Auden's to the last. Hence the famous and extraordinary vocabulary, and the wonderful meters, the alliterative spells and charms. . . .

Richard Howard. *Poetry*. Oct., 1971. p. 38

I think there is a sense in which Auden put himself on a shelf a good many years ago when his verse came reiteratively to proclaim man's incapacities, his inability to take charge, direct his fate; and indeed he has perhaps become our greatest poet of the shelf. But in the new volume [*Epistle to a Godson*] the shelf is even higher in the closet, and on it he sits meditating—with himself, or imaginatively with a few old friends. . . . His verse centers have usually been large and obvious like a statue in a park, with the poet's game one of sitting down in front of the statue and letting the sight of it develop in the mind a series of themes, projections, fancies. Thus it is a contemplative art, an art for a lonely and unbugged visionary on a park bench. Or shelf.

Reed Whittemore. *NR*. Sept. 23, 1972. p. 26

Clarity and carefulness are the essence of Auden's criticism. His perspective is that of explicit Christianity, which is unusual among critics (and therefore valuable), but what is remarkable is the absence of pedantic dithering and obfuscation, the lack of untenable generalizations, the grace (an appropriate word) of his argument. He means to get at the core of the matter and to put it plainly, and he does. Moreover, he shifts gears delightfully, approaching any subject from several disciplines. Civilization, he says, may be judged by "the degree of diversity attained and the degree of unity retained." By that definition, Auden is the most civilized of living writers.

Peter S. Prescott. *Nwk*. March 19, 1973. p. 95B

It is a common opinion among the English *literati* that Auden's later work is a collapse. I am so far from taking this view that I think an appreciation of Auden's later work is the only sure test for an appreciation of Auden, just as an appreciation of Yeats's earlier work is the only sure test for an appreciation of Yeats. You must know and admire the austerity which Auden achieved before you can take the full force of his early longing for that austerity—before you can measure the portent of his early brilliance. There is no question that the earlier work is more enjoyable. The question is about whether you think enjoyability was the full extent of his aim. . . . In his later work we see not so much the ebbing of desire as its transference to the created world, until plains and hills begin explaining the men who live on them. Auden's unrecriminating generosity toward a world which had served him ill was a moral triumph.

Clive James. Cmty. Dec., 1973. p. 58

BALDWIN, JAMES (1924–   )

In *Blues for Mr. Charlie,* Baldwin translates his apocalypse into concrete social terms. The race war is not yet quite upon us, but the play ends with preparation for a Negro protest march in a small Southern town in which its leader-minister keeps a gun in readiness concealed under his Bible. The alternatives are clear: love or violence, the Negro can wait no longer. Baldwin's theater resembles nothing so much—in form and fervor, at least—as the protest dramas of the radical left in the thirties. But the play is effective, for the emotions it arouses are specifically vindictive and personally embarrassing to his white audiences, which partly explains, no doubt, its failure on the Broadway stage. For Baldwin, the preacher, not only thunders at his audience's failure of social and human responsibility, but, far worse, he impugns their sexuality and depicts them as more terrified of the possibilities of life than the Negroes they persecute.

Edward Margolies. Native Sons
(Lippincott). 1968. p. 124

[Baldwin's] rhetorical tactics are immediately clear if we see the essays and the fiction as disjunctive halves of Baldwin's self, as the wish and the reality. The essays envision a community based on love, freedom, and an achieved individual and social identity. Yet in the light of his fiction, one is tempted to call such passages holy fantasy.

Richard H. Rupp. Celebration in Postwar
American Fiction (Miami). 1970. p. 136

I do not take back what I said about Baldwin's having become a great writer—I've said it enough. But no matter how great he is, he does not seem to have anything new or different or progressive to say anymore. This could very well mean that, among other things, Baldwin has unwittingly or wittingly written himself into the very species personage that he has seemingly been trying to destroy, the species personage of The Father. Whether this is true or not, or whether it is true for a certain period, it is clear that he has necessitated if not nurtured into being a radically different set of black writers from himself and, alas, has been eclipsed by them.

Let me make one thing absolutely clear. These writers are not in competition with James Baldwin, nor are they in conflict with him. Nor can anyone take Baldwin's "place" as a writer, and certainly not as a black writer. Baldwin is an individual writer in his own right.

Calvin C. Hernton in *Amistad 1*, edited by
John A. Williams and Charles F. Harris
(Random). 1970. p. 213

Baldwin is saying in effect in this novel [*Another Country*] that we Americans have failed to live up to our professed moral commitments and that the innocence and puritanism of the country are largely at fault. This novel is like the essays insofar as Baldwin's stance is moral indignation. He is simply furious that America possesses the character it has. But what about more pertinent issues such as jobs, housing, health, education, etc.? What of the issues beyond the personal and the private? Baldwin is not so much concerned about these as about the moral issues. Hence his novel is about love, and only a moralist who does not grant the role of politics in determining the quality of life could believe that love is so central. . . . His most recent novel, *Tell Me How Long the Train's Been Gone*, reveals the same position. There Baldwin expresses sympathetic understanding of the political perspective, but clearly enough it is not his own.

Donald B. Gibson in *The Politics of Twentieth-
Century Novelists*, edited by George A.
Panichas (Hawthorn). 1971. pp. 318–9

Baldwin certainly risked a great deal [in *If Beale Street Could Talk*] by putting his complex narrative, which involves a number of important characters, into the mouth of a young girl. Yet Tish's voice comes to seem absolutely natural and we learn to know her from the inside out. Even her flights of poetic fancy—involving rather subtle speculations upon the nature of male-female relationships, or black-white relationships, as well as her articulation of what it feels like to be pregnant—are convincing. Also convincing is Baldwin's insistence upon the primacy of emotions like love, hate, or terror: it is not sentimentality, but basic psychology, to acknowledge the fact that one person will die, and another survive simply because one has not the guarantee of a fundamental human bond, like love, while the other has. . . .

The novel progresses swiftly and suspensefully, but its dynamic movement is interior. Baldwin constantly understates the horror of his characters' situation in order to present them as human beings whom disaster has struck, rather than as blacks who have, typically, been victimized by whites and are therefore likely subjects for a novel.

Joyce Carol Oates. *NYT*.
May 19, 1974. pp. 1–2

To read *If Beale Street Could Talk* as accurate social drama seems to me virtually impossible. I can't care as much as I want to about Fonny and Tish unless the system that victimizes them is described in a way that I can recognize. No one can doubt that terrible things are done to good and innocent black people. But Baldwin writes so flatly and schematically that he drives one to imagining ways in which his story might be more "believable." . . .

So one must try to read this novel allegorically, taking Tish and Fonny as Romeo and Juliet (as they're in fact teasingly called by some of their friends), cop-crossed lovers victimized by a repressive order whose exact workings don't really matter. They are credible and often affecting as lovers, but the fantasy on which Baldwin's allegory relies may disturb some of Baldwin's readers, particularly black ones: blackness in a white system becomes here a condition of helpless passivity, of getting screwed by the man; persecution and violation are emphasized so insistently and despairingly that enduring them becomes a kind of acceptance.

In fairness, I should say that Fonny is allowed to keep what manhood is possible for him by surviving confinement and escaping the homosexual rape he deeply fears that prison has in store for him. . . . But if Baldwin's political meanings carry an essentially sexual message, the frustrated rage in this novel needs a clearer relation to its inner subject. As it is, I unhappily suggest that an important and honorable writer has failed to make us believe in his vision of horrors that surely do exist, but outside his book.

Thomas R. Edwards. *NYR.*
June 13, 1974. p. 37

BARNES, DJUNA (1892–   )

[Barnes's] world is a world of displaced persons—of an Armenian country boy on the lower east side of Manhattan, of Russian emigrés in Paris, Berlin, Spain, or New York, of Scandinavians or English in American farmland. They have abandoned national, racial, and ethical traditions; their human contacts are laceration. They lack even the integrity in isolation that comforts the characters of Hemingway or the early Faulkner, for they are estranged against themselves. Their aborted and ineffectual attempts to find meaning, order, or love are the subjects of the stories. Technique, as well as subject, marks the stories as extraordinary.

Readers who find the verbal pyrotechnics of *Nightwood*, or of the 1927 novel, *Ryder*, or of *The Antiphon* too often merely talky and falsely rhetorical will discover in most of the stories a fusing of experience and idea. Economy is especially characteristic of the revised versions collected in the *Selected Works,* where verbal fat has been pared away, and objects, persons, and actions flash out with chilling precision. This is not to say, of course, that the stories are easy to read; on the contrary, like those of Katherine Mansfield and Katherine Anne Porter—which technically many of them resemble—they retain their meaning in a very dense texture, where each detail is significant and essential to the whole. And in spite of *Nightwood*'s relatively wide circulation they are generally unknown today.

Suzanne C. Ferguson. *SoR*. Winter, 1969. p. 27

BARTH, JOHN (1930–   )

I got into a kind of rage of disappointment when the genius who wrote *The End of the Road* took up the fad for self-imprisonment in funny language. *The Sot-Weed Factor* and *Giles Goat-Boy* are unreadable, and I can swear to this because I read them through. So when John Barth's new collection of short pieces, *Lost in the Funhouse,* arrived my heart sank, and I left it on the shelf for a long time. . . . And now I've read *Lost in the Funhouse* with great pleasure and hardly know where to look. Because of my needless fears, I haven't given the book the attention it deserves, so I can only hazard first impressions. There may be a more significant relation than I have grasped between the folksy short stories about boyhood on the Eastern Shore and the deliberately bizarre excursions into the style of Borges, Beckett, Kafka and mock-epic, but I have a hunch that the structural pretensions are pure put-on. In any case, most of Barth's language has come back to genuine, and very funny, life. The spoofs of "fiction about fiction about fiction" manage, in a way I couldn't have predicted from the laborious imitations of the two previous novels, to be funny on this familiar subject and seriously interesting too, and both in new ways.

Robert Garis. *HdR*. Spring, 1969. pp. 163–4

Since neither *Giles Goat-Boy* nor *The Sot-Weed Factor* is a "proper" novel but "imitations-of-novels," they do not offer representations of reality at all but representations of representations of reality, removing them at least twice from the world of "objective reality" and further emphasizing their artificiality in the process. Thus Barth uses artificiality to expose artificiality. By presenting a farcical and exaggerated version of the world, not as the world is, but as it is erroneously conceived to be, Barth mocks the false conception and suggests cosmic absurdity by inversion.

Charles B. Harris. *Contemporary American Novelists of the Absurd* (College and University). 1971. p. 116

Barth's early narrators demonstrate an independence of mind from the omnipotence of environment which in one sense is a state much to be desired. On the other hand they are presented as suffering from a nihilism which excludes them from confident participation in life, and which is to be seen as a curse or a blight. At the same time that equivocal mental and verbal freedom which they "enjoy," and which allows them to be completely arbitrary in the patterns they choose, is the freedom increasingly exercised by Barth himself. His tendency to sport on lexical playfields increases in his following books. In these "floating operas" signs tend to become more important than their referrents, and the impresario of fictions, John Barth, plays with them in such a way that any established notions of the relationship between word and world are lost or called in doubt. Barth is indeed one of the great sportsmen of contemporary fiction.

Tony Tanner. *City of Words* (Harper and Row). 1971. p. 240

In his last three works of fiction, Barth systematically debunks the idea of progress by showing that life is existentially absurd, by showing that the individual, society, and cosmos are all inherently chaotic. He then demonstrates the foolishness of acting on notions about transcendental correspondence, for such idealism will quickly destroy both man and his society. As an alternate to such notions of idealism and progress, Barth stresses the actuality of cyclical correspondence. According to the cyclical pattern, man and his society must pass from innocent notions about the goodness of life and about the individual's role as a saviour-hero to a more mature, tempered, and somewhat cynical view necessary in order to formulate an appropriate way to create meaning for the individual and harmony for a society. Finally, however, Barth does not demonstrate any permanence or absolute merit in such maturity, for senility, death, and decay are the ultimate rewards for the individual and his civilization. Even so, life will probably continue in correspondingly similar cycles for generations, centuries, millenniums, and substantially longer periods of time.

Gordon E. Slethaug. *Critique*. 13, 3, 1972. pp. 27–8

I had always thought that Barth's mind was more interesting than any of his books so far—it was perceived, through the books, of course, but it could be perceived as being let down. *Chimera* makes me think that this is precisely the impression the books have all set out to create. The texts suggest an author who, for all his narrative meddling and jugglery, is aloof from them, better than they are, and the clumsy gags and the frequent silliness only confirm this feeling. All intentional, an aristocracy of bad taste, a disdain for the world's terms. . . .

Barth is not obscure or difficult, and he can be very funny . . . and the moral dimensions by no means disappear in the trickiness. He is suggesting in *Chimera*, for example, that love is a terrible risk, an almost certain loss, given our own and others' experience in the matter, but that the risk can be redeemed by the quality of spirit with which it is taken. . . .

But Barth won't take this kind of risk with his writing: won't free it and master it, won't let it loose from the safe zones of pastiche. It is as if he would rather not know where the limits of his talent lie, were happier with the thought of being a brilliant man repeatedly betrayed by his books.

Michael Wood. NYR. Oct. 19, 1972. pp. 34–5

In *Lost in the Funhouse* [Barth] transcends the agonizing efforts at self-definition of Ebenezer, Burlingame, and George Goat-Boy, and the equally traumatic biographies of the Maryland tales, and comes to rest in the serene Borgian acceptance of an identity that has no confirmatory existence apart from its fictional entity. Indeed, the mark of Borges's "The Immortal" is everywhere impressed in Barth's paradigmatic renderings of the myths of Narcissus, Menelaus, and the archetypal poet anonymous. His skeptical acceptance of the permanence of multiplicity, of even the possibility that one's self is but the dream of another insubstantial being, becomes the only viable strategy for confronting the Great Labyrinth, both human and cosmic. In parody alone may the artist hope to find a successive form that dissemblingly confirms continuation in time. To retell the old myths, to come paradigmatically ever closer to a great contemporary like Borges (as these stories so patently do), and to lampoon the anti-Gutenberg cries of McLuhan and company (as these stories also do) is to maintain the fiction of continuity and the reality of person in the limited persistence of the word, is finally, if nothing else, to give aesthetic validity to life.

Max F. Schulz. Black Humor Fiction of the
Sixties (Ohio Univ. Pr.). 1973. p. 40

The irony of the novel [*The Sot-Weed Factor*] consists in the fact that it is based on the model of *Tom Jones*, and on all the assumptions the world of *Tom Jones* makes, but that its hero, Ebenezer Cooke, achieves disillusionment, not identity, at the end. The very concept of "identity" is called into question by the novel. No one in the novel is what he appears to be; Bertrand, Ebenezer's valet, poses as Ebenezer aboard ship; Burlingame poses as Lord Baltimore, Colonel Peter Sayer, Timothy Mitchell, and Nicholas Lowe. The overwhelming complexity and richness of the novel derive partly from this substitution of illusion for identity. All of the complicated, shifting interconnections of the plot and the political intrigues it involves are brought a step beyond *Tom Jones*: the threads of the plot never are tied up neatly in *The Sot-Weed Factor*, and facts never do dovetail. The maze of the plot, from the overview of the reader, verges on the condition of a labyrinth, the condition in which the consistent identity of the world exists in a shattered state. The space of *The Sot-Weed Factor* is apparently the same kind of map space as in *Tom Jones*, but cracks in this space are always opening up, and they open into voids.

John Vernon. The Garden and the Map
(Illinois). 1973. pp. 63–4

Barth's solution to his distaste for necessity is to create imaginative alternatives to reality—*The Sot-Weed Factor, Giles Goat-Boy*—with characters whose fictionalizing approach to life he shares. With their own arbitrariness and finality, these alternatives dramatize the irresponsibility of fiction to any man's factual and reasonable truth. They and their heroes, who make their lives into fanciful floating operas, are amoral. The only limiting provision of this value—the fictionalization of experience—is that it work: psychologically to protect, aesthetically to interest. The floating-opera man does not want to give himself away but does want to interest others. For Barth's characters it is a way of living in the world while retreating from it. For Barth as a novelist it is a way of writing a book without the curse of sincerity, a way of having protean secrets protected by protean disguises.

Barth's parody of aesthetic form is one of these disguises. What seems to be an attack on fiction itself is actually a critique of the solidification or rationalization of the aesthetic process into an abstract construct. The aesthetic or fictionalizing process is fluid and willful; it breaks up or ignores traditional values and conventions, which may seem to have a rational basis, to control one's experience.

Thomas Le Clair. TSLL. Winter, 1973. p. 722

• BARTHELME, DONALD (1931–   )

[Barthelme] has mastered many of Joyce's comic devices—though his debt to *Mad* magazine is almost as considerable. Mingled with sharp allusions to Eliot, Kierkegaard, Nietzsche and Pascal [in *Come Back, Dr. Caligari*] there is a lot of Cummings's prankishness. Sartrean nausea is locked in a warm embrace with American gusto. Here is fiction that reaches as far as poetry for its ingredients and verbal forms.

And, at long last, for better or worse, the Absurd has . . . been equated precisely with the Goofy. . . .

His degree of success in rendering the Absurd innocuous could, I suppose, make existentialism as popular an American institution as pizza pie.

R. V. Cassill. *NYT*. April 12, 1964. p. 36

Come Back, Dr. Caligari by Donald Barthelme is a hard wild controlled collection of poker-faced perversities, working a kind of drollery which automatically precludes the intimate effects but pinwheels and sky-rockets spectacularly across its own landscape. Occasionally Mr. Barthelme falls into a mode which can best be described as that of a pop artist in prose; these stories are studded with solemn absurdities from ads, comic-books, mail-order catalogs, record-blurbs, and instruction-leaflets. . . .

The characters rise like automata to their formal speeches and jerky actions, then subside; it makes not only for the cruel funny, but, oddly, for a desolate landscape littered with pathetic fragments of useless speech-patterns. It is a book written as if with verbal components from a used-car graveyard; its most striking effects come from disparity, inconsequence, and incongruity.

Robert M. Adams. *NYR*. April 30, 1964. p. 10

On its most available level *Snow White* is a parodic contemporary retelling of the fairy tale. More accurately, the tale is here refracted through the prism of a contemporary sensibility so that it emerges broken up into fragments, shards of its original identity, of its historical career in our consciousness (Disney's cartoon film is almost as much in evidence as the Grimm story) and of its recorded or potential uses for sociology and psychology—all the Freudian undertones and implications, for example. Placed like widely separated tesserae in an abstract mosaic construction, the fragments serve to give a skeletal unity to the mostly verbal events that surround them, as well as a locus for the book's main imaginative thrust.

The only thing resembling a narrative is that the book does move on to fulfill in its own very special way the basic situation of the fairy tale. But Barthelme continually breaks up the progression of events, switching horses in midstream, turning lyricism abruptly into parody, exposition into incantation, inserting pure irrelevancies, pure indigestible fragments like bits of stucco on a smooth wall, allowing nothing to *follow* or link up in any kind of logical development. . . .

Fiction, Barthelme is saying, has lost its power to transform and convince and substitute, just as reality has lost, perhaps only temporarily (but that is not the concern of the imagination), its need and capacity to sustain fictions of this kind. [1967]

Richard Gilman. *The Confusion of Realms*
(Random). 1969. pp. 45, 47

[Barthelme's] laconic style is maddeningly original, often obtuse. His puzzling prose is a potpourri of free-floating metaphor and enigmatic idiom. His plots meander like an acid-head's triptik. And most of his subject matter seems to have been collected from the aftermath of a psychiatric congress. . . .

At first glance, Barthelme seems to be writing indulgent and surreal nonsense, buttressed by an elegant posture of put-on and a gourmet appetite for the absurd. But beneath the mock-Joycian jabberwocky and rococo fantasy, one discovers in his stories a disarmingly serious relevance to the realities of our anxious present. In fact, society's nail-biting mania is one of Barthelme's favorite fictional springboards.

S. K. Oberbeck. *Book World*.
May 19, 1968. p. 3

Barthelme's stories are . . . unnatural acts. They are attempts—mocking attempts—at narrative in a time that is shapeless and that affords no principle of selection. Like William Burroughs, Barthelme creates a new kind of fiction by frustrating, spoofing, or aggressively ignoring the expectations—of situation, development, denouement—raised by the old. He is light-minded with a vengeance; or, if light-mindedness is indeed an illness, militant mockery is its slightly feverish principle. Hence these stories [*Unspeakable Practices, Unnatural Acts*], though so much like play, are not quite free. They mock contemporary life, they mock the art of fiction itself, not in simple exuberance, and certainly not in full comic gaiety but in a somewhat painful merriment and with ever so slightly a feeling of having to vomit.

Calvin Bedient. *Nation*. May 27, 1968. p. 703

"The aim of literature . . . is the creation of a strange object covered with fur which breaks your heart," said Donald Barthelme some years ago. Fiction then had the power to be outrageous, to create marvels of passion. Barthelme's characters used to hope that the sheer force of imagination could change the world, or at the very least, that they could thwart reality by withdrawing into themselves, into a consciousness that Barthelme usually made witty and ironic. Even his Snow White, who is so tired of being just a "horsewife" for dwarfs, finally saves herself through a mixture of irony and poetry. Barthelme is still writing about literature, but he is not so funny any more.

Barthelme's black humor is now less humorous than black. His latest collection, City Life, is full of chaos and despair. The best stories are about the exhaustion of creative power, the disintegration of individual consciousness—the collapse of inner worlds that are now so fragmented that no one could withdraw into them with comfort—and the failure of fiction to create order or even, perhaps, diversion.

Josephine Hendin. *SR*. May 9, 1970. p. 34

Barthelme's only novel to date, Snow White, is an extended parody, an ingenious "put-on" that is perhaps the purest example of Camp yet published. Barthelme, however, does not emphasize artifice at the expense of meaning, as Sontag's definition of Camp would lead one to expect. On the contrary, Snow White demonstrates as few novels can the indissolubility of form and content in the novel. To be sure, the form of Barthelme's Camp masterpiece—the ways he manages and arranges character and incident and the use he makes of language—does obscure all coherent meaning or "content" in the novel, but this is precisely Barthelme's point. In writing a novel devoid of "meaning" in the traditional sense of that term, Barthelme denies the possibility of meaning in an absurd world. The form of his novel thus becomes an analogue to the absurd human condition.

Charles B. Harris. *Contemporary American Novelists of the Absurd* (College and University). 1971. pp. 124–5

Barthelme's importance as a writer lies not only in the exciting, experimental form, but in the exploration of the full impact of mass media pop culture on the consciousness of the individual who is so bombarded by canned happenings, sensations, reactions, and general noise that he can no longer distinguish the self from the surroundings. Barthelme's metropolis is rapidly reaching the state where the media are the man. As refuge the individual finds only unquestioning acceptance of contradictory states on the one hand, or specialized and meaningless abstractions on the other. Though wisdom and insight may exist here, the mass media have reduced everything to the same level of slightly shrill importance, and thus, paradoxically, to the same level of trivia. In the constant barrage of equally accentuated "nownesses," the individual loses all sense of priorities, and thus, caught between undifferentiated fact and equally meaningless abstractions, his world is that horror envisioned by one of E. M. Forster's characters in *A Passage to India* where everything exists and nothing has value.

As a writer, Barthelme also asks about the arts in such a city and finds the artist too is trapped. Striving to achieve aesthetic distance, to get above the level of mere phenomenon, the artist finds that his works aren't accepted by a world bent on "fact" or that his efforts at perspective have produced only the borrowed, traditional or trivial and are thus unrelated to the world they should represent.

Francis Gillen. TCL. Jan., 1972. pp. 37–8

Barthelme's stories are normally made up of fragments seemingly associated at random; the closer they come to narrative development, character portrayal or any other conventional purpose, the more overtly they signal their fragmentation. Barthelme may separate the parts of a story with numbers or blank space, or interpose graphic divisions. Earlier writers have drawn similar attention to the formal arbitrariness of fiction—one thinks of Sterne, who also favored graphic intrusions and blank space, or Thackeray, who said in *Vanity Fair* that his characters were puppets—but not even contemporary meta-fictionists like Borges go so far in insisting that the reader take the story as a made object, not a window on life.

Although Barthelme's strategies vary in significance from story to story, they all spring from a common impulse. He is very conscious that formulas achieve familiarity and that familiarity breeds inattention. Though he wishes that literature could still provide insight and inspiration as it did in the great, mercifully unselfconscious days of a writer like Tolstoy . . . he is also aware that modern readers have experienced too much literature to respond freely to the old modes, so he free associates to "make it new." While less theoretical contemporaries resort to marginal subject matter, idiosyncratic viewpoints or shocking language, Barthelme uses formal dislocation to achieve this goal.

Charles Thomas Samuels. NYT.
Nov. 5, 1972. p. 27

Donald Barthelme either takes pills, does dope, drinks an awful lot, or has one of the unique literary imaginations of the present age. I think it's the latter. . . .

Calling Donald Barthelme's work fiction doesn't do the job. They're writings . . . in search of their own definition, fiction essays on themes that are secret or haven't been announced. They usually have no plots, no characters we can identify from life, no formal beginnings or endings. They're all event, condition, attitude expressed from the viewpoint of a bright and detached stone-head. Some sentences run on for 200 words in quest of a subject. Like poems, his tales seem to plead for reading aloud. They're for feeling and effect, not narration. . . .

While other writers struggle with identity problems and questions of reality, Barthelme has found the magic. Reality doesn't exist. Identity is a costume. . . . His fairy tales . . . should be viewed as you would modern painting. Enjoy the color. Feast on the textures, shapes, patterns. Muse over the combinations.

Yet like contemporary art and music, Barthelme's writing rides on the back of its social source. The pointless talk and intense self-consciousness of his characters, the barbaric juxtapositions of the sacred and the profane, the expensive junk, laminated vocabularies and suspended judgments of his tales—all point to a cultural cellar in which Barthelme sits thinking. So much so a Skinnerian psychologist could make a case for Barthelme as delivery boy for the dreams of the body neurotic of the U.S.A.

Webster Schott. Book World. Nov. 5, 1972. p. 3

Sadness is a collection of Barthelme's recent stories, his dreams, his toys. Perhaps because he has illustrated one of them with literal montage, it is the art of collage that Barthelme's technique evokes for me—the scissoring and pasting of borrowed images, bringing them into new contexts and thus forming a new reality, but a reality taking half its meaning from the old contexts. Barthelme cites Leninist-Marxist thought knowledgeably, and what we are talking about (not necessarily as a consequence) is a dialectical art, which is to say a revolutionary art. Which is not to say a political art, one that services a revolution, but an art that stages its own strictly apolitical upheaval.

Barthelme is no political man. Mementos abound of Borges and Beckett, who belong also to the grand toymaker tradition of Klee and Calder. The world inhabited by these men is the echo chamber, the hall of mirrors, the palace of art, the House of Usher. Theirs is a closet, a palace revolution. Theirs is a highly objective, even cerebral world, yet these artists make themselves felt nonetheless. We are aware of Barthelme's presence in these stories, whether as an unhappy husband, a man on an operating table, or a mysterious, modern incarnation of St. Anthony. The landscape is bleak, evoking the unpleasant, flat horizons of surrealistic paintings; yet we also detect the familiar features of Barthelme's native East Texas.

John Seelye. SR. Dec., 1972. p. 66

The unforgivable flaw in Donald Barthelme's work is that he is right. He has located the square on which we are cowering, and he has assembled the comedy of our activities on that square, our lives, into an instrument of discomfort. He is the most monstrous writer alive, meaner than Hawkes, nastier than Pynchon, more unfair than Beckett, less forgiving than Ionesco, as cruel as life.

Earl Shorris. Harper. Jan., 1973. p. 92

In the past few years, half masquerading as Thurber's ghost, Donald Barthelme has slipped into the preconscious of contemporary fiction through the pages of The New Yorker. Both Thurber and Barthelme draw on a self-indulgent yet acidly ironic fantasy life in which they triumph over their enemies and find innocent pleasures they prefer to call guilty. . . .

In five collections of stories and one novel, he has established not so much a milieu of places and characters, nor a recognizable style, as an elusive tone. . . . For several years now Barthelme has been sprinkling his texts with modishly doctored engravings and old prints that reinforce his mood [between the fantastic and the comic]. Even without them his most characteristic passages recall Max Ernst's pre-surrealist collages, and also the stunning slow-motion farce-epics of the Bread and Puppet Theater. . . .

For those who prefer to use the handrail of plot when they step off onto the dark stairs of fiction, The Dead Father offers more to hold onto than Barthelme's earlier fiction. Even so, he snatches away our security after only a few steps.

Roger Shattuck. NYT. Nov. 9, 1975. pp. 1–2

BELLOW, SAUL (1915–   )

If [the Bellow hero] is a victimized figure, he is a victim of his own moral sense of right and wrong—his own accepted obligation to evaluate himself by standards that will inevitably find him lacking . . . Bellow's heroes suffer intensely and rehearse their agonies at operatic volume for all to hear. "I am to suffering what Gary is to smoke," says Henderson. "One of the world's biggest operations." But it would be a serious mistake to confuse this characteristic reaction of the Bellow hero with one of passive lamentation or self-pitying surrender. Even in his partly sincere and partly mock self-revilings, he is determined to believe that "human" means "accountable in spite of many weaknesses—at the last moment, tough enough to hold." And in final effect, none of Bellow's heroes actually resigns himself to his suffering. Painfully they climb again and again out of "the craters of the spirit," ridiculing their defeats with a merciless irony, resolved to be prepared with a stronger defense against the next assault that is sure to come.

Perhaps this aspect of Bellow's work has been the least appreciated by contemporary critics. Some have interpreted his thematic preoccupation with the sufferer as a device of compromise, a "making do," or accommodation—an argument which implies that Bellow is gratuitously surrendering the heroic ideal of a fully instinctual life to the expediency of flabby survival within the status quo. But this, it seems to me, is precisely to miss the moral point and to misread Bellow's deliberate irony. Trained in anthropology, Bellow is quite willing to regard the species *man* as merely one of the evolutionary products of nature and natural processes. But Bellow is determined to insist on the qualitative difference between *man* and the other sentient species that nature has produced.

Earl Rovit. *Saul Bellow* (Minnesota).
1967. pp. 12–3

It is a tribute to Bellow's art that he achieves profundity while fixing upon a few basic ideas. Good and evil, the nature of man, his response to love, death and the desire for power, are preoccupations in all the works, and by ringing changes on these classic themes in thoroughly modern contexts he provides a wondrous variety and a source of constant insight. Some readers, baffled by Bellow's astonishing fertility and by the idiosyncratic nature of his central characters, are disaffected by several aspects of his work. The novels are, all of them, essentially plotless, held together by "heroes" whose anxieties are inexplicable, ambiguous, or bizarre, and sometimes laced with zest and comic sensuality. All of the stories end with no sense of finality, as if each man's suffering represents a phase rather than a realization. His fiction thus resembles a juggling act to which more and more slices of experience are added with an almost compulsive virtuosity.

Abraham Bezanker. *YR*. Spring, 1969. p. 359

The last four novels of Saul Bellow are devoted to a single theme: the effort of a perplexed man to discover enough of himself and reality to continue living in a time of personal and public crisis. Introspection, or the nervous exercise of a contemporary consciousness, is the means of discovery for the disturbed hero and forms the substance of the novels. To supply a narrative ground for the intellectualization and verbalization of his introverted characters, Bellow uses the metaphor of the journey of the man of many troubles, Odysseus. Each of his heroes finds himself alienated from father, wife, and children and undertakes a journey of return in the course of which he experiences death and learns important philosophical lessons. . . . It is the development of different kinds of introspection and the astonishing variety of the journey devised for each new wanderer that is the measure of Bellow's genius and the constant delight of his readers.

Leonard Lutwack. Heroic Fiction (Southern
Illinois). 1971. pp. 88–9

This new emphasis on intensity as one of the basic components of the schlemiel-character in American fiction indicates [this character's] main point of departure from European sources. The simpleton of the earlier [European] works was a symbol of unbroken faith against almost universal skepticism and against fierce physical persecution. The American Jewish author is not concerned with faith-rootedness—if anyone is—nor with the survival of a God-centered community. His schlemiel is not even remotely symbolic of a people. He is an expression of heart, of intense, passionate feeling, in surroundings that stamp out individuality and equate emotion with unreason. The schlemiel is used as a cultural reaction to the prevailing Anglo-Saxon model of restraint in action, thought, and speech. What is Bellow's metaphor of Siva moving its many mouths and arms if not the Semitic stereotype of vulgar volubility? The Yiddish schlemiel was an expression of faith in the face of material disproofs. The American schlemiel declares his humanity by loving and suffering in defiance of the forces of depersonalization and the ethic of enlightened stoicism. . . .

The most Jewish of Bellow's heroes, his most typical schlemiel, and most entertaining humorist, is Moses Elkanah Herzog, who is provided with a far more detailed personal history and more substantial biography than such characters usually receive, even in the author's other works. It is only when reading the evocative descriptions of Herzog's childhood and the ample information on his professional and personal life that we realize, by contrast, how poorly documented are the lives of our other characters and how thinly their roots have been sketched.

Ruth R. Wisse. The Schlemiel as Modern Hero
(Chicago). 1971. pp. 82, 93

It is difficult to imagine where Bellow will go from here. The development that is clearly recognizable throughout his work concerns not only language and characterization but also the approach to the form of the novel. As the characters grow older, more mature, and more "human" —a term that means to Bellow an increasing awareness and appreciation of the qualities that enable the individual as well as mankind to "survive"—the language becomes more controlled, more concise, more elegant, with greater emphasis being placed on the subliminal emotional content of each single word. As is natural in this context, the joyfulness and exuberance, the undauntable love of life that characterized *The Adventures of Augie March* and *Henderson the Rain King*, gradually diminish.

This is also the result of the growing importance of ideas in Bellow's later work. Remembering, evaluating, imagining, and reinterpreting become the protagonists' main "business" in life, a development that clearly indicates Bellow's changing attitude toward the novel. Artistic self-expression has become of secondary importance compared to the unending stream-of-thought processes contained in *Herzog* and *Mr. Sammler's Planet*. These novels are not only the comprehensive records that "compulsive witnesses" of their own lives have taken down, they also represent Bellow's effort to turn the novel into a medium of inquiry.

Brigitte Scheer-Schäzler. Saul Bellow
(Ungar). 1972. p. 127

In a lecture given in London in 1971 Richard Poirier attacked Saul Bellow for being "unmodified by reality and unable to admit radical alienation." It is perhaps possible to see something of this rejection of reality in those sections on sex and youth from *Mr. Sammler's Planet*. In the novel not one young person has anything really lasting or positive to offer; they are all flawed for Mr. Sammler by their dirt, their smell, or their slogans. It is at least partly true that in his admiration for the old liberal Bloomsbury values (not so far, perhaps, from some radical ideals) personified in Artur Sammler "the old fashioned, sitting sage" Bellow is unconsciously withdrawing to a safer, more civilized and more reassuring age. There is no doubt that many young Americans do identify Bellow with a Jewish intellectual élite which is just as dedicated to sustaining social inequalities as, say, General Motors. The radical view —implied by Poirier—says that intellectuals like Bellow are cut off from what is going on around them with the consequence that their writing is more or less irrelevant. They are exercising in a void.

The danger in this extreme view of the writer's purpose—the kind of view that Sartre has come to hold—is that the novel must be a social tract keeping up with events of the times and not imaginatively leaping ahead. This can be just as stultifying as leaving important things out. And to ask the novelist to include everything radical groups regard as "significant" would be absurd. Even so, it does seem odd that in a novel that so carefully sets out to describe recent events Bellow makes no mention of the Vietnam War, something which has, by any standard, made an enormous difference to the way Americans feel about themselves.

D. P. M. Salter. CQ. Spring, 1972. p. 64

When all is said and done, Mailer offers us precious little in the way of "salvation." Bellow gives more. We detect in his work a texture and a mellowness lacking in Mailer. Bellow has a practiced sensitivity to the modern longing for non-being; he knows well how our modern idols have failed us one after the other and he knows better than Mailer what the self is up against in the banal and anomic circumstances of life. Revolution is not the solution; nor is hipsterism or Faustian pacts. These are yet further ways of denying limits (Bellow is much like Camus in his analysis of Romantic excess). "You could scarcely get people to long for what was possible," a character observes in *Mr. Sammler's Planet*. And in the same novel we find the affirmation that "the spirit knows that its growth is the real aim of existence." Bellow's characters mature. They come to an understanding of patience and sympathy and laughter.

Bernard Murchland. Com.
May 24, 1974. p. 292

It may be because Bellow cannot bring into single dramatic focus his optimism about man and his pessimism about the conditions of life that his characters so often seem schizophrenic and the endings of his novels disappointingly equivocal. His protagonists are men of goodwill and high hopes who make their way through a hellish wasteland in which they are forced to suffer every imaginable kind of humiliation and injustice. Yet at the end, in spite of everything, they are still seekers and believers. . . .

In *Humboldt's Gift* Bellow has still not found a way of successfully reconciling these contradictory attitudes and the two kinds of material in which they are expressed. But he does manage to cope with them more effectively than he has been able to do in any of his previous novels. The protagonist, Charles Citrine, confirms one's impression that Bellow's views of the nature of human existence are becoming increasingly mystical and may eventually find a formally religious framework. Citrine is a student of anthroposophy, a doctrine which maintains that through self-discipline cognitional experience of the spiritual world can be achieved, and his meditations on such a possibility become a significant yet un-obtrusive leitmotiv of the world. But the critical point is that Bellow treats them throughout as meditations only. They are not required to bear a major thematic weight as are the speculative materials in the earlier novels. Therefore, Bellow's inability to reconcile them with his secular materials does not become problematical, since Citrine merely retreats from time to time into his meditations and at best only holds out hope that they may eventually lead him to a perception of spiritual truth.

John W. Aldridge. *SR*. Sept. 6, 1975. p. 24

In *Humboldt's Gift*, Saul Bellow has written not only the best book of his career (save perhaps that lapidary novella *Seize the Day*) but one of the most vivid, funny, touching and brilliant novels to come along in years.

He has taken the enduring themes of his concern: the exhaustion of the Western mind and its received ideas . . . the difficulty of the ethical and imaginative life in America . . . the maniacal distractions among which people of good will and good minds must live . . . the Yeatsian paradox of aging and dying in the midst of heedless enthusiasm . . . and has orchestrated them in a wonderful, exuberant opera of a novel.

Daniel Stern. *Com*. Oct. 24, 1975. p. 502

● BERGER, THOMAS (1924–   )

[*Crazy in Berlin* is] a first novel of exceptional merit. . . . Indeed, I know of no book by an American that searches more earnestly the meaning of the Nazi convulsion and its aftermath in order to discover their wider applications. . . . Mr. Berger gives us a wealth of characteri-zation, but more of the basis of character read deeply and truly. . . . Behind this work, there is a fine intelligence; this is a book written from the vantage of maturity. The quality of the writing itself is varied. Mr. Berger has a sure sense of the ludicrous; seriousness lights up with mockery; ideas can take the shape of sensual images. Berlin itself, its cellars, streets, and ruins stand before us. If the movement of the book is slow, that, too, may become part of our pleasure in it. But sometimes the writing is unclear or, to put it more accurately, is congested with meaning. Nor has Mr. Berger always organized his materials to best effect; we are threatened with a surfeit of valuable matter. Still, this

book is in most ways a solid achievement, an original novel of unquestionable power.

Gene Baro. NYHT. Oct. 26, 1958. p. 12

Two novels [*Crazy in Berlin* and *Reinhart in Love*] hardly provide an
adequate basis for judgment on an author like Thomas Berger. Criticism
must make allowances for its own errors just as it must allow for the
unexpected turns in a writer's craft. But two novels also amount to a
kind of self-declaration. The declaration, I think, is of a double import:
it reveals something about Berger's singular talent, and it illuminates a
new trend of American fiction.

Berger's primary concern is the individual in a world of cunning
appearances and uncertified realities. Power and Fraud rule that world,
distorting appearances and realities, pressing man to the limits of his
sanity, and pressing on him the guilt-ridden role of victim or aggressor.
But threats also contain their own answer, and shields may be fashioned
of weapons. Man's response, therefore, is to adopt a stance of knowing
craziness, resilient simplicity, or defensive defenselessness. These are the
qualities Reinhart possesses. Nor is it an accident that his patron's day,
so Berger says, is April First, Fool's Day.

Ihab Hassan. Critique. 5, 2, 1962. pp. 14–5

However late or early in the day it may be for the Western novel,
Thomas Berger has just written a really noble one [*Little Big Man*],
something really new. . . . In about the same way that Faulkner delivers
the old South to the ken of a jaded but renewable imagination, Berger
delivers the West. He took on an apparently impossible task and made
the dead bones live, not by stringing them together and jerking the
strings to make them dance, but by showing how we dream "anonymously and communally" as Mann once put it, finding, by a prophetic
leap, the common ingredients our regressive dream of the West shared
with the dreams of those vanished Indians and a boy kidnapped from a
wagon train. And oh, that Wild West dream is funny, magically and
marvelously funny as Berger recreates it, like an embarrassment and a
rapture we never knew quite how to confess.

R. V. Cassill. BW. Oct. 25, 1964. p. 2

Sometimes . . . the new Western anti-heroes shrink in size until they
move through the vastness of the West more like the dwarfed Julius
Rodman of Edgar Allan Poe than any movie version of the Cowboy
Hero. . . . Thomas Berger's Little Big Man is precisely what his name
declares: a shrimp with sharp wits and an enormous spirit—though in a
showdown he prefers to depend more on those wits than that spirit, as,

for instance, in encounters with the sort of large, icy killer he knows he cannot outdraw. . . . Indeed, all of the "historical" characters in *Little Big Man* are undercut and debunked by a kind of merciless geniality that is likely to mislead the unwary reader about the real nature of the novel.

One reviewer, for example, quite inappropriately described *Little Big Man*, just after it appeared, as "exciting, violent, and ribald . . . ranks with *The Big Sky* and *The Oxbow Incident*." But it has neither the moral earnestness of the latter nor the easy realism of the former, only a desire to demonstrate how, for all its pathos and danger, the West was and remains essentially *funny*. . . . Berger is not so brutal and extreme in this regard, so totally nihilistic as David Markson, or even John Barth; but he, too, cannot resist drawing almost anything he happens to know into the circle of his ridicule.

Leslie A. Fiedler. *The Return of the Vanishing American* (Stein and Day). 1968. pp. 160–1

Berger's *Killing Time* is (need I say it?) a picaresque, bleakly comic account of the world's malevolent absurdity, with a Holy Fool at the centre, much bizarre violence and sex, philosophic dialogues, and a style that is mannered and glittering. . . .

The effects Mr. Berger achieves are lurid, yet economical and intelligent. His situations are presented in a bright, harsh light, with a related blackness that you can feel. His tone is sardonic and reflective, aloof, yet without any of the onanistic snickerings of a James Purdy. His characters are all too subtly, even elaborately analysed to be simple grotesques. And yet the effect of the whole book is of a distant and somewhat cerebral brilliance. Our interest is in texture and the to-and-fro of argument rather than in a felt predicament. Even the violence and the misery are appreciated almost as exciting colours, not as human experiences. And the persons and events are so extreme, so spasmodic, that we cease to take even the ideas—the Quest for Being—very seriously. So much novelty and so much inconclusive cleverness defeat their purpose of making us question our lives, and come close to providing a very superior kind of science fiction.

Kenneth Graham. *List.* May 16, 1968.
pp. 639–40

Little Big Man is a great novel because it portrays western "society" in the nineteenth century as it really was—violent, yes, but also absurd, melodramatic, incongruous. Its author never sacrifices his imagination to realism. At the same time it is scrupulously accurate as to places, dates and events, the results of the "60 or 70 accounts of Western reality" which Berger says he read "to reinforce my feeling for the myth." It is also "the Western to end all Westerns" which Berger intended it to be, because it splendorizes the West with love and imagination. Far from discarding any of the choice western properties, Berger has turned them inside out, revealing one by one the possibilities of a western literary art.

Jay Gurian. *WAL*. Winter, 1969. p. 296

Vital Parts confirms Berger's rank as a major American novelist, one whose stylistic fecundity, psychological insight, and social knowledge are seemingly inexhaustible. Reinhart continues to move, clownlike, through his familiar world of "asymmetrical impulses, like a laughter hopelessly mad, hopelessly free," large in physique, generosity, honesty, gullibility, optimism, and capacity for enduring psychosocial wounds. . . .

A comic allegorist of the worthwhile Middle American, skillfully wielding a colloquial diction and rhythm of extraordinary expressiveness, Thomas Berger is one of the most successful satiric observers of the ebb and flow of American life after World War II. His prolificacy promises a continued development of the tragicomic mode of vision, something American literature badly needs to compensate for the over-extended silence of such formerly active writers as Ralph Ellison, Joseph Heller, and Thomas Pynchon.

Brom Weber. *SR*. March 21, 1970. p. 42

In the shifting landscape of Thomas Berger, man is constant, that is to say, hopelessly the prisoner of himself and his pathetically limited vision. All ideology, all hope of genuine change is false since, alas, "The 'public' is a collection of individuals though politicians pretend otherwise." That is the heart of his irony, and that is why his comedy is too bitter for general popularity, though not, in my opinion, too bitter to be called great (despite occasional lapses into archness, occasional strain in the purely slapstick passages). Under the cold, correct surface of his prose—which, employed to render absurdity, creates the fundamental tension of his work—lies one of the most genuinely radical sensibilities now writing novels in this country. Next to the devastation he wreaks in his quiet way, a public anarchist like Reinhart's fellow Cincinnatian, Jerry Rubin, seems pipsqueak indeed. *He* thinks there is hope; Carlo Reinhart and Thomas Berger know there is only the possibility of replacing present delusions with new ones.

Richard Schickel. *Cmty*. July, 1970. p. 80

Berger's settings and characters in all his novels are plausible rather than apocalyptic. His satire refuses to make an alliance between reader and author against an oppressive, ugly "them." Paul Krassner once wrote that "the ultimate object of satire is its own audience," and Berger's integrity arranges that no reader—male chauvinist, militant feminist or in between—can emerge from *Regiment of Women* unscathed. All of Berger's main characters—Georgie Cornell here, Jack Crabb in *Little Big Man*, Carlo Reinhart in *Crazy in Berlin, Reinhart in Love* and *Vital Parts*—are moved more by circumstances than by some passionate belief or lack of belief. Berger's clearest outrage is reserved for anyone who presumes to sit in moral judgment on another, and his central characters are all slammed about by beings more certain than they about the location of truth. . . .

Berger's own style, with its tendency to absorb the speech rhythms of his characters and its unwillingness to stand apart from them, is especially suited for such themes. Since *Little Big Man*, especially, he has concentrated on exploring the possibilities and revealing the secrets of everyday language with a deep wit and feeling that transforms our awareness of the language we really use much more than does the flamboyance of a writer bent on asserting his personal style. *Killing Time* may be Berger's most brilliant effort to engage in this truly poetic task of renovating the language we speak. But *Regiment of Women* is a brilliant flame from the same sources of energy.

Leo Braudy. NYT. May 13, 1973. pp. 6–7

Thomas Berger understands one of the cardinal principles of silent-film comedy, the excruciating approach to an anticipated collision averted by a hair-breadth swerve at the last moment into a fresh kettle of fish. His timing and control are impeccable.

Sneaky People is a book full of secrets and surprises. . . . Each melodramatic twist is short-circuited by an unlooked-for response. . . . Over all this shines the sun of a dusty Midwestern city at the end of the Depression; daily life is lovingly remembered and recreated in exact detail. On a first reading, *Sneaky People* is exhilaratingly bawdy and tricky. A second reading arouses a different feeling: this is Thomas Berger's tenderest, most touching work.

Walter Clemons. Nwk. April 28, 1975. p. 79

BERRYMAN, JOHN (1914–1972)

Despite career-long unevenness in the quality of his work, John Berryman has become a major American poet, has achieved a permanency that places him in a group with Theodore Roethke and Randall Jarrell. Berryman, it seems to me, has taken on the whole modern world and has come to poetic terms with it. At the same time he has taken on himself, and has come to poetic terms with that too. He has seen the wreck of the modern world (or, better, the modern world insofar as it is a wreck) and the wreck of his personal self in that world. He is not a pessimist but has, rather, what we would have to call a tragic view of human life—with good reason for holding it. Yet, not surprisingly, the tragic view finds its complement in a comic view, his wild and so often devastatingly effective sense of humor. He is preeminently a poet of suffering and laughter.

William J. Martz. John Berryman
(Minnesota). 1969. p. 5

The minstrel show was both a genuine kind of folk art and popular entertainment in nineteenth-century America, and a crowning symbol of the oppression of the Negro because it reduced him to the role of comic sycophant. Berryman's use of it is effective because it brings up automatically both the American past and contemporary issues of race, civil rights, and the like; perhaps more important, it also represents the poet as exploited entertainer (though with multiple ironies, romantic and other), making jokes out of his gruesome and harrowing experiences.

The *Dream Songs* are very varied and attractive, often dramatic, with much humor and a vivid awareness of the surfaces (as well as the depths) of contemporary life. There is a "Lay of Ike" and a "Strut for Roethke" and other satiric and nostalgic ones; and there are confessional poems about breakdowns, fears of nuclear war, and the like. . . . But, as the title confesses, there is no unifying structure. In most of them, the method is essentially the same as that of *Homage to Mistress Bradstreet*, a double point of view in which the poet is partially identified with the dramatic character in the past but also retains his focus on the present. But while with *Homage to Mistress Bradstreet* there was the external narrative of Anne Bradstreet's life to serve as framework, with built-in aesthetic and larger relevances in the facts of her being the first American poet and a Puritan, there are no such points of reference in *The Dream Songs*.

Monroe K. Spears. Dionysus and the City
(Oxford—N.Y.). 1970. pp. 248–9

I always thought his earlier poems, with their surface jumpiness, had no metric at all, or scarcely any; they move, not with the basic, consistent cadence of essential poetry but only with their own meretricious push and thrust of hyperbolic and unexpected phrasing. They move, stiltlike, on Berryman's peculiar rhetoric. Now in the new poems [*Love & Fame*], where the language is simpler, I see my feeling confirmed, for with a modified rhetoric the lack of meter is more than ever obvious. . . .

As for diction, we have on the one hand Berryman's well-known colloquial cuteness . . . and on the other his deliberate archaisms, inversions, the use of fusty words like "moot" and "plaint." Archness, what we used to call the sophomoric: in parts of *The Dream Songs* he almost brought it to a pitch intense enough to make an honest effect. . . . Yet must "fresh idiom" mean "twisted and posed"? And does language ever add to "available reality"? We know the danger of that old fatuity; and doubly dangerous it was for Berryman, I think, because it led him, in its arrogance and his own, to infer, by transversion or contraction or mere muleheadedness, that *poetry* as well as verse might be manufactured if only one could invent a fresh idiom in language twisted and posed. This is an oversimplification, more would need to be said in any comprehensive discussion of Berryman's work, but it is still very close to the heart of the matter; and the proof, I believe, lies on every page of his books.

The time has come, surely, to say that Berryman's poetry is usually interesting and sometimes witty but almost never moving, and that in spite of its scope and magnitude it lacks the importance that has been ascribed to it in recent years by many critics, editors and readers.

Hayden Carruth. Nation. Nov. 2,
1970. pp. 437–8

Delusions, Etc. was already in proof when John Berryman jumped off a bridge in Minneapolis onto the frozen Mississippi last January. So there is no question of its being a ragbag of uncollected work hastily gathered up as a memorial. The book is as he wanted it, the order of its poems and the emotional emphasis all his. Which seems to point to the fact that, up to the end, he was fighting against the way of dying he finally chose. For the emphasis is on the faith he had regained after 43 years away from the Roman Catholic Church. So *Delusions, Etc.* begins and ends on a religious note, as though to defend himself against his own depression.

In all truth, it is not the religious note of a genuinely religious man. Berryman's poems to God are his least convincing performances: nervous, insubstantial, mannered to a degree and intensely argumentative. It is as though he had continually to reassure himself of his belief, or to reassure the Deity if He happened to be listening. There is, of course, a distinguished tradition for this kind of verse: John Donne and Hopkins, Berryman's great hero, were continually arguing with God in the tone of voice of men who knew that there was a lot to be said on both sides. But

Berryman had a quirkier sensibility, less rigorous and logical than associative, diffuse, at times a bit scatterbrained. . . .

As the middle sections of *Delusions, Etc.* show, his real gift was
different, less armored, less comforting and emerging only slowly in his
maturity. Essentially, it was a gift for grief. He had always been a poet of
profound unease, touchy and irritable, as if his nerve ends were too
close to the surface.

A. Alvarez. NYT. June 25, 1972. p. 1

No other poem in the twentieth century possesses the scope, the complexity, the grief and joy of life, in quite the marvelous and meaningful
way that Berryman's *Dream Songs* does.

For all its wonder, *The Dream Songs* took its toll on Berryman.
Not only was the composition of it long and painful, but also its completion signaled for him, I think, the end of his most ambitious poetic work.
There was no way at fifty-four that he would ever write another long
poem, and despite the fact that he published two collections of poems
after *The Dream Songs*—*Love & Fame* (1970) and the recent, posthumous *Delusions, Etc.*—he was, at his death in January 1972, engaged in
writing a novel, collecting a group of his literary essays for publication,
and preparing to launch into his long-in-progress critical biography of
Shakespeare—all worthy literary endeavors yet none requiring the talents of the poet.

If *Love & Fame* and *Delusions, Etc.* do not add significantly to
Berryman's stature as a poet, they do provide some excellent individual
lyrics and, more importantly, further perspectives on the themes Berryman developed in his major works.

Larry Vonalt. Parnassus. Fall–Winter,
1972. p. 182

[Berryman] was a full professor now, and a celebrity. *Life* interviewed
him. The *Life* photographer took 10,000 shots of him in Dublin. But
John's human setting was oddly thin. He had, instead of a society, the
ruined drunken poet's God to whom he prayed over his shoulder. Out of
affection and goodwill he made gestures of normalcy. He was a husband, a citizen, father, a householder, he went on the wagon, he fell off,
he joined A.A. He knocked himself out to be like everybody else—he
liked, he loved, he cared, but he was aware that there was something
peculiarly comical in all this. And at last it must have seemed that he
had used up all his resources. Faith against despair, love versus nihilism
had been the themes of his struggles and his poems. What he needed for
his art had been supplied by his own person, by his mind, his wit. He
drew it out of his vital organs, out of his very skin. At last there was no

more. Reinforcements failed to arrive. Forces were not joined. The cycle of resolution, reform and relapse had become a bad joke which could not continue.

Saul Bellow. Foreword to *Recovery* by John
Berryman (Farrar). 1973. p. xiv

There was nothing to keep Berryman from going on with *The Dream Songs*. Two appeared in his posthumous volume; and a thousand more might have come out in his lifetime. Henry might have grown into a public figure like Mr. Dooley, airing his moods and opinions from day to day before an audience that had learnt what to expect. In the way of general ideas and moral insights Berryman has little that is fresh to offer. Neither is he a phrase-maker, nor a magician with words. It is emblematic that a childhood disease should have weakened his hearing, because his ear for rhythm is undistinguished. For all his talent and learning, Berryman could not come near the intellectual style of Auden or the middle-aged Lowell. Once he had circulated the most sensational facts of his private life, his richest treasure was the ironic drama of Henry's diary.

So it strikes one as a hero's mistake that Berryman should have turned his back on this invention and chosen a simpler exploitation of auto-analysis for his last two books. . . .

The coherence of the last books cannot replace the pleasures of *The Dream Songs*: their deliberate humour and indirection; viewpoints that never stand still; a tone that hops from aspiration to bathos. In the last poems, the strongest humour seems unintentional; it would be cruel to deal seriously with their serious argument; their inarticulateness is painfully artless. Having discovered that his sensibility could bewitch us, Berryman made the error of growing solemn about it; and the reader's attention must move back from the poet's attitude to his mind.

TLS. Feb. 23, 1973. p. 195

BIERCE, AMBROSE (1842–1914?)

Bierce's tales of war are not in the least realistic; they are, as he doubtless intended them to be, incredible events occurring in credible surroundings. Triggered like traps, they abound in coincidences and are as contemptuous of the "probable" as any of Poe's most bizarre experiments. Bierce's soldiers move in a trance through a prefigured universe. Father and son, brother and brother, husband and wife, collide in accidental encounters. The playthings of some Power, they follow a course "decreed from the beginning of time." Ill-matched against the outside forces assailing them, they are also victimized by atavistic ones. Bierce's uncomplicated men-at-arms, suddenly commandeered by compulsive fear or wounded by shame, destroy themselves.

Yet each of Bierce's preposterous tales is framed in fact and touched with what Poe called the "potent magic of verisimilitude." Transitions from reality to surreality seem believable not only because the War was filled with romance and implausible episodes but also because of the writer's intense scrutiny of war itself. The issues of the War no longer concerned him by the time he came to write his soldier stories. They had practically disappeared in the wake of history. But the physical and psychological consequences of constant exposure to suffering and death, the way men behaved in the stress of battle—these matters powerfully worked his imagination, for the War was only meaningful to Bierce as a personal experience. If war in general became his parable of pitifully accoutered man attacked by heavily armored natural forces, the Civil War dramatized his private obsessions.

Daniel Aaron. *The Unwritten War*
(Knopf). 1973. p. 184

It was not simply that [Bierce] had learned to despise social ideals of any sort, and to have "a conscience uncorrupted by religion, a judgment undimmed by politics and patriotism, a heart untainted by friendships and sentiments unsoured by animosities." More than this, the world, as he perceived it, took on a threatening aspect; like the musket ball, it attacked his head, his reason. The terrain of reality which he plotted— he was a topographic officer—he saw filled with traps. Where others saw a handsome prospect, he saw danger lurking and always assumed that beneath pleasing appearances was a threatening reality. He was convinced, in short, that reality was delusory. By emphasizing mind he attempted to preserve mind, always threatened by physical obliteration or mental deception; he defended the mind, and in doing so, took as his major theme the *growth of reflection*, the compulsion to scrutinize and observe.

This might have been a tragic theme, for reflection leads to a deeper and deeper penetration of delusion and at last to the conviction that all is delusion—that, ultimately, as Bierce said in a late letter, "nothing matters." Reality, Bierce did conclude in *The Devil's Dictionary*, was "the dream of a mad philosopher," the logical product of irrational minds, and therefore absurd—"the nucleus of a vacuum." But he treated this conviction comically, and employed humor to expose the absurdities of his deluded contemporaries and the institutions delusions created and perpetuated. In short, he preserved his own mind by ridiculing the crazed world that questioned his sense and sensibility.

Jay Martin in The Comic Imagination in
American Literature, edited by Louis D.
Rubin, Jr. (Rutgers). 1973. p. 196

BISHOP, ELIZABETH (1911–   )

[Bishop's] poems often resemble short stories both in the way that she weds action to visual detail, and in the way she makes characters emerge clearly from very few details. She creates people out of scraps of their conversation, pointing it affectionately and ironically with her rhythms. . .

These forty-four poems [*Selected Poems*] show how much she has developed in the twenty-five years they cover. The lines tend to get shorter as she becomes more economical with her adjectives and in "At the Fishhouses" she starts moving out from the immediate experience—an encounter with an old fisherman—to more general questions. . . .

In the later poems, her canvases get bigger and the interrelationships between characters and their physical environments subtler. In the Mexican poems, the sound is no more resonant than before, but the meaning is. Her analyses go deeper and she comes more to evaluate experiences at the moment of describing them, sometimes, as in "Questions of Travel" by the simple expedient of asking what she'd have missed if she hadn't had them.

Ronald Hayman. Encounter. July, 1968. p. 71

The poems in *Questions of Travel*, and some of the new poems first printed in *The Complete Poems* are so clear they seem spoken by someone fresh from dreams, just awake. Many of them describe a country where the truth is almost as strange as dreams and to which the forms of legend and ballad ("The Riverman"; "The Burglar of Babylon") seem entirely appropriate. Humble figures are described in an understated, humorous fashion, and yet take on a mythical air, like the tenant Manuelzinho or the seamstress who grows to be like one of the Fates, Clotho nourished in their midst. But nothing is overdone or beyond the daily exercise of composing oneself. Here, I think, is the point at which Miss Bishop's poems are most provocative. Finally their technique is the opposite of the poetic journal, Lowell's latest urgent attempts at registering character in verse. Registering, transmitting, is the *Notebook*'s strongest effect, these poems which end in blazing nightmares, clear vision frayed by underground warnings. Miss Bishop's instinct—from which so much of the modern poetic interest in character derives—is something else: without ever abandoning the feelings of the moment, continually aware, constantly using verse to master the flood of the particular, she writes poetry to compose rather than expose the self. Doing that, her *Complete Poems* makes us alive again to what poetic *composition* is—both something private and something shared.

David Kalstone. PR. No. 2, 1970. p. 315

When Elizabeth Bishop wished to explain her fondness for George Herbert, she praised his "absolute naturalness of tone" and said some of his poems were "almost surrealistic." She might easily have been describing her own effect. "Naturalness" suggests honesty, lack of artifice. Surrealism suggests fantasy, mystery, witty illusions. The terms are not easy to blend. Yet a combination of natural manner and mysterious matter is the brilliant feature of Miss Bishop's work.

The form her mixture takes is not the traditional retailing of wonders as truths or of the commonplace as wonderful but rather an absorbed loitering in the marches between dream and experience. One could make a book of Miss Bishop's poems about sleeping, dreaming, and early-morning waking. As complements to these there are descriptions of landscapes or objects that become dreamlike as the poet watches them. Finally, there are portraits of people who seem to live in a dream. Few of Miss Bishop's best poems fall outside these classes; and at bottom the poems reveal more humour than satire, more sympathy than fear. The poet masters the mystery by contemplating it.

TLS. Jan. 22, 1971. p. 92

All the way through the volume [*The Complete Poems*] the purpose appears to be one of rendering what [Elizabeth Bishop] sees (occasionally, what she imagines) as accurately as possible. The view, put more plainly though in more complex a manner in the later poems, is of men and all other creatures suspended, incomplete and without complete comprehension, among the beauties and perils of this particular world. . . . Miss Bishop is perhaps willing to circumscribe the limits of our comprehension more straitly than many would like; beyond the immediately visible circumstances, of which she is very sure, the mystery closes in. She has made it her business, though, to make poems out of what does come clear, out of these isolated patches of understanding and vision.

H. T. Kirby-Smith. SwR.
Summer, 1972. pp. 484–5

BLACKMUR, RICHARD (1904–1965)

To identify the tradition that links Blackmur with [Henry] James and [Henry] Adams one could do worse than adopt the term Blackmur himself uses when discussing the 1920s—"bourgeois humanism." This may suggest the New Humanists but Blackmur's struggle with modern literature was not merely polemical like theirs which left them free to dismiss or condemn it. Rather, since he had himself suffered the cultural crises that produced it, he understood how the "malicious knowledges" of the time, notably psychology and anthropology, had undermined man's faith in his rationality, had delivered him over to the "great grasp of unreason," and had set him to inventing the "techniques of trouble." Yet he believed that the great modern writers (particularly Joyce, Eliot, Mann, Yeats, and Gide) managed to create out of the remnants of the humanist tradition an "irregular metaphysics" which secured a measure of control over the irrational forces which had been unleashed.

One of the two major centers of formative power in Blackmur's thinking about America was, then, the literature of the twenties. This book [A Primer of Ignorance] shows that the other was his encounter with foreign, mainly European, culture concretized through his sojourns abroad in the 1950s. These provided the finishing touch to his already wide self-education, not changing his fundamental bourgeois humanism, but only "improving" it. What he found when he began to contemplate America in the presence of European culture can be exemplified in the comparison he draws in "The Swan in Zurich" between the New York City Ballet and the Ballet of Sadler's Wells and other European companies: the American troupe's "excessive commitment to mere technique" in contrast to the technical imperfections but greater human warmth of the European performances. This discovery of American devotion to pragmatic abstractions at the cost of the more personalized values and greater cultural density of Europe strikingly corroborates the earlier testimonals of Hawthorne, James, and Adams.

Ernest Sandeen. *Poetry.* Aug., 1968. pp. 357–8

• BLY, ROBERT (1926–   )

Robert Bly is one of the leading figures today in a revolt against rhetoric —a rebellion that is a taking up of the Imagist revolution betrayed, a reassertion of much of the good sense Pound brought to poetry—but also a movement which has in it much that is perfectly new. The new is found in a pure form in the work of Robert Bly and of his friend James Wright; it is not an easy aesthetic to describe; it can be found only in a response to their poems. . . .

[Bly's] is a poetry, I decided at last, that returns the reader to its subjects, a poetry of excitement primarily about a certain kind of life and vision to which the poem directs attention rather than stealing attention from that experience. Hence, this work is profoundly dependent upon the nature of reality—it reflects a choice of subjects and a judgment on them as experiences. Although all poets take into themselves parts of the exterior world and put them back in what is, to say the least, a rearrangement, Bly is committed more totally than most poets to their subjects for two reasons. The choice of his images, the excitements, the celebrant realities, is a mannered or narrowed one; and the intensity of that choice is such that it is opinionated—it expresses a judgment about what life and poetry should be. If, then, the poet should be one who rejoices at solitude, nature, the sullen beauty of the provinces and of our history, then as advocate of that vision he is not and cannot be the poet who celebrates sickness, glamorizes Miltown, smog and hypochondria. For Bly—and in this respect he is a visionary—the words of poems are real—they *are* expressways or ditches, cornrows or streetlamps, bathtubs or mailboxes; a poem is a chosen world.

David Ray. *Epoch*. Winter, 1963. p. 186

Robert Bly's first collection, *Silence in the Snowy Fields,* impresses because of its purity of tone and precision of diction. It is not until we begin to feel that Mr. Bly could do more, when the monotonous simplicity of many of the poems starts to pall and takes on a programmatic character (after all he edits a polemical magazine, *The Sixties*), that we become dissatisfied. This artful diction is heavily indebted to early Stevens . . . but we miss the cunning backdrop that the simpler poems of *Harmonium* surely have. . . . Bly's characteristic development is to begin a poem with a simple narrative or descriptive *donnée* and then proceed through modulations more or less subtle, to an overwhelmed, even apocalyptic end.

D. J. Hughes. *Nation*. Jan. 5, 1963. p. 17

Though Mr. Bly often takes his themes from the land, they are almost as often in fruitful tension with an imagery of seas and ships. This is no casual rustic versifier but a poet who reaches from his midwestern center to a sophisticated circumference of interest and concern. . . . Sometimes his effects are strained. . . . Seeking simplicity, he protests too much when in a statement on his work he says, "If there is any poetry in the poems, it is in the white spaces between the stanzas." He is better at evocative surfaces than ambiguous depths.

Frederick Nordell. *CSM.* Jan. 23, 1963. p. 9

[Bly] is a poet of Western space, solitude, and silence. He writes poems about driving a car through Ohio, hunting pheasants, watering a horse, getting up early in the morning, and watching Minnesota cornfields, lakes, and woods under the siege of rain, snow, and sun. His distinction in treating these subjects lies in the freshness of his "deep images," which invest the scene he describes with an intense subjectivity and a feeling of the irremediable loneliness of man, who can never make contact with the things of the world. . . .

It is evident that Robert Bly's theory and practice cohere. His poetic voice is clear, quiet, and appealing, and it has the resonance that only powerful pressures at great depths can provide.

Stephen Stepanchev. *American Poetry since 1945* (Harper). 1965. pp. 185–7

Mr. Bly's poems . . . divide into poems of the inner and the outer. He does not deal with the relationship of one to the other, or not very often; usually, he writes of each separately and in opposite tones. His poems about present-day America, especially its political life, tend to be harsh and dissonant, and their sadness has a bitterly sharp edge, except for those dealing directly with the inhumanity of the Vietnam war, which are informed by deep compassion. The poems about the inner world, on the other hand, are slow-moving and quietly, intently joyful; they do not wish to come to grips with experience, but rather to let it flow by, to see it without forcing it. Mr. Bly is trying to free his diction of all rhetorical trappings, whether they be of the long-established or the current orthodoxies, in order to write simply, to render "the light around the body," the *feeling* of the experiences unencumbered by any literal setting. The approach is essentially mystical.

Lisel Mueller. *Shenandoah.* Spring, 1968. p. 70

The Light around the Body is one of the most significant American volumes to be published in years. Maybe literary America is waking up. Maybe it has learned that "inwardness" is not necessarily looking at one's navel, listening to "the way they ring the bells in Bedlam" à la Sexton or tortuously describing the abnormalities of one's aunt or father. The seemingly uncontrollable malignant forces around us do indeed lead us to look inward, but it is at the least sentimental and at the most destructive of the creative self to allow that inward eye complete authority. . . .

There are many poems in the book with obvious and open political content. Such poems as "Those Being Eaten by America" . . . "Smothered by the World," or such poems with specific references to recent and dubious episodes in American history as "Sleet Storm on the Merritt Parkway," "The Great Society," and the whole third section of the book with its poems on the Vietnam war—such poems are not mere propaganda poems, poems like those written freely in the 30's. They are not merely doctrinal. Although they are social protest poetry, they are not simplistic and doctrinaire. They are deeply poetic. They fulfill the needs of art, not those of politics. These poems, it must be remembered, are being written after the symbolists, the post-symbolists, written at a time in all the arts when the chief subject matter is art itself. The aesthetic emphasis is apparent here too, but it is an emphasis not on a sterile impersonality; not on a narrow formalism, or a fetishist autonomy of the work of art; not on disengagement, but on a reality stemming from a concerned, emotional self, inward and released, and from an outward self, yearning for a "glimpse of what we cannot see,/Our enemies, the soldiers and the poor."

Harriet Zinnes. PrS. Summer,
1968. pp. 176, 178

Bly's poems do not wear thin. Our inner lives speak in them, speak out from the silence and solitude of the American midwest. And there is a profound correspondence between "the man inside the body" ("Silence") and the oceans of air and water and land through which he moves. A car is a "solitude covered with iron" ("Driving toward the Lac Qui Parle River") and so is the man moving inside his struts of flesh and bone. For years I felt that Bly's poetry pointed at a mysterious and dissatisfying nothingness that was a non-subject. But he has one subject that speaks out from the spaces between lines, stanzas, and poems and unites them: The Self.

William Heyen. FPt. Fall–Winter,
1969. pp. 43–4

Bly . . . has been in the forefront of the politicalization of contemporary American poetry, and his objectives and his zeal may well have our full sympathy. On the other hand, the apolitical tradition of American poetry since the 1930's has proved very hard to break through. Political ideology and political action have shown a habit of losing the excitement of political oratory in the tight, economic medium of poetry; the effect is often one of simple-mindedness. . . .

Considering the odds Bly is facing, his performance is admirable. . . .

The Light around the Body marks an advance over *Silence in the Snowy Fields*. The advance is perhaps most economically described as a success of subject-matter. There is an attractive and contagious commitment about these poems which occasionally gives rise to a grim, grotesque humor which was absent from the earlier poems. . . .

The best of Bly's poems . . . achieve an original expression of his personal gloom and his sorrow for a world which "will soon break up into small colonies of the saved."

G. A. M. Janssens. English Studies.
April, 1970. pp. 128–31

For those who recognize that it is nations and not individuals that make war, Robert Bly's new book may be the best examination of our motives during the debacle in Vietnam. *Sleepers Joining Hands* looks at the dominion of chaos and death over recent American life and tries to discern its whole meaning, as if at last we have got far enough into it or beyond it to understand what happened, and as if we will not be devastated again by any more surprises. . . .

He can speak quietly of terrible things in a way that produces genuine chills. . . .

The spectacle of power is beautiful, and Bly can illustrate by the ominous unleashing of it that man's frail moral nature is inadequate for the enormous consequences of his acts. Bly can show, calmly, literally, how we writhe to defend our minds against this tragic knowledge, rationalizing, denying and generalizing our sins until viciousness appears demanded of us and we drive ourselves toward insanity.

David Cavitch. NYT. Feb. 18, 1973. pp. 2–3

Bly is . . . the mystic of evolution, the poet of "the other world" always contained in present reality but now about to burst forth in a period of destruction and transformation. Bly's poetry of the transformation of man follows logically from his early poetry of individual and private transcendence. Repeatedly, *Silence in the Snowy Fields* announces an "awakening" that comes paradoxically in sleep, in darkness, in death, an awakening depicted in surrealist images as compelling as they are mysterious, evasive. Bly's sense of mystical transformation is not really completely articulated until, primarily in the 1967 collection, *The Light around the Body*, it achieves an apocalyptic dimension, the awakening no longer individual or private, but part of the spiritual evolution of the race.

This general awakening, like the analogous experience of the isolated mystic, comes in the long dark night of a dying civilization. The poems of ecstatic prophecy in *The Light around the Body* achieve much of their force by juxtaposition with the poems of political despair which dominate the collection. Constantly and convincingly Bly suggests that the psychological impact of Vietnam on America is as destructive as the physical presence of America in Vietnam. . . .

But the confluence of physical and psychological or spiritual in Bly is most striking when he depicts the paradoxically evolutionary aspects of apocalypse, apocalypse now considered not as end but as process.

Anthony Libby. IowaR. Spring,
1973. pp. 112–3

The late 20th century converges on Robert Bly from every side. In *Sleepers Joining Hands*, there is a seething cauldron of ecological devastation, genocide in Vietnam, Consciousness III, the long shadow of the Indian wars, the changing roles of the sexes. He is peculiarly the seer both of the present moment and the possible future.

In a few lines he can catch the essence of vast migrations and enormities. . . .

Alive and terrifying as this poetic vision is, in some ways it is surpassed by the long prose section which adduces vast amounts of anthropological evidence to prove that all societies were originally matriarchal, and that the Great Mother (including the castrating type, the Teeth Mother) is reemerging into the consciousness of Western man after being suppressed for millennia.

Chad Walsh. Book World. April 1, 1973. p. 13

BOGAN, LOUISE (1897–1970)

Where Anne Sexton's poems turn always inward toward the inescapability of the event, toward that hell which is hell because it has no belief in a location other than itself, Miss Bogan's vision is first of the thing, and then outwards; if we are truly responsive, the thing teaches us. The method that teaching takes is a greater understanding and a greater discrimination among the possibilities afforded us by language: as one by one the evasions are recognized and discarded, we may hopefully become more aware of what we can suppose to be permanently true.

I believe Miss Bogan does, often, achieve such permanence. The nature of her decisions and of her exclusions takes her a little way outside clock time, the perennial minutes and their different forms. No more than the convinced hard lyric can she be fashionable or sentimental, choosing the easier moment over the more demanding one. But it is the rigor of that choice that permits finally an upwelling of resonances.

William Dickey. *HdR*. Summer, 1969. pp. 366, 368

Miss Bogan is one of our finest poets. She has written twenty or twenty-five poems that are unforgettable; they may be the best of their kind in American literature. And what we get from them, I think, aside from our delight, is the recognition of her basic poetic wisdom. She has not resisted her temptations, for she has seen that resistance can produce only poems which are crafty and correct but rarely interesting. Instead she has yielded; she has taken her temptations as they came, and has outsmarted them. Let the poem be conventional, public, and occasional, since that is the mask one must wear—so she might have spoken—but let each poem reveal just enough of a private inner violence to make the surface move without breaking. A passionate austerity, a subtle balance; and only perfect poetic attention, far beyond technique, could attain it.

Hayden Carruth. *Poetry*. Aug., 1969. p. 330

Louise Bogan is a poet who generates affectionate approval. Somewhat the same as for Caroline Gordon among the novelists, the feeling pervades that Miss Bogan never received the recognition due her work; and those who write about her verse go extra weight to correct the inbalance. . . .

A Poet's Alphabet is a delight to read. The arrangement takes us from Auden to Yeats, from American Literature to the Yale Series of Younger Poets. The dates of composition take us from 1923 to 1969, the year before Miss Bogan's death in February, 1970. The chief experience one undergoes in *A Poet's Alphabet* is admiration for Miss Bogan's generosity, which however is bestowed never at the expense of truth. Miss Bogan finds the strengths of her writers and emphasizes these in deft, bright, compact, and perceptive analyses.

Harry Morris. *SwR*. Autumn, 1972. p. 627

To write as a woman of things that concern woman would have meant to me [as a young writer] soft prose, fine writing and poetical musings by three-named lady writers. I intended to avoid all of it. But Louise Bogan suggested something deeper: a lack of options as part of the condition of being a woman, a narrow life chosen by women because they were unwilling, if not unable, to take risk. And yet wasn't there something of a risk in the act of being the person who wrote the poem? . . .

For these are the cries of a woman—cries against the turning of luck or of bad timing, and they speak of the ability to face the mirror or the bottle, of the courage to go to the "mad-house" (as she called it in a letter to Theodore Roethke) when life went down on her and she could not pull herself up alone any more. There is a loss implied in these poems for all women who are alone and aging; that final loss when there is no one to turn to again at night in bed under the covers, when there is no one to hold you against the dark.

Nancy Milford. NYT. Dec. 16, 1973. p. 1

BOWLES, PAUL (1910–   )

Reading *The Time of Friendship,* Paul Bowles's new collection of stories, I was aware of a career honest in its aims but only occasionally swinging free of a steady performance. Unlike Tennessee Williams' attempts at unmanageable forms, Bowles sticks with what he can do. Here are the gothic tales with their meaningless violence and seedy Arab settings which repeat the formula established in *The Delicate Prey* seventeen years ago. Here are the macabre Saki endings and the landscapes beautifully tuned to an indefinable melancholy. The stories are always carefully written but, for the most part, they are too self-contained and seldom have anything to match the atmosphere of frenzied desolation that drives through *The Sheltering Sky* to make it Bowles's masterpiece. He is still involved with his ideas of twenty years ago but he has lost his passion for them. The existential experience of *The Sheltering Sky* can never seem dated, but many of the empty exotic scenes in *The Time of Friendship* depend upon a bleak modernity which has worn thin even for Bowles.

Maureen Howard. PR. Winter, 1968. p. 149

[*Without Stopping*] is a pleasure to read for its felicities of phrase, and its celebrity-column distinction is not unlike an album of photographs by Cecil Beaton. But neither its brain-work nor the emotions hinted at go deep. Lots of facts are there, all checked and verified I am sure. But their assemblage and their viewing, their choice and staging are dead-pan. In this sense it is a characteristic work of twentieth-century art, which in its heroic early decades, those in which Paul Bowles grew up, gave to everything, as stylistic priority, an equalized surface tension.

Virgil Thomson. NYR. May 18, 1972. p. 36

• BRAUTIGAN, RICHARD (1935–   )

The best thing about Richard Brautigan's first published novel [*A Confederate General from Big Sur*] is the language, which is consistently more inventive and delicate than you might expect from one of the so-called "beats." . . . His metaphors alone make Brautigan's novel worth reading. . . . Brautigan's characters aren't violent, like Kerouac's. They are selfish, irresponsible, but they harm no one and do not obviously "rebel." . . . The writer is as freely experimental as his characters. He gives us a choice of several written endings, and he dots the narrative with italicized flashbacks to the Civil War, which was "the last good time this country ever had." It all makes for good whimsical reading. Perhaps, however, *A Confederate General from Big Sur* might have been more than merely whimsical if there had been more tension between the imagined society and the one we all live in, or between the writer's fancy and his reason.

Arthur Gold. BW. Feb. 14, 1965. p. 18

Mr. (if I may be so bold and square as to accord him the prefix) Richard Brautigan, in his novel *A Confederate General from Big Sur,* provides as good an account as has come my way of Beat life and humor; though the latter, I have to admit, won from me no more than the kind of wintry smile I habitually wore during the five sad years that I was editor of *Punch*.

Big Sur is, of course, hallowed ground to admirers of Henry Miller's writings, a Beat shrine, if ever there was one. A glimpse is caught in *A Confederate General from Big Sur* of Mr. Miller collecting his mail, and provides the only point in the narrative when the giggling stops and a respectful silence momentarily descends. Otherwise the novel consists of a series of bizarre (perhaps it would be politer to say picaresque) adventures, sometimes salacious, sometimes narcotic, and sometimes pettifoggingly criminal.

Beats, according to Mr. Brautigan's account, are heathen, parasitic, dirty and idle. They are the devil's anchorites, covered with the lice of unrighteousness, and eating the bitter bread of boredom and vacuity. Only an occasional bout of fornication relieves the tedium of their days, and even that is precluded when they are too high to perform. As a protest against the American way of life, theirs would seem to lack point. They are but a waste product of what they affect to despise; refusing to participate in the feast of affluence, they grovel and crawl under the table and about the guests' legs in search of crumbs, cigarette butts and voyeur ecstasies. Poor Beats! Mr. Brautigan has convinced me that we are better without them.

Malcolm Muggeridge. Esquire.
April, 1965. p. 60

Brautigan . . . is funny, but seldom satiric, sometimes bored but hardly ever angry, frequently happier than you but never holier than thou. . . . Alas for the hazards of being reviewed: Brautigan at secondhand is all too likely to sound merely whimsical and cute. He is not; what underlies these games is a modern fatalism, not maudlin fatheadedness. . . . [In *In Watermelon Sugar*] the spun-sugar simplifications of organized happiness and the naïve placidity of the narrator are repeatedly darkened by our perception of real misery, jealousy, frustration and unrequited love. It is more complicated technically and more disturbing emotionally than the earlier works, and it suggests that you should, while reading all the Brautigan now available, look forward to the Brautigan yet to come.

J. D. O'Hara. Book World. Jan. 11, 1970. p. 3

I'll call [Brautigan] a novelist because it is for his novels, *A Confederate General from Big Sur* and *Trout Fishing in America,* that he is best known. There are no books quite like them and no writer around quite like him—no contemporary, at any rate. The one who is closest is Mark Twain. The two have in common an approach to humor that is founded on the old frontier tradition of the tall story. In Brautigan's work, however, events are given an extra twist so that they come out in respectable literary shape, looking like surrealism. *A Confederate General from Big Sur* is a kind of Huck Finn-Tom Sawyer adventure played out in those beautiful boondocks of coastal California where Jack Kerouac flipped out in the summer of 1960. But it is with *Trout Fishing in America* that Brautigan manages to remind us of Mark Twain and at the same time seem most himself. As you may have heard, this one is not really about fishing, but it is really about America. In the book—call it a novel if you will—whopper is piled on dream vision with such relentless repetition that the ultimate effect is a little like science fiction.

Bruce Cook. The Beat Generation
(Scribner). 1971. p. 206

The cover of *Trout Fishing in America* is important. It shows a young couple in front of the statue of Benjamin Franklin in San Francisco's Washington Square. The girl is dressed in a long skirt, high boots, wire-rimmed glasses, and a lace hair band; the man is wearing a nineteenth-century hat, a vest and black coat over his paisley shirt and beads. He too has wire-rimmed glasses. With his vest and glasses, with her boots and lace, they look like something out of an earlier America. They reflect the nostalgia which permeates this book: for a simpler, more human, pre-industrial America. Brautigan knows it's gone. But some of the values in this book are derived from this kind of nostalgia. Brautigan has created a pastoral locked in the past, a pastoral which cannot be a viable social future.

I want to live in the liberated mental space that Brautigan creates. I am aware, however, of the institutions that make it difficult for me to live there and that make it impossible for most people in the world. Brautigan's value is in giving us a pastoral vision which can water our spirits as we struggle—the happy knowledge that there is another place to breathe in; his danger, and the danger of the style of youth culture generally, is that we will forget the struggle.

John Clayton. *NewAR*.
No. 11, 1971. pp. 67–8

Trout Fishing in America is a solid achievement in structure, significance, and narrative technique. For all its surface peculiarity, moreover, the book is centrally located within a major tradition of the American novel—the romance—and is conditioned by Brautigan's concern with the bankrupt ideals of the American past. Its seemingly loose and episodic narrative, its penchant for the marvelous and the unusual, its pastoral nostalgia—all of these things give it that sense of "disconnected and uncontrolled experience" which Richard Chase finds essential to the romance-novel. Brautigan's offhand manner and sense of comic disproportion give to the narrative an extravagance and implausibility more suited to the fishing yarn and tall-tale than to realistic fiction. Lying just below the comic exuberance of the book, furthermore, is the myth of the American Adam, the ideal of the New World Eden that haunts American fiction from Cooper to the present. The narrator of *Trout Fishing in America* is Leatherstocking perishing on the virgin land that once offered unbounded possibility, modern man longing for the restoration of the agrarian simplicity of pioneer America. That a life of frontier innocence is no longer possible adds to the desperate tone and comic absurdity of the narrator's frustrated excursions into the American wilderness.

Kenneth Seib. *Critique*. 13, 2, 1971. p. 71

[*A Confederate General from Big Sur* is] much better than *Trout Fishing in America*, which is the only other [Brautigan book] I have read. Its narrative may be pointless, but at least events follow one another in chronological sequence. Some hippies and their girls and a rich madman settle in a cabin in Big Sur and that's about it. They frighten away the frogs with alligators and have quite a nice time. The dialogue is relaxed, with occasional zany excursions into the pot vocabulary, which I like. Sometimes, even, it is enlivened by the sour wit one finds in Virginia Woolf's saner moments: "I've heard that the Digger Indians down there didn't wear any clothes. They didn't have any fire or shelter or culture. They didn't grow anything. They didn't hunt and they didn't fish. They didn't bury their dead or give birth to their children. They lived on roots and limpets and sat pleasantly out in the rain."

Does this not remind one of Woolf's description of the Great Frost? Whether it does or not, Mr. Brautigan writes five thousand times better than Kerouac ever did, and could easily produce some modern equivalent of W. H. Davies's *Autobiography of a Super-Tramp* with a little more effort, a little more discipline and a little less of the semi-articulate exhibitionism which is what people apparently mean now-adays when they talk of "creative" writing.

Auberon Waugh. Spec. Feb. 27, 1971. p. 287

Right now Brautigan is riding high. He is the Love Generation's answer to Charlie Schulz. Happiness is a warm hippie. . . .

That the young should have taken so passionately to Brautigan is not surprising. He is the literary embodiment of Woodstock, his little novels and poems being right in the let's-get-back-to-nature-and-get-it-all-together groove. His exceedingly casual, off-hand style is wholly vogue, and I readily concede that there is a certain charm about it and him. . . .

[*The Abortion*] is diverting, and Brautiganites will find in it their usual joys. The loveable Brautigan himself is on hand as always, his own hero, talking about love and peace and the beauties of nature. The book is modestly funny, can be read in a matter of an hour or so, and will not hurt a soul.

Jonathan Yardley. NR. March 20, 1971. p. 24

The stories [in *Revenge of the Lawn*], many of them only a paragraph or two long, are characterized by that Brautigan blend of simplicity, humor, surrealism, nostalgia, and bittersweetness that endeared Saroyan to an earlier generation of Americans. The simplicity is sometimes cloy-ing and the nostalgia sometimes veers into the sentimental, but these are small faults if you enjoy Brautigan, as I do, enormously; if you don't, they'll madden you and make him seem dead-pan precocious and wildly self-indulgent. If you're a woman, you will also be maddened by the exaggerated Beat Generation attitudes toward women that linger here.

Sara Blackburn. Book World.
Nov. 28, 1971. p. 2

Revenge of the Lawn is really one vision of people who have drowned their feelings and live underwater lives. For Brautigan's fishermen do not want to catch trout so much as they want to be like them. . . . Going underwater, underground, inside, Brautigan people live with no passionate attachment to anyone or any place and never permit themselves to feel a thing. But in Brautigan's scheme withdrawal can be a strategic maneuver. . . . Brautigan makes cutting out your heart the only way to endure, the most beautiful way to protest the fact that life can be an endless down. *Revenge of the Lawn* is not Brautigan's best book. But it has the Brautigan magic—the verbal wildness, the emptiness, the passive force of people who have gone beyond winning or losing to an absolute poetry of survival.

Josephine Hendin. NYT. Jan. 16, 1972. p. 7

The most laconic of these new writers, Richard Brautigan is perhaps best known for *A Confederate General from Big Sur, Trout Fishing in America*, and *In Watermelon Sugar*, as well as for his poetry. Lucid, precise, whimsical, idyllic, Brautigan develops a unique fragmentary style: his "chapters" are sometimes no longer than his chapter headings. Yet beneath the surface of happy love and naïve humor, the reader feels the lurking presence of loss, madness, death, feels some great blankness enfolding the rivers and wrecking yards of Brautigan's America. Mocking the conventions of fiction, Brautigan engages both silence and speech in his rigorous art, spare as a haiku. A Californian, he has some affinities with the Zen sweetness of Snyder and Kerouac; but his knowledge of the dark also recalls Hemingway.

Ihab Hassan. Contemporary American
Literature (Ungar). 1973. p. 171

On first reading Richard Brautigan's *In Watermelon Sugar*, one senses that something extraordinary has happened to the form of the novel, to the intellectual and aesthetic conventions to which we have become accustomed. Brautigan's work is jigsaw puzzle art that demands more than close reading; it demands an active participation by the reader, a reconstruction of a vision that has been fragmented but warmed by a private poetic sensibility. Three avenues of accessibility, the novel as a utopian instrument, the analogues to the Garden of Eden, and natural determinism converge and create a frame for Brautigan's novel.

Brautigan has created the utopian dream for the post-industrial age of affluence, beyond IBM, and finally beyond curiosity. His longings, unlike other utopian ideals, have no claim on progress, no uplifting of the material condition of man, no holy wars to redistribute the physical wealth, no new metaphors for survival based on the securing of human necessities, and no emotional nirvanas. Other utopian dreamers have responded directly to the events of their age, but Brautigan is responding to the cumulative ages of man, and no response can be significant for him that does not place the entire past on the junk heap (the forgotten works). Nothing will do but a fresh start, with a fresh set of assumptions; *In Watermelon Sugar* takes us back to the beginning, for this is Eden, with its syllabic and accented soul mate iDEATH, reconstructed.

Harvey Leavitt. *Critique.* 16, 1, 1974. p. 18

Like Kurt Vonnegut, Richard Brautigan is beloved by college kids. Each is admired for his tenderness toward human vulnerability, for his pose of the faux naif, for his air of sweet inexpressible sadness. The difference between them is that Brautigan is a singularly careful writer. . . . [He] is a miniaturist who broods about death, who builds his novels from small self-contained blocks. He cannot entirely avoid coyness or dead-end digressions. Yet he conveys a sense of spare economy, of humorous or graceful lines eased in almost imperceptibly. . . . *The Hawkline Monster* is rather more of a pastiche, more of a parody than any of Brautigan's other fictions. It lacks the complexity, the more evanescent refractions of his best book, *Trout Fishing in America.*

Peter S. Prescott. *Nwk.* Sept. 9, 1974. p. 82

BROOKS, GWENDOLYN (1917–   )

It's too soon to say anything definitive about the work of Gwendolyn Brooks. Perhaps she hasn't yet written the poems that will stand out a hundred years from now as her major ones. But she has already written some that will undoubtedly be read so long as man cares about language and his fellows.

There have been no drastic changes in the tactics and subjects she has dealt with over the years. It's doubtful if future critics will talk about the early and the late Brooks, not unless she strikes out into much different territory after 1969. What one observes is a steady development of themes and types.

Her poetry is marked by a number of central concerns: black experience; the nature of greatness; the way in which man expresses his needs, makes do, or lashes out. Ordinarily the view is one of delicate balance, that of a passionate observer. The poems strike one as distinctly those of a woman but always muscled and precise, written from the pelvis rather than the biceps. [1969]

Dan Jaffe in *The Black American Writer*,
vol. 2, edited by C. W. E. Bigsby
(Penguin). 1971. p. 93

Coming to Gwendolyn Brooks, we find a writer avowedly a spokesman, and in this sense a writer who "looks in" to a group. . . . Indulging a fancy to make a point, one could say that Gwendolyn Brooks writes in the confidence and momentum of a tradition that *intends to be* established. Put it this way: there is a language that goes with current city events, or there are languages that attempt to hold that existence in human perspective that is local, indigenous. In Gwendolyn Brooks's writings there is this determination to see what is, not to opt for any falsity, and not to abandon the risk of individual judgment either. The result is a special kind of complexity. Sometimes the poems are confusingly local in reference; they shimmer with strong feelings that surface abruptly. But throughout there is implied a steady view, an insight.

William Stafford. Poetry. March, 1969. p. 424

In recent years . . . Gwendolyn Brooks has abandoned her former integrationist position and moved steadily towards a black nationalist posture. With this ideological change, there has come a parallel shift in verse techniques. Influenced by the young black revolutionary writers of the 1960's, Miss Brooks has given up, not all, but many of the conventional forms used in her early publications. For one thing, like other modern poets, she employs rhyme very sparingly. Perhaps her most popular form now is the kind of flexible, unrhymed verse paragraph found in the volume *In the Mecca*. . . . Perhaps the most effective element in her poetic technique is word-choice. With strong, suggestive, often-times unusual words—words that startle the reader—Gwendolyn Brooks weaves a brilliant poetic tapestry. Never sentimental, never a mouther of clichés, she brings to any subject the freshness and excitement which characterize good poetry—and good poets.

Arthur P. Davis. From the Dark Tower:
Afro-American Writers 1900 to 1960
(Howard). 1974. pp. 192–3

BUECHNER, FREDERICK (1926–   )

Black comedy and benign intentions do not very often mix well in a novel. Frederick Buechner's success in delivering to us the bizarre and the seamy details of the American backlands, with a weird, curiously absorbing, humour, is plain in almost everything he writes; yet the talent is shared by a host of American novelists of his generation and younger, is emulated in scores of zany *pièces noires* about the Great American

Nightmare. Where Mr. Buechner differs is in his anxiety to reconcile, in as subtle and unobvious a way as possible, these horrors with a plausible affirmative view. He is a Christian novelist, taking pains to weave into the sick, alarming, ludicrous fabric of his plots some strand of allegory which will, if one listens with care, make the wretchedness bearable.

In his last novel, *The Entrance to Porlock*, the ghastliness somewhat outweighed the hope. It may be his real gain in technical assurance, in his control of an elegant deadpan style, in sheer entertainment value, which makes *Lion Country* so much more satisfying: a strange, serene balancing act which blends successfully at last the satirical talent and the moral purpose.

TLS. Jan. 10, 1971. p. 1165

Open Heart is an ingenious and glorious metaphor of Christian messianism. But it is both more and less than this: a novel; and its ways are the ways of the novel. . . . Bebb is no theorem or metaphysics. Bebb lives—whether the world is felt to be hallowed or not—with an antic and radiant insatiability; he reminds one a little of Thomas Mann's Joseph. And Buechner is, by his own lights and in some of the most masterly comic prose being written in America, sanctifying the profane. Fraud is only a seeming; suffering and frailty are the means of our purification, and death is not death but eternal life. For me (for whom the Messiah has not yet come), these are illusions, and therefore how hard being a Christian seems!

Cynthia Ozick. *NYT*. June 11, 1972. p. 36

Love Feast, the third volume of a trilogy, completes a process of self-recognition and revelation for Buechner. Its relationship to the earlier books, *Lion Country* and *Open Heart*, is paradoxical, for in those books the precision of language, the strength, inventiveness and whimsy of character, and the story itself promised a resolution Buechner doesn't manage gracefully in *Love Feast*. But it is still a novel of contemporary wit and elegance, full of small truths and unexpected mysteries. As Yeats said, out of our quarrels with ourselves comes poetry. . . .

Buechner's faith seems as stark and mysteriously natural as the desert. No dogma confines his writing, no credo fixes his characters for judgment. He claims to be a part-time Christian, yet to him the messages of Christ show themselves often, even in peculiar, mundane circumstances. In fact Buechner's sense of God and Christian teachings has a vigorous and fanciful quality, born of the Testaments and a conviction that "the language of God is metaphor" and that religion must be learned through story.

It is not surprising, then, that *Love Feast* closes artificially, when we no longer expect resolution to a tale we should have known all along would lead to new chapters and defy conventional ending.

Lincoln Caplan. NR. Jan. 25, 1975. pp. 27–8

• BUKOWSKI, CHARLES (1920–   )

It is not, after all, Bukowski's subjects or his imagery, it is not his point of view or his neostoic attitudes that make his poetry remarkable and almost without parallel in our time—it is his voice, the rhythms and the characteristics of his own idiom that distinguish him from his contemporaries. He has replaced the formal, frequently stilted diction of the Pound-Eliot-Auden days with a language devoid of the affectations, devices and mannerisms that have taken over academic verse and packed the university and commercial quarterlies with imitations of imitations of Pound and the others. Without theorizing, without plans or schools or manifestos, Bukowski has begun the long awaited return to a poetic language free of literary pretense and supple enough to adapt itself to whatever matter he chooses to handle. What Wordsworth claimed to have in mind, what William Carlos Williams claimed to have done, what Rimbaud actually did in French, Bukowski has accomplished for the American language. . . .

There are no sweet endings in Bukowski's world. Because, unlike the Brothers Grimm and their contemporary followers, Bukowski recalls that no one lives happily ever after: there are cancers and bullets; there are psychotic nightmares and tabloids full of excellent suicide motives. There is a world of chrome and neon, concrete and steel in which human beings are trapped like flies, like ants, like dissenters in the collapsing rooms of the Inquisition: sooner or later the question is asked, the answer given—and, the answer always being wrong in the end, the sentence carried out.

John William Corrington. Foreword to It
Catches My Heart in Its Hands by Charles
Bukowski (Loujon). 1963. pp. 5, 9

Charles Bukowski has, during the last few years, become one of the best known of the writers of [the] "sixties" period. The great, perhaps the greatest strength of Bukowski's poetry lies in its powerful imagery and dramatic impact. . . .

The physicality of Bukowski's world comes charging through his work like angry fire trucks, and it does so with an oppressive sense of impending death, destruction (of the material and spiritual), and desolation. All of his world pronounces these terrors, but his protests are not social ones in the traditional sense; they have none of the wild outbursts of the "beat" work.

Lee Holland. *Américas*. Jan., 1964. pp. 30–1

Whether or not one likes [Bukowski's] poems, it is difficult to be indifferent to them. They are energetic, tough, and unnerving. Written out of a driving necessity for expression, they become a battleground on which Bukowski fights for his life, and sanity. Against his enemies, who are grimly, irresponsibly powerful, his words and wit and sour bitterness are fragile weapons. The effort, consequently, is last ditch.

It is also disturbingly ironic. Auden wrote in his tribute to Yeats, "Poetry makes nothing happen." Bukowski is intensely aware of this, laments it because in the world he inhabits it reduces the poet to an ineffectual isolation. Sometimes he almost whines. The implication which continually intrudes itself into his work is that he would like nothing better than to cure the sores he unscabs, yet he realizes, perhaps correctly, they are incurable. It is an ultimately frustrating situation.

Dabney Stuart. *Poetry*. July, 1964. p. 263

No Establishment is likely ever to recruit Bukowski. He belongs in the small company of poets of real, not literary alienation, that includes Herman Spector, Kenneth Fearing, Kenneth Patchen and a large number of Bohemian fugitives unknown to fame. His special virtue is that he is so much less sentimental than most of his colleagues.

Yet there is nothing outrageous about his poetry. It is simple, casual, honest, uncooked. . . .

Bukowski is what he is, and he is not likely to be found applying for a job with the picture magazines as an Image of Revolt. Unlike the Beats, he will never become an allowed clown; he is too old now, and too wise, and too quiet. More power to him.

Kenneth Rexroth. *NYT*. July 5, 1964. p. 5

Some have likened the muscular music of Charles Bukowski to that of the early Sandburg, but the skidrow—mission stiff—greasy spoon—rented room bard is the only one of his kind. He cannot be classified or yoked with any other poet, living or dead.

And poet he is. One who can make words dance and roar like an earthquake or whisper softly like a Spring breeze freshening the fetid air of the streets where men past caring sleep fitfully in flophouse cubicles. In *Cold Dogs in the Courtyard* the death of a cockroach, "blind yet begotten with life, a dedicated wraith of pus and antennae," inspires an eloquent commentary on the human condition. Again, in *Crucifix in a Death-Hand*, Bukowski has "something for the touts, the nuns, the grocery clerks, and you. . . ."

Jack Conroy. ABC. Feb., 1966. p. 5

In Bukowski's world there is little wonder, and beauty has its foundations deeply sunk into ugliness. He took LSD once and was impressed—but not all that much. He drinks a lot but never glows rosily, instead his vision is getting greyer and greyer as he moves further and further into the completely rationalistic view of the mechanics-dominated world that rusts, wheezes and threatens at any moment to completely collapse.

He provides a necessary counterbalance to the hippy lotus-eater worldview of love, long hair and Ultimate Love. He works in the Post Office eight hours a night, he hasn't lost track of the work-a-day (or night) America which is the only reality for too many Americans. At the same time he has avoided that ivy-covered outlook of the college-town-based Platonic poets who read the daily newspapers through the double-layered glass walls of their air conditioned literary museum. He's an authentic, the real-thing, because he talks from the vantage point of the pavement, the dog biscuit factory, the whore house, the park bench, the run-down room with the shabby shade and worn-out rug stretched feebly across the sagging floor. He represents a kind of stepped-up reality in relation to the beats because he never tried to make the running-down American world sing or shout or chant—and they did. He just makes it talk. And if you listen to what it's saying it pays off. You don't go through the looking glass (for a change) but sweat it out in the real world on this side.

Hugh Fox. Charles Bukowski: A Critical and
Bibliographical Study (Abyss). 1969. pp. 94–5

Buk, as he is known to "little mag" readers, is by now an American legend. Even those who merely hover near the underground press know of him as a unique blend of Whitman, Miller, and Dylan Thomas. With two years of college and countless drunks behind him, he now approaches his 50th year as a clerk in a Los Angeles post office—much to the dismay of the postal inspectors. Since he began chopping out poetry at age 35, he has appeared in every important "little" from one coast to the other; the bibliographies read like an ongoing history of the little magazine. Two major books have been published by Jon and Louise Webb of the Loujon press, but he's yet to find a large, established publisher. Thus the work of one of America's most original, hard-hitting, and imaginative poets probably is available in only a few libraries.

The Days Run Away Like Wild Horses over the Hills . . . should now bring Bukowski the attention he deserves. His language is sensitive, harsh, yet always accessible to the most turned-off layman. Even the failures are a hell of a lot better than the works of many modern, better-known poets published today.

Bill Katz. *LJ*. May 15, 1970. p. 1848

Charles Bukowski never did escape from California. Certainly he is quite unimaginable anywhere else, and he is still out there on the West Coast, writing poems and stories about his five decades of drinking, screwing, horse-playing, and drifting around, proving defiantly that even at the edge of the abyss language persists. "A legend in his own time," the cover of his new collection of stories [*Erections, Ejaculations, Exhibitions and General Tales of Ordinary Madness*] calls him, and that seems fair. . . .

He writes as an unregenerate lowbrow contemptuous of our claims to superior being. Politics is bullshit, since work is as brutalizing and unrewarding in a liberal order as in any totalitarian one; artists and intellectuals are mostly fakes, smugly enjoying the blessings of the society they carp at; the radical young are spiritless asses, insulated by drugs and their own endless cant from any authentic experience of mind or body; most women are whores, though *honest* whores are good and desirable; no life finally works, but the best one possible involves plenty of six packs, enough money to go to the track, and a willing woman of any age and shape in a good old-fashioned garter belt and high heels.

He makes literature out of the unfashionable and unideological tastes and biases of an average Wallace voter. And that sense of life is worth hearing about when it takes the form not of socko sex-and-*schmertz* but of blunt, unembarrassed explanation of how it feels to be Bukowski, mad but only north-north-west, among pretentious and lifeless claims to originality and fervor.

Thomas R. Edwards. *NYR*.
Oct. 5, 1972. pp. 21–3

Erections, Ejaculations, Exhibitions and General Tales of Ordinary Madness seems to defy any attempt at a comprehensive label. Bukowski moves in several environments, always a little isolated. He attacks the idols of the underground, but is one; he prefers classical music (late Romantic) to rock, alcohol to marijuana. There are affinities in his work to the Beat poets as well as to writers like Zola with his "delight in stinking" and to Wilhelm Busch, the German cartoonist. Bukowski's own life provides the escapades of Busch's Max and Moritz. He is both the storyteller and the story.

Martha Bergmann. Synergy. Spring, 1973. p. 16

• BULLINS, ED (1936–   )

The American Place Theater has made another important find, Ed Bullins, author of three one acts, *The Electronic Nigger, and Others.* . . . Unlike the general run of young playwrights, Bullins does not spend most of his time showing what a whiz he is at creating monologists who gab endlessly in back rooms about their cranky existences. He gives his attention to the impact of one character on another, the blood of drama, not its gristle.

The least formally structured of his plays, *A Son, Come Home,* happens to be the least effective. . . .

He comes into his own with the title play. *The Electronic Nigger* presents a young Negro novelist, Jones, conducting his first evening class in what prospectuses describe as Creative Writing I. Jones proudly tells his mixed garland of middle-aged and youthful students, "You won't be graded on how well you write, but on how you grow in this class." Unluckily for him, one student turns out to be a verbose know-it-all who disrupts the lesson and steals the allegiance of the other students. . . .

Clara's Old Man, which winds up the trio, is one of the best short American plays I have come across: realistic in manner yet throbbing with weirdness and driven by bursts of extravagant invention that make a definition by genre seem impertinent.

Albert Bermel. NL. April 22, 1968. p. 28

The white problem in America is at the core of all Bullins's work. He denies being a working-class playwright: he is from the criminal class. All the other men in his family have been in prison. He is the only one who went to high school, who went to college; but he claims that working people in Harlem like his surrealist, intellectual plays.

The Electronic Nigger is not straight propaganda. An evening class in literary expression is being gently conducted by Mr. Jones, a novelist: the session is interrupted by a penologist, Mr. Carpentier, who spouts large generalisations in technical language—not unlike Marshall Mc-Luhan's—and takes over the class, until Jones's head is full of noise and

Carpentier is leading pupils in a mechanical goose-step, bawling abstract inanities. (All this is well staged, in-the-round, with life-like acting shifting slowly to an expressionist style, with a climax of disciplined noise and nightmare.) Neither Jones nor Carpentier is white. During the clash, Jones at one point appeals to Carpentier as his "black brother," but the latter denies being black. A white pupil calls him "Uncle Tom" and a black pupil says: "No. It's for me to say that."

D. A. N. Jones. List. Aug. 22, 1968. p. 253

It fascinated me that *In the Wine Time*, produced by an organization consciously devoted to Black Power [the New Lafayette Theater], was the only "black" play I saw this season not obsessed by Whitey. There were, to be sure, occasional references, but the central purpose of the play was "to celebrate the Black experience" *for fellow blacks*. This is no more nor less than the New Lafayette's official credo promised, but it is always a surprise when rhetoric and practice coincide.

Clarity and fidelity of purpose, however, have never yet guaranteed artistic success. *In the Wine Time* does not reverse my opinion of last season (based on an evening of Bullins' short plays done at the American Place) that his reputation has outpaced his performance. On the one hand, *In the Wine Time* is attenuated—a one-acter stretched into three—yet, on the other, its melodramatic ending is insufficiently prepared for, and is even at odds with the desultory humor and fitful tensions that precede it.

Martin Duberman. PR. No. 3,
1969. pp. 489–90

Ed Bullins, out of Genet via LeRoi Jones, writes like a man trying to dislodge a big white monkey from his back. His obsession is the corruption of black integrity by white values. His plays are composed like effigies, specially designed to torture his enemies, and based on the magical assumption that if one destroys the symbol often enough, the reality will also get impaired. Like the vendettas of LeRoi Jones, they belong less to the convention of art than they do to the world of black magic. Which is precisely why they are so fascinating in the theater.

Charles Marowitz. NYTts. April 13, 1969. p. 3

Ed Bullins' *In New England Winter* . . . is compounded of sudden spurts of anger, violence, and passion, and spurts, just as sudden, of wit and humor, tenderness, and, finally, mystery. Like Mr. Bullins' *The Pig Pen* . . . the play opens up, to a certain extent, once it is over—when we realize, for example, that what seemed to be a prologue is actually an epilogue, and that everything that follows leads up to it. . . .

The plot is the least of it. Mr. Bullins' details of character and speech and behavior make up a whole style of living, especially when they are specific and precise. They are so strong that we take everything else on trust, and his language often makes poetry out of the casually obscene vernacular of his actors. The people and their feelings about one another are what give the play its depth.

Edith Oliver. *NY*. Feb. 6, 1971. p. 72

Crazy dark laughter envelops all the proceedings [in *The Duplex*], but the meaning is frightful. It is not simply a matter of revealing the horrid messiness typical of most ghettos, whatever the color of their inhabitants; there is something more damaging beyond the specifics of promiscuous fornication, smoking of pot, gambling, drunkenness, outbursts of physical brutality, irresponsibility and wrecked lives. What is really being exposed is our civilization.

Bullins flatters no one and directly accuses no one. He offers hardly any preachment or "propaganda." His method is largely realistic. . . .

What makes *The Duplex* so telling is that, apart from their native humanity, all of its characters are fundamentally abandoned people. What ails them is not due solely to white indifference, incomprehension or hostility but to a deprivation in the soil of sound values, which are not supplied by America because it has not for a long time actually possessed them.

Harold Clurman. *Nation*.
March 27, 1972. p. 412

In the best of Bullins' work, he is creating a tradition for black drama to follow, helping to create a fearlessness, a self-acceptance. There is no sensational spooning up of filth nor is there sentimentality; instead there is the searing eye of unsentimental analysis. And subtlety, so that when one reads *Clara's Old Man*, one is reminded of the principle that in the presence of artistic greatness, the surface of a play does not necessarily reveal its depths; the depths are suggested rather than stated. And there is implicit direction; though Bullins' working class in his best work does not have conscious direction, one senses a kind of godly principle, a kind of holiness and enormous energy and power, and one perceives that all that is needed is a harnessing force, a wise and compelling leadership, and sweeping changes will be made. There is another artistic principle: that a great work of art must suggest the awesome potentialities of man for growth: this principle too is a spine of Bullins' best work.

There is thus great strength and great confusion in Bullins' working class, of whom one could say: in great chaos, great strength; in great lostness, the potentiality of decisive direction; in compulsive suicide, powerful life.

Lance Jeffers. CLAJ. Sept., 1972. p. 34

Beyond the political activism and the racial consciousness of his plays (which are, of course, what Bullins most values in them), there is another side. *In the Wine Time, In New England Winter, Goin' a Buffalo*, and other Bullins plays create a mood of lost innocence, purity, and beauty that is universally meaningful. In fact, the dramatist creates in most of his work a counter-mood to that which dominates the actual dialogue—there is a sense of once-glimpsed loyalty, sensitivity, and romance which the ghetto reality of the setting makes impossible to attain. This obbligato of tenderness is so overpowered by the brutality of the ghetto that it exists in the plays as something once envisioned, but almost forgotten, by one or two main characters. The theme of a brutal reality destroying human dreams of tenderness and romance is, of course, a common one in twentieth century literature—black and white —and requires no specifically Black consciousness to respond to it. The three Bullins plays are, however, striking illustrations of this theme.

James R. Giles. Players. Oct.–Nov., 1972. p. 32

The Reluctant Rapist is Theatre of Cruelty on every level. And this is especially so when considering the book as a literary object. The writing is *bad*. Not bad-ass. Just bad. It reads like an appointment book (I went here, ate this, fucked that) rather than a work of fiction. It makes no attempts to penetrate to its characters' motivational cores. The prose itself creates no illusions. Neither does it reveal any. Politically, psychologically, linguistically, *The Reluctant Rapist* barely exists.

But at the level of etiology this novel does manage to exert a morbid fascination. The book's cantus firmus—entwined with Stevie Benson's near constant erection—is that not only is it right to humiliate women, but that no matter what they say they actually enjoy it! The idea seems to be that much like a sassy child will love a good whuppin' now and then, so will women love an occasional good raping. Especially the white ones—who have been unfairly denied their full share of degradation by an unenlightened society.

Jack Friedman. VV. Oct. 25, 1973. p. 35

The Reluctant Rapist is a handbook to the plays. As a playwright, Bullins rips, tears, rapes; he blows apart black life. As a novelist, he explains what the ripping, tearing, and raping are all about. They are the acts of a lover in deep need of blasting away the conventional faiths and beliefs to expose the truthful, irreducible center so that he and his beloved may at last be free. Steve Benson the rapist is a metaphor of Ed Bullins the playwright. And Steve's story is a reassembling of the bits from the exploded bombs and tearing beak. . . . The conventional order of events is one of those beliefs that has to be destroyed. And Bullins is successful in destroying it, in fusing the past with the present, in giving us the feeling of living the past again from the standpoint of the present and seeing the future infuse the past.

Jerry H. Bryant. *Nation*. Nov. 12, 1973. p. 504

BURKE, KENNETH (1897–   )

We ask a prosaic question: what kind of book [*Towards a Better Life*] are we reading? It is certainly not a novel, nor was it meant to be. In ascriptions of this kind we are well advised to consult Northrop Frye's account of the several forms of prose fiction. Then it appears that Burke's book is not a freak, a sport of Nature, but an example of a distinguished tradition, the anatomy. . . . The masterpieces of the genre include *A Tale of a Tub, Candide*, the *Anatomy of Melancholy, Headlong Hall*, and *Brave New World*. . . .

It is not enough to say that *Towards a Better Life* is beautifully "written," if by this praise we mean to consign the book to an anthology of Prose Style. However peculiar its origin, it is in fact one of the most moving books in modern literature, as well as one of the purest anatomies.

Denis Donoghue. *The Ordinary Universe*
(Macmillan—N.Y.). 1968. pp. 214–5

If speculative in life, language, or literature, then you can hardly miss with *Language as Symbolic Action*, a rich and culminative work. Burke is still coming on with further developments, in this book and for future ones, but is meanwhile expressing his most important positions, it seems to me, more thoroughly and unmistakably than ever before, with the illustrations and exemplifications sufficient in length and detail, brilliant in quality. Although *Towards a Better Life* has more than enough appeal as art, it will inevitably be of added interest because of its network of relationships to a major career in criticism—one that except for recent memory of KB's pious plumbings around the word itself might have been labelled (rather than libelled) "solid gold." But golden or not, encomiums are not easy to avoid as an unusually productive and unusually successful life's work refines to quintessence, the artificer in fine fettle for completing the contract.

Neal J. Osborn. HdR. Summer, 1968. p. 321

If there is a title peculiarly fitting to Burke in all his work, it is one dear to Burke himself, the title of rhetorician. Burke is a rhetorician in a double sense: whatever he considers, he considers it rhetorically as an instance of rhetoric. Rhetoric, as I am thinking of it, is the use of words to evoke a specific emotion or state of mind. Whatever Burke studies, this is what he finds it to be, whether it is open propaganda, the Constitution of the United States, psychoanalysis, philosophy, or even pure poetry. Dialectics itself he defines as a kind of rhetoric; it is "all enterprises that cure us by means of words." Pure poetry differs from other forms of rhetoric only in the sense that the state of mind it evokes is an end in itself, whereas ordinary rhetoric evokes a state of mind which is to lead to practical consequences.

The objective of Burke's own rhetoric is a consistent one: to evoke a state of oneness among men. If he can convince us that we are all rhetoricians, that we are all using words combatively for our own purposes, he will have purified our warlike natures by evoking in us a feeling of our final oneness.

Merle E. Brown. Kenneth Burke
(Minnesota). 1969. p. 7

Most simply put, [Burke] can get more thoughts out of a book than anyone else can, evoking in his reader time after time a mixed attitude of surprise, gratitude, and chagrin—"yes, of course, why couldn't I have seen it for myself?"—while at the same time, in the same gestures, often in the very same sentences, he is developing a method and a terminology which the reader, if he will, can master for application elsewhere. . . .

There is an enthusiasm in all this that sometimes comes near enough to madness: criticism as rhapsody, or furor poeticus. Nor do I mean that in disparagement, though aware that some writers would; for among the most appealing things about Burke, to my mind, is the sense he has, the sense I get from reading him, that thought, if it is to matter at all, must be both obsessive and obsessively thorough, that thinking, if it is to salvage anything worth having from chaos, must adventure into the midst of madness and build its city there.

Howard Nemerov. Reflexions on Poetry &
Poetics (Rutgers). 1972. p. 84

BURROUGHS, WILLIAM (1914–   )

Burroughs's ideas are serious and interesting, and on the basis of the long interview in *Paris Review* (Fall 1965) one can see that he is one of the most intelligent and articulate writers in America today. And his experiments do produce some distinctive effects. Many passages in his books can catch something of the atmosphere of dreams in which vivid fragments of hallucinatory vividness rise and fade in utter silence, leaving one with the curiously abstract experience of witnessing concretions which do not impinge. Echoes, portents, disturbing details, flicker out at us, not as parts of legible propositions but as parts of a drifting turbulence with intensities and intermittences beyond the grasp of syntax. . . .

To escape from words into silence and from mud and metal into space is Burroughs's version of a well-established American dream of freedom from conditioning forces. It would perhaps be obtuse to ask what mode of life would be adopted in silent space. We are being given the morphology of an emotion as much as a literal prescription, when Burroughs exhorts us to shed all verbalizations and leave the body behind.

Tony Tanner. *City of Words* (Harper).
1971. pp. 130, 134

Burroughs is the great autoeroticist of contemporary fiction, the man who writes to stock up his private time machine. The "absurdity," the world-craziness which he claims to reproduce in its comic disorganization, consists in dislodging all the contents of his mind in a spirit of raw kaleidoscopic self-intoxication. These rapid shifts and indiscriminate couplings of scenes take place in Burroughs's books as if they were violently oscillating and exploding in the telescopic eyepiece of an astronomer who just happens to be gloriously soused.

Alfred Kazin. *Bright Book of Life*
(Little). 1973. p. 263

Burroughs' novels . . . become diabolical maps, maps whose surfaces have been so intersected with conflicting directions, so cut up, that they are unreadable; they are maps of hell. Even the "conflicting directions," the sense of surrealistic contradiction in Burroughs, are finally neutralized by a cut-up world, a world existing in pieces that can't relate to each other enough to contradict. This is more true of the two later novels, *Nova Express* and *The Ticket That Exploded*, than it is of *Naked Lunch* and *The Soft Machine.* In *The Soft Machine* Burroughs makes his best use of cut-ups by establishing with them a dynamic rhythm of cohesion and fragmentation that becomes the experience of the novel. In the later novels, however, cut-ups come to seize their own space, to have less to do with other sections of the novels, except as waste bins to catch those sections when they drop. They become stagnant pools of amputated language and space through which the reader has to wade.

The amputation of language and space becomes also, at its extreme, an amputation of the body. Although the body in Burroughs is reified into two principles, an organic and a mechanical one, the mechanical is the final condition of the body, since even purely organic life, the body as blob, eventually swallows itself and falls into mineral existence, into death. Thus the objectification of the body in realism becomes in Burroughs a total dismemberment of the body, an explosion of it into separate existence, into pieces whose parts are all equal to each other and equal to any other object in the vicinity. This is the final condition of realism: schizophrenic atomism, living in pieces, in a world of pieces.

John Vernon. *The Garden and the Map*
(Illinois). 1973. pp. 108–9

It is an extremely demanding way to write a book, to begin to do something different every five pages or so, and to bring it off requires not only skill but virtuosity of a very high order. The greatest likelihood is that the book will seem frightfully uneven, demonstrating that its author does some things better than others, which seems to me very much the case with *Exterminator!*. Another likelihood is that a book so discontinuous will seem, at its end, not to have been structured but only to have grown by accretion, like a scrapbook, and this too seems to me the case with *Exterminator!*. For all of its brutality, there is so much comic-strip stylization to its whores, pimps, junkies, presidential advisers, and scientologists, that the brutality never seems quite persuasive. The most chilling aspect of the book, in fact, seems to me the dust jacket photograph of Burroughs himself, gaunt, riven, Lazarus returned from the dead. Nothing in the art of *Exterminator!*, despite moments of great verve and inventiveness, seems to me commensurate with the implicit vision behind those hollow eyes.

Philip Stevick. *PR.* No. 2, 1974. p. 306

CALDWELL, ERSKINE (1903–   )

Like most best selling authors, Erskine Caldwell tends to be patronized or ignored by academic critics and serious readers. Many know of *Tobacco Road* and *God's Little Acre,* but tend to dismiss them as merely popular or salacious novels. Few seem to know the full range of the man's work: his text-picture documentaries, such as the remarkable *North of the Danube*; his charming books for children; his neglected *Georgia Boy,* a book that stands with Faulkner's last work as one of the finest novels of boyhood in American literature; and his short stories, some of which rank with the best of our time. A brief study cannot fully redress the indiscriminate neglect of readers and critics (nobody will argue that all Caldwell's works are valuable, or that all need to be considered at length); but I will indicate briefly the achievement of Erskine Caldwell, in an attempt not only to do justice to the writer, but to prevent if possible another disgrace in American letters: the sort of disgrace we visited on Melville, forgotten for years; the sort of disgrace we seem to be visiting on Phelps Putnam, Delmore Schwartz, and other good poets now almost entirely out of print, as well as on Glenway Wescott (who remembers that first novel, so highly praised by Ford Madox Ford?).

James Korges. *Erskine Caldwell*
(Minnesota). 1969. p. 5

Caldwell's portrayal of Southern religion can be summed up . . . in the three themes of fatalism, poverty of ethic, and sexuality, but does Caldwell's account coincide with historical reality? In most of his work Caldwell can plead poetic license, but in *Deep South* he sheds the cloak of the novelist and becomes a combination of reporter, historian, and autobiographer. With surprising consistency, both in *Deep South* and in the fictional works, Caldwell captures the essence of Southern revivalistic religion. The latent sexuality which he brings to the surface has certainly been a feature of the Southern religious scene, especially of the more fervent brands of fundamentalism. Caldwell's emphasis on the ethical barrenness of Southern religion penetrates to the very heart of the South's religious difficulties. Finally, Caldwell ferrets out the curious Southern blend of John Wesley and John Calvin, of evangelicalism tinged with fatalism.

Caldwell's picture is, of course, partial. Southern life and Southern religion are far more complex than they appear in Caldwell's pages. But

Caldwell makes no claim to the completeness of the historian. Rather, he fictionalizes important features of the Southern religious scene, and in so doing creates a fictional religious world which, in its approximation to reality, furnishes an invaluable aid to the historian of the South. . . .

James J. Thompson, Jr. SHR.
Winter, 1971. p. 43

Thirty years divide *Tobacco Road* from *Annette*: Mr. Caldwell's obsession with stunted sexuality remains. The share-cropping paupers of Georgia might seem a far cry from middle-class life in the suburban South, but the differences between Tobacco Road and Flower Street, Zephyrfield, are superficial. The clash continues between baffled male brutality and traumatized female innocence.

Sylvia Millar. TLS. Nov. 15, 1974. p. 1277

• CALISHER, HORTENSE (1911–   )

It is always gratifying to make the acquaintance of a writer of intelligence and feeling; it is these qualities which most clearly mark the work of Hortense Calisher, whose stories in the last few years have made their quiet, cogent bids for our attention. Miss Calisher is an eminently sober writer; without affectations or flashiness. . . . It is a pity that this long view does not take in lighter-hearted areas. Miss Calisher seems quite undisposed toward humor, except of a rather grim sort.

Gertrude Buckman. NYT. Nov. 18, 1951. p. 46

[*False Entry* is] the work of a writer who knows what she wants to do and how she wants to do it. The style, at least at first, seems rather mannered, and indeed it is involved and allusive, but the further one goes, the more one recognizes how beautifully it suits her purpose. . . .

Identity is not given us; it is something that we either do or do not achieve. That Miss Calisher can take this familiar truth and make of it something fresh and exciting is proof of her deep insight and her mastery of a most difficult method. Despite her unconventional method of telling her story, Miss Calisher knows how to make use of the traditional arts of the novelist. . . . If her aim is to explore deeply the mysteries of a particular person, she is able to bring minor characters on the stage in such a way that we can see them clearly. The novel rewards the closest possible reading, but it can give a more casual kind of pleasure, too.

Granville Hicks. SR. Oct. 28, 1961. p. 17

The overall impression of [*Tale for the Mirror*] is that Miss Calisher has settled rather more comfortably and somewhat less excitingly into the mold which she set for herself ten years back. Then, as now, her concern was with the "knell of sadness for something that had been, that had never quite been, that now had almost ceased to be." And this singular concern often involves her in a melancholy sentimentalism that blurs the acuity of her vision by reducing all of life's problems to the lack of communication between human beings. Loneliness—and the inability of people to live in the present because of it—is her theme. . . . If Hortense Calisher's intimate vignettes seem strangely static in a world mad with motion . . . she has at the same time created some of the most discomfortingly vivid writing of this decade.

Gloria Levitas. NYHT. Nov. 4, 1962. p. 13

Hortense Calisher's second novel [*Textures of Life*] attempts, and pretty well pulls off, something of a *Golden Bowl*. This one could not be symbolised by the extravagant *objet d'art*, with its bizarre flaw, conceived by James. Miss Calisher's material is the American bourgeoisie at home, and the textures of the lives she interweaves are homely. Hers is a Golden Bowl in, so to speak, basketwork. But the working is Jamesian indeed in firmness of structure and subtlety of superstructure. Sometimes she uses the master's very idiom—not in pastiche but as legitimately and creatively as Tiepolo used Veronese's. . . .

In James's nexus the Prince is admittedly not up to the other three. Yet it is not simply as a weak character that he lets the dance down. Weak characters can be boldly portrayed; but James is too relenting towards the Prince to make him a Vronsky or a George Osborne; the weakness lies not only in the Prince but in James—where it is perhaps a weakness for Italian young men, or just for princes. Miss Calisher's construction has a comparable flaw, and again in the younger generation. *Jeune premier* parts are always the hardest to do. Her David may not properly exist—there is little to him but a trick of letting his glasses slide down his nose—but he is waved into being by adroit sleight of hand. It is Elizabeth, reacting against her mother's "taste," bohemianly disregarding material objects except such as she herself, as a sculptor, makes, in whom one suspects a lightweightness of character and a college-girl pretentiousness of intellect—which the author seems not to realise. With the older couple Miss Calisher can do no wrong. The vivid, invalid's life of David's father, the vaguer but penetrating vision of Elizabeth's mother—she splendidly creates both and superbly counterpoises them. Miss Calisher is not only that rarity, a talented novelist, but that double-blossomed rarity, a talented novelist who is serious about art.

Brigid Brophy. NS. Sept. 13, 1963. p. 326

Hortense Calisher's *Extreme Magic*, a novella and a number of short stories, is a collection remarkable for uneven achievement. The sensibility is extremely feminine—in the faintly perjorative sense—and the talent diaphanous. . . . The writing is sometimes skillfully evocative, the nuances suggestive, the imagery just; but then there are ornaments (many of them) as trashy as "the river gave a little shantung wrinkle." . . . But there are two stories, "The Rabbi's Daughter" and "The Gulf Between," that are harmoniously true and moving—even substantial—because they rise from authentic experience: in this case cultivated, haute-bourgeois, upper-West-Side Jewish life, a little down on its uppers. Miss Calisher has a real sense of a past . . . she can show where things come from; what people really are; how they feel; how they affect one another; why what happens happens.

Eve Auchincloss. NYR. June 25, 1964. p. 17

[In *Journal from Ellipsia*] Hortense Calisher expends a great many words on a sophisticated science-fiction theme, and these words are not cleanly bolted into clear but complex structures so much as—as though they were all made of some colloidal substance—allowed to stick into great lumps, like long-forgotten sweets shaken out of a paper bag. Admittedly her literary problem is the representation of communion between two worlds—one here, one *out there*—and the effect of cotton wool coming out of, or being stuffed into, desperately communicating mouths may be regarded, by some readers, as appropriate. But the book, besides being very long, is very hard to read, and one wonders whether it was all worth it. What happens in *Journal from Ellipsia* is this: an androgynous creature from beyond tries to break through into this world; it contacts Janice, a beautiful anthropologist, who now wants to break out of this world into the one beyond. Her story is told, as it were, posthumously—the unearthly talking machine, the top arguing scientists, the throwing of the ball of narration to different players (including the one from out there). There are British characters, and they tend to speak in what I call the toodle-pip idiom, an American invention. This, in a book about intergalactic communication, makes everything said seem more implausible than it ought to.

Anthony Burgess. List. April 21, 1966. p. 589

The New Yorkers is a miraculous novel in that it is exactly equal to its ambition. For the first fifty or even hundred pages its ambition is hidden or apparently denied. You think you are reading a futility—another perhaps wise but old-style novel "rich in texture," "closely worked," patient beyond easy disclosure, afflicted with the paradox of a choking capaciousness. Then begins the extraordinary glimmer of Design, and very rapidly there is evidence of something new—newly against the grain of expectation.

The miracle is not in the language, which, though controlled and self-aware, is occasionally formally florid, like porcelain. Sentence by sentence it does not always distinguish itself. Yet the method of its obliqueness, its internal allusions, echoes, and murmurings, all this is uncommonly cunning and thick with the ingenuities of discovery. The miracle is nevertheless not in the language but in the incredible spite—everything is spited, from literary fashion straight up to the existentially-perceived cosmos. If the anti-novel can be defined in part as spiting expectations, then Calisher's concept of it belongs with Nabokov's. Like other "New" novels, *The New Yorkers* is also about itself—which is to say it aspires to fool, to lead, to play tricks with its own substance. But unlike others, especially unlike the most intelligent—for what is more intelligent than a novel by, say, Susan Sontag?—Calisher's novel is *about* intelligence. Or, better yet, Intelligence.

Cynthia Ozick. *Midstream.* Nov., 1969. p. 77

Hortense Calisher . . . is one of our most substantial yet elusive writers. By any narrow or literal definition, she is becoming less and less a strictly narrative artist. Her characters are boundless states of mind. Nor does she structure books conventionally: *Queenie* doesn't move; it spins, pausing for scenes, pausing for ideas. Mrs. Calisher appears also to borrow imaginatively from the other arts, giving the reader the feel of the dance, of the mobile, of sculpture. In *Queenie*, probably the most light-hearted of her novels, she has made a tripping entry into the mind of a present-day young girl, and has with wit and spirit fashioned a kind of ballet around the story of Queenie's coming of sexual and intellectual age.

The story unwinds in the form of tapes addressed to various "interlocutors," including the admissions dean on "Hencoop College" in New York, God, a Hencoop professor in whom for a time Queenie reposes some faith, and finally the President of the United States. . . .

The book overflows with ideas, couched in sparkling aphorisms. Touching on the generation gap, the sexual gap, the abysmal political gap, the communication gap. As the device of the tapes suggests, the story is, among other things, about someone who wants to have a good talk with *Someone*.

Lucy Rosenthal. *SR*. April 3, 1971. p. 34

Like any good writer, Hortense Calisher keeps a reader on the move, She has a "style," though it worries her when people say that, because for some it implies surface, a glib veneer with nothing beneath it. But she needn't worry. Her intelligence shows without aid of italics and block capitals. To be "carried away" is not in her case to be swept off into rhetorical clouds of Chestertonian pomp, but to be led on by the imagination into fresh perception, awe and an occasional all-out celebration. . . .

Hortense Calisher is a creator of voices, moods, states of mind, but not of worlds. Her fiction, like her autobiography [*Herself*], sends us back into the world we know; it may refresh and enhance it, but it does not, even for a moment, obliterate or remake it. This is not to say that she is, in some old-fashioned sense, a realist. On the contrary, rather than fabricating reasonable facsimiles of "things as they are," she takes certain "scenes" for granted and lets her quick wit and marvelous imagination play over them. If we know a bit about the scenes she selects, we're likely to find her works beautifully agile and astute. If not, she is not about to hammer the parts together for us.

Robert Kiely. *NYT*. Oct. 1, 1972. pp. 3, 20

Hortense Calisher is one of those writers whose books are more admired than read. . . . Now the joint publication of her autobiography and her fifth novel may finally bring Calisher the recognition and readership she deserves. . . . *Herself* is Calisher's personal statement about her art—and it is nothing less than a vertiginous guided tour through the mind of a wise and witty woman of 60 who since her childhood knew she would be a writer. . . . Her literary and social criticism is provocative. The comments about Turgenev and Yukio Mishima (whom she admires) and Hemingway, Mailer and literary critics (whom she doesn't) are especially penetrating.

Arthur Cooper. *Nwk*. Oct. 16, 1972. p. 110

Calisher is a shrewd observer of our social ills—displacements of youth, futilities of the rich—but she is more than a naturalist noting easy details, cataloging crimes or sins. She is a maker of fictions; she insists on private consciousness—even when this consciousness is extreme, obsessive, and "poetic." [*Eagle Eye*] is a powerful indictment of social wrongs by an odd hero who may see less (or more) than he believes. . . . Calisher stuns us with the "magic forbidden leaps" of her imagination. She forces us to enter—and withdraw from—her narrator's mind; she offers few clues to his ultimate condition. But by testing us with her sharp vision she emerges here as a true creator—an eagle of fiction-makers.

Irving Malin. *NR*. Nov. 3, 1973. p. 26

CAPOTE, TRUMAN (1924–   )

Why . . . did Capote honor himself by calling [*In Cold Blood*] in any sense a "novel"? Why bring up the word at all? Because Capote depended on the record, was proud of his prodigious research, but was not content to make a work of record. After all, most readers of *In Cold Blood* know nothing about the case except what Capote tells us. Capote wanted his "truthful account" to become "a work of art," and he knew he could accomplish this, quite apart from the literary expertness behind the book, through a certain intimacy between himself and "his" characters. Capote wanted, ultimately, to turn the perpetually defeated, negative Eros that is behind *Other Voices, Other Rooms* into an emblematic situation for our time.

> Alfred Kazin. *Bright Book of Life*
> (Little). 1973. pp. 210–1

It is [Capote's] attention to style, to the extraordinary pull of places, to all the fleeting wisps of the past that give [*The Dogs Bark*] a durability far beyond the perfunctory compendia of pieces with which publishers stay in the graces of their good writers when those writers are between big books. . . . This is less a guidebook for the millions of aspiring journalists and city-room entrepreneurs in the land who wish to break the shackles, than a self-charting of a courageous literary life, a life of stamina, and despite the misleading public appurtenances, of course, of considerable solitude. If the "new journalism," which moves from one symposium to the next, has in fact become something more than we had bargained for (some of its exponents now belittling the act of fiction and poetry as irrelevant, obliterating in one fairly broad sweep some of the deepest impulses of the human blood), then *The Dogs Bark* is an effective answer, for while much of it does indeed stand on "reporting," it is at the core a great deal more ambitious: it is the written geography of an imaginative artist.

> Willie Morris. *NR*. Nov. 3, 1973. p. 22

CATHER, WILLA (1876–1947)

All of what Willa Cather wrote, it seems to me, is ultimately a metaphor of the conflict which Miguel de Unamuno referred to as an "inward tragedy," the conflict "between what the world is as scientific reason shows it to be, and what we wish it might be, as our religious faith affirms it to be." For Willa Cather, this conflict was most broadly expressed in terms of the world she knew in her childhood—the pioneer era which she clearly idealized and ennobled in her fictional re-creation of it—and the post-World War I wasteland she so thoroughly repudiated. It is easy to lose sight of the essentially symbolic nature of this conflict and to read it too narrowly in terms of literal past versus literal present. Her theme was not the superiority of the past over the present, but, as Henry Steele Commager has observed, "the supremacy of moral and spiritual over material values, the ever recurrent but inexhaustible theme of gaining the whole world and losing one's soul."

Rather than being irrelevant to the modern world, the moral thrust of Willa Cather's art, her concern with pioneers and artists as symbolic figures representing the unending human quest for beauty and truth, places her among the number, not of the backward-looking (which she saw herself as being one of), but of the true spiritual pioneers of all ages in whose lives or work other men continue to find inspiration.

Dorothy Tuck McFarland. Willa Cather
(Ungar). 1972. pp. 4–5

It is love's partner, affection, that warms the life in [Cather's] work, and love's opposite, hate, that chills it. We meet pity and reconcilement there, and we meet obsession, and the hunger for something impossible. But what her characters are most truly meant for, it seems to me, is to rebel. For her heroines in particular, this is the strong, clear, undeniable impulse; it is the fateful drive. It is rebelling not for its own sake so much as for the sake of something a great deal bigger—that of integrity, of truth. It is the other face of aspiration. . . .

The desire to make a work of art and the making of it—which is love accomplished without help or need of help from another, and not without tragic cost—is what is deepest and realest, so I believe, in what she has written of human beings. Willa Cather used her own terms; and she left nothing out.

Eudora Welty. NYT. Jan. 27, 1974. p. 20

CHANDLER, RAYMOND (1888–1959)

There are all gradations of class and milieu and speech and diction in Chandler's novels. For these reasons, Chandler, through Marlowe, succeeds as no one else has succeeded in portraying Los Angeles, including Hollywood, and it seems at times that it is neither the violence nor the solution of the mystery Chandler is interested in as it is the city and the people, through the whole range of which, in the solution of the crime, Marlowe moves. . . . Emphasis is usually placed on the portrayal of Southern California, including Hollywood, and on the interrelation in this society between power and crime; and the unexpected relation of one segment to another, from the bottom (the little, helpless, incompetent, and hurt), to the top (usually the ruthless, rich, and spoiled). . . . In Marlowe's world, disunity, disruption, mobility, immorality, rootlessness and ruthlessness provide the constant motif. Marlowe himself is an old-fashioned character, chivalrous, with an individual sense of conduct and of justice; he judges his world, implicitly at least, from a point of view as conservative as Chandler's upper-class English education and his own cheerful admission that he was a snob would suggest.

> Herbert Ruhm in *Tough Guy Writers of*
> *the Thirties*, edited by David Madden
> (Southern Illinois). 1968. pp. 178–9

The action of Chandler's books takes place inside the microcosm, in the darkness of a local world without the benefit of the federal Constitution, as in a world without God. The literary shock is dependent on the habit of the political double standard in the mind of the reader: it is only because we are used to thinking of the nation as a whole in terms of justice that we are struck by these images of people caught in the power of a local county authority as though they were in a foreign country. The local power apparatus is beyond appeal, in this other face of federalism; the rule of naked force and money is complete and undisguised by any embellishments of theory. . . .

  In this sense the honesty of the detective can be understood as an organ of perception, a membrane which, irritated, serves to indicate in its sensitivity the nature of the world around it. For if the detective is dishonest, his job boils down to the technical problem of how to succeed on a given assignment. If he is honest, he is able to feel the resistance of things, to permit an intellectual vision of what he goes through on the level of action. And Chandler's sentimentalism, which attaches to occasional honest characters in the earlier books, but which is perhaps strongest in *The Long Goodbye*, is the reverse and complement of this vision, a momentary relief from it, a compensation for it. . . .

The detective's journey is episodic because of the fragmentary atomistic nature of the society he moves through. . . . The form of Chandler's books reflects an initial American separation of people from each other, their need to be linked by some external force (in this case the detective) if they are ever to be fitted together as parts of the same picture puzzle.

Fredric Jameson. SoR. Summer,
1970. pp. 632–3

Chandler had a fine feeling for the sound and value of words, and he added to it a very sharp eye for places, things, people, and the wisecracks (this out-of-date word seems still the right one) that in their tone and timing are almost always perfect. . . . It is impossible to convey in a single quotation Chandler's almost perfect ear for dialogue, but it comes through in all the later books whether the people talking are film stars or publicity agents, rich men, gangsters, or policemen. To this is joined a generous indignation roused in him by meanness and corruption, and a basic seriousness about his violent entertainments.

Julian Symons. Mortal Consequences
(Harper). 1972. p. 142

[*The Big Sleep*], and the six other novels by Chandler, are in the tradition of a negative romanticism which is perhaps the dominant mode of American literature from Hawthorne to our contemporary black humorists—that power of darkness which Hawthorne, Poe and Melville explored—which Mark Twain could not laugh away, and which created a mythical landscape in Faulkner. Poe's "The Fall of the House of Usher" can be regarded as the rehearsal for the saga of the Sartoris-Compson-Sutpen families in Yoknapatawpha County. And the predecessor of Chandler's Californian nightmare had his hero Dupin "be enamored of the night for her own sake." But where Poe brought inductive light to moral darkness, Chandler refuses to cheat his vision in like manner. When Marlowe has solved a dilemma, he has not explained the enigma. All of Chandler's books end on a note of dissatisfaction. The purported solution does not tidy things up since there is no end to a waking nightmare.

This dark vision has lost none of its power today. The excess of violence of which Chandler has been needlessly accused is now hardly noticeable, nor was it lovingly attended to for shock effect, but rather described because life is simply that cheap in this truly egalitarian society: literally, a matter of fact. And so Chandler does not laud death with the lyrical mesmerism of Hemingway, nor does he play metaphysical games with it in Sartrean ingenuity. A death is a waste of life.

E. M. Beekman. MR. Winter, 1973. p. 164

CHEEVER, JOHN (1912–   )

The two Wapshot stories reveal John Cheever's growth as a novelist. The first of them dwells at length on the natural ceremonies of a coherent, traditional past. The style has only to recall them in order to reveal their value. But the style in *The Wapshot Chronicle* is too often merely winsome and nostalgic. Like Henry Adams' *Mont St. Michel and Chartres, The Wapshot Chronicle* indulges the wish for a coherent present by idealizing the past.

The ceremonies of *The Wapshot Scandal* are less nostalgic and more relevant. If a Fourth of July parade typifies the first novel, a rocket launching typifies the second. Cheever faces the conflict of past and present in the second book and reveals a crucial paradox: in a time of highly-organized social effort, the individual is more isolated than ever. In order to live he must find significant ceremonies.

Richard H. Rupp. Celebration in Postwar
American Fiction (Miami). 1970. p. 39

The novel [*Bullet Park*] is bleak, full of danger and offense, like a poisoned apple in the playpen. Good and evil are real, but are effects of mindless chance—or heartless grace. The demonology of Calvin, or Cotton Mather. Disturbing or not, the book towers high above the many recent novels that wail and feed on Sartre. A religious book, affirmation out of ashes. *Bullet Park* is a novel to pore over, move around in, live with. The image repetitions, the stark and subtle correspondences that create the book's ambiguous meaning, its uneasy courage and compassion, sink in and in, like a curative spell.

John Gardner. NYT. Oct. 24, 1971. p. 24

Now, because Mr. Cheever has written a volume of stories [*The World of Apples*] which tend to show people as being motivated by old-style feelings like love and loyalty and kindness and consideration for others and protectiveness toward the weak (e.g., children), one doesn't want to represent him as preaching. It is merely that every work of art, like every creation of any kind, comes out of a system of values and preferences, and this is a book by a gifted and established writer which doesn't, for once, seem to come out of negativism, alienation, despair of the human condition and frantic self-gratification in whatever horrifying ways suggest themselves. One meets people in everyday life who have these old-fashioned values, and perhaps the shortest way to convey the rare quality of Mr. Cheever's book is to say that here, for a wonder, we have a modern work of literature in which people behave as decently as they generally do in real life, rather than behaving like sick fiends.

John Wain. *NR*. May 26, 1973. p. 26

With one or two exceptions, these stories [in *The World of Apples*] chronicle the sadness and futility of suburban and moneyed existences. In several the sound of the rain is intended as a balm for the bruised spirits of those grown more accustomed to the sounds of traffic. And perhaps this is one of Cheever's shortcomings. Writing strictly of one class, his books cannot compare with those attempting a Balzacian cross-section of humanity. . . . Cheever's humor and irony make him a greater writer than, say, Louis Auchincloss, whose humorless novels also examine the professional classes to the exclusion of all others. But the limitation is there.

Roland Laird. *Com*. Nov. 30, 1973. p. 246

CHOPIN, KATE (1851–1904)

Greater attention, it seems to me, has to be given to the integral relationship between local color in [*The Awakening*] and the development of its theme, as well as to Kate Chopin's use of related symbolism. There is no doubt a certain irony in suggesting a new reading of *The Awakening* in terms of its local color. It was precisely because of diminished interest in regional literature that many commentators feel it was so long ignored; there is the obvious implication that regional literature is somehow incompatible with universal appeal. In exploring both local color and related symbolism more fully though, it seems to me that critics will do greater justice to the profundity of Kate Chopin's theme. For the novel is not simply about a woman's awakening need for sexual satisfaction that her marriage cannot provide; sexuality in the novel represents a more universal human longing for freedom, and the frustration that Edna experiences is a poignant statement about the agony of human limitations. . . .

There is a wealth of sensuous imagery in the novel, and this has been noted consistently by the critics; but what has not been noticed . . . is that sensuousness is a characteristic feature of the setting, a product of climate and the Creole temperament. And thus it must be considered primarily as constituting the new environment that Edna marries into, and not as directly supporting a preoccupation with sexual freedom. It is this environment that becomes the undoing of the American woman.

John R. May. SoR. Fall, 1970. pp. 1032–3

It does not seem probable that [Kate Chopin] will burst into glory with the reissue of her complete works . . . but she is deserving of a good deal more attention than she has received, partly because she was long before her time in dealing with sexual passion and the intricate familial and personal emotions of women, and partly because she is an uncommonly entertaining writer. The stories, a good many of them only a page or two long, are frequently no more than anecdotes or episodes or even tricks; but, like Maupassant, whom she translated and by whom she was much influenced, she usually embedded her skeleton in sufficient flesh and musculature to conceal the joints. . . .

Mrs. Chopin's landscapes and her interiors, metropolitan or rural, are animate and immediately perceived; there is no self-indulgent clutter in them, just as her characters rarely are cartoons, generally recognizable as they may be. She is sparing and precise whether she is dealing with simple folk or people of elaborate construction, and she seems to have known and to have comprehended fully a great variety of people in a variety of strata.

Jean Stafford. NYR. Sept. 23, 1971. pp. 33, 35

CONDON, RICHARD (1915–   )

In <i>The Vertical Smile</i> Richard Condon, like many of his compatriot writers, has much to offer in brimming energy and expertise while displaying a complex and varied background. He sub-titles this long comprehensive novel as an "entertainment" but not everyone will accept this as an accurate description of the provocative disclosures and sexual deviations, sufficiently "off-beat" to alert even the most "permissive" reader. Ada Harris and Osgood Noon, lovers who met fortuitously by night in a hotel corridor and embarked upon a passionate affair without the formality of an introduction, are both in their "seventies." . . . This curious situation could have been sufficient content for the novel. In fact it is only the jumping off point for a commentary on the American manner of conducting national policies. . . .

Clearly, Richard Condon is genuinely concerned at the pace, the corruption and the general craziness of so much in the American way of life. Like James Hanley, he sees people as being irrevocably divided into separate camps, but his technique of putting this across is totally different, in that he draws outsize, self-obsessed characters and places them in exaggerated situations. He offers no solutions. The reader may be so appalled by the frankness and crudity that he will reject the jolting disturbance of reading *The Vertical Smile*. If he persists he will emerge from the experience shaken but wiser, having enjoyed quite a few laughs on the way.

Rosalind Wade. *ContR*. July, 1972. p. 46

One has to piece together the Condon life—its details being inseparable from data about bathtubs in Indianapolis and zoning laws in Portugal—but the confusing evidence suggests that he got into writing late (except for an early monograph for *Esquire* on Mickey Finns) via a curious Hollywood route. He had been "chief braggart" for a number of films, then decided one day to leave press agentry, scribble up some scripts and thereby "be fitted for gold toenails"; but when he sat down to his Olivetti he slipped inadvertently into the past tense and so turned novelist.

Maybe some of the extravagance of such tales as *The Manchurian Candidate* and *The Vertical Smile* derives from his Hollywood braggart period, but more likely it goes further back; as he says somewhere in this crazy new book [*And Then We Moved to Rossenarra*] he was perfectly modest until he was six. Anyway you would think that in dealing with dear old reality rather than fiction he would slow down. He is not noveling in the new book—and he is nearer 60 than six—but it makes no difference; he is still a glorious verbal braggart.

Reed Whittemore. *NR*. June 2, 1973. p. 26

Winter Kills is . . . a triumph of satire and knowledge, with a delicacy of style and a command of tone that puts Condon once again into the first rank of American novelists. Condon's hero is the lineal descendant of the ineffectual avengers who stalked the movie world of the 1950's. But while they were trying to hold onto a warped dream of individuality, Nick Thirkield is merely trying to find a fact. And Condon goes with him, less interested in facts than in nonfacts and superfacts, not historical truth but the Macy's parade of history, the overblown images from which we have all manufactured our own paranoid vision of the true connections of American society. . . .

Winter Kills, then, is "some kind of bummer through American mythology," in which almost all of Condon's characters, from highest to lowest, are driven by the American dream of being someone, making a difference, having power and control. *Winter Kills* isn't the world; it's the way we think about the world, the distortions and how they are created, "the application of the techniques of fiction playing like search-lights on a frenzied façade of truth." Condon has created a paranoid novel that does not leave us trapped inside its world, but functions instead as a liberation, exposing through the gentler orders of fiction the way we have been programmed to believe anything in print. By mingling historical reality with his own fabulous invention, Condon savagely satirizes a world in which fiction and reality are mingled to manipulate, exploit and kill.

Leo Braudy. NYT. May 26, 1974. p. 5

● CONNELL, EVAN S., JR. (1924–   )

The writer who tries to create art with the story must . . . take a position. He must feel deeply (passionately, I suspect) about why the human beings he is telling about operate as they do. It's not a matter of striking a pose or rising to a moral. It is a matter of finding motivation that prevails, getting at a piece of truth.

This is what makes Connell's short stories worth considering seriously. His people are captives within themselves. They are isolated—so isolated that we wonder whether Mr. Connell wouldn't like to make this isolation one of those "eternal verities" or whatever they are that William Faulkner insists on throwing at us. For when Mr. Connell's characters reach out from their isolation to make contact with the world and its inhabitants, they are either rebuffed, entangled in the debris of other lives, turned further inward or simply destroyed.

Webster Schott. NR. Oct. 14, 1957. p. 20

It seems to me that Evan Connell could become one of our best writers. . . . The Bridges [in *Mrs. Bridge*] are as vivid a family as I have encountered in modern fiction, and as individuals they are scarcely less immediate. But they are terribly, deliberately and predictably limited. . . . Mr. Connell knows so much more than he is willing to tell that he has failed us by remaining partially silent. . . .

But whether Evan Connell writes up, down or sideways he is a joy to read for he employs a prose style that is his own and yet not grotesque in its singularity nor dense in its idiosyncrasies. It is clear, it is clean, and it communicates. Finally, Mr. Connell is able to do easily—

so easily—the one thing that it has always seemed to me hardest and most important for a novelist to do. He can make his characters change.

Robert Gutwillig. *Com*. Feb. 13, 1959. p. 525

[Mrs. Bridge] is a startling performance, one of brilliant wit and, despite a surface coldness of satire, a sympathetic one. Mr. Connell's characters are not notably depraved or wicked or even ungenerous, but they are small. They seem bent upon making spiritual midgets of themselves, or perhaps it is the thin air they breathe that makes them so small, so disappointing to themselves. . . . In spite of the superb technique many readers may find this a chilling book, but for others that very astringency will be part of its individuality and impact.

Riley Hughes. *CW*. March, 1959. p. 509

Evan Connell has written a curious and original book about an American at war. Everybody knows the intensity with which American writers have studied the experience of the last war, but *The Patriot* avoids their inclination to regard the experience as somehow too big to be moralized over. Such novelists have concluded that the war was fearsome, that it was "real" in an unprecedented way and altered understanding and attitudes, but only the squarest characters in their fiction discuss it in terms of good and bad. Cadet Isaacs, by contrast, escapes with his moral faculty just intact. . . . Mr. Connell and his hero rend their innards in the effort to digest an experience conventionally indigestible.

Neal Ascherson. *NS*. Feb. 16, 1962. p. 235

In a remarkable, long poem [*Notes from a Bottle Found on the Beach at Carmel*] written in prosaic lines chocked and often choked with facts, containing all manner of odd, bizarre and quaint information, Evan S. Connell, Jr. states the condition of our times. . . .

Evan Connell is a Spengler for declining the West. The speaker of the poem is a speculative protagonist, a meditative man, a philosopher who goes on a vast odyssey of seas, libraries, and histories to discover the meaning of life and final meaning. . . .

It is enjoyable to read the poem for its philosophy. The author never raises his voice as he traverses his fabulous seas, lands, histories, and life cycles. He poses no solutions. He is unprophetic. He warns and remonstrates, baring his calm, rational, all-observant wisdom throughout.

Richard Eberhart. *NYT*. Nov. 10, 1963. p. 18

A recent and extraordinary book which has a growing underground reputation is *Notes from a Bottle Found on the Beach at Carmel* by

Evan S. Connell, Jr. [It] is a long (238 pp.) beautifully executed narrative poem of the size and scope of Pound's *Cantos*. It is a learned and subtle poem, yet written in a style of great clarity and precision, all its virtuosity gracefully concealed. This poem could easily be the most important single poem of our period when we have enough perspective to see things clearly. That it has, so far, been ignored by most of the critics of poetry may charitably be attributed to the fact that Connell enjoys a considerable reputation as a prose writer and has published very little verse in the magazines. Meanwhile, strange as it seems, without fanfare or controversy, *Notes from a Bottle Found on the Beach at Carmel* has sold quite well in the bookstores.

> George Garrett in *American Poetry*, edited by
> John Russell Brown, Irvin Ehrenpreis,
> and Bernard Harris (St. Martin's).
> 1965. pp. 237–8

The sensational but truly descriptive title of Mr. Connell's fine new novel [*The Diary of a Rapist*] may lead readers who do not already know his work to expect a lurid sex adventure concocted for the best-seller and paperback trade. This is very far from the case. The diary is a low-keyed, pointillistic rendering of the needs and despairs of a young clerk working in a federal employment bureau, married to a woman who has rejected him, and seeking refuge in hopeless ambitions, fantasy, and petty violence. The quiet piecing together of incident recalls Mr. Connell's *Mrs. Bridge*; the jeremiads against civilization, *Notes from a Bottle Found on the Beach at Carmel*. On the whole, however, Mr. Connell's book is closer to Keith Waterhouse's *Jubb* than to any of his own previous books. The mood is British, restrained, melancholic; the prose highly polished, elegant even in its occasional inelegancies.

> Dorothy Nyren. *LJ*. April 15, 1966. p. 2084

Before attempting a novel, Connell mastered the short story. His first book was *The Anatomy Lesson, and Other Stories*. He has acknowledged debts to Proust, Mann, and Chekhov, has studied under Wallace Stegner and Walter van Tilburg Clark, and has expressed his admiration for the historical fiction of Janet Lewis. The tone of a Connell story is unmistakably American; the perception is European. He can evoke a heightened moment of experience, relying less on plot than on innuendo. With Joyce and Flaubert, he shares a predilection for epiphanic detail and "the ineluctable modality of the possible."

A Connell story is like the sieve of Eratosthenes: everything nonessential is filtered out until only what is prime remains. Grace and equipoise are properties of his work, and he is adept at rendering the ambiguity of an emotion or situation. Avoiding the beginning-middle-end artifice of narrative fiction, Connell creates the illusion that his stories are nothing more than textures or surfaces. Smooth overall, the narrative armature of a Connell story is oblique, helical, and sinusoidal. Here his affinities with Chekhov and Proust are apparent, particularly in his preference for the rough-edged story of mood. Shunning any realistic imitation of life, he unerringly achieves intense verisimilitude. With Joyce's godlike author, Connell remains aloof from his creations, completely outside them, in apotheosis, paring his fingernails.

Gus Blaisdell. NMQ. Summer, 1966. p. 183

Ten years ago Evan S. Connell, Jr., published a first novel entitled *Mrs. Bridge*. It consisted of 117 related vignettes in which Connell, with great skill, laid bare the privileged yet empty life of his white Protestant, upper-middle-class heroine. . . .

Mrs. *Bridge* was a tour de force, a well-written, bittersweet book in which the author's despair for the fate of his people was nicely balanced by his love for them.

Now, ten years and several books later, Connell has returned to the materials of his early success. In *Mr. Bridge* the characters are the same, as is the technique, but this time the spotlight is trained on the husband. . . .

The vignettes in *Mr. Bridge* are readable, often insightful, sometimes brilliant; but they lack the consistent precision and dazzle of the earlier work. The story itself has less of a cumulative effect. . . .

Taken alone, *Mr. Bridge* is not a bad book, in spite of its defects. But it is not as good a novel as the one with which it will inevitably be compared.

Peter L. Sandberg. SR. May 3, 1969. p. 32

Like many of his contemporaries, Connell is no storyteller. Writers like Roth and Bellow, however, find cunning façades for their jerry-built structures (through Portnoy's psychoanalysis or Herzog's letters), whereas Connell is ingenuous in disguising his inability to construct a tale. *Mrs. Bridge* is written in a series of very short chapters (some paragraph-long) that simply slice up the heroine's life, while *The Diary of a Rapist* employs the oldest and least convincing plot evasion known to literature.

Evan Connell, then, is a novelist who can't construct stories about uninteresting or remote people told in characterless prose. Why give him any attention? Because in everything he writes, he is admirably serious and painstaking and because, like a character actor who disappears into his role, Connell always has the potential for turning imitation into insight.

Charles Thomas Samuels. *NR*.
June 7, 1969. p. 21

Ten years ago, when everything was different, the novel *Mrs. Bridge* by Evan S. Connell, Jr. attracted attention as one of those few American books which succeed in telling us something about that mysterious realm, the American Middlewest of the middle classes. . . .

In *Mrs. Bridge* Connell named the artifacts of that place and that time, spoke the dialect, rehearsed its folkways, all with the inseparable mixture of love and horror we must each of us have had for our parents and for our own childhood. Its form was ingenious. A major part of the success of the book was that Connell had found a solution to the problem of making a whole book out of lives whose only story, whose entire theme and plot and texture, is simply that they have no story.

John Thompson. *Cmty*. July, 1969. p. 63

[*Points for a Compass Rose*] is a book—plainly and simply that, gracefully written in fine ironic style expressing very well the moral tensions of the inner man who is the author. The work most like it, of course, is Connell's earlier *Notes from a Bottle Found on the Beach at Carmel*, for both of these must have found their origin in his journals. But *Points for a Compass Rose* also calls to mind J. G. Ballard's collection of grotesqueries, *The Atrocity Exhibition,* and William S. Burroughs's *Naked Lunch.*

His purpose is didactic—and now beware, for we are into the meaning of it all. Connell seems constantly to be adjuring us to "look" or "listen," or challenging us, "Do you understand?" Clearly, he wants us to understand, for this work which he calls "a gnomic book about America" has been written to show us what we have become. "Of what value is life," he asks, "if it's not woven on history's loom into other lives?" Well, in *Points for a Compass Rose*, Evan S. Connell, Jr., attempts to do just that. Our civilization, our culture, our lives are on his loom here. We may not like the pattern of moral disaster that emerges, but there is no denying a certain cruel accuracy in the lineaments of his design.

Bruce Cook. *Book World*. May 27, 1973. p. 10

When I first heard that Evan S. Connell, Jr. had brought out another epic-length poem [*Points for a Compass Rose*], I was exhilarated for days. We have here on the planet with us a man of such courage and strength of spirit that he has not lost what Alfred Adler calls "the nerve for excellence." He has kept it despite the burden of an awareness not only of the enormity of his project and of the limitations of his own human understanding, but also of the abject ignorance and indifference of his audience. . . .

It is time—past time—to approach Connell's poetry seriously, with meek heart and due reverence. . . .

[*Points for a Compass Rose* and *Notes from a Bottle Found on the Beach at Carmel*] are masterpieces. You could bend a lifetime of energy to their study, and have lived well. The fabric of their meaning is seamless, inexhaustible. . . .

Their language is steely and bladelike; from both of its surfaces flickering lights gleam. Each page sheds insight on every other page; understanding snaps back and forth, tacking like a sloop up the long fjord of mystery. Thinking about these poems, one at a time or both together, is a sweet and lasting pleasure to the mind.

Annie Dillard. *Harper.* Jan., 1974. pp. 87, 90

A certain kind of novel has always reported on reality for us, told us things we didn't know; has let us into feelings and places we haven't had and haven't seen; and it is probably the current scarcity or ineptitude of this kind of novel which is driving us to biographies for a sense of how other people live (or used to live) their daily lives. *The Connoisseur* admits us into a man's mind, persuasively evokes the beginnings of a mild mania, takes us to Taos, brings us back to New York, propels us through a party, a museum, an art gallery, and a Mexican restaurant. But its major development is an extended description of an auction held in a motel in Queens. . . .

The effect is not that of a documentary, but it *is* that of a novel: an unfamiliar world is made present, real enough for us to feel that our experience of life has been extended by our reading. It doesn't matter whether Connell invented the auction or transcribed an actual event more or less faithfully. It is the business of many novels to make such distinctions seem trivial. . . .

Connell's writing . . . is discreet, efficient, sometimes flat, quite often verging on cliché. . . .

The Connoisseur seems to be asking whether this kind of fiction— the imaginative exploration of a moment of change in a none too representative life—has any future.

Michael Wood. *NYR.* Nov. 28, 1974. pp. 29–30

• COOVER, ROBERT (1932–   )

Robert Coover writes [*The Origin of the Brunists*] as if he didn't expect to make it to a second [novel]. Everything goes into it, including plots for several grim short stories and more social novels and notes for a juicy essay. . . .

En route . . . Mr. Coover takes apart the economy, power structure, social order and sexual codes of a small town berserk with holiness. Burning with ambition, *The Origin of the Brunists* achieves much that this young teacher at Bard College hopes for. It is a novel of intensity and conviction. . . . If he can somehow control his Hollywood giganticism and focus his vision of life, he may become heir to Dreiser or Lewis. . . .

The strength of this novel derives from the old tradition. It brings us the news about mining, petty journalism, small town nonculture and the weird fusion of truth and wish that sometimes underpins religious belief. It's impregnated with stories. It creates characters. But it offers no new or terrifying revelations.

Webster Schott. *NYT*. Sept. 25, 1966. p. 4

[*The Origin of the Brunists*] is a remarkable effort of the imagination, concern, and a sheer creative force—sustained and elaborated from beginning to end. . . . Mr. Coover's characterizations are sharply wrought and remarkably multi-dimensional. . . . The handling of so many characters so masterfully is virtually unknown in first novels. In addition, Mr. Coover sustains the intensity and readability of his narrative joining and moving his people and their dilemmas toward a final effort that is compelling and lasting. . . . This is fiction as it should be, the product of high emotion and dedicated talent; real, hot with life in conflict, filled with the bizarre and the commonplace.

William Mathes. *BW*. Oct. 9, 1966. p. 14

A sense of metaphysics . . . pervades Robert Coover's book [*The Origin of the Brunists*]. . . . Coover's is a major work in the sense that it is long, dense, and alive to a degree that makes life outside the covers almost pallid. As a first novel it is extremely impressive in massive architecture, assurance, texture and invention. . . .

The chief merit of the novel is the reality of the characters. . . . There is much irony in the book, but it is never facile, and is made the deeper by the compassion with which the characters are felt and drawn. . . . If Coover can equal this book with his second novel he will be quite formidable. In fact he is formidable already.

Miles Burrows. NS. April 14, 1967. p. 514

It would be a pity if the baseball buffs were put off by this mythology [in *The Universal Baseball Association, Inc.*] or the mythology rooters dismayed by the baseball. Coover has in fact written a fine baseball novel, the best I can remember in an admittedly thin field, and based obviously on a study of the texts. The atmosphere is turn-of-the-century early Lardner, when the game was in full swagger, but his averages are lively-ball 1930. The best of both worlds, in my opinion. The language is just right—colorful but not fancy. Take away the big metaphor in the middle, and the book still stands up. Conversely, not to read it because you don't like baseball is like not reading Balzac because you don't like boarding houses. Baseball provides as good a frame for dramatic encounter as any. The bat and ball are excuses. Baseball almost involves a real sub-culture, a tradition, a political history that were in some sense pre-ordained when the first diamond was laid out, that were implicit in the distance between bases, and that continue to make ball parks seem like unfrocked churches, places where even the boredom is of a finer quality. That the players and fans might be shadows in the mind of a Crazy Accountant up there is not only believable but curiously attractive.

Mr. Coover's admirable novel adds to our stock of benign legends. And how many books have you read lately that do that? [1968]

Wilfrid Sheed. The Morning After
(Farrar). 1971. pp. 81–2

Robert Coover has published two novels. . . . What makes these books something more than rattling good tales is the fact that they treat in a loose, semi-allegorical way the origin and nature of religion. They say something about the meaning or lack of meaning of history. And they make a tentative statement about supernatural possibilities. The books are grounded in an impressive knowledge of religion, history, philosophy, theology, black arts and assorted crafts.

Though much of the factual detail in Coover's books appears to rest on Christian tradition, ritual and faith—on the Bible particularly—the books are in no way arguments for Christianity. They contain no pietistic strains, no gentle instruction, no comforting hope. A slangy, cocky, hip tone characterizes Coover's treatment of religious themes; the writer is above his subject, a kind of literary-theological folk-rock thing straight out of a hustler world that would rather not be conned. Perhaps Christians have consistently misunderstood human experience and its relationship to a creator: "I'm afraid, Gringo, I must agree with our distinguished folklorist and foremost witness to the ontological revelation of the pattern of history," says one character towards the end of the baseball book, "and have come to the conclusion that God exists and he is a nut." The flip and playful tone in no way diminishes the seriousness of the observation.

Lee J. Hertzel. Critique. 11, 3, 1969. pp. 12–3

"Strange creatures abide here," says Robert Coover as he muses in mid-story, trying to extricate himself from the brilliant maze of ghoulishness and Charles Addams shenanigans he has wrought. Strange creatures they are indeed. In the very title of *Pricksongs and Descants* the reader will sense the bizarre juxtapositions of sexual and death forces in Coover's excellent collection of twenty stories and sketches. . . .

The author has obviously been brought up on [*Finnegans*] *Wake* rather than A. A. Milne, and it's a good thing. For style saves his chamber of horrors from degenerating into gratuitous savagery and morbidity. Coover masters several technical and stylistic modes in the collection, from the conventional rhythms of Edith Wharton's graceful prose to the wildest Wolfean flights and Joycean spasms of language. . . .

Using techniques varying from folk fantasy to Sterne-like intrusion into realistic narratives, alternating chronologies and points of view with Faulknerian suddenness, Coover achieves highest excellence in a scintillating variety of short fictional forms.

Frank Cunningham. SR. Oct. 25,
1969. pp. 40–1

Coover doesn't care what his characters feel about radical politics, not even what they did last summer; he is concerned with them only as types which put readers on, onto "new modes of perception and fictional forms." To that end he reconstructs fairy tales—"The Ginger-Bread House," "Jack and the Beanstalk" and "Little Red Riding Hood"—and Bible tales: Joseph and Mary, Noah's flood. All this is done to flow our minds out of their ruts of conventional responses to traditional formulations, demonstrates to our satisfaction that "anything can happen," in art if not in life. . . .

We are not asked to be concerned with resolutions in his characters' lives, but with resolutions in his technique. Coover has written fine fiction before . . . fiction which deals with people who create their own fictions (religion, baseball), they live and die in them. But these novels were located in the world, not in the anti-world of *Pricksongs and Descants* where, if anything can happen, anything and nothing happens and it all doesn't matter much anyway.

Shaun O'Connell. Nation. Dec. 8, 1969. p. 640

John Barth looms behind the crude fatuities and linguistic boisterous-ness of Mr. Coover's "Morris in Chains," and Donald Barthelme is likely to be at once brightly attentive and slightly bored in the face of the whimsical-sinister tales which adapt Red Riding Hood and Hansel and Gretel. . . .

Fortunately there is the benign influence of Beckett. *Pricksongs and Descants* has affinities with *More Pricks than Kicks. S*ometimes the debt is a bad one, creating nothing but the pastiche of a tone of voice. . . . But Mr. Coover—who is manifestly very clever indeed, and very sensi-tive despite his decision that it is *de rigueur* to alternate between glower-ing and twinkling—has caught much more than mannerisms from Beckett or from the zeitgeist. . . .

"The Wayfarer," "The Marker," "The Babysitter," "The Hat Act": these are not vacant surrealisms, and even those who feel that the sick joke has been an unconscionable time dying may yet like Mr. Coover's bedside manner. The glacial hauteur is designed to ward off any possibility of finding out whether or not the words are heartfelt, but there can be no doubt as to their being headfelt.

Christopher Ricks. NYR. Feb. 12, 1970. p. 22

In his fictions, long and short, Coover has always been primarily concerned with the power of the imagination and its inextricable involve-ment with religious and sexual urgings, not in the argumentative chicken-egg primacy sense of Freud and Jung, but with an understanding of how they are all one, all manifestations of the principle of growth at the center of all being, the continual motion flowing from the universal's love of the particular. And he is as aware of the danger inherent in that power as of its creative and moral potential. In *The Origin of the Brunists*, he approaches the force of sex and the imagination in the birth of a religious sect; the blood and violence on the Mount of Redemption in a night of religious frenzy are as essential to the creative union of the lovers in the novel as the Beast's rage is to the curing of its poisonous head. In *The Universal Baseball Association, Inc.,* he celebrates the reality of the living moment in all its inscrutability even as he admits the danger of the imagination to the dwellers in that moment. In both books, he cares truly for the creation with all its madness and disaster.

R. H. W. Dillard. HC. April, 1970. p. 3

Like a child who pats a pile of wet sand into turrets and crenelated ramparts, Robert Coover prods at our most banal distractions and vul-gar obsessions, nudges them into surreal and alarming forms. His fictions—novels, stories and . . . plays—sound at times like incantations which, as they progress, mount to frenzy. What began slowly, seemingly grounded in homely realistic details, lurches, reels a bit, becomes possessed by manic excitation; the characters' faces dissolve to reveal archetypal forms beneath; time and direction come unglued; the choices a writer makes to send his story one way or another are ignored so that simultaneously all possible alternatives occur and, at the end, as often as not, we find our laughter contracting in our throats because some of Coover's stories can be fearsome indeed.

Peter S. Prescott. *Nwk*. May 15, 1972. p. 98

[*A Theological Position* is] a collection of four plays by an author whose works of fiction have been highly praised. Like the fiction, these plays go beyond the absurd to the ridiculous. All of them are wildly extravagant satires on theatrical and social standards and norms—*The Kid* is the ultimate deadly statement on the Western epic; *Love Scene* should leave no director or actor unshaken; *Rip Awake* turns the legend of Rip Van Winkle entirely inside out; and the title play says all that need be said about the fatuousness of religious drama. Although there are some things in all the plays that may offend someone, there is something in the title play to offend everyone.

Richard M. Buck. *LJ*. July, 1972. p. 2426

COWLEY, MALCOLM (1898–   )

For all the integrity and skill in these poems [*Blue Juniata*], Mr. Cowley's verse in each decade partakes of the colors of the period style. Yet what, in another man's book, might seem imitative of Frost or Masters in the early poems, or echoes of Eliot or Fearing later along, are in Mr. Cowley's part of the texture of his subject, the literary sensibility of the past half-century. Mr. Cowley's gifts as interpreter of that sensibility, most memorable perhaps in *Exile's Return*, make *Blue Juniata* a book whose value as a witness of our culture outweighs its not being beaten into a markedly personal language or rhythm. The quality of perception behind the poems seems more vivid than the lines in which it is embodied. Yet I cannot imagine a reader who will not read this book without being moved, or finding pleasure in it.

Daniel Hoffman. *Poetry*. Aug., 1969. p. 336

It is possible to approach a work like [*A Second Flowering*] with just a touch of resentment. We have read about the Lost Generation until our heads are water-logged with its self-congratulation, its nostalgia. One broods over the gallons, the tuns, the tank cars of ink spilled out on the lives and work of these men—Hemingway's bibliography alone must be on its way to several volumes requiring sturdy book ends—and one thinks: enough. . . .

These are not just thrice-told tales, they seem by now to be so numbingly familiar as to be almost personal—tedious old gossip having to do with some fondly regarded but too often outrageous kinfolk. And if the work also affects a critical stance, do we look forward to still more commentary on "The Bear" or Cummings's love lyrics? Or another desolating inventory of the metaphors in *The Great Gatsby*? In *A Second Flowering* all of these matters are touched upon, yet it is testimony to Cowley's gifts both as a critic and a literary chronicler that the angle of vision seems new; that is, not only are his insights into these writers' works almost consistently arresting but so are his portraits of the men themselves.

William Styron. *NYT*. May 6, 1973. p. 8

CRANE, HART (1899–1932)

Some one thing is steadily happening in *The Bridge*; something is not only being disclosed and revealed, but some positive activity is pushing ahead. If *The Bridge* does not, certainly, contain a clear narrative sequence, neither is it a haphazard meandering of the Quixotic or picaresque imagination. What gives the poem its momentum, I suggest, in an *unflagging process of permeation*. . . . The plot of *The Bridge* is the gradual permeation of an entire culture by the power of poetic vision— by that ever-pursuing, periodically defeated but always self-renewing visionary imagination which, as I have said, is the true hero of the Romantic epic. When this heroic force has invaded and uncovered and transformed as much of the culture as it knows, beauty and harmony have come again; it gives voice to its ultimate hymn of praise, and the poem is done. . . . The pulsations of *The Bridge* intimate a world not ending but a world reborn, or about to be reborn, out of the enormous creative struggle of the imagination.

R. W. B. Lewis. *The Poetry of Hart Crane* (Princeton). 1967. pp. 381–2

In one way perhaps Whitman's example, which seemed to offer [Crane] validation, did him more harm than good. Temperamentally, perhaps, especially in the final years of his short life, Crane had more in common with St. John of the Cross than with Whitman. If he had lived earlier and elsewhere, he might have trusted his mystic experiences, and interpreted them as "a flight of the alone to the alone." "The way down," into the depths of consciousness, was very possibly the only mystic way Crane had ever personally and strongly experienced. His life was too anguished, his experience too scarifying, to encourage frequent perceptions of "immanent divinity." But Whitman's "way up," his nature mysticism, was the only *example* Crane knew. He was forced to interpret his experiences of illumination in terms fundamentally alien to his temperament.

Hyatt H. Waggoner. *American Poets*
from the Puritans to the Present
(Houghton). 1968. p. 509

In modern American poetry the lyric customarily records the confessional impulses of a tormented sensibility, often in an overwrought rhetoric, in a poem of and about self-consciousness. In these journals of pain, the poet's forcing of feeling sometimes induces a forcing of syntax and a taxing of language. Each poem is an unfolding of contraries, a religious-erotic experience. In Crane's poems, the points of pressure are often the sublimated equivalents of the pressure of feeling in his life: the swings from hurt to joy and from exaltation to despair, the air of tense, distraught eagerness to will love into being and to war with death in the self. This drama of both unfulfillment and transfiguration is played out to a dazzling, driven music. The language sweeps along lyrical currents —jammed, excited, buoyant, involuted, majestic.

The immediacy and verve of Crane's poetry or its complicated verbal surface cannot be denied. Many of his readers feel that they are looking through a frosted window and are only dimly if tantalizingly aware of what is behind that window. But, as T. S. Eliot said, it is a test that "genuine poetry can communicate before it is understood." What is not sufficiently accepted is that Crane was a good poetic workman, devoted to his craft and continually refining his tools. He is not an unschooled rhapsode. There are pattern, sense, and method in his poems. . . .

Herbert Leibowitz. *Hart Crane*
(Columbia). 1968. p. 21

Each episode [of *The Bridge*] presents directly rather than symbolizes a different kind or stage of consciousness. All contribute to the "world dimensional" of the poem, the world in which the poet, after the fashion of Satan in the epigraph from *The Book of Job* that prefaces *The Bridge*, goes to and fro in the earth and up and down in it, enacting in his movement the doubleness and balance that distinguish so many elements of the poem. To follow him is to learn of heaven and hell, of vast continents and seas, of immense elemental energies (nebular, volcanic, meteorological) and processes (diurnal, seasonal, vegetative), of evolutionary and human history. It is indeed to know the constituents of chaos—and of cosmos.

Sherman Paul. Hart's Bridge
(Illinois). 1972. p. 300

The synesthesia, synergy and syncopation [Crane] so brilliantly mastered were the shifts of a peculiarly naked temperament supported by a first-rate intelligence.

In all the many willingly submissive acts he had to perform, acts of graceful homage to masters genuine and spurious, to Stieglitz, Stein, Whitman, Blake, Rimbaud, Hopkins, Dante and Eliot on the one hand (I've left out a dozen), to Ouspensky and Spengler on the other, his keen mother wit told him that he had arrived somehow just off the beat—by a hair. It had already cost him a mighty effort to break free of the myths laid down by the great Midwestern novelists. Once free, like Keats he seemed to embrace and swallow all his own time, releasing it only in a poetry so splendidly ambiguous about most of the things that harried his time-bound friends that to this day it guards its wisdom with a positively Delphic severity.

Not bridges, harbors, Manhattan or the Indians, not Columbus or Pocahontas or the tropics or jazz or the sea, were his private discoveries. But it was a measure of his genius that his finest verse in *The Bridge* dared to rival Twain on the Mississippi and Whitman on New York, achieving in his serviceable contracted iambic pentameter almost the same magnificence. No models, then, but the best and least widely understood.

R. W. Flint. NYT. July 21, 1974. p. 5

CREELEY, ROBERT (1926–   )

Of Creeley's language much has been written elsewhere, and it will suffice here to make a few generalizations based on a close reading of these new poems [*Words*]. Basically he develops a context of speech in which the substance of flat, ordinary conversation becomes immediate and recognizable as what one would call archetypal language. For instance, although I do not remember Creeley using this specific example, the simple question "What is the matter?" becomes in Creeleyese the ultimate, extraordinary question, rather than a mindless, surface solicitation. His language dramatizes the quiet desperation of automatic speech, and the seemingly flat, prosaic talking in these poems actualizes the screamings of the modern soul. (It seems to me no accident that Hemingway's publisher has presented this stylistic innovator.) The language here is presentational, and the statement, often a fragment in line form, is never isolated, depending on the previous line and growing from that line as well as from itself, beyond itself to the next line. What appears as flatness is in reality the groping mind.

Donald Junkins. MR. Summer, 1968. p. 601

Read at a sitting, these pieces [in *Pieces*] grow together, live together, after the manner that Creeley describes in one of his best poems. . . . This is a strenuous volume, requiring the most intense effort on the part of the reader to actualize the abstractions through which this poetry works, in its search for "a locus of experience, not a presumption of expected value." . . . It is impossible, I believe, to become more abstract without destroying the very presence of poetry. Yet Creeley manages to hold himself at the taut edge of poetic existence. It is a dangerous technique, impossible, I imagine, to imitate successfully, but a unique and worthy achievement in its own right.

Louis L. Martz. YR. Winter, 1970. p. 261

Pieces is a very wise and very beautiful book of verse. It enacts the piecemeal achievement of a vision so scrupulous and catholic that what by method is merely muscular and aesthetic becomes in the end profoundly moral. . . . Ordinary objects . . . locate extraordinary experiences in Creeley's poetry because he is so careful about his words and the expressive possibilities of line length. . . .

The stunning quality of such spareness can perhaps only be fully appreciated in the context. This means, in the fullest sense, as part of the entire book, for Creeley has carefully constructed the whole thing as a unit of beautiful discretions: "My plan is/these little boxes/make sequences." Which is to say, every word, every line, every poem, is forced to absolute separateness, for Creeley believes that real unity can only come when the pieces possess their own radical integrity. . . . Language here is perfectly articulated—if the poem courts a danger it is that all the pieces will collapse and scatter, like a stack of blocks—yet the whole accumulates itself in a collective refusal to swallow up any of its parts. We see the pieces and the sequences with equal clarity, as Creeley planned us to do. Such a devotion to language is a double pleasure, of purpose, of result. One does not achieve this easily: a poet must know his place and see to it.

Jerome McGann. Poetry.
Dec., 1970. pp. 201–3

In *St. Martin's,* a small collection of poems occasioned by a visit to the West Indies, Mr. Creeley maintains his normal austerity of manner. Clipped and quiet, his speech combines a mild surface with sharp signs of turbulence below. His strenuous allegiance is to reality, to the truth of his unyielding nature and the bleak limitations of all human existence. The colourless imprecision of his language directs the reader to those burdens and pleasures of friendship and love that supply Mr. Creeley with his special themes. The most appealing poems in the book are the two longest, a pair of love poems addressed to his wife. In them the poet manages to follow the exact, sudden shifts of his mind while he rises subtly through a patterned sequence of images and attitudes (linked but unpredictable) to a beautifully prepared ending.

TLS. July 23, 1971. p. 855

The basic organizational plan [of *A Day Book*], the jacket explains, is of "a record of experience." The implicit aim is to embody poetic process, the way we get from our daily empirical consciousness into a self-transcendent art. Almost half the book's approximately 165 pages is made up of prose entries in a journal; the rest consists of poetic entries, often parallel or at least reciprocal to the prose. Since the book is unpaginated (an annoyance, given its size, whenever one wants to go back and find anything in it), and since no time divisions within its span of more than thirty months are specified, we have the impression of an almost undifferentiated drift of consciousness. Yet the sequence retains a fundamental, sometimes absorbing *promise.* Who can tell what will show up next in the float, partly confessional and partly atmospheric, of events, conversations, gossip, crumbs of literary or philosophical thought, introspective moments, *aperçus,* outbursts of erotic fantasy and memory, and moments of defeat by or triumph over depression that the drift carries along with it? If we take into consideration the poet's varied interests in jazz, drugs, varieties of sexual behavior, being on the move, and the confusions of love and family life, we have an ambience not unlike the television documentary *An American Family,* with modulations—would God that side were more consciously striven for!—toward Proustian recollection. When that Proustian effort does occur, as in the long poem "People," we see how moving the whole work might have been.

M. L. Rosenthal. *Parnassus.* Fall–Winter,
1973. pp. 205, 207

CULLEN, COUNTEE (1903–1946)

A strong academic orientation is apparent in most of [Cullen's] poems. Eschewing racial themes for the most part, Cullen worked a rigorous technical mastery over meter and rhyme and won plaudits and publication even while an undergraduate. Cullen modeled most of his verse on John Keats, whom he invoked on more than one occasion. But despite his efforts toward "universality," Cullen's most successful poetry is distinctly racial—something he himself subsequently came to realize.

> Edward Margolies. *Native Sons*
> (Lippincott). 1968. p. 42

[Cullen] was, and probably still is, considered the least race-conscious of the Negro poets. . . . Nevertheless, it was because of the color of his skin that Countee Cullen was more aware of the racial poetry and could not be at all times "sheer poet." This was clearly a problem for Cullen—wanting to write lyrics on love, death, and beauty—always so consciously aware of his race. This can be seen, for instance, in his poem "Uncle Jim," where the struggle is neatly portrayed through the young boy, thinking of Keats, and his uncle, bitter with thoughts of the difference between being a black man or a white man in our society. . . .

For Cullen, then, the racial problem was always there, even when one was thinking of odes by Keats, and he was impelled—*in spite of everything I can do*—to write about this subject. This was the cause of much weakness in his writing, as well as some strength; for there are poems about race which have an emotional intensity that most of his white peers could not have matched.

> Margaret Perry. *A Bio-Bibliography of*
> *Countee P. Cullen* (Greenwood).
> 1971. pp. 26–8

Few of the notable Negro poets of the 1920s worked with the pagan-primitive theme as much as Cullen (indeed, it appears in only a few of his poems). . . . And Cullen's efforts were confused as well, because they were not merely attempts to explore the source of African nativity, the wellsprings of Negro spirit and identity. But for that poet, Africa and "paganism" were instruments in his personal rebellion against the Christian church. His religious skepticism was always voiced as stemming from race consciousness: "Lord, I fashion dark gods, too." Cullen's attitudes about Africa and primitivism are enigmatic because they are only tools of this deeper revolt. "The Shroud of Color," which is free of primitivism, is a far more successful statement of his problem with Christianity than "Heritage." And while the latter is probably the author's best known work, the former is far the better poem for its clarity. Actually, even his struggle with faith was emblematic of a far deeper and more traumatic rebellion which his training in the genteel convention ill-equipped him to handle. Both as a person and a poet, Cullen tried to free himself of an unusually close relationship with his adoptive father, a minister. His personal rebellion was slight and genteel. Searching always—and futilely—for an adequate *persona*, Cullen toyed with the self-image of the pagan poet.

Nathan Irvin Huggins. *Harlem Renaissance*
(Oxford—N.Y.). 1971. pp. 164–5

In his earliest poems, Cullen . . . wanted to believe that impulses of his African heritage surged past his censoring consciousness and forced him to repudiate the white gods of Western Civilization. Cullen's Africa, however, was a utopia in which to escape from the harsh actualities of America, and the heritage a myth on which he hoped to erect a new faith to comfort himself in a world seemingly dedicated to furthering the interests of white men. . . .

As the African impulse waned, Cullen knelt before the altar of love, but there also false gods demanded sacrifices he would not offer. Like a wanderer disconsolate after a worldwide search, Cullen turned back to Christ. But he still could not rely upon the white god who governed the Methodist Church in which he had been reared; he could not believe a white god capable of comprehending the depths of a black man's suffering. Therefore, he fashioned for himself a black Christ with "dark, despairing features." This image, however, furnished scant comfort; Cullen knew that his own creation could not correct mankind's transgressions. Without faith, without vision, Cullen, whom Saunders Redding has compared with Shakespeare's ethereal Ariel, lost his power to sing and soar above the fleshly Calibans.

Darwin T. Turner. *In a Minor Chord: Three
Afro-American Writers and Their Search for
Identity* (Southern Illinois). 1971. p. 61

CUMMINGS, E. E. (1894–1962)

[Cummings's] poetry and prose give us the purest example of undiluted Emersonianism our century has yet provided. In his Introduction to the new poems included in *Collected Poems* (1938) Cummings had placed himself unequivocally in the Emersonian tradition, but there has been a subsequent failure of even his most sympathetic interpreters to understand this. The paradox must be explained by the fact that in the recent past critics young enough and "modern" enough to be interested in Cummings have had no real firsthand and extensive knowledge of Emerson.

Hyatt H. Waggoner. *American Poets*
from the Puritans to the Present
(Houghton). 1968. p. 516

Generally we may say that Cummings' typographical inventions are instruments for controlling the evocation of the poem in the mind of the reader; they are means of mitigating the temporal necessities of language with its falsification of the different, temporal rhythms of experience itself. Cummings is a painter, of course, and most of his poems are two things, auditory art and visual art, nonrepresentational pictures whose appearance on the page is essential to the artist's intention.(His correspondence with his publishers confirms this.) There is, typically, an intimate connection between the poem's appearance and the proper control of reading rate, emotional evocation, and aesthetic inflection. Indeed, one has the sense, reading these "picture poems" (his phrase) aloud, that one is translating inadequately from one language to another, with proportionate loss to the mere listener. This is an especially striking realization when one remembers that Cummings himself read his poems memorably, indeed read his own work better than any other living poet. One wonders what the greatness would be if he could hear in Cummings' voice what is added in the eye.

John Logan in *Modern American Poetry*,
edited by Jerome Mazzaro
(McKay). 1970. p. 260

I certainly don't think Cummings' reputation is helped by the persistent preservation, inviolate, of all 739 poems in the new edition [of *Complete Poems*]; for his was a narrow art; he repeated himself shamelessly and went through practically no development of theme or method once he had settled into a niche. If poems were paintings the 739 could be bought and sold and hung with joy in 739 individual parlors, but since they are not paintings they huddle together uncomfortably in this heavyweight volume and represent him as a heavyweight poet, which he was not; he was a gloriously special poet who could do what he could do.

Particularly since he prided himself on his uniqueness—and in fact thought of any act of creation as primarily an individual's assertion of uniqueness—it seems a mistake to have the 739 wandering around forever in a lump. He deserves a slimmer, brighter image, for he remains a delight for youth. It doesn't matter that while he tells youth not to pay any attention to the syntax of things he is himself infatuated by the syntax of things; he comes over loud and clear as an indefatigable promoter of spring, love and the private life, and an equally indefatigable condemner of most of our faceless modernity.

Reed Whittemore. NR. Oct. 21, 1972. p. 32

Where Emerson was essentially a Neoplatonist, Cummings was a scoffer in his youth, then more and more a Christian. He does not think of Christ as the most perfect man, in Emerson's way of speaking, but rather prays to him as a divine intercessor. In theological terms his God is less immanent than Emerson's and more transcendent. He says in a poem addressed to God—here I translate into prose—"How should any tasting, touching, hearing, seeing, breathing, merely human being—lifted from the no of all nothing—doubt unimaginable You?" As regards a future life, one of the subjects on which Emerson remained ambiguous, Cummings lets us infer that he believes in the resurrection of the flesh.

Malcolm Cowley. YR. Spring, 1973. p. 352

The mystery of E. E. Cummings's great aborted talent is not solved, only deepened, by his *Complete Poems.* His brave quixotry . . . has made him one of the poster gurus of a new generation: "one's not half two. It's two are halves of one," says the motto shining poignantly on a brilliant yellow-orange background, with a single flower as shy adornment of this revealed truth. In fact, Cummings's first and last lines are nearly always, as in this case, his memorable ones, and most of his poems sag in the middle. While we all go round remembering "nobody, not even the rain, has such small hands," or "the single secret will still be man," or "there's a hell of a good universe next door, let's go," we rarely recall what led up to these declarations. Something is wrong with the relation of parts to wholes in Cummings: we do not receive, as Coleridge thought we should, "such delight from the *whole,* as is compatible with a distinct gratification from each component *part.*" Cummings was capable of stunning parts, and these parts glitter on the page like sparklers, float up like scraps of hurdy-gurdy music—but the sparks don't organize into constellations, the music falls apart into notes and remains unorchestrated. "Our genuine admiration of a great poet," says Coleridge, "is a continuous *under-current* of feeling; it is everywhere present, but seldom anywhere as a separate excitement." Whether this is true or not, it is certain that for the most part Cummings provides only separate excitements, and is for that reason beloved of the young, who vibrate to his local effects and ask no more.

Helen Vendler. YR. Spring, 1973. p. 412

DAHLBERG, EDWARD (1900–   )

Dahlberg's early novels dealt with the theme of alienation, loneliness, separateness. They showed Lizzie clinging to society by the precarious handhold of other people's bunions, double chins, sagging breasts, stubby chins, and unwanted pregnancies, and her son forced by the hailstorms of the world into a relationship with her that was too close for comfort, so that he longed continually to be free; yet when circumstances did free him for a time, it was always into some hell like the Cleveland Jewish Orphans' Home. These disadvantages would have sunk an ungifted man, turned him permanently into a grumbling failure. In Dahlberg's case, the disadvantages became the title-deed to his own birthright. During his period of re-thinking, he rejected the dominant assumptions of the modern world, including its cultural assumptions, and by a paradox this catapulted him into the imaginative world of Yeats, Eliot, Joyce and Rilke. That he drew his own map of the world is owing to another important element in Dahlberg's character as an artist: his Jewishness.

John Wain. NYR. Jan. 2, 1969. p. 13

Dahlberg's *"Walden"* is his masterpiece, the autobiography *Because I Was Flesh*. In it the American of *The Carnal Myth* (and *The Sorrows of Priapus*) is personified as Dahlberg and his mother, who are mythologized as Ishmael and Hagar wandering in the American urban wilderness. Through the vision and style forged in *The Carnal Myth* (and other works) Dahlberg is able to assimilate their story into the universal aspects of man's nature and its embodiment in the western cultural tradition (especially its classical and Biblical aspects) and thus make of it a specific exemplification of that nature and that tradition. In so doing he overcomes that alienation from other men which all Americans suffer from, he believes, but which he suffers more acutely and with more awareness because of his illegitimacy. The book is also an act of expiation, he says, through which he embraces in love the mother he could not fully accept in life. He calls the book "a memoir of my mother's body." In it she is both a human being and an image of the earth, that ultimate source which all of his adventurers in *The Carnal Myth* unknowingly were searching for. In making her such an image and in finally embracing her, Dahlberg has, again, implicitly achieved—in the work at least—release from the American fate; instead of a sterile "treeless ghost" he is a living man in vital connection with man's source, as well as with other men.

Melvin Lyon. PrS. Spring, 1970. p. 83

Can These Bones Live is a remarkable example of criticism that is as creative as D. H. Lawrence's *Studies in Classic American Literature*, or as William Carlos Williams' *In the American Grain*. Like its generic predecessors, Dahlberg's book reveals the author's heart and temperament as much as it illuminates the literature it analyzes. Mythological influences are also responsible for the reshaping of the material in *Bottom Dogs* and in *From Flushing to Calvary* in a nonfictional mode. *Because I Was Flesh* is a reexamination of the drab world presented in the earlier novels; but this time it is presented with a rich and allusive prose style—one which reflects Dahlberg's continuing attempt to make the writing of prose the art it was in the age of Elizabeth I.

Fred Moramarco. Edward Dahlberg
(Twayne). 1972. p. 19

DE VRIES, PETER (1910–   )

The secular humanism . . . effectively places De Vries outside the purlieus of the black humorists, though he is often erroneously classified as one. He has none of the commitment to an apelike grotesquerie so characteristic of the black humorists. He is on the side of spirit and intelligence as against a cynical, naturalistic animality. The bitternesses and baffling frustrations of life he quite knows and agonizes over, but the despairing mood is never quite final, never quite absolute. The conclusion must be a torn wavering between optimism and pessimism, the needle more often quivering toward the philosophy of Wally Hines in *The Vale of Laughter*: "guarded pessimism." . . . For all its slapstick comedy, *The Mackerel Plaza* has a serious underlying theme, which I would phrase as follows: Without denying the existence of a designing intelligence in the universe, faith in a personal God is irrelevant, and the fruit of human wisdom is, in Hester Pedlock's words, "to be as humane as is humanly possible."

Louis Hasley. SAQ. Autumn, 1971. p. 474

De Vries is fun, and the humor is the most obvious element of his work. I have neglected this more obvious element to get at other sides of his characters, their individuality, sensitivity to human need, and moral self-consciousness. I have tried to point out that the atmosphere of his work changed so that these personal qualities in the second half of his corpus are grounded not on some transcendent power which supports human life but are established against transcendent powers which are impersonal and disruptive. . . .

In the later fictions, De Vries's characters see evil occurrences as not such singular, isolated events. They suffer so many losses that they give up God's world of deprivation and death and opt for the human world of joy and intimacy, a world which stands opposed to the world of change or decay. God is associated with evil; mirth and human beauty, holy moments which redeem life from sadness, are human creations.

Wesley A. Kort. *Shriven Selves*
(Fortress). 1972. pp. 55, 61

Perhaps it is because [De Vries's] unrestrained use of outrageous puns and similar verbal low comedy is so dazzling that we tend to slight his other talents as a humorist. But the range of his performance is hard to equal.

His phrasing, for instance, can be as deft as Waugh, Benchley or any of the other great comic manipulators of English, where the fun lies principally in the precise choice of words and their precise order in a sentence. He is a master of booby-trapping paragraphs. He will come on in a style as elegant as Edward Villella in a *pas de deux* and shift abruptly into some verbal pratfall in the Groucho Marx manner. He strings together narrative sequences, novel length as well as short pieces, that are as happily zany as anything Wodehouse or Mack Sennett ever dreamed up. . . .

His parodies never miss a note of the originals, and they are funny as well as accurate, which is not always the case with well-wrought parodies. The samples in this book [*Without a Stitch in Time*] run from Faulkner and Waugh to Katherine Anne Porter and Ring Lardner. He long ago showed us how to turn out the classic short piece on a light subject, with the theme stated clearly in the first sentence or two and a snapper at the end echoing back to the beginning.

Yet with all this virtuoso clowing, De Vries produces something that is more than brilliant entertainment. Like the Elizabethan fool and like all great comic writers, he is continually presenting us with the sharpest, wholly unillusioned insights into the intricacies of human relationships.

Paul Showers. *NYT*. Dec. 24, 1972. p. 3

Amongst most American novelists, even those who urgently foster a sense of the ridiculous, there exists an undermining inability to question the tenets of bastardized and expensive Freudianism. These writers, who occasionally and heroically manage to be funny in spite of it all, are in the situation of snobbish members of the English ruling classes who think to satirize the things they love and only make them shine. De Vries has evidently approached the knotty topic of analysis from the point of view of an outsider who knows that it has a certain amount in common with the devout notion of warfare between the flesh and the spirit, though it lacks the tetchily august presence of the Godhead, which is not replaced by journalism about dreams or by paperbacks about experiences on the couch. It is De Vries' Dutch Reformed background in the Christian form of the conflict, mixed with an exquisite knowledge of what everyone doesn't know about Freudian theory, that helpfully makes him an onlooker in this land.

Penelope Gilliatt. *NY.* July 16, 1973. p. 78

DICKEY, JAMES (1923—   )

[Dickey] has a powerful sense of ritual and myth, which lies behind most of his poems: a sense of the action as embodying powers larger than life, forces beyond the will of the individual. Many poems show tranced, exalted figures, seen from a distance, engaging in ritual actions. The basic perception that lies behind the poetry is thus often Dionysian, more than human. Though his central concern is with vision, not form, he is aware that the problem of form is inescapable; and we have seen how carefully he evolves the kind of rhythmic structure that he needs. Dickey began as an extremely difficult and often obscure poet; his striving toward greater openness and accessibility may be regarded as an Apollonian quality.

Monroe K. Spears. *Dionysus and the City*
(Oxford—N.Y.). 1970. p. 258

The two chief obligations of the responsible reviewer are to expose frauds (in Dickey's phrase, the "suspect poets"), and to badger the good poets out of any tendency to self-complacency, demanding that they give their best, and perhaps a little bit more. With these criteria in view, I can see that it is no accident that Dickey has been for the past ten years (until recently, when he seems to have tired of the task) the most influential poetry reviewer of his generation. Particularly the reviews he wrote in the early Sixties appear to have hit the mark. . . . In some cases, Dickey's influence—if any—may have been no more than a matter of fortifying a poet's resolve to continue to exercise powers as yet only gingerly tested, half-discovered. His chief merit, I feel, is his knack for catching a writer in the early stages of experimentation with a new style—at the precise moment of optimum daring when the urge to turn back is strongest—and chiding him into a full mastery of latent, or as yet unripened, potential.

Laurence Lieberman. Poetry. Feb., 1970. p. 347

Many quite venerable narrative devices are employed with conspicuous success in Mr. Dickey's first novel [Deliverance]: a journey into the unknown, a conflict to the death between man and man, the spectacle of man pitted against the inexorable forces of nature. All of these elements are projected against a background of fear, dread, and anxiety, manipulated with commendable skill and effectiveness to enhance the effects sought by the author. As a result he offers us a first-rate shocker, compulsive and persuasive. The book should make a successful motion picture. For Mr. Dickey, a poet of established reputation, it represents a formidable departure and a pleasant, if unexpected, diversion.

VQR. Summer, 1970. p. lxxxviii

At the core of James Dickey's Deliverance is a primal fable of intense power. The four unlikely city slickers who ride down the wild Cahulawassee River learn, in horrifying detail, what survival means and how cheap and expensive life can be. While it stays with these men and their journey, Deliverance partakes of the bardic magic that has held audiences in thrall for thousands of years, the magic of a narrative more insistent, while it lasts, than the concerns of life itself. When its battered canoe touches shore and civilization, though, Dickey's novel raises questions that cannot be ignored.

Chief among these is the retrospective attitude of the narrator, Ed Gentry, toward his experience. At the outset, the trip holds the brief promise of "another life, deliverance" from his soft urban life, from his job as art director of a commercial photography studio; it also promises Gentry another chance to study the challenge of Lewis Medlock, an intense, compelling fanatic who believes that "the whole thing is going to be reduced to the human body" and who lavishes a lover's care on his own body so as to "be ready." The disastrous journey downriver fulfills both of these promises, but it also introduces a new factor [the meaning of survival] that obliterates their importance. . . .

Paul Edward Gray. YR. Autumn, 1970. p. 104

DICKINSON, EMILY (1830–1886)

[Dickinson] was first of all true to herself and her wits. Whether from Church or Science, she would accept nothing by hearsay or on Authority, though she was tempted every way. She reserved herself in some final suspension of judgement. So her poems record not only her ecstatic devotion, but her sharp, sceptical independence, her doubt, and what repeatedly opens under her ecstasy—her despair.

However important for her poetry her life of love, with all its difficulties, may have been, there is another experience, quite as important, which seems to have befallen her often, and which had nothing to do with her outer life. It is the subject of some of her greatest poems, and all her best poems touch on it. It is what throws the characteristic aura of immensity and chill over her ideas and images. She never seems to have known quite what to think of it. It seems to have recurred to her as a physical state, almost a trance state. In this condition, there opened to her a vision—final reality, her own soul, the soul within the Universe —in all her descriptions of its nature, she never presumed to give it a name. It was her deepest, holiest experience: it was also the most terrible: timeless, deathly, vast, intense. . . . The one thing she was sure about, was that it was there, and that its speech was poetry. In its light, all other concerns floated free of finality, became merely relative, susceptible to her artistic play. It was a mystery, and there was only one thing she relied on to solve it, and that was death.

Ted Hughes. Introduction to *A Choice of Emily Dickinson's Verse* (Faber). 1968. pp. 12–3

The mythic Emily Dickinson was a shy primitive, a recluse whose retirement from the active world was due to an act of renunciation of an unattainable lover. The poet Emily Dickinson does not fit the woman of this myth. The poems she left to the world, the best evidence we have today, are the speculations and contemplations, the queries and outbursts of a tough-minded, independent woman whose self-doubt and timidities were a mask. She was a woman who allayed her despair at the world's rejection of her as a poet by composing hymns to herself and hymns to God. Emily Dickinson knew the sacrifice she was making, knew why, and was willing to gamble on an imitation of Christ for the sake of a victory like His—immortality.

Ruth Miller. *The Poetry of Emily Dickinson* (Wesleyan). 1968. p. 3

124   DICKINSON, EMILY

The voice that we hear in Emily Dickinson's poetry may be defiant, as when she challenges the God of the orthodox, or proud, when she feels confident of the soul's integrity. Sometimes we *know* that the "I" represents Emily Dickinson the person, at other times that may be our conjecture. In both of the two types of poems: the highly personal "speech"-poem, which often has a stated "I" as speaker, and the less personal "thought"-poem, there are instances of great poetry, and much unsuccessful verse as well. The dangers are sentimentality and "cuteness" on the one hand, dryness and a mechanical repetition of set formulas on the other. The glories of one are vividness, immediacy, exuberance, and originality; those of the other type are terseness, concentration of energy, and acuteness of observation.

Britta Lindberg-Seyerstad. The Voice of the
Poet: Aspects of Style in the Poetry of
Emily Dickinson (Harvard). 1968. p. 57

Rage at her abandonment and all the heightened libidinal expectations aroused by [her brother] Austin's courtship were the emotions which [Emily Dickinson] had to discharge somehow. And the rage was not mere anger but was enormously intensified, one must recall, through the addition of revived feelings of deprivation associated with her father and mother, of whom Austin and Susan [his wife] were unconsciously representative. Emily, as abandoned child, was furious, and containing wrath of such virulence, she was dangerously vulnerable to prostrating depression. If the murderous rage cannot be satisfied outright (as it cannot, usually), there are only two recourses: it can be repressed—that is, turned toward the self, which means depression and death-obsession —or the rage can be totally nullified through satisfaction of the frustrated needs which provoked the anger in the first place. The choice was made for Emily Dickinson when Samuel Bowles, or Charles Wadsworth, or whatever male acquaintance was destined for this role as "Master," offered his strength and sympathy and opened the floodgates upon himself. The release brought the poet a wave of anguish and ecstasy that dispersed itself in the creative tide that reached its crest in 1862, never afterward to be approximated.

Emily Dickinson had made the momentous discovery that the organization and symbolic intensity of poetry relieved and channeled her pent-up feelings to a degree afforded by no other avenue open to her. In this poet, creativity and psychic disorganization came within a hair's breadth of each other.

John Cody. After Great Pain: The Inner Life of
Emily Dickinson (Harvard). 1971. pp. 387–8

There was, of course, only one highly industrious Emily, who took suggestion, as was said of Coleridge with much less reason, as a cat laps milk; who was possessed of extraordinary mimic powers and a preternatural gift of language remarkable for its condensed power to arrest, to stun. And it was, finally, through a fiercely dedicated use of this admittedly unbalanced equipment that she was able to steal, though belatedly, into the company of the immortals. That is the unavoidable conclusion dictated by the facts and the inescapable inferences from them. She is attributable to no school, or is attributable to all of them, because she took from one and all indiscriminately, in full consciousness of what she was doing. She contradicted herself because it was not thought that concerned her but the expression of thought, lack of system being of no consequence to her essentially unreflective mind. Most of her work fails because it did not rise up in the heats of her own imagination, but was taken cold from the printed page, transmuted and transferred, mechanically and without personal involvement, to her own breathless phrases and flitting stanzas.

John Evangelist Walsh. *The Hidden Life of Emily Dickinson* (Simon). 1971. pp. 154–5

At the outset, and knowing well how qualified it will have to be, I should like to emphasize the degree to which [Emily Dickinson's] way of life represented a conscious choice. I think we should at least walk into the mystery standing up. More than is true of almost any other poet . . . her life, like the major vehicle of her poetry [the riddle], was metaphoric; and as she grew older, it became more and more deliberately so. From girlhood on, she enjoyed that way of conveying truth, whether by word or action. . . . Superficially, this led to not a little archness, posing, keeping the world at bay. She enjoyed riddles, apparently enjoyed being one, and was keenly aware of the dullness of the easy riddle: "The Riddle we can guess/We speedily despise—."

On a higher level, the "riddle" became metaphoric of cosmic questions that, though they haunted Emily Dickinson throughout her life, provided her very reason for being and for writing poetry. "In a life that stopped guessing," she wrote her sister-in-law, "you and I should not feel at home." But she grew up in a community and in an atmosphere in which the cosmic questions (at least officially) were all answered; "guessing" was out of order. A sentence in one of her letters to her spinster cousins would have sounded strange to orthodox Amherst ears (and perhaps to her cousins, had it not been buried in a whimsical context): "It is true that the unknown is the largest need of the intellect, though for it, no one thinks to thank God."

Thus, I think it can be said that Emily Dickinson's manner of life and her way of telling about her life were symptomatic of her sense of the mystery of things. Central to this mystery (certainly central to the biographer) was the mystery of herself.

Richard B. Sewall. *The Life of Emily Dickinson*, vol. 1 (Farrar). 1974. pp. 4–5

• DIDION, JOAN (1934–   )

First novels are the occasion of hope and prophecy. A new talent must be assessed, pigeonholed, labeled. Miss Didion [in *Run River*] writes superbly; her prose is her servant; she has an uncommon grasp of place and character. All is suavely understated, preventing melodrama, the pretense of epic dimensions, and tedious symbolism. The novel is reasonable and true. The landed gentry in California are like that. Yet— . . .

A big *yet* indeed. . . . The book is *too* even, *too* smooth. It sticks to its business with the determined regularity of minor art. All humor, all irony have been pared away. And where is invention? Must realism with all its sincerity be so flat? The English novel is eccentric, irregular, at once pathetic and ridiculous. Miss Didion has polished her prose too well for her own good. She should have put in some touches with her left hand, or attempted some little impossibilities here and there, so that we could appreciate the smudges.

Guy Davenport. *National Review*. May 7, 1963. p. 371

As melodramatic as [her] material may appear . . . it is not at all so as Joan Didion handles it. She is, above all, cool, and an impressively skilled writer. Even in this first novel [*Run River*] there seems to be nothing technically that she cannot do. . . . Her reader suspects that the author, with all of her power—to present character, to manipulate time, to suggest significance through detail and symbol, to be aware—might herself not know what she wants, or might not see life, as Philip Roth does, as possessing a tang.

Robert Maurer. *NYHT*. May 12, 1963. p. 10

Joan Didion is one of those brilliant new-breed journalists who wander sadly and watchfully across the United States as if touring a disaster area. . . . The subjects [of *Slouching towards Bethlehem*] are conventional, given Miss Didion's temperament: Las Vegas weddings (an essay on American vulgarity); San Francisco hippies (the American dream gone to pot); backstage Hollywood à la Lillian Ross; Joan Baez ("a girl who might have interested Henry James"); Howard Hughes (subversive hero of the middle-class underground). A substantial element of spiritual biography is present in these pieces of wary skepticism. Though she has a journalist's weakness for converting her themes into "myths," "dreams," and "folk" symbols—she is an original observer and even better, an original thinker. Has anyone ever written a better treatment of that overexposed topic of the year—hippies?

Melvin Maddocks. CSM. May 16, 1968. p. 11

There hasn't been another American writer of Joan Didion's quality since Nathanael West. She writes with a razor, carving her characters out of her perceptions with strokes so swift and economical that each scene ends almost before the reader is aware of it; and yet the characters go on bleeding afterward. A pool of blood forms in the mind. Meditating on it, you are both frightened and astonished. When was the wound inflicted? How long have we to live? . . .

It is the condition of a woman's mind that is her subject; it is the "nothingness" after one has been used as an object that she explores; it is the facts beyond "answers" or "explanations" that she plays with.

John Leonard. NYTd. July 21, 1970. p. 33

To read Joan Didion is to worry about her. There is in most of her work the terrible feeling that this latest pained and painful examination of whatever is on her mind right now is only the freshest installment in some epic suicide note to the world. The premonition of personal loss is apocalyptic. . . .

Here, in her second novel and first departure in almost a decade from the first-person reportage she does so excruciatingly well, are both disappointment and relief. Disappointment, because [*Play It as It Lays*] is nothing like the gorgeous caterwauling tour de force that might have been expected; relief, a personal relief, because at the end she explicitly rejects suicide as an alternative—for her—to the miserable goings-on so sparely chronicled. . . .

Familiarity with her autobiographical work makes it impossible to read this novel without recalling on almost every page the other memories, the real ones.

It doesn't seem important finally, whether this is a good book or not. Those who care about Joan Didion will have to read it. For one thing, it is a compelling exercise in literary pathology; but, most of all, it is a matter of devotion.

Nicholas A. Samstag. SR. Aug. 15, 1970. p. 27

Nullity, nothingness, human negation, *nil*—these are merely variants of the same phenomena, the essential emptiness of experience, that great hole at the middle of things. Single as the phenomena may be, the characters in novels can make varying approaches to it, as novelists themselves can have various feelings about it. It can be seized in a kind of hungry embrace, in the fashion of the moral idiots who people the world Miss Didion creates in [*Play It as It Lays*], a novel written with such bitter wit that the reader feels at the end that it must have been acid that he has been drinking. . . .

I am tempted to say that this novel is a triumph not of insight as such but of style, meaning by *style*, of course, the linguistic embodiment or, rather, actualization of imagination. . . . If Miss Didion had made one false move, the whole thing would have collapsed like a pricked balloon. But she didn't.

Mark Schorer. *AS*. Winter,
1970–1. pp. 168, 174

Didion's great talent lies in her ability to evoke the stunning abstractness of southern California "dying in the golden light." Her images of people alone on freeways, beside mansion pools, in supermarkets at three in the morning, at despairing beach parties, on blistering streets with curlers in their hair and wedgies on their feet are remarkable and compelling. And indeed, much of this sense of things pervades *Play It as It Lays*. . . .

I could not escape the sensation, as I read *Play It as It Lays*, that Maria's language was not her own: that her telescoped responses and significant silences had been placed in her mouth and behind her eyes by a generation of literary references created by an experience that was not the primary experience of the author. Thus, the story of Maria's life fails to become a convincing portrait of emotional removal; on the contrary, the story *itself* becomes an act of emotional removal. One feels oneself in the presence of a writer who believed it good to be told she wrote like a man, and has—with the tools of talent and intelligence—knocked that belief into place: a shield between herself and her work.

Vivian Gornick. *VV*. May 31, 1973. p. 32

Play It as It Lays depends upon an intimate connection between setting and theme; but also . . . its overriding thematic concern is man's relationship with himself and with existence in general. Didion's novel is neither primarily a sociological commentary on the values of contemporary American society nor a psychological case study of its heroine. It is, rather, a picture of personal dread and anxiety, of alienation and absurdity lurking within and without. For although Hollywood is her setting, nothingness is Didion's theme. . . .

The facts of Maria's life are the basic material of thousands of soap opera situations. What saves *Play It as It Lays* from degenerating into banality is Didion's control over her material, her skill in focusing attention not on the events in Maria's life so much as on her cumulative response to them. The real action of the novel takes place in the mind and heart of Maria as she is forced to deal with her experiences. Viewed from a medical point of view, she might well be classified as a near schizoid personality whose experiences have precipitated a severe emotional crisis resulting in the loss of an integrated personality. In a more profound sense, however, her sickness is neither emotional nor psychological; it is ontological. She is suffering not from a nervous breakdown, but from the breakdown of a world around her which threatens to engulf her whole being with nothingness. . . .

With relentless attention to telling detail, a perceptive eye for sharply-etched characters, an unerring ear for the absurdities and non sequiturs that pass for daily conversation, and a diamond-hard unsentimental style, Joan Didion has fashioned a remarkable novel which never misses in its portrayal of a modern woman caught in a mid-twentieth-century crisis. She has cast anew, in her unique idiom, one of the prevailing concerns of modern literature: confrontation with the void. Despite its preoccupation with death, suffering, boredom and despair, *Play It as It Lays* is always fresh and alive. The novel not only touches the heart of its reader through its sensitive treatment of Maria Wyeth but also assaults the mind in its investigation of the heart of darkness too often discovered lurking behind the fundamental questions about existence in the modern world.

David J. Geherin. *Critique.*
16, 1, 1974. pp. 64–5, 78

• DOCTOROW, E. L. (1931–   )

Thematically, E. L. Doctorow's [*Welcome to Hard Times*] is concerned with one of the favorite problems of philosophers: the relationship of man and evil. Its structure is appropriately dramatic and simple. . . . Perhaps the primary theme of the novel is that evil can only be resisted psychically: when the rational controls that order man's existence slacken, destruction comes. Conrad said it best in *Heart of Darkness*, but Mr. Doctorow has said it impressively. His book is taut and dramatic, exciting and successfully symbolic.

Wirt Williams. *NYT*. Sept. 25, 1960. p. 51

Doctorow [in *The Book of Daniel*] has written the political novel of our age, the best American work of its kind that I know since Lionel Trilling's *The Middle of the Journey*. . . . This is an artwork about the idea of the Rosenbergs and the people like them, how they came into being in this country, why their trial was needed, what their legacy is, and the intertexture of that legacy with the social-political climate today. I haven't looked up the facts of the Rosenberg case; it would be offensive to the quality of this novel to check it against those facts. This is a work of historic and psychic currents.

Stanley Kauffmann. *NR*. June 5, 1971. p. 25

The Book of Daniel is a purgative book, angry and more deeply felt than all but a few contemporary American novels, a novel about defeat, impotent rage, the passing of the burden of suffering through generations and "the progress of madness inherited through the heart." It is a novel about Daniel's struggle for detachment, his need to put a distance between himself and his story. We know he will never make it, in spite of his taking fixes from history. Daniel's suffering is the matter of this story, though he hardly recognizes it, and Doctorow, in a ferocious feat of the imagination, makes that suffering appallingly real. There is no question here of our suspending disbelief, but rather how, when we have finished, we may regain stability.

Peter S. Prescott. *Nwk*. June 7, 1971. p. 110

To E. L. Doctorow politics is clearly a matter of life and death if men can be executed for their beliefs and actions. . . .

By focusing on Daniel and his family from the end of the Second World War to the peace march on the Pentagon in 1967, Mr. Doctorow creates a sharp, harrowing vision of people dedicated to ideologies that both heighten and betray their best impulses. Despite its questionable approach, *The Book of Daniel* is a plangent reading of recent history in which private and public events can clash and destroy human beings. . . .

Mr. Doctorow is that rare American novelist who is completely serious about politics, at ease with large abstractions, and capable of welding deeply human concerns with reverberant historical notes.

Joseph Catinella. *SR*. July 17, 1971. pp. 32, 61

[*The Book of Daniel*] seems to me extraordinarily sensitive both about the past that his narrator-protagonist, Daniel Isaacson, shared with his parents and about the present in which he searches for further clues to their true identities and his own. The book begins and ends in ambiguity, with Daniel refreshingly unsure about the meaning of anything. All we know for sure is the agony of his quest—and its importance. The book jumps madly, constantly from the first to the third person and back again, pauses for quiet, scholarly little dissertations on political and social questions, catching more truly than any fiction I have ever read the quality of the Stalinist mind, voice, and life-style, without sacrificing our human sympathy for the elder Isaacsons. . . .

[This] is the work of a novelist trying desperately to catch hold of at least a fragment of the truth of our time and succeeding in getting hold of more than most have lately managed to capture.

Richard Schickel. Harper. Aug., 1971. p. 94

A method for giving us the *feel* of a historical moment—as distinct from information about it—is something that more and more of our novelists may soon be after, now that Thomas Pynchon and Doctorow have shown us how it is done, now that the millennial sixties are over and we are looking back to see what happened rather than forward to see what next. . . . The method of [Doctorow's] new novel [*Ragtime*] is dictated by the lives and times of America during that moment between the turn of the century and World War I, the moment of the arrival of the Model T, the assembly line, the moving picture, and Scott Joplin's rags. *Ragtime* succeeds entirely—as his three earlier books did not—in absorbing rather than annotating the images and rhythms of its subject, in measuring the shadows of myth cast by naturalistic detail, in rousing our senses and in treating us to some serious fun. . . .

It incorporates the fictions and realities of the era of ragtime while it rags our fictions about it. It is an anti-nostalgic novel that incorporates our nostalgia about its subject. It is cool, hard, controlled, utterly unsentimental, an art of sharp outlines and clipped phrases. Yet it implies all we could ask for in the way of texture, mood, character and despair.

George Stade. NYT. July 6, 1975. pp. 1–2

Ragtime is blandly and confidently assertive, laying its short sentences like steps on the road to nowhere, so we can't see ahead, anticipate; the characters are rhetorical ploys, but splendid. Doctorow is never confused by life, though he is often dismayed, and his impudence is both witty and grave, so we can be pleasantly caught between feeling that he is only a novelist on holiday and that all other visions of the period before his may be the really irresponsible ones. Even the ironic juxtapositions that Doctorow loves almost sentimentally may be right, necessary. Because so many of the juxtapositions are of nasty rich and suffering poor, his politics tend to seem leftish, but Doctorow tells with amusement and affection the story of a radical starving Jewish artist on the Lower East Side who becomes Baron Ashkenazy, movie maker and millionaire. His vision is of the Seventies more than of the Sixties, and the juxtapositions themselves entrance him more than any political view of history. . . .

It's hard to make a whole book out of what Doctorow does best here; it's excellent in vignettes and short passages but unsuited for plots where we come to know the characters too well. . . . Still, no one has written a book quite like *Ragtime*, just as no one had written one quite like *The Book of Daniel*. Doctorow's restless and witty thoughtfulness seems like some combination of Pynchon, Edward Gorey, and William Appleman Williams, and certainly no one ever was *that* before.

Roger Sale. NYR. Aug. 7, 1975. pp. 21–2

DOOLITTLE, HILDA (H.D.) (1886–1961)

Calling these early lyrics H.D.'s best also entails recognizing that their stature is modest. They are excellent poems but minor in range and technique. In substance they are limited to outcries of desire for beauty and love, of scorn for complacency and compromise, and of grief at the distance between her experience and her dreams. They bespeak a strong will and a rich imagination but a narrow play of intelligence. In expressing moods varying from exhilaration to misanthropy, they strike the reader as naïvely self-centered. . . .

Despite [their] promising intentions, her later works are generally less successful than the early lyrics. Although she addressed herself to larger, more compelling themes—such as the problem of loyalty and self-interest, the problem of evil and suffering, and the existence of God—her writing became less distinguished. Whereas the hallmark of her early poems had been a luminous brevity, her later work tended to be wordy and banal.

Vincent Quinn. Hilda Doolittle (H.D.)
(Twayne). 1967. pp. 146–7

H.D.'s strength lies in her rendition of detail: her weakness is in structuring those details into a poetic, characterological, or, still more acutely, fictional whole. Poems, fiction, even essays like *Tribute to Freud* or *By Avon River* become a series of isolated images or events linked by free associations, often through mythological themes. At the very sentence level, her boundaries tend to be ill-defined. A sentence modifier from one sentence will seem to apply to the next. Lists (of which H.D. uses many) will be oddly broken between sentences. The word to which a pronoun or adjective refers may be one or two sentences back; the reference itself may be twinned or multiple. Often, for structure, she will resort to a series of parallel structures to be summed into a totality. Sometimes she will use negations—a series of *not*'s or *nor*'s to strip off the extraneous and come to the final, finely rendered residue as a climax.

Doubtless no small part of H.D.'s propensity for myth is a quest for similar organizing structures. If one can see present people, events, and feelings as projections or continuations of a simpler, more structured mythic past, they become more manageable and, for H.D. at least, somehow more real. She uses for living people the image of a palimpsest or a series of old photographic negatives on top of one another; the sign one sees on the surface implies a deeper reality underneath. She seeks to turn herself, her very body, into an hieroglyph or emblem—as in the use of her initials for a seal or sign. Her poetry, like the myths she emulates, manifests that which is spiritual, abstract, and timeless by the hard, the real, the objective, the exact.

Norman Holland. *CL*. Autumn, 1969. p. 475

The poems in this new book [*Hermetic Definition*] date from circa 1960, when [H.D.] was 74. She had been inserted into literary history at 26, when Ezra Pound invented "Imagism" to supply a context for five poems of hers. A normal context would have been a book of poems, but Pound sensed that a book's worth would be a long time getting written. He had didactic uses for a "movement" anyhow, and "Hermes of the Ways," "Orchard," a few others might as well exemplify it as wait for an *oeuvre*.

Unhappily the invented movement that was meant to float her reputation encapsulated it, and though she lived many more decades and extended her self-definition through many volumes, she has remained totally identified with the very little she had done when she was first heard of. It is as though five of the shortest pieces in *Harmonium* were to stand for the life's work of Wallace Stevens.

Her psychic life was contorted. Freud himself analyzed her, and she lived her last years at Küsnacht on Lake Zurich under care that was partly psychiatric, partly directed toward the corporeal needs of an old woman who had broken her hip and walked only with difficulty. She kept resin and pine-cone burning in her room, and pondered books of hermetic symbolism. . . .

These poems are "about" her phantasmagoric self, in part her sense of having become a myth prematurely. . . .

Hugh Kenner. *NYT*. Dec. 10, 1972. p. 55

In short, writing under the pressure of war in London, the bombs falling around her, H.D. brought together all her powers in one marvelous synthesis [*Trilogy*]: her verbal power in its superbly workable maturity, her spiritual and cognitive powers, the power of her concern for the humanity of the world. If she said things about the "holiness" of the "scribe" which I as a young man in that same war learned to distrust and fear, she nevertheless grounded them firmly in the actuality of the human condition; and in doing so she created one of the great works of her time in poetry. It has been out of print for many years. Now its publication in one volume is an event to be celebrated by us all.

Hayden Carruth. HdR. Summer, 1974. p. 311

DOS PASSOS, JOHN (1896–1970)

In functioning as an "architect of history" and attempting by means of the work of art to mold the course of social history, Dos Passos turned his fiction into a series of critical documents on the age, confronting contemporary problems from the time of his attack upon war in *Three Soldiers* to that of his assault upon labor in *Mid-Century*. His "documents" have been based upon a firm set of principles, sustained from first to last. Contrary to popular opinion, which has labeled him a political apostate, a liberal-become-conservative, his values have remained constant. Simply put, they comprise a hatred of "collectivisms," with their concomitant of centralized power, an admiration for the "proletarian soul," and a persistent desire to protect this "soul" from the aggregates of power.

If Dos Passos were willing to accept any label for himself, it might be that of an "independent seeker," a nebulous term, to be sure, but one that suggests his perpetual focus both on individualism and on searching, with its implications of change. The various stereotypes that have been attached to him—the lost-generation aesthete, the fellow traveler, the ex-radical—have fitted only for a time. Underlying the "phases," however, has been an unflagging credo, a faith in the individual sturdiness of the plain people. "Individuality is freedom lived" (*Occasions and Protests*, p. 52).

W. Gordon Milne in The Politics of
Twentieth-Century Novelists,
edited by George A. Panichas
(Hawthorn). 1971. pp. 264–5

Dos Passos went on producing—many novels, reportage of the World War II period, and long semipopular histories of the growth of American democracy. But he felt isolated; he had lost his faith in people. This is even more striking a change than the long swing to the political right that went with it. . . . At the same time that he had, so to speak, come back to "The American Way" politically, he lost the openness, inventiveness and optimism that had made him so American when he was still a rebel. . . .

Dos Passos was one of the key figures in a literary lost generation that found itself and then lost itself again. It is a story still not fully told or understood, but these letters [*The Fourteenth Chronicle*], with their glimpses of an entire man who was so much more complex than his political notions or even his fiction, take us imaginatively and morally closer to understanding it.

Robert Gorham Davis. NYT.
Oct. 14, 1973. p. 4

By its intricacy and by its comprehensive sweep the trilogy *U.S.A.* comes close to being the great American novel which had been the aspiration of writers since the turn of the century. It is one of the ironies of our times that when the great American novel did arrive, it turned out to be condemnatory and pessimistic rather than a celebration of the American way. Yet there is an underlying affirmation in Dos Passos' denial. The American dream, battered and corrupted by men of ill will, or little will, still manifests itself—though in anguish—not completely stifled by the trappings of empire and the machinations of self-interest that the author describes.

What first aroused the enthusiasm of readers and critics was the technical virtuosity of the work. Dos Passos was clearly the heir of Balzac, Zola, and Galdós in his attempt to mirror contemporary society —as he was the competitor of Jules Romains, whose *Hommes de bonne volonté* was appearing during the same span of years. It is equally evident that the idea of multiple perspectives is something he owed to *Ulysses*. But the techniques he employed and the balance of elements he achieved are his own and stamp him as the last of the great inventors in the field of the social novel. He welded together four separate, even disparate, types of material, each of which is necessary to the statement the novel ultimately makes.

George J. Becker. John Dos Passos
(Ungar). 1974. p. 58

Century's Ebb may be unfinished, or at least unpolished, but it deserves to be published. It contains some good Dos Passos writing: the first, moving lyric about Walt Whitman, several impressionistic passages like one entitled "Turnpike" and another about George Eastman and his Kodak camera, and parts of the long narratives. But, finally, whether *Century's Ebb* is complete and whether it stands with Dos Passos' best fiction are not the main points to be made about the book. It is the last work of one of the major American writers to emerge during the 1920s. Most important, it brings down the curtain on Dos Passos' remarkable effort throughout his literary career to convey the panorama of 20th-century society. His later novels are partly right wing polemics, but anyone wanting to dismiss Dos Passos should remember that he was not a crank, a Westbrook Pegler, but an intelligent, thoughtful man of letters who agonized about his politics.

Townsend Ludington. NR. Nov. 22, 1975. p. 24

DREISER, THEODORE (1871–1945)

I soon found that Dreiser did straddle two worlds of time, our own and the past. His first novel, *Sister Carrie*, was begun in the nineteenth century and finished in the twentieth—a fact of which Dreiser was highly conscious. His masterpiece, *An American Tragedy*, was published at the midpoint of the 1920s, the decade when American writing assumed an importance on the international scene that had been un-imaginable when Dreiser began. He was one of those—in America, the most important of those—who put their shoulder to the wheel turning past into present; one of the great international company of *survivors*, men formed before the turn of the century but dominant after the First World War—among them Mann, Gide, Stravinsky, Joyce, Wright, Valéry, Yeats.

For someone like myself, brought up in New York, the world of Dreiser's fiction is immediately familiar, and for all of us his subject matter remains the most important. He wrote about the child who comes alive in the American city, that ugly, intoxicating center of the modern world. Yet when I first read Dreiser I found him quite unlike any American novelist before him (and most after), in his rooted urbanism first of all. He seemed to accept the American situation as the norm—an un-usual state of affairs for an American writer—and his style was peculiar. He handled words, sometimes brilliantly, sometimes wretchedly, without the sound of pebbles in the mouth—the nervous rattle of insecurity that makes much American fiction, for me at least, a provincial phenomenon even at its most brilliant. The publication of *Sister Carrie* in 1900 marks the boundary line not only between the old and the new, but between the European and the American century.

Ellen Moers. Two Dreisers
(Viking). 1969. p. viii

We have been speaking as though *Sister Carrie* were important primarily as an historical and social document and as a record of the psychology of Dreiser. But it is more than a document, it is a vivid and absorbing work of art. In dealing with a novel, the most obvious question is what kind of material the author has thought worth his treating, what kind of world stimulates his imagination. For Dreiser this was the world he lived in and the world he was, and by accepting as fully as possible this limitation, he enlarged, willy-nilly, by a kind of historical accident if you will, the range of American literature. The same kind of compulsive veracity that made him record such details of his own life as masturbation and theft, made him struggle to convert into fiction the substances of experience at both the social and personal level that had not been earlier absorbed. The kind of realism that is associated with William Dean Howells had little relation to the depths that Dreiser inhabited, and even if Frank Norris had shocked the country with the realism of *McTeague*, he had, in the end, gratified the moral sense of America by converting the novel of greed and violence into a cautionary fable. But *Sister Carrie* was different from anything by Howells or Norris. What was shocking here was not only Dreiser's shamed willingness to identify himself with morally undifferentiated experience or his failure to punish vice and reward virtue in his fiction, but the implication that vice and virtue were, in themselves, mere accidents, mere irrelevances in the process of human life, and that the world was a great machine, morally indifferent.

Robert Penn Warren. *SoR*. Spring, 1971. p. 359

Dreiser would have us see that Jennie [in *Jennie Gerhardt*] is caged from the beginning of the novel, just as Clyde Griffiths in *An American Tragedy* is imprisoned by "tall walls" from first to last. In that work the wall images take on a variety of forms defining the exact nature of Clyde's physical and psychic entrapment. Analogously, the boundaries of Jennie's confinement increasingly come into focus throughout the book until we see that, as is typical of Dreiser, the social, material barrier the author overtly refers to in this second chapter stands for a more universal condition. All of Dreiser's protagonists share Jennie's initial instinctive sense of belonging to a particular world, except that for most it is symbolized by the city and not by Jennie's pastoral landscape. They somehow feel that their world—the city that looms magical, dreamlike, and compelling in the opening pages of Dreiser's novels—is rightfully theirs, as if by inheritance, and that they must achieve a more *perfect* harmony with this exciting "conformable" world, must come fully to possess and be possessed by an environment whose mores and processes they accept as the law of their behavior. Yet Dreiser's characters yearn infinitely, and therefore even if their world were not flawed, there is no Eden which can really be a refuge and a fulfillment for them—not until the bulwark Solon Barnes [in *The Bulwark*] comes to terms with a snake.

Warwick Wadlington. *SoR.*
Spring, 1971. p. 422

Most of his early novels, *Sister Carrie, Jennie Gerhardt, The "Genius,"* reveal the young Dreiser searching, puzzling, finding what life can give or take, learning the caprice of existence. His family memories are all in these books. But the [Cowperwood] Trilogy is different, being based less upon Dreiser actualities than upon Dreiser dreams. Into *The Financier* and its sequels poured Dreiser's most grandiose imaginings of the wonders of sex and money that just might have been his, presupposing a more propitious beginning and more favorable impelling "chemisms."

Philip L. Gerber. *PMLA.* Jan., 1973. pp. 118–9

Dreiser's artistry is difficult to discuss because so much of it must be attributed to natural tendencies. Certainly it is Dreiser's natural tendency to let his dark symbols float and to draw his narrative out that works to his advantage in *An American Tragedy*. Where in *The Financier* the long section devoted to Frank's trial serves only a slight purpose aesthetically, in *An American Tragedy* the drawing-out of Clyde's trial becomes, finally, a superbly masterful treatment of suspense. The lengthiness of the trial section also corresponds to the lengthy deliberations Clyde goes through in deciding what he is going to do about Roberta. It is structurally fitting that as much space be given to the legal decision eventually made concerning Clyde's crime as Clyde gave to his own agonizing meditation over whether or not to commit the crime. Despite the many negative things that must be said about the way Dreiser handles the form of his other novels, his technique, his style, and the essentially sentimental power of his imagination work together to produce in *An American Tragedy* a narrative that is at once a folk-epic and a complex work of something other than art—a "psychology of reality," perhaps.

James Lundquist. *Theodore Dreiser*
(Ungar). 1974. pp. 103–4

• DREXLER, ROSALYN (1926–   )

This vital, intense "diary" [*I Am the Beautiful Stranger*] of one Selma Silver, who was growing from ages 13 to 16 in the 1930's, is swift, complete, individual, and universal. You can mock its occasional sillinesses, but you're left holding its truths. For Selma is wholly convincing even when you can hardly believe her. . . . Back then, when "teenager" hadn't yet been invented, I don't think anybody talked the way Selma sometimes does. But nobody back then (except maybe Saroyan) wrote as spiritedly as Mrs. Drexler does, either.

Maggie Rennert. BW. June 27, 1965. p. 22

Rosalyn Drexler's plays suggest, more than anything else, the early Marx Brothers. Wayward, full of lip, fantastic yet anchored in domesticity, they work at reordering all those matter-of-fact details, from the date on the calendar to the necessity of putting on one shoe after another, which obstruct us in our pursuit of significant whim and appetite. . . . All her dialogue issues from an imagination which has previously discovered the uses of language for new guise, for bluff, feint, decoy and red herring—all necessary properties and instrumentalities of the crucial game that goes on in most of her work. The game might be called "keep them guessing" or "never give a sucker an even break." For Mrs. Drexler's imagination holds that the world is forever trying to impose roles and identities upon us which it is our duty and pleasure to resist and repudiate by outwitting the identifiers and the casting directors.

Richard Gilman. Introduction to The Line of
Least Existence by Rosalyn Drexler
(Random). 1967. pp. ix–xi

In addition to writing plays, the libretto for *Home Movies* which won the off-Broadway award known as the "Obie," and two successful novels, Rosalyn Drexler is a successful painter. This visual orientation may explain her highly untraditional view of theatrical language, a quality evident in all her plays. Like Koch, she conceives of language as most engaging when least eloquent, and closest to a state of pure "flatness." In *Hot Buttered Roll* the dialogue is in the prose style of the girlie magazine. The play is about a certain Mr. Corrupt Savage, whose most passionate wish is to go on spending his days in contemplation of the supposedly inspiring pictures and text characteristic of this genre. . . . In

Drexler's reality, the eternally flesh-contemplating Corrupt Savage is the nearest thing to a true saint, or hero. It is the cold calculators who surround him, those contemptuous of human fantasies however odd or pathetic, who are the real villains of the piece.

Michael Benedikt. *Theatre Experiment*
(Doubleday). 1967. p. 197

The Line of Least Existence is a joy to read, as are all Rosalyn Drexler's plays in the collection recently published by Random House. Few contemporary playwrights can equal her verbal playfulness, fearless spontaneity, and boundless irreverence; few in fact, share her devotion to pure writing, preferring their language functional, meaningful, or psychologically "real." Whether her plays amount to anything, whatever that means, is hard to say: hers is obviously an up-to-date sensibility, and I read considerable off-hand, tough, supercool wisdom about human relationships into her fantastifications, knowing all the time that they may be as frivolous as they look.

Michael Smith. *VV*. March 28, 1968. p. 50

The new literary voice comes from some odd and perilous psychic area still being charted, some basic metabolic flashpoint where the self struggles to convert its recurrent breakdowns into new holds on life and reality. It is the voice of writers like Donald Barthelme, Thomas Pynchon, and Rosalyn Drexler. In her new book [*One or Another*], Mrs. Drexler monitors the voice of Melissa . . . married to Mark. . . . In these lives madness is no longer a possibility—it is a note in their chord of being that automatically sounds with every breath they draw. . . . What counts now is the delicate new apotheosis, a new transcendence that accepts the mad world as the only human habitat, while plotting shrewdly against its madness. Few writers have been able to suggest this new transcendence. Mrs. Drexler is one of them: funny, scary, preternaturally aware, she is at the exact center where the new sensibility is being put together cell by cell.

Jack Kroll. *Nwk*. June 1, 1970. p. 87

One or Another is a very funny book; moreover, it is both funny "ha-ha" and funny "weird," an observation Melissa Johnson, the novel's heroine-narrator, would be likely to make herself. In *One or Another* reality and unreality are merged; the borderline between dreams and actual events has been erased; shadows are indistinguishable from substance. Obviously, a novel of the interior is not concerned with plot. Mere sequences of events hold no interest. Style alone sustains *One or Another*. With careful economy and wit (that rare commodity bludgeoned out of so much of contemporary literature), Miss Drexler guides the reader through the tortured dreamscape in which Melissa Johnson finds both refuge and exile.

William Hjortsberg. *NYT*. June 28, 1970. p. 5

[In *To Smithereens*] the relaxed sleaziness and community of the lady wrestling world alternates with the frantic, tired chic of the plastic New York art scene, in which here-barely-disguised New York artists and hangers-on act out their own fantasies of power, success, and grandeur. Does it all sound slightly sick, weird, ugly/sad, and obsessed-with-violence? It's exactly the opposite. . . . [Rosalyn Drexler] has a marvelous talent for taking this kind of material and imbuing it with qualities of great warmth and wicked satire, pathos, and a haunting aura of nostalgia for a world most of us have never known. . . . She's an absolute original who can take all the ingredients that usually characterize "serious fiction" . . . and use them with inventiveness, playfulness, and even hilarity.

Sara Blackburn. *Book World*.
March 19, 1972. p. 5

The scene of [*To Smithereens*] is less a time and a place—New York, mainly in the late Sixties and early Seventies—than a condition of consciousness. New York becomes a name for a brand of hysteria, for a circus of crazies, comically seen and perfectly human and manageable as it turns out. Paul and Rosa, individual and well-defined as they are, tend to disappear into this collective portrait. Paul is the twitchy, ruined modern male from an R. Crumb comic ("the *universal* Paul," Rosa thinks), and Rosa is the resurgent female, all immediacy, innocence, and half-nelsons.

"You're not as crazy as you seem, are you?" a character says in Rosalyn Drexler's play *The Line of Least Existence*. "None of us is. We're all rational people." The specific context of the words makes them sound like a desperate pleading lie; we are just as crazy as we seem, if not crazier, but please let's not admit it. But the play itself, and in particular the character of the woman speaking the lines, suggests that what the words say is literally, drably true. We are dull people, and any semblance of vivid craziness we may present is an illusion. Mrs. Drexler knows that we really are crazy, and in very bad shape; but she also knows that the forms of our craziness have a conformity, a banality all of their own. Between madness and grayness, or out of a gray madness, we have to put something together.

Michael Wood. *NYR*. Aug. 10, 1972. p. 14

The raunchy and the ridiculous are Drexler's home territory—you feel she spends a lot of time in all-night cafeterias. Her word-play is like sword-play—with rubber swords that still deliver a stinging slap. Her set-pieces—newspaper clippings, radio interviews, beauty advice—are among the delights of [*The Cosmopolitan Girl*]; her one-liners are memorable. . . . She weaves a seamy web of parodies that covers the situation perfectly. Moving back and forth between the absurd and the everyday Drexler puts both in their place—on the same plane. *The Cosmopolitan Girl* is a send-up and send-off for the New Woman.

Sara Sanborn. *NYT*. March 30, 1975. p. 4

DUGAN, ALAN (1923–   )

The poems of Alan Dugan come nearer [than those of Howard Nemerov] to a deep bitterness. They are enormously skillful and terse, and have been carved out in an idiom which Dugan has made entirely and identifiably his own. It is a strange but effective juxtaposition of lofty poetic diction and straight, unpolished, low-down vernacular. When his aim is satiric, as, for example, in "Self-Exhortation on Military Themes," this double-tone can obviously be used ingeniously to exhibit the cheapness and transparency of Noble Postures. But this is not the only way he uses it, and this book [*Poems 3*] is by no means a simple confrontation of "poetic" shams and ugly truths. Dugan is at least as much attracted by the possibilities of grandeur as by the need to confess disappointment; and I would be willing to bet that there's not a poet writing today who uses the exclamatory "Oh" more frequently.

Anthony Hecht. *HdR*. Spring, 1968. pp. 214–5

The poet Robert Graves in a memorable lecture series once criticized Ezra Pound's unabashed ambition of writing great poems. For Graves, it is more than enough simply to try to write good poetry. Such a view may perhaps be too easily explained by the fact that it represents the advice of a minor poet to a great poet. Alan Dugan is a good poet who has in his own peculiar way proven what Graves was getting at. By cultivating what is by any standard a confining style, and by exercising his caustic intelligence on a relatively narrow range of subjects, Dugan has created a significant body of work that speaks with authority to a variety of modern readers. One does not get terribly excited about Alan Dugan's work, but one nevertheless returns to it with increasing regularity, for it successfully inhabits that middle ground of experience which our best poets today seem loathe to admit, as though to do so would somehow in itself constitute a denigration of their talents and a disavowal of intensity. . . .

His predictable low-keyed humor, so often remarked upon by others, does little to mitigate the stinging venom of self-contempt that courses through so much of Dugan's work. His is a bitter eloquence. If the cadence is austere, it is rarely impoverished, and the muscular flow of his terse diction is rarely purchased at the expense of complexity. Dugan invites us to witness with him, without any redemptive qualification, the sordid spectacle of our common humiliation.

Robert Boyers. Salmagundi.
Spring, 1968. pp. 43, 52

In this third collection [*Poems 3*], Dugan's electric, eccentric charge survives, intensifies, clarifies; something dead and defeated beyond rage in *Poems 2* . . . has been drummed or charmed or bled away. The exhibits are the same: emblems of husbandhood, of war, of *The Working World's Bloody Flux*, of the body of this death and the sordid capitalism of desire: a persistence of excruciation over "the fall to flesh," over "goods, deeds, credits, debts." But the Dugan of *Poems 3* is less bitterly private, less grudgingly obscure than before, less impelled to dump on his own performance as a proof of cynic sincerity. The uncompromising honor of audacity remains; the forged ironies have mellowed here and there to the outright coolth of good humor; poem after poem assaults us with the astonishment of lyric beauty.

Barry Spacks. Poetry. July, 1968. p. 270

Days like these, to take Alan Dugan from the shelf is like finding another grownup at a birthday party for kiddies. An intelligent being! You want to fall to your knees in gratitude. Warfare versus Peace, for example, is a major theme in *Collected Poems*; unlike other writers who have been to the wars, Dugan neither boasts nor sobs, but like a man suckled on Virgil, Horace and Tacitus, he is businesslike and undeluded: war is interesting, but it is still hell. . . . There are no hawklike or dovelike answers in Dugan. He merely pays grim and merry attention to basics, whether he sings of childhood, lust, liquor, the dusty life of offices, city streets, domestic tranquility, birth, as in "Coat of Arms." . . .

As a craftsman, Dugan is extraordinary. He loads every rift with concrete; he makes a hard, crunching music; and his control of momentum is peerless: the poems, one after another, come barreling down the alley like big black bowling balls and down you go.

Alicia Ostriker. PR. Spring, 1972. pp. 272–3

DUNCAN, ROBERT (1919–   )

The publication of Duncan's book, *Bending the Bow*, is an event exceeding questions of quality. I cannot imagine my friends, the poets who gather to dismember each other, asking of this book, as they would of the others in this review, those narrower in scope, smaller in style, "Is it good or is it bad?" The question doesn't arise; not because Duncan is a good poet, though he is superb, but because the comprehensiveness of his imagination is too great for us. Here is an event; for the present our only question is, can we respond to it?—can we respond adequately to its most important feature, a new open sequence called *Passages*? We are given the first thirty sections of it, from which we see immediately resemblances to Pound's *Cantos*, but also differences, and the differences are the more salient. Duncan has learned from Pound's failures. . . . For the present I read the *Passages* not only with admiration and envy, and not only with a responsive depth of feeling, but with a wondering intuition that new force and clarity have come into the poetic imagination of America. When I reflect that Duncan, although he has already written a great deal, is only now, at age 49, riding the crest of his power, and that he still has years to go, the future of our poetry looks much more attractive to me than it has at any other time since the generation of the elders desisted.

Hayden Carruth. *HdR*. Summer,
1968. pp. 402–3

The Opening of the Field had announced the birth of a surpassingly individual talent: a poet of mysticism, visionary terror, and high romance. Duncan's work is outstanding among his contemporaries' in having rehabilitated from three hundred years of relative disuse and stagnation the emblem—not the image, or the symbol—as the central vehicle of the poem's drama. Duncan's emblems are populated by flaring presences, who, like crucified angels, blazingly dance out of the "black pit" of blindness, and into "the beginnings of love." But in his recent books he has produced numerous exercises—lacking all vividness—while he waits for the return of his demon. These many autotelic performances are like prayers to the absent spirits urging their return: they may serve, for us, as a record of soul-priming, the readying of fallow poetic ground for the next major theme, whenever it may strike.

Laurence Lieberman. *Poetry*. April, 1969. p. 43

Despite Duncan's admiration for Projective Verse, his own seems restrained, often dense, hermetic except in melody. His early works—illustrated by Jess Collins, who prompts Duncan to experiment with collage techniques—are privately printed. *Selected Poems* (1959) indicates the range of his poetic complexity as of his quirks and mannerisms. More impressive, *The Opening of the Field* and *Roots and Branches* develop his central themes: immanence, mythopoesis, homosexual love, despondency. . . . The method of the poems is far more musical than dramatic; for music, the author believes, moves at the heart of nature. Aesthetic, erotic, mystical, the poetry of Robert Duncan wants to create itself from the intellectual order not of one mind but of existence; it does not always succeed.

Ihab Hassan. *Contemporary American
Literature* (Ungar). 1973. p. 116

● EASTLAKE, WILLIAM (1917–   )

This witty, exhilarating novel [*Go in Beauty*] displays some remarkable powers. Perhaps its major achievement is that William Eastlake's hilarious sense of irony allows him successfully to bathe a story that is essentially tragic in a calmly majestic humor. In the book's course he illuminates in passing the problems of sibling psychology, expatriation, primitivism, the artist's fidelity to truth, distributive justice (Emerson on the mesa!), the nature of integrity and a few others. . . .

Since somebody is bound to point to Eastlake's debt to Hemingway, let us say the mimicry has been metamorphosed here into mastery. The story is coherent, readable and told with a precisely right sandpapered style.

Lon Tinkle. NYT. Oct. 21, 1956. p. 4

After reading [*Go in Beauty*] once, one is impressed and puzzled; after reading a second time, one is still impressed but less puzzled. I think this is an important first novel. The author has written distinguished short stories; he has a definite style; and if he is not yet at home with the novel, he is perfectly at ease with each chapter. Instead of hanging out a list of complimentary adjectives, let's say that he is a writer worthy of close reading. . . .

The action is powerful, the conception is serious and the prose is lean and clear. . . . The sad beauty of Mr. Eastlake's tale is that reality, whether of the world or of the self, may be ignored or defied, but never thwarted.

Thomas F. Curley. Com.
Jan. 4, 1957. pp. 363–4

William Eastlake's second novel [*The Bronc People*] makes definite the arrival on the scene of a new, hard, dry, tender, very contemporary talent. Eastlake has been writing about cowboys and Indians and the Southwest for several years; a small group of readers has noticed him, some of them puzzled by the kidded debt to Hemingway and a subject matter which edges up against that beer-and-pretzels category, "the adult Western." Now, however, the Hemingway trick is bared for a joke and the proximity to the portentous teevee or movie Western is made a part of the comic action. A free-swinging playfulness and a deep nostalgia for the truths of sensual experience give us something we always need—a storyteller of wit, compassion and venturesomeness in both language and fantasy.

Herbert Gold. Nation. Sept. 20, 1958. p. 158

I do not really know how to describe Mr. Eastlake's new book [*Portrait of an Artist with Twenty-six Horses*]. . . . His characters seem to me small, remote, yet very clear, presented through a reversed telescope that yet brings them right to the reader. Their motives, on the other hand, are a trifle larger than life size. . . . The plot is developed into a masterpiece of the kind of suspense that makes the reader want to reach into the story and yell at the oblivious characters on whom the outcome depends. . . . At another level, we have a second story. . . . It develops almost surreptitiously. As the story ends its resolution and the young man's fate become parts of one another. This is technically a neat trick, a nice job of construction. . . . Discard any thought of realism and accept this book for what it is, and it will give you real pleasure.

Oliver La Farge. NYT. April 28, 1963. p. 5

In a sense, it is unfortunate that all three of William Eastlake's novels have been set in the West, more specifically the Southwest, even more specifically New Mexico and the surrounding areas. *Go in Beauty* and *The Bronc People* have gone the way of all "Westerns" and are at present out-of-print. Eastlake's most recent novel, *Portrait of an Artist with Twenty-six Horses,* also is set in New Mexico and unfortunately may follow the same pattern despite its delightful title—unfortunately, because Eastlake's novels are neither the stereotyped "Westerns," nor are they regional Southwestern novels any more than William Faulkner's novels are "Southern" or regional novels of the South.

Just as Faulkner created his Yoknapatawpha County out of the area surrounding Oxford, Mississippi, William Eastlake is creating a fictional area in the "Checkerboard" region of the Navajo reservation and its adjacent areas in northern New Mexico. His characters live and die in a physical setting that often has dominated the works of lesser writers, turning their expressions into regionalistic descriptions. . . .

Eastlake is a writer who, like the Ernest Hemingway of *The Sun Also Rises* and *A Farewell to Arms,* keeps a tight rein on his materials, using physical descriptions to suggest or enlarge ideological content. He *uses*, then, the New Mexico landscape, history, and people not for ornament but, for the enhancement of meaning. Reading Eastlake, one is always aware of the desert, the mesa, the mountain, the sky, in all their color and beauty, their proudness and mercilessness, but one is also

148   EASTLAKE, WILLIAM

aware that they may be the symbol of "home," or of the "cradle" or the "coffin" of civilization.

Delbert E. Wylder. *NMQ.*
Summer, 1965. pp. 188–9

I find *Castle Keep* impressive, though sometimes difficult. William Eastlake tells his story of American soldiers, defending a castle in the Ardennes in 1944, with a multiplicity of narrators. Get used to one and it's time to change over. But there's something appropriate in this guard-duty approach; it also gives one a kind of castellar impression, as though each narrator were a wing or wall. The big question is: what are they all defending? Abandon the stronghold and you preserve the fragments of civilization it guards; hold it, and you risk a sort of destruction of history. The interweaving of opposed attitudes is intricate, and, for a tale which involves so much sheer waiting, there is an unfailing sense of movement. Mr. Eastlake is strong on the dialectic and, eventually, on the action, and he has a considerable mastery of diverse American speech-rhythms. I think this is one of the really good American war-books. Soldiers' talk is sweetened by tapestries.

Anthony Burgess. *List.* March 3, 1966. p. 325

William Eastlake writes as though Vietnam could still be explained. *The Bamboo Bed* makes *Catch-22* look like a comic strip. One suspects that Vietnam, a war conceived and illustrated by Chester Gould, makes *The Bamboo Bed* look like a comic strip. But Eastlake went over there to see, and came back and wrote *The Bamboo Bed*. If he left anything out, it was because he didn't think our civilian credibilities could stand any more. He is one of the best American novelists writing today and if he thinks that we can't stand more absurdity than he has written into *The Bamboo Bed* he is probably right. Even though there was probably more to tell. He tells enough.

Richard Rhodes. *Book World.*
Nov. 9, 1969. p. 5

The Bamboo Bed is not a political novel, hardly even a war novel. It is neither realistic nor (in the ordinary sense of the term) hard-hitting. A brilliant, strange, wondrous performance: it is the kind of feather that knocks you over. It has something of the black humor of *Catch-22* which it superficially resembles. But Eastlake has done something more than spawn a sequel to Joseph Heller's novel. *Catch-22* is set in World War II—*set in*; any conflagration could have been used as the backdrop to its madness. *The Bamboo Bed* is the war in Vietnam. . . .

A myth is a fiction that makes it possible to deal with the ineffable.

Some myths are pernicious, which is why, as Mailer tells us, we are in Vietnam. *The Bamboo Bed*, a mythic exercise in its own right, deflates the myth behind our involvement in Vietnam by mythologizing that war out of existence.

Beverly Gross. *Nation.* Nov. 24, 1969. pp. 576, 578

Most of [the poems in *A Child's Garden of Verses for the Revolution*] are introduced by skillfully written prose passages that establish the contexts. Eastlake . . . is deeply concerned about our time of violence, hatred, ignorance, and war—foreign and domestic. . . . For observation, detail, scope, and shattering insight into social ills, his poetry is among the best. Yet I think he is a better prose writer than a poet; the brevity of his language, the sense of detail, and the rhythm of his narration have the impact of engrossing journalism, not poetry.

Jon M. Warner. *LJ.* Nov. 1, 1970. p. 3785

If Eastlake is—though he wastes no time making a show of it—a deeply intellectual writer in that he confronts serious ideas with both depth and wisdom, he is also a most unusual intellectual, for he actively applies a tempering modicum of myth and magic to his work, thus achieving a dimension of ken unusual midst the singleminded technological thought patterns so widely praised today. And all these things are manifest in an impressionist manner that suggests rather than gouges. Eastlake's major triumph as a writer has been, at his best, to instill in his readers his own unique sense of life, a sense just different enough from their own to create important questions concerning man and the direction of contemporary life. His reintroduction of myth and magic may seem a step into the past, but these aspects of human experience are perpetually modern; Eastlake differs from many contemporary thinkers in his rejection of an all-or-nothing philosophy—all reason or all magic—in favor of a balance of both.

By presenting unusual perspectives and stimulating questions, Eastlake has triggered new feelings and new insights. In exploring the fictive world of William Eastlake, one confronts a portrait of the artist as shaman.

Gerry Haslam. *WR.* Spring, 1971. p. 12

William Eastlake is the funniest, most profound, most musical writer I have read in years. He has the greatness of soul not only to kid the characters in his book [*Dancers in the Scalp House*] (Navajos, semi-Navajos, quasi-Navajos, lunatic-fringe Navajo-sympathizers and anti-Navajos) but also to kid himself and his own style and thought as a writer. He has the confidence, in other words, of a man half-bard and half-bum, yet undeceived as to the truth in all the confusion. Eastlake is wise: a poet in the best sense. . . .

His mind is tough, reasonable, and crawls simply everywhere in the connections he makes. Funniness, last resort of the Indian, he has aplenty. . . . Eastlake is a fine American humorist, and he is wise. The last beautiful passage strikes in no uncertain tones one of the finest dirges I've seen.

Barry Hannah. NYT. Oct. 12, 1975. p. 43

EBERHART, RICHARD (1904–   )

The most frequently noticed, and by this time surely obvious, quality in Eberhart's work [is] his "Romanticism." His reliance upon inspiration, his insistence upon the primacy of intuition over intellect, and his clearly expressed assumption of the existence of a noumenal world—these all point in this direction, as all of his critics have perceived. Complicated, frequently strained discussions of his "Romanticism" are sufficiently abundant, and it is not necessary to belabor the point here. They are so abundant that it may be well to conclude this discussion in simplicity, with the perception of Philip Booth, who is "sure beyond doubt that he is fundamentally a religious poet, and that at his best his religion and poetry are one." For Eberhart does not, perhaps cannot, indulge in the tortuous philosophy of a Coleridge, nor is he the elegant theoretician that Eliot was. He does not attempt to reassemble the sensibility shattered in the seventeenth century; at the deepest level of awareness, he simply takes it for granted.

Thus it is not surprising to find that the most fashionable thing to say about Richard Eberhart is that he is unfashionable. Coming to maturity during a period that stressed discipline and craft, he relies unblushingly on inspiration.

Joel Roache. Richard Eberhart
(Oxford—N.Y.). 1971. pp. 252–3

[Eberhart] continues after forty years, two *Selected Poems* and one *Collected Poems*, to be the vigorous, idiosyncratic visionary his many admirers have come to cherish. As Kenneth Rexroth remarked, Eberhart always *appeared* to be a poet of the academies, perhaps because of his long teaching career, while his work has actually been the articulation of a quite independent intelligence and imagination, fascinated by physical nature and metaphysical speculation, by the contrariness of human behavior and the elusive traceries of the Divine. Stylistically, Eberhart has developed after his own fashion as well, early absorbing Hopkins, Donne, Blake and others, but always putting what he learned to his own uses. As a poet of inspiration, one who often relies on the moment of perception and its rapid dictation, he has taken risks which more polished poets would avoid, yet the uniqueness of his poetry resides in this visionary intensity that throws caution to the winds in order to seize the given insight.

Fields of Grace, his poems of the past four years, shows that Eberhart has lost none of his power and exuberance; his imagination ranges widely and with keen receptivity over the surfaces, declivities, the abrupt transitions between life and death in the natural world. . . .

Ralph J. Mills, Jr. Parnassus. Spring–
Summer, 1973. pp. 215–6

ELIOT, T. S. (1888–1965)

For me, the poetry [of *Four Quartets*] is saved by the scruple. The way in which it is saved may be indicated, perhaps, in a passage from *Varieties of Religious Experience,* where [William] James discusses the character of sanctity, particularly its ascetic quality. He remarks that while it is normal and, apparently, instinctive for us to seek "the easy and the pleasant," at the same time it is also normal "in moderate degree" to seek the arduous: "Some men and women, indeed, there are who can live on smiles and the word 'yes' forever. But for others (indeed for most) this is too tepid and relaxed a moral climate. Passive happiness is slack and insipid, and soon grows mawkish and intolerable. Some austerity and wintry negativity, some roughness, danger, stringency, and effort, some 'no! no!' must be mixed in, to produce the sense of an existence with character and texture and power."

Perhaps this is how *Four Quartets* lives, and how it communicates with those readers who do not share its Christian belief; by giving us the sense of an existence with character and texture and power. This is the tone of its "approach." Eliot has always implied, incidentally, that the satisfactions of poetry are in this tone. The great poet helps to purify the dialect of the tribe by making our stupidity unendurable.

Denis Donoghue. The Ordinary Universe
(Macmillan—N.Y.). 1968. pp. 265–6

Those who are put off by Eliot's religion unconsciously agree with the pharisaical among churchgoers, for they, too, adopt the heretical opinion that the faith is a set of lucid propositions and the God of the faithful fully known. Their objection is not really to Eliot's idea of reality but to his calling this reality "God." They have in this a confidence about the meaningfulness of words which Eliot is innocent of. He supposes that all languages are approximations, imperfect versions of reality, so that words are proved true only pragmatically, by their power to order experience. His is the least dogmatic and the most skeptical of religious poetry. To judge it fairly, one must ask not whether in the abstract the Nicene Creed is a true statement, but whether the experiences Eliot depicts hang together as credibly consistent.

This question soon brings us to that of Eliot's limitations—the kinds of experiences he leaves out. For a poem's self-consistency must appear to us, as readers, and it will do so only if it can draw a circle wide enough to include our major concerns. For most thoughtful readers Eliot's circle has seemed almost too wide. It is hard to name an aspect of modern life which his poetry does not touch, and we praise him, therefore, for his sense of *his* time. But I suspect that it is more generally his sense of time that matters.

John F. Lynen. *The Design of the Present* (Yale). 1969. p. 437

The conversational tone of most of Eliot's work invites the reader to accept the persona in a more or less equal relationship. The persona does not speak down to the reader—even in *Four Quartets* he addresses the reader as a friend except in a few falsely humble, rather patronizing lines that tend to weaken the equal relationship. But while the conversational base defines the rapport between reader and persona, within the conversational tone the persona reveals a pattern of emotional response appropriate to his role as questing man. The talk of *The Waste Land* reflects in turn the speaker's aspiration and despair, his capacity for ecstasy and humor, his union of sense and sensibility which makes him a representative man.

George T. Wright in *Modern American Poetry*, edited by Jerome Mazzaro (McKay). 1970. p. 237

The *Four Quartets*, I believe, has not been adequately examined in terms of Eliot's own early criticism. His career altogether reverses itself. Whether good or bad, the art of his later poems is almost an exact contradiction of his early theory and practice. Indeed, if he could have read his own late poetry early in his career without knowing that it was his own, the *Four Quartets* would have been a good example of what he was revolting against.

Floyd C. Watkins. *The Flesh and the Word* (Vanderbilt). 1971. p. 75

In Eliot's "The Love Song of J. Alfred Prufrock" and *The Waste Land*, myth discloses the personal terror and the feelings of impotence and despair which the protagonist objectifies in relation to society and history. Like Yeats and Auden, Eliot is ever aware of the seeds of death within the experience of love, but for Eliot there is no contest between the two; in *The Waste Land*, love retreats before its enemy as the protagonist takes on the role of the passive and maimed mythical king. Perhaps the most significant disclosure of unconscious feelings lies not in the actual myths Eliot uses in *The Waste Land*, but in the way mythical figures merge into each other. Like creatures in a dream, they depict the conflict and suffering of the protagonist and his distaste for the self which is finally defined by all of them. No doubt Yeats was correct in placing Eliot among those who attempted to exclude "the personal dream" from their work; certainly Eliot avoided the deepest psychological revelations of the very myths he employed. The conflicts and terrors that dream reveals, however, and indeed its very methods of condensation and merging, of disguising the self in a variety of forms, are present in his use of myth.

Lillian Feder. Ancient Myth in Modern
Poetry (Princeton). 1971. p. 347

From first to last in Eliot's poetic career, from the undersea vision of Prufrock through the Hyacinth garden of *The Waste Land* to the rose garden of "Burnt Norton," it is a quintessentially Jamesian experience which lies at the heart of his work. The tragedy is that of one who can perceive but cannot act, who can understand and remember but cannot communicate. "I could not/Speak, and my eyes failed, I was neither/Living nor dead . . ./Looking into the heart of light, the silence." At one time Eliot thought of titling the second part of *The Waste Land* "In the Cage," an obvious reference to [Henry] James's novella where the little telegraph girl, shut into her wire cage, can only live vicariously through the communications that pass across her desk. She knows everything, and can act upon nothing: she is like Tiresias, who knows all, fore-suffers all, and can prevent none of it.

This is the vision of personal isolation that Eliot shares with James, and that lies at the deepest reaches of all his works. And yet, like James, Eliot was possessed with the complementary "vision of an ideal society"; the result was an art aware at every turn of the "disparity between possibility and fact." In his later works Eliot does explore ways of breaking the "closed circle of consciousness," through discipline or through grace.

A. Walton Litz in Eliot in His Time,
edited by A. Walton Litz
(Princeton). 1973. p. 21

No other poet in the history of the language, with the possible exception of Pound, has revalued so many reputations, or domesticated so many foreign poets in English taste. In accepting Eliot as my generation did, wholesale, we accepted not only "The Love Song of J. Alfred Prufrock" and *The Sacred Wood*, but an attitude toward the entire European past, a modification of its "pastness," and a spirit of inquiry that seemed to us life-giving. Perhaps that was only one of his two or three ideas, but it was a big one—too big, the critics now seem to feel, to have been expressed with full success in Eliot's first go at expressing it ("Tradition and the Individual Talent"); but with the passing of the years, it has been worked out to really enriching and liberating conclusions.

Robert M. Adams in *Eliot in His Time*,
edited by A. Walton Litz
(Princeton). 1973. p. 135

The haunted characters in Eliot's drawing-room plays are pursued by phantoms of connectedness—actions committed in the past, family secrets, old associations, lovers—the social, sexual, and psychological determinants that are the ghosts of modern drama. But in the end these baleful connections are revealed to be illusory, and the characters are seen to be truly haunted by an inability to connect. The crowded drawing room, the carefully prepared meeting of principals, the statesman's diary are all empty—a cheat and a disappointment. The exact quality of this emptiness is frequently and carefully described—the sudden solitude in a crowded desert, the exacerbated isolation in the midst of an apparent connectedness. It is an isolation that appears inevitable and also miserably unreal because connectedness is felt as the only reality.

Michael Goldman in *Eliot in His Time*,
edited by A. Walton Litz
(Princeton). 1973. pp. 163–4

ELLIOTT, GEORGE P. (1918–   )

Elliott calls himself a writer-critic rather than a scholar-critic or philosopher-critic. He deserves the name, not only because he has published novels, stories and poems as well as another volume of essays [*Conversations*], but also because he writes well. His manner (when not oracular) is attractively informal, neat yet colorful, and he combines cultural-literary comment with a kind of personal reminiscence that offers us a few glimpses into the role his temperament played in the formation of his opinions. But a little more of the philosophic and scholarly spirit might have strengthened his reasoning, and impressed upon him the fact that his dissatisfaction with a present in which he feels alienated, and his idealization of a past in which the artist enjoyed more sense of community, are fundamental characteristics of the very modernist tradition he deplores. . . .

It is too bad these essays are shot through with an unconvincing social polemic because Elliott does some things especially well. His praise of the art he loves—Dante's, Chekhov's or Tolstoy's—is fine indeed. His comments on teaching, pornography and the novel—subjects on which a sensible position is lent force by radical fashion—are consistently engaging and nicely balanced. Radical fashion also helps to explain why his pages on such extremists as McLuhan, Robbe-Grillet and Genet are exceptionally satisfying.

David J. Gordon. NYT. Feb. 6, 1972. p. 29

Elliott is often an appealing critic, mostly because his finest qualities, his honesty and gentleness, can set him off to advantage against splashier and more professional academics. But of his fiction some of the early stories in *Among the Dangs* are the best; his novels always seem to struggle to be born, to be expressive in the flat style, to be interesting about characters not in themselves interesting—to struggle, but never to work.

Roger Sale. NYR. May 4, 1972. p. 3

[*Muriel*] moves along so smoothly that its wisdom, quiet strength and range of inclusiveness pass unnoticed. *Muriel* is alive clear through. Whereas most sagas of farming life are long and burly, *Muriel* needs only 154 pages to release its force. Where, then, does its strength come from? It depicts a small world; its characters do not struggle dramatically; no argument is broached, let alone proved. Like the rich Kansas plains where much of it takes place, the novel epitomizes the archetypal female, who is both motionless and brimming with motion. . . .

The shortness of the novel, finally, reflects the haunting brevity of life; life slips past Muriel before she can make sense of it. And, as in all good primitive art, no authorial intrusion mutes dramatic immediacy. Each character has a mystery life beyond the one presented to his family and friends, a life that Elliott respects too much to codify. Thus the structure of the novel helps shape Elliott's view of life: human existence is both fixed and free; although the whole fits into a (four-part) pattern, the individual parts move at random.

Peter Wolfe. Nation. June 5, 1972. pp. 730–1

ELLISON, RALPH (1914–   )

Ellison's hero [in *Invisible Man*] has nowhere to go once he tells us he is invisible. He does indeed, in the Epilogue, say that he intends to rise again and try his hand at life, that he has faith in democratic principles, and that life itself is its own excuse despite the blows it has dealt him. But there is no evidence in the text to fortify his beliefs. The blues singer has depths of feeling to begin with, but Ellison's hero has just begun to learn to feel as the novel ends.

One dwells on these issues because *Invisible Man* is so very nearly a great book. Perhaps Ellison himself, caught somewhere between Negro blues and the symphonic complexities of Western experience, has yet to find his footing. Or possibly his position as an American Negro, an invisible man, will make it impossible for him to find his way.

Edward Margolies. *Native Sons*
(Lippincott). 1968. p. 148

Ellison makes greater use of the blues than Baldwin does; he finds them vital and authentic celebrations of Negro experience. More important, though, is the range of his language. No one since Mark Twain is so rich, so varied, or so comic in his re-creation of oral speech. Bracing peals of laughter echo on and under the surface of *Invisible Man*. The whole is an elaborate musical and verbal joke, celebrating love, sacrifice, and self-knowledge as our ultimate resources against the vicissitudes of life.

Richard H. Rupp. *Celebration in
Postwar American Fiction*
(Miami). 1970. pp. 163–4

If one is a black individual (as the central character [of *Invisible Man*] is, while at the same time emblematic of everyone) in a society whose people denigrate (the pun is intended) blackness, then the institutions, dedicated as they are to the preservation of the status quo, must of necessity be in large measure against him. What, then, does the black person do? Does he support that which thwarts the realization of his potential? Does he seek to destroy the institutions, the only protection from chaos? These are the questions which Ellison's novel poses and in its own way answers. There are no solutions to such questions. One can only withdraw, thus solving the problem privately. No action is possible, for there is no basis for action. This seems to be the implication of

Invisible Man. He is as invisible at the end as he was at the beginning, and he is invisible because he *feels* he is. The conception of invisibility exists only as a response to a society which tells individuals they are invisible. There may be alternatives different from accepting as fact that one is invisible; at least many people think so, people who believe in the possibility of significant change.

It is in the area designated by the above considerations that *Invisible Man* makes a political statement. Insofar as it suggests that significant changes of a social nature are not possible and in many ways not even desirable, it is a vehicle for a particular political bias, for that sentiment happens to be held by large numbers of people who express it by means of political actions. Hence, despite Ellison's intentions, despite his professions about being an artist and that alone, he expresses ideas and attitudes which, once freed into the world, are likely to have political consequences.

Donald B. Gibson in *The Politics of
Twentieth-Century Novelists,*
edited by George A. Panichas
(Hawthorn). 1971. p. 315

Ellison's artistic sense . . . was far more developed than [Richard] Wright's—he never conceived of his own fiction as a device for exclusively expressing social protest, although protest mars some of his early work. After 1943 he ceased to concern himself primarily with politics and turned to the theme that dominates all of his later work: the need of white Americans to recognize Negro identity in all of its diversity. "Mister Toussan" (1941), a short story published in *The New Masses,* had already explored that idea, and later stories approached it from various points of view. Within a few years he had published several stories: "That I Had the Wings" (reprinted as "Mr. Toussaint"), "In a Strange Country" (1944), "Flying Home" (1944), and "King of the Bingo Game" (1944). These stories, together with "A Coupla Scalped Indians" (1956), have not yet been collected, but they indicate that Ellison is an impressive short story writer as well as a novelist and essayist.

Theodore L. Gross. *The Heroic Ideal in
American Literature* (Free). 1971. p. 159

FAULKNER, WILLIAM (1897–1962)

White critics of William Faulkner and their black fellow travelers—Ralph Ellison and Albert Murray are the best known—have praised him for his "realistic portrayal of Negro people." However, his Negro characters, whose function is to satisfy the demand of white Americans for racial peace, are remnants of the plantation tradition.

Dilsey of *The Sound and the Fury* is one example. Like the "mammies" of Paul Laurence Dunbar's *Strength of Gideon*, her literary lineage goes back to Thomas Nelson Page: she attempts to hold the white family together, she is the foundation of a dying institution. While suffering insult and abuse, she survives by virtue of patience and submissiveness. The Greek ideal is safe with the Dilseys of the earth. Knowing and accepting their places, they face each tomorrow with a Bible under their arms, not with Molotov cocktails under their skirts. They are, to be sure, far different from the Harriet Tubmans and Sojourner Truths of true American history.

Addison Gayle, Jr., in *Amistad 1*, edited by
John A. Williams and Charles F. Harris
(Random). 1970. p. 20

If Faulkner was "a perfect case of split personality," it was not as he intended; Faulkner the writer and Faulkner the "denizen of the world" were never very far apart. His "polar" imagination empathized with the Negro and liberal as he criticized the segregationist, with the Southerner as he criticized the Negro and liberal, maintaining all too often, instead of a firm middle-of-the-road position, a mere political schizophrenia. Faulkner was not the hero who can successfully say, "This stinks and I'm going to do something about it"—he was no Chick Mallison or Nancy Mannigoe, daring existential action in the face of blind unreason and failed communication. He was not even an Isaac McCaslin, swearing "at least I will not participate in it myself." He was still very much the author of *Go Down, Moses* who found Isaac's stand painfully ambivalent; the author of *Intruder in the Dust* and *Requiem for a Nun* unable to portray heroism except in terms of fantasy and sensationalism. The same endowments which insured his success as a novelist insured his failure as a political voice.

Walter Taylor. *SoR*. Fall, 1970. p. 1092

In his prefatory note to *The Mansion* Faulkner comments that " 'living' is motion, and 'motion' is change and alteration and therefore the only alternative to motion is un-motion, stasis, death." Man must act conditionally, must be adaptive. In the language of "The Bear," man must examine the Grecian urn, acknowledge the truth and beauty of its depictions, and then transcend the static moments captured there. He cannot transport himself into a bygone frieze, into an historic moment like the past hunt for Old Ben or into an artistic design like the Nazarene of messianic teaching. It is important that Old Ben in death "almost resembled a piece of statuary" for he resembles both beauty and non-life. Any fixed moment or grand design is contrived, a kind of death; life for Faulkner is in becoming rather than being; ripeness is all. That is why truth for Faulkner embodies intuition as well as intellect and why conceptualization must ultimately give way to the primacy of the heart. . . . Ike McCaslin illustrates that for Faulkner heroism lies not in the vision of a new Canaan nor even in the sacrifice of a corrupted heritage, but in an ability to suffer, in Ike's remarkable capacity to grieve.

Arthur F. Kinney. SoR. Fall, 1970. p. 1124

In *Light in August* Faulkner had presented individuals who were victimized by history largely without knowing it. But in *Absalom, Absalom!* he advances to a much more complex presentation of history. Before, history had been treated as a static, simple, essentially known quality which finally weighted down its unalert human vehicle. Now, however, history becomes a dynamic, highly volatile quality that presents first an aspect of startling clarity, then an aspect of shadowed obscurity, teasing and confusing the mind it penetrates while at the same time demanding that the mind subdue it. . . . It is the confrontation that is significant in the novel; neither the legend of Thomas Sutpen, which is really a capsule history of the South, nor the meager account of Quentin Compson hearing and then telling the story of Thomas Sutpen provides the final significance of the work; it is the rendering of the process of historical interaction between myth and recipient, a process now vivid and dramatic, now obscure and ambiguous, which causes many readers to regard the novel as Faulkner's best.

Lewis A. Lawson in The Politics of
Twentieth-Century Novelists,
edited by George A. Panichas
(Hawthorn). 1971. pp. 288–9

As Faulkner's styles and techniques become more moralistic in the later works, the martyrdom of the protagonists becomes more extreme, the martyrdom is decreed by a legal system established by the forces of civilization, the protagonist is less guilty and criminal, his virtues are greater, and he has fewer flaws. To put it simply, the moral systems of the later novels are great oversimplifications; principle or meaning is placed far above the concreteness, credibility, and particularity of character. . . .

In the older works the character worked out his life in the events in the novel, and the reader was left to deduce the principle if he could.

Floyd C. Watkins. *The Flesh and the*
Word (Vanderbilt). 1971. p. 263

It appears that in his last two novels Faulkner's comedy has lost its satiric edge. His miser, Flem Snopes, was murdered almost gratuitously in *The Mansion*, long after he had been turned from an incarnation of Mammon into the country boy who made good. It is a measure of Faulkner's final reconciliation to human frailty that the most apt exemplars of Snopesism we can find in *The Reivers* are a country farmer who plows mudholes in the Memphis road so that he can use his mule team to pull out mired automobiles for a fee, and a depraved little boy, Otis—Ned calls him "Whistle-britches"—whose greatest feat is to steal the gold tooth from a sleeping Negro maid in a whorehouse. It's all good fun, but for great satiric comedy, with a Swiftian bite and Rabelaisian pungency, we must still turn back to *The Hamlet*, surely one of the great comic creations of our time. In it Faulkner proved himself a master of the comic mode, as *Absalom, Absalom!* had proved him a master of the tragic.

Robert D. Jacobs in *The Comic Imagination*
in American Literature, edited by Louis D.
Rubin, Jr. (Rutgers). 1973. p. 318

To both Hawthorne and Faulkner, "maturity" signifies the acceptance of a corrupted humanity with its sin-flecked history, not an insulation from it. . . .

The "ultimate essence" of the Civil War Faulkner extracted from a welter of fact and fantasy and myth about a ruined land, a brave but fallible people, and an outraged race. Like Mark Twain, another sardonic and compassionate observer, he made no partisan pronouncements. Neither side won Faulkner's War. A great wrong was extirpated in a clumsy, bloody, and perhaps necessary way. Then a new set of chains tightened about the race John Brown elected to redeem. The War, like the portent of Brown himself, remained a mystery susceptible to any man's interpretation after quickly crumbling into myth.

Daniel Aaron. *The Unwritten War*
(Knopf). 1973. pp. 324, 326

[Faulkner] had been advised . . . by his mentor Sherwood Anderson, to write about his own Mississippi, and in 1926 he set out to do that. He wrote *Flags in the Dust*, but the finished manuscript was rejected left and right. Finally Harcourt Brace agreed to publish it on the condition that it be severely cut, a task Faulkner could not bring himself to do; the cuts were made by his agent, Ben Wasson, and the novel was published as *Sartoris*. Faulkner's affection for the original never faded, however, and he preserved the manuscript and typescript; we have it now in an edition edited by Douglas Day and, though he is credited only in the introduction, Albert Erskine.

Obviously *Flags in the Dust* will be of great value to Faulkner scholars (though presumably many of them have already had access to the manuscript), but the book is of broader value. It offers the opportunity to observe, by comparing it with *Sartoris*, what happens to a manuscript when it comes into the hands of an intelligent and demanding editor. Of far more importance, *Flags in the Dust*, because it is much more intricate than *Sartoris*, makes clear that everything that would engage Faulkner for three and a half decades had formed in his imagination at the outset.

Jonathan Yardley. NR. Sept. 8, 1973. p. 32

Passages of [Faulkner's] prose bubble up in [Joseph Blotner's biography] to frighten and amaze us . . . the sonorous opening chords of *Absalom, Absalom!*, for instance, with their impressive adjectival orchestration, the careful fastening of consciousness to its object, and Faulkner's characteristically increasing rhetorical beat, a precise local observation blown through a metaphor like a herald announcing . . . what? always . . . the palpable appearance of Time. . . .

It is as if remembered things themselves had memories, as if matter *were* memory. The muscles that hoed the garden remember the moves they made. To *see into*—for Faulkner—is to *think back*. . . .

He was rarely among people who understood his achievement, not that this might have lifted his loneliness very much (solitude was the space of more than his imagination), and the needs, sensations, and feelings—the pity, the pure fury—which one time had created those incredible lengths of language, those new and powerful forms, became themselves rhetorical habits, last rites, passionless gestures of passion. . . .

William Gass. NYR. June 27, 1974. pp. 4–5

FIEDLER, LESLIE (1917–   )

I don't think that Fiedler's way of treating myth is as easily transferable into prescriptive program as he wants it to be. His methods do damage not just to literature, by breaking up whole works to salvage the "authentic" fragment, but to life, making it only a kind of *materia mythica* to be arranged and manipulated without entering very deeply into the particular experiences that compose it. He doesn't mean to do this, and his career is a deserved and salutary rebuke to those who would insulate art from its human motives and consequences; but *The Return of the Vanishing American*, for all its admirable intentions and its achieved pleasures and illuminations, is finally bad medicine.

Thomas P. Edwards. *PR*. Fall, 1968. p. 610

Fiedler has certain subjects—being a Jew in America, American Jewish writers, liberal politics and taste, the mythology of chaste homosexual relations at the center of classic American literature—to which he returns over and over, and about which he has had, essentially, one idea. He has gone on liking the idea, and gone on giving himself contexts in which it can be used. . . .

The real point about Fiedler, which we can make praise or blame as we choose, is that he is always a political writer, always putting himself into situations where he is speaking against this fashion or that obsolescence, deriding some official line, jockeying for some new position. He always acts as though we might be deceived by some other hawker of myths and contexts if he did not set us straight, and he loves doing this so much that he will take any opportunity that presents itself to keep us informed, protected, reminded. But he also just plain loves to hear himself talk, too, and as long as he is excited by an idea he will go on saying it.

Roger Sale. *NYT*. Oct. 10, 1971. p. 10

FITZGERALD, F. SCOTT (1896–1940)

Why does Gatsby exist . . . to a far greater degree than Joyce's Stephen? We know from *Tender Is the Night* and "The Diamond as Big as the Ritz" that Fitzgerald entertained his fantasies to a degree dangerous in anyone and peculiarly so in a writer; his daydreams of the beauty and style of wealth are not unlike Stephen's proud exertions. But in *The Great Gatsby* and again in *The Last Tycoon* the dream is rendered in all its beauty and "placed"—not discarded. A distinguished intelligence that yielded to the dream in *Tender Is the Night* now insisted upon its rights. But the real explanation is that for Fitzgerald the person existed; *The Last Tycoon* is all person.

Denis Donoghue. The Ordinary Universe
(Macmillan—N.Y.). 1968. p. 67

Even Nick's own wishful vision of beautiful futility [in *The Great Gatsby*] recognizes the continual phoenix-rebirth of dream and aspiration as the fountainhead of human history. It was Amory Blaine, the hero of Fitzgerald's first novel [*This Side of Paradise*], who discovered and accepted the moral philosophy that one must, after defeat and failure, pick up and go on to "the next thing." Putting behind him Nick Carraway's rendering of a blind-end world in *The Great Gatsby*, and taking with him that part of it which has value as usable human truth, Fitzgerald went on, as an artist, to the "next thing" in *Tender Is the Night*, which is the story of a man who, with much fuller knowledge of the inexorable laws of reality than innocent Gatsby had, nevertheless pitted his character, his integrity, his personal vision and energy, flawed and imperfect as they were, against the futility and despair that he knew were the ruling truths of his world.

Richard Foster in Sense and Sensibility in
Twentieth-Century Writing, edited by Brom
Weber (Southern Illinois). 1970. p. 108

What fascinates people so about Fitzgerald? For one thing, it seems important that his writing can't be separated from his life; so seen, his novels aren't impenetrable façades, to be viewed from in front and below, but labyrinths to be explored. Like Proust and Joyce, he left a rich documentation of his life, viewing himself from a bewildering variety of angles and describing his own fantasies and preoccupations under many different guises. He created for himself, and for those who follow in his trail, not simply a personality but a society, a fictive world.

Robert M. Adams. NYR. Jan. 27, 1972. p. 28

FREDERIC, HAROLD (1856–1898)

In literary quality, the stories [*Stories of York State*] are competently handled for their time, with a surprising lack of mannered extremities: the clichés of feeling and expression, the incredible manipulations of plot and motivation, and the frequent sentimentality strike one as much less offensive than they might be. Although these seem to be negative virtues, the relative unobtrusiveness of the "period" features gives the stories a durability certainly not evident in the minor works of Mark Twain, for example.

The positive value of the stories lies in their appeal to Civil War enthusiasts, to antiquarians of the area, and to those who enjoy regional literature in general (if such readers exist at all). . . .

The stories possess two particular features which we often have assumed to be either the invention or the personal property of one or another contemporary writer; but this ghost, when he hears boasts of newfangled inventions, replies, "Oh, we had the same thing when I was young." For example, the persistence of the naïve, usually orphan, adolescent narrator . . . suggests that Hemingway and Salinger are a bit later in the field than is often realized. In addition, Frederic's treatment of a semi-imaginary county and its towns in these stories as well as in three of his novels, where place and family names recur, takes a bit of the edge off enthusiastic claims for Faulkner's giant achievement in the same kind of effort.

Frank Baldanza. *SoR*. Winter, 1969. pp. 250–1

The novels of Harold Frederic have a breadth that clearly goes beyond what the epithet "pioneer realist" suggests. Although much of his fiction was set in the same small area of upper New York State, his concerns were far from regional. He often returned to the hills and valleys of his home, but he always looked beyond them. His reputation must rest most heavily on *The Damnation of Theron Ware*, a work whose greatness has yet to be fully appreciated, despite the current revival of interest. As long as it is commonly thought to be what Van Wyck Brooks' edition proclaims it, a classic of realism "which exposes the cultural barrenness of the small town," the novel will probably never attract the kind of reader who would most appreciate its fine and subtle ironies, its complex and original treatment of the most American of themes—the ambiguous relationship between innocence and experience.

The other novels deserve wider attention too. Not all of them, to be sure, not *In the Valley, The Return of the O'Mahoney*, and *March Hares*. But the remaining works have in rewarding measure the artistry and intelligence which distinguish *The Damnation of Theron Ware*. From *Seth's Brother's Wife* through *The Market-Place* they tell a story worth telling, a paradoxical tale of an innocence that discovers itself endowed with new ideas, new opportunities, new powers, only to discover itself as still innocent, still limited, still banal.

Austin Briggs, Jr. *The Novels of Harold Frederic* (Cornell). 1969. pp. 211–2

Frederic tended on occasion to write dramatized essays rather than novels. Not only that, but he was curiously inept with essay materials and in these novels he was often betrayed by the unresolved conflict between his ideology and the dramatic reality which embodied most faithfully his deepest understanding of the nature of men. It was only in his last three years that this conflict was resolved and his mature genius found expression. When it did, his achievement was too far in advance of current attitudes to be comprehensible to his public. . . .

Frederic's achievement lies in the sensitivity and power with which he probed the naïveté and inconsistency of the American Dream and announced its inevitable collapse in the face of the new order of complexity of the twentieth century. In this he surpassed all his contemporaries in his ability to dramatize, allegorize, and mythicize the coming fall from innocence. In addition, testing his vision against his own experience, he understood that a loss of innocence might not bring a dignified, saddened wisdom, but might transform youthful egotism into debased cynicism, and ultimately into predatory rapacity. Thus Frederic wrote for the twentieth century, not his own, and in his greatest works achieved a vigorous and alarming vision of the civilization to come which has, as we can now see, verified his worst fears and proved him to be one of the most perceptive and important novelists of his time.

Stanton Garner. *Harold Frederic* (Minnesota). 1969. p. 45

My own view is that *Gloria Mundi* illustrates an unresolved ambivalence toward the issue posed by all three of the principal women—and especially by Frances Bailey—that of female emancipation, and also a self-contradictory attitude in Frederic between his observations of human behavior and his will to believe in the possibility of human fulfillment. Furthermore, these problems of ambivalence as regards both topics are characteristic of his work more generally, and they account both for certain cruxes in individual works and for much of the intellectual interest and tension of the novels. An instance is Frederic's shifting moral attitude toward Celia Madden between *The Damnation of Theron Ware* and *The Market-Place*. The structure of *Gloria Mundi* is a negative example. We have here a portrait of human frustration upon which the will to be happy, to believe that love conquers or resolves all, is superimposed in the form of the fairy tale. The traditional resolution of the romance (with the inheritance, the title, and the marriage) partially obscures both the architectonic structure, the dialectical character, and the irresolution of the novel of ideas.

Jean Frantz Blackall. *MarkhamR*.
May, 1972. p. 46

Frederic's War stories expressed all that [Stephen] Crane said they did. They also reflected a tacit bias that Crane left unmentioned. Far from celebrating the War as a holy cause, Frederic treated it as unmitigated disaster, and his stories are probably among the earliest examples of fiction written by a Northern writer of distinction which was not simply against war, as Crane's was, but against *the* War. . . .

Frederic is at his best in depicting the confused reactions of the villagers to the distant savagery. The ferocious casualties suffered by Oneida County contingents in the Peninsular campaigns alone stunned their families and friends. How much of these times Frederic actually remembered and how much he simply reconstructed from latter-day recollections of others it is hard to say, but he recreates as few writers have ever managed to do the atmosphere of a bereft community mourning its dead and swept up "in a hysterical whirl of emotions—now pride, now horror, now bitter wrath on top."

Daniel Aaron. *The Unwritten War*
(Knopf). 1973. pp. 220–1

FRIEDMAN, BRUCE JAY (1930–   )

Friedman's humor is more reductionist than [Saul] Bellow's or [Isaac] Rosenfeld's; that is to say, it is less humane. In works of complex irony, like Italo Svevo's *Confessions of Zeno*, the narrator offers several alternative explanations for his actions, contrasting his motives with others' interpretations of those motives, and with the unanticipated end results. The idea emerges of man as an intricate, irreducible being who is both funnier and more precious than he ordinarily appears. But the black humor of *Stern* explains away all motives, presenting a view of man that is necessarily meaner and more circumscribed. The final pages of the book show Stern's overflowing sympathy, which is *almost* recognized as the manifestation of a great soul. . . . Stern's capacity to admit the humanity of his adversary, his vision of the enemy as just another "refugee," could have made him a moral hero. Instead he is cut down to size in the final paragraph where all this emotion is exposed for the theatrical extravagance the author finds it to be.

The book remains critical of the protagonist and uses the weapons of satire to deflate him. Nevertheless, even Stern's ineffectual sensitivity is healing. If at the end he is still not at home in the world, he is at least more at home in his home, as husband and father and man.

Ruth R. Wisse. *The Schlemiel as Modern Hero* (Chicago). 1971. pp. 89–90

Friedman's world is ominously dependent on chance, a world of inconsequential meetings and partings. The future ceases to exist as an estimable series of actions. The categories of time and space fail to define the limits of perception, leaving Stern and Joseph forever vulnerable to the indefinites of unfolding experience. As in the involved world of television defined by Marshall McLuhan, so in the would-be conformist worlds of *Stern* and *A Mother's Kisses* discontinuity and simultaneity have displaced uniformity and consecutiveness. Hence the absence in Friedman's stories of family history, of sense of place, of names (what is Stern's first name? Joseph's last? Joseph's father's?), of anything other than the rudiments of narrative succession; and contrariwise an emphasis on the terrifying involutions of the moment. Under the circumstances not to feel anxiety is not to be human.

Max F. Schulz. *Black Humor Fiction of the Sixties* (Ohio Univ. Pr.). 1973. pp. 107–8

A number of our toughest novelists have gone so far in the direction of comprehensive in-joking, cosmic cynicism, urbane oversoul that they've out-toughed themselves, out-orbited modernity, and checked themselves back in with the basics—parents, children, marriage, friendship, gutted tradition. Their over-experienced, flailing heroes have reeled through all the circles of our hip Inferno and are now ready to retest their reactions to certain establishment values even if the retesting process hurts. And it does hurt.

Case in point: Bruce Jay Friedman's unheroic but swinging compendium of vulnerabilities named Harry Towns [in *About Harry Towns*]. . . .

A book . . . of brilliant chapters, a series of episodes with little development, change that is no real change, irresolute resolution. Harry writes scripts for Hollywood and scripts for the lives of himself and everyone else. The professional scripts sell and are evidently successful; the others are aborted by flaky circumstances. Friedman solves nothing

for his well-meaning protagonist, who, on the last page, senses that maybe he ought to go to Sofia and knows that he must "try like hell not to get hit with a brick." Even Ulysses might settle for that in 1974.
James R. Frakes. NYT. June. 23, 1974. p. 32

FROST, ROBERT (1875–1963)

In a great many of Frost's poems, particularly in those published before his wife's death in 1938—that is, up through *A Further Range*—we find ourselves in a diminished version of an Emersonian world. The familiar Emersonian emphases are here—the concentration on the individual searching for himself and for meaning, on nature as a resource, on immediate experience as a way to some kind of truth. But the mood is autumnal, the tone ironic or noncommittal, and the very categories of thought that are being played with have been scaled down in size.
Hyatt H. Waggoner. American Poets
from the Puritans to the Present
(Houghton). 1968. p. 300

Frost once said that he had never written a nature poem. He was fully entitled to speak as he did. Those poems of his that deal with what we commonly call nature are concerned with human nature, from the turns and whimsicalities of mood in response to natural occasions to our perilous "hold on the planet" and our faith or lack of it in human destiny. He could find in woods and flora and spring pools parables of the human situation, but he did not mystically or romantically identify man with nature. He kept the distinction between them sharp and clear. Frost was not so much a nature poet, if there is such a thing, as a country poet. The difference is considerable. A poet can dredge landscape and seascape for images, can offer a philosophy of nature and man's relation to it, without in any profound sense being a countryman. Frost, on one side, was profoundly a countryman. His own description, "versed in country things," defines one side of him and his work with the naturalness of his own mode of phrasing.
Theodore Morrison. YR. Winter, 1970. p. 179

Throughout Frost's poetry the reader senses a struggle between the natural and human realms that is demarcated by a host of familiar emblems —walls, brooks, bridges, ice—which simultaneously separate and link the combatants. The oft-noticed conservatism of Frost's statements— the refusal to tread either out far or in deep, or the fact that the swinging birches never swing out too far but always return to a middle range—is in fact a kind of phenomenological "trimming." For the problem of defining a poetic "self," with all its attendant vocational questions, while simultaneously exploring the contours of the self-in-the-world, provides the charm for so much of Frost's personal and artistic reminiscence, while simultaneously giving his poetry a unique spatial configuration.

Jan B. Gordon in *Modern American Poetry*, edited by Jerome Mazzaro (McKay). 1970. pp. 61–2

One may regret in Frost that delight leads him so much into bleak finalities, thumbs down, with only small tunes for momentary touches of comfort. It has to be accepted, it is him (or the way he became), it explains some of the attraction now so widely found in his poems. Not for Frost, let us say, that melody beyond, above himself like rising air, that inexplicability of verbal deliciousness and directness which Wordsworth (another poet also who lived on the touch-line of melancholia) constructs in "Among all lovely things my love had been" or in the self-surrender of

Oh! Might I kiss the mountain rains
That sparkle on her cheek.

It is a weakness, all the same ("Come with me," says Frost. "I go to you," says Wordsworth). . . .

Some poets make poems which are like unripe persimmons, bitter outside, with a true sweetness internally. Frost does the reverse. The outside is often sweet—the inside hell. . . . Frost, a poet fascinated by the capturing, directive power of roads, paths, tracks, and by the steady indifference of everything from rock to birch, a poet whose delight leads to the repeated revelation of self-centered bleakness, a poet intermittently sure in the manipulation of limited means, is neither beast nor angel. Nor major poet—a claim which is ridiculous.

Only now, when movement within form is neglected, could the teasing limited subtlety of Frost, strong as he may be in *North of Boston*, be supposed to match or surpass the teasing subtlety of the ranging humanity of his friend Edward Thomas (whose sentimentalities, too, give less offence).

TLS. April 16, 1971. p. 434

"Humor is the most engaging cowardice." Although Frost's manner is not always humorous, and although much of his ironic defensiveness represents . . . a conscious pragmatism, an awareness of the moral and psychological value of a humorous perspective, this statement perhaps sums up best of all why Frost is not among the great poets, though he is among the very good ones. We reserve greatness for "believers"—in no matter what. Frost's concern "not to set down an idea that is of [his] own thinking," but rather "to give it as in character" certainly made for liveliness, immediacy, and variety in his work. He greatly extended the "sound" of poetry. But all too often the "voice" of a poem acts as a mask, "simply a kind of guardedness," shielding the poet from the full implications of his serious subjects and preventing any real intellectual grappling with them. . . .

Apart from the interpretation of individual poems, a proper attention to the tones of voice in his poetry enables us to appreciate more exactly the nature of Frost's distinctive contribution to American literature. The sheer variety of sound in Frost's poetry makes most other poets seem one-dimensional. Working with the cadences of New England speech, and declining "music" in favor of "the sound of the talking voice," Frost ranged in tone from the lyric to the narrative, from the dramatic to the meditative, from the "terrifying" to the humorous. All the fun's in how you say a thing.

Elaine Barry. *Robert Frost*
(Ungar). 1973. pp. 15–7

FUCHS, DANIEL (1909–   )

If *Summer in Williamsburg* presents a dilemma, and *Homage to Blenholt* is a high-spirited attempt to delay or evade the problem of choice, *Low Company* marks an acceptance of the burdens of commonplace reality. For what constitutes both a major strength in Fuchs' work and a reason, perhaps, for the abrupt termination of his career as a young novelist, is his grim and ironic appreciation of the power of the commonplace, everything in daily existence that erodes ambition and spirit. As Albert Halper, a novelist who is Fuchs' contemporary, remarked of him: "he is a man with a burden. I do not envy him . . . he is a child of sorrow."

Perhaps so. But this child of sorrow, this poet of the Williamsburg streets, wrote some of the most winning fictions we have about American Jewish life. His scope narrow, but his tone pure, Fuchs was that rarity, a "natural" writer with a gift for spontaneous evocation and recall.

Irving Howe in *Proletarian Writers of the Thirties*, edited by David Madden
(Southern Illinois). 1968. pp. 104–5

Daniel Fuchs's *Summer in Williamsburg* is a tale of the second generation like [Meyer Levin's] *The Old Bunch*. Fuchs's first novel, it was
published in 1934, three years before Levin's. *The Old Bunch* looks
back to the tradition of the Naturalist novel and clearly belongs to a
closed chapter in literary history. Fuchs's book, on the other hand,
anticipates the ironic novel and is contemporaneous in spirit. Fuchs
represents the refusal to sink into self-pity and hysteria. His irresistible
urge toward sad comedy creates such contrasts as that between Cohen,
the posturing unfortunate, and Sussman, the gas-inhaling suicide.
Fuchs's acrid humor, akin to that of his contemporary Nathanael West,
looks forward out of the dreary solemnity of Albert Maltz and Farrell to
the tense serio-comedy of Malamud and Bellow.

> Bernard Sherman. *The Invention of
> the Jew* (Yoseloff). 1969. p. 102

West of the Rockies is a novel about Hollywood, though the people and
events it deals with are as far removed from the stardust image as the
book itself is from the "blockbuster" treatment accorded to that strange,
artificial community by writers less talented if more widely known, than
Daniel Fuchs. It is a tightly controlled, perceptive piece of writing which
tells of the tenuous, perturbed relationship between a world-famous
Hollywood actress—a star—and a youngish man who works for her
agency; and though it is no part of Mr. Fuchs's purpose to reveal sensational examples of tat behind the glamour or vicious backstage wheeling and dealing, we are given, with no sense of strain or contrivance, a
sense of the realities of "stardom": of the personal failures which have
led to the crisis the characters now face. . . .

Mr. Fuchs develops this notion of dependence and muted anguish
with considerable skill, relying not only on what he tells us but on what
he deliberately omits in order to convey the pressures and decidedly
unglamorous aspects of stardom on Hollywood's terms.

> *TLS*. Oct. 15, 1971. p. 1290

How different . . . from any other Jewish fiction of the forties and fifties
is a book like Daniel Fuchs's *Summer in Williamsburg*, first published in
1934, ten years before [Bellow's] *Dangling Man*. When Fuchs's novels
were reissued in the early sixties much was made of the fabulistic,
"poetic" side, as if they could only be appreciated in the wake of a
moral allegorist like Malamud. Actually, the great strength of the books
is their feeling for the life of the streets, the Runyonesque "low company"
of youthful gangs in Williamsburg and Jewish mobsters in the Catskills,
a chapter of social history quickly forgotten when the Jews became more
respectable and the Jewish novel more morally austere. In Fuchs the

moral temperature is low—he is notably ham-handed in portraying the
religious life of his Jews, a more inward subject. He is a folklorist, an
anthropologist of street life rather than a purveyor of moral parables.
For all his freedom from the cant of proletarian writing he remains in
essence a 1930s realist; for him life is with the people.

Morris Dickstein. *PR*. No. 1, 1974. p. 42

• FULLER, R. BUCKMINSTER (1895–   )

Buckminster Fuller—you are the most sensible man in New York, truly
sensitive. Nature gave you antennae, long-range finders you have
learned to use. I find almost all your prognosticating nearly right—much
of it dead right, and I love you for the way you prognosticate. . . .

To say that you have now a good style of your own in saying very
important things is only admitting something unexpected. To say you
are the most sensible man in New York is not saying much for you—in
that pack of caged fools. And everybody who knows you knows you are
extraordinarily sensitive. . . .

Faithfully [I am] your admirer and friend, more power to you—
you valuable "unit."

Frank Lloyd Wright. *SR*. Sept. 17, 1938. p. 14

At a time of crisis in his life Fuller set himself, like Descartes in his
Dutch stove-heated compartment, to survey the whole of the human
dilemma—all the obstacles that stood in the way of man's survival and
in the way of man's potential development. His philosophical starting
point was the totality of possible events—"universe," as he called it,
defining it in terms of the way it impinges on the human mind. . . .

Fuller's definition of "universe" is an attempt to treat *all* experience as finite. . . .

Fuller makes cumulative experience a pivotal factor in change.
Experience is finite; it can be stored, studied, directed; it can be turned
with conscious effort, to human advantage. . . .

Real wealth to Fuller is thus nothing more than the extent to which
man, at a given moment, has harnassed forms of universal energy and,
in the process, has developed a re-employable experience.

Robert W. Marks. *The Dymaxion World of*
Buckminster Fuller (Reinhold). 1960. pp. 9–10

Through the more immediate results of Fuller's work, structures of great elegance affording dramatic, functional performance may be viewed around the world. Its greater value, however, may lie in the wide influence of his philosophical approach. His coherent system of thought is a creative synthesis which embraces many significant areas of the social, industrial, scientific, and individual aspects of living. It represents a major attempt to outline a workable and comprehensible cosmology which endeavors to account for all physical and psychophysical phenomena behaviors within a field system of relations encompassing all known scientific laws and hypotheses.

In assuming a finite universe, permeable to human thought (which though not simultaneously "knowable" may yet be comprehended through its rationally co-ordinate patterns), Fuller restores man to a comprehensive position in which he may exercise his full evolutionary initiative toward controlling his destiny. He avoids previous philosophical dilemmas of paired antitheses, like materialism versus idealism, by assuming an integral polarity in phenomena relations, in which apparently exclusive opposites are resolved into places as complementary interactive aspects of a whole process. Within this approach, Value is not ultimately material, but like thought may be externalized in a materially operable principle. Hence ethical assumptions gain new dignity as the embodiment of such Value principles, materially and durably evident in man's universal experience.

John McHale. *R. Buckminster Fuller*
(Braziller). 1962. p. 42

Ideas and Integrities is a difficult book to read from start to finish. It is a much better book to read from finish to start. Each page is, in a sense, a statement of a contemporary problem, followed by a series of incisive, unexpected, wildly imaginative questions. The genius of Richard Buckminster Fuller is that he knows exactly what questions to ask, and in which order. What makes him more than a walking computer is his humanity and his imagination. For whether he likes it or not, Bucky is, above all, an artist and a poet—that rare contemporary poet who does not despair of the human condition.

Peter Blake. *NYT*. July 28, 1963. p. 7

Buckminster Fuller, whose name is high on the campus lists of favored environmental persons, is a comprehensive, all-purpose, long-distance, world-around genius talker who teaches everything to everyone everywhere. Wherever you look, there he is in his blue suit, with wide-open magnified eyes, pouring out his ideas in a flood of words, intoxicated by the universe and fed by an internal stream of energy that re-creates itself as it is used, and that may very well be a conscious effort by the universe to use Fuller to illustrate its own principles. For him, the universe is simply an endless, beginningless, wrap-around environment, "a non-simultaneous complex of unique motions and transformations."

Forty years ago when he first began talking on a broad scale about the universe, what it contained, what to do with it, and how to live in it, he was seldom understood and only rarely appreciated. His thoughts, and the language he used to express them, occasionally reached the outer limits of inscrutability. . . .

Fuller over the years has found his own way to clearer and deeper expression of a philosophy of science, art, and society—an expression that uses the imagery of a fully developed poet, the ideas of a scientist, designer, and practical engineer, and the spiritual energy of an authentic prophet.

Harold Taylor. *SR*. May 2, 1970. p. 56

It is impossible to convey the density of illustration or the copiousness of Buckminster Fuller's thought in a brief synopsis. Nor is it possible to draw a hard line between those points in Fuller's thinking where description leaves off and prescription takes over. Science fact and science fiction blur, perhaps by design, in [*Intuition*]. . . . Written partially in English, partially in space-think, the art of saying more with less words, Fuller's non-poems are a sort of physics refresher course cum brain-storm cum moral epistle.

Victor Howes. *CSM*. May 10, 1972. p. 11

There is an earnestness in Buckminster Fuller's attitude to life that is direct and manly and that inclines a critic to relent from too exclusive a concern with the aims of the poetic craft. . . .

One sees evidence [in *Intuition*] that Buckminster Fuller is indeed exquisitely sensitive to certain forms of beauty. . . . But framing seemly, shapely speech is not among his gifts. That is a misfortune. There is no instrument save language for giving expression to his doctrine, and dressed in the language that he has devised for the purpose that doctrine seems childish and embarrassing. Mr. Fuller is plainly a man who must be judged by his actions, for his intuition fails him when he sets out to speak to his fellow man.

Emile Capouya. *SR*. June 24, 1972. p. 67

Bucky had discovered something about the way of his own thought. Though he did not, like Thoreau, polish aphorisms till they resemble souvenirs, yet like the aphorist he thought in discrete energy packets, linear in sequence. The key to clarity was to make these boundaries somehow evident. From this time even the sentences he prints as ordinary prose have a new awareness of internal marking points.

He had discovered, in his own roundabout way, a mode of American poetry, the straightforward sentence collected out of energized units, and analyzed into them again by a visual aid. . . .

Bucky Fuller's satisfactions are conceptual: the domes, a general case, and the worldwide process he has envisaged for so long, a general case as well.

Similarly, the satisfaction he takes from writing (mostly verse now —the published prose comes from lecture transcripts) is that of conveying with clarity the most accurate general statement he can manage. Beauty does not concern him. It is not banished, though, by those enjambed polysyllables. The 1956 poem he dedicated to Dr. Jonas Salk not only resembles Roman and Elizabethan attempts to versify advanced knowledge, it is the nearest thing we have to a Metaphysical poem.

> Hugh Kenner. *Bucky: A Guided Tour of*
> *Buckminster Fuller* (Morrow).
> 1973. pp. 219–20, 222

Whatever Bucky has built or tried has been a demonstration that it is possible, in a practical way, to break out of the limiting conceptions supplied by common knowledge and the standard operating procedures. And . . . in form and structure whatever he has built or tried to build, derives from the views he has developed of the form, structure and play of forces in the universe. Repeatedly he tells his devoted audiences to start with Whole Systems. "Dig wholes!" . . .

How far along has Bucky gotten in the fulfillment of these excellent intentions, bringing all the parts of our special knowledge and interests to bear on our well-being? In verbal precision and definition he gets more successful every year. But there are not yet many practical returns. . . .

In a time of specialization, alienation, divisiveness, dissonance, fragmentation of knowledge and all the rest of it, Bucky has come forward with demonstrations, in artifacts and schemes, of healing possibilities. His task, like Thoreau's, has been to work outside the customary practices, as a maker of metaphors and paradigms "meeting our deepest needs," freeing us a little from limiting conceptions, giving us new points of departure.

> Elting E. Morison. *NYT*. March 11, 1973. p. 6

In performance what is wrong seems to matter little, because Fuller when performing makes the particular points minor, and the star-spinning from one to the next entrancing.

This may indicate why Fuller is so beloved, and scorned, and even feared. He seems to cast a spell that makes interested listeners into something like followers, and those who seek to dismiss him know that spell-binders have been suspect for a number of centuries. Those who claim to chart the universe are often known for having too easy answers; in response to such people, specialists, who could be trusted, came into being, and they soon demonstrated that the universe could not be charted. They piled up such huge storehouses of specialized knowledge that any one person's knowledge of more than a little bit of it would have to be inaccurate, or superficial, or trivial. So let us accept this. As a knower, as someone speaking about history or chemistry or physics or architecture, Fuller is seldom going to be as accurate, as subtle, as comprehensive as at least some and maybe many specialists in each of these "subjects" might be. But is there nothing left? What is left is Fuller's faith. . . .

Sitting on bleachers, watching him at a distance of at least a hundred yards, one could nonetheless feel his presence as something more than charismatic or soothing. He asked and so received and deserved, only for time and patience, not for belief, or if he asked for that, it was only as a way of asking us to believe more in ourselves. That was memorable, and listening to Fuller as he spins his stars is an experience one should have, and probably more than once.

Roger Sale. *NYR*. Feb. 7, 1974. pp. 30, 32

• GADDIS, WILLIAM (1922–   )

This 956-page first novel [*The Recognitions*] is easily the most exasperating mélange of genuinely scathing and merely random satire, of shrewd dialogue and chaotic fragments, of apt allusion and pretentious display, of suggestive prose and turgid outpourings that this reader has come upon. With such virtues of good avant-garde writing as audacity, freshness and independence it mixes such faults of the bad as obscurity, formlessness and intellectual arrogance. Inevitably it echoes the devices of *Ulysses* and resembles it in its attitude toward contemporary life, except that Joyce's vision of the decline of man from a godlike Ulysses to a commonplace Dublin Jew seems by contrast wistful and whimsical. For Mr. Gaddis (who, by the way, began this book eight years ago, when he was about twenty-five years old) sees ours as literally a society of forgeries, counterfeits, plagiarisms and fakes. . . .

It would be unjust to treat Mr. Gaddis' book as though it were in any way intended as a conventional novel. Structurally it is a series of symbolic episodes calculated not to tell a story but to suggest the sterility of contemporary life. Like a poem it coheres only in spirit, and this it does by exemplifying throughout half a million words man's degeneration to a point where he can no longer recognize the genuine, no less create it.

Unfortunately *The Recognitions* does not persuade us that it is based on any but a narrow and jaundiced view, a projection in part of private discontent. It is a clinical collection of slides showing organisms of decay magnified grotesquely and stained to an unnatural vividness. Somewhere in this book there is material for a novel and somewhere behind it is a writer with remarkable equipment, but *The Recognitions* itself is a grandiose curiosity.

. ·Milton Rugoff. NYHT. March 13, 1955. p. 6

What [*The Recognitions*] lacks, like all claustrophobic works of art, is imagination. It has plenty of invention and fantasy, but that is something different. Imagination in art is the ability to select significantly: to select in order to communicate a vision.

This book has no vision because the writer can see no way out of the vicious environment he describes so obsessively. The facts are piled up because they may contain a clue to the way out—but he does not find it. The book lacks perspective both socially and psychologically. And in the end it is this, I think, that explains the awkwardness of the style in which much of it is written and its inordinate length. Because the writer is trapped, he barely envisages the existence of the reader; unlike that of James Joyce his prose is unoral, heavy, silent; unlike a great but lengthy writer like Thomas Mann he has no desire to convince by accumulation; one finds oneself after nearly 1,000 pages in exactly the same place as one started.

John Berger. Nation. April 30, 1955. p. 378

It is only belated recognition of *The Recognitions* that may now indicate some definite guidelines to the course open to the contemporary novel. And for those who consider the achievements of James Joyce in perfecting many vital aspects of the modern novel—only to bemoan the absence of any major successors to Joyce—a closer examination of Gaddis's first and only novel to date should do much to emphasize the pervasiveness of the Joycean influence and perhaps indicate tendencies of what is to come. . . .

When imitation becomes impossible, it usually follows that a reaction develops instead, but in the case of James Joyce such a reaction could hardly be fruitful: against which Joyce is one to react? the naturalistic Joyce? the symbolistic Joyce? the Joyce of "scrupulous meanness" or the Joyce of "mandarin" involutions? the poet? the storyteller? the chronicler? the moral amoralist or the immoral moralist? With James Joyce, I am suggesting, the twentieth century has produced its most consummate literary artist, and it is to William Gaddis's credit that he has sought and found in Joyce both a direction toward the future and a definite delineation of what has been accomplished, so that *The Recognitions* at once acknowledges its debt and proclaims its individuality. Gaddis is able to do this because the basic element of his work is the delicate balance between originality and imitation, and the book itself as such is able to *be* a living example of what it *means*.

Bernard Benstock. WSCL.
Summer, 1965. pp. 177–9

Even the most indulgent well-wisher is likely to pick up any novel, especially a first novel, three hundred pages longer than *Ulysses*, with reluctance and read it to the end only with stalwart perseverance, even if stimulated, as in Gaddis's novel, by excellence in conception and execution. Stretches of vexation, frustration, *déjà vu*, and frank boredom make the first reading sluggish; but I read it a second time much more willingly and have perused it again and again eagerly. . . .

Gaddis has published no other novels; but a chapter from a new one appeared in the fall of 1970 in *Dutton Review*, No. 1. At forty-nine,

Gaddis is a classic example, apparently, of a young writer of genius shooting the works in his first novel—equal in length, range, and complexity to five novels. Appalled by the disconnectedness of time, Stanley, a character in the book who has devoted his life to finishing a massive composition for the organ, makes a statement that describes *The Recognitions* itself: "It's impossible to accomplish a body of work without a continuous sense of time, so instead you try to get all the parts together into one work that will stand by itself and serve the same thing a lifetime of separate work does, something higher than itself."

David Madden in *Rediscoveries*, edited by
David Madden (Crown). 1971. pp. 292–3

Tony Tanner recently concluded his critical survey of American fiction between 1950 and 1970 [*City of Words*] by claiming that William Gaddis' *The Recognitions* (1955) inaugurated an entire period of American fiction. Tanner's conclusion culminates a long, largely underground history for Gaddis' gigantic novel about forgers and counterfeiters, phony art, onanistic sex, and the false rhetoric of all kinds of religions. Still, few outside of a coterie of devoted followers have read or even heard of *The Recognitions*. Although it surfaced briefly at various times during the last twenty odd years, making its way onto an occasional college reading list, relatively little has been written about the perplexing novel since the initial, antagonistic reviews. A satire so fastidious in its condemnation of the entire modern world—a deliberate counterfeit which itself borrows at random from hundreds of sources and satirizes such living persons as then Senator Richard Nixon—of necessity had to provoke exasperated responses. Because reviewers attacked the novel as being too long, complicated, and nihilistic, the public at large ignored it. We have now had, however, access to some of Gaddis' manuscripts, which may help *The Recognitions* find its rightful aboveground reputation.

The manuscripts reveal Gaddis' intent to satirize the book reviewing world of the 1950s for preferring the kind of work being done by Hemingway and other popular writers of the time. Thus he made no attempt to accommodate reviewers or readers and went so far as to predict they would not read his 956-page long, involuted, fragmented, self-consciously demanding novel. . . .

Peter William Koenig. *CL.*
Winter, 1975. pp. 61–2

The most radical feature of *JR* (and the one that may limit its audience to readers possessing powers of super-human endurance) is the form in which it is presented. The book consists of 736 pages of virtually unin-

terrupted monologue and dialogue, an almost continuous outpouring of
language embellished scarcely at all by descriptions of character and
setting. People by the dozens move back and forth through thick mists
of verbiage, talking to and at and around and behind one another. Yet
somehow nobody really listens or quite understands what is being said.
This, as it turns out, is entirely appropriate to the subject, which is the
debasement of language as both cause and symptom of the corruption of
a society which has been abstracted by technology from the concrete
realities of feeling and being, and in which the totalitarian obfuscations
of bureaucratese, the gibber and jargon of the computer, and the lying
Newspeak of Watergate politics, corporate finance, and multimedia education have severed the connection that is supposed to exist between
words and the truths they are intended to describe. . . .

Gradually there emerges out of this babble of jargon-demented
tongues the perfectly sane, merely obsessive figure of JR, logical end-
product of the ongoing situation, supreme example of the utilization
potential of a meaningful learning experience. A good old American boy
from his perpetually runny nose right down to his torn sneakers with the
flapping soles, JR has learned his lessons well and knows by instinct
how to apply them manipulatively to achieve, in the classic rags-to-
riches tradition, the only goals he has been taught to respect: money,
fame, and power. . . .

It is undoubtedly inevitable that the novel promises at almost every
point to fall victim to the imitative fallacy, that it is frequently as turgid,
monotonous, and confusing as the situation it describes. Yet Gaddis has
a strength of mind and talent capable of surmounting this very large
difficulty. He has managed to reflect chaos in a fiction that is not itself
artistically chaotic because it is imbued with the conserving and correcting power of his imagination. His awareness of what is human and
sensible is always present behind his depiction of how far we have fallen
from humanity and sense. His vision of what is happening in our world
is profound and extremely disturbing. If it should ever cease to disturb,
there will be no better proof of its accuracy.

John W. Aldridge. *SR*. Oct. 4, 1975. pp. 28–30

Whereas *The Recognitions* was like *The Waste Land* in its apocalyptic
fears and longings ("we have entered the period of final woe at last,"
says one character), *JR* is like *Ulysses* in its sustained comedy and clear-
eyed regard for the homely virtues. . . .

Certainly, no recent satire or black comedy is so entirely devoid of
the satirist's congenital vice, which is heartlessness. The appalling and
hilarious fates of this novel's characters are also moving, partially because in them we see our own possibilities, but mostly because Gaddis is
aware that suffering is real, because his imagination has reach enough to

participate and make us participate in the suffering of real people of whom his characters are images. Behind the wild comedy, the frantic pace, the precise satire, the rigorous art, there is the somber mood of something that for want of a better word we might just as well call tragedy.

George Stade. *NYT*. Nov. 9, 1975. p. 50

• GARDNER, JOHN (1933–   )

Taut, ruminative and in its dignity never solemn, [*The Resurrection*] is an ordeal to read—but a rewarding one. . . . I was reminded here and there of Hermann Broch's *Death of Virgil*, but Mr. Gardner's protagonist is altogether more in this world. The children (to whom he hardly knows how to speak) are deftly drawn in the insouciance of their daily energy; the frozen panic of the wife comes through movingly, and one character—Horne, the mad law-librarian—embodies the notion of malfunctioning demiurge. Mr. Gardner subtly combines them all through devices of hallucination and dream, tense-switching, and italicized thoughts-within-thoughts.

Paul West. *BW*. July 17, 1966. p. 12

At times Agathon [in *The Wreckage of Agathon*], whose name in Greek means the Good, stands for the whole Western tradition of humane tolerance, now threatened by the twin fanaticisms of repression and revolution. At others, he is some kind of primordial natural force, a witness to age-long woe and fatality. At still others, when what he calls facticity catches up with him, Agathon is just a slobbish old lecher smelling of onions. In this guise he represents the irreducible, incorrigible lump of humanity that always jams up the bright theoretical machines continually being invented by one Lycurgus or another, and thus saves mankind from betterment.

In this guise, Agathon saves the book too. With his rambling wit, his irrelevancies, rages, blunderings, unfairnesses, with his tender-rough efforts to jerk his friend Peeker to wisdom through the muck of the world, he emerges as one of the scapegrace saints who have adorned literature from Socrates to Gulley Jimson.

Robert Wernick. *Time*. Nov. 9, 1970. p. 86

John Gardner's [*The Wreckage of Agathon*], like [Dan] Jacobson's [*The Rape of Tamar*], is a *tour de force* dealing with ancient historical legend in modern idiom. The resemblance is even closer in that his central figure, a sublimely ridiculous seer named Agathon (a mixture of "Crito" and Joyce Cary's Gulley Jimson, with a touch of Marguerite Yourcenar's Hadrian), believes that, in a world where truth is unknowable and where time's wreckage makes prisoners of us all, vividness of being is the highest wisdom. . . .

The novel is narrated alternately by Agathon and his disciple and mixes the concerns of public and private life. Gardner is ambitious to make his book a statement not merely about justice or about time but also about sex, growing old, and the art of living. His rhetoric and invention maintain considerable energy, but on second reading the liveliness appears more facile than at first. . . .

And the book's numerous aphorisms, though potentially forceful in the proper context, are a good deal less original than the author seems to be claiming, hence a little embarrassing.

David J. Gordon. YR. Spring, 1971. pp. 433–4

In Gardner's updating Grendel becomes a symbol of ultimate nihilism. . . . But this novel is no mere allegory. Its forces are more flesh than metaphysics, and *Grendel* is a tale full of action, observation, poetry, and strange to say humor. Grendel possesses, for all his negativism, a sort of Holden Caulfield charm. In his eyeball-to-eyeball and ethos-to-ethos confrontation with Hrothgar's law and order, Grendel perceives a wry comedy. . . . The world Mr. Gardner seems to be suggesting, in his violent, inspiring, awesome, terrifying narrative, has to defeat its Grendels, yet somehow, he hints, both ecologically and in deeper ways, that world is a poorer place when men and their monsters cannot coexist.

Victor Howes. CSM. Sept. 9, 1971. p. 13

Mr. Gardner's *Grendel* is interpretation and elaboration rather than translation—a sophisticated version of what *Beowulf* is ultimately *about* in modern terms. The device that he uses is to present us with a subjective autobiography by an extremely self-conscious Grendel before and immediately after Beowulf's arrival in Denmark. . . .

Mr. Gardner has a disturbing talent. There can be no doubt about that. Grendel, in addition to being the narrator, is much the most sympathetic figure in *Grendel*—in spite of his outrageous behavior and often deplorable opinions. What remains questionable is whether the literary object upon which *Grendel* is parasitic can carry the weight Mr. Gardner imposes on it. *Beowulf*, for all its historic interest, remains obstinately second-rate as a work of literature.

F. W. Bateson. NYR. Dec. 30, 1971. pp. 16–7

One approached Mr. Gardner's new novel [*Grendel*] with caution, suspecting another literary word-game. In the endless search for new objects of compassion, he has taken the monster from *Beowulf* called Grendel, and asks us to examine its predicament: how can Grendel's anti-social tendencies (eating all those brave Scandinavian soldiers) be explained except in terms of childhood deprivation, social rejection on account of physical deformity, horrible smell, etc.?

However, from this whimsical, monumentally silly idea for a novel Mr. Gardner has constructed something of pure delight. Grendel's grudge against humanity may originate in the pique of a rejected suitor when, on his first encounter with men, he is mistaken for a tree fungus, but Mr. Gardner invites us to believe that Grendel had a point. We examine the Beowulf legend for a start, and through it all the legends with which mankind sustains belief in his intrinsic nobility, and see the whole structure as a pack of lies. Squalid, bloodthirsty encounters between frightened men are built into epic battles; ignoble and furtive lusts become by the telling something beautiful and good. Mr. Gardner's book is as funny and as elegantly written as anything I have read for a long time.

Auberon Waugh. Spec. July 1, 1972. p. 14

The Wreckage of Agathon, an inventive if rather baroque meditation on the status of imaginative freedom within an oppressive political order, and *Grendel,* a dazzling revision of the Beowulf story that injects nightmare into the complacencies of our cultural and historical self-imaginings, seemed for all their brilliance more like strokes of theater, bright ideas carried off by extraordinary powers of execution, than fully explored fictional territories. Both, though thematically "relevant" enough, took place in a remote past, letting us see ourselves in them only around a corner. One wondered if Gardner's art might not require such a corner, if he mightn't be doomed to being a writer who could address us only in asides, winking knowingly from a long way off.

Two readings of [*The Sunlight Dialogues*] now convince me that Gardner is much more than a sleight-of-hand man. Where *Grendel* was, within its limits, virtually perfect, like a masterfully practiced stage-turn, *The Sunlight Dialogues* is ambitious, heroically flawed, contemporary (though with rich mythic resonances), absorbing moment by moment and darkly troubling after it's over.

Gardner is that rare creature, a philosophical novelist.

Thomas R. Edwards. NYT. Dec. 10, 1972. p. 1

Of course, Gardner's novel [*The Sunlight Dialogues*] can be faulted. Just as he shares with John Updike (and many other American writers) an obsession with entropy, so he reveals something of Updike's straining for self-vaunting but redundant simile. They both should be banned from using the word "like" for a decade. It could also be argued that some of the very long tirades detach themselves from the speakers' characters and swarm around like unattached mists of angry words. But these cavils are minor compared with the high degree of success achieved by this ambitious novel. It is a major fictional exploration into America, no less—the America that is vanishing and the problematical America of today. And without abandoning its fictional premises, it draws us into a sobering meditation on the possible shapes of our immediate future. It tells no lies yet ends with a refusal to accept despair. It does all this at the same time as it involves us in an absorbing and intricately interwoven story. This is a great deal for any one novel to do, and it should be recognized immediately for what it is—a very impressive achievement.

Tony Tanner. SR. Jan., 1973. pp. 79–80

John Gardner's last two novels, *The Wreckage of Agathon* and *Grendel*, were short and beautifully compact. They, too, were philosophical novels; that is, they addressed themselves to contradictions and irrational miseries in our society, and they make splendid sense. *The Sunlight Dialogues* is too wordy, too vague of design, to sustain and deliver the same kind of energetic meaning.

Mr. Gardner is a medievalist (he teaches Old and Middle English at Southern Illinois U) and his mind would seem to have been on the sagas of Iceland when he undertook this novel. The sagas wander off in just this way, appending digression to digression, ending up with all the design of a monkey-puzzle tree. And yet John Gardner writes a bold, flexible prose, and his mastery of vernacular is superb. The book is too good to bore; it overwhelms, it hides its climaxes, it strays; it is too damned long.

Guy Davenport. National Review.
Feb. 2, 1973. p. 159

Like a proper allegory, Gardner's novel operates on two levels. In its frame of realism, *The Sunlight Dialogues* takes place in Batavia, New York, in 1966. The Sunlight Man proves to be a member of a prominent local family, and in his detailed chronicle of the generations of Hodges, Gardner can perform like a veritable Galsworthy toward his Forsytes.

But, like a morality play, the novel constantly moves from specific people and events toward a sort of staged warfare of good and evil. Clumly is the last tired Apollonian, struggling fecklessly to enforce the law's jot and tittles as small boys let the air out of his tires and, in fact, the old American order deflates around him. The Sunlight Man, a poet, a magician, is in essence a daemonic figure: the embodiment of all that is newly restless, newly rebellious in the American spirit.

Melvin Maddocks. At. March, 1973. p. 100

Jason and Medeia [is] a tour de force of literary nostalgia and imitative form.

Jason and Medeia is nothing less than an epic poem in 24 books (the full Homeric complement) on one of the major cycles of Greek legend. . . .

Gardner's ambition is evidently to fabricate in English a fourth "ancient" epic to complement the *Iliad*, the *Odyssey*, and the *Aeneid*, as well as a book to stand beside his own novels, which are very much concerned with myth, wonder and historical fantasy. . . . Gardner, himself an ingenious translator from the Middle English, has invented a bizarre variant . . . the open hoax, the instant classic, a translation without an original. . . .

What remains unclear . . . is why Gardner should have undertaken such a hybrid project. The answer, I'm afraid, lies near at hand: Gardner is a prolific and learned writer of amazing virtuoso dexterity, but with little power of judgment or depth of inspiration. Like another superb technician, Ezra Pound, he needs to hang his hat on another man's rack, to unravel and reweave someone else's thread. Always the clever student, full of boyish bravado, he sets tough tasks for himself—hurdles, challenges—and polishes them off effortlessly, without really pondering if they were worth doing at all.

Morris Dickstein. NYT. July 1, 1973. p. 4

Now John Gardner, having tried his hand at a brief rifacimento of heroic myth in *Grendel* (*Beowulf* retold from the monster's point of view), brings Jason to these shores. *Grendel* he wrote in prose; Gardner is a novelist and prose is his medium. *Jason and Medeia* is in verse, not as *Time*'s critic believed, in blank verse but in the freely syllabled six-beaters which Richmond Lattimore used to translate Homer. A shambling, ungainly measure at best, it yields in Mr. Gardner's hands some thirteen thousand lines not one of which is so worded or cadenced that it gives pleasure on first encounter or remains in the memory afterward. The decision to cast his narrative in verse may be in large part responsible for what I take to be a full-scale disaster.

D. S. Carne-Ross. NYR. Oct. 4, 1973. p. 35

In *The Sunlight Dialogues*, John Gardner . . . has aimed high and won. . . .

Resembling more 19th century writing in its ability to create a totally absorbing world, *The Sunlight Dialogues* has a power rare in modern fiction, on all levels, wheeling through different points of view in Faulkner-like incursions into private consciousnesses. The language itself is impressive, holding the barely disguised primitiveness of our world in its images: "a house as black as dinosaur bones," the first of many; and there is a poet's eye for the symbolic detail.... But most forceful of all is the opposition of the dialogues themselves, and the indictment of law and order as a chillingly negative impulse that finds its apotheosis in the funerals that Clumly attends with unfailing regularity.

Susan Knight. *NS.* Oct. 19, 1973. p. 570

Gardner's reverence for ancient forms and permanent truths was clear enough in his earlier novels, but only in their doctrine, not in their multiple styles, which were insistently original. He has always been a man with a message. But like other serious modern novelists, he finds it hard to express his message directly. So he put it where he could be absolved from responsibility for it, in the mouths of crack-brained seers, monsters, madmen—his Agathon, his Grendel, his Sunlight Man. These characters and the novels in which they appear were often garrulous and sometimes cute. To the extent that they were, the severity and restraint of *Nickel Mountain*, the inarticulateness of its characters, is an implicit criticism of them, or at least a moving away or on.

Nickel Mountain, that is, has the look of being the result of certain conclusions Gardner had written himself toward: that "what was important was unspeakable," but perhaps susceptible to embodiment in a form; that in art, at least, less is more; and that at this point in the history of fiction, originality may lie more in the recovery of ancient forms than in the invention of new ones. These conclusions may or may not be true, but that good fiction can be written out of them is proved by *Nickel Mountain*, which is shapely and moving enough to make you believe, while you are reading it, in ancient forms and permanent truths.

George Stade. *NYT.* Dec. 9, 1973. p. 5

A serious case can be made for how little John Gardner resembles himself. Now he's an epic poet, now an epic novelist, now a medieval monster, now a simulated Poe or Melville. He is the latter two, and more, in this new collection of his short stories [*The King's Indian*], the title story a remarkable novella, full of marvels.

Gardner is the Lon Chaney of contemporary fiction, a writer without a personal psychography in his work. He seems sprung not from life but literature, history and ideas, a man making books with other books as a starting point, but a writer of enormous range and inventiveness. His prose is regal.

What he is is a splendid show-off.

William Kennedy. *NR*. Dec. 7, 1974. p. 19

GARRIGUE, JEAN (1914–1972)

Miss Garrigue is perhaps more skilled than any other poet writing today with the power to dramatize emotional thresholds between jeopardy and renewal. She has a genius for returning to life's viable starting points following defeats, disappointments, hovering over the twin craters of frustrated love and failed art, owning up to the bleakest shortcomings in the self. In poem after poem, her subject is the failure of events in daily life ever to measure up to her spirit's esthetic craving for perfectability. . . . She relentlessly subjects her keenest life-experiences to the refining "restless eye" of her dream-life. It is because she is able to enjoy all living beauties so much, strictly for themselves, that one is assured of the tragic heroism of her deprivations, of the demands her theology imposes on her responsive being. Her triumph is one of restraint, a succession of inured resistances to all pleasures easy of access, delaying and forestalling her natural gift for spiritual uplift until she has reached the supreme moment in which we are able to "think all things are full of gods." She will settle for nothing short of that arrival, and if she has had to sacrifice the more fashionable virtues of poetry in our time—expressiveness and immediacy—to evolve a middle range, a plateau, of vision (halfway between the language of feelings particularized and the language of elusive dream-states), we can only be as grateful for the qualities her art withholds as for those it affords, for there are rewards to be secured in reading her best poems of a kind that can be found in no other body of work.

Laurence Lieberman. *Poetry*.
May, 1968. pp. 121–2

The sumptuary must convince the skeptical reader that so much strenuous emotion is warranted and not just self-indulgence. The overingenious design of Miss Garrigue's poems cannot support so much emotion.

When she restrains her impulse to shock, however, when her self-consciousness is in abeyance, she writes finely and movingly. My favorite poems are "This Swallow's Empire," "A Fable of Berries," most of "Pays Perdu," "Address to the Migrations," with its controlled oratory, "Of a Provincial City," and "Nth Invitation." Miss Garrigue has a gift for song, and many of her best pieces are love ballads which either *Christabel*-like blend romance with black irony, or in the manner of songs in Jacobean plays express a macabre love-wit ("The Strike of the Night" and "Gravepiece"). Beginning with *Country without Maps*, she achieves a comely lyrical calm; the shorter lines provide a welcome enlivening of the rhythm.

Herbert Leibowitz. *HdR*. Autumn, 1968. p. 560

It emerges gradually that Miss Garrigue has taken up her rich, mannered style with her eyes open. There are prose stanzas in this book [*Studies for an Actress*] in which that style is dropped, and they are good. But they do not contain those lines of poetry which appear in her other verse. Her style, then, is the only way in which she can realize her potential for certain thoughts; thoughts which cannot form in the mind unless the emotional conditions are propitious to them and the clock is turned back. They cannot form in this mind and be recognized as poetry unless they resemble what has already been poetry. For she has no vision of a lyric poetry which is new in kind. . . .

In her last book she has made an effort to bring both sensibility and manner up to date; possibly she had at last woken up to the fact that her traditional poetic abilities were strangling her. The mixture is of old and new. But she begins to know herself well enough to hear her own voice.

Rosemary Tonks. *NYR*. Oct. 4, 1973. p. 10

Once in a while [in *Studies for an Actress*] there are echoes, strains of the old magic, of the enchantment her poems can convey when she mingles dream and reality, magic and fact. "Pays Perdu" from *Country without Maps* may sum up and distill that essence more perfectly than any other poem of hers. In this volume [*Studies for an Actress*] though I find a diffuseness and uncertainty that may not have been a matter of "failing powers" but rather a function of a new start, an engagement with new material. To our loss Jean Garrigue did not live to finish what she began.

Louis Coxe. *NR*. Oct. 6, 1973. p. 28

● GASS, WILLIAM H. (1924–   )

The world with which Mr. Gass works [in *Omensetter's Luck*] has long been exhausted, you would think, not only by Sinclair Lewis but by the likes of Sherwood Anderson and Edgar Lee Masters. Certainly all the hip little novelists nowadays have abandoned it for the chic regions of drug addiction and alcohol trauma, jet-set sodomy and the dropout's novel of ideas. Mr. Gass, though he leads us into many a terrifying vision, does not resort to a single routine apocalypse. And yet while the costumes of the book may be historical, its impact is compellingly modern. . . .

Mr. Gass's prose is equal to his design. Among novels I've read in recent years, only Norman Mailer's *An American Dream* has been able to pound such wild music out of pain. Gass, like Mailer, finds the very melody of dread. But whereas Mailer uses the current counters of urban despair, Gass reaches back to the language of the Bible, of Cotton Mather and the Farmer's Almanac.

Frederic Morton. NYT.
April 17, 1966. pp. 4, 53

Here on my desk is William H. Gass's *Omensetter's Luck*, which I have no hesitation in calling the most important work of fiction by an American in this literary generation. . . . On the one hand Gass's novel is marvelously original, a whole Olympic broad jump beyond what almost any other American has been writing, the first full replenishment of language we have had for a very long time, the first convincing fusion of speculative thought and hard accurate sensuality that we have had, it is tempting to say, since Melville.

Yet there is also something refractory, stiff, retrograde. For *Omensetter's Luck* hangs back at times. . . .

Yet just because of this, this freedom caught by the tail, it seems to me to make up that kind of incomplete, contingent and vulnerable miracle which can renew an art more powerfully than total revolutions, those hermetic masterpieces whose price is always a sterile autarchy.

Richard Gilman. NR. May 7, 1966. p. 23

Gass's fiction may be phenomenological as all get out, and if phenomenology is what you want, more power to you. Myself, I like his stories because they are interesting as narrative and verbal constructs and because at their best they can say something strange and worth listening to about the world.

In all five of these stories [in *In the Heart of the Heart of the Country*], Gass has modified Robbe-Grillet's technique for representing the contents and motions of a highly abnormal mind; but then Gass has put this technical facility to the service of what seems to me a worthy fictional end—not "new" but not old exactly either and certainly not old-fashioned: just literary, human.

George P. Elliott. Nation.
April 29, 1968. p. 573

Gass's first novel [*Omensetter's Luck*] . . . received remarkable critical acclaim from all shades of the critical spectrum, and Gass immediately became one of the important writers of his generation. This collection [*In the Heart of the Heart of the Country*] . . . serves to focus the distinctive qualities of his sensibility and style. . . . Gass is "old-fashioned" in his insistence that language is an immediate extension of human feeling and cognition. But what makes him modern is how much he knows—like John Barth, Thomas Pynchon and Walker Percy he is one of the philosopher-novelists who bring a new intellectual power to the basically transcendental American sensibility. It is writing like this that will achieve, if it is at all possible, a saving continuity with tradition as it attempts to save human feeling and individuality for art.

Jack Kroll. Nwk. April 1, 1968. p. 92B

Gass is a fiercely eloquent writer, and in the kind of discovery toward which he moves there are inevitable opportunities for a talented man. All ordinary things, events, and characters, given the initial conception, virtually vibrate with metaphor. All ordinary things are equally open to exploitation, for the simple reason that God is everywhere and awaiting only the language that will unlock the secret. Language itself is the greater part of the action and the likely logic of the action in Gass's fiction is, indeed, rhetorical: tropes, parodies, vertiginous verbal associations make the movement and the drama. Moreover, the fictions at the outset are provided with great freedom, because everything is grist for the obsession with which they begin—Gass is alternately furious and fluent, caretaking and cool; his materials are alternately Biblical and low pornographic, and in each instance serviceable to their end.

Marcus Klein. Reporter. May 16, 1968. p. 36

For anyone who writes fiction, or writes about it, or reads fiction for the solacing sense of potential reality it can provide, [*Fiction and the Figures of Life*] is the most important and bracing theoretical study that I know of. Like Aristotle describing the processes of tragic poetry from root to flower, Gass begins at the very beginning (the only interesting place ever to begin) to create for the medium a "comprehensive esthetic." His ambition is grand and noble and, if he doesn't quite redeem it with these essays, he comes close, and closer yet with the example of his own fictions.

Geoffrey Wolff. Nwk. Feb. 15, 1971. p. 86

The reviews, articles and esthetic meditations which appear [in *Fiction and the Figures of Life*] are, in their own way, edifying, theoretical and perhaps even trend-setting. But what should be said first is that they are by a man who loves words more than theories. . . . Nearly all of the essays in this collection of occasional pieces are a pleasure to read and some . . . are works of beauty. . . . The unlikely combination of criticism, philosophy and metaphorical inventiveness has resulted in a kind of poetry. . . . In a variety of ways—by means of startling metaphor and philosophical cajolery—[Gass] does the same thing in each essay: he calls our attention to art. It sounds like a simple enough achievement until we remember how few critics do it or, as Gass suggests, how many seem bent on doing the contrary.

Robert Kiely. NYT. Feb. 21, 1971. p. 3

[Gass] is not much interested in the kind of mirror before which preens that dandy Nabokov whose novels, Gass says, are used "to hold the mirror up to Nabokov." Nor is his interest that blasted cliché, which he staunchly rejects, old friend though it may be, of the novel as a mriror to the world. . . .

Gass's own looking glass is like Alice's, not a plane off which images bounce but a medium through which one passes lightly and easily from one realm to another, between the world of God's creation and the world of, say, Henry James's, between philosophy and art, criticism and fiction, phenomena and words. What interests Gass most of all is the relationship between these realms, the boundary (he knows it is there) that one has crossed, and the slightly bumpy sensation one feels at the precise moment of passing through.

Beverly Gross. Nation. March 22, 1971. p. 376

[In *Fiction and the Figures of Life*] the fictionist, trained as a philosopher, examines the art of fiction, its tools, and its relation to philosophy with thoroughness, speaking always to the point until the consistency of the essays becomes the flaw in the collection.

Though the essays are written with unfailing grace, the reader of Mr. Gass's fiction will find them redundant, for the subject of the fiction is often fiction. In his essay, "The Concept in Fiction," Gass is erudite and analytical about the names of characters. In *Omensetter's Luck* he is convincing. . . .

In the essays he deals brilliantly with a Platonic vision of language and reality, calling for a fiction in which characters, "freed from existence, can shine in essence, and purely Be." But the difference between the stories spilled like all-too-digested dinners from the mouths of old women and the fiction that can "shine in essence, and purely Be" is *demonstrated* in Gass's fiction.

Earl Shorris. Harper. May, 1972. pp. 98–9

The Midwest . . . in William H. Gass's story "In the Heart of the Heart of the Country" . . . becomes a metaphor for loneliness, for a sense of the self as stranded in a symbolic geography, almost before the writer has done anything to make this happen. Lives are "vacant and barren and loveless," Gass writes, "here in the heart of the country." "Who cares," he asks later, "to live in any season but his own?"

I suspect that it is because this last question is so central in American writing, and so perfectly rhetorical, not expecting an answer, that the Midwest, with its physical spread and relative emptiness, slips so easily into allegory, has a hard time sustaining itself as a real place in fiction. There is no mention of the Midwest in Gass's *Willie Masters' Lonesome Wife*, but the location is recognizably that of Gass's earlier story: the heart of the heart of the country, the lonely heart of a person looking for love, a lonely mind reaching out for us, then shrinking back, complaining of its isolation even as it wriggles further into solipsism. . . .

Behind the fussiness of much of his book there is a real urgency, a powerful vision of the loneliness inherent in writing (you write because you can't speak, for whatever reason) and of writing as a useful and articulate image for loneliness of other kinds.

Michael Wood. NYR. Dec. 14, 1972. p. 12

GINSBERG, ALLEN (1926–   )

Allen Ginsberg is a notoriety, a celebrity; to many readers and non-readers of poetry he has the capacity for releasing odd energetic responses of hatred and love or amused affection or indignant moralizing. There are even people who are roused to very flat indifference by the friendly near-sighted shambling bearded figure who has some of the qualities of such comic stars as Buster Keaton or Charlie Chaplin. And some of their seriousness.

His latest book *Planet News* grants another revelation of his sensibility. The usual characteristics of his work are there, the rhapsodic lines, the odd collocations of images and thoughts and processes, the occasional rant, the extraordinary tenderness. His poetry resembles the Picasso sculpture melted together of children's toys, or the sculpture of drift-wood and old tires and metal barrels and tin cans shaped by enterprising imaginative young people along the polluted shores of San Francisco Bay. You can make credible Viking warriors from such materials. Ginsberg's poetry works in parallel processes; it is junk poetry, not in the drug sense of junk but in its building blocks. It joins together the waste and loss that have come to characterize the current world, Cuba, Czechoslovakia, the Orient, the United States, Peru. Out of such debris as is offered he makes what poetry he can.

Thomas Parkinson. *CP*. Spring, 1969. p. 21

What is engaging about *Planet News* is the personality of Allen Ginsberg. This King of May and guru presides over a gentle saturnalia. He is believably "tranquil in his hairy body," his bawdry devotional and his homosexuality as casual and empathic as Whitman's. The poems have a friendly clutter and humor. For those who expect the howls (and howlers) of a Beat publicist for buggery and expanded consciousness, *Planet News* will prove surprising in its chaste and controlled lyricism. Ginsberg is more Ganymede than Jove. From a poet as erotically gregarious and "prophetic" as Ginsberg, one is prepared for a certain amount of the "Gasbag," and his long shaggy prose lines droop at times from all the cosmic weight they must bear. Still, in such poems as "Galilee Shore," "Describe: The Rain on Dasaswamedh," most of "Wichita Vortex Sutra," "City Midnight Junk Strains" (a fine elegy for Frank O'Hara), and in particular, "Wales Visitation," he may not "make Mantra of the American language," but he certainly makes "old human poesy."

Herbert Leibowitz. *HdR*. Autumn, 1969. p. 501

Allen Ginsberg . . . is the figure who preeminently represents the link between right now and back then; and in a single remarkable poem called, of course, "America," becomes the living memory of our dying memory of the mythological thirties. He included the poem in his first slim collection, *Howl*, a little book which raised a lot of hell, out of which there emerged finally a new life-style and a new metapolitics that has remained at the center of the cultural scene ever since.

Leslie Fiedler. *The Collected Essays*, vol. 2
(Stein and Day). 1971. p. 253

Ginsberg is one of the most traditionalist poets now living. His work is an almost perfect fulfillment of the long, Whitman, Populist, social revolutionary tradition in American poetry. In addition he is a latter-day *nabi*, one of those Hebrew prophets who came down out of the hills and cried "Woe! Woe! to the bloody city of Jerusalem!" in the streets. *Howl* resembles as much as anything the denunciatory poems of Jeremiah and Hosea. After Ginsberg, the fundamental American tradition, which was also the most international and the least provincial, was no longer on the defensive but moved over to the attack, and soon, as far as youthful audiences were concerned, the literary Establishment simply ceased to exist. It's not that Ginsberg is the greatest poet of the generation of the Fifties, although he is a very good one, it's that he had the most charismatic personality. The only poet in my time to compare with him in effect on audiences was Dylan Thomas, and Dylan Thomas was essentially a performer, whereas Ginsberg meant something of the greatest importance and so his effects have endured and permeated the whole society, and Thomas's have not.

Ginsberg is the only one of his immediate associates who outgrew the nihilistic alienation of the Beat Generation and moved on to the positive counter culture which developed in the Sixties. He was the spokesman of the lost youth of 1955 and he remained a spokesman of the youth who were struggling to found an alternative society in 1970. His influence is enormous, as great in India or Sweden or underground behind the Iron Curtain as it is in America.

Kenneth Rexroth. American Poetry in the
Twentieth Century (Herder and
Herder). 1971. pp. 170–1

Should it not be declared that with the publication of [Ginsberg's] *Howl* (1956) and [Lowell's] *Life Studies* (1959) our poetry was indubitably changed and indispensably enriched? Before that, it now seems, there were the giants (Eliot, Pound, Williams) struggling with their long poems, and the veteran lyric craftsmen (Frost, Stevens) presenting us with many fine shorter ones. But beyond that—a handful of well-made, intelligent, quite respectable lyrics that, after taking an English course or two, one could produce dutiful analyses of and admire for their well-wrought shapes. Ginsberg and Lowell changed all that, thrusting upon us in their immensely different ways the poem as personal performance. . . .

Often with Ginsberg the solemn and the silly are in too close company for this reader's comfort; it is the lack of complex ideas that for all its incidental virtues finally make his poetry mean less to me than it does to some. But the very idea of reviewing Ginsberg, certainly our most incorrigible poet, has its ludicrous aspect. . . .

William H. Pritchard. HdR.
Autumn, 1973. pp. 592–4

Largely because of his deep feeling for [Neal] Cassady, Ginsberg's tender lyrical voice is well-represented in *The Fall of America*. But his ambition in this book to speak, like Whitman, from the self-transcendent perspective of a prophet doesn't come off very well. The data remain data, conceptually unmanaged; the mood of outrage seems childishly insufficient as a mode of emotional mastery over the horrors he describes. As in *The Gates of Wrath*, Ginsberg's strength in this latest book is the strength of his belief in the art of poetry itself. Ginsberg remains an imitator, a disciple whose work is always reminding the reader of the 19th-century Romantic masters. As their disciple, however, Ginsberg has no peer: perhaps it is his own form of maturity as a poet. In any case, Ginsberg's whole working life has been an illustration of the capacity of that poetry to revitalize itself in the consciousness of people seeking through every mode of communal effort to find grace, a way to survive with others.

Diane Middlebrook. *Parnassus.*
Spring–Summer, 1974. p. 135

• GOODMAN, PAUL (1911–1972)

Paul Goodman's dance poems are based indirectly on the Noh-plays. These are not intended to be dramatic, in the Western sense, of unfolding an action. Their aim is rather an "initiation into a true awareness." . . .

The style—a loose blank-verse interspersed with short lines and with prose—is fluid; the thought is always interesting, and the stylized form allows him to make use of such phrases as "how curious this is!"—"how strange!"—with full effect. A poet with such a strategic sense as these dance-poems reveal may develop along unexpected lines.

Lloyd Frankenberg. *NR.*
March 16, 1942. p. 371

Among writers of the non-realistic persuasion, Mr. Goodman is unusually well-educated, imaginative, and witty, and even though, as we follow him from piece to piece, his unremitting literacy and cleverness become a bit wearing, this virtuosity must be to some extent excused as an excess of virtues. [*The Facts of Life*] contains at least one story, the title story, which is entirely delightful, and a play, "Jonah," about the prophet of doom, which is both comic and wise. The fact that the collection as a whole falls short of these two items doesn't of course diminish Mr. Goodman's stature in relation to other writers of his convention. It does, however, tend to confirm an old suspicion that even the method of non-realism cannot forfeit story-telling to disputation and still be sustaining.

Diana Trilling. *Nation.* July 28, 1945. p. 90

In a sense . . . *The Empire City* is what can always be called "coterie literature." More often than necessary, it is frankly, intimately addressed to the intellectual who has had Utopian dreams, read or written for *Partisan Review*. . . . At the same time, it is a book originating in good will, mature candor, and an urgently fermenting, more than secular morality. . . . The spirit inside, and the text itself, which seems not so much written as whistled, laughed, teased, prayed, come as close to imparting a man's gratuitous love for his own kind as mere language ever can.

Robert Phelps. NYHT. June 28, 1959. p. 3

The Empire City unfolds as a series of incidents, antic, lyrical, wry or elegiac, but informed by high spirits that counterbalance a terrifying awareness of degradation. . . . Nothing that we have lived or lived through during the past generation escapes having its absurdities uncovered. . . . It is all funny and sorrowful and not to be denied. . . . Yet Goodman, unlike Kafka, who was content to let the humor, ruefulness and terror speak for themselves, has an irrepressible taste for oratory, a thirties-like itch for declamation that introduces great stretches of tedium into an otherwise fertile landscape.

Richard Gilman. Com. July 31, 1959. p. 401

The Community of Scholars beautifully exemplifies Goodman's virtues as a social critic, in a less dramatic way, perhaps, than his classic study of juvenile delinquency, *Growing Up Absurd*, but no less impressively: this is a book that deserves comparison with Newman's *The Idea of a University* or Veblen's *The Higher Learning in America*. The theme here is the disruptive effect of administration and administrative mentality on the proper relation between college students and their teachers in America today, and on the proper relation between the college itself and the surrounding society. As usual with Goodman, the approach is philosophical rather than narrowly political. That is, he does not begin by asking what choices are allowed by the apparently ineluctable forces of the present (in this instance the growth of an administrative apparatus extraneous and even hostile to the process of learning); he begins by asking what are the essential properties and purposes of a college, under what arrangements historically have these properties found their fullest expression, and under what conditions can we plausibly imagine that they might be better realized in the future. [1962]

Norman Podhoretz. Doings and Undoings
(Farrar). 1964. pp. 99–100

Goodman is by temperament optimistic and busy; one wonders whether he cares very much about seeing his demands realized or whether just making them is sufficient satisfaction. His habit of attributing the evils and neglects of society to mental inadequacy . . . is, to my mind, an evasion of the real resistance to change arising from people's historically acquired attachments to property, conventions, superstitions. . . . Though, if things were up for a vote, I should oppose most of Goodman's recommendations, I do not doubt that arguing against them would lead me to better opinions than agreeing with almost anyone else. This is another way of saying that Goodman is making an indispensable contribution to democratic thinking.

Harold Rosenberg. NYT. Jan. 14, 1962. p. 6

Essentially, all of Paul Goodman's poems are about himself, and social and political concepts are present, not programmatically, but because they are interwoven with his private concerns. Thus the erotic is just as likely to be present in a political context as the political in an erotic context, and we gain some beginnings of insight into their still obscure interaction. The relationship between sexual fear and the politics of murder and suicide, and the alternative relationship of an architecture of community and the use of human energy for peace and pleasure: these concepts are as integral to his poetry as Pound's insistence on the reciprocity of monetary reform and just government with precision and vitality of language are to the Cantos.

Denise Levertov. Nation. April 13, 1963. p. 310

Intimacy really means everything to [Goodman]. Placing the sharpest value on the spontaneous utterance, the thing to be said, yet schooled, helter-skelter, in the classical tradition, Goodman, predictably, is a glorious mixer. Politically, he blends, I think, Kantian morality with Humean expediency; personally, he "publishes thirty books and rears three children," and indulges his idiosyncrasies. If Hebraic truth is prophetic and for the race, and Christian truth confessional and individual, Goodman irresistibly responds to both. In the novels, whether the naturalism of Making Do or the surrealist tinting of The Empire City, his heroes, devastatingly impressionable, keep fingering the chinks in the armor, the holes in the fences, wrestling with those parts of the economy, or the self, unexplored or unwanted. They are, like Goodman, both pariahs and charioteers.

Similarly, the poems. These are rallying songs of innocence and experience—querulous, anecdotal, prayerful, salacious. Often they are hymns to overcoming that which cramps, celebrating that which heightens, or brings together: "Creator Spirit, come." The best, it seems to me, are unpruned or unornamental, zesty and life-giving, if only for the moment. The worst (and, happily, that means the minority) lack every-thing—fullness of language, flow of images—that poetry must be if it is not to be cactus.

Robert Mazzocco. NYR. May 21, 1970. p. 4

America's inability to accommodate and profit by the whole of Paul Goodman is, for Goodman, properly a sign and symptom of her inabil-ity to deal with *any* experience in a spontaneous and inclusive way (though it should be said, in America's defense, that to accommodate the whole of Paul Goodman is a considerable undertaking, one that might make any republic fractious). Goodman's emphasis on a reading of his *Collected Poems* as a whole, as a *Leaves of Grass*-type experi-ence, rather than as a series or even as a scattering of beautiful realiza-tions, lucky hits and near misses, is part of the same impulse towards convergence, unity, completion, connections within the self. . . .

Goodman [is], more than any American poet alive, the true heir and disciple of the Good Grey Poet, mining the verge of the inclusive experience; and if he does not have Whitman's genius for suggesting that he is a Cosmos in himself, relying of necessity on the received forms to stiffen his talent, he is apter to catch his own posture, even his own imposture, in a reflexive and restorative irony. The other, public irony is that Paul Goodman's poetry has been obscured—cancelled, as a Sacred Book—by its situation in his canon—if he had written only poems, he would I think have held the place in American poetry today that sexuality, say, has in our assessment of human possibilities—central, flawed, affording occasions for joy and fulfillment.

Richard Howard. Alone with America
(Atheneum). 1971. pp. 155–6, 162

[Goodman] had been a hero of mine for so long that I was not in the least surprised when he became famous, and always a little surprised that people seemed to take him for granted. The first book of his I ever read—I was sixteen—was a collection of stories called *The Break-up of Our Camp*, published by New Directions. Within a year I had read everything he'd written, and from then on started keeping up. There is no living American writer for whom I have felt the same simple curi-osity to read as quickly as possible *anything* he wrote, on any subject. That I mostly agreed with what he thought was not the main reason; there are other writers I agree with to whom I am not so loyal. It was that voice of his that seduced me—that direct, cranky, egotistical, gen-erous American voice. . . .

Paul Goodman's voice touched everything he wrote about with

intensity, interest, and his own terribly appealing sureness and awkwardness. What he wrote was a nervy mixture of syntactical stiffness and verbal felicity; he was capable of writing sentences of a wonderful purity of style and vivacity of language, and also capable of writing so sloppily and clumsily that one imagined he must be doing it on purpose. But it never mattered. It was his voice, that is to say, his intelligence and the poetry of his intelligence incarnated, which kept me a loyal and passionate addict.

Susan Sontag. NYR. Sept. 21, 1972. p. 10

There was always a coarse-grained Hasidic magic about Goodman's stories, novels and poems. As with Buber, his peak moments were events that happened between people and in community. The Gestalt group work pioneered by Goodman and Perls is really a therapeutically ritualized search for Buber's I-Thou experience—with a heavy admixture of Reichian body mysticism to give it an even greater earthiness and weight. Like Buber, too, (and like the Taoist sages who are so similar to the Hasidic mystics) Goodman had a shrewd eye for how miraculously transfigured the commonplace substance of life might be—if only for one zany instant—if only to be followed by the business as usual of benightedness, folly, nastiness and failure. . . .

The patient acceptance of human frailty, the constitutional melancholy and broodiness, both are drawn from the Hasidic masters. . . . The whole nobility of Judaism has always lain in its stubborn trust that the world, such as it is, and people, such as they are, are unique manifestations of the Lord's will and so here is where we must make do.

Theodore Roszak. Book World.
Oct. 15, 1972. p. 10

Belatedly, in August, I heard of Paul Goodman's death. Shortly before, I'd been reading his last book of poems, Homespun of Oatmeal Gray, a book full of frustration and loss. I had thought again, as often in the past ten years, of writing him a letter. His "Drawing the Line" was one of the writings that changed my way of being in the world in the early '60's; that, along with Simone Weil, moved me toward politics. All his work, poetry and prose, was full of vital energy and courage and love for good craft, "healthy speech," the natural world and the human body. Goodman was one of those few contemporary poets for whom there was no apparent split between himself and nature—in his own person he did not seem to suffer from that division, although he certainly suffered from and struggled with its effects on politics and the social order. His sensuality—at least as I read it in his poems—seems all of a piece: grass, water, a Cape Cod beach, city streets, the embrace of another body, the taste of food, are parts of one whole for him, much as they were for Whitman. Like Whitman, he seems to have come by this wholeness through bisexuality (though I think of Whitman as a more truly feminine nature). Whether he was as capable as Whitman of respecting wholeness in others, I do not know.

Adrienne Rich. APR. Jan.–Feb., 1973. p. 16

[Goodman] belonged among those authors who are remembered less for what they wrote than for who they were. As a teacher he did not bring a new message but evoked the voice that had been slumbering in the imagination of his audience. His thought was neither very original nor in any way systematic. A eulogy that were to try a summary of his ideas could only reveal their contradictions. I can honor him only by continuing in his own aphoristic, somewhat freewheeling style, to free-associate some ideas which might please or displease him.

I believe that Paul was first of all a poet, and the youth of the 1960's listened to him not because he or they were politically radical, but because he opposed Wordsworth to General Motors, free love to the Board of Education, community to big organizations. He was neither a socialist nor an anarchist in the strict sense of those terms, but a rebel who had the courage to say what others dimly guessed or did not admit to themselves: that they did not understand the world into which they were supposed to grow up; that they felt crushed by the demands made on them by their parents, their teachers, their future employers; that all this seemed absurd. Many who, before he said this, had felt stupid, felt free because he had said it.

Henry Pachter. Salmagundi. Fall, 1973. p. 54

Many years ago I said in a review that if Paul Goodman had written in French or German he would have been well known all over the world before he was thirty. In a recent book on American poetry I said of him that he taught at Black Mountain a part of the year for many years. The second statement is a mistake. As a matter of fact, the squares on the Black Mountain faculty, particularly the most reactionary (putatively Far Left) German refugees, demanded that he be fired because he was what they considered a "sexual deviant." One thing he certainly was for many years was a leading think tank for the editors of the Partisan Review, along with Harold Rosenberg and Lionel Abel. Had Rahv and Phillips not taken exhaustive notes on the conversations of these three mentors, the Partisan Review would have had great difficulty ever rising above the intellectual level of the Reader's Digest. . . .

All his life he wrote poetry. Did he think of himself as a poet? Was he a poet? . . . One thing he certainly is not is a poet of the international modernist idiom. Twelve dollars and fifty cents worth of poems [*Collected Poems*], four hundred and sixty five pages. There is little evidence that anybody from Baudelaire to many of the youngest poets of the *American Poetry Review* ever existed. The work of a life in poetry—it's the life that matters. This is confessional poetry in a different sense than the use of the term invented by A. Alvarez. He meant the autobiographical case histories of the more or less mad. I think he first applied the term to Sylvia Plath. Paul was far from mad. He was sane and sad. He is one of the very few Americans with a genuine tragic sense of life, that sense that comes from six thousand years of culture, the abiding realization that life is heartbreakingly comic. Never forget, Chekhov called his plays of disorder and early sorrow, suicide and decay "comedies." Paul shared that point of view, a hard thing to do in a country where you are either an optimist or a pessimist or unpublishable.

Kenneth Rexroth. APR. 3, 3, 1974. p. 48

• GORDON, CAROLINE (1895–   )

Penhally is the triumphant tragedy of a house and the vindication of a mode of life. It is an achievement at once of erudition and of sombre and smouldering passion. It is distinguished by the afterglow of the Greek-Roman-Anglo-Saxon classicism that marked the Old South off from all other lands. . . .

Penhally differs from other historical works which are written from the outside and are at best *tours de force*—more or less re-constitutions. It unites itself to the living school of autobiographic writers in that it is a piece of autobiography. Mrs. Tate [Caroline Gordon] has from her earliest days so lived herself into the past of her race and region that her whole being is compact of the passions, the follies, the exaggerations, the classicisms, the excesses, the gallantries and the leadings of forlorn hopes that brought the Old South to its end. She does not have to document herself in order to evoke Morgan's cavalry raids or conditions of life amongst the slaves in the be-hollyhocked Quarters. She has so lived in the past that it is from her own experience that she distils these things.

So *Penhally* is a chronicle of reality. . . . Her characters have none of the historic over-emphasis that distinguishes the usual romance of escape. Her Southern girls are not over-dimitied, her gallants not over-spurred, her great proprietors not over-lavish. They are in short every-day people—but people of an everyday that is not today. That is a great literary achievement—and a great service to the republic the chief of whose needs is to know how life is constituted.

Ford Madox Ford. Bkm. Dec., 1931. pp. 374–6

None Shall Look Back fills out by a . . . discursive method the fortunes of the family in the midst of a war which destroys the social basis of its way of life. *The Garden of Adonis* has for scene the country community about the time of the last depression, when the full effects of defeat have had time to show their marks. *Aleck Maury, Sportsman* is not outside [Caroline Gordon's] subject but treats it in a very special way; and her most recent novel, *The Women on the Porch*, shifts the location to the city, the full-blown symbol of the western progression, or more specifically in American mythology, the end of pioneering. The heroine, the first to marry outside the connection (and this is significant), in her flight from the City with no intention of returning to the family seat instinctively finds her way back, but this time to a place of ghosts and sibyls. But the startling disclosure of the book is the crystallization of what has been gradually emerging, the theme of prevailing interest. To isolate such a theme . . . is an act of violence and distortion to the work as a whole. Briefly, this theme is what Life, the sly deceiver, does to womankind but particularly to the woman of great passion and sensibility. It is not that men do not come in for their share of sorrows and disappointments; it is, rather, that Life, represented in the only possible hierarchy of institutional and organized society, has a masculine determination. Very subtly the White Goddess reasserts herself as Miss Gordon's Muse. The young girl in "The Brilliant Leaves," the various heroines of *Penhally* (Alice Blair, the dark sister), Lucy of *None Shall Look Back*, and most eloquently the wife of Aleck Maury, are all the same woman. Very few of the male characters—Forrest, Nicholas, Mister Ben the possible exceptions—are able to measure up to the requirements of what the heroine thinks a man should be.

Andrew Lytle. SwR. Autumn, 1949. p. 578

[Caroline Gordon] has not accommodated the austerities of her method to that cultivation of violence and oddity for its own sake, whether in subject-matter or style, which is one of the more distressing infantilisms of an otherwise vital and growing Southern expression in literature. And while there is nostalgia and backward glancing in her early novels of the old South, she sternly reminds herself in the title of one of them that "None shall look back." Thus she loses out, as well, at the popular romancing level of Southern fiction, for she has not gone with the wind.

Caroline Gordon, whose prose is perhaps the most unaffected and uniformly accomplished that is being written by any American woman today, should be seen as the conservator in contemporary Southern fiction of the great classical tradition of the nineteenth century novel as formulated by Stendhal, Flaubert and somewhat later, Henry James. . . .

Miss Gordon's allegiances are clearly formulated [in the preface to the anthology *The House of Fiction*] and in her last novel, *The Strange Children*, her fidelity to the tradition of "naturalism" as she has defined it emerges with a mature authority. It is in this finely thoughtful work that her real service to the realm of Southern letters as the conservator of the heritage of "naturalism" and thus of the mainstream of the great fiction of the western world is most powerfully demonstrated.

> Vivienne Koch in *Southern Renascence: The
> Literature of the Modern South*, edited by
> Louis D. Rubin, Jr., and Robert D. Jacobs
> (Johns Hopkins). 1953. pp. 325–7

The Malefactors marks a new departure in Miss Gordon's fiction. Yet it does have a connection with four novels which precede it. It also illustrates strikingly a change in outlook which these nobels represent. *Penhally* and *None Shall Look Back* are full of regret for the vanished order of the Old South where men and women knew their place in the social hierarchy and could depend all their lives on values which their ordered society taught and supported. With *The Garden of Adonis* Miss Gordon moved into the modern Southern world which has lost its connections with the old order. Her men and women must now struggle through the crises of their lives helped only by a sense of decency and the necessity of reconciliation to forestall disaster. There is no way back, not even through nostalgia and grief for a vanished order.

In *The Strange Children* a new note is faintly sounded. . . . This muted emphasis on a religious theme prepares us for its full development in *The Malefactors*. Among the wastrels of talent whom we meet at the fête of the prize bull only Tom and Vera discover the way up and are reborn. Will this, then, be the pattern in Miss Gordon's fiction hereafter? As the South has faded from her novels, religion has taken its place, and the way is up.

> Willard Thorp. *BuR*. Dec., 1956. pp. 14–5

Most of the critics who have written about Miss Gordon have discussed her as a Southern writer—and of course she is. Some of her characters are deracinated Southerners or Middle Westerners, usually intellectuals who have left home. They are invariably unhappy; trouble and disorder trail along their foreign paths and remain with them when they occasionally return home. Miss Gordon has also written many passages, even whole novels, about the land and its healing moral power, which gives one a sense of belonging. She especially likes land that has not given up its fruits and rewards too easily; one appreciates what one has sweated to achieve.

Is Miss Gordon's preoccupation with Art also Southern? Perhaps, but her style is closer to Willa Cather's than it is to Southern rhetoric, even the quiet rhetoric of Katherine Anne Porter. Respect for form is in part Southern—for example, in manners, which cover and control personal likes, dislikes, drives, and ambitions; possibly too in a fairly general disregard for scientific principles and a preference for the arts that bear on personal relationships; and in a more open respect and liking for "elegance." But change comes on apace, and the Southern world of Miss Gordon's youth is no longer what it was. North and South grow more, not less, alike, and at least one or two of her novels seems to acknowledge that this is so.

William Van O'Connor in *South: Modern
Southern Literature in Its Cultural Setting*,
edited by Louis D. Rubin, Jr., and Robert
D. Jacobs (Doubleday). 1961. p. 321

Most of Miss Gordon's fiction belongs close to the heart of the new tradition; in fact, she and her husband [Allen Tate] are responsible for the term, symbolic naturalism, and for its definition. Miss Gordon conspicuously lacks the spontaneity and originality of the more widely read artists in the mode, but she has been one of the most conscientious students of technique and has constantly sought to broaden the range of her subject matter and philosophic understanding. Committed, like her husband, to the conservative agrarian ideal and opposed to modern "progress," she turned immediately to a fictional examination of her heritage, which centers in a rural district on the Kentucky-Tennessee line, adjacent to that of Robert Penn Warren. Only gradually, after an excursion back into Virginia beginnings, did she work her way into the modern era.

Miss Gordon's instinct is for pattern; she works most effectively, therefore, with the historical movement, the family group, the typical, rather than the individual, character. Not until her later novels does she attempt any deep penetration into her protagonists' minds or psychological processes and seldom then does she enter into them with any strongly participative warmth. Her quality as an artist depends upon objective observation and analysis, on a sure control of technique and symbolic extension, rather than upon the arousal of an empathic response to her characters. Perhaps largely for this reason, she has never achieved great popular success, though her work has stood high in critical esteem.

John M. Bradbury. *Renaissance in the South: A Critical History of the Literature, 1920–1960* (North Carolina). 1963. pp. 57–8

In 1953 Caroline Gordon remarked that a trend toward orthodoxy in religion was apparent among fiction writers as it was in the world at large. . . . It is no more surprising that in her quest for the universal myth she should have come to Catholicism than that she should have found, before her conversion, the touchstones of her being in the southern past. She is not, in the forties, a Catholic writer. But the entire, combined force of her need—for order, for tradition, for piety, for absolution and grace, for a shaping world view that would take the place of the shapeless chaos of the world—forced her inevitably and logically toward the Roman Church; and at the end of the decade, in 1951 to be precise, she published her first overtly Catholic novel. She had made the open commitment augured in all her predispositions. The wonder is that writers like Faulkner and Warren, who, for the same reasons, seemed to press toward the same end, had not yet entered the Church a decade later.

Before the Church there were the South and the Past. The elegiac tone Carolina Gordon adopted toward the past derived from her conviction that a total conception of life, life as good, stable, and continuous, had disappeared or been destroyed. A pervasive sense of cultural loss flows through her work. The fragmented lives of her characters are a reflection of this destruction of a whole and coherent cultural pattern that might define life. No force appears in the secular world to act as anchor for man, since neither the cosmopolitanism of urban culture nor the intellectualism that flourishes there provides a satisfactory center for human existence. Nor is the world of nature in itself sufficient. The urgent pessimism of her fiction is the result of her conviction that man's hope and his fate are equally blasted.

Chester E. Eisinger. *Fiction of the Forties* (Chicago). 1963. p. 186

It is the strength of Miss Gordon's work to suggest continually new facets of significance as one lives through the books in his mind. The characters and the incidents form new configurations with the result that the significance of any one of her books enlarges constantly as one reviews it. Her purpose has been from the beginning to suggest that reality is spiritual as well as empiric, immaterial as well as material. Accordingly, she has presented the experience of her characters in time and then again as it reaches beyond time. The ineffable dimensions of her materials she suggests through a discerning use of myth; and in her later books Christianity reinforces their universal implications. . . . As a writer Miss Gordon is the inquiring moralist even before she is the religious writer. Because of her passionate concern with the way life should be, her books are rooted in social realities even as they look toward the visionary. Intelligence, compassion, psychological insight, depth of vision, and stylistic distinction inform a canon of work that impresses always by its comprehensiveness and strength.

Frederick P. W. McDowell. *Caroline Gordon* (Minnesota). 1966. p. 45

[Caroline Gordon's] fiction dramatizes the myth of the South, as Cooper's does that of the Western migration, James's of Old and New World culture, Proust's of French social change at the end of the nineteenth century. Beginning, in thematic order, with *Green Centuries* and ending with *The Malefactors*, Miss Gordon's fiction shows the movement from loss to acquisition, from rootlessness to stability, from chaos to order, from matter to spirit. In *Green Centuries* the antagonistic natural world drives the exile to certain destruction as he escapes his past (finally, himself) in the pursuit of the unknown. This theme of the natural world as opponent reappears later in *The Garden of Adonis* and particularly in *The Women on the Porch*, as does the central concept of the failure of love between man and woman, in part the result of destroyed cultures or man's warped view of new and different economic systems.

James E. Rocks. *MissQ*. Winter, 1967–68. p. 10

Penhally is a completely "rendered" novel, as [Ford Madox] Ford would have said. Its method of presentation—the shifting post of observation in the line of succession among the Llewellyns—allows a remarkable degree of control for such a large subject. Its author has seldom written better. But she was not content with the perfection of a method, and her subsequent books have realized her subject by a variety of means. Her second novel, *Aleck Maury, Sportsman* (1934), for instance, is based on the convention of the old-fashioned memoir. Aleck Maury is the only one of her major characters whom Miss Gordon has granted the privilege of telling his own story, and she thus departs from what with her is a virtual principle. This, the most popular of her novels, can stand by itself, but it gains something from those written after it, as though it were cutting across a territory whose outlines are more fully revealed later on.

Ashley Brown. *SHR*. Summer, 1968. p. 283

No more than a handful of modern writers have produced short stories which are both technically sound and rich in fictional values.

Such a writer is Caroline Gordon, whose artistic discipline has always been adequate to control the wide range of vision she brings to her fiction. Indeed she tends to crowd into her stories more than their formal limitations would seem to permit: the total experience of a region's history, the hero's archetypal struggle, the complexity of modern aesthetics. In every instance, however, she succeeds in bringing the broad scope of her narrative into focus and in creating the ideal fictional moment, when form and subject are at war and the outcome hangs forever in the balance.

Yet there is a classic simplicity in most of her short stories, an unusual economy of incident and detail which decorously masks their essential thematic complexity. Even the prose is, for the most part, spare in its diction and syntax, particularly in the first-person narratives, dominated by a tone that is quiet and conversational, the intimate language of the piazza on a warm summer evening.

And it is in this quality that one finds a clue to the origins of Miss Gordon's narrative virtue. For she is still in touch with the oral tradition which in her formative years was a vital element of family life. Like William Faulkner and Katherine Anne Porter, with whom she has much in common, her experience of the nature of being begins in the family, with its concrete relationships, its sense of wholeness, its collective memory.

Thomas H. Landess. Introduction to *The Short Fiction of Caroline Gordon: A Critical Symposium*, edited by Thomas H. Landess (Dallas). 1972. p. 1

The Glory of Hera is a matchless book—a peak, I think, in the career of a writer devoted to a too familiar, and often belittled, vocation. The uniqueness of the book consists in this: that its author stretches the capacities of the novel so that it can operate authentically in the protean land of ancient Greek myth. It can take on the shapes and assume the colors that make it resemble a luminous mosaic depicting the exploits which were attributed to the god-engendered hero, Heracles. Beginning with Homer's account of the burly bowman, the myth, though revealed piecemeal in many arts, remained the special property of the poets, so astonishing was it, so unbounded, ranging as it did from Heaven to Hell and over all of the perilous borderlands of Earth. The ancients would argue that whatever else might occur, this ineffable stuff could never be captured by a writer of mere prose, by which they would have meant, of course, a chronicler or encyclopedist of some sort. That Caroline Gordon has captured it—indeed she has delivered it quivering and alive from the monstrous darkness of the past—is a triumph for the modern art of prose fiction as well as for the far from modern arts of revivifying immemorial legends.

Howard Baker. *SoR*. Summer, 1973. pp. 523–4

HAMMETT, DASHIELL (1894–1961)

The characteristics of Hammett's "daemonic" tough guy, with significant variations in the last two novels, can be schematized as follows: he is free of sentiment, of the fear of death, of the temptations of money and sex. He is what Albert Camus calls "a man without memory," free of the burden of the past. He is capable of any action, without regard to conventional morality, and thus is apparently as amoral—or immoral—as his antagonists. His refusal to submit to the trammels which limit ordinary mortals results in a godlike immunity and independence, beyond the power of his enemies. He himself has under his control the pure power that is needed to reach goals, to answer questions and solve mysteries, to reconstruct the (possible) motivations of the guilty and innocent alike. Hammett's novels . . . present a "critique" of the tough guy's freedom as well: the price he pays for his power is to be cut off behind his own self-imposed masks, in an isolation that no criminal, in a community of crime, has to face.

Robert I. Edenbaum in *Tough Guy Writers of the Thirties*, edited by David Madden (Southern Illinois). 1968. p. 81

What [Hammett's] stories have, even the earliest and least of them, is a flavor wholly individual. This flavor comes partly from the bareness of a style in which everything superficial in the way of description has been surgically removed, partly from his knowledge of actual criminal investigation, and partly from the wistful cynicism with which he wrote. . . .

With all his innovations of form and language, Hammett kept the puzzle element from the orthodox detective story. . . . The problems are composed just as skillfully as those in an orthodox detective story, but in the best of Hammett they are the beginning and not the end of the book's interest. *The Maltese Falcon* and *The Glass Key* offer a gallery of characters and scenes unexcelled in the crime story, all of them seen with a Dickensian sense of the truth in caricature.

Julian Symons. *Mortal Consequences* (Harper). 1972. pp. 137–9

The rebellion in crime fiction started . . . with Dashiell Hammett. From *Red Harvest* (1929) to *The Thin Man* (1934), his books used the hero as a man who was not far removed from the criminal elements he combatted. No fancy pants, he was ready to shoot or hit and to use illegal means to finish a case. Solutions were less important than the need to settle a job: that's what he got paid for. Nor was this an intellectual mandarin outwitting the stereotypical dumb police, but a professional of crime who knew that the police are—seriously—either incapable of solving certain crimes because of the orthodoxy of their methods or unwilling to solve them for political reasons. Organized crime became part of the world of fiction so that the miscreant was no longer a peculiar individual with even remote socially acceptable motives, but a faceless cog in a large machine which used violence with a ruthless neutrality.

The writing itself changed. Hammett's style is bare and terse, with a delivery that is direct and to the point, while the tone is cynical. Action and style support each other: both have a relentlessness which makes events seem inevitable. Though the detection puzzle remained, there was now more emphasis on atmosphere and characterization. This was the saving grace of the particular development, variously called the "thriller," "private-eye fiction," the "hardboiled school of writing," or the "crime novel." In terms of literature it made something mandatory which only talent can provide: style.

E. M. Beekman. MR. Winter, 1973. p. 151

When Hammett turns [from criminals] to the respectable world, the world of respectable society, of affluence and influence, of open personal and political power, he finds only more of the same. The respectability of respectable American society is as much a fiction and a fraud as the phony respectable society fabricated by the criminals. Indeed, he un- waveringly represents the world of crime as a reproduction in both structure and detail of the modern capitalist society that it depends on, preys off, and is part of. But Hammett does something even more radical than this. He not only continually juxtaposes and connects the ambi- guously fictional worlds of art and of writing with the fraudulently fictional worlds of society; he connects them, juxtaposes them, and sees them in dizzying and baffling interaction. He does this in many ways and on many occasions. One of them, for example, is the Maltese Falcon itself, which turns out to be and contains within itself the history of capitalism. It is originally a piece of plunder, part of what Marx called the "primitive accumulation"; when its gold encrusted with gems is painted over, it becomes a mystified object, a commodity itself; it is a piece of property that belongs to no one—whoever possesses it does not really own it. At the same time it is another fiction, a representation or work of art—which turns out itself to be a fake, since it is made of lead.

It is a *rara avis* indeed. As is the fiction in which it is created and contained, the novel by Hammett.

Steven Marcus. Introduction to *The Continental
Op* by Dashiell Hammett (Random).
1974. pp. xxiv–xxv

● HANSBERRY, LORRAINE (1930–1965)

The supreme virtue of *A Raisin in the Sun* . . . is its proud, joyous proximity to its source, which is life as the dramatist has lived it. I will not pretend to be impervious to the facts; this is the first Broadway production of a work by a colored authoress and it is also the first Broadway production to have been staged by a colored director. . . . I do not see why these facts should be ignored, for a play is not an entity in itself, it is a part of history, and I have no doubt that the knowledge of the historical context predisposed me to like *A Raisin in the Sun* long before the house lights dimmed. Within ten minutes, however, liking had matured into absorption.

Kenneth Tynan. *NY*. March 21, 1959. p. 100

It is a sound rule in the theatre that excellence is inversely proportional to tears shed; that is, the bigger the catch in your throat as the curtain comes down the more suspect the play will seem half-an-hour later. On this account *A Raisin in the Sun* is highly questionable. At the end of it the handkerchiefs were out in force and the audience, though they elbowed each other as savagely as usual through the doors, were speechless. True enough, Miss Lorraine Hansberry's play has most of the ingredients of the classic tear-jerker: a poor but honest family on the wrong side of the tracks; a benevolent despot of an Old Mum; her ageing son who is eating his and his wife's heart out for lack of an opportunity in life; his pert kid sister who goes to medical school and has a couple of admirers in tow, one intellectual, one rich. There is also a large insurance cheque, most of which the son is promptly conned out of. More than that, the dialogue is occasionally as predictable as the situations: the mother hands the cash over to her son with the words, "It isn't very much, but it's all I got in the world." He, presumably, passed it on to the con man murmuring, "Take it, it was my mother's."

Yet, although *A Raisin in the Sun* occasionally slips over into triteness, it makes an extraordinarily compelling evening's theatre— which shows once again, I suppose, the degree to which drama is an extra-literary activity. As a play it may be patchy, but as a vehicle for the actors it is superb. One reason is that a powerful rhetoric comes naturally to Miss Hansberry. This puts her in a rather small club of writers, most of the other members of which are Celts. But with a difference: the rhetoric of a talented Negro writer always gives you the impression that it is about something, which is certainly not true of the Irish or the Welsh. Miss Hansberry has more than a gift of the gab; she also has a great deal to say on questions that deeply concern her. So her rhetoric is not just colourful; it has a natural dignity, which presumably has something to do with the fact that the rhythms and diction of passionate Negro speech come straight from the Bible. The language is felt and meant to a degree where it can afford to be simple. Finally, Miss Hansberry's characters continually talk about the subjects which concern all Negroes: the jobs they can get, the areas they can live in, the strategies by which their pride is preserved or undermined, the problem of assimilation and racial independence. This means that the otherwise nice, rather sentimental family life, with its humdrum quarrels, ambitions and pieties, is continually strengthened by outside loyalties and outside hatreds.

A. Alvarez. NS. Aug. 15, 1959. p. 190

The Sign in Sidney Brustein's Window is not compactly written or tightly staged or performed. The chances are that its structure would have been strengthened and its wordiness thinned out if Miss Hansberry had not been gravely ill during the final weeks of preparation. . . .

In spite of its imperfections *The Sign in Sidney Brustein's Window* can stimulate and please. Unlike so much piffling stuff on Broadway, Miss Hansberry's work reflects passion, intelligence and a point of view. It has an appreciation of character and it knows how to be earnest without pomposity or sobriety about the corruption that threatens every corner of our lives.

Howard Taubman. NYTts. Nov. 1, 1964. p. 1

Lorraine Hansberry's greatest achievement lies in her ability to avoid what Saunders Redding has called "The obligations imposed by race on the average . . . talented Negro." The obligation to limit one's scope to the immediate but parochial injustices of racial intolerance has for long sapped the creative energy of the Negro writer. Having paid her debt to this tradition with the poor *A Raisin in the Sun*, however, Hansberry achieves a significant break-through with *The Sign in Sidney Brustein's Window*, which is clearly in the mainstream of contemporary drama. The Negro is no longer seen as the victim of a savage social situation but becomes an endemic part of a society desperately searching for a valid response to the human condition. Lorraine Hansberry's death at the age of thirty-four has robbed the theatre of the one Negro dramatist who has demonstrated her ability to transcend parochialism and social bitterness. . . .

Lorraine Hansberry' commitment . . . transcends the merely parochial for her rebellion is directed less against intransigent racialism than against the sterility of the absurd and the inconsequence of a theatre founded on distraction.

C. W. E. Bigsby. *Confrontation and Commitment: A Study of Contemporary American Drama 1959–66* (MacGibbon & Kee). 1967. pp. 172–3

Structurally, Lorraine Hansberry remains essentially within the bounds of the conventional realistic well-made play, something almost anachronistic amidst the styles of the 1960s. The term "well-made" can be misleading because of its unfortunate connotations with the emptiness of nineteenth century tradition, but we need only look at the plays of a modern dramatist such as Lillian Hellman to recognize that orderly development of plot and a neatly planned series of expository scenes, complications, and climaxes can greatly assist in thematic and character development of a superior nature. Plot in Miss Hansberry's plays is of secondary importance, for it is not her main dramatic purpose. Nonetheless, because the audience has considerable interest in *what* is happening as well as *to whom*, both *A Raisin in the Sun* and *The Sign in Sidney Brustein's Window* are thoroughly enhanced by well-ordered revelation of the events which are so important in the lives of the characters. The straightforward telling of a story remains a thoroughly honorable literary accomplishment, and Miss Hansberry has practiced this ancient dramatic art with eminent respectability. Moreover, the scene, incident, and dialogue are almost Ibsenesque, avoiding overt stylization for its own sake and performed within the standard "box" set that progressively becomes more rare.

Jordan Y. Miller in *The Black American Writer*, vol. 2, edited by C. W. E. Bigsby (Penguin). 1969. p. 161

Ed Bullins occupies much the position in today's vanguard of black writers that Lorraine Hansberry did ten years ago. The differences between their generations—as well as some surprising similarities—were highlighted this season by an evening compiled from Miss Hansberry's work, entitled *To Be Young, Gifted, and Black*. The differences are matters more of content than form. Some of Miss Hansbery's attitudes (though not all) are decidedly out of fashion with black playwrights now. For example, the self-portrait she draws of herself as a young coed is far closer to the heroine of any standard McCall's serial about life in a white college dorm than to the experiences of today's black collegians. And her love of country ("I walk in my American streets again"), hedged with whatever doubts and increasingly superseded in the last years of her life by concern for her fellow blacks, would be unthinkable for a Bullins or a LeRoi Jones—as would her ambivalence about whether she considered herself a revolutionary.

Martin Duberman. PR. No. 3, 1969. p. 490

[Hansberry] knew that *naturalism* began in *determinism*, and she wanted no part of that. For her, for her play, human possibility was what counted. She wanted, as her remarks on Sean O'Casey in *To Be Young, Gifted, and Black* indicate, to create the life of the Chicago she knew, but more than that she wanted to organize her creation so that her play and her hero could opt for what was best and most spirited in that life, not give in to all that was destructive. Her second play, *The Sign in Sidney Brustein's Window*, was primarily an attack on a particular kind of fashionable determinism, the assumption that nothing can be done about the evils of the world and the resulting "great sad withdrawal from the affairs of men," as one of the characters puts it.

Gerald Weales. Com. Sept. 5, 1969. p. 542

When so bright a light goes out so early, when so gifted an artist goes so soon, we are left with a sorrow and wonder which speculation cannot assuage. One is filled for a long time with a sense of injustice as futile as it is powerful. And the vanished person fills the mind, in this or that attitude, doing this or that. Sometimes, very briefly, one hears the exact inflection of the voice, the exact timbre of the laugh—as I have, when watching the dramatic presentation, *To Be Young, Gifted and Black*, and in reading through these pages. But I do not have the heart to presume to assess her work, for all of it, for me, was suffused with the light which was Lorraine. It is possible, for example, that *The Sign in Sidney Brustein's Window* attempts to say too much; but it is also exceedingly probable that it makes so loud and uncomfortable a sound because of the surrounding silence; not many plays, presently, risk being accused of attempting to say too much. . . . Lorraine made no bones about asserting that art has a purpose, and that its purpose was action: that it contained the "energy which could change things."

James Baldwin. Preface to To Be Young,
Gifted and Black by Lorraine Hansberry
(New American Library). 1970. pp. xiii–xiv

To Be Young, Gifted and Black is the portrait of an individual, the workbook of an artist, and the chronicle of a rebel who celebrated the human spirit. It is also, I believe, a prophetic chapter in the history of a people and an age.

It is worthy of some emphasis here, therefore, that Lorraine Hansberry's particular view of life did not emerge in one by nature given to celebration, to excessive confidence in the universe or the magnanimity of her fellowmen. What for others may have come with the weight and majesty of profound "existential" revelation—the discovery at some point in life that the universe is not particularly man's friend; that there is an inherent and inevitable tragedy in all men's fate; that there is within every human being an ego which will not be denied without fundamental havoc to himself or those around him; that to fulfill that ego, man is capable of the most incredible acts of transcendence or abasement, sacrifice or aggrandizement, humanity and inhumanity; that even so, our aspirations must ever outstrip our achievements; that we are, in simple fact, all born *dying*; and that, in short, there is a quite impossible, untenable, built-in absurdity to life—all this to her was *assumed*: was already assumed, it seemed to me—though I could neither appreciate nor handle such knowledge at the time—when I first met her as a girl of twenty-one. Had somehow been assumed, I sometimes think—though I know of course this is not possible—from the time she was a very little girl. Perhaps because of her intrinsic sense of vulnerability as a woman in a violent universe; perhaps because of her multifold experience as a *black* woman . . . perhaps because of her intuitive view of human frailty and the comedy of errors and compendium of terrors that is the average human life—it never could have occurred to her to think otherwise.

Robert Nemiroff. Foreword to *To Be Young, Gifted and Black* by Lorraine Hansberry (New American Library). 1970. p. xviii

Lorraine Hansberry was no "black panther," but an intelligent, compassionate human being with a gift for lucid dramatic writing which, when well acted as was the case of Sidney Poitier in *A Raisin in the Sun* and as now in a new kind of characterization by James Earl Jones [in *Les Blancs*], commands attention and inspires respect. To wave aside *Les Blancs*, a more mature play than *A Raisin in the Sun*, as old-fashioned and obvious—it may be "old-fashioned," obvious it is not—is an evasion which I am inclined to ascribe to bad faith, especially in view of what certain folk call "good theatre."

Harold Clurman. *Nation*. Dec. 7, 1970. p. 606

Imaginative, unified, easily documentable, and intensely interesting story that it is, and being good theater as well as good dramatic literature, *The Drinking Gourd* is in the best tradition of historical dramas—much more so than *Les Blancs*, which is also an historical drama. In both of these works, nevertheless, as in the drama which first won her acclaim as a playwright, Miss Hansberry skillfully used original and vivid dialogue to reveal character and develop action. In *Les Blancs* she wrote all of the dialogue in standard informal spoken English, having no reason to use any other kind. In *The Drinking Gourd* she used the same kind of English to represent the speech of literate characters but changed to substandard usage to represent the speech of semiliterate and illiterate people. This she did convincingly without resorting to mutilated English, which has so often been perpetrated as "dialect," whereas it represents nobody's actual speech.

W. Edward Farrison. CLAJ. Dec., 1972. p. 196

My God, how we need [Lorraine Hansberry] today! She knew that politics was not ideology, but caring. Politics is that quality of becoming more and more human, of persuading, cajoling, begging, and loving others to get them to go with you on that journey to be human—and defending yourself against those who seek to prevent that journey.

Perhaps the greatest irony is that so much humanity should have come from the life and work of a black woman. Then again, it is quite logical. She had been tempered by the fire and emerged briefly to let her own light shine. She knew that blackness was the basis for her existence, not the totality, and that if it becomes the whole, one can only become consumed by the fires of one's own rage and frustration. Lorraine Hansberry is the black artist who lived beyond anger, which is not to say that she wasn't angry. Her plays are an expression of rage against the outrages perpetrated against humanity. Anger did not define her art, but motivated and informed it. The quality which pervades her plays is compassion, the kind of compassion which can slap a face as easily as it can tease. She didn't make the mistake of hating white people. She hated what people did to each other.

Julius Lester. Introduction to Les Blancs
by Lorraine Hansberry (Random).
1973. pp. 31–2

HAWKES, JOHN (1925–   )

Regeneration as a theme will probably never cease to interest the novelist, however much the contemporary dramatist may have abandoned it. But as a counterweight to sentimentalism, the writer must be prepared to demonstrate that regeneration is not without its cost. The tragic implications of the theme may be, in fact, so stark that many recent critics have come to regard a work like *King Lear* as a portrait of almost unrelieved existential despair.

John Hawkes in his recent novel, *Second Skin*, chooses a comic development, but if his imagery and part of his setting owe something to *The Tempest*, the horror and brutality of many events recall the sterner stuff of *Cymbeline* or *A Winter's Tale*. And in other important respects Hawkes' novel departs from the overall pattern of those romances: the evil past and hopeful present are not so sharply separated, and there is no prospect of a glorious reunion or a joyful return to one's native land. Though the surrealism of Hawkes' earlier work has all but vanished, a system of interfolded flashbacks keeps the realities of both past and present constantly before our eyes.

Jay L. Halio. SoR. Winter, 1968. pp. 236–7

Feasibly our best writer, Hawkes has written six books which have gained him only a narrow readership—and that at a time when being a writer's writer and gaining attestations of one's immortality in the scholarly journals are of no earthly use in reciprocating an artist's energy. Every book Hawkes has written is a work of uncommon intensity and originality, to put it mildly. Of the first six, *The Lime Twig* and *Second Skin* are the most extraordinary. *The Lime Twig* typifies Hawkes's earlier work in its psychotic and unswerving narrative. In *Second Skin*, on the other hand, a certain amount of light and relief are admitted for the first time; a queer and bucolic surrealism reigns over much of the novel. Hawkes's newest book, *The Blood Oranges*, is another step in the same direction. It is the most accessible novel to date of this difficult writer.

Out of a gentle recidivism, Hawkes slips the reader a dwarf from time to time; but in general, this is a different kind of book from that we had come to expect from Hawkes before *Second Skin*. Impressively, *The Blood Oranges* uses a cultivated diction reminiscent of Anglo-Mediterranean literature—Norman Douglas, Gerald Brenan, E. M. Forster—in the service of a distortive vision and narrative. This time, though, the book is less about death and violence than it is about sex and love. In an atmosphere deliberately reminiscent of *Twelfth Night*, Hawkes contrives a sequence of lyrical and narrative meditations on sexual multiplicity.

Thomas McGuane. NYT. Sept. 19, 1971. p. 1

John Hawkes' sixth novel, *Death, Sleep & the Traveler*, cat-footed, makes the first five seem heavy. It walks on psychic eggs, sucks them, leaps off. Not a whit too much or little, nothing too violent or tame, almost nothing too obscure or obvious . . . sophistication could not go further. Clear and impeccable, free of the infra-realism and dreamsogged surrealism of the first books, composed in time-shifting short sequences, each with the throaty resonance of a vibraphone key, each with its soft psychic percussion, in a style at once deliberate and delicate, it is an esthetic performance of the first order. . . . The narrative *encases* life in its own perfection. Its ruthless detachment makes life itself academic. . . .

Since his third novel, *The Lime Twig*, Hawkes' fiction has dwelled upon not only sexual guilt but also the guilt of the artist as such—the dreamer whose dreams leave life untouched, the spiritual Narcissus. The new book sours on marriage and sexuality . . . as well as on myth, dreams, pornography—*representations* of sexual life. . . .

Death, Sleep & the Traveler is a beautiful achievement, unique and elegant in form, brilliantly judged, and likely to endure as a small classic. To be sure, Europeanized, Bergmanized as it is, it may not seem *our* classic, except in being an intense romance and (what for us is hardly separable) its Puritan backlash, its ambivalence toward the raw stuff of life.

Calvin Bedient. NR. April 20, 1974. pp. 26, 28

Although [Hawkes] is still not much read by the general public, the steady, perennial voice of his supporters, and still more, of course, the novels themselves, have won from many a conviction of the centrality and importance of his work at the present time. It is clear, too, that Hawkes has merited his reputation for aesthetic purity: he is a singularly committed and devout practitioner of the fine art of the novel at a time when that austere discipline totters with disregard. There can be no quarrel with his seriousness and integrity.

Still, as is perhaps inevitably the case when a due measure of respect has been long withheld, compensating claims for Hawkes's stature tend to be exaggerated, implausible. If the general public has remained unimpressed, the reason may be that they are genuinely baffled and discouraged by the difficulties of Hawkes's presentation, or that they are offended, justifiably or not, by the harshness, the dread, the bitter violence of such earlier works as *The Cannibal* (1949), *The Beetle Leg* (1951), and *The Lime Twig* (1961). His latest novel *Death, Sleep & the Traveler*, and its immediate predecessor, *The Blood Oranges*, both seem to be mellow, erotic fictions, but in fact neither the horror of his earlier visions, nor their difficulty of access, has truly abated, though they have been transmuted and refined.

John Romano. Cmty. May, 1974. p. 58

Although Hawkes writes a maze-like work [*Death, Sleep & the Traveler*] about maze-like reality, he surely does not remain a passive creator. *He delights in his maze.* He shapes it so cunningly that although it resists thematic analysis, it remains a unique construction. There are many dreams . . . which dazzle me. There are the recurring, brilliant images of water, mirror, and animal. I realize that I am unsure of events . . . but I am confident that this fiction (about fictions) will continue to enlighten me for a long time. In reading it I meet "various unfamiliar shadows," "psychic sores," the batlike terrors of sleep. I appreciate the cleansing anxiety it provokes. I accept its wise violations. I am, consequently, very grateful to Hawkes.

Irving Malin. *Com.* May 3, 1974. p. 222

HELLER, JOSEPH (1923–   )

Its technical innovations notwithstanding, Heller's novel does operate within an established literary tradition. *Catch-22* is finally a radical protest novel. Like *The Grapes of Wrath* and *An American Tragedy*, its protest is directed from the left toward the prevailing centers of power in America. But whereas Steinbeck and Dreiser aimed their polemics at the trust and the tycoon, Heller's target shifted. As C. Wright Mills points out, the new images of power in modern mass society are the interlocking bureaucracies of industry, the military, and the political administration. Heller apparently feels that the power shift must be countered with new patterns of protest.

Charles B. Harris. *Contemporary American
Novelists of the Absurd* (College and
University). 1971. p. 34

Taken as a whole, the Yossarian-Milo relationship [in *Catch-22*] concretely illustrates Norman O. Brown's thesis that capitalism is a sublimation of the death instinct, that money converts the world to matter (feces). Before a world organized into commodities to be accumulated, Eros withdraws. "This withdrawal of Eros hands over culture to the death instinct; and the inhuman, abstract, impersonal world which the death instinct creates progressively eliminates all possibility of the life of sublimated Eros, which we nostalgically so admire in the ancient Greeks." *Catch-22* is as rich in meaning as any novel written in our century. It bears up under continuous rereading; and the multi-layered structure demonstrated here indicates simply that a work of art as varied and true as *Catch-22* is not the work of a prophet, but the creation of an artist so richly endowed by the sensibilities of his time that he knows unerringly where his culture is going.

Jess Ritter in Critical Essays on "Catch-22,"
edited by James Nagel (Dickenson).
1974. p. 56

Something Happened succeeds massively in sucking the reader into the claustrophobic world of the narrator. The despair Slocum feels when he thinks of his job, his pitiful attempts to defend his work against the onslaught of his children, who are afraid they will follow in his footsteps, makes us take inventory of ourselves, our work, and what we did to our own parents. Slocum's fights with his daughter, from which both emerge bloodless and desperate, make Arthur Miller's conflicts between father and son in *Death of a Salesman* seem anemic and unreal. The cannibalism, the relentless cruelty of the loving family has never been better portrayed.

Susan Fromberg Schaeffer. Book World.
Oct. 13, 1974. p. 1

It would be easy to dismiss *Something Happened*, and probably wrong. For as he did so unforgettably in *Catch-22*, Joseph Heller pushes at us here a deadly moral and we may well find ourselves impaled on it. This is not just another punishment of the same old organization man. No, Slocum's scummy, slimy nature is calculated to trap us in his horror as surely as Yossarian's adorable boyish farce did in *his* horror. *Something Happened* does not have anything like the marvelous clowning, the poignant camaraderie, the wild caricature, the pure acetylene contempt of *Catch-22*; large corporations are pretty funny but nothing can be as funny as an army. Nor does business life provide quite such shocks as can the military. . . .

But the ruminations of Slocum do become as insidious as muck. The voice is so familiar. . . . These sketches and snatches of vision, which we ought to be ashamed to share, slowly work on one another and fester richly as we learn of their sources in what happened to Bob Slocum since he was born, and then the whole mess begins to give off an elemental stink of life.

John Thompson. NYR. Oct. 17, 1974. pp. 24–5

Something Happened has a more rambling, formless structure than *Catch-22*. It is much longer—far too long. It is far more uneven. But it has the same vivid sense of absurdity. It contains many insights, descriptions, and flashes of humour which are as devastating and brilliant as anything in Mr. Heller's first novel. He gives a wonderful portrait of the huge, nightmarish, claustrophobic company where Bill Slocum works. He takes a brutal joy in dissecting every abominable aspect of this ever-expanding American company. He enjoys exposing all its cancerous innards. He carves up the neurotically tormented middle-class American family in the same way. . . . Mr. Heller's disembowelments are ferocious, gory and memorable. In *Catch-22* he satirized the horrors of war: in *Something Happened* he has attempted something more ambitious and difficult—an exposé of the horrors of prosperity and peace.

Caroline Blackwood. TLS.
Oct. 25, 1974. p. 1183

HELLMAN, LILLIAN (1905–   )

Her accounts [in *An Unfinished Woman*] of her loves and of her work are oblique, as if neither aspect of experience were vital to her (although the real meaning of the fact may be that both are too vital to be shared). Her summary comment on [Dashiell] Hammett, with whom she spent thirty years, is deliberately but disturbingly flat: "He was the most interesting man I've ever met." Her most analytical comments about herself are that she was "difficult" or "headstrong"—adjectives which classify her as her parents might, from without, but which provide little insight into her inner workings.

The cumulative effect of her lack of self-penetration, her apparent uneasiness in love-relationships, her reluctance to contemplate her own writing, her acceptance of a travelogue version of her experience, is to suggest that her central effort has been to create, for her own benefit as well as for others, a character to meet masculine standards. This is not a mere "image": her life substantiates it. The life of constant action (in this case "masculine" rather than "feminine" accomplishment) rests on a foundation of intense self-concentration. Lillian Hellman's work has been to make a self, rejecting in the process many traditional concomitants of femininity.

Patricia Meyer Spacks. HdR.
Winter, 1971–72. p. 561

The dramatic quality [in *Pentimento*] is everywhere evident, not only in the background of social intrigue before which many of these lives are enacted; but rather more importantly in the author's sense of timing, a kind of poised power over the units of scene that few writers of fiction possess. But there is also the extraordinary gift for the precise detail which is a fictional quality, and then again, for the often comically explicit detail. . . . She seems always to find precisely the right word, the right combination. . . .

She has called herself an unfinished woman, and she concluded the book of that title with what is probably the most open-ended sentence in literature: "However." Open to the rest of her experience in life, as she has been to it in the past, is the only sense in which we can accept the word "unfinished." But be that as it may, she writes what seems to me a prose as brilliantly finished as any that we have in these years.

Mark Schorer. NYT. Sept. 23, 1973. pp. 1–2

[Hellman's] instinct for careful work has paid off in prestige as well as currency. Authoring only 14 plays, two of them adaptations, she has found a place among the foremost dramatists of the century. An Unfinished Woman, her autobiography, won a National Book Award and Pentimento should widen her reputation as a storyteller. The earlier book covered sizable areas of her life with seven-league boots. In Pentimento she returns to some of those areas and does profiles of obscure people she knew (permitting herself a solitary exception in her chapter on "Theatre"), even throwing in a sketch of a reptilian hero who clung to life with a fury that would do credit to a two-legged hero.

Writing of men and women she loved and who have in nearly all instances died, she tries to see them in perspective. Hence her title: an artist's term for a painting that was reworked but whose original details emerge as the paint thins out. The profiles don't go deep; cautious in her art, Hellman is wary about attributing motives or dabbling in conjectures. One character stands forth sharply from her pages however— L. H. herself. In short, apart from its readability, Pentimento is valuable as a picture of a woman and writer in the making.

James Walt. NR. Oct. 20, 1973. pp. 27–8

HEMINGWAY, ERNEST (1899–1961)

Whether we accept Hemingway's personal solutions to survival—the therapeutic value of work that will not go stale, the need of a rather rigid code of behavior to meet an irrational and threatening universe, the profound significance of love—is finally personal; but as conveyed in Hemingway's best work—in the short stories, The Sun Also Rises, A Farewell to Arms and The Old Man and the Sea—they are solutions that derive organically from the tragic condition of man which he describes so credibly. Hemingway has not only modified our attitudes toward language, although that would surely be accomplishment enough; he has recorded permanently the conditions under which twentieth-century man has lived in the western world.

Theodore L. Gross. *The Heroic Ideal in American Literature* (Free). 1971. p. 220

Jordan [in *For Whom the Bell Tolls*] regretted that he had no one to whom he could pass on what he had learned in his brief heroic hour, and his own model hero was his grandfather, not his father. In *The Old Man and the Sea* Hemingway ends his long series of father-son failures with a relationship that is as nearly perfect as it can be in an imperfect world: Manolin is the beneficiary of Santiago's heroism although Manolin is another man's son. Hemingway cherished the relationship of hero-father to son more than the relationship of epic hero to society, the isolated more than the public act of heroism. Like [Frank] Norris before him, he finally rejected the idea of heroism in war, the idea of the *Iliad* epic.

Leonard Lutwack. *Heroic Fiction* (Southern Illinois). 1971. p. 87

Hemingway's last novel, *The Old Man and the Sea*, is the single exception in his general decline. In many ways it turns back toward the older manner of the nineteen twenties. It is certainly more restrained than its predecessor, *Across the River and into the Trees*, even more than *For Whom the Bell Tolls*. *Across the River and into the Trees* is ruined by the hero's sentimental meditations on events of the past; *The Sun Also Rises* and *A Farewell to Arms* were books of acts; *The Old Man and the Sea* falls somewhere between the two. The old man struggles with the fish, but also he thinks a great deal, perhaps too much. The code of the good characters of *The Sun Also Rises* was to have personal values, to see them in the facts and the deeds, but not to state them. Colonel Cantwell in *Across the River and into the Trees* dwells on old events and deeds, talks about them in order to see universal meanings.

Floyd C. Watkins. *The Flesh and the Word* (Vanderbilt). 1971. p. 152

Frederic Henry [in *A Farewell to Arms*] is the first completely developed example of what was to become Hemingway's dominant motif: a man, often of military or para-military status, who is forced to recognize the inevitability of death and the concomitant frustration of trying to secure something of value from its onslaught. What makes Hemingway's presentation in *A Farewell to Arms* a brilliant achievement—one never surpassed in any of his later variations on the theme—is his subtle presentation of the process of discovery and the near-perfect fusion he maintained between the theme and his narrative method. . . .

In Frederic Henry's growing imagination death is not merely a single, final act of surrendering life—although the absurdity of such death weighs on him; what makes death intolerable is the knowledge that, like life, it is a continuous process, the reduction of experience in the very act of living. It is the inexorable loss of one's capacities by subtraction to nothing for nothing—*nada*. How, the novel asks, can one find value in life which is best described as an "occasional temporary avoidance" of death?

Dewey Ganzel. SwR. Autumn,
1971. pp. 577, 582–3

HIMES, CHESTER (1909–   )

Chester Himes is one of the most prolific of all Negro novelists. At this writing, he is the author of six major novels and a number of lively potboilers about a couple of Harlem detectives. Although he enjoys a good reputation in France, where he now lives, for the most part the American critics have dismissed him as being of the Wright school of naturalism, whose "protest" is no longer fashionable. Such criticism is not altogether fair. Himes's interests are considerably different from Wright's, and his firsthand knowledge of certain areas of American life is more developed. His protagonists are generally middle-class, fairly well-educated, somewhat sophisticated in the ways of the world, and often intellectually oriented. They are concerned with ideas and the application of ideas to their experience; they are constantly searching out rational explanations for the irrationalities of their lives. They move with considerable aplomb among white liberals and radicals of both sexes, and engage them in dialectics on their own terms. Himes is also a more deliberate prose stylist than Wright. He seldom intrudes, moralizes, or explains. His characters are usually sufficiently articulate to say what they mean—and what they mean issues often enough from their character and intelligence. Himes does parallel Wright in his bitterness, fury, and frustration. He has given up on America, and rarely returns now on visits.

Edward Margolies. Native Sons
(Lippincott). 1968. pp. 87–8

Himes is perhaps the single greatest naturalistic American writer living today. Of course, no one in the literary establishment is going to admit that; they haven't and they won't. Reviews of his books generally wind up in the last half of the Sunday *New York Times Book Review,* if they are reviewed at all. Himes will tell you that he doesn't care; that all his career he has been shuffled under the table. Perhaps this is, after all, the smallest of hurts he has suffered.

John A. Williams in *Amistad 1*, edited by
John A. Williams and Charles F. Harris
(Random). 1970. p. 27

In the crime novels of the black writer, Chester Himes, [Raymond] Chandler's blend of realism and exaggeration is exuberantly developed. His series of novels paints life in Harlem, including all levels of society from the pimps to the rich, in a direct, brusque style which is so very American that it is amazing Himes' reputation had to be particularly established in France (where he is considered the "Balzac of Harlem"). Himes likes grotesque exaggeration, and his gallows humor is very vitriolic indeed. But despite their humor, their superb dialogue and poetic realism, these crime novels are angry books. Violence has a quality of grim delight here, born of a barely repressed hatred. In his explosive ferocity, Himes has an authenticity that a paper-shredder like [Mickey] Spillane completely lacks and for which Chandler did not have the personal motivation. I am surprised that Himes is so little appreciated in his own country while in Europe he is well known and seriously appreciated—surprised because his work is a pioneering document of black experience which, in many ways, is far more incisive than some recent autobiographical statements on the subject.

E. M. Beekman. *MR.* Winter, 1973. pp. 170–1

● HOROVITZ, ISRAEL (1939–   )

The Indian Wants the Bronx . . . is funny and terrifying. . . .

The actors in this play brilliantly reveal the incipient ferocity born of moral isolation that can be observed in persons who still possess some of the charming folly of untrammeled youth. In [*It's Called the Sugar Plum*] it is innocence coupled with schooled dumbness that the actor conveys with apt ease.

Horovitz's writing of *The Indian Wants the Bronx* demonstrates a perfect ear for the speech of his two punks. He is not slumming: he has made himself part of their spirit. But like other playwrights of his generation (those between 21 and 30), he should not dwell too long or too lovingly within that sphere; it is narrow and shallow for lack of a more complete understanding of the world outside it. The world may be equally ferocious, but it is nevertheless the *world*, and all of it must be explored to make art splendid and life worth the strife.

Harold Clurman. Nation. Feb. 12, 1968. p. 221

On the evidence of these two plays [*The Indian Wants the Bronx* and *It's Called the Sugar Plum*], Horovitz is a conventional playwright compared to some of the other graduates of the off-off-Broadway scene—Van Itallie, say, or Sam Shepard. He works in tight dramatic scenes in which the confrontation of character and situation dictates the action. The characters are not quite realistic (his hoods are too patterned in their articularity, and the hero of *It's Called the Sugar Plum* is not so much a Harvard student as a pastiche of campus fashions) and his situations are as unlikely as they are arbitrary. Yet his work is a variation on the realistic line that has always dominated in the American theatre. If *The Indian Wants the Bronx* is a fair sample, he may provide several more interesting stops on that line.

Gerald Weales. Reporter. May 2, 1968. p. 35

There are perhaps two surprising, antithetical qualities in the work of the playwright Israel Horovitz, and both were evident in his latest double bill, grouped under the title, *The Honest-to-God Schnozzola*. . . . Mr. Horovitz is clearly imaginative and yet, in a sense, conventional.

He has a good ear for the way people talk—always the first test of any playwright—and he combines this with a very just sense of fantasy and feel of doom. Yet he also has a shrewd streak of theatricality running down his back. I don't object to it, but I think it might confuse firmer and less pliant minds. You see here, theatrically speaking, both pieces are set-ups for a final stroke of theater that arrives with the predictable unexpectedness of the pay-off to an O. Henry short story. Yet when the trick has been turned, even though we have an idea of how it has been done, it remains pretty effective.

Clive Barnes. NYTd. April 22, 1969. p. 40

The Honest-to-God Schnozzola . . . was more properly "Honest-to-God 'Cabaret,' " but with a change in point of view; this time, the contempt has shifted from depraved Germans to even more depraved Americans. . . .

If any man has earned the right to go his own way, it is Mr. Horovitz, but I do wish he would change his course. As he has already proved in *It's Called the Sugar Plum,* which shared a bill with his *The Indian Wants the Bronx,* and which seemed to me much the stronger and more original of the two, he can delineate a character with a flick of a line or a piece of business, he can write dialogue that is dramatic and rings true, and he can explore an atmosphere or state of mind. I wish he would leave studies of corruption, evil, Fascism, mindlessness, and other abstract nouns to the lesser talents among us.

Edith Oliver. NY. May 3, 1969. pp. 108–9

I think something fine has been achieved in *Cappella.* I think. The novel has absurdist affiliations: these irritate. . . .

A good deal is frankly impenetrable and annoying. God and gastronomy have the same liturgical significance. This comes with the absurdist franchise after all. Yet, quite reluctantly at first, I forgave. *Cappella* is also an entertainment.

This is the first novel of Israel Horovitz, a double-OBIE [award] playwright. As might be expected, Horovitz has a glib knack for soliloquy. His words decant without sediment; they purl. And it is here that the enjoyment of *Cappella* is located: up front, on the apron edge, in a single spotlight.

Three quarters of the book is an extended story telling. And the stories engross, they make thick laughter; their tone and accent, their circular movement is suave, accurate.

D. Keith Mano. NYT. Feb. 25, 1973. p. 2

Mr. Horovitz [in *Dr. Hero*] is summarizing a life . . . though he has a distinctly oblique way of coming at it and a parodistic tone that ties its glimpses of everything from toilet-training to abandoned friends to ultimate defeat together. . . .

Mr. Horovitz has taken his familiar materials . . . and tossed them at us like so many eccentrically weighted basketballs. . . .

In short, the evening is a game, insouciant mockery throughout. . . . [The play's] contours are bold, its horrors are swiftly defined and swiftly dispensed with, its fantasy-quotient is consistent, its lens—the one we are allowed to look through—is sharply focused. If it fails, as I think it does, it is because Hero's ambition is much too generalized, nothing we can visualize with him, and because "the contest" in which he is defeated is similarly without an immediate, graspable base. Mr. Horovitz has got his outlines clean, his tonalities all in order; it's the ultimate innards of the piece that are spongy.

But his surface, at least, is controlled, pulled together; and that keeps us from drifting off on our own down memory's rag-tag lane.

Walter Kerr. NYTts. April 22, 1973. p. 11

Israel Horovitz, of course, comes under the category of "famous young playwright." He is a winner of two [*Village Voice*] "Obies," and the seriousness of his commitment comes through in *Cappella*. What distinguishes his book is the chances he is willing to take. His dramatic skill (if that's the right word) works itself out in Cappella's brilliant monologues. Each story contains a half-truth that turns itself inside out to become a double character revelation as Cappella defends himself against his own life. The old man rants, boasts, wails, and wrings every possible change and, finally, self-condemnation out of each experience. . . .

As Franz Kafka said, "From life one can extract comparatively so many books, but from books so little, so very little life." The copyist is that old thing, "a literary conceit," through which Horovitz tries to impart another time dimension to his book. That dimension is unnecessary. *Cappella*, while it's working, exists beautifully in its own time.

Corinne Robins. VV. May 10, 1973. p. 32

[*Alfred the Great*] is the first of a trilogy, to be called *The Wakefield Plays* by the American playwright [Israel Horovitz] best known for *The Indian Wants the Bronx*. Dedicated to Samuel Beckett, *Alfred the Great* is a domestic drama, but much more than that. No doubt Horovitz has been influenced by Beckett, O'Neill, Albee, and Pinter—and that is good; however, this four-character work set in the playwright's hometown contains no new vision beyond the basic themes and ideas of these masters of personal fears and terrors—and that is bad. Truly, much of the dialogue is brilliant, as are the silences; and the play is beautifully structured. But the plot, "the return of the native," is quite familiar except for some particularly grisly twists which are not really surprising; and some of the stage directions are a bit pretentious. Despite anything it lacks, though, we should all be thankful for *Alfred the Great*; it bodes well for the trilogy, and no other American playwright of Horovitz' caliber seems to be doing anything worthy of publication (or production) at all.

Richard M. Buck. LJ. March 15, 1974. p. 772

● HOWARD, RICHARD (1929–   )

Richard Howard is a poet of substantial gifts who has in addition most of the negative virtues; he is not prolix, not overdecorated, not pseudo-referent, not bardic, not otherwise affected. *Quantities*, if all of it maintained the level of its first poem, would be an impressive achievement indeed. "Advice from the Cocoon" sets a high standard. . . . Mr. Howard knows the diction of conversation may become poetry, but the rhythm of it cannot. Most of his collection is in strict meter, and . . . rises to a strength no accidental measure can. The moral is obvious: if conversation is what you want, converse.

Turner Cassity. *Poetry.* Dec., 1963. p. 192

In almost every poem in his recent book *The Damages*, Howard exhibits that Proustian capacity for attention to other people and to their quick gestures and the surrounding bric-a-brac which so relentlessly reveal them. . . . Howard has a talent which has lately come to seem the novelist's exclusively: the ability to observe social surfaces and manners accurately and to make the inessential suddenly seem essence. Such a talent does not in Howard's work result in satire. Instead, Howard's total attention leads to a kind of sympathy with things he sees. . . . Howard . . . has another of the talents normally associated with the novelist's art: the patience to let the judgments of situations apart from oneself arise from the situations themselves. He therefore asserts as an aesthetic premise the novelist's view of reality: "Reality/had to be happened on,/one had to *find*,/not create it." Paradoxically, then, the energy of attention in Howard's work stems from a deep respect not for the formal medium of poetry but for the world of reality which is the material of art. . .

It would be easy, I think, to undervalue Howard's poetry, since one of its deepest impulses is toward diminution of vision, modesty of technique, and respect for reality. Yet this very impulse is Howard's great strength, for it simultaneously permits his poems to assume the honesty, gaudiness, and energy of genuine art. For above all, Howard attains within the terms of his work the formal coherence which is the end of all poetic technique.

Donald Sheehan. *CL.* Spring, 1969. pp. 293–5

Mr. Howard's criticism is distinguished for the breadth of its sympathies and the size of its appetite. He enjoys the advantage, of course, of being in a position to assume the very existence of that appreciation of modernist poetics that [the] older and more stringent body of criticism made possible. But he approaches this advantage with an admirable confidence, and exploits it with an uncommon energy and almost prodigal intelligence.

He is, above all, an enthusiast. He places no distances between himself and the poetry he is writing about [in *Alone with America*]. He immerses himself in it totally, and does so without apology or facile invocations to the zeitgeist. He not only likes this poetry—most of it anyway—but is clearly prepared to live by it. And he brings to it a vocabulary of praise far larger, less inhibited and more illuminating than any we have had from a critic of contemporary poetry since R. P. Blackmur wrote his early essays on the poets of his own generation.

Hilton Kramer. *NR.* Dec. 20, 1969. pp. 24–5

This collection of essays by Richard Howard [*Alone with America*] is at once a valuable (to date perhaps an indispensable) in-depth survey of forty-one contemporary American poets and a large, at times exasperating reminder of both the strengths and weaknesses of contemporary criticism. Its value springs from the fact that Howard not only has produced substantial essays on all forty-one of these poets (a formidable feat in itself), many of which have received no up-dated critical attention or virtually no attention whatever, but also he has managed to write at least a handful of good, incisive studies. . . .

Howard's reasons for writing these essays, or, in his words, for this "accounting" of these American poets, reveals that he too has chosen that brand of personalism characteristic of contemporary criticism. . . . Howard, then, implicitly admits that *Alone with America* isn't as much an assessment of "the art of poetry" since 1950 as it is a recording of individual entries. . . .

The advantages and perhaps inevitable excess of personalism in criticism are quickly and eminently obvious. These essays are marked by an energetic vibrancy and verve, a *joie de poésie* seldom encountered in criticism. Himself a poet and the author of three books of poems . . . Howard responds to the work of his contemporaries with an involvement and excitement which is often literally breathless and in a style implicitly packed with the zing, bang, and pow of contemporary rhetoric. And because he approaches each poet as a free standing figure, because his response is not predetermined by a complex of critical premises, he can and does respond to the poetry, in large part, on its own terms.

However, those are also the sources of excess. Admittedly, there is little more dreadful than that bloodless criticism of dissertation scholarship. But Howard's exuberance becomes so breathless, an endless sequence of dashes and ellipses, that at times it is also virtually unintelligible and can be conservatively described as grotesque rococo; it is as felicitous as that which might result from a chance coupling of Hannah Arendt's high Anglo-German and Jack Kerouac's spontaneous bop prosody on Lautréamont's dissecting table.

A. Poulin, Jr. *JML.* 1, 1, 1970. pp. 111–2

At a time when most poems being published—our best and our worst—are confessional, *Untitled Subjects* is an extraordinary collection not at all committed to that kind of exposure. Richard Howard's are "life studies" of another sort, wonderful monologues involving fifteen great, or sometimes obscure, figures from the Victorian past. . . .

Howard's is . . . an astounding book. We might have met the figures treated here as subjects in his two earlier books of verse. But now he abandons the role of literate spectator and with it the presumed security of both poet and audience stalking, with some awe, a superior historical figure; there are no privileged observers, the voices, with one or two exceptions, are only those of "other lives"—vulnerable and resourceful. . . .

If the characters are redeemed from rather than reduced by history, it is because of the bravado with which Howard makes them want to account for themselves.

David Kalstone. NYT. April 12, 1970. pp. 4, 22

Howard has emerged in ·his two latest books, *Untitled Subjects* and *Findings*, as perhaps our first consummate archeologist poet. He, too, would leave for history not words, but findings. Findings, unearthed in that literary archeology of scholarship and translated into a language of invisibility. A language divested of all surface glitter, style reborn as a pure instrument for transmittings, sacrificing all glamour of performance for functional rigor. An unimpeding, uninterfering, unmediated natural language of pure function best suited for the roles, the masks of mediumship. Findings wrestled into the heaped-up mounds of poems, abandoned by the mound builder at last, leavings yielded to us and our progeny.

These are the poems of a man who has stood squarely at the crossing roads between self-demolition and self-reconstruction . . . and in taking unflinchingly the longest single stride across that chasm of lost identity of any contemporary he has imported into his remodelings of the self, resources that no American poet before him had guessed could be sponsored by a thoroughly modern intelligence. Howard has discovered a mode for mating a heterodox creative scholarship with the art of poetic composition. His method is a form of impulsive treasure hunting and sleuthing that recalls Virginia Woolf's ingenious skirmishes—widening the scope of the familiar essay—in her *Common Readers*. Howard's free-ranging eye, like hers, in choosing finds, sources, magical touchstones in the writings of other authors to be assimilated into his own voice, seems to have been guided alternatively by idle curiosity, heart's impulse and a high bold sense of pioneer adventuring.

Laurence Lieberman. YR.
Autumn, 1971. pp. 85–6

Cashing in, one might say, on the contemporary boom in Victorian studies, [Howard] gives us [in *Untitled Subjects*] a series of nineteenth-century portraits, mostly historical, some imaginary but historically typical, in the form of the intimate journal, the verse letter, or the Browningesque dramatic monologue. He takes some bits straight from actual surviving prose. . . .

The very prolixity, the overabundance, the innocent self-exposure of great nineteenth-century figures, Scott, Thackeray, Ruskin, the pre-Raphaelite group for instance (and other figures imaginary, but representative and typical, and given to us with the same density of reference), are used by Howard as an ingenious and original tactic for making us read on (as we would all read, for instance, an unpublished manuscript journal, curious about keys to character, alert for a whiff of scandal). And Howard's real and imaginary Victorians are "characters"; so much themselves that they are more than themselves, towering into noble or absurd self-caricature. But this fine volume is reverently if sometimes humorously exploratory. There is no touch of Lytton Strachey's sniggering superiority. One might almost say that Howard has invented a new type of historical poem, or perhaps has invented the historical poem properly (as we talk of "the historical novel") for the first time. He helps us to know the Victorians because, in G. M. Young's phrase, he lets us "hear them talking."

G. S. Fraser. *PR*. Winter, 1971–2. p. 474

Richard Howard brings to poetry the eavesdropper's uncanny ear for nuance, the memoir-and-faded-letter reader's love of gossip. In these "two-part inventions" wherein, according to J. S. Bach, "lovers of the instrument are shown a way to play clearly in two voices," lovers of poetry may overhear what Walt Whitman said to Oscar Wilde, what Rodin said to a stranger on the train to Marseilles, what Edith Wharton said to a friend of her late lover and Mr. Henry James. . . .

Two-Part Inventions is the Pulitzer Prize-winning poet Richard Howard's fifth book of poetry, a subtle, evocative book of confrontations and revelations. It is Mr. Howard's announced intention to "recuperate for poetry some of the energy that has leaked into fiction, into theatre."

He succeeds well enough to engage the interest of anyone looking for new straws in the literary wind.

Victor Howes. *CSM*. Oct. 16, 1974. p. 12

HOWELLS, WILLIAM DEAN (1837–1920)

Just as Howells's "psychic sensitivity" took the form of muffling his antagonisms to his father or to the Brahmins who invested this Western outlander in the archepiscopal robes of Boston's moral ideals by installing him as editor of the *Atlantic Monthly*, the highest accolade New England culture had to bestow, so his fiction shied away from reporting fully the ugly polarities of American reality.

In the best pages of *A Modern Instance* (1882), *The Rise of Silas Lapham* (1885) and *A Hazard of New Fortunes* (1890), Howells is the dryly ironic observer of the vicissitudes and "anxious respectability" of the newly monied. He understands the comic folkways of all the classes in the social scale: the churchgoing which trivializes the old Puritan faith, the scatterbrained benevolence of the rich, the leeway given by parents to young couples courting, the cozy chatter of landladies and the leers of hotel clerks. One time Howells approached the greatness of George Eliot and Henry James, only to retreat with imaginative cowardice from what he saw so clearly.

Herbert A. Leibowitz. *NYT*.
June 20, 1971. p. 27

One of [Howells's] most trenchant critiques of plutocratic values, *A Hazard of New Fortunes* (1890), links the Civil War directly with the class war of the Gilded Age, chattel slavery with wage slavery. . . .

Yet if Howells had deep reservations about the War's impact on American society as a whole, he was sure its influence on American literature would be incalculable, not because it inspired much writing of permanent value, but because it signalized a victory of nationality over provinciality. It "fertilized the fields of thought among us," he concluded, "as well as the fields of battle with the blood of its sacrifice." Before the War, Howells argued, American literature was New England literature; after 1865, a truly native literature nourished by European vitality animated the American consciousness.

The War provided him, as it did Whitman, with valuable evidence for his social and aesthetic credo. Howells's subsequent campaign against romanticism in literature employed some of the same words and arguments he used against the chivalric creed of the professional "Southrons." Read in this light, the defeat of the South inadvertently assured the triumph of literary realism, for the War's authentic record was embodied in the annals of the common soldier, in the careers of a handful of officers unbeguiled by military glamour, and in the lives of a few statesmen.

Daniel Aaron. *The Unwritten War*
(Knopf). 1973. pp. 130–1

To understand the psychic demands *Literary Friends and Acquaintance* made on Howells—to gauge the pressures hidden by his unassuming manner and genteel politeness—we have to recognize its place, emotional and thematic as well as chronological, in the Howells canon. The book has a complex inner dimension of meaning, belying its simple appearance as a pleasant, nostalgic recollection of the golden New England world of the author's early and middle-aged successes. *Literary Friends and Acquaintance* is a chief aspect of a larger story Howells was engaged in writing much of his life. This story—told in letters, essays, reviews, editorial columns, short stories, novels, and memoirs—constitutes an irregular history of literary and intellectual life in America for a period of sixty or more years. Taken altogether—in both its direct and implicit dimensions—it is one of Howells' major achievements, having a significance comparable to the lifelong records of the literary and intellectual life in America afforded in the writings of an Emerson or, in our own day, of an Edmund Wilson.

Lewis P. Simpson. *The Man of Letters in
New England and the South* (Louisiana
State). 1973. p. 86

HUGHES, LANGSTON (1902–1967)

It is difficult to give a proper assessment of Hughes's work because so much of its effect depends on an oral interpretation and the physical presence of an audience. Oddly, this is almost as true of his poems as of his plays, despite the fact that from the beginning he experimented with verse forms, diction, and typography. In a general sort of way he is in the Whitman-Lindsay-Sandburg free-verse tradition, yet despite this and his university education and wide cosmopolitan background, he is primarily a folk artist who writes *for* the people he is writing *about*. Even at his most ideological and didactic, he speaks with directness, honesty, and understanding to those whose experiences he loves to share and record. There is something unmistakably genuine about his pride in the "little people" whose lives, strivings, and endurance he celebrates, most often in their own voices, in jazz and gospel rhythms and in visual patterns that dance before the eye and demand to be read aloud.

Edward Margolies. *Native Sons*
(Lippincott). 1968. p. 37

Langston Hughes's new poems [*The Panther and the Lash*], written shortly before his death last summer, catch fire from the Negro American's changing face. To a degree I would never have expected from his earlier work, his sensibility has kept pace with the times, and the intensity of his new concerns—helping him to shake loose old crippling mannerisms, the trade marks of his art—comes to fruition in many of the best poems of his career. . . .

Laurence Lieberman. *Poetry.*
Aug., 1968. p. 339

While his poems appealed to an audience which included whites, Hughes created for himself a black audience, especially school children. And he expected his poems to be taken on the simple and unpretentious level on which they were written. One would be right in saying that Langston Hughes backed out of the Negro-artist dilemma by choosing not to deal with art as serious "high culture." His casual and almost anti-intellectual attitude about art permitted him a wide freedom of subject and a personal honesty. It allowed him to make the very important point that the people's language, and voice, and rhythms were legitimate stuff of poetry. But this same freedom deprived him of the control and mastery that might make each (or indeed any) of his poems really singular. Langston Hughes avoided the Scylla of formalism only to founder in the Charybdis of folk art.

Nathan Irvin Huggins. *Harlem Renaissance*
(Oxford—N.Y.). 1971. p. 227

The name, Jesse B. Semple [called Simple, in Hughes's Simple sketches], was a combination of advice and imperative, and in his so-called simplicity Simple joined the corps of American folk hero humorists—Uncle Remus, Josh Billings, Mr. Dooley and others—who drew laughter out of the shock and novelty of common sense. Simple may not always have been as funny as his predecessors, but he was richer and much more complicated.

He was an urban folk hero, equipped with city tastes and a city vocabulary, yet he was as ardent a regionalist as Sam Slick, Jonathan Oldstyle, Hosea Biglow, or any of the rural American humorists. It made no difference that Simple's region was Harlem and that his dialect was Harlem argot; his attitude toward his section of the country was as elaborately loyal as a Westerner's or Down Easter's, and he was just as purely a home-grown philosopher. He was brash, as are all literary regionalists, he was anti-authoritarian, and in spite of his critical stance and occasional doomsday visions, he was an optimist at heart. Where he differed from his fellow regionalists is that his region was continually under attack, because in a larger sense than Harlem his region was blackness; and so the criticisms he leveled at the nation were often informed by a sense of urgency and frustration which, until the emergence of contemporary black comedians such as Dick Gregory and Godfrey Cambridge, was unique in American humor. There was also the difference between a cracker barrel and a bar stool. The fact that Simple did his philosophizing from a local dive was designed to be one of his comic properties, but it also suggested that in order to sustain his hopeful view of the world it helped to be high, if only on beer.

Roger Rosenblatt in Veins of Humor, edited by
Harry Levin (Harvard). 1972. pp. 226–7

During the twenties there arose the first large-scale manifestations of black pride: concern for the beauty of blackness, interest in black history and culture, and political awareness of poetry as a means of exploring and celebrating blackness.

Foremost among such writers is Langston Hughes, who has perhaps the greatest reputation (worldwide) that any black writer has ever had. Hughes differed from most of his predecessors among black poets, and (until recently) from those who followed him as well, in that he addressed his poetry to the people, specifically to black people. During the twenties when most American poets were turning inward, writing obscure and esoteric poetry to an ever decreasing audience of readers, Hughes was turning outward, using language and themes, attitudes and ideas familiar to anyone who had the ability simply to read. He has been, unlike most nonblack poets other than Walt Whitman, Vachel Lindsay, and Carl Sandburg, a poet of the people. He often employs dialect distinctive of the black urban dweller or the rural black peasant. Throughout his career he was aware of injustice and oppression, and used his poetry as a means of opposing or mitigating them.

Donald B. Gibson. Introduction to Modern
Black Poets, edited by Donald B. Gibson
(Prentice-Hall). 1973. p. 7

JAMES, HENRY (1843–1916)

At the end [of *The Portrait of a Lady*], Isabel feels again, talking to Ralph, "the good of the world." To reconcile the demands of the imagination with the impositions of the world is a delicate exercise; especially if the natural idiom of the imagination is a language of freedom, mobility, and range, and the idiom of the world is, for the most part, deception and abuse. In the great conversation with Madame Merle, early in the book, Isabel said that she could not consider herself expressed by anything. "Nothing that belongs to me is any measure of me; everything's on the contrary a limit, a barrier, and a perfectly arbitrary one." But she does not insist upon a Platonic poetry. Indeed, the momentum of James's fiction works against that recourse. To be an old woman without memories is dreadful, but the worst escape is in transcendence, where the good of the world, such as it is, cannot be felt. James was sure of little, but he was sure of this. It is the informing principle of his fiction.

Denis Donoghue. *The Ordinary Universe*
(Macmillan—N.Y.). 1968. p. 74

In most of the late fiction, the real focus of James's story is on the effect experience has upon a "registering consciousness," upon what this sensitive observer and participant can make of what he slowly, gropingly "sees" happening to him. However, though many readers of James fail to grasp this, "seeing" is never enough; the Jamesian hero, to be a hero, necessarily utilizes his newly gained insight in some kind of ethically meaningful action. . . . These positive actions which occur after awareness has been achieved counter a common view that James's heroes are "trapped spectators" of their fate. Correspondingly the *Autobiography* argues that as both artist and man James did not consider himself a passive victim of his intelligence.

William Hoffa. *SwR*. Spring, 1969. pp. 288–9

In Proust's major work and in Faulkner's finest novels—*The Sound and the Fury* and particularly *Absalom, Absalom!*—James's experiments with unreliable narration, the romance of subjective perception, are magnificently adapted and vindicated. But in *The Sacred Fount*, one finally says to oneself, precious little else is going on; the story of a story that fails to become clear makes, in the absence of other interests, a thin literary diet. Passion and intimacy—the subjects of the obsession—are absent from the novel in all but the most attenuated, cerebral forms. In fact, passion and intimacy are so muffled that the reader may wonder if the distance of reverent protection is not also the distance of abhorrence and repulsion, if the narrator's inexperience of these things is also the novelist's, and if the imagination is the only prism through which he can come at them, both by default and by design. Is the obsessive imagination of passionate experience a substitute, through fear, for the experience itself?

The vision of life posited by the sacred fount theory, if taken seriously, is a fearful one—surely more appalling than sublime—and there is every reason to believe that James was consciously experimenting with it. The gain and loss implied by its version of passion and intimacy—the profit and the cost of a close personal encounter with others—were soon to reappear in Chad and in Marie de Vionnet [in *The Ambassadors*]. And the gain and loss that come from merely imagining rather than undergoing such experience, from being repelled by its violence and thus substituting the *vision* of intimacy for intimacy itself—this only too clearly continued to fascinate James. If he painted a partial portrait of himself and his artistic stance toward experience in the narrator of *The Sacred Fount*, he was within the next year to envisage his two most haunting figures of the imagined as opposed to the realized life: John Marcher in "The Beast in the Jungle" and Lambert Strether in *The Ambassadors*.

Philip M. Weinstein in *The Interpretation of Narrative*, edited by Morton W. Bloomfield (Harvard). 1970. pp. 208–9

James's moral manichaeism is the basis of a vision in which the social world is made the scene of dramatic choice between heightened moral alternatives, where every gesture, no matter how frivolous or insignificant it may seem, is charged with the conflict between light and darkness, salvation and damnation—where people's destinies and choices of life seem finally to have little to do with practical realities of a situation, and much more to do with an intense drama in which consciousness must purge itself and assume the burden of moral sainthood. The theme of renunciation which sounds through James's novels—Isabel Archer's return to Gilbert Osmond, Strether's return to Woollett, Densher's rejection of Kate Croy—is incomprehensible and unjustifiable except as a victory within the realm of a moral occult which may be so inward and personal that it appears restricted to the individual consciousness, predicated on the individual's "sacrifice to the ideal."

Peter Brooks. *PR*. Spring, 1972. p. 200

That James found the Gothic tradition a means of quelling personal fears and tensions is further borne out by his activities after the shock of his theatrical venture in 1895. About this period of failure, James remarks, ". . . I have the imagination of disaster—and see life indeed as ferocious and sinister." Not coincidentally, thus, the powerful middle group of supernatural tales—among them, "The Friends of the Friends" (1896), "The Turn of the Screw" (1898), and "The Real Right Thing" (1899)—appear in the nineties after the failure of *Guy Domville*. In fact, the first entry in James's *Notebooks*, one week after the opening of the play, contains the germ of "The Turn of the Screw." To this extent, at least, James routs and exorcises his own "ghosts" in his tales of terror.

Pamela Shelden. SLitI. Spring, 1974. p. 125

JAMES, WILLIAM (1842–1910)

His deep sympathies and great imagination gave him the command of a prose style unequaled in vigor, clarity, and colloquial spontaneity by any other philosopher writing in English. His literary reputation kept his name alive long after his psychology and philosophy had faded in popularity. . . .

It is hardly surprising that rediscovery of James had to take place in Europe, where he was first appreciated and had never been as forgotten as in his own country. . . . This rediscovery of James by the phenomenologists has come about mainly by a more understanding reading of *The Principles of Psychology*. Thus it is James the psychologist (which of course also includes much of his radical empiricism and pluralism) who, in the twentieth century, has become a stronger seminal influence in philosophy than he ever was during his lifetime.

Gay Wilson Allen. William James
(Minnesota). 1970. pp. 41, 45

In spite of being a better arguer than Emerson, James was just as prepared as the Concordian to give sentiment a central place in his theory of knowledge. Although James followed Locke on certain issues in his *Principles of Psychology* of 1890, James in that work gave sentiment a decisive, un-Lockeian role in the acceptance of metaphysical beliefs. In *The Will to Believe*, a collection of essays, published in 1897, he gave sentiment a similar role in religion. In his *Pragmatism* of 1907 he went further and made sentiment a factor in the acceptance of *all*

beliefs; and in *A Pluralistic Universe*, published in 1909, one year before he died, James defended a form of anti-intellectualism which was
very close to that of Bergson and the tradition of philosophical Romanticism. In *Pragmatism* James went well beyond Edwards and Emerson
in making claims on behalf of the heart and the "whole man," and
thereby brought to a climax one of the most powerful strains in the
history of philosophy in America.

Morton White. *Science and Sentiment in*
America (Oxford—N.Y.). 1972. p. 172

JARRELL, RANDALL (1914–1965)

Randall Jarrell was difficult, touchy, and oversensitive to criticism. He
was also a marvelous conversationalist, brilliantly funny, a fine poet,
and the best and most generous critic of poetry I have known. I am
proud to remember that, although we could rarely meet, we remained
friends for twenty years. Sometimes we quarreled, silently, in infrequent
letters, but each time we met we would tell each other that it had meant
nothing at all; we really were in agreement about everything that mattered.

He always seemed more alive than other people, as if constantly
tuned up to the concert pitch that most people, including poets, can
maintain only for short and fortunate stretches.

Elizabeth Bishop in *Randall Jarrell, 1914–1965,*
edited by Robert Lowell, Peter Taylor, and
Robert Penn Warren (Farrar). 1967. p. 20

All the voices in all of Jarrell's poems are crying, "Change me!" The
young yearn to be old in order to escape from their nocturnal fears; the
old long for the time of their youth, no matter how poor and miserable it
was, for "in those days everything was better"; life is moving toward the
death; the dead are moving back into life, and wherever they come, they
come in disguises. It is a world of shifts and changes, as in a fairy tale,
and the only reason you suspect it is more is that Cinderella and the
Dwarfs and the Frog Prince have had a curse put on them: they have
real memories and real fears. Karl Shapiro once acutely observed that
Jarrell's "almost obsessive return to the great childhood myths is sometimes as painful as psychoanalysis," and that the subtitle of his work
might well be "Hansel and Gretel in America." What Hansel and Gretel
tell us is that the woods are dark and that the creatures who inhabit

them change their skins. In the mythic imagination metamorphosis is the great theme underlying all others. To the individual psyche it is the way out of the cage.

Stanley Kunitz in *Randall Jarrell, 1914–1965*,
edited by Robert Lowell, Peter Taylor,
and Robert Penn Warren (Farrar).
1967. pp. 99–100

I will always go on writing for Randall: that is, for an attention, ear, and spirit on which nothing was wasted, and which nothing escaped. A poem—including those very different from his own—was a natural environment for him; he entered a strange poem as a great naturalist might enter a strange forest, every nerve awake—but as a naturalist who was himself part bird, part liana, part jaguar. His influence on the poetry of his time has yet to be fathomed: it worked through his own poems, his published criticism, his teaching, his involvement with the work of his friends. For many of us, if asked that old question: "To what or whom do you address your poems?" the truthful answer would be: "To the mind of Randall Jarrell."

Adrienne Rich in *Randall Jarrell, 1914–1965*,
edited by Robert Lowell, Peter Taylor,
and Robert Penn Warren (Farrar).
1967. p. 183

Jarrell was not good with raw wounds. He needed, for the good of the poetry, a wound not quite healed and yet as close to healing as it would ever come. He needed to be able to go a little way off, far enough to talk about the experience. He was not a dramatic poet. Reading his poems is not like seeing *King Lear*: it is like the relief of breaking a wounded silence, letting the pain drain away in words, in companionable talk. When we say that his idiom is conversational, we mean that it is like the conversation that helps, in trouble; balm to hurt minds. . . .

Jarrell is a little Proust to whom, as someone has said, the only real paradises are lost paradises, spectrally recovered in memory and vision. Memory is compulsive in this poet, as if he feared that by losing anything he would lose everything.

Denis Donoghue. *The Ordinary Universe*
(Macmillan—N.Y.). 1968. pp. 34, 37

At the center of [*The Third Book of Criticism*], and of Jarrell's critical achievement as a whole, are his essays on modern poets: in this volume Stevens, Auden (twice) and Robert Graves. The "method" is unvarying: a setting out, from evidence of the poems and the biography, of the poet's main attitude (in Auden, it is the changes of attitude which interest Jarrell); an attempt to distinguish the best poems from the second or third-best (with Stevens and Graves, as in the Frost essays, Jarrell provides lists—the invitation is to check out the list, not memorize it); an attempt to sum up and salute the poet's work, i.e. why and how it has given Jarrell so much reading pleasure. Nothing could be simpler; nothing more difficult of accomplishment. Throughout the essays, always in an offhand, metaphorically illustrative manner, run analogies with music that suggest why Jarrell is so secure in his taste, especially when it involves listening to effects. . . .

Then there are the satisfying ways that common sense, what any fool should know if he had a thought in his head, is made to reveal about the poet something we didn't quite know. . . . This common sense, which usually means for Jarrell comic sense, is not merely turned against an easy target like "critics"; he is sure enough of his admirations to know that full and convincing praise of a poet's work means that some adverse comment on it, however slight, must also be involved.

William H. Pritchard. *HdR.*
Summer, 1970. p. 375

JEFFERS, ROBINSON (1887–1962)

[Jeffers's] theory of the world was not borne out . . . by his behavior in it. He was two men in one—at least two—as Thomas Hardy was. Hardy had the bleakest possible view of nature and man, yet many of his poems seem to be written by a warm-hearted man who has forgotten what he was supposed to think. Few things are more attractive than this: than feeling in someone who has put feeling aside, than tenderness in a person of tough mind. The mind of Jeffers had been hardened in hot fires—just when, it may be possible some day to determine. In his Foreword to *The Selected Poetry of Robinson Jeffers* he spoke of two "accidents that changed and directed my life." One of these was his meeting with Una, and the other was their coming to live near the Monterey coast mountains. There must have been other "accidents," too, including a collision with ideas that transformed him from the more or less commonplace poet of his first two volumes into the stunning one of "Tamar," "Roan Stallion," "The Tower Beyond Tragedy," and the other long poems that followed.

Mark Van Doren. Foreword to *The Selected Letters of Robinson Jeffers*, edited by Ann N. Ridgeway (Johns Hopkins). 1968. p. viii

For a number of reasons, Jeffers devoted a great deal of his time and energy to the cultivation of a subgenre—narrative poetry—to which his gifts were not especially adaptable. What is also distressing, though, is that the attention Jeffers has received has been so disproportionately weighted in the direction of these failed narratives and that his stock has fallen so badly as a result. What more signal instance have we of the capitulation of criticism to what is most gross and obvious in a man's work, and in a generation that has had the temerity to exhume and to sanctify an Emily Dickinson, a body of work at once fragile, restrictive, and yet upon examination singularly exotic and intense both in formal and human qualities? It is as though there had been a tacit agreement among all influential parties that Jeffers' shorter poems should be looked upon as nothing more than an adjunct to the narratives, perhaps even as something less, as filler for the volumes his publishers issued with remarkable regularity for so. many years. As it is, Jeffers' short poems, many of them rather lengthy by standards of the conventional lyric, will fill an enormous volume when they are collected, and an impressive volume it will be; for at his best Jeffers could blend passion and restraint, image and statement, contempt and admiration, as few poets of any time have been able to, and often with a music so ripe and easy that it is able to impress itself upon our senses without our ever remarking its grace and majesty, its sureness of touch.

Robert Boyers in Modern American Poetry,
edited by Jerome Mazzaro (McKay).
1970. pp. 187–8

Robinson Jeffers used the various concepts of Nietzsche's philosophy to clear away outworn intellectual traditions and religious preconceptions in order to develop his own doctrine of Inhumanism. That Nietzscheanism was a useful—though sometimes limited—tool for Jeffers is now obvious. That his Lucretian-derived Inhumanism and its insistence upon transhuman magnificence flourished from inception is equally clear. Hence readers acquainted with both Nietzsche and Lucretius may achieve a more sensitive appreciation of the tumultuous grandeur and severe individualism of Jeffers' poetry.... The proper study for the reading of Jeffers, then, is *Thus Spoke Zarathustra* and *De Rerum Natura*.

Arthur B. Coffin. Robinson Jeffers: Poet of Inhumanism (Wisconsin). 1971. pp. 257–8

• JOHNSON, JAMES WELDON (1871–1938)

The Autobiography of an Ex-Coloured Man, of course, in the matter of specific incident, has little enough to do with Mr. Johnson's own life, but it is imbued with his own personality and feeling, his *views* of the subjects discussed, so that to a person who has no previous knowledge of the author's own history, it reads like *real* autobiography. It would be truer, perhaps, to say that it reads like a composite autobiography of the Negro race in the United States in modern times. . . .

Mr. Johnson . . . chose an all-embracing scheme. His young hero, the ostensible author, either discusses (or lives) pretty nearly every phase of Negro life, North and South and even in Europe, available to him at that period. That he "passes" the title indicates. Miscegenation in its slave and also its more modern aspects, both casual and marital, is competently treated. The ability of the Negro to mask his real feelings with a joke or a laugh in the presence of the inimical white man is here noted, for the first time in print, I should imagine. Negro adaptability, touchiness, and jealousy are referred to in an unself-conscious manner, totally novel in Negro writing at the time this book originally appeared [1912]. . . . Jim Crow cars, crap-shooting, and the cake-walk are inimitably described. Colour snobbery within the race is freely spoken of, together with the economic pressure from without which creates this false condition. There is a fine passage devoted to the celebration of the Negro Spirituals and there is an excellent account of a Southern camp-meeting, together with a transcript of a typical oldtime Negro sermon. There is even a lynching. But it is chiefly remarkable to find James Weldon Johnson in 1912, five or six years before the rest of us began to shout about it, singing hosannas to rag-time (jazz was unknown then).

Carl Van Vechten. Introduction to *The Autobiography of an Ex-Coloured Man* by James Weldon Johnson (Knopf). 1927. pp. v, xii–ix

The problem of the actual writing of these folk sermons [*God's Trombones*] is admittedly difficult: complete identification with the themes and idioms of a by-gone generation, a thoroughly incandescent revitalizing of its mood and faith, are perhaps impossible. At this late distance rhetoric must come to the rescue of a lapsing diction and poetic fictions re-kindle the primitive imagination. It is a question of Ossian all over again. The comparison with genuine folk-poetry is constantly in mind and the poet judged by the hard epic standard of objectivity, impersonality and the extent to which he approximates the primitive originals or reproduces their authentic quality. That Mr. Johnson succeeds as often as he does in passages of really fervid and simple folk poetry is great credit to his artistry. At least three of these poems in my judgment have this quality and are really great: "The Creation," "Judgment Day," and in the main "Go Down Death." To proclaim too enthusiastically the perfection of poems like the last-mentioned is to forget, in an age of personalism, the touch and tang of epic poetry. These are folk-things, and the epic standard must apply.

Alain Locke. *The Survey.*
Aug. 1, 1927. p. 473

Published anonymously in 1912 with a preface by Brander Matthews and reissued under the author's name in 1927 with an introduction by Carl Van Vechten, *The Autobiography of an Ex-Coloured Man* is noteworthy because of its restraint, its comprehensiveness, and its adumbration of the Negro Renascence of the 1920's. At a time when most Negro fictionists were giving blow for blow and painting extravagantly favorable pictures of members of the race, Johnson set out neither to glorify Negroes nor to malign whites but to interpret men and conditions as he knew them. . . .

Besides being more detached than any preceding novel of American Negro life, *The Autobiography of an Ex-Coloured Man* is groundbreaking in its introduction of a well-realized cosmopolitan milieu. Unlike most earlier Negro fiction, it is not localized in the South but moves out into the broader field of European and Northern urban life. . . .

In addition to being more impartial and more comprehensive than any earlier novel of American Negro life, *The Autobiography of an Ex-Coloured Man* is a milestone because of its forthright presentation of racial thought. Admitting the dual personality which some Negroes assume—one role among their own group and the other in the presence of whites—Johnson is himself not guilty of such a two-sided character. Not attempting to "wear the mask," he gives a calm, dispassionate treatment of people and situations as he sees them.

Hugh M. Gloster. *Negro Voices in American Fiction* (North Carolina). 1948. pp. 79–80

Johnson indisputably anticipates the Harlem School by subordinating racial protest to artistic considerations. For the most part, the racial overtones of [*The Autobiography of an Ex-Colored Man*] form an organic part of its aesthetic structure. While in one sense the racial identity of the protagonist is the central fact of his existence, in another, it is almost irrelevant. The protagonist faces a series of situations from which he flees; his flight into the white race is merely the crowning instance of his cowardice. To be sure, his tragedy is heightened because there are good objective reasons for his final flight, but these reasons in no sense constitute a justification. The focus of the novel is not on the objective situation but on the subjective human tragedy.

Compared to the typical propaganda tract of the period, *The Autobiography of an Ex-Colored Man* is a model of artistic detachment. Yet even Johnson cannot wholly repress a desire to educate the white folks. Artificially contrived discussions of the race problem mar the novel, and at times the author is needlessly defensive. But despite an occasional lapse, he retains a basic respect for his function as an artist.

Robert A. Bone. *The Negro Novel in America* (Yale). 1958. pp. 48–9

In the language of *God's Trombones* Johnson found a much more flexible medium than Dunbar dialect for the interpretation of folk material. Traditional dialect attempts (sometimes unsuccessfully) a strict fidelity in metre and in rhyme scheme; Johnson adapted to an artistic form the rhythms of an actual sermon, the accents of actual speech and intonation. He freed himself from the necessity to rhyme, thus subordinating strict poetic form to the artistic interpretation of his subject matter. In *God's Trombones* Johnson approximated the vivid imagery of the folk, an imagery far superior to any he attained in the *Fifty Years* dialect poems and certainly an imagery which rivaled the best of Dunbar's. Johnson used all the tricks of the folk preacher's trade—hyperbole, repetition, juxtaposition, personal appeal to his listeners, the knack of making Biblical happenings have an intense meaning to current life. Johnson even used punctuation and capitalization to achieve his effect— dashes to indicate the frequent and dramatic pauses, capitalization to emphasize important words, such as "Old Earth" and "Great White Throne." The sensitive reader cannot fail to hear the ranting of the fire-and-brimstone preacher; the extremely sensitive reader may even hear the unwritten "Amens" of the congregation.

Eugenia W. Collier. *Phylon*. Winter, 1960. pp. 358–9

Although Johnson wrote no other novels, his achievement in *The Autobiography of an Ex-Coloured Man* deserves recognition. The book has a significant place in black literature because it overthrows the stereotyped black character, employed even by early black writers, in favor of one that is complex and many-sided. Johnson gains depth and subtlety by using the first-person point of view rather than the third-person favored by his contemporaries. Moreover, his skill in using an unreliable narrator who reveals more than he intends—indeed, more than he knows—adds important psychological dimensions to the main character and his story. Finally, Johnson's skill in conveying his vision of black life in America through irony rather than by means of the heavy-handed propagandistic techniques of his predecessors marks a new, more artistic direction for the black novelist.

Robert E. Fleming. AL. March, 1971. p. 96

Johnson had read and been greatly impressed by Du Bois's [*The Souls of Black Folk*], and it is not surprising that the mulatto status and the varying musical inclinations of his narrator act as symbolic projections of a double consciousness. The narrator modulates between the black world and the white (often with less than equanimity) and seems torn between the early melodies of his mother and the Chopinesque style that wins his white beloved. In a sense, *The Autobiography of an Ex-Colored Man* is a fictional rendering of *The Souls of Black Folk*, for Johnson's narrator not only stresses his bifurcated vision, but also his intellectual genius. He maintains an open, critical attitude toward the many sides of black American culture, condemns in unequivocal terms the limitations of the black situation, and assiduously records his movement from a naïve provincialism toward a broad cosmopolitanism. The narrator, in short, is a black man of culture recording the situations and attitudes that have succeeded in driving him underground, to a position the larger society might define as criminal. . . .

The Autobiography of an Ex-Colored Man is both the history and the confession of one of the "talented tenth" (that class of college-bred black Americans in whom Du Bois placed so much faith); it offers the rehearsal of a "soul on ice" who draws substance from a world that could not recognize his true character nor sympathize with his longings. Each of its episodes is an effort at personal definition and a partial summing up of the black American past.

Houston A. Baker, Jr. VQR.
Summer, 1973. pp. 438–9

The main story line of the work [*The Autobiography of an Ex-Coloured Man*] delineates the progress from childhood to maturity and marriage of the offspring of a Southern gentleman and his light-skinned mistress. In this progress Johnson gives us realistic pictures of Negro life seldom, perhaps never, treated in fiction up to that time: the activities of Pullman porters on the job and off; the life in a Key West cigar factory; a good old-fashioned camp meeting; and, most important, the bohemian night life of black New York before it moved to Harlem. In his night-life sketches Johnson was a precursor of much Renaissance literature of the next two decades. Johnson, again, was not the first to write about this life. In Dunbar's one Negro novel, *The Sport of the Gods*, he touches on the theme. But Johnson, as a part of the theatrical world of the era, had a much better knowledge of Black Bohemia than any other writer. . . .

   The Autobiography of an Ex-Coloured Man is different from earlier black fiction in other ways. First of all, his protagonist is almost an anti-hero. A decent person in every respect, he is also a weak and vacillating human. Facing a series of important choices in his life, he takes the easier way every time. Starting out to become a distinguished part of the Negro world, he ends up as an ordinary middle-class white citizen. First, his "averageness" and his humanness suggest that the protagonist's individual characteristics, and not race, shaped his career. And second, Johnson does not belabor the race issue as practically every other black novelist before him had done. He has to talk about segregation and discrimination, but he does not lose his perspective. He has to discuss the black-white sexual liaison that produced the protagonist, but he does not become bitter over the plight of black womanhood. There is no moral condemnation here, no lecturing. This race mingling is described as a fact of Southern life.

Arthur P. Davis. *From the Dark Tower:*
Afro-American Writers 1900 to 1960
(Howard). 1974. pp. 30–1

JONES, JAMES (1921–   )

James Jones writes abominably, like Dreiser, which is to say that his sentences are dismal monstrosities of kitsch, while his novels (some of them, anyway) render the world with great power. Jones is a typical product of a culture that finds it so easy to sneer at the mandarin finesse of Henry James and believes in its heart of hearts that the only art worth cleaving to at all is rough-hewn, untutored, and springs not from emotion remembered in tranquility—where in the true American life is that? —but from action remembered in the midst of still more action. In short, art becomes journalism, the writing that gets done with the guns still pounding outside: Stephen Crane, Hemingway . . . and James Jones at his best.

Raymond A. Sokolov. *NYT*. Feb. 14, 1971. p. 7

Virtually alone among World War II novels, *From Here to Eternity* gives us a view from within of the old regular army, of the "thirty-year man" who enlisted because he was a Harlan County miner's son

(Prewitt) who could not find work; a natural leader and organizer (Warden) who could play the game in the army; an old Wobbly (Jack Malloy), or a gutter rat (Maggio) who had nowhere else to go. These tough morsels—even the sadist, Fatso, who happily tortured prisoners in the Stockade—are ultimately a judgment on a society whose men have no real work, whose skills are the real lament of the book. Men are employed by the army, but *they* are not used.

> Alfred Kazin. *Bright Book of
> Life* (Little). 1973. p. 79

Jones is accused of uncouth writing, sensationalism, and naïveté; but though he sometimes gives evidence of these faults, he possesses gifts greater than subtlety: a capacity to respond to life in narrative terms, enduring honesty in statement, a covert uncanny sensitivity. Nor is his achievement limited entirely to war fiction; *Some Came Running* (1957) is set in the small·towns of postwar, midwestern America, and *The Merry Month of May* (1971) in Paris during the May riots of 1968.

> Ihab Hassan. *Contemporary American
> Literature* (Ungar). 1973. p. 66

JONES, LeROI [AMIRI BARAKA] (1934–   )

Since all [Jones's] work is heavily autobiographical, his poetry and his fiction (particularly *The System of Dante's Hell*) show his attempt to escape the middle-class background which makes him feel like an oppressor of his own kind. It is in *Home*, however, that his journey can be seen most clearly. A collection of essays written at random over a five-year period, the book is given a shape of its own by the chronological arrangement of the pieces. They move from "Cuba Libre" (1960), in which he can still use the pronoun "we" meaning "we Americans," to the essays of 1964 and 1965 where his identification is purely black and the prospect is destruction.

> Gerald Weales. *The Jumping-Off Place*
> (Macmillan—N.Y.). 1969. p. 137

LeRoi Jones's *The System of Dante's Hell* . . . ostensibly consists of disconnected scenes and random thoughts or observations. Some early reviewers asserted that Jones used a pretentious title as an appeal to intellectuals. Yet, with meticulous precision, with broken but somehow poetic sentences, Jones does expose a Hell, a black ghetto thriving on incontinence, violence, and fraud, surrounded by "white monsters" who add to the torment of the Inferno and prevent escape. . . .

Yet in a very real sense Jones believes that he belongs in the Inferno which he himself has helped to build. He has witnessed and participated in the basest evil: "heresy against one's own sources, running in terror from one's deepest responses and insights . . . the denial of feeling." . . . In this urban Inferno the victims are not only tormented by their environment and their monsters but by each other, thereby removing the last trace of humanity. It is a city dominated by the Gorgon of Despair.

Olga W. Vickery in *The Shaken Realist*,
edited by Melvin J. Friedman and
John B. Vickery (Louisiana
State). 1970. p. 157

In [Jones's] poetry, fiction, drama, criticism and scholarly works there is but one constant hammering—to be BLACK in America is to be REVOLUTIONARY. In *Dutchman, The Toilet*, and *The Slave*, three plays by LeRoi Jones, there is all the hatred, venom, brutality, profanity and downright insanity that whites have traditionally heaped upon the Negro; but now turned back upon whites. Whitman once said, "A poet enlisted in a people's cause can make every word he writes draw blood." Jones, and those gathered about him, are not begging white society to love them. No. They are out to take their freedom and dignity as black men and to harass the white world while, at the same time, inspiring the masses of big-city Negroes to the affirmation of their inherent beauty and worth, not as middle-class-oriented integrated Negroes, but as Black People.

Calvin C. Hernton in *Amistad 1*, edited by
John A. Williams and Charles F. Harris
(Random). 1970. pp. 214–5

The prose tracts Jones has written in recent years, since the publication of *Black Magic Poetry*, have consistently urged a firm moral position for the black man, one which unites him with his Black brothers and one that turns its back on white corruption. The logic of this position was begun in the earliest poetry and developed through the struggles with [T. S.] Eliot's conception of God, and through the ultimate creation of an alternative to Eliot's moral view.

It may be said that one of Jones' solutions to the dilemma of what to do about Eliot's God, and what to do about the existential heroes of his comic book youth, is to supplant them both in his own person. . . . It may not be realistic to see Jones imagining himself as a kind of God, though he has seen black men as gods; but there is a curious passage near the end of *Black Magic Poetry* that suggests the temptation may be present. . . .

Perhaps it is merely a vatic pose Jones adopts in these poems, and he does not apotheosize himself at all. But there is a curiosity that lingers in the imagination regarding the name he has assumed since the publication of his poems, the Islamic name which appears in the "Explanation" to *Black Magic Poetry*. One wonders if God and the comic book heroes are dead forever, or if they have been absorbed into Jones' poetic unconscious wanting to poke out again. His name, Baraka, like Lorca's Duende, means many things. Its root is Hebrew: Brk, and it means a number of things: lightning, the blessed of God, virtue, inspiration, the muse.

Lee A. Jacobus in Modern Black Poets, edited
by Donald B. Gibson (Prentice-Hall).
1973. pp. 125–6

There are enough brilliant poems of such variety in *Black Magic Poetry* and *In Our Terribleness* to establish the unique identity and claim for respect of several poets. But it is beside the point that Baraka is probably the finest poet, black or white, writing in this country these days. The question still has to be asked whether he has fulfilled the vocation set for him by his own moves and examples. He has called himself a "seer" (one familiar with evil is the way he defined it) and holy man, but hesitates to claim (while vying for it) the fateful name of prophet.

The prophet differs from the poet and other word-men in his role of awaking and sustaining among his people a vision of their destiny set beside the criteria of their deepest values in the most fundamental though significant language. A poet's obligation, by contrast, is to the integrity of his verbal rendering of his individual sensibility. The problem is whether Baraka's creative impulse, which is essentially underground, hip, urban, and avant-garde, can be made to speak for a nation of black people rather than for a set of black nationalists. Can he transcend the inclination to ad-lib on the changes of black consciousness . . . toward redefining that consciousness in the light of enduring values and in major works of sustained thought and imagination?

Clyde Taylor in Modern Black Poets, edited
by Donald B. Gibson (Prentice-Hall).
1973. pp. 132–3

The Jones play [*A Recent Killing*] is uncouth in texture and performance, but it is nonetheless a play of considerable scope, power and, despite its harshness, sensibility. . . .

It seethes with passionate anger, with bursts of wild humor, with a consuming desire for expression. It explodes all over the place and, as usual with such hectic efforts, there is a quantity of debris—some of it ugly. But ugliness may also serve art's purposes: what is more important in this case is that the play teems with life. . . .

Most of the twenty-five scenes in this long play depict the world which creates the inevitability of its conclusion. Obviously cutting is required and loose ends should be tied up, and there are other things which may be argued against the play. Still, the faults are less significant than that the play is an American drama wrought from the bitter blood struggle of a man who can write, and writes not only about himself and his race but about the immediate environment in which we all dwell.

Harold Clurman. Nation. Feb. 12, 1973. p. 218

A good many poets and critics don't like what's happened to the old LeRoi Jones, promising young Negro poet of *Preface to a Twenty Volume Suicide Note.* Baraka, obviously, is not interested in their opinions. Nevertheless, it is a mistake to dismiss him as an angry propagandist, as so many have done, because he appears to run against the literary grain. The old art of LeRoi Jones was written to be read. The new writing of Baraka is calculated to be heard—*how we sound*, he would say now— and his audience must have some sense of the Afro-American perspective from which his new writing issues. The black aesthetic which shapes his writing is neither lacking in artistic taste (strident, anti-poetic, uncontrolled, say the critics) nor in itself startlingly new. It only appears that way from a literary point of view, one that is in many respects incongruous to the cultural context upon which his stylistic rationale is based. What is remarkable, from a literary standpoint, is the range of innovation his political ideology and altered cultural consciousness have required of him as a writer. For Baraka, though, it is not remarkable at all, but only the result of an inevitable artistic transformation, the sure spelling out of his specific placement in the world as a black writer.

William C. Fischer. MR. Spring, 1973. p. 305

KEROUAC, JACK (1922–1969)

Given [Kerouac's] past habits as a writer, one knows what to expect from him. Although some have seen *Vanity of Duluoz* as a more disciplined work—Kerouac now uses commas because, as he says in the opening pages, no one liked his factotum dash—it is really the same old heap of prose. . . . All this we've had before, and, indeed, depending on one's mood, the awkward exuberance could even be fun and of some interest. But there is something else going on in *Vanity of Duluoz*, which may well have been present in Kerouac's earlier books, though hidden beneath the Love, scenedigging, and beautiful people: a bitterness and a petulance that change the top-heavy prose from an almost pleasant semiliterate excess into an ominous insistence that attention be paid to the man suffering and writing these lines.

Perhaps it is because Kerouac is getting middle-aged and beginning to worry about the younger generation that this cantankerous attitude peeps through more often than it did in the past. Perhaps he now suspects that a preference for the weird and subrational does not necessarily make one an artist. Perhaps he means now really to tell it to us like it is. Whatever the reason, I could not get over the notion that with every metaphor and incident in this autobiography, the author was desperately insisting that things *will* be as he intends them—even though his genius is not up to proving it.

Jack Richardson. NYR. April 11, 1968. p. 34

What about him inspired a generation of followers to idealize him as a rebel of social and political meaning? Was it because he told how he did not like the "mean old cops" he encountered on the road? Or that he did not like suburban houses and TV sets—though proud of having bought both for his mother? Was it because he liked Krazy Kat, hiding in an alley with a brick for the cop? But that, patently, is childish social criticism. When infrequently he faced political problems straight on, he resolved them by simple and sudden intuitions that "everything would be all right." It just would. . . .

Political commitment assumes the possibility of power, and through power, of change. Kerouac lived with a profoundly defeated sense of helplessness, reflected in his prolonged, or rather his unending, adolescence. He had an appalled vision of life as empty, meaningless, and futile. His readers saw him as a modern Whitman affirming life and beckoning them to its open roads. But his obverse side was nihilistic, and his refrain that of Beckett—born to die.

Blanche Gelfant. CL. Summer, 1974. p. 417

● KESEY, KEN (1935–   )

Written on two levels of meaning, composed in two keys together, [*One Flew Over the Cuckoo's Nest*] tells the direful tale of a struggle for survival in an institution for the mentally disordered, and it also presents a parable of life in a world presided over by a tyrannical junta of compulsion and conformity. . . . This is allegory with a difference, the difference being found in the very method of composition, in the bi-tonal technique of terrible realism in conjunction with a profound and searching parable of government and the governed.

R. A. Jelliffe. CST. Feb. 4, 1962. p. 3

One Flew Over the Cuckoo's Nest by Ken Kesey is a Gothic novel. . . . It is not simply imitative. The important theme is . . . the compulsive design. The "Big Nurse"—as the narrator calls her—is an authoritarian, middle-aged woman who tries to impose her will upon her lunatics—she must make them fear and respect her so that she can feel superior. She exerts power not to help others but to help herself: her compulsive design cannot stop—except through violence—because it is all she has. . . .

"Humor blots out the pain." Mr. Kesey gives us many amusing scenes which are "black"—Big Nurse for example, informs Billy, the whore's betrothed, that she is going to tell his mother!—but he knows that if we can laugh at the unreality around us, we retain our humanity. Gothic and comedy are Janus-faced. *One Flew Over the Cuckoo's Nest* is an honest, claustrophobic, stylistically brilliant first novel which makes us shiver as we laugh—paradoxically, it keeps us "in balance" by revealing our madness.

Irving Malin. Critique. 5, 2, 1962. pp. 82, 84

In his first novel, *One Flew Over the Cuckoo's Nest,* Ken Kesey demonstrated that he was a forceful, inventive, and ambitious writer. All of these qualities are exhibited, in even greater degree, in *Sometimes a Great Notion*. Here he has told a fascinating story in a fascinating way. . . .

Many novelists have experimented with the rapid shifting of point of view, and some have tried to blend past and present. . . . But I can think of no one who has made such continuous use of these two methods as Kesey. And he has made them serve his purpose; that is, he has succeeded in suggesting the complexity of life and the absence of any absolute truth.

Granville Hicks. *SR*. July 25, 1964. pp. 21–2

Beyond the P.T.A. and the beer commercials, beyond the huge effluvium of the times, exist people who live by the ancient passions, and Mr. Kesey, in the fullness of his material, discovers them for us. . . .

What convinces me of Mr. Kesey's virtue as a novelist is his obsessiveness. He views the same basic mysteries again and again but from different angles. He is never satisfied with surfaces, throwing away revelations that would do less ambitious writers for a decade. The mysteries drive him, as they do all the best writers, because they are unanswerable. . . .

[The] conception, sharp-edged and vivid, of the unreconstructed, unterrified individual serves as the mainspring of Mr. Kesey's force, and his wonderment provides the extra momentum.

Conrad Knickerbocker. *NYT*.
Aug. 2, 1964. p. 4

One Flew Over the Cuckoo's Nest works better [than *Sometimes a Great Notion*] to the degree that it is dreamed or hallucinated rather then merely written—which is to say, to the degree that it, like its great prototype *The Leatherstocking Tales*, is Pop Art rather than *belles lettres*—the dream once dreamed in the woods, and now redreamed on pot and acid.

Its very sentimentality, good-guys bad-guys melodrama, occasional obviousness and thinness of texture, I find—like the analogous things in Cooper—not incidental flaws, but part of the essential method of its madness. . . .

Everywhere in Kesey, as a matter of fact, the influence of comics and, especially, comic books is clearly perceptible, in the mythology as well as the style. . . . What Western elements persist in Kesey are, as it were, first translated back into comic-strip form, then turned once more into words on the conventional book page. One might, indeed, have imagined Kesey as ending up as a comic book writer, but since the false second start of *Sometimes a Great Notion*, he has preferred to live his comic strip rather than write or even draw it. . . .

But *One Flew Over the Cuckoo's Nest* survives the experiments and rejections which follow it; and looking back five years after its initial appearance, it seems clear that in it for the first time the New West was clearly defined: the West of Here and Now, rather than There and Then—the West of Madness.

Leslie A. Fiedler. *The Return of the Vanishing American* (Stein and Day). 1968. pp. 183–5

Kesey seems to have been one of the first voyagers into psychodelia to come back with tales of a spiritual Eldorado that made the world of ordinary consciousness seem a stale, inchoate, constricted imitation of reality. He rose up among the wandering tribes of California, found his disciples and became a leader to those drifting out of social gravity into their own orbits. Until running afoul of the police, Kesey led his little band across America staging impromptu "Acid Tests" as he went along. These tests, hip camp meetings where the local populace was invited to turn on, began finally to rub society wrong, even before LSD had been declared illegal, and after several bumps against the terrene police force of California, Kesey was snared on a marijuana charge and skipped across the border into Mexico.

Jack Richardson. *NR*. Sept. 28, 1968. pp. 30–2

We are left [in *One Flew Over the Cuckoo's Nest*] with a somewhat sentimentalized over-simplification of moral problems. Admittedly, Kesey's opposition of Good and Evil is less bald and the Victory of Good less clear than might seem. The superhero McMurphy is sacrificed to the machine culture and Big Nurse remains in the ward. . . .

The book's beginning is too easily forgotten and we are pushed along by Bromden's optimism. We are to hope, not despair, and, more importantly, not define the line between. Kesey believes in the comic book world in spite of himself. This is the moral ground on which critical faultfinding must begin. Kesey has not avoided the dangers of a simplistic aesthetic despite his attempts to complicate it. He forgets that the comic strip world is not an answer to life, but an escape from it. The reader finds Kesey entering that world too uncritically in defense of Good.

Terry G. Sherwood. *Critique*. 13, 1, 1970. pp. 108–9

If hippies are, as Alan Harrington suggested to me, "no more than Beats plus drugs," it may be worth studying the quantities of that equation to see just how they happened to fall into place. It all began, legend has it, with Ken Kesey. He had a far more substantial and direct influence on events than did Timothy Leary. It was Kesey, they say, who made it all happen. . . .

Ken Kesey was . . . enrolled in the Stanford University creative writing program as a graduate student. He had come down from Oregon, where the year before he had come out as a champion wrestler in the AAU's Northwest Division and had barely missed qualifying for the Olympics. That was Kesey then, sort of an All-American boy in the old Kerouac mold. He had, in fact, out-Kerouacked Jack both as an athlete and a scholar, for he had managed not only to graduate from the University of Oregon, but had done so with distinction and had gone on to Stanford as a Woodrow Wilson scholar. And there he intended to prepare himself to write great American novels.

And he did produce a couple that, if lacking greatness, were at least grand, before turning his back on writing and becoming guru to a group of wacked-out psychedelic gypsies who called themselves the Merry Pranksters.

Bruce Cook. The Beat Generation
(Scribner). 1971. pp. 196–7

One Flew Over the Cuckoo's Nest is a modern fable pitting a fabulous kind of good against a fabulous kind of evil and making use of many of the traditional devices of American romance. . . . It does not return to the past, gaze toward the future, or travel to the unknown to get its "romance" setting. The setting is the static institution which sums up both the preoccupation of our age with the mystery of power, and the substitution of an image of the waste land for the image of a journey between Eden and Utopia. It is shot through with the vitality of its use of the here and now. We are constantly shocked into discovering how the book is really tied to the recognizable, not to the distant or strange, but to our very own—to technology we know of, to clichés we use, to an atmosphere possible only in the atomic tension of our times. Just as no one can confidently say who is mad and who is not in Kesey's novel, no one can say in what sense his story is real and in what sense it is fiction.

Raymond M. Olderman. Beyond the
Wasteland (Yale). 1972. p. 48

It is not surprising that in *The Making of a Counter Culture* Theodore Roszak should be interested in Ken Kesey, the organizer of public LSD trips, rather than Ken Kesey, the author. For Roszak is correct in his assumption that, like J. D. Salinger's admirers in the 1950's, Kesey's admirers in the 1960's were concerned primarily with the style of life he seemed to represent, not the substance of his work. The difficulty is that in Kesey's case public admiration and the image of him created by Tom Wolfe in *The Electric Kool-Aid Acid Test* have obscured the depth of his accomplishment: specifically, the importance of *One Flew Over the Cuckoo's Nest*, the novel on which his literary reputation depends.

The marrow of Kesey's art in *One Flew Over the Cuckoo's Nest* lies in his description of a struggle for sanity that in its political implications denies the sufficiency of escapism or primitivism. Indeed, Kesey has found it necessary to reverse the myth of the Indian introducing the white man to a way of life that goes back to nature. Unlike Cooper's Chingachgook with his "red skin and wild accouterments of a native of the woods" or Faulkner's Sam Fathers, a "wild man not even one generation from the woods," Chief Bromden, Kesey's Indian narrator, has lost complete touch with his tribe.

Nicolaus Mills. CentR. 16, 1, 1972. p. 82

To understand [*One Flew Over the Cuckoo's Nest*] is to experience ... at least three themes which the book has in common with other major works of literature. First, there is the idea that we must look beyond appearances to judge reality. . . . Second, there is the idea that fools and madmen have wisdom. Writers from Shakespeare to Kesey have suggested that the world is sometimes so out of joint that it can only be seen from some perspective so different that it cuts through illusion to truth. . . . And through this madness, in Kesey's book, the third theme emerges: the idea that the bumbling fool may be transformed into a worker of good deeds. . . .

The book, then, works through the eyes and action of madmen to go from a vision of the world where all things are profane to a vision of the world where all human things are potentially sacred.

Janet R. Sutherland. EJ. Jan., 1972. pp. 29–30

The contemporary cultural reaction against the ethic of the rational intellect, including an overriding distaste for "content" art, and the correspondingly pervasive commitment to sensorial experience, are exemplified in the career of Ken Kesey, erstwhile novelist and psychedelic superhero. Whatever became of that boisterous and brilliant young diamond-in-the-rough novelist who commanded the attention of middle-class American youth during the Haight-Ashbury era as prophet of the feverish *Now* religion? In 1962 Kesey published his bitter fable, *One Flew Over the Cuckoo's Nest,* still an extremely popular novel, and he was immediately included in the slate of highly regarded, challenging young American writers.

Like so much of the important literature of this century, Kesey's first book laments the destruction of America by the monstrous organizational Combine, and it defines that retreat to private, "irrational" satisfactions which has in the past decade become an extraordinarily widespread response to claustrophobic rational life in the social mad-house. Kesey then personally rejected the painfully logical, but thoroughly berserk machinery of orthodox space-age existence and followed his Indian refugee Chief Bromden back to the tribe. Of course, Kesey's noble savages were Indians only in spirit, social drop-outs who had discovered the primitive in themselves and who preferred the random life to the servile treadmill of community responsibility and business as usual. Kesey went native, went mad by society's definition, which labels any man insane who is unable or unwilling to conform, and he found a new life as charismatic chieftain of the Merry Pranksters.

James O. Hoge. SHR. Fall, 1972. p. 381

Kesey and Vonnegut occupy different pulpits but both speak to the same congregation and proclaim similar messages of redemption. The two novelists are addressing themselves to those who, amid the conformity and barrenness of our time, are searching for some vestige of personal integrity and some measure of human kindness.

For Kesey the key word is "courage." . . . Kesey grants that a Cross may be the price of personal integrity, but he also proclaims that crosses can be redemptive and that resurrection is always the final word. . . .

Kesey and Vonnegut would never be classified as "religious writers." Yet each of them in his own way has made an important contribution to a contemporary understanding of Christian redemption.

James R. Tunnell. CC. Nov. 22,
1972. pp. 1182–3

My own problem with this catch-all collection [Kesey's Garage Sale] is not that some of the material was twice published but rather astonishment that most of it, largely detritus, was published in the first place. The more I see of the counter-culture, the more it seems to me an inverted Rotary, with its own tiresome rituals, glad-handers, oafs and uniforms. . . .

And filling something like Billy Graham's office in the inverted Rotary we have Ken Kesey, betting not on prayer and hard work, but chemistry (LSD-25) and idleness to save souls.

The largest chunk of Kesey's Garage Sale is given over to a sprawling, occasionally charming, more often inchoate, screenplay, "Over the Border," starring Kesey and the Pranksters, thinly disguised as Devlin Deboree and the Animal Friends, on the lam in Mexico. . . .

Not every child raised on Wheaties grows up a champion; neither does every tripper return with "Kubla Khan." Some merely check in with "Over the Border." Engaging, and redeemed by humor here and there, but no more than a trifle.

Mordecai Richler. NYT. Oct. 7, 1973. pp. 6–7

• KINNELL, GALWAY (1927–   )

I liked Galway Kinnell's poems mainly for their wholehearted commitment to themselves, and for what I can only call their innocence. Mr. Kinnell cares quite openly and honestly about almost everything he has ever seen, heard of, or read about, and finds it rather easy to say so. There is nothing very tragic or tearing about him, or nothing very intense, either. He seems to me a natural poet: humanly likeable, gentle, ruminative. But he is dishearteningly prolix. Prolixity is, of course, the foremost and perhaps only natural enemy of the natural poet, and Mr. Kinnell is going to have to do battle with it if he is to realize himself. . . . Kinnell realizes the difference between knowing something because you have been told it is so and knowing it because you have lived it. And this latter kind of knowing is what good poetry can give, and what Kinnell in some of his work gives, too. . . . Mr. Kinnell has made an authentic beginning, and many poets die without getting even this far. Perhaps to a degree more than is true of other poets, Kinnell's development will depend on the actual events of his life. And it is a life which I think we should watch. [1961]

James Dickey. *Babel to Byzantium*
(Grosset). 1971. pp. 134–5

[Kinnell] writes in looser cadences than Wright or Snodgrass: free verse, often conversational, and seldom rhymed. Following the advice of Dr. Williams and Robert Bly, he seems to prefer accentual rhythm to the time-hallowed iambics they resent so much. The syntax, as important a factor in his poetry as it is in Merwin's, is relaxed, save in a few poems where it swells into complex units for special effect; the clauses generally align themselves in the simple patterns of coordination, subordinate constructions being relatively infrequent. This makes for ease rather than tautness in his diction and rhythmical movement. One could say he tends to build his poems by accumulation and expansion, not by compression as so many of his contemporaries do; an extreme example of this is the long descriptive piece on New York which concludes [*What a Kingdom It Was*], "The Avenue Bearing the Initial of Christ into the New World." A Whitmanic spirit moves this expressionist endeavor to seize the throbbing and shrill variety of New York life, and the incidental failures of thickness, loose diction, and commentary are Whitmanic too. Failures or no failures, however, the poem represents a gesture of courage; one can see in it the pledge of greater future accomplishments on the part of a young poet who dares to write richly instead of curling up in early preciosity. Kinnell brings a gust of fresh air into American poetry, without indulging in vulgarity.

Glauco Cambon. Recent American Poetry
(Minnesota). 1962. pp. 30–1

In much of Kinnell's poetry . . . the intuition of the sacred sets matter against spirit, concrete against abstract. But working against this instinctive dualism is an equally instinctive kinship with all suffering, an impulse which finds expression in his short story as the wish to serve. Countering the upward spiral of transcendence, of the "flesh made word," his poetry also moves outward, horizontally, in sympathy with the commonest forms of life. This is the expanding consciousness of Whitman, who found the sacred not among the stars but in the streets. So in "The Avenue Bearing the Initial of Christ into the New World," the kingdom is realized among the perishing humanity of Avenue C. It is a vision of desolating ugliness. Kinnell has ceased to make claims for the beauty of life. . . . So in this poem the poet has disappeared; the observer has become one with his subject; there is only the Avenue and the fullness and movement of its life. The tragic illumination of the poem does not come in any cumulative revelation but in "moments of transcendence" drifting in "oceans of loathing and fear," traffic lights blinking through darkness and rain.

Sherman Hawkins. PULC.
Autumn, 1963. p. 64

Galway Kinnell and Dickey belong together like yin and yang, like a parable of North and South, Catholic and Protestant. It is encouraging to think the continent still has room for two "nature poets" as different and as good. Where Dickey's poetry seems a condensation of light and space, a Wordsworthian openness to wonder and terror, Kinnell's is as cool as a proposition in Aquinas. His first book, What a Kingdom It Was, opened with a half-dozen or so very accomplished conventional miniatures fashioned from the matter of Frost by the sensibility of an early Lowell: Catholic, New England, tragic and apocalyptic. It closed with a long poem about New York of extraordinary freshness—the long crowded day of a Whitman in a late mid-twentieth century October. The metaphysical fever of modern Catholic poetry had vanished into a rigorous, modest, athletic attachment to the world. In Flower Herding on Mount Monadnock he develops this gift for a kind of luminous, feeling sobriety, especially in two long poems, "The Homecoming of Emma Lazarus" and "For Robert Frost."

R. W. Flint. NYR. June 25, 1964. p. 13

Galway Kinnell is a rhapsodic poet with restraint, a Whitmanesque bard with a more rarefied sensibility. Many of the poems in *Flower Herding on Mount Monadnock* are steeped in the American scene but without the dull wash of local color, many are ripe with the flavor of American idiom without descent into vulgarism. The harbor and Bedloe's Island, the immigrant, the hitch-hiker, the poets from Dickinson to Frost, the seasons and the corners of the continent—these are all beheld with insight and with wonder. Intermittently are poems about the Orient—a meditation in Calcutta, delicate renderings of Kyoto prints. Kinnell's new poems are poignant and emotive, with feeling that breaks near the surface and only occasionally flirts with banality.

Fred Bornhauser. *VQR*. Winter, 1965. p. 150

Mr. Kinnell makes his hero's journeying [in *Black Light*] moral as well as physical. Perhaps immoral would be a better word, for despite long desert rides and mad adventure, the real story is in the stripping away of all Jamshid's fragile, self-righteous little virtues. Mr. Kinnell offers no conclusions and no explanations. Jamshid's misdeeds simply appear, as colors appear in a dull rock under black light, although this may not be what the author intended by his title. Regardless of its ambiguity, the book holds one's interest, for the writing is condensed, austere, and effective, and Mr. Kinnell's Iran is described out of actual experience in the country.

Phoebe Adams. *At.* May, 1966. p. 132

Even when he operates on just two cylinders (in disproportionately many of his new poems, unhappily), Galway Kinnell is the poet the young writer will now watch—for tips of voice and stance—as he might have watched W. D. Snodgrass five years ago. There are individual lines, images, and whole passages in nearly every poem in *Body Rags* that are unforgettably poignant. Kinnell's generosity of spirit—a keenly piercing reverence for society's derelicts—and his self-scalding empathy for the mutilated souls of the crushed, the beaten, the solitary proud victims of back alleys and backwoods, give all of his work the rare quality of that which has been profoundly seen, witnessed, lived to the bones, before being translated—however fumblingly or gracefully—into words.

Laurence Lieberman. *YR*.
Autumn, 1968. p. 137

Each generation looks about to see who the great ones are in the arts, and in our time we can single out Galway Kinnell as one of the few consummate masters in poetry. His third book, *Body Rags*, is uniformly strong beside *What a Kingdom It Was* and *Flower Herding on Mount*

Monadnock, and it takes some risks those books do not. In two of the three poems in the final section of the new book, "The Porcupine" and "The Bear," there is some of the best poetry to be found any place today while the long, civil rights-concerned poem, "The Long River," which makes up the entire second section, is one of the most pertinent and ambitious poems of the time.

John Logan. Nation. Sept. 16, 1968. p. 244

Body Rags . . . should continue the disagreements between [Galway Kinnell's] English critics. The one large-scale poem, "The Last River," is a baffling mélange of personal experiences, horrid anecdotes and social comment. This reviewer can take it, and admire it, in sections: the places where the poet manages (as in a number of shorter, less ambitious poems) an achieved clarity of image and statement that doesn't get mawkish or pretentious. Kinnell is least good where his point gets lost in gloomy, portentous scrutiny of the scenes and topics that most fascinate him, things about which he is often asking rhetorical questions that one wants to answer in a ribald way: dank rivers, frog-ponds, nastier bits of insect life. Kinnell has a precise, Roethke-ish sense of the natural processes, a disquieting feeling for the relation of these things to a thinking human being who feels part of them (see the very fine "Night in the Forest"). He is best where these perceptions stay clear and unmelodramatic. And in the one or two places where he allows himself a little wit, it rather unexpectedly works.

Alan Brownjohn. NS. Sept. 12, 1969. p. 347

With the advantages of hindsight we should not be surprised when we notice that the initial poem of *What a Kingdom It Was,* aptly entitled "First Song," is located out of doors—in Illinois corn fields with frog ponds nearby—and that in the course of its three stanzas there is a movement from "dusk" into night. A large proportion of Kinnell's poetry is involved with the natural world, for he is drawn to it in profound ways, has been since childhood, and it provides him with an inexhaustible store for his imaginative meditation, if that phrase will do to distinguish a kind of thinking through images and particulars that is integral to the poetic act. But Kinnell's images from nature will become increasingly stark and rudimentary, their bonds with the ordinary range of human sympathies ever more tenuous, as he matures; for indeed his poems about killing a bird for Christmas dinner, shooting buffalo with a murderer for companion, mountain climbing, camping out alone in the mountains during winter, examining fossils in the cliff above a frog pond, seeking to define himself by identifying with porcupine and bear, bring him finally to the contemplation of what it is to be human in an extreme, one might say primitive situation. Under such fundamental circumstances he faces himself and the conditions of the world simultaneously, without mediation or disguise. It should be said, however, that Kinnell employs other means than nature for cutting to the bone of existence, though intimate acquaintance with other living creatures and with the earth is of primary importance to his work.

Ralph J. Mills, Jr. IowaR.
Winter, 1970. pp. 67–8

Kinnell has echoed all the great, sad questions of the past concerning our destiny, and he has summoned up the famous masks of the poet, especially the crucified, freely confessing sinner-saint and the sufferer beyond all telling. Something like an astrologically oriented prophetic role attracts him too, and so we have a renewal of the poet as seer. But the real power of [*The Book of Nightmares*] comes from its pressure of feeling, its remarkable empathy and keenness of observation, and its qualities of phrasing—far more than from its structural thoroughness or philosophical implications. It needs stripping down. But no matter. Whatever its weaknesses, *The Book of Nightmares* grapples mightily with its depressive view of reality and with essential issues of love, and it leaves us with something splendid: a true voice, a true song, memorably human.

M. L. Rosenthal. NYT. Nov. 21, 1971. p. 77

Galway Kinnell's *Body Rags* (1968) was a major poetic event. "The Bear" and "The Porcupine," which have already become anthology pieces, seem to me to have a peculiar excellence that goes beyond anything in *Crow*, for unlike [Ted] Hughes's witty but essentially one-dimensional moral allegories, Kinnell's animal poems are explorations of the poet's deepest self, a self he can only discover by identifying imaginatively with the sufferings of wild, alien creatures. Both poets are haunted by violence, but whereas Hughes views violence as an abstract concept, generic to the contemporary human situation, Kinnell sees it always in terms of himself.

Kinnell's new book, *The Book of Nightmares*, is somewhat uneven. It consists of ten long meditative poems, in form like irregular odes, each made up of seven sections of varying length. In each case, the poet begins with an actual situation—trying on old shoes in the Salvation Army Store (III), trying to fall asleep in a flophouse (V)—and then begins to meditate, moving backwards and forwards in time, as he tries to come to terms with the nightmares that confront the living. As in his earlier poems, Kinnell uses images of nature in its most elemental forms

—bloody hen feathers, spiders, bare black rocks, skulls, the corpses of animals—to discover the deepest instincts of the submerged self.

Marjorie G. Perloff. CL. Winter, 1973. p. 123

Kinnell's poetry [in the 1960's] involves itself with a virtual rediscovery of how to view objects intensely, while continuing to avoid any pre-scribed system. Even as early as his long poem, "The Avenue Bearing the Initial of Christ into the New World" . . . Kinnell's poetry has been celebratory and inclusive in its characteristic attitude toward the world of objects. "There are more to things than things," says one modern French philosopher, and the contemporary poet instinctively agrees, but how to discover that "more" without falling into mere attitudinizing remains problematic. Pound taught his successors, which include most American poets, that no authority could replace personal testament, especially when such testament involved accurate perception and atten-tive apperception. . . . Kinnell took from Pound . . . only so much as could fruitfully be grafted onto the traditions of Blake and Whitman, and though for some Pound's concern with "technique" might seem inimical to inspiration, such need not be the case. Pound's concern with objective "vision" on the physiological level corrects rather than re-places the "visionary." But Kinnell was still faced with the problem of how to bring his poetry out of the modernist cul-de-sac of irony into a post-modernist aesthetic. He does this in large measure by two actions, which may appear contradictory, but are in fact complementary: self-discovery and self-destruction, the heuristic and the incendiary actions of poetry. Kinnell became a shamanist, rather than a historicist, of the imagination.

Charles Molesworth. WHR.
Summer, 1973. pp. 226–7

● KOSINSKI, JERZY (1933–   )

This semi-autobiographical account of a small Polish boy who was sep-arated from his parents at the beginning of World War II traces his wartime wandering from village to village, horror to horror. *The Painted Bird* is unique among such chronicles in that scarcely any Nazis figure in it, nor are there any descriptions of concentration camps; nonetheless no book has delved so deeply into the "Nazi mentality" in its truest sense—which is to say, not confined to the narrow limits of a uniform or even a nationality.

So awful (in the gravest meaning of that word) is this book that I can scarcely "recommend" it to anyone, and yet, because there is enlightenment to be gained from its flame-dark pages, it deserves as wide a readership as possible.

Andrew Field. BW. Oct. 17, 1965. p. 2

Jerzy Kosinski was born in Poland in 1933. He lived through the war and then the Stalinist occupation of his country; at the age of twenty-four he came to the United States. He has since published two works of social commentary and two of fiction, *The Painted Bird* (1965) and *Steps* (1968). He writes in English, and by some miracle of training, which recalls the linguistic bravado of Conrad and Nabokov, he is already a master of a pungent and disciplined English prose. Simply as a stylist, Kosinski has few equals among American novelists born to the language. And I have also become convinced, after reading *Steps*, that he is one of the most gifted new figures to appear in our literature for some years.

Steps is an experimental work, which is partly to say that it follows upon the "tradition of the new" that has dominated Western writing for the past century but that it also deviates sharply in tone and technique from that tradition—otherwise it could no longer be described as experimental. It is a work highly problematic in aesthetic strategy and moral implication, and even after two careful readings I do not pretend to grasp it fully.

Irving Howe. Harper. March, 1969. p. 102

Steps has great impact the first time through. Much of this is due to its relentless Grand Guignol horror and perverse sexuality—and perhaps from our own realization that we are so fascinated by it. On a later reading the novel seems much more limited. It does not acknowledge the power, or even the reality, of individual and social forces which are opposed to the constant degradation and degeneration which it depicts. Admittedly, every reader will see the episodes of *Steps* in the light of his own personal norms, and will therefore join Kosinski in condemning what the episodes show. My point is that the human range of the episodes is not large enough to be the whole truth, or even to permit the whole truth to emerge from the reader's judgment of them.

Howard M. Harper, Jr. CL.
Spring, 1971. p. 214

I would think less of *Being There*, I am sure, if I did not know Kosinski's previous works. On the basis of those works, we have a right to grant Kosinski the maximum presumption of intention in this work. It becomes more than an analogue to chess problems or crossword puzzles to seek out in *Being There* the implications of various relations, repeated phrases and allusions. And it is a legitimate pleasure, if that is the accurate term, to contrast and compare this exploration of the abyss which separates people, making communication between one person and another almost impossible, with what Kosinski has previously done.

For if the vision which Kosinski has projected in his earlier works is not ours—and it is not, finally, mine—we cannot deny either its power or its attraction nor the knowledge that it derives from deep experience rather than a modish, cranked-up literary imagination. Although Kosinski has attempted less in *Being There* than in his first two novels, it approaches these works in its control, its finish. We keep a close eye, in America, on "our writers," particularly if they have hit it big with a first novel, and take an almost perverse satisfaction in seeing a giant tumble. *Being There* is not a sign of that tumble, as I am sure it will be read by some, not even a stagger. Quite the reverse, it is a sign that Kosinski is able to work in different forms, take risks of different kinds.

James Finn. *NR.* June 26, 1971. p. 33

In the decades since the close of World War II, both contemporary fiction and drama have recorded the devastating effects of that global conflict on man's moral consciousness. . . . Kosinski's brilliant fiction, like the works of Nietzsche, stand as a vivid warning to mankind, a warning to be heeded lest we too, like Dionysus Zagreus, suffer the fate of being torn apart. The moral descent of Kosinski's protagonists portrays the failure of both community and communication.

Unlike the plaintive hero of Shelley's poem, "Alastor," Kosinski's figures do not seek to evade the gross and "unseeing" multitude; they do not yearn for communion or "intellectual intercourse" with kindred spirits. The powerful quest of the rejected and alienated romantic soul is not at stake in his fiction; nor is the Faustian desire for unbounded knowledge a striking motive. The world of the Kosinskian hero has a closer parallel to the dark irrational universe of Kafka—man trapped in a world of dissolving meaning, in which there are few fragments to shore up against his ruin. Without Kafka's power for symbolic absurdity or a similar rich vein of rational irrationality, Kosinski's imaginative writings proceed out of a varied and dense past of vivid and personal nightmare.

Daniel J. Cahill. *TCL.* April, 1972. p. 121

In his "attempt to peel the gloss off the world," Jerzy Kosinski [in *The Painted Bird*] so successfully reveals man's depravity that the reader is more affected by the shock of the intense cruelty depicted than aware of its real effect upon the boy-narrator. In fact, so intense is our response to the depraved world of the Eastern European peasantry that we are reminded of the universality of Yeats' profound poetic vision in "The Second Coming": "Things fall apart, the centre cannot hold;/Mere anarchy is loosed upon the world." But what was a vision of "mere anarchy" for the poet is an accomplished fact for the novelist who is in part dramatizing the larger setting that permitted the occurrence of the grotesque, final solution of the Nazis. Without an understanding of the deep racial hatred of the Jews by the common people of Europe, we can never begin to apprehend the "blood-dimmed tide" (Yeats) loosed by the Third Reich; without an understanding of the human tendency to project guilt feelings on others considered alien, Kosinski is saying, we can never still the tide of hatred. . . .

Perhaps one of the most puzzling and persistent impressions one has upon first reading *The Painted Bird* is the curiously detached descriptions of brutal and perverted actions. This response by the boy is typical of the affective anesthesiatic who repels terror by aloofness, though the narrator's story demonstrates that he never becomes an anesthesiatic. Through his detachment, he creatively insulates himself against insanity by becoming remote from those events which he is utterly helpless to change in any way.

Meta Lale and John Williams. *Ren.*
Summer, 1972. pp. 198–9

The content of *The Future Is Ours, Comrade* is now less interesting than its method, for one reads it in 1972 not for Joseph Novak, Russian specialist, but for Jerzy Kosinski, incipient novelist. The structure of the book suggests the later novels, the gathering of parts that never quite become a whole. In *The Future Is Ours, Comrade*, Kosinski introduces a number of exemplary characters, each of whom contributes to the immediate subject of the chapter and the overall theme of Soviet conformism. There is, however, no attempt to bridge between figures. One conversation simply stops and the next begins. In form, then, if not in material, there is a suggestion of the self-contained tales in *The Painted Bird* and the fragments that make up *Steps*.

Each person in *The Future Is Ours, Comrade* is presented through what we are supposed to take as his own words, although, later, in *No Third Path*, Kosinski admits that he uses "condensed and composite" interviews and that "the subjectivity of the quoted comments" is filtered through "the subjectivity of the author." This implies that the reported speeches are artificial concoctions which, even if one accepts the substantive truth of the interviews, are designed for a particular effect.

Certainly, Kosinski manipulates his material in other, more obvious ways, uses journalistic tricks which are also novelistic devices. The two most in evidence, both ironic, are juxtaposition and the too-neat tagline closing off an anecdote.

Gerald Weales. HC. Oct., 1972. pp. 3–4

Kosinski's dramatic framework remains the struggle toward personal identity complicated by his own acceptance of a new land, a new language, and consequently a "new" self. His dramatic centers continue to be the self, that mysterious and impenetrable entity, and collectivism, that increasingly omnipresent and modern reality. The radical secularism of his art triumphs only when his sense of self is ascendant; otherwise it traps him in a kind of collective impressionism from which he cannot extricate himself. His genius lies in his ability to recreate an elemental sense of primitive and dark reality inherent in his violent and sexual images. From this dark well his art must be drawn. Yet it is a dangerous and frightful well into which to descend, for we who admire him are aware of the stark and terrible contours of his unrelenting imagination.

Samuel Coale. Critique. 14, 3, 1973. pp. 36–7

Today, nearly ten years after its appearance, *The Painted Bird* continues to arouse fascinated horror, outrage and concern. Yet none of these responses is equal to its complexity. . . .

   The Painted Bird is narrated by an unnamed boy who wanders during World War Two from village to village in Eastern Europe, suffering, witnessing, and inflicting atrocious cruelty. In all this, the novel evinces a high degree of fictional consciousness. This consciousness is explicit in an extremely interesting essay, the "Notes of the Author on *The Painted Bird*," which appears at the close of the German edition of *The Painted Bird* and has been published in English by Scienta-Factum in New York (1967). In it Kosinski enlists writers like Proust, Valéry, and Artaud to organize his theoretical account of composing his novel. Their names furnish the work with the right resonances and the affinities which are its due. These writers, whose work is marked by a thematic concern with the act of writing, evoke a poetic consciousness essentially Romantic. Kosinski's novel shares in this tradition and helps define it further. This consciousness, for one thing, finds its correlative in the genre of the fictional autobiography, one, moreover, which affirms the constitutive activity of the act of writing in the self it narrates by concluding with the origin of this very enterprise of writing an autobiography.

Stanley Corngold. Mosaic. 6, 4, 1973. p. 154

Reading *The Devil Tree* one is aware of those things that Kosinski does with consummate skill: the mode that lies somewhere between Kafka and our own sense of daily reality; the flat, underplayed, uncomprehending style; the use of a kind of narrative parataxis, all of those short, unrelated bits of narrative, much of whose force lies in the art with which they are detached from each other. . . . It is a unique fictional method, so starkly inimitable that anyone who had ever read anything by Kosinski would know who had written those lines. The narrative parataxis, moreover, is a marvelously expressive device for Kosinski's purposes in *The Devil Tree*: wishing to show the rootlessness of his central character, he is able to move him from Manhattan to Nepal without transition or modulation; wishing presumably to show the particular shallowness of his quest for sensation, he is able to show unfulfilled sex, unmotivated drug use, and unresolved encounter sessions by the rhythms and omissions of his narrative segments.

Kosinski evidently intends for his novel to embody American myth and American reality, American dreams and American limitations, which means that *The Devil Tree* aims in a somewhat different direction from *Steps*, which locates all of its scarifying brutality in no particular place, and *Being There*, which projects a fatuous extension of American power without much attempt to place that movement in the solid texture of American reality. What such a purpose requires is a certain consistency of mode. Yet the book moves among a variety of modes: at one time it is neopicaresque, the central figure a bemused invisible man in the world of petty functionaries; at other times it seems a rather unfocused and old-fashioned piece of satiric realism; and at still other times it is cut loose altogether from social fact, in a country of the mind like Kafka's *Amerika*. So it is that its import is diffuse, its ability to move the reader is intermittent, its parts are better than its whole, and its voice is greater than its vision.

Philip Stevick. *PR*. No. 2, 1974. p. 305

KUNITZ, STANLEY (1905–   )

Most of Stanley Kunitz's poetry is in two concentrated books, *The Testing-Tree*, just out and green, and his familiar *Selected Poems*, published in 1959. There is a difference, not just in lapse of time; the books are landmarks of the old and the new style. The smoke has blown off. The old Delphic voice has learned to speak "words that cats and dogs can understand." Others have grown clear, it is the drift of the age, but the powerful manner in which it is done here goes beyond my shrewd-ness.

I have read through the *Selected Poems* many times and at inter-vals, marking fine lines with a pencil. I have cut my way, and earned my exercise. The more ambitious poems are mostly in the toughest and densest style of the thirties and forties, and have the heroic concentra-tion used forcibly by Allen Tate, Hart Crane, Dylan Thomas, William Empson, some of Auden and Roethke. Kunitz stands with the fiercest and most musical. Sometimes I find when I have worried out his deep meanings, the surface will again grow troubled. . . . What remains is the passionate gnarl. The slow, clinging fog and the stark bang of syllables are not in Kunitz but mostly in the reader's mind.

The Testing-Tree throws away the once redoubtable armor. All is unencumbered and trustful. One reads from cover to cover with the ease of reading good prose fiction, reads with such fresh confidence that even Kunitz's versions of Osip Mandelstam, darkest of the realistic masters, seem as open as Whitman.

Robert Lowell. *NYT*. March 21, 1971. p. 1

Stanley Kunitz has had to go away further to exile, and to stay away longer, than perhaps any other major poet of his generation. *The Testing-Tree*, Kunitz's first book in the thirteen years since the publication of his Pulitzer Prize-winning *Selected Poems*, resounds with the upheaval of a spiritual recluse coming back to the world, to voice, after a long self-banishment: the voice surprised at its own return from muteness with intense shocks of awakening like those of a body amazed to have ex-humed itself from a premature burial. . . .

Kunitz's repatriations in his new book are wrenchings of the "crea-ture self" ("he is not broken but endures") out of its stony sleep of slow recovery from the ravishment—which drove his friend Mark Rothko to suicide—by the worlds of country, family, "adversaries." His recovery occurs with the violence and rage of a self-disinterment, no less than a full return at the age of sixty-four to the "fugues of appetite" of his lost youth.

Laurence Lieberman. *YR*.
Autumn, 1971. pp. 82–3

In a clear sense Akhmatova was lucky with her translator [in *Poems of Akhmatova*]. Stanley Kunitz turns out to be a person who is spiritually and technically qualified for the task. If he makes mistakes, the mistakes are more in technical details than in conveying the spirit of the poems chosen. And these mistakes, if they do lead the reader astray, at least do not take him in the opposite direction. . . . I repeat, this is a good book, but I would like to think that it is only the beginning. For the successes of this particular tandem are quite obvious, and I speak of the oversights which have occurred with a certain harshness, precisely because they are in such contrast to the generally high level of the work.

Joseph Brodsky. *NYR*. Aug. 9, 1973. p. 10

LARDNER, RING (1885–1933)

Lardner's great force in portraying the baseball world lay in his recognition that its essence, instead of being mythical or serious, was indeed play. It was not a play element in culture, but culture as play. Totally comprehending its meaning and fully committing himself to it, he accomplished the difficult task of humorously inverting his language and perspective, thereby equaling the genuine social reality he recognized in the world of sports. Freed from symbolic strategies of representing the serious reality behind the face of the game, Lardner gained the fine economy of having the game as it was. Thus, his players, except for his central characters, are "real," bearing their historic names, personalities, and legends. And his bats, instead of being the phallic symbols which Malamud's characters swing [in *The Natural*], seem always to be genuine Louisville Sluggers.

It is not his world which is fictive, but his narrator, whose language must perpetually render the world of baseball not as his fiction but as his life—that form of childhood pleasure indulged by the adult society where, from within the confines of the ball park, adults both in the stands and on the field helplessly convert loss, despair, and boredom into direct and overt gains of pleasure. In the process of such a major conversion, it is small wonder that Lardner converted, and thereby redeemed, the epistolary novel, which Richardson had boldly used to keep middle-class virgins precarious maidens, into a form for keeping adult children from becoming mere adults.

James M. Cox. *VQR*. Spring, 1970. p. 325

Lardner was a superb master of the spoken language and he created a long line of characters whose idiom was recorded with great precision, while the frequently vain and empty man behind the words stood forth sharply revealed. Lardner had a wild, delightful, manic quality that could erupt into nonsensical laughter. . . . In the early part of his career, this language gift was employed in drawing comic pictures of small-town people. His first collection of stories, *You Know Me Al* (1916), is a series of letters written by a baseball player Jack Keefe to his best friend. These letters capture perfectly the half-literate Middle Western speech of the protagonist, who is gullible, stupid, conceited, and totally ignoble. Hilariously funny, the tales can almost sicken the reader with their picture of human depravity. Lardner followed this book with many others, among the best being *Gullible's Travels*, in which Mr. Gullible recounts in the exact language of his Middle-Western world the tortures of a vacation trip that he and his wife make. . . .

As Lardner's career developed, he moved further and further from the provincial life which he began by depicting with precise ironic truth and he wrote more and more about the world of suburbanites and of life on Long Island, in New York City, and in Florida, but he never lost his skill with language, his comic sense of incongruity, or his pessimistic despair.

> C. Hugh Holman in *The Comic Imagination*
> *in American Literature*, edited by Louis D.
> Rubin, Jr. (Rutgers). 1973. pp. 250–1

LATTIMORE, RICHMOND (1906–   )

The high stance and the grand manner are a distressingly large element of this 30-year sequence [*Poems from Three Decades*] but, happily, not all of it. Spare, hard-eyed, tersely spoken kinds of observation crop up now and then, and these signals, momentary at first, become something to watch for. The vigil is long but finally rewarding. To follow the progress of these three decades of work is to witness not merely a parade of poems from this year or that but a process of reduction and discard. Revelation follows upon surprise: somewhere in the professorial purview of Richmond Lattimore there lurks a little Caliban-shaped figure who wants to tell it straight and like it is.

When this slouching *Doppelgänger* gets going, the rhetorical bubbles break, things replace concepts and the scene observed is not merely emblematic of some idea but alive in its own details. Poems like "Game Resumed," "Scene from the Working Class," "The Last Train out of White River Junction" show the man as the poet he is and can be: sane, tough, graceful and on the lam from the "bright captures" and "wing-shimmers" of all of his summery sestinas.

> John Malcolm Brinnin. *NYT*.
> Nov. 19, 1972. p. 48

The range of Lattimore's comment includes both Troy and Vietnam, small-town America seen from an airplane and Elpenor's identity crisis in Circe's cellar. But Lattimore is most comfortable in the occasional poem—more specifically, the academic address poem. One wants to hear him at Phi Beta Kappa or commencement ceremonies, for he fulfills such tasks perfectly: lucid on first hearing yet never trite, defending no insidious establishment, affording the young none but existential truth. . . .

If Lattimore finds himself in the same abyss as other poets, he falters by deciding that singing would be beside the point. And so one cannot point to anything wrong, certainly never to anything bad, in his poetry; but something is definitely missing, or at least missing in the new poems here [*Poems from Three Decades*]. . . .

Lattimore wants neither to condemn nor to celebrate, but to tame. He has the proper respect for our inscrutable savagery and our exhilarating inner demons, but he distrusts or ignores what he cannot ultimately domesticate. That this taming process is no glib academic evasion, but a necessary act of hardening and surviving for Lattimore, is best expressed in the early poem "Invictus," which, in a survey of his career, stands out so outrageously as the most intensely realized of all his poems that one wonders why it is not famous on its own. In this vision, and a few other early lyrics, perhaps Lattimore has earned the right to be as dry as he has been in recent years. . . .

Robert Weisberg. Parnassus. Spring–
Summer, 1973. pp. 166–7

LEVERTOV, DENISE (1923–   )

In her newest book, *The Sorrow Dance*, Denise Levertov beautifully demonstrates the mastery over her medium—words and the silences between them—which she has been able to achieve. . . .

She has an instinctive feeling for shaping a poem, letting out the lines easily. Her poems seem to flow effortlessly, nothing jars, you cannot imagine them contrived or rounded any other way. She knows the rhythm of the language, and when to end a line, when to end a stanza. How does she know so well when to say and when to stop saying? It's a kind of tact unspoken in the placing of each word, each line and stanza.

Miss Levertov has learned a great deal from [William Carlos] Williams, and pays tribute in the poem "For Floss." But she has her own voice, and a European discipline underlying an American idiom and expansiveness.

Kathleen Spivack. Poetry.
May, 1968. pp. 123–4

The Sorrow Dance, by Denise Levertov, is a striking collection, and one which is a welcome addition to her already significant body of work. Her rhythms here are unerring, her voice true and original. She forces her

reader to read at her pace, to emphasize the words she wants emphasized, to participate in the poem. . . . Word by word there is transformation as her poems take shape. Her voice is delicate, feminine, but
rugged, not the voice of the ladies Roethke saw as stamping a tiny foot
against God.

In her best work she creates a concrete physical world. The structure of her precise imagery becomes the thematic center of her work,
and she instinctively knows when it is necessary to stop talking. She
does not burden us with comment, does not underestimate her audience's ability to taste and see, or to think.

William Heyen. *SoR*. Spring, 1970. pp. 547–8

The contrast between Denise Levertov and the women poets of the early
part of the century is startling. In comparison with her poetry, theirs
makes being a woman in itself at the best a form of neurasthenia. Denise
Levertov writes at ease as a woman about love, marriage, motherhood,
deaths in the family. The universal round of domestic life is transformed
by the sensibility and moved into the transcendent setting of "wholeness,
harmony, and radiance," yet this is only a portion of her work, a group
of subjects lying naturally to hand and left easily for other subjects as
diverse as can be—poems of social protest, of nature, of meditation and
contemplation, of vision. The last three categories are the experience of
a visionary at home in the world, with a wider range of knowledge and
more different kinds of experience than most poets, let alone most
women poets in the past. It's almost invidious to so accentuate her sex,
but it is very significant because her poetry, in a far different sense from
that of the distraught contributors to *Pagan*, is a poetry of sexual liberation of a human person moving freely in the world.

Kenneth Rexroth. *American Poetry in the
Twentieth Century* (Herder and
Herder). 1971. p. 163

[*To Stay Alive*] resolves itself into a rehearsal of common twentieth-
century experience, but is unaware of the fact. It is as if the poet's self
intervenes in an ongoing horrible process, needs to bear witness, and
needs self-immolated people as lights "to show us the dark we are in."
One point of view would say bluntly that this is the crux of ego-tripping
liberal consciousness-raising. Who is this "we" that needs burning
human bodies for enlightenment? How come nonrevolutionary liberals
are awakening to the nature of totalitarianism as late as 1968? . . .

But, immediately, one feels reluctant to continue like this: the poet
is in genuine anguish and that is to be respected, especially since suicidal
impulse is always encroaching. Part IV of the first "Entr'acte" is an

instance of her strength: the careful record of thinking and feeling processes, placed within careful intonational controls. But this is immediately followed by the kind of insistence on traditional universals which
withdraws attention. . . .

A chronicle of political coming of age depends on accurate understanding of the global attack on totalitarianism—*To Stay Alive* is too
parochial to convince through such detail and analysis.

Eric Mottram. *Parnassus*. Fall–
Winter, 1972. pp. 158–9

Any new work by Denise Levertov should awaken the reader's anticipa-
tion. No poet of her generation, it seems, not even Robert Bly, has been
more involved in political activism or the anti-war movement and they
have naturally enough dominated her writing in the last few years. Yet
this involvement, which she has defended in essays and prefaces with
eloquence, has not fundamentally damaged her poetry—though some
may think so—by engaging it with public themes. Miss Levertov is a
poet of flexibility, depth and imaginative growth. She has become one of
those figures around whom a large part of our sense of what has occurred in American poetry in the past fifteen or so years revolves.

Footprints is Miss Levertov's tenth book; it picks up threads of her
work which had been partially set aside in favor of the urgency of
political commitment prevailing in *Relearning the Alphabet* and *To
Stay Alive*. It is, however, false and misleading to compartmentalize her
poetry, with one place for a more rhetorical kind of writing, *engagé*, and
another given to the sacred speech of the true imagination. The poet
herself would deny any division of this sort, for in her opinion the
artist's involvement with public affairs is part of a total involvement with
the life he lives and the world in which he lives it.

Ralph J. Mills, Jr. *Parnassus*. Spring–
Summer, 1973. p. 219

The Poet in the World is an interesting, uneven, occasionally exasperating and always sincere collage of essays, criticism, fiction, political
statement, articles on teaching and on other poets.

Of its five sections—"Work and Inspiration," "Life At War," "The
Untaught Teacher," "Perhaps Fiction" and "Other Writers"—by far the
most interesting is the first. Miss Levertov can, and does, write lucidly of
the blunders, prizes and tenacities of the poet sweating out her poem;
and her discussion of other writers (Creeley, Williams and Duncan are
those she most admires), though highly subjective, is alive and uncompromising. She is at her most happily typical when she takes on the
questions of the nature of poetry, and when she describes poetry in

terms of a *translation*, a word defined in her 1865 Webster's as "being conveyed from one place to another, remove to heaven without dying." . . .

But that earlier word "uncompromising" shades uncomfortably, in other sections, into the sort of single-mindedness more admirable in a crusader than in a writer. However compassionate or enraged she may be, the difference with which a writer wears her rue must be the evidence of an openness to the unwelcome intrusion of the conditional, to that complexity which is always cutting down the self-indulgence of the simplistic. In Levertov's prose, this problem is mixed up with the absence of that sense of proportion which is humor. Irony, slapstick, self-mockery and wit are temperamentally uncongenial to her. Unwilling to distinguish between that healthy skepticism which ultimately is the protection against cynicism's dry rot, once she quits prosody, her conclusions are often accompanied by a disconcerting overkill.

Josephine Jacobsen. NR. Jan. 26, 1974. p. 30

LEWIS, SINCLAIR (1885–1951)

Many critics have pointed out that [Lewis's] middle-class world was a nightmare world; at times his vision resembles that in *The Waste Land* of people walking meaninglessly around in a ring, or the Orwellian image of drawn and cowed people in an Airstrip One. But his florid, loud-mouthed representatives of the class which spins not and toils chiefly at salesmanship proved to be richly varied and full of life and gusto. Lewis was never happier than when a Marduc or a Pickerbaugh, a Windrip or a Blausser, had sprung full-blown into existence in the world of his imagination and begun to wax eloquent. These were characters to be treated with satiric humor; some of them were menaces, some of them were conspiring to destroy all freedom and individuality, but except in his gloomier moments, Lewis never believed that they would succeed. He kept his faith in the American dream. . . .

D. J. Dooley. The Art of Sinclair Lewis
(Nebraska). 1967. pp. xv–xvi

The continuing debate over Lewis' ambivalence—his savage ridicule as against his "happy endings," his deadly effects as against his protestations of sympathy—is perhaps due to the fact that Lewis was a humorist first and a satirist only secondarily. Furthermore, he was attempting to transform the brief hit-and-run method of newspaper humor into the sustained form of the novel—a feat at which no one but Mark Twain had really succeeded before him. . . .

It is not necessary to exclude other views in order to view Sinclair Lewis as a humorist. But it helps to clarify our conception of his total achievement to see him as a novelist working with the journalistic and folk materials of native American humor to arrive at a culminating expression of that humor as it had developed in the upper West. Like much of the humor of that region, Lewis' humor reflects the contradictory pulls of regional loyalty and realistic clear-sightedness, of pride and complaint, of a dream and a disillusionment with that dream.

James C. Austin in *American Dreams,*
American Nightmares, edited by
David Madden (Southern
Illinois). 1970. pp. 104–5

Lewis' leaden irony about style is misplaced, for it calls attention to the fact that his impulses were sociological rather than novelistic. Like some sociologists, Lewis used the technique of bombarding the reader with data transferred bodily from his "research" notebooks. Thus the inordinate length and tediousness of his work, and thus its popularity with readers who honor what they think is fact and reality, rather than mere fiction. Yet the order of "fact" that Lewis selected lacks even sociological validity. His Gopher Prairie is not true to the historical midwestern village of the years 1910–1920, nor is his Zenith true to the historical reality of the small American city just after the First World War. In each instance, the truth is far more complex, at once more appalling and more interesting, than Lewis' method of burlesque indicated.

John McCormick. *The Middle*
Distance (Free). 1971. p. 81

It has often been observed that one of the great contributions of [*Babbitt*] was that it succeeded in naming an American phenomenon, and the act of naming, of course, has always been one of the primary functions of the poet or artist conceived in the widest sense. By this I do not mean that all Lewis did was to catch the essence of the smug, complacent booster or joiner, the self-satisfied and unimaginative small-town businessman. This he did, of course, but if that were the limit of his achievement, *Babbitt* would be to us today a faded novel, its chief character a mere curiosity of second-rate American literature. The truth is that Lewis had hit upon, and long struggled to understand, a deeply rooted disease of the American spirit. . . .

It has often been remarked that he could never work up a fair and complete portrait of his fellow Americans because he despised them so heartily that he had no detached perspective on them. But he was no Jonathan Swift. Indeed, he was an imperfect satirist precisely because he could never really hate the Babbitts and Elmer Gantrys he went after, but was always searching for something good to come from them, a search which, nevertheless, continually proved futile.

George H. Douglas. *Nation*.
May 22, 1972. p. 661

There is a level of accomplishment in Lewis's five major novels that cannot be explained in terms of the way he used the tools of his trade as a popular novelist (although it must be remembered that he, more than any other twentieth-century novelist, is responsible for developing those tools). He conceived heroes who became essential reference points for students of American culture. He wrote at least four novels (*Main Street, Babbitt, Arrowsmith*, and *Elmer Gantry*) that are *tours de force* and that have not been outclassed by any subsequent novels on the same topics. He successfully responded to and caught the mood of his times, a point that is underscored by the first Mrs. Lewis who asks and answers: "Were the 1920's really the Jazz Age except for a few? Most Americans at that time lived more like Sinclair Lewis characters; there was more substance to life than Fitzgerald's glossy version." Our idea of the 1920s as an era is likely to be influenced by Lewis's depiction of it for a long time to come. And the range of his interest, the primal quality of his imagination, and the sense of plight that is pervasive in his writing, all in combination with a style that however erratic nonetheless fits the clattering internal-combustion society he describes, add up to an achievement that demands, yet defies, appreciation.

Perhaps the best way of all to deal with Sinclair Lewis is to think of him as a one-man *Sturm und Drang* movement; such a conception would at least allow for a justification, in terms of art, of the strong nationalistic and folk element, the adolescent fervor, the restlessness, the agony of repressed passion and the spiritual struggles in his writing. It would also enable one to accept a critical fact about Lewis that might otherwise be difficult to swallow; that he is a law unto himself.

James Lundquist. *Sinclair Lewis*
(Ungar). 1973. pp. 85–6

LONDON, JACK (1876–1916)

The writings of London which have shown the greatest vitality are ... his books about the Far North. Products of a winter in the Klondike during the great rush, experienced when London had not yet started on his writing career, they constitute not only the earliest but the best of London's contribution to letters. They are great adventure stories partly because they catch the spirit of the last (and the most insane) mass rush towards a new frontier, partly because they embody London's perceptive view of the difference between the wilds and civilization. They appeal because they embody every man's desire to get away from daily routine, to gamble on a quick success, and to cope with nature in its more rugged aspects.

Whether London's hero is a man, or a man disguised as a dog, he is full of vigor, there is a sparkle in his eyes, and he escapes the dull features of a humdrum existence. So it is that there continues to be a steady world audience for *The Son of the Wolf*, *The Call of the Wild*, *White Fang*, short stories such as "Love of Life" and "To Build a Fire," and even *Burning Daylight* and *Smoke Bellew,* in spite of their weak endings. London's Yukon fiction reveals him at his best.

Franklin Walker in *Essays on American Literature in Honor of Jay Hubbell,* edited by Clarence Gohdes (Duke). 1967. p. 261

Judging by the number of his titles that remain in print, some in editions of quite recent vintage, Jack London is still widely read more than a half-century after his death. His stories and novels of adventure in the Far North have lost none of their vigor, and his depiction of the "dominant primordial beast" in man still touches the American psyche—the Russian psyche as well, since for years he has been as popular in that country as any other American writer.

But if London's reputation rests upon his swashbuckling tales of men and animals battling each other and nature, he was considerably more than a mere storyteller. He was one of the most ardent and controversial Socialists of turn-of-the-century America, whose philosophy was a fascinating and unresolved jumble of Nietzsche and Marx. He was a bitter critic of the American middle and upper classes, yet he cruised the world in an extravagant yacht, the *Snark*, and built himself a $70,000 mansion in California. He wrote about the underside of society in which as a young man he had lived, but his popular success as a writer enabled him to move among the well-situated and powerful.

Nowhere in London's fiction are the complexities and contradictions of his life and mind more intimately revealed than in *Martin Eden*, the most personal of his novels. It is a curious and in some respects unsatisfactory work, but it has all the power of his more popular fiction and a poignancy with which he is not ordinarily associated.

Jonathan Yardley. *NR*. June 2, 1973. p. 31

LOWELL, ROBERT (1917–   )

I am not faulting Lowell's characters because they are not true-to-life, as the cliché has it, but because they lack theatrical validity. They are somewhat hedged in by his virtues—his intellectuality, his irony, his sense of language, his emphasis on theme, his preoccupation with the major concerns of our or any time. It may be that this deficiency will limit him as a playwright, not let him break through to a large audience where he can work on several levels at once. Even so, it is already clear, on the evidence of the two "imitations" [*Phaedra* and *Prometheus Bound*] and *The Old Glory* that Lowell is one of the most impressive dramatists to turn up in the 1960's.

Gerald Weales. *The Jumping-Off Place*
(Macmillan—N.Y.). 1969. pp. 179–80

The fact is that in this book [*Near the Ocean*] Mr. Lowell is concerned less with the mystery of man's destiny than with the dilemma of the times in which the poet finds himself, or, perhaps more accurately, the times in which the poet seems to be lost. Clearly Mr. Lowell wishes to interpret our time. His desire for a way is an anguish for which one feels sympathy and respect. His agony and his sense of inadequacy and loss are truly what hold this book together. Yet his is not the agony of a Juvenal watching the wanton destruction of something fine by men of egregious appetites for the material and the carnal, but rather that of a man who cannot decide, who cannot make up his mind, who sees nothing to believe in, who is forced back on his own reserves and judges these to be too slender. Mr. Lowell searches the present without understanding and without at all liking what he sees. He searches the past without comfort; all he finds there are ancestors whom he cannot follow, whose love he has lost or somehow forfeited, and for whom he has found no substitute.

F. H. Griffin Taylor. *SwR.*
Spring, 1969. pp. 300–1

[Lowell] has moved with his culture. Like earlier New England poets, his sensibility first found itself in opposition; but unlike them, he has been forced by the rapid changes in American life repeatedly to reconstitute his principles of opposition, and thus always to define freshly his relation to his fellows. He has developed three basic directions for his work: a critique of public action and attitude in America; a critique of the state of the individual ego; and a sense of the historical, religious, mythological, and literary contexts which provide perspectives whereby to understand the possibilities of public or private life at any time. As his society has shifted during the last twenty-five years, Lowell has emphasized various combinations of these. . . .

His work, in short, has been a mirror to his culture, supplying society with elements for advance. He has criticized the poets of his generation whose "writings seem divorced from culture." Culture, he came to see, provides the necessary background for art: neither, without the other, can endure. Constantly updating old poems for inclusion in new volumes, he moves with culture and refuses to let society catch up with him.

Jay Martin. Robert Lowell
(Minnesota). 1970. pp. 44, 46

It is this successful marriage of ancient and modern that makes *Prometheus Bound*, like *The Vanity of Human Wishes*, a truly autonomous work of art, and not merely an interesting footnote to Robert Lowell's own poetry, as certain "imitations" are. Yet I am tempted to see the language of the play not only as a successful immediate tool, but as an indispensable stage in Lowell's stylistic development; its atemporality, its ability to incorporate surrealistic vividness into sentences fluid enough for the stage, all prepare the way for the weird yet comprehensive style of *Notebook, 1967–68*. *Prometheus Bound* in turn seems to derive from the recovered grand style of *Near the Ocean*—a most appropriate interplay, for the two original books undertake an inquiry into the first causes of our civilization, more than a little Aeschylean in its scope.

Alan Williamson. Poetry. Jan., 1970. p. 282

In *Life Studies*, which marked the beginning of what has been called confessional poetry, Lowell's techniques of self-discovery exclude myth; he concentrates on the personal and intimate episode, and his language is direct and sometimes colloquial. Important as this volume is as an expression of Lowell's new voice and his growing power to elicit from the absurd remark or the pathetic incident a link to the deepest levels of human suffering, and vital as it was in influencing younger poets, such as Sylvia Plath and Anne Sexton, it represents only one phase of his development as a poet. Lowell has gone on in later works to combine the mythical method of his early poetry with the direct and sometimes shocking psychological revelations of *Life Studies* and, in so doing, has reached beyond the compulsive inner probings of that book for a deep and intimate knowledge of human feelings as they are manifested in the larger realm of natural, social, or political life.

Lillian Feder. *Ancient Myth in Modern Poetry* (Princeton). 1971. p. 408

While all these aspects of *Notebook 1967–68* recommend notice for their own sakes, one comes away from Lowell's latest volume with the conviction that he has, in effect, drawn together, in both content and technique, the essential unity of his whole work. One of Randall Jarrell's early reviews of Lowell . . . speaks of the "conflict of opposites" in his work, a conflict between what Jarrell calls "the stasis or inertia of the stubborn self" and "everything that is free or open, that grows or is willing to change." Jerome Mazzaro in his book on Lowell sees the same dichotomy in Nietzschian terms, a division between the Apollonian and Dionysian drives in man. The Robert Lowell who emerges at the end of the 1960s still offers no reconciliation between the two forces that he sees as constituting the nature of man, but neither has he abandoned the search for it. In the larger sense, all of Lowell's verse is "confessional" in that he has found the truest metaphor for the division of the nature of man to be within himself—though the same tensions extend outward to embrace American, and particularly New England, historical predecessors; his own family, both ancestors and now descendants; his literary colleagues; and, finally, the whole of twentieth-century society.

George Lensing. *SoR.* Winter, 1971. p. 344

It is impossible to make the transition . . . to Robert Lowell's revised *Notebook* without insisting that in fact there is no just transition, that the world of Lowell's poems is utterly more engrossing, dazzling, breathtaking even than could be believed on the evidence of his previous volumes. The *Notebook*'s sonnets are incredibly audacious and roomy in their willingness, their eagerness to speak about all the things a fully alive person should care about. . . . The speaker of *Notebook* is more nearly always "half-balmy," devoted to "unrealism" (Lowell earlier called it "surrealism") which is "about" something, though always obliquely and often puzzlingly.

The last adverb is meant seriously, since many of these poems resist the intelligence very successfully indeed, sometimes in a manner similar to moments in the *Cantos* when Pound is muttering on about something into which we're not quite let; other times when Lowell entertains what he calls some "bent generalization" that lodges in the mind, yet whose precise weight doesn't reveal itself. The poems ask to be read again and yet again; never have I moved through a book the second or third time with less of the feeling of familiarity, confident that I'd "done that one" before.

William H. Pritchard. *Poetry*.
Dec., 1971. pp. 166–7

On the one hand, the will to discredit and destroy the past; on the other, prophetic denunciation of or sorrow over that destruction. Our past destroys us, but we must not lose the past. Here, it seems to me, is the tragic center of Lowell's work, the moral stance that dominates his later writing, brings the political and the personal into a single perspective, and perhaps accounts for the elegiac tone that, in *For the Union Dead* and *Near the Ocean* particularly, has largely displaced the erupting violence of *Lord Weary's Castle*. . . . Something has been resolved, if only in the sense that the poems of these late volumes admit of no resolution, whether in religion, in psychotherapy, or in a moral understanding of history. These things remain important, in their way; but their way is not, as in "At the Indian Killer's Grave," to transform circumstances or to provide answers. The past is irrevocable, as it was for Milton in his later years; as with Milton, human history is a record of disasters, and the problem is to survive, remaining sensitive to both personal and public terror but resisting those forms of destruction that can be resisted. . . .

Lowell's real subject in these later poems is, finally, the difficulty of remaining individually human and morally responsible in a world that offers increasingly compelling occasions for surrendering either or both.

George W. Nitchie. *SoR*. Winter,
1972. pp. 126, 130

[In *The Dolphin*] Lowell no longer quite succeeds in transforming his life into art, and his revelations, sometimes embarrassingly personal, sometimes boring, should indeed have remained "sealed like private letters." Here, if anywhere, the famed confessional mode, inaugurated by Lowell's beautiful *Life Studies* of 1959, reaches its point of no return. . . . The complex web of realistic images and evocative proper names that characterized the *Life Studies* poems is replaced by flat statement: "I cannot play or sleep," "We have our child." The lines give us no particular image of the speaker; he is simply what Yeats called "the bundle of accident and incoherence that sits down to breakfast," a real-life Lowell addressing his real-life wife. . . .

For Lizzie and Harriet contains, in revised and rearranged form, what may loosely be called the "love poems" of the *Notebooks*. *History* incorporates the remaining *Notebook* poems, again in revised form, and adds 80 new topical sonnets. The organization is now chronological:

History begins with Biblical themes and ends with Lowell's most recent history, the book's final sonnets thus overlapping with those in *For Lizzie and Harriet*.

Future bibliographers will have a monstrous time with these books. Since neither the *Notebooks* nor *History* have alphabetical indexes, it is often difficult to find which *Notebook* poem turns up where in the new volumes. Titles have been changed, sequences altered, lines from one poem stuck in the middle of another, and it takes a good bit of detective work plus some simple arithmetic to figure out that everything in *Notebook* (1970) is used again somewhere in the two "new" volumes.

In itself, this procedure is perfectly acceptable. Lowell, as Stanley Kunitz has said, "doesn't so much write his poems as rewrite them . . . he is never done with a poem." The impulse to rework and improve a poem is surely admirable—Yeats, say, did it all the time—but the depressing truth about the revisions in *History* and *For Lizzie and Harriet* is that they almost invariably make the poem in question less effective.

Marjorie G. Perloff. NR. July 7
and 14, 1973. pp. 24–6

The casual reader will hardly bother to search the varying editions of *Notebook* for Lowell's changes. But to do so is a lesson in sharpening and clarification: "Mary Stuart" and "Revenants" are only two examples out of many in which final success has been brilliantly won. Lowell goes as far back as *Lord Weary's Castle* to recast his earlier rhetoric into barer, demotic speech. He has condensed some of his controversial "imitations" of poets from other languages—notably his Sappho, his Villon, his Heine dying in Paris—into definitive Robert Lowell poems.

In all this work of the last six years, he can be seen exercising and renewing his power over the basic line of English poetry most congenial to him, the Marlovian-Shakespearean pentameter. During a difficult period of his life, safety-belted into his fourteen-line stanza, he has been playing with it, deepening his grasp, seeing what it can accommodate in the way of mundane fact, prose loosening, supple understatement.

Walter Clemons. Nwk. July 16, 1973. p. 86

Each edition of *Notebook* carried a clear warning that in Lowell's usage, "plot" was an unusually capacious notion: "Single poems and sections are opportunist and inspired by impulse. Accident threw up subjects, and the plot swallowed them—famished for human chances." . . . Which enables us, leaving all sorts of questions unanswered, at least to begin answering one question we've posed already: what sort of game Lowell is playing with us. We can begin by saying that it's an exceptionally *intimate* game: we are to be with him, we *have* to be with him, as he runs a distracted hand through his hair, leafing through his old files and trying to see what his recent writing amounts to; where and how, if at all, it "adds up." As much with *History* as with any of the *Notebooks* we are really left to do the adding up for ourselves—*if we can*, the poet himself having virtually admitted that for his part he can't. And so, for "intimate" in this sense we might as well read "democratic." From that demotic idiom which has become, since Williams, ever more *de rigueur* for American poets, Lowell is excluded because of his early schooling in the drumming decasyllable, "the mighty line"; his coquettish habits of publishing are his way of achieving by other means a sort of unbuttoned welcome of the reader in the workshop, something that other American poets have achieved through a low-key idiom that he's debarred from.

All the same, "coquettish" is an abusive word, and it has to be. For as readers we just don't know where we are, or what is expected of us. For instance, if from one point of view these procedures are democratic, in another light they are just the opposite, for the poems seem to come to us under the lordly rubric, "Never apologize, never explain."

Donald Davie. *Parnassus*. Fall–
Winter, 1973. pp. 51–2

McCARTHY, MARY (1912–   )

[McCarthy's] work is about the painful mixed blessing of freedom for her kind of people—for intellectuals—and in particular, about how hard it has been for intellectuals in our time to behave decently and humanly. For to be free and clever has often meant only to be able to escape from difficult, limiting reality into the realm of flattering abstractions. And yet—for I have said that to speak of what she dislikes is to speak of only half her subject—if she shows what makes her kind go wrong, she shows just as vividly what makes them go right. She shows that sometimes, even in intellectuals free to please themselves, there arises a love for reality that is greater than love of self. This development, because it means that the self must be willing to suffer for something it values more than its own ease, can be one of the moving and beautiful events of a human life—it can be heroic.

At any rate, the conflict between these two tendencies of the mind is at the center of all Miss McCarthy's novels. Because this conflict is her own, her reports on it have the variety, complexity, and intensity of personal experience. But because the freedom to live by ideas, ideas which may lead away from the real as well as toward it, is what distinguishes the whole class of twentieth-century intellectuals, her tales of the troubled Mary McCarthy heroine have developed naturally into social satire.

Irvin Stock. *Mary McCarthy*
(Minnesota). 1968. p. 9

To read Mary McCarthy you have to be constantly awake. There is no filler that can be skipped, or relaxed winks to the reader assuring him he needn't work too hard for the next page or two; whatever you miss is to your disadvantage, and most of the essays [in *The Writing on the Wall, and Other Essays*] need to be reread, preferably after a second look at the particular book under consideration.

What keeps one awake is the sound of a voice always talking *to* you, varying itself in pitch and delivery as the subject demands. This is not to praise her for lively shock-value, as in the phrase "I'll bet Mary McCarthy would do a job on *that* one." In fact readers with the image foremost of the Lady Mary as wicked wasp will find it quite irrelevant to this book; whatever cleverness there is, and there is plenty, operates in the service of literature.

William H. Pritchard. *HdR.*
Summer, 1970. p. 372

The big news about Miss McCarthy's new book [*Birds of America*] would seem, anywhere in the course of reading it, to be its warmth. A novelist noted for her use of acid and vitriol has here produced, not precisely a novel but a work, didactic in tone, whose principal characters are a loving son and a lovable mother, in which even divorced husbands are likeable, the ugliness of modernity is hateful, and home, art, old days, old ways, lovely and to be valued. . . .

Not till [the end] does the realization begin seeping into the reader's mind of what Miss McCarthy may really have been about here. Far from extolling established values, she has destroyed them, by putting in their place a new archetype: the woman of the future. . . . The whole of Miss McCarthy's career—rebel against religious orthodoxy, sexual nonconformist, intellectual and political iconoclast, falls into place: *Birds of America* is a parable of her development. Louder than the loudest protests, clearer than the coolest psychological logic, this warm, readable narrative liberates the cold 'truth about her mind, unique in its own right.

VQR. Autumn, 1971. p. clx

As in her earlier books about the war, *Vietnam* and *Hanoi*, the most impressive quality that Mary McCarthy brings to bear on her subject is a keen moral sensibility. This is her real guide as she picks her way through the legal debris in the Georgia courtroom, sorting its facts, examining its participants, and salvaging the key issues. What emerges [in *Medina*] is not a document that vilifies the rather shallow figures of the trial but a polemic that tries to pull us closer to recognition of the nature of our involvement in this action.

Basil T. Paquet. NYR. Sept. 21, 1972. p. 37

The first seven chapters [of *The Mask of State*] are on-the-spot accounts of the Ervin Committee hearings. Their factual accuracy proves that Miss McCarthy listened carefully and absorbed the substance of the testimony. When she tells us what happened her perception is fully adequate to providing an understanding of the events.

Admittedly, one whose hunger for facts, accusations and quotations is insatiable would do better to plunge into the brain-addling flood of undigested information which is visited upon the reader of *The New York Times*. Mary McCarthy's aim is to interpret what is being said, and by what manner of men.

What better evidence of Mary McCarthy's journalistic skill can we ask for, than the fact that almost a year later nothing has happened which seriously contradicts her conclusions and perceptions. Despite the energetic ingenuities of all the king's lawyers and all the king's pressmen, we see them shattered now as she described them then.

It is no deprecation of Mary McCarthy's other talents to say that she is one of America's finest journalists. It is good for all of us that she has turned her powers to the inner tribulations of this country which, despite a long exile, she appears to care for very much.

Richard Goodwin. NYT. June 30, 1974. p. 6

McCULLERS, CARSON (1917–1967)

In a recent survey, *Fiction of the Forties*, Chester Eisinger has traced the main flaw in *The Member of the Wedding* to "its focus on the child's self-centered world in which the macrocosm plays no part." But this, I think, is precisely the source of its strength. Throughout this essay, I have argued that Mrs. McCullers is fundamentally a master of bright and melancholy moods, a lyricist not a philosopher, an observer of maimed characters not of contaminated cultures. That she writes best of uncomplicated people in fairly straightforward narrative forms is proven positively by *The Member of the Wedding* and "The Ballad of the Sad Café," and negatively by the failure of her last full-length work of fiction. Published in 1961, after ten years of painful composition, *Clock without Hands* tries to link the existential crisis of a man doomed by cancer to the sociological crisis of the South poisoned by racial strife. But because Mrs. McCullers was ill and working against her natural grain, the novel is deficient both in psychological intuition and cultural analysis.

Lawrence Graver. Carson McCullers
(Minnesota). 1969. p. 42

In Mrs. McCullers' writings, even when bodies are not freakish, souls are. Souls, she remarks, have colours and shapes like bodies. Indeed, these shapes are so marked that they give the impression of abnormality even in a normal body. Contradictions in the mind show in the body of Jake Blount [in *The Heart Is a Lonely Hunter*] as though he were a man who had served a term in prison, lived for a long time with foreigners in South America, or gone to Harvard. Something was different from the usual. The great question here is whether fulfilment obtained at the expense of normality should be considered wrong. Should such fulfilment be allowed to bring happiness? The soul of man is small and grotesque. It seeks to love its grotesque counterpart in the flesh. The flesh, however, does not recognize its soul and hates it.

What Mrs. McCullers is offering in this regard is a strange variant of neo-Platonism. In classical neo-Platonism beautiful soul cries out in longing to beautiful soul, finding its happiness in a union beyond the flesh as it reaches out to the bliss of the Transcendent Good. Mrs. McCullers' affirmation is that a Creator has formed an incomplete humanity, one that can only trust that there is sense in creation. Some good, rather than total good, is the meaning available for man.

Radiance, nevertheless, exists in the world and cannot be denied.

Alice Hamilton. DalR. Summer, 1970. p. 216

In McCullers what fills the space usually occupied by man-and-woman love is a sensitiveness that charges other people with magical perceptions. She radiated in all her work a demand for love so total that another was to become the perfect giver, and so become magical. The world is so bleak that it is always just about to be transformed.

Alfred Kazin. Bright Book of
Life (Little). 1973. p. 52

MACDONALD, ROSS [KENNETH MILLAR]
(1915–   )

Archer from the start has been a distinguished creation; he was always an attractive figure and in the course of the last several books has matured and deepened in substance to our still greater pleasure. Possessed even when young of an endless backlog of stored information, most of it sad, on human nature, he tended once, unless I'm mistaken, to be a bit cynical. Now he is something much more, he is vulnerable. As a detective and as a man he takes the human situation with full seriousness. He cares. And good and evil both are real to him.

Archer knows himself to be a romantic, would call it a weakness— as he calls himself a "not unwilling catalyst" for trouble; he carries the knowledge around with him—that's how he got here. But he is in no way archaic. He is at heart a champion, but a self-questioning, often a self-deriding champion. He is of today, one of ours. *The Underground Man* is written so close to the nerve of today as to expose most of the apprehensions we live with.

In our day it is for such a novel as *The Underground Man* that the detective form exists. I think it also matters that it is the detective form, with all its difficult demands and its corresponding charms, that makes such a novel possible.

Eudora Welty. NYT. Feb. 14, 1971. p. 29

The development that one hoped for has not quite taken place. Macdonald's later books are in many ways better than the early ones. They are composed with less violence, more subtlety, more satisfactory plots. The quality of the observation gives pleasure; the view of California as a place of immense beauty made ugly by man is expressed with passion; there is a lot of sympathetic and discerning characterization, particularly of the young. . . . Yet an impression that Macdonald has repeated too often the quest for personal identity and the investigation of the past that marks these books, that he has been too easily content with the things he can do well, remains.

Julian Symons. *Mortal Consequences*
(Harper). 1972. p. 191

In *The Underground Man* Macdonald keeps entirely within the formula but broadens it by providing a great California fire as the background of his book. This fire is an "ecological crime" linked more than fortuitously to the cigarillo dropped by Stanley Broadhurst, the murdered son. Stanley belongs to a "generation whose elders had been poisoned, like the pelicans, with a kind of moral DDT that damaged the lives of the young." By combining ecological and moral contamination Macdonald creates a double plot that spreads the crime over the California landscape. . . . Superb in snapshot portraiture of California life, Macdonald gives us a sense of the wild life flushed out by the smoke, the way people lean on one another when they fear crime and fire.

Geoffrey Hartman. *NYR*.
May 18, 1972. pp. 31–2

As always in the Lew Archer novels a great many people [in *Sleeping Beauty*] are linked together by avarice, adultery and anger; all are suspect because in the closed world of a family's affairs those who do not breed corruption are eroded by it. In this novel, too, we see all of Macdonald's other motifs elegantly developed—the search for the lost child; the idea that family determines fate; the need to restore order to the past as well as to the present; the balance between natural and moral disaster; scattered images suggesting the imminent end of man and his endeavors; and a harmony of structure: the bird that is washed up from the oil-slicked ocean at the book's beginning is paired a little later with a man who is similarly oiled and destroyed.

Peter S. Prescott. *Nwk*. May 7, 1973. p. 101

• McGUANE, THOMAS (1940–   )

A sense of dizziness, of speed, of a peculiarly cerebral combination of drollery and sadism will carry the reader some distance in *The Sporting Club*. An accelerating plot and apparently straight passages of trout-fishing will carry some readers a further distance. . . .

Thomas McGuane has a sprightly, knowing ear for dialogue, and an eye for the "absurd," and a light, fashionably cool touch that tires us only occasionally, and an obvious intelligence that has plotted all this out, crazy pranks and jokes and all, with vigor and enthusiasm. And it is always possible that we are to take the destruction of the Club (and even the scandalous revelation of its founding members' depravities) as a moral act. Quinn asks Stanton: "Just tell me why you're going after everybody." Stanton replies: "Because I hate it all."

The hatred is hard to take seriously, but the comedy is engrossing and at times ingenious. Thomas McGuane is, at 28, that notorious and difficult creature—a writer of promise.

Joyce Carol Oates. NYT. March 23, 1969. p. 5

Taking America apart is a game that the Americans themselves are accustomed to play with quite as much gusto as any critical observer from outside. . . . Mr. McGuane's [*The Sporting Club*] is set in the lush hunting-grounds of the Centennial Club, where trout and grouse and deer fatten themselves for the rods and guns of relaxing tycoons and back-to-nature enthusiasts. The Club has its mystique. As the hacking-jacketed ex-president Fortescue says: "There are still some of us alive for whom life in the forest means a return to older virtues, not just a vacation." Pomposities ripe for puncturing cluster round, and the puncturing instrument is Mr. McGuane's hero, the half-mad, idle-rich, pistol-collecting, duel-provoking, buttocks-baring and totally anarchic Stanton. . . .

The alarming and violent fun of the book makes it very much a document for the Sixties, and although its target was not, perhaps, too hard to hit, it shows imaginative verve in its action, and the bouts of near-absurdist comedy are nicely interspersed with sketches of the natural background, the "warm and creaky" night, the "raccoons rinsing mussels."

Edwin Morgan. List. Dec. 4, 1969. pp. 799–800

Put simply, McGuane has a talent of Faulknerian potential. His sheer writing skill is nothing short of amazing. The preternatural force, grace, and self-control of his prose recall Faulkner. He is as assured in elegantly elaborate description as in the outrageously bawdy comedy first revealed in *The Sporting Club*, an account of the rich at play in the Michigan wilds, and now come to full bloom in *The Bushwacked Piano*, the saga of a young man at large in an America wallowing in its own vulgarity. At 31, McGuane is a virtuoso.

His intelligence is as great as his style. His persistent thematic concern is the defilement of America, land and people alike, the advent of what he calls "a declining snivelization." This is no easy bow to ecological or political fashion. In his exploration of man and nature he is solidly within American literary tradition; his depiction of man's encroachment upon the land is as eloquent in its way as Faulkner's, in "Delta Autumn" and "The Bear."

Jonathan Yardley. NYT. March 14, 1971. p. 6

Nicolas Payne [in *The Bushwacked Piano*] is a young man who refuses to be, unlike D. H. Lawrence, "at one" with things. He fights against life's Waring Blender, and lives constantly under its "awful shadow." Payne is a young man with awful problems and when Ann, his girlfriend, tells him, "It's all in your head," it's the kind of information that he knows can't help anyone. Payne sometimes goes around "for no reason" on crutches. He sometimes hears nonexistent dogs, he never knows their number. He would like to become a legend. He carries a pistol for warmth and believes in "horses that will not allow themselves to be ridden," terror, fraud and God who's smart as a whip. He reviews his options every day and when he longs for the life inside the Waring Blender, and he does sometimes, he does not carry a pistol, and tries not to limp. What he wants out of life is something as impressive as fun. . . . *The Bushwhacked Piano* is gorgeously written, sad and terribly funny, and says a lot about love and violence in America in this, the so-called Twentieth Century.

Jane Richmond. PR. Fall, 1972. pp. 627–8

Thomas McGuane is one of our best young novelists, and it's cheering to watch him approach his apogee. From the beginning, he has seemed the heir apparent of two interlocking schools: in his conscious concern with aspects of American virility, as in his tool-like, purpose-built prose, he is a more modern, more ironic Hemingway; in his eye and ear for the perversions of American life and (hence) language, he is the successor, in narrative and dialogue, of Twain and Lardner and Richard Bissell. . . .

Ninety-two in the Shade is a short, tight, dense tale of the classic

American confrontation between waste of time, waste of life, and death, on the one hand, and sublime mastery of a talent, gift, skill, or trade, on the other. In short, the subject is the heights and depths of human possibilities. . . .

The book is a black comedy that has the grinding inevitability of tragedy.

L. E. Sissman. NY. June 23, 1973. pp. 88–9

In a completely deadened world there *is* an excitement, as [McGuane's hero] Skelton finds, in the thought that somebody wants to kill you. In a totally meaningless and unnatural world there *is* a moral beauty in following your instincts, even if your instincts issue instructions to kill or be killed. At the same time, all killing is clearly senseless, a stupid trap for both you and your victim, and that is why we have to see the humor of murder. It is cruelly funny, because the joke is on both of you, and no one is left to laugh. These are the thoughts, though, it seems to me, of a culture absolutely at the end of its tether, and the ironic, defeated moral of *Ninety-two in the Shade* belongs with them. . . .

The book is a flippant, lucid, somber American allegory, and between the bleak, neat deaths of two men and the slow anarchic slither into lifelessness of the rest of the country, there is only the alert, breezy talent of the allegory's author. . . . McGuane mobilizes all these meanings with such verve and intelligence that the end of America can't really be as nigh as his book suggests it is.

Michael Wood. NYR. Dec. 13, 1973. p. 20

McGuane's novel [*Ninety-two in the Shade*] is set in the riverrunning heart of America, in that vague and pulpy geography of marshes, inlets and creeks. It is here that Nichol Dance, a Caliban in Ariel's clothing, and a cold sole known as Carter ply their skiffs, for the benefit of visiting fishermen. Into their icthyolatrous womb sinks Tom Skelton, a young man who has at last escaped from life and is looking for the real thing among what Americans call "nature." He, too, takes up with a skiff, but you cannot go very far or very fast in an Ameridiluvian swamp and *Ninety-two in the Shade* describes that overwhelming sense of place which invades someone who cannot move. . . . *Ninety-two in the Shade* is full of small, bright objects leaning slightly to one side, and they wink all the fiercer in a setting sun. It is a funny and talented novel.

Peter Ackroyd. Spec. July 13, 1974. pp. 52, 54

MacLEISH, ARCHIBALD (1892–   )

MacLeish in phase is a poet who deals most congenially with affirmation, nostalgia and their delicate affinities. In the crisp, emotionally charged shorthand which, for a time, was his own personal convention, he recorded—and, to a degree, created—the semimythical character of the well-bred, well-heeled young American who lived in that state of mind called Paris at the end of World War I. . . .

When MacLeish did finally embrace America and became in person, in rhetoric and in Washington the most "official" of our poets, something essential had been sacrificed. Since much of what he wrote was easily consigned to that limbo where a determined will toward the poetic results only in poesy, many of his admirers felt that the poet had lost himself to his *view* of himself. Much of his "public speech," they felt, was crimped by grating assumptions about the nature of America, "brotherhood" and the audacity of Communist fellow travelers; that many of his vatic utterances were memorable not because they were persuasive but because they were just so darned pretty.

Yet, even in the midst of his speeches to the multitude, MacLeish's earlier voice was still able to register, like a needle on a graph, those nicer nuances that had once defined his talent.

John Malcolm Brinnin. *NYT*.
Nov. 19, 1972. p. 6

MacLeish has, finally, fashioned an eminently readable poetry in a considerable number of his poems, endowed as he is with linguistic and musical facility and a gift for the suggestive image. But he lacks an innovative poetic imagination. If we place his poetry next to that of Eliot, Pound, Williams and Stevens—to all of whom he appears indebted—we will perceive that it takes over features and practices from theirs to make a pleasing work that yet neither sustains nor engages the intelligence and sensibilities of the reader in the manner of those pioneers. We may delight in MacLeish's lyrical gifts, be drawn into the celebratory or elegiac moods he casts, but where in his writing can we locate—except at second hand—anything like the dynamic, individual, complex wrestling with language and form, with history, myth, personality, mystical experience and the modern environment so prominent, so much a shaping force (though differing in disposition and degree) of artistic practice for such poets as Yeats, Eliot, Pound, Stevens, or Williams? Theirs was the deep, desperate, wholly engaging struggle which brought about innovation, often from an eccentric, unpopular, isolated, or even wrong-headed perspective. MacLeish has lived and written from a more commonsense center, as befits a man of long and distinguished public service.

Ralph J. Mills, Jr. Parnassus. Spring–
Summer, 1973. pp. 214–5

MAILER, NORMAN (1923–   )

Norman Mailer is the most stubbornly political of living American nov-elists, a fact that explains a certain element of tough strength in most of his work as well as the increasingly problematic status of his fiction since <i>The Naked and the Dead.</i> He is shrewdly realistic about political actualities yet doggedly hopeful about man's possibilities, and this pe-culiar mix of wry knowledge and romantic faith has made it progres-sively more difficult for him to write in the fictional modes of conventional realism about a play of political forces whose chief effects seem to him the destruction of human meanings, the institutionalization of unreality, the mass production of inobtrusive and bottomless despair.

Robert Alter in The Politics of Twentieth-
Century Novelists, edited by George A.
Panichas (Hawthorn). 1971. p. 321

The public life of the past decade has not only given [Mailer] subjects worthy of the most vehement ambition, it has had the effect also of justifying themes, attitudes, that earlier seemed freakish or fantastic. Mailer has been saying for years that the great contemporary subject was totalitarianism. Now we are all saying that, or something like it, and feeling it with a paralyzing oppressiveness. His obsession, as it used to seem, with conflicts of power and brute force, with pitting himself against rivals (not just other writers but more ferocious antagonists like Sonny Liston, the Kennedys, Lyndon Johnson), with combat to the death against some vast imaginary Thing called various names but most ominously "cancer," no longer strikes us as ersatz Hemingwayism but as a kind of nervy common sense; and we read him now with all the interest a witness-bearer deserves whose obsessions have been borne out by the explosion of actual events. . . .

In both <i>The Armies of the Night</i> and <i>Walden</i> the use of the writer's own self-projected image or self-conceit—in large part through comic exaggeration and a broad yet dead serious social mockery—is tactically central. Mailer is not the first American literary talent to be accused of throwing itself away in egotistical rant. . . .

Warner Berthoff. Fictions and Events
(Dutton), 1971. p. 303

Few writers tell us more [than Mailer] about the America in which we live, its impulse toward indiscriminate power, its need for idealism and personal courage. And after all, after the mist of Mailer's own rhetoric and self-indulgent bombast clears, the works do bear close attention: *The Naked and the Dead* and *The Deer Park* are among the finest novels since the Second World War; essays like "The White Negro," "Superman Comes to the Supermarket," and the commentary on *The Deer Park* in *Advertisements for Myself* are composed with great care and perception; "The Man Who Studied Yoga" and "A Time of Her Time" are successful accounts of the conflict between the will and the idea, remarkable pieces whatever Mailer's larger ambitions may have been; and his recent political journalism, *The Armies of the Night* and the report of the political conventions, illuminate the terror of authority in contemporary America with an immediacy and eloquence not felt in other writers—he makes so many of his contemporaries seem simply dull.

Theodore L. Gross. The Heroic Ideal in
American Literature (Free). 1971. p. 273

Mailer is a writer as yet without the ultimate serenity that is probably needed for the great book he wishes to write. I say this out of the conviction that he is nonetheless the only writer of prominence in English who can be expected to deliver a work that deserves comparison with the best of Faulkner or James. Some of his contemporaries have written more shapely books, almost everyone who might be compared with him has avoided his excesses, but none has displayed his mastery of contemporary English as it has been fashioned not only in literature but in a multitude of media. No one now gives more hope that language may still be the potent instrument of human need in its confrontations with the benign as well as the wicked forces of institutionalized life.

Mailer's writings are best considered as one large work. However thematically repetitious, it is a work which constantly comes alive with extraordinary accumulations of intensity and brilliance. It is nonetheless a chaotic mixture that awaits some larger redemptive effort, so that despite *The Armies of the Night* and *Why Are We in Vietnam?*, Mailer now is like Melville without *Moby Dick*, George Eliot without *Middlemarch*, Mark Twain without *The Adventures of Huckleberry Finn*. The present danger is that he is applying to new issues and circumstances methods that he has already worked to exhaustion and, even more, that his achieved self-explanation has come to precede him to experience. In treating the moonshot, the Ali-Frazier fight, or women's liberation, he seems locked into a system that one hoped he could have transcended.

Richard Poirier. *Norman Mailer*
(Viking). 1972. p. 3

To say that Mailer has learned through writing novels how to continue as a writer and a man does not, of course, turn the novels themselves into laboratories or gymnasiums—I think them more important and valuable than any of the nonfiction, as it happens, if only because they are so much more offensive, more challenging to our conventional wisdom about art and life. Novels, however, have been healthy for him in the past, making possible the brilliant performances as essayist and reporter from *Advertisements for Myself* to *The Armies of the Night* and *Cannibals and Christians*, and it might not hurt him to get back to the old drawing board yet again.

Thomas R. Edwards. *NYR.*
June 15, 1972. p. 22

[Mailer] uses his gifts meanly [in *Marilyn*]—and that's not what we expect of Mailer, who is always billed as generous. This brilliant book gives off bad vibes—and vibes are what Mailer is supposed to be the master of. *Marilyn* is a feat all right: matchstick by matchstick, he's built a whole damned armada inside a bottle. (Surely he's getting ready to do *Norman*? Why leave it to someone who may care less?) But can we honor him for this book when it doesn't sit well on the stomach? It's a metaphysical cocktail-table book, and probably not many will be able to resist looking for the vicious digs and the wrap-up on the accumulated apocrypha of many years, many parties. To be king of the bums isn't really much. What are we actually getting out of *Marilyn*? Good as the best parts of it are, there's also malevolence that needs to be recognized. Is the great reporter's arrogance so limitless that he now feels free to report on matters to which he's never been exposed? Neither the world nor Marilyn Monroe's life should be seen in Norman Mailer's image.

Pauline Kael. *NYT.* July 22, 1973. p. 3

[Mailer's] method [in *Marilyn*] is simply to track Marilyn through the stages of her life as recorded by other men, sermonizing, hypothesizing, rhapsodizing as is his wont. He calls it a "Novel Biography," presumably to stress its conjectural and innovative rather than its factual quality, and as in all that Mailer undertakes, what ensues is characterized by verve even when all else is lacking. If the demands of time made for haste, hence for an expense of style in a waste of material, the resulting performance is hardly negligible. An aside by Mailer after all is worth a whole essay by many another, and Mailer carries it all off, however imperfectly, with such brio that one is reminded of John Barrymore in his later years, when the play was less important than the performance. . . .

Early on nearly destroyed by the quick fame and notoriety of *The Naked and the Dead*, and having suffered a decade of critical neglect and personal *angst*, Mailer has spent the second climacteric of his creative life wrestling with just those protean forces ("the orgy of publicity" of chapter VII) that were the death of Marilyn Monroe, with the result that though he somehow bested [Arthur] Miller he is now *contending* with Marilyn. The movies—his own in particular—have become very nearly an obsession with him, but in a much larger sense he has identified himself with the ephemera of our popular culture, the periodic brouhaha of championship boxing matches and elections, the monumental explosion of flackery that was the moonshot, the flotsam and jetsam of our generation taking its shape from the informing presence of . . . Trashman!

John Seelye. NR. Sept. 1, 1973. pp. 25–7

Mailer's finest critics, like Poirier and Leo Bersani and Tony Tanner, tend to err by adopting him for their gentler, more complex vision of the world. They make him more humane than he probably is. They see him as critical of the magic and machismo of which he is more likely the victim. They insist on his mastery of the shifting tones and meanings of his prose, whereas I think he has bravely and erratically delivered himself up to the vagaries of language in his time. . . .

Mailer is right to prefer his multiplicity to a more artful unity. There are evils and energies in America which will not speak at all unless they speak through Mailer. He is the ordinary guy as bad guy, he is the indiscreet charm of the American bourgeoisie. But then he speaks so well for the enemy because he is in large part the enemy, and we can't have him as our hero as well. We cheat Mailer and ourselves by pretending he is tamer than he is.

Michael Wood. NYR. Sept. 20, 1973. p. 22

MALAMUD, BERNARD (1914–   )

Each of Malamud's three major novels is concerned, I believe, with the *being* of the central character, with his decision to discover a new life, with the subject matter of the search, which in every case begins with the search for self. And in each novel, despite ironies, usually ludicrous, the hero succeeds—never, however, in the terms in which he had envisioned his quest.

William J. Handy. *Modern Fiction: A Formalist Approach* (Southern Illinois). 1971. p. 133

Anti-heroes from the pens of Henry James through James T. Farrell have reached the point of no return by climbing to the doom at the top. But some moderns, Malamud especially, have stated the case positively, for the failures, rather than negatively, against the successes. In Malamud's stories, the protagonist usually has the raw potential for becoming a schlemiel, that is, the potential for suffering, submitting to loss, pain, humiliation, for recognizing himself as, alas, only himself. This potential is sometimes realized, sometimes not. The hero of *A New Life*, S. Levin, wins what the title promises because he takes burdens on himself and follows the bungling path of the loser. A relative, H. Levin, in a story called "The Lady of the Lake," changes his name and, as he hopes, his status to Freeman, but ends as a slave to his own deception, embracing "only moonlit stone," the symbol of deception. The character courageous enough to accept his ignominy without being crushed by it is the true hero of Malamud's opus, while the man playing the Western hero without admitting to his real identity—Jewish, fearful, suffering, loving, unheroic—is the absolute loser.

Ruth R. Wisse. *The Schlemiel as Modern Hero* (Chicago). 1971. p. 111

The Tenants is a superb novel, whose mastery of tone, language, and characterization can only enlarge the stature of Bernard Malamud, one of our best writers. . . . A writer's frustration, ecstasy, and enforced solitude, his envy of people who seem to lead happier, more useful lives, are themes invoked by Mr. Malamud in a book that quickly assumes greater dimensions.

As Harry [the chief character] sits at his desk, wondering why he can't finish his novel, or as he roams through his deserted building, listening to the wind make almost human noises, *The Tenants* broadens its focus to contain material more violent than anything in *The Assistant*, though far less expressive of man's power to redeem himself than in *The Fixer*. A magnificent story is told with grieving insight into some of life's more damaging conflicts and betrayals. . . .

There seems to be little love in this taut, highly concentrated novel. Its fierce symbols—jungle vegetation, flora that surrounds human beings who stalk each other like beasts—create an Eden not so much lost as ravaged by man's passionate enmity toward his kind. The complex integration of symbolism and realism reminds us how prophetic *The Nat-*

ural, Mr. Malamud's first novel, was in influencing the direction his writing would take.

Joseph Catinella. SR. Sept. 25, 1971. p. 36

In Bernard Malamud's fiction the characters are often in deep need of a world ordered and enriched by reference to transcendent will and design. They are often people on a journey looking for what they do not have, an ordering or life-giving center. They are often on a quest or a pilgrimage. . . . They conclude that there is no ordering or life-giving center. The holy is gone, and they conclude their journeys by standing still, by affirming what remains despite that loss or by holding their own during the absence of sacredness. . . . It is fair to say that, in his juxtaposition of journey and stasis, journey is generally found to be a disillusioning and ineffective tack. It is so because there are no life-giving, ordering centers which a man can find or toward which he can move. More promising is standing, grasping the present, being true to what is within, and making the most of possibilities which lie at hand. The modest optimism which emerges from his work depends on the austerity and integrity which can be secured by faithful endurance in the face of the absence of grace.

Wesley A. Kort. Shriven Selves
(Fortress). 1972. pp. 101, 106

As short fiction goes, middling Malamud is merely exemplary—models of artisanship aglow with a special vision; at its best it works magic: Malamud is our principal necromancer and fabulist.

The eight tales of his new collection [*Rembrandt's Hat*] run the course from middling (he has never written below that mark) to spectacular: a few fine, though repeat, performances, variations on themes reverberating from *The Magic Barrel* and *Idiots First*, as well as the novels; a few tentative departures—delicate, interesting, admirable, though not particularly memorable; and at least two, which happen also to be the longest in the volume, that are commanding examples of his art. . . .

But what is most notable here is a quality as much moral as artistic: Malamud's distinguished grace of absolute integrity, his refusal to evade a story's smallest inner necessities: his requirement of himself that he *write*, where he could have elided, each turning and gesture of the spirit.

NR. June 6, 1973. p. 32

In *Pictures of Fidelman* Malamud sets out to turn the tables on himself and, gamely, to take a holiday from his own obsessive mythology: here he imagines as the hero a Jewish man living without shame and even with a kind of virile, if shlemielish, forcefulness in a world of Italian gangsters, thieves, pimps, whores, and bohemians, a man who eventually finds love face-down with a Venetian glassblower who is the husband of his own mistress—and most of it has no more impact than the bullet that Yakov Bok fired in his imagination had on the real Czar of Russia [in *The Fixer*]. And largely because it has been conceived as a similar kind of compensatory daydream; in *Pictures of Fidelman*, unfortunately, natural repugnance and constraints, and a genuine sense of what conversions cost, are by and large dissolved in rhetorical flourishes rather than through the sort of human struggle that Malamud's own deeply held sense of things calls forth in *The Assistant* and *The Fixer*. It's no accident that this of all the longer works generates virtually no internal narrative tension (a means whereby it might seek to test its own assumptions) and is without the continuous sequential development that comes to this kind of storyteller so naturally and acts in him as a necessary counterforce against runaway fantasy. This playful daydream of waywardness, criminality, transgression, lust, and sexual perversion could not have stood up against that kind of opposition.

Philip Roth. *NYR*. Oct. 3, 1974. p. 26

MENCKEN, H. L. (1880–1950)

As one of the most influential critics of his period [Mencken] led the battle against the Puritan tradition, against the disproportionate influence of rural America, the "Bible Belt" that produced what Herbert Hoover would call the "noble experiment" of Prohibition. He attacked the censorship that then made it hard to treat sex at all honestly. . . . Similarly Mencken beat the drum for the leading writers of the '20s. Like him, Dreiser, O'Neill, Sinclair Lewis, Sherwood Anderson, and the rest are now generally patronized when not ignored, because they were overrated in their day; yet they helped to mark America's "coming of age," a maturity that our young people can take for granted. Although they were all writers to outgrow, they enabled us to outgrow them—and then too easily to grow ungrateful. . . .

Mencken is more than a museum piece. He left some solid work, notably his thorough, loving study of the American language, but also in his contributions to literary criticism. He is still enjoyable reading because of the verve with which he attacked shams that are by no means extinct. His gusto can be more refreshing because his declared prejudices are easier to discount than the more fashionable prejudices of the '70s.

Herbert J. Muller. *NR*. Feb. 12, 1972. p. 32

Alas, there is no Mencken. He is gone for good. Furthermore, if his counterpart were to appear before us today and take up the vigil of the master where he left off, he wouldn't be able to get away with it for very long. For the conditions that made a Mencken possible and plausible back in the 1920's, when he was in his public heyday, simply do not exist any more. Nor do the conditions obtain that in the decade of the 1910's permitted him to achieve preeminence as a critic of literature and champion of the bold moderns who opened up American fiction to the insights of the twentieth century. Mencken was of a specific time and place, and when the time ended and the place took on a different look, he was out of it. What most of those who lament his absence today forget is that Mencken ceased to perform his now-legendary function as Lord High Executioner of American Poltroonery several decades before he suffered the stroke that ended his literary career in 1949. The vintage Menckeniana that everyone quotes and longs to have duplicated today was almost all composed in the days of Presidents Wilson, Harding, and Coolidge. By Herbert Hoover's time he wasn't able to bring it off nearly so well, and the Roosevelt years were definitely not for him. Wisely, he realized it soon enough, and turned to other and more fruitful pursuits.

Louis D. Rubin, Jr., in *The Comic Imagination in American Literature*, edited by Louis D. Rubin, Jr. (Rutgers). 1973. pp. 217–8

● MEREDITH, WILLIAM (1919–   )

It is kindest to pass over briefly the earlier pieces [in *Love Letter from an Impossible Land*], which inevitably and quite frankly derive from the Latin and Metaphysical poets, or are sheer imitations of Auden, Spender, Rukeyser and other contemporaries. The more formal or traditional the pattern, the more cramped, mannered, and rhetorical they are. Too often they bear the awkward burden of abstract intellectual concept, seldom the exact, salty flavor of genuine experience. But when William Meredith leaves the book-shelves and becomes the flyer, he becomes also a poet in his own right.

Ruth Lechlitner. *Poetry*. July, 1944. p. 227

Mr. Meredith's poetry is cool, intellectual, and self-contained. . . . His detachment bespeaks no incapacity for more overt emotional expression, but a deliberate decision to set down his observations and conclusions as clearly and succinctly as possible, in the reasonable expectation that the reader who admires this poetry for its intelligence and elegance will have the wit to see through to its emotional strength.

Milton Crane. NYT. August 22, 1948. p. 10

Mr. Meredith's art is tough-minded, delicate, and impatient with slovenly writing in himself and in others. . . . [The Open Sea] is as solid an accomplishment in the actual composition of a book (as distinguished from the composition of a single poem) as I have seen in a long time. The very consistency of excellence makes it difficult to single out single poems for praise, but I have a personal favorite, in any case. It is a sonnet called "The Illiterate." Its virtues, as I feel them, are precision, grace, and a profound depth of human feeling which is curiously conveyed through the daring experimental spirit. . . . We have been told by Vested Interests that you can't write sonnets any longer, that you can't do this and you can't do that. The only answer to the theoretical absolutist is the living and embarrassing evidence of a beautiful poem.

James Wright. YR. June, 1958. p. 609

In connection with William Meredith's verse, the two words that come most often to mind—that is, to my mind—are "balance" and "relaxation." He is introspective and a little diffident, grave and perplexedly troubled, particularly when he can't do anything about what is happening, what has happened. He is the kind of poet who stands looking at the ocean where the atomic submarine Thresher went down, meditating, speculating, grieving intelligently. Things of this nature hurt him into poetry, but not poetry of great intensity. Instead, it seems muffled and distant, a kind of thin, organized, slightly academic murmur. One keeps listening for Meredith's voice, and is baffled at its being, although one is surer and surer it is there, so consistently elusive. . . . At his best he is a charming poet, cultivated, calm, quietly original, expansive and reflective, moving over wide areas slowly, lightly, mildly and often very memorably. [1965]

James Dickey. Babel to Byzantium
(Grosset). 1971. pp. 197–8

The elegance which is compounded of compassion, intelligence, and linguistic precision once again characterizes the work of William Meredith. In The Wreck of the Thresher he is fascinated by the ironies in our assumptions and by the paradox of our identities. There is a recurrence of upside-down, inside-out mirror imagery, as of the branches and the roots of a tree. Meredith is sane and exploratory, yet subjective and nostalgic. And he maintains a simplicity of form which works nicely in behalf of his richly complex grasp of the nature of things. One only wishes for the elimination of such gaucheries as "At the Opera."

Fred Bornhauser. *VQR*. Winter, 1965. p. 150

"Art by its very nature asserts at least two kinds of good—order and delight." So William Meredith, in his introduction to a selection from Shelley, a poet who interests this decorous American for his patience with established verse forms, being "otherwise impatient of everything established." Meredith's declension of order and delight as versions of the good, a pairing susceptible of a whole range of inflections, from identity to opposition, is the generating trope of his own poetry, its idiopathy or *primary affection*.

In his four books of poems, even in his translations of Apollinaire, a curious restraint, a self-congratulatory withholding that is partly evasive and sly, partly loving and solicitous, testify, like so many essays in emphasis, to the war between delight and order, and yet to the necessity of divising them in each other: if order is not found in delight, the world falls apart; if delight is not taken in order, the self withers. Success, for Meredith, is provisional—he does not ask more. . . .

The persistent modesty of this disarming poet makes an assessment of his achievement—its value, and in the old sense its virtue—something of a violation of his very temper. The arms of which he would strip us are self-importance and heedlessness, those devices we employ to get through life more cheaply. Meredith's voice now, submissive to his experience and the representation of a discipline at a higher frequency than itself, recalls us to a more expensive texture.

Richard Howard. *Alone with America*
(Atheneum). 1971. pp. 318, 326

[Meredith] is often compared with Richard Wilbur for imposing, with considerable grace, the most rigorous formal demands upon his verse. Such writing had a notable boom in the 'fifties, and following the usual sea-change in literary taste is viewed with suspicion now. But it seems unfair for Meredith or Wilbur to be held accountable for the refined disasters produced by their imitators. Meredith's best poems are elegant but not precious, ordered but not finicky, deeply thoughtful but not recondite. . . . The new poems [in *Earth Walk*] . . . show that Meredith is still making advances at an age when most writers are traveling in tried-and-true ruts. . . . Time and again Meredith has discovered dignity where other men have ceased to look for it, and given it new life in his poems. I am happy for him that he has seen such things, and for us that he has written them down.

Robert B. Shaw. Poetry. July, 1971. p. 233

Like Frost, Meredith portrays a natural landscape of fields and woods, the clearing where "a whippoorwill calls in the dark," the hill where the poet has "planted spruce and red pine." But Meredith's poetry also incorporates the contemporary city where a man's wallet is snatched from him on a stairway by a boy who, running away, "turns a brown face briefly/phrased like a question." And whereas, in Frost, the land-scape of farm and countryside has significance as part of an ethical drama, in which man pits his strength and courage against inimical nature, in Meredith the props of the natural scene stand for a deeply intuited consciousness of an identity between our physical selves and the earth we inhabit and are made of. If Meredith's poetry has a signature, it is the tree, which appears over and over again as a literal object in a scene, an emblem, a self, rooted in earth and growing outward to air and sun.

The poet of *Earth Walk* chooses to place himself squarely in real-ity, conveying to us a sense of the mind's rootedness in a body against whose weight we struggle to raise up decent lives.

Marie Borroff. YR. Winter, 1971. p. 285

If he is really too disciplined and adjusted an individual, too genial, too much the hero of the buried life harumping among the hydrangea bushes, he is, nevertheless, a poet who knows, deep to his fingertips, what the tiger or the nightingale always forgets, that the dispassionate, domestic, monogamous world has its dramas and sorrows, that rectitude itself can be an adventure, a moral adventure almost as Kierkegaard dreamed.

Robert Mazzocco. NYR. June 15, 1972. p. 32

Mr. Meredith places [in *Earth Walk*] his most recent poems first in line instead of last—a wise decision, I think. . . . I do not mean to suggest that Mr. Meredith in his early period was ever a bad poet; too often, however, he was not a very exciting one. Yet, curiously, from the begin-ning he was writing just outside the camp of "modernism," for the most part speaking in a subdued, almost timid voice directly to the reader and making of personal experience a fitting subject for his low-key medita-tions. He may have looked more to recent poets than to Whitman for inspiration, but he was, in one sense, writing in the 'forties the way most people are now writing in the 'seventies.

By making this point I do not argue that he is one of the true pioneers of the new era. There is little of the pioneer spirit in his work. And today, as the boisterous crowd surges forward, chanting, shouting, and waving banners, Mr. Meredith marches along a hundred yards behind, quietly playing his flute.

Thomas H. Landess. *SwR*. Winter, 1973. p. 148

MERRILL, JAMES (1926–   )

James Merrill's *First Poems* had already revealed an accomplished technician, intricately teasing out paradox and symbol in a metaphor-bejeweled language at once dazzling and opaque. Themes were developed in an imagery rich in suggestions of pain, illness, malice, perversity, a cruelty flashing out in the midst of lyric celebration: "As girls love daisies, love dismembers hours." From the start, Merrill's imagination has been fascinated by the interplay between the real and the artificial, tempted to prefer the latter to the former: the mirrored reflection to the actual face (the mirror in his poetry becomes virtually a signature), a man in a painting to a real man, a stage scene to a scene in the living world. In *The Fire Screen*, we see these early powers and tendencies fully matured. All the brilliance of the early poems remains, all the virtuosity; paradox, symbol, image, literal statement coalesce in densely meaningful forms which have also, strangely, become less opaque, more accessible.

Marie Borroff. *YR*. Winter, 1971. p. 282

Critics have made too much of Mr. Merrill's seriousness. Every good writer is "serious." Mr. Merrill gives ample evidence of emotional depth and of an irrepressible conscience poking through his agreeable frivolity. Privately he has undergone more than his fair share of anguish, and he uses painful incidents as a point of departure for many poems. But their effect is rarely pathetic. Mr. Merrill's charm lies in his ability to fit a profound and complicated human relationship into the form of a fascinating analogy developed through word play, elegant conceits, and gentle self-ridicule. It is his very success and his ease that dissipate the pathos. Anyone who reads and understands these beautifully-made poems will not be sorry to exchange the element of pathos for so much intellectual brilliance and aesthetic power.

TLS. Jan. 22, 1971. p. 92

In this volume [*Braving the Elements*], Merrill has found a use, finally, for all his many talents. His surreptitious fondness for narrative, which issued rather badly in his early novel *The Seraglio* (1957) and his later sketch for a novel *The (Diblos) Notebook* (1965), has now found a clear medium in his wonderful short narrative lyrics; his almost unnaturally exquisite gift for euphony has become unobtrusive but no less exquisite, in fact more so; his ironic and wayward humor has been allowed to surface in poetry as well as in prose; his single best subject—love—has found a way of expressing itself masked and unmasked at once, instead of hiding almost mummified in swathings of secrecy.

Helen Vendler. NYT. Sept. 24, 1972. p. 5

Merrill may well be our subtlest examiner of waking nightmares, some of them apparently his own. The usual protagonist of a Merrill poem is an individual who bears (I suspect) certain likenesses to Merrill himself: a less innocent Lambert Strether moving uneasily through an era of hard acid rock and public assassinations. Sensitive, middle-aging, he skims along the border of his society, skeptical of self-dramatizing public statesmen, distrustful of the daily newspaper and its "bulletin-pocked columns," unwilling to be Aquarianized by his counterculture neighbors. . . .

A superiority of Merrill's is that, along with a crushing burden of sophistication, he carries a childlike freshness of observation, a certain ability to look back into his boyhood with detachment.

X. J. Kennedy. At. March, 1973. pp. 101–2

No poet of our moment has finer formal gifts with which to make his affirmation. Merrill is at ease and very good in free verse, but his most stunningly beautiful work comes when the greatest number of restrictions have imposed themselves. The different forms and styles he uses now are the ones he has used for years; he simply gets better and better at doing what he always did well. Because there is nothing of a formal nature that he cannot do, nothing is accidental, everything was meant to be exactly as it is. His use of meter and rhyme is anything but "old-fangled"; he takes liberties with the classic forms—a Merrill sonnet sequence, ballad, or villanelle may be too flexible for the purist—and bends with pleasure and finesse to the double-dactyl invented by Anthony Hecht and John Hollander. . . . Virtually all his reviewers have justly lavished praise upon the range of Merrill's cultivated mind among the music, art, language, and customs of many countries, his delicacy, elegance, wit, polish, euphony, and descriptive powers. In *Braving the Elements* all this is as true as ever.

Judith Moffett. HC. June, 1973. pp. 8–9

[Merrill] is a poet in a situation of leisure, travel, civilized friendships, airplanes, motor cars, Mexico, Greece. He can be unashamedly "camp" and he has fun and wit, but his brittleness is redeemed by his sympathy. His themes are often those of pathos, a rather unfashionable emotion today. But the subjects of his poems (which can be extremely obscure) are really only excuses for the very rich harvest of a purely poetic— imagistic, allusive, word-jocular—world.

Stephen Spender. NYR. Sept. 20, 1973. p. 11

When Braving the Elements won the Bollingen Poetry Prize for James Merrill, the New York Times published an ill-informed editorial criticizing the foundation for making the award in troubled times to a genteel and private poet. It is true Merrill has avoided confessional poetry and topical or fashionable subjects. But for readers who understand Merrill's highly-informed language, the poems of Braving the Elements deal more memorably and more incisively with liberation, radical violence, kidnapping, space travel, the assassination of political leaders, and the effect of mass-media on the English language than any poetry written in America today. More importantly, Merrill is the finest poet translating the tradition of French symbolism into the English language. On the European continent, the predominant force in contemporary poetry is still the symbolist movement. In the English speaking world other currents have deflected that potent language because Yeats found few successors sufficiently gifted in the style. Merrill is fluent in it. And if we are to understand lyrical poetry in the etymological sense of rootedness in musical expression, Merrill is one of its few preeminent masters.

Richard Saez. Parnassus. Fall–
Winter, 1974. pp. 183–4

MERWIN, W. S. (1927–   )

[Merwin's] words are literal, yet far-out; like musical chords extended into their far sequences. Yet it is no accident that Merwin's forerunners, as they occurred to me, are all French; Merwin is a long way from the dominant objectivism of American poetry today, in spite of superficial resemblances. Looking back to Merwin's earlier books, one can see many phases in his progress, including some prolonged spells of wasted, pedestrian writing, during which he might have gone in several directions. He chose, or was chosen by, this one: a sacrifice of the conventional harmony of words, which dominated *The Dancing Bears* (1954), for a gain in the subtle atonality of ultra-meanings; though his longer poems, in spite of subtlety, are complex and strong. Poems like "The Moths" and "The Widow" are among the most advanced work being done in America.

Hayden Carruth. Poetry. Sept., 1968. p. 422

The Selected Translations of W. S. Merwin is a collection of superbly accurate renderings into contemporary American English of the poems of 87 men ranging from an anonymous Egyptian of the 20th century B.C. to a brilliant Russian poet still in his twenties. As such the book is something far richer, more various, more awesome than a book of "imitations" that might have given us 87 of the voices of W. S. Merwin rather than an incarnation of the single voice of Man.

It was from Pound, Merwin tells us in his introduction, that he learned to respect "the greatest possible fidelity to the original, including its sounds." But of course, we say, that's obviously *how* one translates, but anyone who has ever attempted translation knows how nearly impossible it is to practice the obvious, how difficult it is simply to *prefer* the voice of Neruda or Alberti or Pasternak, to name a few of the recently mutilated, to one's own. So entirely absent from the present collection is Merwin's own style as a poet that one begins to suspect that this is a book written out of the love of poetry rather than the love of self.

Philip Levine. Poetry. Dec., 1969. p. 187

In his more recent poetry, Merwin uses classical myth only occasionally, but in the volumes *The Lice* and *The Carrier of Ladders* myth itself is as important a poetic device as it is in his earlier work. In *The Lice*, Merwin develops his method of probing within the structure of myth for the unconscious forces that motivate its creation through an exploration of the nature of generalized "gods" or "divinities" rather than through allusions to particular ancient mythical figures or narratives. . . .

Gods also hover over the lives of the speakers in Merwin's latest book of poems, *The Carrier of Ladders*: naked and abstract in "Plane," tainted by a history of loss and violence in "Psalm: Our Fathers," and reduced to the most essential form or equation of myth and ritual in "Words from a Totem Animal," in which the sacrificial beast and the participant in rite become one in their relation to the silent, cold, unreachable self which these gods so clearly represent.

Lillian Feder. Ancient Myth in Modern
Poetry (Princeton). 1971. pp. 414–5

W. S. Merwin is a distinguished and difficult poet who writes distinguished and beautiful prose. Although *The Miner's Pale Children* consists of almost ninety prose pieces on everything from stones and spiders to bandages, eggs, and love, the work as a whole has a curious and pervasive unity. It is the kind of unity that can be achieved only by a strongly creative personality viewing the world in its own way. Merwin views the world as living—shoes contain memories and a stone put in its proper place eases man's tensions; tight-rope walkers meditate on their craft until the excitement and danger of their performance is lost in the vitality of their equipment; gardens suffer, literally suffer, the ravages of war. In Merwin's view of the world, everything lives; and his talent is such that in his prose, everything comes alive.

PrS. Winter, 1971–2. p. 370

A lot of Merwin's poems are like variations on the theme of what Ruskin termed "the pathetic fallacy," the projection upon nature of our human passions. The repetitiousness of this attitude makes them a bit monotonous: more, I think, than the form, which has little variation.

However when all this is said, these poems communicate a sense of someone watching and waiting, surrounding himself with silence, so that he can see minute particles, listen to infinitesimal sounds, with a passivity of attention, a refusal to disturb with his own observing consciousness the object observed. It is as though things write their own poems through Merwin. At their best they are poems of total attention and as such they protest against our world of total distraction. He gives the reader the feeling that the things we see in nature can be withdrawn from our eyes and restored to their integral separateness; and that, in doing this, rituals and sacraments which have been lost, and a sense of the sacredness of living, are restored. He gives things the invisibility of covering darkness and then watches light re-create them for us.

Stephen Spender. *NYR*. Sept. 20, 1973. p. 11

MILLER, ARTHUR (1915–   )

I had mixed feelings about Miller's new play [*The Price*], but on the whole thought better of it than most reviewers did. It is, as many have said, moralistic, talky and frequently contrived. . . . Despite these inadequacies, and they do seriously compromise the evening, I was impressed by Miller's intermittent insights ("we invent ourselves to wipe out what we know") and moved by the play's central dilemma: "who's to take care of the helpless old father?" Such a theme, concerned as it is with retesting the boundaries of personal obligation, has seemed to many merely old-fashioned. In terms of current taste it is, but when that shifts, as it must, Miller's subtle inquiries will be more fully appreciated.

Martin Duberman. PR. Summer, 1968. p. 419

Although what Miller has to say in the new plays is philosophically suspect, it is not his theme but his commitment to it that has crippled his work. His new truth is not an impetus to creativity, but a doctrine that must be illustrated. . . . Miller's most recent play [*The Price*] is set in the same thematic country as *After the Fall* and *Incident at Vichy*. . . . If this were all there were to *The Price*, it would not be that welcome a change from *After the Fall* and *Incident at Vichy*. Its strength lies in the character of Gregory Solomon, who dominates the play when he is on stage and, through well-timed intrusions during the brothers' discussion, continues to be a formidable presence even when he has moved to the periphery of the central action. A man almost ninety years old, a retired appraiser, who finds in the furniture an opportunity to begin again, he is an embodiment of the idea that life is the product of belief beyond disbelief. More important he is Arthur Miller's first real comic character, a creation that realizes some of the possibilities implicit in Willy Loman's happier scenes.

Gerald Weales. The Jumping-Off Place
(Macmillan—N.Y.). 1969. pp. 19, 21–3

In all [Miller's] works, despite crushing obstacles, something is achieved, the possibility of responsibility and action is restored. Dignity is reaffirmed.

And because this possibility permeates his work, Arthur Miller is one of the most rebellious writers in the modern drama. His continuing exploration of the ramifications of determinism and free will, guilt and responsibility, drift and action, represents his revolt against a theater singing dirges of woe. Miller rebels against the fashionable complacency and chic lamentation that dominate so much of the contemporary stage, on, off, or below Broadway. His consideration of responsibility and free will is a challenge to the paralyzing morbidity of a drama which views man as trapped in a cosmic straitjacket, thrashing about in his pettiness and helplessness. His characters are not defined in terms of hysteria, but of history; they are not only affected by their world, they are able to affect it as well.

Miller does not invite his audience to luxuriate in a velvety cloak of universal despair and self-pity, nor does he subject us to sadomasochistic barrages under the shrill slogans of joy, freedom, and liberation. In a

theater of angry young men, frustrated old men, and precocious ado-
lescents of indeterminate age, Miller goes his own way, committed to a
drama of communication, based on the reasonable assumption that the
stage may still be the place for an aesthetic and civilizing act.

Benjamin Nelson. *Arthur Miller: Portrait of*
a Playwright (McKay). 1970. pp. 318–9

In spite of personal dedication and public optimism, Miller's plays are
remarkably full of suicide. Larry Keller crashed his airplane, and Joe
Keller shot himself. Willy Loman crashed his car and did not die his
dream death of a salesman. John Proctor (and several lesser characters)
of *The Crucible* went to death to assert their integrity, as Eddie Carbone
met death in a vain effort to assert his integrity. Lou and Maggie killed
themselves in despair in *After the Fall*. Prince Von Berg sacrificed his
life to prove his faith in individual life, and Gregory Solomon lost his
daughter by a suicide that is not particularized. For all these misfortunes, Miller seeks our pity, and pity is what he evokes when most
adept. Though Miller is said to specialize in the inarticulate, all his
victims are articulate; they talk. Incisive dialogue etches Miller's low
men in our minds; Joe Keller, Willy Loman, Eddie Carbone, Gregory
Solomon are vigorous with concrete colloquialisms, Jewish inflections,
or rhythmic repetitions of everyday words. Often, however, Miller tries
to convert his low man into Everyman, or—worse—into the Tragic
Hero. Then Miller is betrayed by his weakness for sonorous abstraction
or incongruous image. He finds it hard to accept that he is most true
when most trivial.

Ruby Cohn. *Dialogue in American*
Drama (Indiana). 1971. p. 95

[Miller's] avoidance of intellectual heroes has made it even more difficult for him to articulate his own ideas. While writing *The Crucible* he
felt that "the historical moment seemed to give me the poetic right to
create people of higher self-awareness than the contemporary scene
affords." But the contemporary scene affords people who are very much
more self-aware than the ones he chooses. Returning to modern times in
A View from the Bridge he burdened himself with a hero who was so
unaware of himself and so inarticulate that a choric lawyer had to be
introduced to explain the significance of what was going on. *After the
Fall* went to the opposite extreme with a hero who unnecessarily
swamped the play with self-explanation. *Incident at Vichy* also suffered
from a surfeit of exposition: both Von Berg and Leduc are attitudes
dressed up as men. In *The Price* Miller tries to get the best of both
worlds by taking as his hero a policeman who had opted against devel-

oping his initial potential as an intellectual. But because his decision to join the police was taken twenty-eight years before the action of the play, it is hard to bring it into focus.

> Ronald Hayman. *Arthur Miller*
> (Ungar). 1972. p. 118

MILLER, HENRY (1891–   )

If the heart of the American Dream is the image of the unfettered man "making" himself by accumulation of goods and credit, assuring a place for himself at the American banquet, Miller has detached the activity from any social end, and celebrated the act of accumulating experiences, especially sexual experiences, as an end in itself. Instead of a duty, life becomes an adventure—but still an adventure of self-aggrandizement and self-creation. . . .

The excitement in Miller's early work is its authentic emotion of release, its unhindered explorations of the suppressed fringes of middle-class fantasies, where respectability fades into criminality. It is a literature of pure disengagement and self-assertion, an act of aggression against all confining values.

> Alan Trachtenberg in *American Dreams,*
> *American Nightmares*, edited by David
> Madden (Southern Illinois). 1970. p. 142

Miller has spent a long industrious life grinding slow and exceeding fine, also coarse. He is a world literary figure, and it is proper to ask where—apart from the long-banned candor—his achievement lies. With whom shall we compare him—Lawrence? Joyce? Beckett? He is not as important as any of these because he has not created a world that is recognizably his own. He has not really created at all. He lacks architectonic skill, a making or shaping drive. He has had only one real subject—himself—and he has not been prepared, or endowed with the ability, to convert himself into a great fictional myth. Called a novelist by some, he has the novelist's ear and eye but not the novelist's power to create great separable artifacts. He has done what any man with his endowments and deficiencies is forced to do—produce autobiography that begs at the door of fiction.

> Anthony Burgess. *NYT*. Jan. 2, 1972. p. 10

MOORE, MARIANNE (1887–1972)

The function of a poem, when Miss Moore writes it, is to provide for distinctive energy of mind a sufficient occasion; a direction. The mind moves from its presumed rest; ranges abroad through materials congenial to its nature; comes to rest again. This is the figure the poems make; a sequence, a curve, the trajectory of a mind well aimed. If we ask why one curve is chosen in preference to another, there is no ready answer: it is so. The assumption is that energy of mind is good, and its release in action is good. The note is experimental, exploratory.

> Denis Donoghue. *The Ordinary Universe*
> (Macmillan—N.Y.). 1968. p. 47

Epigrammatic brilliance, intellectual fastidiousness, and an unwillingness to falsify one's sense of one's own limitations may have an exemplary value of their own, in art as well as in life. Marianne Moore does not tell us the meaning of history, the nature of sin, or the right way to conduct our lives. She keeps things in order; she observes and annotates; she exercises the courage of her peculiarities. She gives us imaginary gardens with real toads in them; she also gives us the sick horror of decency trying to confront honestly the fact of modern war, and the undramatic, faintly humiliating, matter-of-fact discovery that decency recovers from that confrontation.

> George W. Nitchie. *Marianne Moore*
> (Columbia). 1969. p. 178

Critical writings about the work of Miss Moore fall into two sharp divisions: clear-minded essays—[T. S.] Eliot and [Hugh] Kenner are cases in point—where an exact perception of what she is about eschews all floridness; and, on the other hand, a host of "tributes" in which the poet is reduced to the status of a kind of national pet and where the intellectual stamina finds no answering attitude in the appreciator but calls forth instead sentimental rhapsodizing. One of the more depressing thoughts to cross the mind of anybody who has read such criticism in bulk is to wonder whether Marianne Moore has not suffered more from lax adulation than almost any other significant poet of our century. Perhaps the reason for this lies as much in the nature of the work as in the nature of Miss Moore's more indulgent public. This work is morally "armoured," like some of her favourite animals, but suppose that armor should come to seem quaint, a carapace of knowing quiddities? This is the way many people have apparently read it, and this is the basis for Miss Moore's popular success. Thus the one potential defect in a brilliant oeuvre passes for its virtue in a body of critical writing that seldom engages with the reality.

Charles Tomlinson in Marianne Moore,
edited by Charles Tomlinson
(Prentice-Hall). 1969. p. 12

Marianne Moore and Emily Dickinson do not stand to each other in a relationship as undeniable as that between Miss Moore and Henry James. I doubt if one who had mastered the urbane obliquity of James would care altogether for the abrupt and unceremonious withdrawals into enigma of Emily Dickinson. It has often been remarked that Marianne Moore's style develops out of highly civilised prose. Her sentences are beautifully articulated, more condensed than prose normally is, and with an odd sidelong movement that in prose would probably disconcert; but no one could mistake the element from which they have arisen. Their affinities are with conversation. . . . Emily Dickinson was afraid to converse: she utters a few astonishing words from behind the door and then closes it in palpitation. She too wants her "heightened consciousness" to find its response—but from whom? . . .

And yet, given this all-important distinction between the two poets, their choice of language seems to unite them unexpectedly. Both are incontrovertibly American—or perhaps one should say American of a certain tone and temper which, like much else in the modern world, may be dissolving. They are individual, ironic, and above all fastidious. They place a high value on privacy and know the power of reticence. Their poetry is exact and curious like the domestic skills of the American woman in ante-bellum days. It has the elevation of old-fashioned erudite American talk—more careful in its vocabulary, more strenuously aiming at correctness and dignity than English talk of the same vintage.

Henry Gifford in Marianne Moore, edited by
Charles Tomlinson (Prentice-Hall).
1969. pp. 172–3

I think it has been insufficiently emphasized that a good deal of Miss Moore's verse, particularly the earlier, is not stanzaic at all, or rhymed —or, indeed, regularly, or approximately regularly, syllabic. Nevertheless, perhaps it is here that her contribution to modern experimental poetry may be seen at its purest and most remarkable, for what she is writing is not prose or the prose-poem but poetry with prose's rhetoric, complexity and ease, poetry without adventitious musical aid, whose units are arguments and paragraphs. . . . The baroque cleverness and ornament is to delay and enrich a closely-argued journey towards the clinching spire or altar of meaning and emotion.

> Roy Fuller. *Owls and Artificers*
> (Deutsch). 1971. pp. 49–51

The word "precious" is usually a term of condemnation. For Marianne Moore it is the highest possible praise. Life itself is seen as "An Egyptian Pulled Glass Bottle in the Shape of a Fish" and she does not permit it to be seen in any other way. She, like Stevens, has often been compared to Edith Sitwell, but Edith Sitwell's bric-a-brac universe is a form of rather savage metaphysical sarcasm. Marianne Moore approves of hers. She not only likes it that way but she is incapable of seeing it otherwise. This in itself is an ironic and witty commentary on the world as it really is. It even has a scarcely audible note of tragedy, but it's doubtful if that is intentional. I've often wondered if Tennessee Williams got the idea and the title for his play, *The Glass Menagerie*, from the contemplation of Marianne Moore and her poetry. Certainly the play could stand as a perfect criticism of both person and poems. . . .

Other women of her generation, notably Elinor Wylie, tried to claim the heritage of Emily Dickinson, but today their verses seem thin stuff indeed, while Marianne Moore's survives. More apparently inhuman poetry has probably never been written. . . . There is a progression in the development of a carapace for the sensibility. Emily Brontë, Christina Rossetti, Emily Dickinson, Marianne Moore. They all write about the same thing, the vertigo of the sensibility in a world of terror.

> Kenneth Rexroth. *American Poetry in the*
> *Twentieth Century* (Herder and
> Herder). 1971. pp. 68–9

MORRIS, WRIGHT (1910–   )

Wright Morris has been the most consistently original of American novelists for a quarter of a century which has borne witness to his originality by refusing to keep his novels in print. Faulkner once occupied the same position, though not for so long a time; and Morris' longer stay may have been his own fault, as Leslie Fiedler once remarked, because he would never join a gang. Perhaps he could not because he had anticipated and discounted too many of them.

He discovered early that life, from any rational point of view, was absurd but took the discovery as a matter of fact rather than as a revelation of philosophical truth. He developed a sympathy for common humanity and an eye and ear for its peculiarities without becoming an alienated or angry young man. He realized that the American archetype of the self-sufficient hero was inappropriate to the modern world and simply avoided the traditional character instead of preserving the cliche with an "anti-hero" or some other man of straw. He lit out for the Territory, in the words of Huck Finn, ahead of the rest and made it, in his own play on the words, a territory in time rather than in space. Because of this he may prove to be not only the most original but the most important American novelist of the mid-century.

Leon Howard. Wright Morris
(Minnesota). 1968. p. 5

Despite its brevity, *Fire Sermon* is simon-pure, dyed-in-the-wool, honest-to-God Wright Morris of the very highest grade. I am not saying that it is his best book—but it is a radiant expression of the art he has developed through 30 years and 14 earlier novels. Although it is anything but preachy, it will stick in the minds of some members of the congregation for a long time. . . .

As he has frequently done, Morris takes his time in showing his characters before he sends them into action. He isn't much interested in the kind of audience whose attention must be (as the blurb writers put it) gripped by the first paragraph. The more patient reader, if he will let himself, comes to admire the skill with which, stroke by stroke, the characters are given form and substance. He will also discover, among other things, that the book is funny, one of Morris's funniest.

Granville Hicks. NYT. Sept. 26, 1971. p. 52

In a jacket plug for *One Day*, Eudora Welty said, "Laying sure hands on the *daily* is Wright Morris's *forte*." His "sure hand" is at work again in *Fire Sermon*, particularly in the first third of this very short novel, in which slowly, deliberately he defines his two main characters, the twelve-year-old Kermit and his 82-year-old "next of kin," his great-uncle Floyd, and sets up the relationship that develops when the old man takes the boy in after the death of his parents. . . .

To someone who grew up on movies in which Jackie Cooper reduced Wallace Beery to sudsy softness and Shirley Temple penetrated the iron exterior of Lionel Barrymore, there is something dangerously familiar about some of the early scenes in the book. . . . Both funny and sentimental, then, these early scenes, but the novel is not going to end—as the movies I invoked usually did—in a smilingly tearful two-shot. This novel is not a hands-across-the-generations schmaltzer, but another enactment of inevitable replacement of the old by the young. . . .

Although the book ends with the young watching the dawn (yes, Morris really does that), with Kermit sorting himself out as best he can, the pervasive quality of the novel lies in Uncle Floyd and the nostalgic sense of loss in him.

Gerald Weales. HdR. Winter,
1971–2. pp. 725–6

Solitary, prolific, enjoying fitfully public acclaim, laboring more often in obscurity, [Morris] seeks to repossess American reality by penetrating its past, stripping its myths. Morris is native to the plains of Nebraska; his characters, frail, inward people, return to their Midwestern past in order to find some viable identity of their own.

His novels vary in quality. Some seem opaque, tedious, or frivolous; a few attain permanent distinction. Certainly Morris is an artist; conscious of his material, he struggles continually against its flatness. . . . Isolation, silence, memory, and above all the muteness or failure of love, the inability to respond, are the concerns of his best work.

Ihab Hassan. Contemporary American
Literature (Ungar). 1973. pp. 37–8

MUMFORD, LEWIS (1895–   )

Lewis Mumford sees *The Pentagon of Power* as his last book, the culmination of a life's work of criticism and prophecy: it is a critique of our civilization through an extended historical analysis deep in conception and popular in exposition. As such it demands respect; and the critical question is whether its inevitable shortcomings vitiate its message. . . . Professor Mumford rightly takes credit for a very considerable achievement. This is to have demonstrated, by a multitude of arguments and examples, that our science and technology are made by man, the product of human presuppositions and choices. We can have a different sort of technology, serving a better sort of society, if we but will it and master its achievement.

In his attempt to find a positive unifying theme for the provision of a simple moral, Professor Mumford may well have neglected the deeper significance of his materials. The confluence of various unpleasant things described as Megamachine is likely to be temporary; and its replacement will doubtless include other things pleasant and unpleasant. History is not a curve that measures goodness as a function of time: nor is it a cosmic drama in which the last act is now beginning. As materials for an appreciation of the deeper dialectic of history, where wonder and tragedy are intermixed, where the liberation of one generation is the oppression of the next, Professor Mumford's anecdotes and insights, extending to science and its ideologies, are undeniably rich and suggestive.

TLS. July 9, 1971. p. 795

[*Interpretations and Forecasts: 1922–1972*] is hardly the occasion for a full assessment of Mumford's achievement; we need, as I have said, the companion volume on cities. But I know few in the next generations who combined the grace, the breadth of inquiry, the urgent yet urbane disinterestedness that one finds in Mumford, in [Edmund] Wilson, in [Walter] Lippmann, in [V. L.] Parrington, although none of these figures, I think, conveys either the rich sense of individual personality or the enduring wisdom that one finds in the greatest English prose writers of the late eighteenth and mid-nineteenth centuries. It may be too soon to judge what Mumford and the others have left us. They have no heirs of anything like their stature, and few even want to celebrate their virtues. . . .

One way of praising the early work of Lewis Mumford is to say that as he leaps across the apparent boundaries offered by countries and centuries and subjects, he also confronts each person, book, and event as something fresh, by itself, not fodder for generalization, though perhaps an occasion to celebrate the possibilities of generalizing. . . . [R. Buckminster] Fuller, like the later Mumford, seeks not just generalization but masterful generalization. Both are decent, on the side of life, but both are imperial, commanding. One can admire them, and live at the heart of empire too, and yet not necessarily want to join in the chorus.

Roger Sale. *NYR*. Feb. 7, 1974. pp. 30, 32

NABOKOV, VLADIMIR (1899–   )

Nabokov's gift is for the creation of these small-scale effects, rather than for larger structures. His best books, among them *Pnin, Lolita* and *Speak, Memory*, have relatively little of the anagrammatic hide-and-seek and fussy pedantry that usurp the center of later and apparently more ambitious works such as *Pale Fire* and *Ada*. They are certainly not powerful, all-encompassing visions like those of Proust and Joyce; in fact, their structure seems slight and rather negligible. They are held together primarily by a sensibility—a texture of delicately perceived sensuous particulars, of radiant moments of poetic feeling tempered by a dandified wit; their affective core is nostalgia, the poignant sense of a lost past. Such a core of feeling exists in *Ada*, but it is lost beneath a grotesquely elaborated "structure" which remains largely superficial. The book is a bit like a seashell, extravagantly involuted, knobbed, covered with all kinds of random incrustations. What is most striking about it is the fantastic disproportion between that hard external carapace and the small living creature inside it.

Elizabeth Dalton. PR. No. 1, 1970. p. 158

Both Proust and Nabokov establish clear boundaries between past and present, provide elaborate and meticulously drafted maps for their realms of recollection, and carefully choose the grounds, or privileged moments, at which past and present will be allowed, briefly and dangerously, to meet and commingle. The goal of these artists is something more important than self-discovery or the discovery of cultural and regional identity. It is the discovery and definition of human consciousness, conceived as the master key to the riddle of reality, conceived also as providing limited, transitory glimpses of the realm of essence.

Neither Proust nor Nabokov permits this essentially metaphysical quest to sterilize his fictional art. Both remain great tragicomic novelists in close touch with the actualities of man in contemporary society and with central issues of modern history. Thirst for the eternal never alienates their loyalty to the human condition although it may constitute the deepest source of their great originality and power as stylists and fabulists.

Julian Moynahan. Vladimir Nabokov
(Minnesota). 1971. p. 6

Writing mostly in Russian during nearly two decades of exile in the West and then transforming himself in middle life into an Anglo-American novelist, Nabokov improvised a stylistic manner of extraordinary verbal ingenuity, having, one feels, all the properties of masterliness except natural fluency and natural resonance. Precisely because his effort was not only to establish a new working medium (and thus a new readership) but to preserve himself as a human being solidly rooted in life, an element of strain and artificiality cemented itself into his work, deadening the active flow of it. V. S. Pritchett . . . (a specialist in these matters) has defined the case well: "Vocabulary, grammar, syntax and the fashions of epithet" had themselves to take the place of the country and culture Nabokov had lost, and as a result he became "a superb exploiter" of the historical languages he adopted to this end but not, like Joyce, their master. He now writes English, including various odd sorts of jargon and slang, with remarkable virtuosity and inventiveness, but he writes it as if it were about to become a dead language; the texts of his novels are scenarios, awaiting realization.

Warner Berthoff. *Fictions and Events*
(Dutton). 1971. pp. 90–1

In what sense . . . do Nabokov's writings mirror his own émigré environment and personal background? That Nabokov's own life and the life of the Russian emigration provide frequent themes and images in his novels and stories is not surprising. . . . Virtually every one of Nabokov's characters is an émigré living in Europe or the United States. More interesting, however, is the pervasive appearance of the "double" motif in Nabokov, not simply as a repetition of the old *Doppelgänger* tool of modern European and Russian literature, but as a reflection of that essential duality suggested by the life of a Russian émigré in Germany.

Nabokov's own denial notwithstanding, the double theme is present throughout his writings. . . . "What made Nabokov choose the theme of the Double as most congenial to the truths he wanted to dramatize?" a recent critic, Claire Rosenfield, asks. The two answers usually suggested are that the double is a standard literary device, employed by Dostoevsky ("Dusty") among others, or that it reflects the sense of alienation from society experienced by artists and writers in general. The Russian emigration's contribution has not been explored in any detail.

Robert C. Williams. *YR*.
Winter, 1971. pp. 246–7

Nabokov is a writer who wants neither to eradicate time through logic nor to outflank its consequences with claims to a spurious immortality.

For him, conventional time is not so much a mortal enemy as it is a dull, cloddish conception that takes no account of the prodigious feats of which an imaginative memory is capable. In his autobiography, *Speak, Memory*, he gives a blunt warning: "I confess I do not believe in time. I like to fold my magic carpet, after use, in such a way as to superimpose one part of the pattern upon another. Let visitors trip." Well, one remembers that there were certainly quite a few barked shins among even the well-intentioned visitors of *Ada*, the price paid for leaping at conclusions when there is no terra firma underneath.

Jack Richardson. *NYR*. March 25, 1971. p. 19

The suffering of Nabokov's characters comes both from within and from without. Agnostics like their creator, sure of nothing but the steady flow of sensations, his characters are, in fact, desperately dependent on the external world. Through their passion for intensity they victimize themselves; and hence their suffering is in part self-created. Yet, at the same time, their suffering has a corresponding source in the external world. Not only is the world devilishly seductive and tantalizing, but also the impressions one receives from it seem at times to form themselves into significative patterns and designs, leading one to the momentary hope that the world holds a meaning of its own, an innate meaning not imparted to it by the perceiver. As these patterns form and dissolve, so the hope quickens and dwindles, leaving the perceiver with nothing but memories. The humanity of Nabokov's characters is based on no philosophical, political, or religious system, on no creed or ideology, but simply on the dignity with which they confront this mirage of hope.

This is surely a view of life born of Nabokov's personal experience. Having seen how fate plays games with man, leaving traces here and there, clues that hint at a whole design or pattern, at a coherent and rational meaning innate in the external world, Nabokov plays the part of fate in the world of his fiction. In the style and form of his fictional worlds, countless moments of aesthetic bliss are available to the reader willing to alter his habitual mode of perception, willing to take—if only temporarily—the aesthetic stance.

Donald E. Morton. *Vladimir Nabokov*
(Ungar). 1974. p. 12

Behind the often delightful invitation to play of mind there lurks a persistent didacticism. In correcting any mistaken ideas we may have about fiction and reality, Nabokov means to demonstrate that if fiction is not Reality, then neither is so-called "reality" outside of fiction. Reality, as he is fond of saying, always belongs in quotation marks. The ground thereby claimed by Nabokov's own fictional enterprise is, to say the very least, exorbitant—and he chooses to govern it all by himself.

As we've seen in the past ten years, any number of little Nabokovs will be ready to make such an investment in a book of this kind [*Look at the Harlequins!*] that they end up admiring it as their own handiwork, their own "invention." To some extent this is always and quite properly the case. But the kind of exegetical efforts we are invited to make here need to be distinguished from those we are willing to make while reading Melville or Joyce or Pynchon. At their many puzzling moments those writers direct the attention of the reader not principally to their own literary texts and lives but to the life and texts of the existent world, with all its inheritances, in which they live and write. Theirs seems to me an altogether more exciting and important venture than Nabokov's, even if he has sometimes been called—and sometimes deserves to be called—our greatest living writer.

He stands on the periphery of the great tradition of American literature since Hawthorne and Melville, and of 20th-century literature since Joyce, in that he is, despite his terror of solipsism, its most awesome practitioner. He is not sufficiently vulnerable to—and his style is only infrequently enriched by—the power of the social and literary institutions by which man continues to invent himself.

Richard Poirier. NYT. Oct. 13, 1974. p. 4

NEMEROV, HOWARD (1920–   )

There is nothing on the dust jacket [of *The Blue Swallows*, Nemerov's seventh book of poems] to indicate he has ever been awarded a major prize. If this is true, it is shocking, for he continues to be one of the very best poets writing in English. His poems are not normally marked by the extreme severity of ["Small Moment"]; but I chose it anyway because it seemed to me absolutely awesome. More commonly, his poems are compassionate, witty, and immensely civilized. . . . Nemerov in his poetry shows himself to be clear-headed, unillusioned and affectionate; wry, critical, often funny, and just as often deeply moving. Which is to say that he presents us with a highly intelligent and flexible viewpoint which is busily inspecting what is constantly passing for "civilization" right before our eyes. And there is not much that escapes notice. There is scarcely another poet who can show us so well how futile and ridiculous we are.

Anthony Hecht. HdR. Spring, 1968. p. 214

A man so able to delight in extended comic metaphor is a wise man and desires and easily makes the transition to a more encompassing expression. Over the years, Nemerov has managed to merge his self-satire and satire of the world through the maturation of a special tone—disarmingly colloquial and casual—and sustained irony. The tone, entirely his, allows him to write simply or complicatedly, sarcastically or casuistically. The ironic method, also entirely his, eschews the usual tricky and "incongruous" lines whereby we normally decide that a poem is ironic; Nemerov's better poems are ironic *line-for-line*. They build; they do not destroy themselves for their effect.

David Galler. The Carleton Miscellany.
Summer, 1968. p. 112

The difference between the early *Salt Garden* and [Nemerov's] most recent work is not the frustration of vision but its movement directed along a scale reaching from psychology to ontology. Indeed, direction turning into presence felt through all the senses becomes a major overt theme; and although *The Salt Garden* possibly contains more extraordinary poems than any single later volume, a sense of substantial presence increasingly informs his style. In this sense, *Gnomes & Occasions* is clearly an advance. . . .

Nemerov's stylistic parallels his thematic development. His first two books displayed a certain elegance, even a dandyism, derived from Ransom and early Stevens. Although this tone has never been completely dropped, it is in sharp abeyance by *The Salt Garden* and is mostly relegated to satirical uses. What has taken its place and been evolved into a powerful discriminatory instrument, a language to gauge "the pressure of intelligence" (in Leavis' phrase), is the plain style, a matter of diction and tone. The foremost practitioners of the plain style in our day are [J. V.] Cunningham, [David] Galler, and Nemerov. The line of descent is from Gascoigne, Fulke Greville, Ben Jonson and tribe, Churchill, some Byron, Landor, some Hardy, Robinson, much Frost, and later Yvor Winters. Plain style must not be confused with so-called "American Speech" (comparison of Nemerov's "Storm Windows" with just about any William Carlos Williams will write the difference large) nor slang (i.e., the bulk of our poetry since circa 1956). Plain style seldom if ever has recourse to colloquialism or the poetical. It tends away from local resonance, though it may be resounding enough as it builds up its effects over the whole of a poem.

Robert Stock. Parnassus. Fall–
Winter, 1973. pp. 158, 160

If one could choose a word to describe Nemerov's art, one would have to settle for a coinage somewhere between *civilized* and *right*. But it is invariably civility with flair. You sense it whether he is writing about a recording of Casals playing Bach . . . or commenting on that void that is more than mere absence. . . .

Perhaps one of the strongest facets of Nemerov's talent emerges in his satirical poems, many of them quite short but all with the pith that characterized a poem of his called "Boom!" some years back. It is here that the poems flourish with the kind of inevitability and ineluctability that poems must have to leave us thinking that they are absolutely beyond improvement or paraphrase.

Samuel Hazo. *Com.* Oct. 19, 1973. p. 67

NIN, ANAIS (1903–   )

A few preliminary words need to be said about some of the typical characteristics of Miss Nin's novels and style. It may be observed that the unity which Miss Nin achieves is accomplished largely through three devices: (1) recurring characters, symbols, and motifs; (2) direct and indirect psychological analysis; and (3) the result of the first two: the definition of a single primary character. Curiously, each of these devices is used in Miss Nin's *Diary* also, but . . . with much more success than in her fiction.

Style, an amorphous subject at best, is conspicuously and consistently one of the attractive qualities of Miss Nin's art. The originality of her diction, imagery, and symbolism has led some to charge her with being too esoteric, but I think that one will find, upon close examination of her works, that she seldom introduces extraneous words and images into her writing, and that unity is a chief characteristic of nearly all her works. Miss Nin's rich vocabulary enables her, especially in the *Diary*, to make her pronouncements and descriptions clearly and precisely. In all of her writing she is sensitive to rhythm (and the idea of rhythm, movement, is a key symbol in her art), sensitive to rich and sensual images.

Duane Schneider. *SoR.* Spring, 1970. pp. 506–7

Miss Anais Nin has acquired during the past thirty years a hothouse image, like some rare orchid—exotic, delicate, yet rich with voluptuous promise, a writer whose *Journals*, of which further volumes are promised, have become a literary legend to many who will never read a word of them. It's therefore likely to surprise anyone familiar with such an image to find that this slim . . . reissue of a novel [*A Spy in the House of Love*] which first appeared in 1954 is, beneath the dreamlike imagery and modish, tentative exploration of emotional disturbance, an impassioned cry for Women's Lib. Not that Miss Nin would dream of wasting fine writing on blueprints for economic independence, the burdens of domesticity, or the recognition of a woman's capacity in a man's role; she is concerned here with the obsessive guilt and bewildered longings of a woman who cannot bear to be caged by one man, one home, one personality, who will lie and cheat to retain sexual independence and who, above all, recognizes and is appalled by her desire for passion without responsibility, sex without love, for the game of "defeating life's limitations" by "passing without passports and permits from one love to another."

TLS. Jan. 29, 1971. p. 113

Miss Nin's diaries emphasize her resort to frequent bouts of psychoanalysis to rescue her from the desperate restrictions of an untrammeled life. Absorbed in narcissism, she flounders among the multitude of selves she perceives. Committed to fantasies of feminine power, she involves herself therefore in endless responsibilities to others. Her self-display requires an audience, her audience makes demands, her freedom eludes her. Her relationships lead her back only to herself. It seems a strangely symbolic fact that her husband has disappeared, apparently by his request, from her published diaries. The stillborn fetus might, for all we are told, be a virgin birth: the figure of Anaïs Nin, surrounded by others, exists nonetheless in a terrifying isolation of self-concern.

Patricia Meyer Spacks. HdR.
Winter, 1971–2. p. 564

Anais Nin is one of the most extraordinary and unconventional writers of this century. Her vast diary, which encompasses some 50 years of human relationships, resembles no other in the history of letters, and as a novelist she has been distinctly catalytic. With her direct knowledge of the mechanics of psychoanalysis, she conveyed the even flow of uncensored speech in a series of prose writings which constitute one continuous novel. Collected under the title, Cities of the Interior, these writings in fiction are so detached from historical epoch, and the topography of her inner spaces so remote from the naturalistic landscapes of her fellow novelists of the 1940's and 1950's that they might well have been left untouched as a legacy for future generations, had not the publication of her diaries, beginning in 1966, brought her into full public view, earned her a sizable American audience, and a particularly remarkable popularity with younger readers. . . .

If conversation and letter writing project the psyche outward, a continuously flowing interior monologue provides the channel for self-analysis. The splicing of dialogue and monologue, and the determining of their relationship to each other, are important features of Anais Nin's artistry. As she reports people's confessions, as she reveals their letters to her, she manages to bypass the kind of gossip and anecdote that we have learned to expect from diarists. Imagine a conversation in which nothing unimportant is ever uttered, where each bit of dialogue is crucial, digs deep into vital issues, where each meeting occurs at times of heightened awareness!

Anna Balakian. *NYT*. Jan. 16, 1972. p. 28

• OATES, JOYCE CAROL (1938–   )

Unlike many collections whose short stories have been gathered arbitrarily to manufacture a book, Miss Oates' book [*By the North Gate*]
has emotional consistency and thematic unity that produce a single
effective fictional experience. It is one that, at times, seems too painful
to bear. Yet it is also too interesting to ignore, too perceptive to turn
away from and too honest to reject.

> R. D. Spector. *Book World.*
> Nov. 17, 1963. p. 32

One of the excellent qualities of this novel [*With Shuddering Fall*] . . .
is an unswerving fidelity to its theme. The theme is violence, beginning
with a minor automobile accident, then accelerating swiftly to a nearly
mortal flight, an immolation, onward and downward into an ever faster
and stronger whirlpool of violence, until the entire world of the novel is
caught in a paroxysm of hate and destruction. . . . This material is not as
garish as it sounds because of the clarity, grace and intelligence of the
writing.

> John Knowles. *NYT.* Oct. 25, 1964. p. 5

The question is no longer whether Miss Oates is a very good writer—she
is, indeed—but just how far and high she can thrust the trajectory of
brilliant accomplishment she has begun. It appears to me that her gifts
are at least equal to Flannery O'Connor. If she is not absolutely more
serious than Nabokov—whose *Lolita* this present novel [*Expensive
People*] resembles in its virtuosity—she is more obviously "ours" and
therefore to be taken more seriously by us. Everything she touches turns
to such blistering gold that sometimes I suspect she must have had
Rumpelstiltskin in to help her spirit in the night.

    Expensive People contains and exploits a little of everything. It is
satire, confession, dream, report on suburbia, gothic tale in contemporary dress, with even some touches of the pop novel thrown in to
show that the author can find a valid use for the screech of that untuned
fiddle, too. But though her technique is eclectic, parodistic, sheer magpie, her bits of everything are fused into a prophetic novel as singular in
effect as the night cry of a hurt animal.

> R. V. Cassill. *Book World.* Nov. 3, 1968. p. 5

Even though all her technical faults remain untouched, *A Garden of Earthly Delights* not only fulfills her early promise, it makes her, for me, the second finest writer in America. Wright Morris is a better writer because I think aesthetic values are of more lasting importance. I am unable to explain in aesthetic terms the mystery of Miss Oates's genius for sustaining the intensity of her vision and for creating such totally alive characters and situations. I know of no other young novelist who succeeds in creating life with an apparent absence of art. She seems to make criticism irrelevant; it elucidates her work very little beyond offering an introduction. (The opposite is true of Wright Morris.) Joyce Carol Oates is a phenomenon, an original, a natural—not a mentor, as Joyce, Morris, Hemingway, and sometimes Fitzgerald and Faulkner are. She must be experienced, not analyzed—this is simply a brute observation, not praise. The young writer who cites Miss Oates's writing as justification for his own faults disguised as virtues can only suffer, and may not survive.

David Madden. *The Poetic Image in Six Genres* (Southern Illinois). 1969. p. 46

At this hour in her career Miss Oates resembles, speaking harshly but I believe truly, a female James Jones donning and doffing, by turns, an unseductive doctoral hood. There is nothing mysterious about her emergence as writer or teacher, nor are the anti-elitist elements of contemporary culture responsible for that emergence without exception negative, regrettable influences. But seeing Miss Oates merely as part of a whole cultural configuration is, in the end, unjustifiable; hers is an individual human situation and, as such, deserves respect and understanding. The primary fact about that situation is, perhaps, that only an exceptional creature—someone combining in himself extraordinary will, intelligence, and humility—could, given its nature, win through to a significant literary achievement. There could be richer rewards than have ever been forthcoming from prodigies, publishing phenomena and the like if Miss Oates could find such resources within herself. Best therefore not to quote odds; best simply to wish her well in what cannot fail to be a long and arduous search.

Benjamin DeMott. *SR*. Nov. 22, 1969. p. 89

Heart is Miss Oates's part. Though she speaks of irony, she is skeptical of it. Fortunately there is in *them* itself no counterpart to the uneasy self-depreciation which warps her Author's Note, with its concluding curtesy about "the rather disdainful and timorous title *them*." Disdainful and timorous Miss Oates is not, and knows she is not. She has a proper dislike of self-depreciation, and pities those who have been unnerved out of confidence. One of her earlier stories, "Archways," speaks bitterly of how the young are "educated now into knowing their unworth"; this story has clear affinities with the end of *them* and a sense of "unworth" is Miss Oates's true and desolating concern. She would not adopt the old pompous ways of speaking of self-respect . . . but she has a staunchly old-fashioned, and salutary, sense of the relations between self-respect and respectability. The degradations of city life are so intense, and so intensely created by her, that respectability can be seen as vital to self-preservation; one remembers Steven Marcus's fine account in *The Other Victorians* of respectability and urban brutality, and of the amount that respectability made possible that was not just worthwhile but a matter of life and death.

Christopher Ricks. NYR.
Feb. 12, 1970. pp. 22–3

Miss Oates's work presents a mixture of two styles—one of them a large, earnest naturalism from which come detailed scenes of rural and urban desolation, the other a tendency to push beyond these life scenes toward transcendent meaning, an urge that expresses itself in the eruption of hallucinatory violence. . . .

There is an authentic feeling in her stories for the physical ambience of poverty, for the grease stains, the stale smells, the small pathetic decorative objects of plastic. . . . What seems less authentic, however, is the violence itself, and the rather programmatic way it is used to resolve every situation.

Elizabeth Dalton. Cmty. June, 1970. p. 75

[Oates's] virtues aren't difficult to sum up: a native gift for "story telling"; a more or less clean narrative line, taking her from recognizable starting-points to conclusions very solidly on the same track; a passion for, amounting to an obsession with, what we like to call inner life; a good, almost photographic eye and ear for the minutiae of ordinary existence; a concern with some central human issues and conditions: the myths of love, the nature of female morale, the oppressions of family life, the aridity of urban and suburban existence; the quest for communion; the struggle against others.

In any conventional accounting for literary potentiality and achievement this cluster of attributes would rank high. And that in fact is the point about Miss Oates: in a time of uproar and uncertainty in literature, a period of violently shifting standards and aggressive new imaginative proposals together with a counteracting erosion of confidence about writing itself, she satisfies a longing for familiar ground, for what literature is supposed "to be about," for the appearance of stability, continuity and graspable seriousness. And she does this handsomely, with few blatantly false steps, no inept images or gross failures of rhetoric, and with just the right degree of "experimentation" to keep her from resting too complacently in the bosom of the familiar.

Richard Gilman. NYT. Oct. 25, 1970. p. 4

The details in Oates' fiction follow each other with a humble truthfulness that makes you wonder where she is taking you, that is sometimes truly disorienting, for she is all attention to the unconscious reactions of her characters. She needs a lot of space, which is why her short stories tend to read like scenarios for novels. The amount of concentration this involves is certainly very singular, and one can well understand the vulnerability, the "reedlike thinness," the face and body tense with listening that her appearance gives off. My deepest feeling about her is that her mind is unbelievably crowded with psychic existences, with such a mass of stories that she lives by being wholly submissive to "them," the others. She is too burdened by some mysterious clamor to *want* to be an artist, to make the right and well-fitting structure. . . .

Yet admiring her sense of reality, so unpresuming, honest, and truly exceptional, I have to add that the problem of dealing with Oates is that many of the things she has written are not artistically ambitious enough. They seem written to relieve her mind of the people who haunt it, not to create something that will live.

Alfred Kazin. Harper. Aug., 1971. pp. 81–2

Wonderland reaches its peak early and sustains it for almost 400 pages; but it's as precarious as the fat girl's tower of numbers holding itself up by the force of its own motion and the novel finally collapses and ends in shambles. The book begins to fail when Oates tells us that her characters are emotionally shaken and their lives changed by JFK's assassination; as in her use of the Detroit riots in *them*, the reality the narrative has created is so strong that actual events we ourselves have witnessed seem bland in comparison, and we can't believe that they could affect the characters' lives. The savage personal vision is lost and not regained; and *Wonderland*, the most involving, the most poetic, the greatest of Oates's novels so far becomes the most deeply flawed of her long works, because it has reached a higher plane than her other books and therefore must fall through a longer distance. Its ultimate failure seems inevitable and even admirable, since anything that exists at this degree of heat must burn itself up if it keeps going, and Oates isn't one to quit when she's ahead.

John Alfred Avant. LJ. Aug., 1971. p. 2545

Joyce Carol Oates doesn't pick at her characters' brains. Having escaped the fascination that motive and mental state have for other contemporary writers, she keeps the unfortunates who populate her novels so busy they have hardly a moment for introspection. Miss Oates tells what happens to her characters and what their experiences—usually terrible —do to them but she rarely explains what they are thinking about their plights. . . .

A number of the major themes of literature are recognizable in Miss Oates's work. She has Tolstoy's sense of history as it overwhelms the individual, and she reveals a classical affinity for fatalism and lost innocence. Her characters are afflicted with the anomie explored by the French existentialists. On a lesser scale, she shares James Agee's reverence for the terror and frailty of childhood and, like D. H. Lawrence, she scorns the life of the mind as ineffectual and irrelevant.

But, most of all, Miss Oates's ties are to the twentieth-century school of American naturalism, particularly Theodore Dreiser. Although she is less concerned with sociology than he was, Miss Oates's stories unfold in the same harsh settings, and her characters fight to survive with the same befuddled amorality as those of *An American Tragedy*.

Brian P. Hayes. SR. Oct. 9, 1971. p. 38

Wonderland is about a cluster of deeply related things—a cluster that seems to writhe frighteningly from a single source. It is about the spirit's hunger for strength and identity, its consequent need to possess others, its terror of the anonymity of flesh, of the blank nothingness of death. Oates seems uncannily up with all of us, the very young, the middle-aged, the old; and though her three "gook" titles sound tritely pretentious—"variations on an american hymn," "the finite passing of an infinite passion," "dreaming american"—she is to my mind one of the most comprehensive and knowing American novelists now writing. . . .

The supreme attraction, the essential originality of *Wonderland*, as of *them*, is its dramatic unpeeled quality. Everything in it seems loaded, exposed, veined and vulnerable yet opaque, like a skinless plum. The scenes and characters (even the minor figures) are fully there without being contained. They are uncovered rather than delineated, broken into, never packaged. Oates's style, correspondingly, is inventive and continually fresh without being sharp or self-alerting—it is not a stylist's style. Seriously, steadily, it reveals; it is the perfect medium for her empathic imagination.

What a shame were *Wonderland* to be neglected or resisted because *them* made so recent an impact. In achievement it is more or less the equal of the earlier book, and the two together, like the gifted and enormous Pederson children, are distinct yet related wonders.

Calvin Bedient. PR. No. 1, 1972. pp. 124, 127

Wonderland is an ambitious novel, and a fascinating exploration of an area which has always been at the core of Miss Oates' work, but which she has never approached so boldly: the matter of identity in a world whose reality is questionable. To my mind the most telling portions are those in which the setting is vivid; they render most clearly the disparity between the interior life and the objective world. . . . However, the whole novel is successful; to have rendered such complex material with such simplicity is the mark of a fine artist. It is perhaps a measure of my own living condition as a living particle of Miss Oates' America that I feel such a marked preference for the located individual, and a certain distaste for the slipperiness of the purely interior flow of feeling.

Ellen Hope Meyer. MedR. Spring, 1972. p. 54

Joyce Carol Oates has come out with another book of poetry, her first [*Anonymous Sins, & Other Poems*] having met in many quarters with gentle critical disapproval. It is often difficult for an artist to move from one *genre* to another. Miss Oates is a novelist and short story writer of enormous power and widespread recognition; her prose skillfully re-creates for us the chaos of our lives, the empty sentimentality of our hopes. Though her second group of poems, *Love and Its Derangements,* is an improvement over the previous book, it is not as consistently satisfying as the prose works. The least skillful characteristics of her novels and stories appear in the poems; there is little remaining space for the dramatic virtues she does possess. There are stunning poems in the volume, but they appear all too infrequently.

The essence of Miss Oates' poetry is emotion—intense, but unat-tached, free-floating. Poetry, to be truly effective, must "organ-ize" emo-tion in two senses: it must give coherent organic form and direction to feeling and it must make that emotion felt in a direct, internal, and particular way. One of the worst criticisms one can make of a poem is to say that it abounds in vague emotion or empty verbiage. Unfortunately, a few of Miss Oates' poems do just that. Others employ stale or illogical metaphors. Some, however, probe deeply the moving themes of her novels—the psycho-sexual framework of love, the disappearance of concrete personal identity in our world, the need to achieve an existen-tial relation between man and woman which forever lays the ghost of the old absolutist romantic notions which inevitably betray the hopeful be-ings who hold them. At these moments Miss Oates is at her poetic best.

Sally Andersen. Spirit. Fall, 1972. p. 24

Critics slight Joyce Carol Oates when they tag her as merely, or pri-marily, a "gothic novelist" (i.e., lurid, grotesque, grisly). Some have clucked suspiciously about how much she manages to write and publish . . . hinting quality must suffer. Some find her work repetitious in theme and content, even (somehow) more like refined but still sensational journalism rather than carefully crafted fiction. These demurrers shy from the most astute challenges posed by Oates in her lushly tense, often wounding novels and stories. She is no more "gothic" than today's headlines, no more violent than the nightly bloody canapes served up on the six o'clock news. But her focus and creative impulse tend to deinstitutionalize the blood-letting, causing the impact to bite deep, even in media-narcotized minds. If there is any "journalism" in her writing, it is in the crushing immediacy of contemporary atmospheres and details which coupled with her unabashed fictional virtuosity, makes the terrifying aspects of American life vivid for her readers. Certainly there has been no absence of acute high quality in anything she has recently undertaken in fiction. And rather than repetitions in her work (are Matisse's nudes or Picasso's satyrs repetitious?), I think one discovers Oats has a brazenly disciplined and audacious methodology for attacking metaphysical problems while integrating the real, or apparent, textures of modern life into the equation.

S. K. Oberbeck. *Book World.*
Sept. 17, 1972. p. 4

In the landscape of the contemporary American short story Miss Oates stands out as a master, occupying a preeminent category of her own.

It was as a writer of stories that she began her career in the early 1960's, and she has continued to write stories ever since, not as a diversion or spinoff from the writing of novels, but as a central concern in her work—a fortunate recognition that the shorter form is peculiarly suited to her. There is a sense of tension, of nerves stretched to the breaking point, of "the pitch that is close to madness" in much of what she writes. Sustained too long, it would lose its emotional effectiveness and intellectual credibility. As it is, a story such as "The Dead," which tells with the utmost conviction of a young woman writer going gradually to pieces, is not only harrowing to read but unfaltering in its control, written as close to the edge as possible without crossing over it.

William Abrahams. *SR.* Sept. 23, 1972. p. 76

The life people live in the fiction of Joyce Carol Oates is both drab and electric, full of melodrama and yet curiously dull. Life is mysterious, a character thinks in her novel *them* . . . and then wonders why the mystery is cast in the forms of such diminished people. The suggestion is that melodrama is not nearly as unusual as we think, is hardly extraordinary at all. It is all too often merely a familiar instance of life's heavy hand as a scenarist. We live with it, lose our friends and children by it, but we acquire none of the glamour that seems our due, we are as diminished as ever.

Yet there is also the suggestion in much of Miss Oates's work that the glamour refused to us in reality can nevertheless come to us as an irrational promise, an exhilaration in the midst of mess and despair. We can tell large, important lies to ourselves even when we are at our most diminished, and they are not entirely lies, because they arise out of feelings we really have. Melodrama fuels these feelings, seems to confirm them, but stops short of making them come true, leaves us with a bright mood only, stranded this side of transfiguration.

Michael Wood. NYT. Oct. 1, 1972. p. 6

Much of the power of Joyce Carol Oates' fiction lies in her disturbing ability to identify and expose the fears we have deep within us. Through her art she touches these dark, personal fears: those we admit, those we deny, and those we dimly perceive—but perhaps refuse to confront.

Many of Oates' stories explore two major fears. One is the individual's fear of physical or emotional damage inflicted by another person. . . . The second is man's secret fear of the consequences of a sudden eruption of hidden psychic forces—forces which he suspects lie within him but which he can neither fully anticipate, understand, nor control. . . .

Most interesting of all, perhaps, is Oates' treatment of the fear of being the Outsider. No matter what else the story is about, nearly every one touches on this particular terror. The Outsider is a person who perceives himself as somehow cut off from, shut out of, the human race. He suffers from being uncontrollably different, an aberration. . . .

Given the horror of his situation, where does the Outsider in Oates' fiction look for comfort and solace? With genuine love unavailable, many of the characters look to art and the act of writing, desperately hoping to stave off disaster by fashioning pattern out of flux and sense out of absurdity.

Carolyn Walker. Critique.
15, 1, 1973. pp. 59–60

With her torrent of words, her absorption in feeling and her pitch of drama, why shouldn't [Oates] succeed as a poet too. Melville did; Hardy did; Lawrence did; Emily Brontë did; it is possible; it even, on the face of it, seems natural. . . .

These poems [<i>Angel Fire</i>] have an awkward gait and an ungainly structure, an incoherence of parts and a lack of conclusiveness in the whole. They are the poems of someone with ideas enough to make poems and with words enough to make poems but without the mysterious power to create the voluptuous surfaces, the original cadences, or the visual juxtapositions of words which alone convince us of the existence of a genuine new poet.

Helen Vendler. NYT. April 1, 1973. pp. 7–8

Is Joyce Carol Oates, the only American woman writer of talent who has matched the industry of her British counterparts such as Doris Lessing, Muriel Spark and Margaret Drabble, to be cubbyholed as they have been? Is this remarkable novelist, a woman who is never afraid to take risks, a woman whose fictional works confront our contemporary scene, doomed to suffer the fate of Lessing, for example, and be seen only as an authority on the role of women? To do so would be to miss what she is all about.

In novel after novel, story after story, Oates gives us her own tragic America, a personal vision as perceptive as it is instructive and terrifying. She does not so much preach as show us ourselves on an exaggerated screen. Her damaged women, her haunted men are grotesques but always under her firm artistic control. They are as old fashioned as the wild, secretive loners who roamed the streets of Winesburg, Ohio at twilight. But, as with Sherwood Anderson's folk, Oates' swollen characters are relevant to and complement the horror and dangers of our American landscape. The truths of our lives are exhibited in the excesses. In no work of hers is this as evident as in her latest, lengthy novel, *Do With Me What You Will*.

Charles Shapiro. NR. Oct. 27, 1973. p. 26

At first the novel [*The Assassins*] seems a murder mystery: who killed Andrew? But to develop that topic would require at least one well-meaning, rational investigator. Stephen means well but is helplessly irrational; no one else is rational, well-meaning, or even well. The novel therefore reaches only coarse conclusions. By its end one of the leading characters has been set wandering aimlessly; another is deaf, blind, dumb, and paralyzed as the result of a suicide attempt; the third has been shot; and the fourth has been shot and hacked to pieces with an ax. Why? What does it mean? Such questions are pointless. Motivation is unknowable and finally irrelevant in this world of paranoid neurosis: "they" make things happen, and these suspicious, isolated, hysterical victims merely flounder as their sickness bids.

J. D. O'Hara. NYT. Nov. 23, 1975. p. 18

O'CONNOR, FLANNERY (1926–1964)

Flannery's early stories met with . . . unreflective criticism. Why, people wanted to know, did she have to write about such unattractive characters? And why write only about the South? Were there no other parts of the country worth portraying? From the point of view of sales, however, her stories had one thing in their favor: violence. Ours is an age which may be said to specialize in violence. Flannery's characters live in a matrix of violence and some of them meet violent ends. People continued to wish that they could meet at least one "attractive" person in her stories, but they kept on reading. She began by writing stories which few people could understand. She ended by writing stories which everybody —or almost everybody—professed to "love."

This pattern seems to recur over and over in literary history. It usually signifies the emergence of a strong and original talent. In Flannery's case there is no question of the strength and originality of the talent.

Caroline Gordon. SwR. Spring, 1968. p. 267

In Miss O'Connor's fiction, the religious vision is markedly apocalyptic. According to this vision, everything in life leads to death, and death is revelation. It is exactly in the instant of passing out of time and life and into eternity that her characters seem to live most fully: they *begin* their humanity exactly when it is ended in time. She quietly insists on viewing death, however horrible and violent, from the perspective of eternity. If the reader resists this view, there will seem to be no moral or emotional resolutions to her stories: only the arbitrary, violent, and meaningless "resolution" of an equally arbitrary, violent, and meaningless death. If he accepts her view, he will be asked to see that the death of any character is supremely valuable as a means to his awakening to reality. . . .

The particular view of death that we find in Miss O'Connor's fiction is related to her presentation of the operation of grace. In this fiction, the effects of grace are rarely visible in the active and fruitful union of the human with the divine will, and redemption does not seem to happen *in the world*. Grace is usually seen to operate as a powerful but hidden force which is entirely separate from human will and intention. It seems as though God is out to accomplish His salvation in spite of the sinner's willful drive against Him.

Ruth M. Vande Kieft. SwR. Spring,
1968. pp. 345–6, 350–1

The work of Flannery O'Connor is remarkably free of morbidity because, like Greek tragedy or Christian myth, her attention is less on catharsis and loss than on transfiguration; less on the fact of death than on its attendant circumstance and aftermath—the apocalyptic vision of possibility. . . . The thrust of Flannery O'Connor's work . . . is into the heart of paradox, epitomized by serious consideration that man's mortality might be an act of grace and the occasion of death a prophetic sign. . . .

Flannery O'Connor undercuts the more sensational or melodramatic aspects of dying, because she is concerned less with documentary realism than with the aura of understanding effected in the agonist himself or in a bystander.

Leonard Casper in *The Shaken Realist*,
edited by Melvin J. Friedman and
John B. Vickery (Louisiana
State). 1970. pp. 290–1, 293

Flannery O'Connor's Catholic celebration is unique in contemporary literature. Her literal, banal style disguises a sense of participation in the sacred action of the universe: the salvation of man. She remains firmly grounded in the physical scene, the rural, biblical South, but she shows us the mystery on which that scene is built. At times communal, more often personal, the hidden celebration in her work is perhaps the finest testament of her ability to connect fact and mystery.

Although Flannery O'Connor and Eudora Welty are both southern ladies (Miss O'Connor would be amused at the term) whose literary imagination is thoroughly grounded in the rural South, they are not really comparable. Eudora Welty's countryside is rich, historical, and mythical; her lyric style has its closest affinities with poetry; her essential subject is the incommunicable uniqueness of life. Flannery O'Connor's South is all red clay and pinewoods—often aflame in one way or another; she used ugliness, grotesquerie, suffering, and Old Testament violence to point up the need for a salvation greater than ourselves. To this end she was anti-humanist and conservative, fearing the false comforts of liberal compassion and urban civilization. Her closest affinities are not with southern literature at all, but with French literature. One hears in her work the tragic echoes of Pascal, the prophetic thunder of Leon Bloy, and the dying words of [George] Bernanos's country priest —"Does it matter? Grace is everywhere."

Richard H. Rupp. *Celebration in Postwar
American Fiction* (Miami). 1970. p. 98

• O'HARA, FRANK (1926–1966)

This is the poetry of flat, dead-pan colloquialism. . . . This does not mean that O'Hara is easy or trivial. It is just as hard to be casual and amazing as it is to be catchy and profound. . . . I am not sure that his direct, "hear me talking to you, I just want to say this and get going" speech always rises above the flatness of its own colloquialism, but when it does, it is moving in the way that only simple communication can be moving. Certainly his poems always manage a fresh start, free from the dreadful posturings of the conventional verse of his generation.

Kenneth Rexroth. NYT. Oct. 6, 1957. p. 43

Most writers about New York exaggerate or sentimentalize; the city has qualities that don't lend themselves easily to lyric expression. I think Mr. O'Hara is the best writer about New York alive, perhaps the only good one; he succeeds in conveying the city's atmosphere not by writing directly about it but by writing about his emotions, all of them somehow filtered through its paint supply stores and its inspiring April smog. . . .

Second Avenue's language has a good deal to do with its success. Like that of [William Carlos] Williams—from which it differs in other respects—Mr. O'Hara's language is convincing and natural. (There isn't a tedious "literary" use of a word in the whole poem, except when Mr. O'Hara is parodying the built-in solemnity which has been a chief horror of our poetry for twenty years.) Stilted academic language (in which animals are "beasts" and "trust" means only "have faith in" and not "a bank") has never been able to say anything about New York. "Beat" language has done a little better; but, accurate as it may be, it remains a jargon which limits the meanings of words (*cool, bust*), and which is not nearly comprehensive enough to deal with "the most substantial art product of our times." Mr. O'Hara's language is hugely comprehensive and capable of the widest and most surprising effects. . . .

Kenneth Koch. PR. Jan.–Feb., 1961. pp. 130–1

Everything (experienced) is in the imagination. First impressions focus on this: anything can be taken up and said. O'Hara had the ability, and the power, to use in a poem whatever occurred to him at the moment, without reflection. It is not that he lacked selectivity or discrimination, but rather that his poems grew out of a process of natural selection— discrimination conjoining civility of attention—so that any particle of experience quick enough to get fixed in his busy consciousness earned its point of relevance. He was always, in the painter Willem de Kooning's words, "out buying some environment." All kinds of things: the departure of one friend and the arrival of two others, the headlines (Khrushchev, Lana Turner, the mugging of Miles Davis, the death of Billie Holiday, Marilyn Monroe), smog, sexual notions and unpermissiveness of childhood, idiotic notions of manhood, "the cheap tempestuousness of our time," sainthood, toothpicks, "arcane dejection," Bayreuth, Canada, Park Avenue, Kenneth, Vincent, Joe and Jane (the ancient and magical custom of naming names and seeing your friends turn sacred on the page), fantastic realities ("we are all rushing down the River Happy Times . . . signed, The Saw"). It is a poetry of nouns and pronouns; the verbs often doubtful, in quotes, adornments after the fact (for names contain actions), or simply useful connectives, reduced to prepositions —this is an age which insists that the substantive is the last thing you can bank on!

Bill Berkson. Art and Literature.
Spring, 1967. p. 55

No one could have guessed ten years ago that the poems of Frank O'Hara would be among the most seminal influences on the work of the youngest generation of American poets now in their 20s. So much of the work collected in *Meditations in an Emergency* and *Lunch Poems* appeared at first flat, prosaic odds and ends of commonplace events, thoughts, gossip, locations and clichés. . . . Today, one has come to see why such poems are considered pioneering classics not only by the young but by some of O'Hara's contemporaries. Such poems are classics for the obvious reason: O'Hara was probably the first poet to ignore taking the traditional step away from undigested daily experience in order to refine it into formal art. In brief, he was the first and he remains the best of the poets of the impure. . . .

Once one learned how to appreciate this impure quality, the reading of an O'Hara poem was usually like trying on a new pair of glasses. What had been dim or ignored out of habit or prejudice or preconception suddenly became incandescent with poetry. . . .

Wit is another part of his example and legacy. Again, O'Hara's edgy, sometimes corny but always very genuine wit is as commonplace as the time of day or the mildly good high one can feel at a cocktail party. It is, as he might say, "real."

At other times, however, O'Hara hides behind a kind of adolescent Wow! and smarty-pants posturing and fails to get at or get across the complex of feelings which clearly originated the poem. Instead, he remains entangled by New York chic and hysterical activity—an acting-out of feelings on the page instead of an exploration into their reality.

But at his best, the man speaking in many of O'Hara's poems possesses that rare quality: charm.

Paul Carroll. The Poem in Its Skin
(Follett). 1968. pp. 221–2

As a poet, [O'Hara] was able to impart existence to things merely by naming them. And he could breathe life into art, or at any rate call attention to the life that was already there, in a way which is hard to pin down but whose aura continues.

"Picasso made me tough and quick, and the world," begins an early autobiographical O'Hara poem. . . . Tough *and* quick in order to turn back to Picasso and the world and get the good out of them, this time to remake them in his image, putting something in the empty space between the world and Picasso. He discovered how to do this along with a generation of American artists.

John Ashbery. Art News. Jan., 1968. pp. 50–1

During the halcyon days of the Abstract Expressionists and Imaginative Realism movements, Frank O'Hara was the laureate of the New York art scene. . . . A fascinating amalgam of fan, connoisseur and propagandist, he was considered by his friends, in an excess of enthusiasm, the Apollinaire of his generation, an esthetic courtier who had taste and impudence and prodigious energy. . . .

A Pan piping the city streets, he luxuriates in the uninhibited play of his imagination. . . .

Between the lines of his prankish behavior and his celebrations of love and art and friendship, of "all dear and singular things," one reads a plaintive anxiety. The brittle, decorated surfaces of his poems, the droll humor, cloak a Pierrot who is easily wounded. As a distant cousin of the Dadaists, he indulges a talent for spoofing all that intimidates him: the fear of death and failure, the loss of love. . . .

His gift was best expressed in a civilized poise that enabled him to glimpse in sensual chaos the mysterious springs of love and grace. . . . The pleasures of the *Collected Poems* confirm his place as one of our best minor poets.

Herbert A. Leibowitz. NYT.
Nov. 28, 1971. pp. 7, 28

[O'Hara's] intense involvement with so many different levels of work, so many different kinds of artist, naturally created great demands on his personal loyalties. But it was part of O'Hara's genius to be oblivious to these demands, to treat the whole thing as if it were some big, frantic, glamorous movie set. To us he seemed to dance from canvas to canvas, from party to party, from poem to poem—a Fred Astaire with the whole art community as his Ginger Rogers. . . .

It is only now that one sees the truth of this intellectual's intellectual—this Noel Coward's Noel Coward—only now one realizes it was his capacity for work, his stamina, his passion for work, that was the energy going through his life. . . .

Who but the dead know what it is to be alive? Death seems the only metaphor distant enough to truly measure out existence. Frank understood this. That is why these poems [*Collected Poems*], so colloquial, so conversational, nevertheless seem to be reaching us from some other, infinitely distant place. Bad artists throughout history have always tried to make their art like life. Only the artist who is close to his own life gives us an art that is like death.

Morton Feldman. Art in America.
March, 1972. pp. 53–5

Until very recently . . . O'Hara was regarded as something of an *enfant terrible*, a Pop Poet who claimed, in his "Personism: A Manifesto," that "I don't even like rhythm, assonance, all that stuff. You just go on your nerve." The *Collected Poems* belies this brash assertion at every turn. O'Hara was nothing if not learned. His command of language and verse forms, his knowledge of European literature rivaled not only Lowell's but Eliot's and Pound's; he could, when he wanted to, write fine sonnets . . . aubades . . . or eclogues. . . . His aesthetic, for that matter, was no more revolutionary than Wordsworth's. "It may be," O'Hara wrote, "that poetry makes life's nebulous events tangible to me and restores their detail; or conversely, that poetry brings forth the intangible quality of incidents which are all too concrete and circumstantial. . . ." One thinks immediately of Coleridge's famous statement, in Chapter XIV of the *Biographia*, that Wordsworth's aim in *Lyrical Ballads* was "to give the charm of novelty to things of every day . . . by awakening the mind's attention from the lethargy of custom, and directing it to the loveliness and the wonders of the world before us."

But although O'Hara's poetics is essentially romantic, he parts company with Wordsworth on one important point. For him, poetry, far from having its origin in emotion recollected in tranquillity, is the expression of what is happening *now*. Unlike the confessional poets, who find the meaning of their present existence to be firmly grounded in the past, O'Hara seeks to remove what Coleridge called "the film of familiarity" by placing the poet's self squarely at the center of the poem, in the very process of discovering his world. Not analysis of feeling but its coming into being is what counts, and the reader's job is, accordingly, to participate in the poet's act of discovery.

Marjorie G. Perloff. CL. Winter, 1973. p. 99

O'Hara himself is one whom other poets love for saying yes but do not actually believe. His influence and popularity are considerably greater than his achievement—a phenomenon attributable to many factors including his sheer entertainment value and the notoriety of his pathetic and unexpected death. But most of all I think his popularity stems from his sybaritic stoicism, or perhaps affirmative skepticism, and from his articulation of strategies, attitudes and values which other poets find themselves momentarily sharing. In addition, many of O'Hara's strategies can be adapted to qualities of experience less camp and aggressively superficial. While O'Hara reduces the present to sheer surface and the creative play of the individual consciousness, he also points to materials and attitudes which might constitute a genuine moral vision free of the systematic and abstract distortions of most philosophical attempts to define value.

Charles Altieri. IowaR. Winter, 1973. p. 98

O'HARA, JOHN (1905–1970)

There are more elegant stylists, more profound thinkers, more sensitive spirits. There is no working writer who matches O'Hara's importance as a social historian. When the next century wants to know how Americans lived between 1920 and 1940, it will find what it wants to know in O'Hara. It will find the names of things—the right names—but it will also find accurate analyses of the social structure and characters who are both real and representative. The stories and people may not always fall within the individual reader's experience, but it is difficult to doubt that O'Hara's wide knowledge and deep commitment to the truth would permit him to falsify his material.

Matthew J. Bruccoli in Tough Guy Writers of
the Thirties, edited by David Madden
(Southern Illinois). 1968. pp. 129–30

Searching among the basic elements of fiction—story, character, idea—for the secret of O'Hara's tremendous *interest*, one may be puzzled. Often the story is not expertly dramatized, yet the reader is very curious to know what will happen next. The characters may be talented, testy, unpredictable, and only superficially known, yet the reader will be fascinated in the process of getting to know about them. The ideas are limited in range and very elusive when they pretend to depth, yet they *live* compellingly in the character-action nexus. Somewhere in this complex lies the secret of O'Hara's readability—of the fact that millions of readers find it impossible to lay a story of his aside once they have started it. Perhaps the heart of it is that the characters come alive because the reader is completely involved in the living instant when he sees them responding—often surprisingly—to the problem and the situation through which they exist and grow.

Charles Child Walcutt. *John O'Hara*
(Minnesota). 1969. p. 46

The most interesting question raised by O'Hara's death (in 1970) is whether he will be replaced, whether we will get another high-grade popular naturalist pouring out one heavily detailed novel after another, ostensibly giving us the low-down on American society, making his ruthlessness plausible by his commanding technique, his frightening eye and ear, his pleasantly insulting insistence on the dirtiness of sex; and yet for all his Diogenes air, a celebrant of the status quo.

Seventeen novels and eleven volumes of short stories. (Among the latter are some of the best stories ever written about Hollywood, not just a writer's revenge on the studios.) When a man has written that much as well as O'Hara and has been as widely read, his disappearance leaves a gap. My chief curiosity about that gap is to see whether any new author has the energy to fill it—not to mention the professionalism—to patrol that area of the print spectrum; because the popularity of an adroit, nasty, industrious, superficial but intelligent writer like O'Hara was a tribute, in its way, to the very idea of the novel.

Stanley Kauffmann. *NR*. Feb. 26, 1972. p. 26

• OLSON, CHARLES (1910–1970)

The radicals have devoted reams of paper, splashed gallons of ink in discussing form, their form to be sure, but form nonetheless. Meanwhile the claim that the conservatives were too academic is vitiated by the fact that almost all of the radicals are highly educated men. The grand pooh-ba of the lodge, the big daddy, is Charles Olson, who attended the best private schools and colleges, has spent most of his adult career as a scholar-professor and as an official at various colleges; and he writes a complex, allusive, learned poetry, replete with classical allusions and quotations. They, as much as their enemies, write poems about statues, museums, painters and old myths.

George Garrett in *American Poetry*, edited by
John Russell Brown, Irvin Ehrenpreis, and
Bernard Harris (St. Martin's). 1965. p. 228

The Maximus Poems clearly reflects Olson's grassroots radicalism and humanism, which provide the emotional charge for much of the book. The work belongs to the great tradition of long poems of epic intent, of noble voice, in which the theme is of national scope: the founding of a state and the ordering of a good society. Since Olson's politics is not narrowly programmatic, the book escapes the rigidity that often mars works of dogma and persuasion. If anything, it needs a measure of dogma; dogma might have helped the poet to achieve a structure. As it stands the book is shapeless. It has neither beginning nor end; it is all middle. It reminds one of wallpaper rather than of a formally complete, framed picture. One assumes that Olson intended this effect, as corresponding to his sense of reality. . . .

Any student of the work of Charles Olson is bound to come away with respect and admiration for his humanity and his sense of the importance of the workshop and all elemental activity. But, because much of his work is fragmentary and has the character of notes for poems, jottings, "pre-poetry," it rarely provides a sustained experience of either language or reality.

Stephen Stepanchev. *American Poetry
since 1945* (Harper). 1965. pp. 143–5

In *Mayan Letters* we have unequivocal evidence of a *kind* of intelligence which cannot propose the assumption of content prior to its experience of that content, which *looks*, out of its *own* eyes. This does not mean that conjecture is to be absent, insofar as *jacio* means "throw" and *con*, "together"—however simply this point may note the actual process. It is a consistent fact with Olson that he does use his legs, and does depend on what his own instincts and intelligence can discover for him. In this way he *throws together* all he has come to possess.

But humanism, as a system of thought or ordering of persons in their relations to other things in the world, is distinctly absent. Even the most sympathetic ordering of human effects and intelligence leads to unavoidable assumptions, and the test—which is the reality of one's quite literal being—denies any investment of reality prior to its fact.

Robert Creeley. Introduction to *Selected
Writings* by Charles Olson (New
Directions). 1966. p. 4

The *Maximus Poems*, Olson's major work to date, presents a vision of history obviously modeled on that in [Pound's] *Cantos* and a vision of place (the fishing port of Gloucester, Massachusetts) modeled on that in [W. C. Williams] *Paterson*. . . .

Just as Pound's vision of "paideuma" is ultimately characterized in Arcadian terms, as the ideals of Williams and Crane are characterized in terms of a nature myth, so we find Olson speaking of "polis," Plato's ideal state (specifically the spiritual essence of Gloucester, presently degraded), in terms of pastoral images, such as the "tansy," a local flower. The heroes, the so-called root-men, of "polis" are the men who lived close to nature and faced its perils with equanimity and purpose: explorers, map-makers, founders of colonies, settlers, and fishermen (all in contrast to "owners" and exploiters). But the point is that the technique appropriate to revealing natural-historical truth is purported to be itself natural, and a natural technique involves the "breath" of the poet, speech force, personal idiom, and, inevitably, personal experience. . . . Olson's editor calls Maximus "the man in the Word," an accurate enough epithet if it is taken to suggest poetic-colloquial revelation of nature, history, and self—or, conversely, the expansion of personal speech to universal logos.

L. S. Dembo. *Conceptions of Reality in
Modern American Poetry* (California).
1966. pp. 211, 213–4

Our traditional response to poetry is to receive consciously the meaning of the words, letting their sounds, including rhythm, affect us at a level beneath that at which our intellect is engaging the meaning. Olson, it seems, wishes us to invert this response: we are to listen to the sounds and let the meaning work upon us as it will, just as we direct our attention to the movement in a ballet, while the changes in lighting provide nuances; at least this, as a rule of thumb in reading Olson's poems, will serve provisionally as a corrective against our more usual and indeed more natural responses.

By receiving the poetry thus, it will be the energy that is transmitted, the process Olson seems to think to be the proper one for a poem. . . . According to Olson's precepts all verse, not just certain passages, conveys energy; and that energy is contained in all the features of the poem, the objects as he calls them—syllable, line, image, sound, and sense. And our response to the poem is not an intellectual one, modified by feelings, but what we must think of as felt energy, in the transmittal of which meaning plays a part but not an overbearing one. Or, to put the same matter another way, we must try to "see" the images of the poem as if by way of the touch of our hands, as a child may say, "Let me *see*," as he puts forward his *hand*.

A. Kingsley Weatherhead. *The Edge of the
Image* (Washington). 1967. p. 204

Charles Olson is a poet of the first rank. In his poetry . . . he speaks as a man who has formulated exactly what he needs for his work to survive. . . . His one theme is energy—how a man's energy is expended in history and in space. . . . Often the forceful beauty of Olson's writing comes from his devotion to accuracy in the strict sense of history and archeology. . . . I am happiest in Olson's work when I read it quite apart from his esthetic pronouncements. I like the Maximus poems because they are private and domestic.

David Ray. *BW*. March 19, 1967. p. 6

Notably, Olson and those congenial with him have worked on the possibilities of the line in poems. Punctuation can signal the reader, and many conventions and habits in language enable a reader to adjust to sequential requirements as he reads; additionally, in poetry, the break or continuance of the line is a usable element. Olson varies line length extremely, and forces the breaks to perform many functions. Others often do this in practice; he has made himself a spokesman for treating the opportunities seriously and with sustained attention.

William Stafford. *Poetry*. March, 1968. p. 415

We might think that Olson chose to concentrate on Gloucester simply because it happened to be the poet's home-town, out of some familiar Romantic notion of mystical properties available for a man in his native origin, his "roots." This is not the case; Olson *chose* to make Gloucester his standpoint, there was no mystical compulsion upon him to do so. This is where it's instructive to remember his essay on Melville, with its title *Call Me Ishmael*. Ishmael—the archetypal nomad and wanderer. And in fact Olson's argument about Melville's *Moby Dick* shows once again with what desperate seriousness he takes the matter of geographical location; for his argument is that the greatest character in Melville's great and strange romance is the Pacific Ocean, that the book as a whole celebrates the imaginative discovery and appropriation by Western man, specifically by American man, of that great waste of waters in the West, the Pacific—one more territory which the pioneers could light out into when they had crossed the entire continent and found themselves faced by the sea. The standpoint which Olson . . . [is] concerned to investigate is not characteristically a fixed point, the place where roots are sunk; it is a moving point, the continually changing standpoint of a man who is on the move across continents and oceans.

Donald Davie in *The Survival of Poetry*,
edited by Martin Dodsworth
(Faber). 1970. p. 224

After years of destructive intestinal fighting, Black Mountain College, the dishevelled progressive school in the Southern mountains, had been reduced to poverty, a handful of students and a tiny covey of teachers. Charles Olson survived, a disciple of William Carlos Williams and Ezra Pound, an extremely infectious teacher. In a few years he gathered a definite school. I don't think any of them read French, certainly not for pleasure, and like almost all American poets, had heard of no one later than Jules Laforgue. Basing themselves on the few Americans of the international avant-garde of the older generation, Louis Zukofsky, the early Walter Lowenfels, Parker Tyler, Gertrude Stein, Walter Conrad Arensberg, Mina Loy, and myself when young, they found their way out of narrow provincialism and pseudo-British insularity, the enforced orthodoxy of the Reactionary Generation and their quarterlies. Olson's outstanding disciple who for a while surpassed his master was Robert Creeley.

> Kenneth Rexroth. *With Eye and Ear*
> (Herder and Herder). 1970. pp. 71–2

Writing under the shadow of Pound's Cantos and Williams' *Paterson*, Olson [in *Maximus Poems, IV, V, VI*] has tried to delve back further than Pound into pre-history and to create a more sharply defined image than Williams of a modern city.

There are passages where Olson succeeds very well in evoking and satirising the realities of urban living. He focuses on Gloucester (Massachusetts) and, to quote [Robert] Duncan's summary of the central conceit, "Homo maximus wrests his life from the underworld as the Gloucester fisherman wrests his from the sea." Gobbets of local history are lovingly dredged up and patiently reassembled. Modern wit sometimes flashes brightly through the historical material but the poem as a whole is maddeningly uneven. His method prevents him from providing linkages. The material must be allowed to speak for itself without any explanation of its relevance, and he incorporates long stretches of (apparently) verbatim quotation from documents which have a bearing on local history, assuming that his placing of them inside his structure will suffice to make them meaningful. It doesn't. At its best, though, his writing has a vitality in common with Duncan's. He is often very successful in making the movement of the verse imitate the movement he is describing.

> Ronald Hayman. *Encounter*.
> Feb., 1970. pp. 85–6

Next to his excellent, somewhat oracular poetry, Olson's great influence rests on his formulation of the process of "projective" or "open" verse. This provided a new and very usable system of prosody to a whole generation of poets, who may well have felt that a development of some sort was needed from the poetics of Pound and Williams, yet sought something in the same context of freedom. Some took projective verse directly as their own; many more shaped and adapted Olson's theories to their own ends. But what is remarkable is the number of poets—and eventually critics, as well—who were finally deeply affected by this enthusiastic and somewhat eccentric man. Charles Olson mattered greatly. He changed their minds. . . .

Olson's projective verse ideas are in close harmony with the general artistic principles of the Black Mountain group—the emphasis on the organic ("A poem is energy transferred from where the poet got it") and on the process and act of poetry. One is haunted by the notion that if Rauschenberg had been the composer, Cage the poet, and Olson the painter, it might all have come out the same.

Bruce Cook. *The Beat Generation*
(Scribner). 1971. pp. 120, 122

There is always some amount of fascination in seeing what things have been made available to another's mind "by accident" and have emerged in print as the details of a poem. In presenting his material, Olson is both observant of the way his world, including its history, looks and feels, and determinedly bookish, with the cantankerous and pedantic bluster of his self-educated colleagues Rexroth and Edward Dahlberg. But with or without the help of his theories, he has managed to write a few moderately interesting sections of a long, unsuccessful poem which must have been the labor of years, and these are worth reading. The structure of the poem is only the structure of fortuitous association plus the more obvious devices and literary mannerisms of Pound and Williams, but his mind seems to me quite a capable one, and at all points is working hard to say what has been given it. That is enough, because it has to be.

James Dickey. *Babel to Byzantium*
(Grosset). 1971. pp. 138–9

The character, the bearing, and the affect of Olson's verse, its human involvement with the issues of poetry *in extremis*, makes it a telling witness to that continuing pressure which has extended the limits of the poetic almost unrecognizably in our century. It is a curious gathering, the congregation of American poets of our moment, trying in their separate yet related ways to see their own inner selves, and the volatile historical situation, and the crisis of art, in the same single organic vision. They must define the very landscape of their lives, the very language they are to use, the very sense of personality. Here is Lowell, whose frenzied sense of his own suffering is meant to be the key to reality for all of us. Not far off is the late Sylvia Plath, who marked out a pure, all but obscene curve of death, naked and beautiful—that was a kind of suicide of poetry. And Jarrell, who kept reaching for a lost individual possibility, buried somewhere perhaps still in the neglected common life. But the list need not be further proliferated here and now. Charles Olson, who snapped his sentences open like twigs as he wrote, and whose mind moved outward in a series of intersecting ripples pushing against his syntax, sought to mobilize all that he could of language and local human reality and the most cherished memories of tradition against the new "pejoracracy." He was conceivably the unacknowledged leader of all these unacknowledged legislators. Poetic leadership, I suppose, consists not in directives and programs but in accurate perceptions. . . .

M. L. Rosenthal. MR. Winter, 1971. p. 56

Olson is unique, and probably the most difficult of recent American poets. No other poet requires such an effort, equivalent to learning a new language, or rather to adjusting the sense we have of the old one, so that we hear the precision of his, and learn to experience a world through it. There are Olson poems I doubt anyone will ever understand except in their general aspect. Others are line and sunlight clear. The best of them hover between formal clarity and the larger obscurity of the man's mind, a mind so rich that hosts of poets not of his school have paid him the tribute of a Socrates.

His shifts are subtle though major. It is as though in his hands the American language is once again in touch with its roots. He is not quite archaic though he is full of archaisms. His syntax is too alive to be archaic. His focus stops in the noticing of something where you least expect it, and the sudden concentration that is felt brings about a rearrangement of all that has gone before.

Matthew Corrigan. NYT. July 18, 1971. p. 6

Charles Olson's name comes up often in discussions of the influence of Pound and Williams on younger poets, and rightly so. Shortly before Olson's death, Gerard Malanga asked him whether he could have written <i>The Maximus Poems</i> without having known Pound's and Williams's work. Olson answered: "That's like asking me how I could have written without having read." But there has been so little notice taken of the matters that divided Olson, Pound, and Williams that at least one Poundian has glibly dismissed Olson's poetics as almost wholly derivative and surely inferior to Pound's work. Anyone interested in understanding the course of American poetry over the last sixty or seventy years and the directions open to it in the future is likely to be frustrated by this myopic blurring of distinctions. In truth, the story of Olson's relationship to Pound and Williams is a detailed and complex one that casts light on all three poets and especially on their long poems.

Robert von Hallberg. CL. Winter, 1974. p. 15

O'NEILL, EUGENE (1888–1953)

In 1934, after the failure of *Days without End*, Eugene O'Neill left the theatre and went into the desert, an appropriate place for meditation. His career was already a success, but it was attended by an air of ambiguous achievement. The work was impressive, one play added to another, but it was not good enough. O'Neill had tried everything. He had gone to school with Strindberg, Ibsen, and Chekhov; he had taken formal lessons from the Greek tragedians, he had studied the resources of symbolism. But it was not enough. By temperament, he took his themes where he found them, in places, conditions, facts, people. He tried to give his characters a representative dimension so that they would not be merely themselves; they would acquire a glow, a quality of radiance, making them memorable. But the sum had not come out right. The more he put into the plays, the less they retained. Making his characters more than themselves, he made them less than anybody. The more elms he added, the harder to believe in the desire. So he went into the desert and, eight years later, wrote *Long Day's Journey into Night*. . . . The main difference between *Long Day's Journey into Night* and the earlier plays is that now, in a far deeper sense than before, O'Neill has committed himself to his own experience.

Denis Donoghue. The Ordinary Universe
(Macmillan—N.Y.). 1968. p. 151

Again and again in [O'Neill's] plays he wrote about himself and his family, drawing his own and their portraits under various guises, exploring their relations with one another, dramatizing his varying, indeed conflicting feelings toward the others. Of course a great many writers have made literary capital of their personal histories, of their families, but this is more common with novelists, and even among them few have been so obsessive about it as O'Neill.

Tracing relationships between O'Neill's life and his work, viewing one through the other, throws fresh light on both, though not with equal strength. Since his plays originated not only in outward circumstance, in things that had happened to him, but in his inner self, the plays tell us more about the man than his personal history tells us about the plays. His history yields external manifestations for the most part, only occasional glimpses of the inner man; it was the inner man, the essential O'Neill, who wrote the plays. Care is of course imperative in reading him for autobiography: under the functioning of the creative imagination and a writer's opposed drives for self-disclosure (self-justification) and self-concealment (born of self-doubt and guilt feelings), the inner flux and outward reality of his life have undergone transformation, are interwoven with fiction. But it is there, the autobiography, as bed-root throughout his writings.

Louis Sheaffer. *O'Neill: Son and
Playwright* (Little). 1968. p. 79

Emperor Jones's ultimate fall [in *The Emperor Jones*], although superstition is involved, occurs because the artifices that have propped him up have been removed. So, exposed and defenseless, Jones—like any other man—falls victim to his fear and his essential, primitive nature. In certain ways, therefore, this is only incidentally a Negro play; it could well have used any man. O'Neill's insight into the human condition is, if anything, marred by the play having a Negro subject. The analogies to *Othello* were too tempting for the reviewers to miss, and few of them understood the play as more than an artful and powerful treatment of travesty of Negro pretense. *The Hairy Ape* treats the same insight in a different way, this time with a white subject. And on this occasion, the reviewers revealed that they had missed the original point entirely. Lawrence Remner, writing in the New York *Herald* (March 10, 1922), felt that *The Hairy Ape* lacked convincing motivation. He noted a "dramatic form" similar to *The Emperor Jones*, but confessed, "it was a much more exciting game to see the negro usurper beaten by fate. He was a clever rascal in his way. The hairy ape is only a feeble giant who is bowled over by the first blow of fate." Seen as conventional tragedy, the Negro was more convincing because of this "clever" pretense. But the hairy ape was assuming to be a man and civilized, and once the props that sustained him had been challenged—taken away—he was reduced to his essential animal. Perhaps Remner's failure was that he could not see that for a white man humanity might be a pretense. Notably, no critics complained about *The Emperor Jones* for its reduction of the Negro to primitivism; that, of course, was not strange.

Nathan Irvin Huggins. *Harlem Renaissance*
(Oxford—N.Y.). 1971. p. 297

One characteristic is consistently evident throughout O'Neill's career: an unusual technical flexibility, a readiness to experiment and take risks, which he never lost even in his later years. His plays explore the full range of dramatic expression, which continued to fascinate him as long as he lived. Parallel to this runs his experimentation with ideas. Many writers have left their mark, stylistic or philosophical, on his work; they include Spengler, Nietzsche, Marx, Freud, Aeschylus, Shakespeare, Ibsen, Strindberg, Gerhart Hauptmann, and Georg Kaiser. While O'Neill's work in its totality indicates chaos and helplessness, the individual plays show a tentative reaching out, quickly overcome, toward nihilism and Catholicism, determinism and the triumph of human freedom. This is what St. John Ervine meant when he said that O'Neill does not develop, he just expands. But it was precisely this infinite reluctance to declare or commit himself that constituted the artistic as well as the philosophical and religious freedom so indispensable to O'Neill. This predilection for epic completeness—or rather "all-embracingness"—is just as evident in the total *oeuvre* as in the individual later plays and dramatic cycles, which can no longer be contained within conventional limits.

Horst Frenz. Eugene O'Neill
(Ungar). 1971. pp. 104–5

All the fury and anguish, all the vital agony of living, which had been dissipated in his earlier plays by undigested bits of philosophy and unearned attempts at lyricism, had this time [in *Long Day's Journey into Night*] been given clear, hard outlines. Perhaps because the Tyrones had been constructed around personal remembrance, they were freed from the tendentiousness that fettered so many O'Neill characters, and the terrible truths they told to each other were not statements about life but embodiments of it. They were released also from the need to speak to each other in the fustian vernacular of a Hairy Ape or, like Lazarus, in cloudbursts of grandiloquence. When they argued, teased, cajoled, confessed, and complained, they did so in precise, rich human speech that was colored just enough by the dramatist's art so that it remained both unobtrusive and remarkable. Having overcome the need to prove himself a thinker and poet, a fuzzy combination of Shaw and O'Casey spiced with a bit of Nietzschean suffering, O'Neill was free to be what he superbly was: a dramatist of courage and force who understood very well how to construct the tensions and rhythms of a play so that it becomes infused with crude theatrical life and capable of sustaining the needs of the singular vision that gave it birth.

Jack Richardson. Cmty. Jan., 1974. pp. 52–3

There are other problems [in *A Moon for the Misbegotten* besides the obsolete language]: in the way the exposition is handled, for instance;

in the heavy, recalcitrant humor that often seems dragged in like an unhappy child torn from its slumber and obliged to do recitations for its parents' guests. But in O'Neill's last plays the flaws dissolve before the onslaught of all those feelings the unhappy man could not put into his life, only into his final works. There is in *A Moon for the Misbegotten*, as in the rest of them, a passionate compassion, a torrential pity that isn't lessened by being in large measure also self-pity. For it is hard-won and genuine, based on unswerving insight and on true perception of the ultimate incommensurateness between what we would make of life and what it makes of us. The failings of the ear and the sporadic creakings of the construction are overwhelmed by that tragic vision that nothing extenuates, nor sets down aught in malice.

John Simon. *HdR*. Summer, 1974. p. 265

• OZICK, CYNTHIA (1928–   )

Trust introduces a novelist of remarkable intelligence, learning, and inventiveness—qualities that make the book an uncommonly rich reading experience, yet qualities so lavishly displayed they frequently hobble Miss Ozick's muse. . . . For all of its high-powered philosophizing, sparkling dialogue, fine characterization, literary allusions, symbolism, and cutting satire, *Trust* is a curiously old-fashioned piece of realism. The brilliant bits seem to be waiting for a vision potent enough to fuse them into an important work of the imagination. It never arrives. Yet lacking the powers of a Günter Grass, Miss Ozick still manages a considerable achievement of passion and skill.

R. Z. Sheppard. *BW*. June 19, 1966. p. 8

When Cynthia Ozick clears the Jamesian hurdles she has set up for herself in her large first novel, *Trust*, we realize that she has a voice of her own, and that it is direct, poetic, inventive, playful, and, more often than not, full of wisdom. But first we must dismiss, as a dismal bore, a great part of the pseudo-Jamesian concerns of her book. Mrs. Ozick offers a world of high finance and policy-making, a world not entirely supported by the author's craft despite her verbal skill. . . . In this densely populated book filled with characters and caricatures who insist upon their right to be endlessly clever with each other, only the heroine and her stepfather, Enoch Vand, achieve real life. His odyssey from ambition to theology is worldly but personal, and Mrs. Ozick handles it movingly. For she is a committed, serious writer, concerned with the world but also with the word. She has written an interesting and sometimes brilliant first novel.

Elinor Baumbach. SR. July 9, 1966. p. 34

The sense of gratuitousness [in *Trust*] extends to the very existence of the characters. For instance, for all the detail in the rendering and the energy with which she is invested, the heroine's mother seems more like an hallucinated projection of the heroine's resentment than a credible mother or wife or woman. Mrs. Ozick, on the other hand, is successful in creating her arch-conservative first stepfather, particularly in the long episode in which he reveals to the heroine the truth of her past.

One wants to mitigate the harshness of the judgment of the novel, because the novel shows symptoms of power and talent. But the inescapable impression that the novel makes, despite every desire to wish it well, is that the book is a performance from ambition, that if Mrs. Ozick is to write a successful novel she must achieve a more authentic accommodation between her language and her feeling.

Eugene Goodheart. Critique. 9, 2, 1967. p. 102

There is now in this country a generally unrecognized renaissance of the short story, and for one writer to put three of the best into her first collection [*The Pagan Rabbi, and Other Stories*] is extraordinary. Cynthia Ozick works with fantasy, or with engaging conceits. Her stories, nudged on to the track, accelerate, change gears, turn at alarming angles from their predicted courses. . . . Living fraudulently, whether by ignorance or design, is one of [her] major themes. . . . Nothing happens in her stories that is not bound up into the whole. Nearly all of them, for all their wit and their absurdities, turn out to be both funnier and sadder than we expected at the start. She builds her stories carefully and she writes them very well. They will be with us, I think, for some time.

Peter S. Prescott. Nwk. May 10, 1971. p. 112B

Miss Ozick's first book, the novel *Trust*—rich, convoluted, even virtuosic—revealed a rare quality of mind and a joy and a facility in language that was almost literally staggering but, because of its very complexity, tended at times to be opaque. In [*The Pagan Rabbi, and Other Stories*] . . . all that was best in the novel—that relentless, passionate, discovering and uncovering intelligence—is present and instantly recognizable, but there is now a difference in the prose. It is sharpened, clarified, controlled and above all beautifully, unceasingly welcoming. . . . Cynthia Ozick is a kind of narrative hypnotist. Her range is extraordinary; there is seemingly nothing she cannot do. Her stories contain passages of intense lyricism and brilliant, hilarious, uncontrollable inventiveness—jokes, lists, letters, poems, parodies, satires.

Johanna Kaplan. *NYT*. June 13, 1971. p. 7

Cynthia Ozick comes forward in [*The Pagan Rabbi, and Other Stories*], not as a Jewish writer, but as a Jewish visionary—something more. All of her characters are, to begin with, distraught, distended by the world, trapped by misunderstanding, incommunicativeness, loneliness, exhaustion. But their distraction is only a starting-point. The stories are never simply descriptive or evocative. . . .

Cynthia Ozick is always refining and winnowing obsessions and for the projection and substantiation of obsessions, thought is indispensable. A writer has to mind the language when obsession is at stake. It isn't enough to record the experience, because the experience is not given. It is wrested from the encumbrance of normal perception and wrenched apart, examined like the entrails of a haruspex and sewn up again differently. For this work all of the literature, philosophic, moral, mythological, and all of the language, its unfamiliar words and its delicious words have to be used. And Cynthia Ozick does all this, the language textured by a network of associations, reminiscences, allusions to the vast intellectual tradition of the West which has tried to crack the hard nut of thought with its bare teeth.

Arthur A. Cohen. *Com*. Sept. 3, 1971. p. 462

PERCY, WALKER (1916–   )

As in Faulkner's novels, Percy's fiction takes place in a prolapsed world, often cut off from the ordinary workaday world, where characters are haunted by the past and bound by the absurdity of their situation. To this, Percy adds two states of narrative consciousness—one of perception and another of reflection—and also a sense of the grotesque. Percy's strength as a novelist—his brilliant sense of the grotesque, his ability to depict the estranged mind, his sense of coincidence—is also the source of his weakness because it leads at times to far-fetched situations, especially in *The Last Gentleman*. . . .

Richard Lehan. SoR. Spring, 1968. p. 309

Percy seems unwilling to stray from certain orthodox principles; and throughout [*Love in the Ruins*] there is an excessive interest in symmetry, an urge to give chapters and sections little endings toward a larger denouement that makes the "end" of the book. Not that this isn't a serviceable schema; but the looped progress of his first novel [*The Moviegoer*] still seems the way Percy's extraordinary percipience ought to be arrayed. Even at that, *Love in the Ruins* moves in a sidling way, by analogy and evasion, only occasionally falling into direct statement. . . .

Throughout, the book is written at an extraordinary level of physical perceptions; and Percy's attempt to offer an image of a supple Christianity is impressive. All of his claims, artistically and philosophically are embedded in a windrow of rendered and carefully watched fiction. It is only because Percy focuses our attention at a very high level that large reservations about the success of this novel can be expressed. Percy is easily one of the finest writers we have, capable, moment by moment, of being better than one can quickly see.

Thomas McGuane. NYT. May 23, 1971. p. 37

Although [Percy] is a natural writer, downright, subtle, mischievous, his novels seem to be essentially the self-determination of a religious personality, of a seeker who after being ejected from the expected and conventional order of things has come to himself as a stranger in the world.

A disposition to look at things in a radically new way is very much what happens in *The Moviegoer, The Last Gentleman, Love in the Ruins.*

Alfred Kazin. *Bright Book of Life* (Little). 1973. p. 66

Of Percy's three novels *Love in the Ruins* is most explicitly the work of a Christian writer. The Christian writer's dilemma . . . is that, although his truth may still be there for the comfort of all, he seems close to being the last of his kind. Percy persists in telling us, however, that we will have to renounce the deification of our lusts and our pretensions to spiritual supremacy and confess that, alas, we are only men. For, even if the predicted end did not come, we are still divided against ourselves. Reviewers complained that something had gone drastically wrong with Percy's art but what seems to have happened is that he has developed a taste for prophecy and has been persuaded that an increasingly fantastic world calls for new fictional forms and fantastic inventions.

Eugene Chessnick. *HC*. Oct., 1973. p. 5

● PLATH, SYLVIA (1932–1963)

Sylvia Plath [in *The Colossus*] writes clever, vivacious poetry, which will be enjoyed most by intelligent people capable of having fun with poetry and not just being holy about it. Miss Plath writes from phrase to phrase as well as with an eye on the larger architecture of the poem; each line, each sentence, is put together with a good deal of care for the springy rhythm, the arresting image and—most of all, perhaps—the unusual word. This policy ought to produce quaint, over-gnarled writing, but in fact Miss Plath has a firm enough touch to keep clear of these faults. Here and there one finds traces of "influences" not yet completely assimilated ("Snakecharmer," for instance, is too like Wallace Stevens for comfort, and the sequence "Poem for a Birthday" testifies too flatly to an admiration for Theodore Roethke), but after all, this is a first book, and the surprising thing is how successful Miss Plath has already been in finding an individual manner.

John Wain. *Spec.* Jan. 13, 1961. p. 50

These last poems of Sylvia Plath's [*Ariel*], once read, hang around one like the smell of morphia, impregnating everything. As the expression, or rather unmodified articulation, of raw pain, with its precommittal intensification of vision and its heightened sharp-edged clarity, they are unique in contemporary poetry. There is little regret or bitterness in them, certainly there is no hope. They are of the moment, looking neither back nor forward, last-gasp cries that long since lost any note of tenderness, or even ironic, self-directed amusement. They are poems for the most part beyond art, as they are also beyond consolation or compassion. Their tone and manner are almost brusquely objective, gestures of vivid dismissal made by someone immune from rescue and without either the mood or the time to modulate or conciliate. Acceptance of conventional, meaningful reality is token, the references to continuing, ordinary life scant. . . .

This is not the sort of book discussable, at this stage anyway, in normal critical terms. It belongs, ironically, to life rather than to literature, its nerve-ends still squirming. In any poetry of such swerving trajectories and imbalance it is easy to lose track: the horrors flap off the walls like vultures, awareness breaks and recedes in hypnotic waves of semi-consciousness. Each of these poems stands recognizable as an act of courage, as a cleanly-struck blow against a superior adversary. But the nature of the conflict is never clearly defined nor the wounded areas properly probed. The ambulance bells are still ringing.

Alan Ross. Lon. May, 1965. pp. 99, 101

Are these final poems [*Ariel*] entirely legitimate? In what sense does anyone, himself uninvolved and long after the event, commit a subtle larceny when he invokes the echoes and trappings of Auschwitz and appropriates an enormity of ready emotion to his own private design? Was there latent in Sylvia Plath's sensibility, as in that of many of us who remember only by fiat of imagination, a fearful envy, a dim resentment at not having been there, of having missed the rendezvous with hell? In "Lady Lazarus" and "Daddy" the realization seems to me so complete, the sheer fineness and control so great, that only irresistible need could have brought it off. These poems take tremendous risks, extending Sylvia Plath's essentially austere manner to the very limit. They are a bitter triumph, proof of the capacity of poetry to give to reality the greater permanence of the imagined. She could not return from them.

Already there are poets writing like Sylvia Plath. Certain of her angular mannerisms, her elisions and monotonies of deepening rhyme, can be caught and will undoubtedly have their fashion. But minor poets even of a great intensity—and that is what she was—tend to prove bad models. Sylvia Plath's tricks of voice can be imitated. Not her desperate integrity.

George Steiner. Reporter. Oct. 7, 1965. p. 54

In these poems [in *Ariel*],written in the last months of her life and often rushed out at the rate of two or three a day, Sylvia Plath becomes herself, something imaginary, newly, wildly and subtly created—hardly a person at all, or a woman, certainly not another "poetess," but one of those super-real, hypnotic, great classical heroines. This character is feminine, rather than female, though almost everything we customarily think of as feminine is turned on its head. The voice is now coolly amused, witty, now sour, now fanciful, girlish, charming, now sinking to the strident rasp of the vampire—a Dido, Phaedra, or Medea, who can laugh at herself as "cow-heavy and floral in my Victorian nightgown." Though lines get repeated, and sometimes the plot is lost, language never dies in her mouth.

Everything in these poems is personal, confessional, felt, but the manner of feeling is controlled hallucination, the autobiography of a fever.

Robert Lowell. Foreword to *Ariel* by
Sylvia Plath (Harper). 1966. p. vii

Often, very often, Sylvia and I would talk at length about our first suicides; at length, in detail and in depth. . . . Suicide is, after all, the opposite of the poem. Sylvia and I often talked opposites. We talked death with burned-up intensity, both of us drawn to it like moths to an electric light bulb. Sucking on it! She told of her first suicide in sweet and loving detail and her description in *The Bell Jar* is just the same story. It is a wonder that we didn't depress George [Starbuck] with our egocentricity. Instead, I think, we three were stimulated by it, even George, as if death made each of us a little more real at the moment. Thus we went on, in our fashion, ignoring Lowell and the poems left behind. Poems left behind were technique—lasting but, actually, over. We talked death and this was life for us, or better, because of us, our intent eyes, our fingers clutching the glass, three pairs of eyes fixed on someone's—each one's gossip. [1966]

Anne Sexton in *The Art of Sylvia Plath*, edited
by Charles Newman (Indiana). 1970. p. 175

In [Sylvia Plath], as with perhaps few poets ever, the nature, the poetic genius and the active self, were the same. Maybe we don't need psychological explanations to understand what a difficult and peculiar destiny that means. She had none of the usual guards and remote controls to protect herself from her own reality. She lived right in it, especially during the last two years of her life. Perhaps that is one of the privileges, or prices, of being a woman and at the same time an initiate into the poetic order of events. Though the brains, the strength, the abundance

and vivacity of spirits, the artistic virtuosity, the thousand incidental gifts that can turn it into such poetry as hers are another matter. [1966]
Ted Hughes in *The Art of Sylvia Plath*,
edited by Charles Newman
(Indiana). 1970. pp. 187–8

If Sylvia Plath's performance [in *Ariel*] were not so securely knowledgeable, so cannily devised, so richly inventive and so meticulously reined, it would be intolerable. Many of these poems are magnificent; a whole book of them is top-heavy, teetering on that point where the self-created figure threatens to topple over into self-expression and the diversions of psychopathology. Reaching for a poet with whom to compare her, or in whose sphere of influence to "place" her—and only the illustrious will do—one hesitates before Blake (too "big," too masculine, too mythopoeic), before Baudelaire (too much the *poseur*, too *raffiné*, perhaps too comfortable in his rancor), and stops at Emily Dickinson. But anguish in Emily Dickinson is a consequence; it partakes of a classical notion of anguish: the great heart victimized by its own humanity. In Sylvia Plath, by contrast, anguish is not a consequence but the whole relentless subject itself. . . . Anything pursued far enough is likely to turn into its opposite: a shriek maintained for eighty-five pages becomes, to say the least, a bore. Nevertheless, what we have here is not, as some bewildered critics have claimed, the death rattle of a sick girl, but the defiantly fulfilling measures of a poet. Taken in small—one is almost forced to say, medicinal—doses, she is a marvel.
John Malcom Brinnin. *PR*.
Winter, 1967. pp. 156–7

The poetry of Sylvia Plath's *Ariel* is a poetry of surrender, surrender to an imagination that destroys life instead of enhancing it. Nowhere in our literature has a finely wrought art proven so subversive as hers, so utterly at odds with those designs, those structures within which we customarily enclose ourselves to hold experience off at a distance. Emerging from encounter with her poems, as from the murky, subterranean depths of a well, one feels not so much emotionally raped as simply breathless with weariness and confusion. It is as though we had been flung into hideous contact with another order of being, suffocated by a presence too driven and hungry to be supported by the thinness of the air we breathe, a presence thrashing about, taking no notice of us, poor mortal creatures, a presence, finally, reaching, touching, shrieking on a scale that dwarfs into insignificance the familiar scale of our activities. It is with caution and humility that we must approach her art, for it is vaporous with potions that do not intoxicate, but depress and confound. If we listen humbly, there are insistent voices trembling beneath the surface of the poetry, voices which beckon to us, suggesting that we lift our heads from the page and answer the poet in kind, assenting to manipulation by that imagination which has taken everything around it for its own, wringing experience to satisfy its hungers.

Robert Boyers. CentR. Spring, 1969. p. 138

Passions of hate and horror prevail in the poetry of Sylvia Plath, running strongly counter to the affirmative and life-enhancing quality of most great English poetry, even in this century. We cannot reconcile her despairing and painful protest with the usual ideological demands of Christian, Marxist, and humanist writers, whether nobly or sympathetically eloquent, like Wordsworth, breezily simplified, like Dylan Thomas, or cunning in ethical and psychological argument, like W. H. Auden or F. R. Leavis. Her poetry rejects instead of accepting, despairs instead of glorying, turns its face with steady consistency towards death, not life. But hating and horrified passions are rooted in love, are rational as well as irrational, lucid as well as bewildered, so humane and honourable that they are constantly enlarged and expanded. We are never enclosed in a private sickness here, and if derangement is a feature of the poetry, it works to enlarge and generalize, not to create an enclosure. Moreover, its enlargement works through passionate reasoning, argument and wit. Its judgement is equal to its genius.

Barbara Hardy in The Survival of Poetry, edited
by Martin Dodsworth (Faber). 1970. p. 164

Little enough has been said of Sylvia Plath—but perhaps Robert Lowell's description of her poetry as "controlled hallucination" (in the introduction to Ariel, 1966) is worth volumes. Hers is a sensibility disturbed, which sees reflected in the exterior world the very tensions, conflicts, and fears that haunt the inner spirit. Her power as a poet derives from her capacity to express this state of mind through the evocation of profound horror. The sense of horror springs from many sources: from her habit of dredging up historical atrocities, from the violent intensity of her expression, from the accuracy and hardness of her language, and most significantly, from the nature of her perception. Always she is aware of the doubleness of things, the shark beneath the surface, the tumult beneath the calm, the glitter beneath the veil. The gaze which she turns outward upon the world is schizophrenic; of the things she perceives, her mind asserts, with the speaker in "Death & Co.," "Two, of course there are two."

This perception leads first to fear and eventually to despair, for it forces upon one the recognition that the world is disjointed, that things are not what they seem. Among Sylvia Plath's works run two rather different ways of expressing poetically the theme of doubleness. One method—the more obvious of the two—proceeds by revealing horror amid an atmosphere of apparent security. This is a somewhat traditional device, certainly not unique with Miss Plath, although in her hands it is capable of vivid effects. A second and somewhat more subtle method illustrates the validity of Lowell's comment: doubleness is conveyed by a sort of hallucinatory vision, a way of seeing simultaneously, the opposing qualities of a thing.

Lynda B. Salamon. Spirit. Summer, 1970. p. 34

Sylvia Plath's only novel, the autobiographical The Bell Jar, is a deceptively modest, uncommonly fine piece of work. First published in England under the pseudonym Victoria Lucas . . . the book is more than a posthumous footnote to her career as a poet. . . . The novel is in its own right a considerable achievement. It is written to a small scale, but flawlessly—an artistically uncompromising, witty account of the experiences, inner and outer, that led to Miss Plath's earlier breakdown and recovery.

The book is humorous and dramatic, the prose for the most part lean but sometimes, suddenly, full of a transforming imagery. . . .

Miss Plath doesn't claim to "speak for" any time or anyone—and yet she does, because she speaks so accurately. . . .

The novel has a sharp and memorable poignancy. With her classical restraint and purity of form, Sylvia Plath is always refusing to break your heart, though in the end she breaks it anyway.

Lucy Rosenthal. SR. April 24, 1971. p. 42

The novel itself [The Bell Jar] is no firebrand. It's a slight, charming, sometimes funny and mildly witty, at moments tolerably harrowing "first" novel, just the sort of clever book a Smith summa cum laude (which she was) might have written if she weren't given to literary airs. From the beginning our expectations of scandal and startling revelation are disappointed by a modesty of scale and ambition and a jaunty temperateness of tone. The voice is straight out of the 1950's: politely disenchanted, wholesome, yes, wholesome, but never cloying, immediately attractive, nicely confused by it all, incorrigibly truthful; in short, the kind of kid we liked then, the best product of our best schools. The hand of Salinger lay heavy on her.

But this is 1971 and we read her analyst, too wily to be deceived by that decent, smiling, well-scrubbed coed who so wants to be liked and admired. We look for the slips and wait for the voice to crack. We want the bad, the worst news; that's what we're here for, to be made happy by horror, not to be amused by girlish chatter. Our interests are clinical and prurient. A hard case, she confounds us. She never raises her voice.

Saul Maloff. NR. May 8, 1971. p. 34

I feel in [Sylvia Plath] a special lack of national and local roots, feel it particularly in her poetry, and this I would trace to her foreign ancestors on both sides. They were given and she accepted them as a burden not as a gift; but there they were, somehow cutting her off from what they weren't. . . .

For all the drama of her biography, there is a peculiar remoteness about Sylvia Plath. A destiny of such violent self-destruction does not always bring the real person nearer; it tends, rather, to freeze our assumptions and responses. She is spoken of as a "legend" or a "myth"— but what does that mean?

Sylvia Plath was a luminous talent, self-destroyed at the age of thirty, likely to remain, it seems, one of the most interesting poets in American literature. As an *event* she stands with Hart Crane, Scott Fitzgerald, and Poe rather than with Emily Dickinson, Marianne Moore, or Elizabeth Bishop.

Elizabeth Hardwick. NYR. Aug. 12, 1971. p. 3

In some strange way, I suspect [Plath] thought of herself as a realist: the deaths and resurrections of "Lady Lazarus," the nightmares of "Daddy" and the rest had all been proved on her pulses. That she brought to them an extraordinary inner wealth of imagery and associations was almost beside the point, however essential it is for the poetry itself. Because she felt she was simply describing the facts as they had happened, she was able to tap in the coolest possible way all her large reserves of skill: those subtle rhymes and half-rhymes, the flexible, echoing rhythms and offhand colloquialism by which she preserved, even in her most anguishing probing, complete artistic control. Her internal horrors were as factual and precisely sensed as the barely controllable stallion on which she was learning to ride or the car she had tried to smash up.

So she spoke of suicide with a wry detachment, and without any mention of the suffering or the drama of the act.

A. Alvarez. The Savage God
(Random). 1972. p. 20

"Such a dark funnel, my father," Sylvia Plath cries out in her "Little Fugue." And Otto Plath is a funnel indeed, leading her psyche from the openness of youth down toward the small dark point of death. . . . To date no one has traced the trajectory of her father's memory in the body of Plath's work. We suggest that a pattern of guilt over imagined incest informs all of Plath's prose and poetry. When Otto Plath dies of natural causes in a hospital on November 2, 1940, he might just as well have been a lover jilting his beloved. Indeed, in all her poems Plath makes of this separation a deliberate desertion. In poem after poem the father drowns himself.

This is the central myth of Plath's imagination. Critics have called hers a poetry of annihilation, poetry in which her own suicidal impulses are set against the larger framework of a world which deliberately destroys—the Nazi genocide of the Jews, the Kamikazes, Hiroshima. Even a train is said to eat its track. A favorite Plath image is that of the hook: from the bend in a road, to the corner of her son's smile—both traps for the unsuspecting. Plath's is a terrible, unforgiving nature; in feeling victimized by her father's early death, and later by an unsatisfactory compensatory marriage, she makes no distinction between her tragedy and those of Auschwitz or Nagasaki. [1972]

Robert Philips. The Confessional Poets
(Southern Illinois). 1973. p. 128

Given the fact that in a few poems Sylvia Plath illustrates an extreme state of existence, one at the very boundary of nonexistence, what illumination—moral, psychological, social—can be provided of either this state or the general human condition by a writer so deeply rooted in the extremity of her plight? Suicide is an eternal possibility of our life and therefore always interesting; but what is the relation between a sensibility so deeply captive to the idea of suicide and the claims and possibilities of human existence in general? That her story is intensely moving, that her talent was notable, that her final breakthrough arouses admiration—of course! Yet in none of the essays devoted to praising Sylvia Plath have I found a coherent statement as to the nature, let alone the value, of her vision. Perhaps it is assumed that to enter the state of mind in which she found herself at the end of her life is its own ground for high valuation; but what will her admirers say to those who reply that precisely this assumption is what needs to be questioned?

Irving Howe. Harper. Jan., 1972. p. 91

Winter Trees is the slimmest as well as the last of Sylvia Plath's collections; there are nineteen poems here on forty printed pages. But there is ample further evidence of her endless imaginative resource in the restatement of her familiar themes; all proceeding, ultimately, from the "divided self," the self which is alienated, oppressed, disembodied, dissolved. We meet again the familiar images, particularly the (characteristically schizoid) image of the mirror, which appears in all but two of these poems and seems to haunt them with its inevitability and its destructiveness. . . . We are dazed again by the complicated use of colours, almost as a symbolism, to signify states of mind, attitudes; the alienating absolutes of black and white, the terrifying violence red almost always means, the uncertainty of blue, which can signify the cold night-blue of the moon ("What blue, moony ray ices their dreams?"), blue angels— "the cold angels, the abstractions," or the sky-blue of a child's eyes; and the occasional consolation of the organic colours, brown and green.

Damian Grant. CQ. Spring, 1972. pp. 92–3

The poems we write are the only poems we can. We pretend they are choices when, in fact, they may be so only in the obverse sense: that we are the chosen. Many times we may not even be free to leave them unwritten. This is especially true in a poet as obsessive and emblematic as Sylvia Plath, whose most noteworthy book was produced in something equivalent to Keats' "great year" which preceded, like his, a premature death.

Now, ten years later, surely enough time has passed that we can dispense with the "Plath myth," an obscuring glitter around *Ariel* and *The Bell Jar* which wraps them in biographical data. After all, the novel is little more than a psychologically meager but socially accurate portrait of the 1950's. Plath's last poems, however, project a mythic world which is not "confessional" in an autobiographical but a sacramental sense. What they achieve, finally, is even beyond their treatment of the persona as "woman"—a combination saint and witch in Ariel's speaker —a new dimension for the contemporary lyric in which tragedy is again possible because seen from a perspective both comic and magic.

Peter Cooley. HC. Feb., 1973. pp. 1–2

Tragedy is not a woman, however gifted, dragging her shadow around in a circle or analyzing with dazzling scrupulosity the stale, boring inertia of the circle; tragedy is cultural, mysteriously enlarging the individual so that what he has experienced is both what we have experienced and what we need not experience—because of his, or her, private agony. It is proper to say that Sylvia Plath represents for us a tragic figure involved in a tragic action, and that her tragedy is offered to us as a near-perfect work of art in her books *The Colossus* (1960), *The Bell Jar* (1963), *Ariel* (1965), and the posthumous volumes published in 1971, *Crossing the Water* and *Winter Trees*. This essay is an attempt to analyze Miss Plath in terms of her cultural significance, to diagnose through her poetry the pathological aspects of our era which make a death of the spirit inevitable—for that era and for all who believe in its assumptions. It is also based upon the certainty that Miss Plath's era is concluded and that we may consider it with the sympathetic detachment with which we consider any era that has gone before us and makes our own possible: the cult of Sylvia Plath insists that she is a saintly martyr, but of course she is something less dramatic than that, though more valuable. The "I" of the poems is an artful construction, a tragic figure whose tragedy is classical, the result of a limited vision that believed itself the mirror held up to nature—as in the poem "Mirror," the eye of a little god that imagines itself without preconceptions, "unmisted by love or dislike." This is the audacious hubris of tragedy, the inevitable reality-challenging statement of the participant in a dramatic action which he does not know is "tragic." He dies, and only we can see the purpose of his death—to illustrate the error of a personality that believed itself godlike.

Joyce Carol Oates. SoR. Summer,
1973. pp. 501–2

PORTER, KATHERINE ANNE (1894–   )

For years, [Katherine Anne Porter] was praised by discerning critics as the cleanest, clearest, and as they say of vines, most shy-bearing of the writers of our times: which in my opinion she probably is. Then, after writing the best seller *Ship of Fools*, she came to be regarded in wider circles with a certain uneasiness, as being negative, skeptical, prejudiced, formalistic: which in my opinion she is not. She is no more negative, I must argue, no more skeptical, et cetera, than it is very good to be. . . .

Miss Porter is a Modern, a beneficiary of a discipline which has been known as Modernism, just as surely as any of a number of writers who can be grouped together because of their affinities with James and Proust and Joyce. She is akin to Ezra Pound and Pablo Picasso. She grew up in a period in which the mastery of an art was held to be a lifelong, exacting discipline. It was a period, we can say from this distance, which accepted constraints and past history, as well as freedom and modernity.

Howard Baker in Sense and Sensibility in
Twentieth-Century Writing, edited
by Brom Weber (Southern
Illinois). 1970. p. 76

In the stories that have usually been considered Miss Porter's finest work, the central figures are people whose desperate preoccupation with themselves cuts them off from effective communication with all other human beings. In some instances, a family situation, present or remembered, may be responsible for the protagonist's alienation or provide its particular dramatic circumstances. But whether the setting is a New York rooming house, where the protagonist is a long way from home and alone for most of the time of the story's action, or a Texas farmhouse, with the family present most of the time, the reader's attention is fixed upon a totally private agony.

In all but one of these stories, the protagonist is a woman. . . . Especially in the stories about women, it may be in the failure of a sexual union that the fatal pride chiefly shows itself. But sex is ultimately of no greater importance than social class or occupation or level of literacy. What all these characters have in common, from the Miranda of "Pale Horse, Pale Rider" to Royal Earle Thompson of "Noon Wine," is a consuming devotion to some idea of themselves—of their own inestimable worth and privilege—which the circumstances of their lives do not permit them to realize in actuality but which they are powerless to abandon. The idea lives in them like a demon, directing all their thoughts and actions. Whatever it may be in which they invest that most precious and indefinable sense of self—a cherished grievance, a need to justify a fatal action, an ideal of order and mental discipline— they pursue it relentlessly, through all discomforts and deprivations, even to death—and if not to the death of the body then of the spirit, incapacitating themselves not only for love but for the enjoyment of any common good of life, to walk forever among strangers.

John Edward Hardy. *Katherine Anne Porter* (Ungar). 1973. pp. 62–3

POUND, EZRA (1885–1972)

I would propose . . . as a way-in to the *Cantos*, that the unity of the poem is that of its dominant figure, Pound himself, the controlling intelligence, teaching the moral significance of history as a mirror for magistrates. His role is that of the great counsellor, close to the strong Prince, governing his state in terms of a coherent political intelligence. This will explain, to start with, why the form of the poem is not a real problem: as long as the words issue from the single controlling intelligence, and as long as the speaker's role remains unchanged, the unity of the poem is built-in, thus guaranteed. The speaker is deemed to be a fixed point, centre of an ever expanding circle of reference; himself immutable. This marks the main difference between Pound and his nearest relative Walt

Whitman. Whitman assumes that the self "is" through the collusion of its world, the objects it makes its own. Hence these objects, because they contribute to the opulence of the self, should be as vivid and manifold as possible. The equation in this case is $X = A$ plus B plus C plus D, and so on. Each object apprehended enriches the observer. But Pound conceives the self as a being, immutably set off against a world upon which it imposes—or in which it sometimes finds—an idea of order congenial to its nature.

Denis Donoghue. *The Ordinary Universe*
(Macmillan—N.Y.). 1968. p. 293

Over and over, in "Arnold Dolmetsch," in "Psychology and Troubadours," and pre-eminently in *Guide to Kulchur*, [Pound] has insisted that each man must define his own microcosm and that erecting subjective validities into putatively universal dogmata does violence to human needs and to truth. For Pound, poetry begins in an interest not in the nature of the ruling deity, but in human experiences. This is one reason why his peculiar sort of neo-Platonism *had* to issue in a polytheistic religion, and why his mysticism did not emerge as specifically Christian —or even as religious, as one expects to think of that word. The more fortunate among us participate in the energy of the Supreme Intelligence, and since each individual is unique (owing to his own *logos* or *virtù*), each man's participation will be objectified in a unique way; yet the "gods" representing these objectifications will all be genuine.

Pound's religious concern, therefore—or, better, his moral philosophy—points inward, to one's true self and to the ordered exercise of one's natural energies—ordered and restricted sufficiently to avoid injuring or interfering with other people, but not limited by arbitrary (dogmatic) exclusions and repressions. These observations suggest again that the most important characteristic of Pound's cosmology is what we may call its metaphorical possibilities and that it is primarily a mechanism for the expression of purely subjective concerns.

Thomas H. Jackson. *The Early Poetry of
Ezra Pound* (Harvard). 1968. pp. 84–5

Pound's psychological theory of myth may be summarized as follows:
(1) The psychic experience is extraordinary, brief, and yet subjectively true. It is beyond the generally shared realm of common experience, but it is "vivid and *undeniable*." Pound often calls it an "adventure."
(2) It is no more than *experience*. It does not reveal an objective, transcendental order. Myths are primarily "explications of mood," and Pound almost never chooses to "probe deeper."

(3) The myth or work of art is made out of this rare emotion.

(4) It is an objective verbal *equation* for a basically incommunicable experience. Language cannot convey the primary intensity of the experience itself; it can only reconstruct something else as the "nearest equation" that the myth-maker is "capable of putting into words."

(5) The myth-maker (poet) cannot relate his experience by speaking out directly in the first person. He must "screen himself" and speak indirectly through "an impersonal or objective story." Hence the need for masks and personae.

All of these ideas are central to Pound's theory of poetry as a record of delightful psychic experience.

Hugh Witemeyer. The Poetry of Ezra
Pound (California). 1969. p. 24

Form was one of the values to which Pound was utterly committed. Not a form of objects—not "well-wrought-urn-ism"—but a form of events, of process, of lines of force as Fenollosa apprehended them: "Transferences of power." Sight alone can never come to the conception of a universe so full of vital energies that forces are being transferred constantly, but without sight we would have only a vague roaring in our ears from such apprehension. Form, for Pound, is an attempt to focus on the loci of these transferences. His is dynamic form, to be sure. . . . Reading a line from a Canto, we must have a sense that something is "going on" all the time; the words do not simply lie in limp patterns, the poem is something happening rather than something over with. But it also has a fixedness, a dance, even in its movement: Pound was a Vorticist, a man who believes that powerful force creates and maintains form. The vortex is a figure for the reconciliation of those mighty opposites, dynamic and static, in a shape whose fixedness is dependent on a certain intensity of movement.

Herbert Schneidau. Ezra Pound: The Image
and the Real (Louisiana State). 1969. p. 195

Quite apart from Pound's idiosyncratic technique of fragmented rather than sequential presentation (which has long been the subject of criticism), the shifts in his viewpoint and in his preoccupations during the three decades covered by the first eighty-four cantos inevitably detract from the unity of the poem as a whole. But these changes, which sometimes are very abrupt, as in the new direction assumed in the *Eleven New Cantos* (1934), are perhaps more appropriate for a modern epic than a classical unity of subject and tone would be. For *The Cantos* is obviously a poem written "in process" by a poet aware of the problems of historical novelty and change and of the difficulties of maintaining his sea legs as a voyager in the stream of twentieth-century culture. When one considers the misfortunes that befell him, one recognizes the achievement of this Odyssean wanderer in surviving at all.

Walter Sutton in *Sense and Sensibility in*
Twentieth-Century Writing, edited by
Brom Weber (Southern Illinois).
1970. p. 128

It is Pound's conception of a world in memory sustained within the mind of one man that makes the Cantos one of the great poems in English. Pound calls it, here again, his "palimpsest," and indeed there is no better word to describe the effects of these [*Drafts and Fragments of Cantos CX–CXVII*] as of all the earlier Cantos. Pound's poems are a manuscript written over the faintly discernible words of others, a shifting, glittering, glimmering memory of creative achievement that gleams through the ugliness of existence and makes what Pound here humorously calls "a nice quiet paradise over the shambles"—a paradise within the mind, holding together man's cultural achievements, retaining the old scripts, making them legible again. It is, of course, the romantic conception of mind that DeQuincey summed up when he said that the human brain was "a natural and mighty palimpsest." Deriving from Wordsworth's *Prelude* and Whitman's *Leaves of Grass*, Pound's Cantos pick up and sustain the cultures of the world within the apprehension of an individual mind and pass them on to poets such as [Robert] Lowell.

Louis L. Martz. *YR.* Winter, 1970. p. 263

Pound's structures, like Jefferson's plough, were meant to be useful: to be validated therefore not by his opinions but by the unarguable existence of what exists. . . . He constellates Luminous Details, naming them, as again and again in the *Cantos* he names the signed column. For the column exists; what it proves about forgotten possibilities it proves by simply existing. And five hundred more such columns would not intensify the proof. Again and again in the *Cantos* single details merely prove that something lies inside the domain of the possible. It is not necessary to prove that the possibility was ever widely actualized; only that it exists. What was done at Wörgl—once—by one mayor, in one village—proves that stamp scrip will work. What was done in San Zeno, once, on one column, proves the possibility of a craftsman's pride in an unobtrusive structural member. And any thing that is possible can again be. The *Cantos* scan the past for possibilities, but their dynamic is turned toward the future. And they enumerate so many places, so many stones, so many buildings, because nothing is so irrefutable as a stone.

Hugh Kenner. *The Pound Era*
(California). 1971. p. 325

The poem upon which "Near Perigord" is based, "Dompna Pois," illuminates another important aspect of *The Cantos*: Pound's method of presentation, especially as it applies to his epic hero. In the epigraph preceding "Na Audiart," Pound speaks of "Dompna Pois" as a poem in which the artist creates " 'Una dompna soiseubuda' a borrowed lady or as the Italians translated it 'Una donna ideale.' " In our discussion of that poem we noticed that it symbolized Pound's poetic method (the creation of an ideal through the accumulation of fragments); this is also the method of *The Cantos*. Pound later called this the "ideogrammatic method," but he discovered it in Provence long before he came across the Fenollosa manuscripts. Pound's epic hero can also be defined in these terms, for he is really "un om soiseubut," a "borrowed" (and "ideal") man, the composite *persona* who undergoes a series of significant metamorphoses. When considered in this context, the similarities of the individual personae of *The Cantos* become quite apparent.

Stuart Y. McDougal. *Ezra Pound and the*
Troubador Tradition (Princeton).
1972. pp. 146–7

Toward the end of his life, Ezra Pound, 86, has found yet another eloquent new voice: silence. This American bard whose *Cantos* transformed the language of English poetry . . . this early champion and benefactor of James Joyce, Robert Frost, Ernest Hemingway, D. H. Lawrence and T. S. Eliot . . . this inspired midwife to Eliot's *Waste Land* . . . speaks now mostly in monosyllables—when he speaks at all.

Some say this has to do with the fatigue of age plus a physical collapse that followed his thirteen years of incarceration as a political prisoner of his own United States. . . . Some say Pound's silence, which deepens from year to year, expresses the profound sense of anti-climax that came with freedom. Some say it spells his disgust with life and mankind. And others say Pound has discovered that words have more to do with lies and misunderstanding than with communication.

Alan Levy. *NYTmag.* Jan. 9, 1972. p. 14

● PURDY, JAMES (1923–   )

[*Malcolm* is] the first novel proper by the author of those brilliantly unsettling short stories, *Color of Darkness*; and it is a work of baffling, perverse and very real distinction. . . . *Malcolm* . . . can no doubt be placed in that fine old comic picaresque tradition to which Anglo-

American fiction has recently returned. Still, such laughter as it evokes sounds a little like the beginning of a death-rattle. And this is what confirms the earlier impression that James Purdy is a writer of exceptional talent, who must be acknowledged in the company say, of Saul Bellow and Ralph Ellison. . . . Mr. Purdy possesses a demonic originality, but it is an originality chiefly of angle of perspective and selection of detail. The themes he sounds are the great ones. . . . There is something large and comprehensive in this hectic little book.

R. W. B. Lewis. *NYHT*. Oct. 11, 1959. p. 5

James Purdy's *Malcolm* comes to us with loud huzzas from Dame Edith Sitwell, Dorothy Parker and David Daiches. I'm afraid that Purdy loses rather than gains from these high claims; he is certainly a writer of considerable interest, as his two previous books, *63: Dream Palace* and *Colour of Darkness*, have already shown, but there is nothing in *Malcolm*, his best book so far, to show him to be anything but a most delightful but surely not yet major talent. One is reminded of the brittle comedies of Carl Van Vechten and, further in the background, the work of Ronald Firbank. Yet while I think the dominant note of the book is its playfulness, it does certainly have overtones of something larger.

Mr. Purdy depends on a large imagination and a sharp wit—a wit which is sometimes moral and reflective and sometimes malicious. This, I think, divides the book, for one is uncertain of the solidity of the symbolic structure. Most critics have not made much of the symbolic purposes, preferring to delight in Purdy's prose; and I cannot help feeling that they do this because the symbolism is largely fanciful, and provides structure as much as explanation for the book. It is best seen, I think, as a succession of loosely-knit episodes, each of them moral fables (fables in the Aesop sense) about maturity, and linked by the innocence and openness of the central character, Malcolm.

Malcolm Bradbury. *Lon*. July, 1960. pp. 81–2

With the publication of *Malcolm*, James Purdy has left no doubt that he is a writer of integrity with a voice of his own. In America today, when most novels seem to be hurriedly manufactured with standardized patterns and interchangeable paragraphs, Purdy's work stands out as something of a rarity. He also has a highly personal vision of his own—bitter, ironic, and grotesque. Perhaps it is this combination of qualities that reminds us of Nathanael West. In two short novels, *Miss Lonelyhearts* and *The Day of the Locust*, West revealed more of the inner rot of the America of his day than several shelves of the naturalistic "political" novels produced by his more popular contemporaries. Similarly, Purdy, in *Color of Darkness* and in *Malcolm*, has said more in fewer words about the hunger and horror of our fragmented, business-cheapened life today than a whole chorus of best-selling, grey-flanneled voices from Irwin Shaw to Herman Wouk.

Much of Purdy's unusual achievement is made possible by his flat, bald style. It is precise and deceptively simple. He uses few of the rhetorical devices available to him in English; he is even sparing of adjectives and adverbs. In *Malcolm* especially his prose is terse, almost naked, sometimes matter-of-fact, dry. His individual voice comes through in a strange twist of a phrase here, an odd choice of a word there, and in a peculiar tension that vibrates from even his least tightly structured paragraphs.

Paul Herr. CR. Autumn–Winter, 1960. p. 19

It is indeed a pleasant surprise to find that James Purdy can produce a compelling and compassionate picture of everyday life within the framework of [*The Nephew*]. . . . No one else could have written this version of small-town American life. For Purdy sees the familiar, the ordinary, with a vision that lies somewhere between that of Blake and Grant Wood. So his picture of the inhabitants of Rainbow Center is, naturally, with all its surface similarity, a far cry from either *Main Street* or *Winesburg, Ohio*.

Richard McLaughlin. SpR. Oct. 30, 1960. p. 4D

Like Salinger, Purdy is a writer of love, "pure and complicated." But there all analogies end. For Purdy is a true original within the area where, neither windswept nor entirely claustral, his sensibility dwells. The area, as in so many works of Kafka, is sharply defined in its details and weirdly ambiguous in outline. His focus in human relations is the paradox of love and loneliness in our age, illuminated time and again by terror and humor. This is why Purdy's language, precise, simple, and spare as it seems, often glows in a surreal haze. The originality of Purdy may finally rest in his profound insight that language and feeling, in our day, have severed their connections.

Ihab Hassan. SR. Nov. 17, 1962. p. 29

I think it undoubted that James Purdy will come to be recognized as one of the greatest living writers of fiction in our language. . . . It is extraordinarily difficult to review [*Children Is All*], because it is impossible to convey the subtlety, depth on depth, that lies beneath what Mr. Angus Wilson, writing of another of Mr. Purdy's works, has described as his "magnificent simplicity." . . . In his precision, avoidance of superfluity, vagueness or romanticism, Mr. Purdy may be regarded as a draughtsman. He has enormous variety. At least three masterpieces in this book, "Everything Under the Sun," "Daddy Wolf," and the almost unbearably anguishing play *Children Is All*, are studies in loneliness, but the movements in which that loneliness is conveyed are entirely different. . . . *Children Is All* is, to my mind, a sublime work of pity and tenderness. It could only have been written by a great writer.

Edith Sitwell. NYHT. Nov. 18, 1962. p. 6

I was startled when a perceptive friend of mine abroad wrote that Purdy's first novel *Malcolm* struck him as "degenerate." I had never thought of it as that; but the fact that I hadn't may be simply a deplorable symptom that Americans are beginning to accept as normal the loveless state of affairs in which talk is incessant but communication nonexistent. While there are few signs of truly human feeling anywhere today, elsewhere the educated may bear less resemblance than Americans to Purdy's Fenton Riddleway, who "was able to accept nearly anything . . . the immense 'dreariness of things as though there were no other possibility."

The surrealistic world of *Malcolm* is degenerate, but what has made the novel popular is not that it makes this grotesque world appealing, but that it shocks readers into recognizing that it is unmistakably theirs. It is a vastly different matter whether a book's degeneracy results from the writer's offering an enticing escape from reality (as in *Gone With the Wind* or *Lady Chatterley's Lover* or *On the Road*) or from his attempting to make us face unpleasant realities (as in *Suddenly, Last Summer* or *Cards of Identity* or *The Sound and the Fury*).

Warren French in Essays in Modern American
Literature, edited by Richard E. Langford
(Stetson). 1963. p. 113

Among the many labour-saving devices employed by reviewers, one of the commonest is to discuss a writer in terms of his relationship with other writers, alive or dead, and to deduce the influences which have contributed to his style and technique. Applied to such a book as *Children Is All*, however, this method would be the reverse of labour-saving, for Mr. Purdy is not *like* any other writer I can think of, and the task of influence-spotting, in his case, would be an arduous and unrewarding one. In other words, he is a true original, and these stories seem to me quite startlingly effective. Mr. Purdy's method is to spotlight a situation at the moment of its maximum intensity: what has led up to it is deftly and economically implied, usually by means of dialogue, and what comes after is left, as often as not (and sometimes most disquietingly), to the reader's imagination. The stories have an admirable compactness, and Mr. Purdy never uses two words where one will do.

He is also remarkably versatile, both in style and content; he can be witty, macabre, touching, and whimsical (in the best sense) by turns. In one of the best stories, a woman's character is built up and her weaknesses cruelly exposed merely through the random chatter of two female friends; the short "Sermon" is a devastating little piece, the preacher being, apparently, no less a person than God Himself. This collection also contains two playlets which, apart from the omission of "he said" and "she said," read like the stories, which are themselves written almost entirely in dialogue.

Jocelyn Brooke. List. Aug. 15, 1963. p. 249

The terrible, destructive private self each one of us possesses, reflected in the suppressed violence of contemporary social life, is a central subject in the works of James Purdy. . . . Purdy shows us the "Nightwood" Djuna Barnes had to explain; he reveals the loneliness Marguerite Duras has attempted to elucidate, but without the latter's cloying self-conscious approach. He never intrudes as he makes us see the desperation with which we live; and the objectivity of his observation finally extends to the furthest limits of grief.

What makes Purdy's stories so vital is the hard esthetic veneer in which he freezes the violent emotions his stories contain. . . . Because his style is so rigid and matter-of-fact, the reader, in Purdy's characteristic device, is shocked as an apparently meaningless event in a character's life reveals a tragic and irreversible truth. . . .

Despite this hard "veneer," Purdy is still capable of exploring innumerable and subtle gradations of character motive; and his unswerving eye for the small gestures of daily existence beautifully penetrates those most private recesses of feeling that few contemporary authors have been able to disclose.

Jonathan Cott in On Contemporary Literature,
edited by Richard Kostelanetz
(Avon). 1964. pp. 498–9

The assumption is that all of us, in so far as Purdy really has the word on us, live in a world divided. For the most part the interior room, the "real" one, the one where we live, is sealed off from the ones in which we meet other people, talk to them, desire them, marry them, kill them, construct them in our own image. Once in a while we open the door ever so slightly and let someone look in, but what he sees there is a reflection. . . . Since the man in the interior room is so hard to get to, since he can be seen infrequently and then only obliquely, the suspicion begins to grow that he is not there at all. He becomes a kind of silly putty that assumes the shape of whatever it lies against. He becomes whatever another person, in a scramble to escape his own facelessness, wants him to be. . . . Boyd (in *The Nephew*) says, "We none of us, I'm afraid, know anybody or know one another." His words could be an epigraph not only for *The Nephew*, but for all of Purdy's work.

Gerald Weales in *Contemporary American Novelists*, edited by Harry T. Moore (Southern Illinois). 1964. pp. 144, 146

It appears to be generally believed that James Purdy is an important American writer. The publication of his third novel, *Cabot Wright Begins*, offers an occasion for dissent. Purdy is a terrible writer, and worse than that, he is a boring writer. . . .

The early stories are ineptly written, but several of them have a raw power that comes from Purdy's imagining domestic hostility and potential violence as *overt* violence. Thus a son kicks his father in the groin, a husband beats his wife bloody at a party, a boy breaks the neck of his younger brother, and (in "Why Can't They Tell You Why?", the best story in *Color of Darkness*) a mother drives her son literally mad.

The later stories, in *Children Is All*, have lost even this power. In its place there is only verbal violence. . . .

Ultimately, Purdy is neither a novelist nor a fiction writer. He is a social satirist, and at times a funny and effective one. The last third of *Cabot Wright Begins* suggests that he missed the true vocation for which his combination of passion and bad taste qualify him, that of sick comic. [1964]

Stanley Edgar Hyman. *Standards* (Horizon). 1966. pp. 254, 256–7

Purdy is a naturalist of unusual subtlety and a fantasist of unusual clarity. . . . A wild, flailing, and finally hysterical attack on everything that bugs him, from *The New Yorker* to Miss Subways to Orville Prescott, [*Cabot Wright Begins*] is redeemed by a brilliantly controlled spoof on American sexuality and book publishing. . . . The first two-thirds or so of *Cabot Wright Begins* is a rich, resonant, and deadly accurate satire on American values, as good as anything we have had since the work of Nathanael West. . . . Through a marvelously flexible and clearly drawn plot line, moreover, Purdy keeps the narrative steadily on the track of its subject. . . . It remains to say, of course, that a writer who takes on our culture today is hard put to maintain his wits amid the witlessness of his subject. But much of *Cabot Wright Begins* is evidence that it can be done, that the detachment and deliberateness of art still remain the best defense against the grotesqueness and biliousness that infect our mind. The main thrust of Purdy's career has been to make us aware of this truth.

Theodore Solotaroff. *BW*. Oct. 18, 1964. p. 3

Ten years ago James Purdy was, in the words of the composite kudos, a "young, bold, individual, arresting and irritating talent." Today, four novels and three volumes of short stories later, he is considered part of the older new-guard in American fiction—a "voice," but one that has lately been greeted by diminished bravos, at times cat calls. The critical hatchet job by Stanley Edgar Hyman (memorable, but somewhat in excess of even a purist's obligation to the public) was a reaction partly prompted by Dame Edith Sitwell's pronouncement that Purdy is "one of the greatest living writers in our language." . . .

However Purdy's original brilliance may have dimmed of late, however his inventiveness may have flagged, the feeling that he has said all he has to say . . . is not universally shared among critics. Like all writers obsessed by certain themes Purdy does repeat himself. Yet I suspect both the obsession and repetition are lodged in the impossibility of solving the problems he has set for himself through any single artistic coup. . . .

Every character lives the myth of the isolated self, a stranger to himself and to others, locked in his own private hell that seals off the world outside.

Robert K. Morris. Nation. Oct. 9, 1967. p. 342

James Purdy with a Christian vision of love tells in *63: Dream Palace* the story of "the least among us," Fenton Riddleway, "dumb and innocent and getting to be mad," and his little brother Claire, helpless, puny and seemingly feebleminded. To love them means to be shaken with pity and terror. It means to know utter despair, for there is nothing anyone can do to save them. They are doomed.

The "least" in Purdy's work is the exiled wanderer, abandoned in a strange world where nothing makes sense, where he can find no hold. Once he leaves his natural home, the golden bench of Malcolm, the West Virginia farm of Fenton, or Cousin Ida's cottage of Amos Ratcliffe, he is Ulysses faced with monsters at every turn. But unlike Ulysses, he cannot slay them. If he is like Bennie of "Daddy Wolf," with no money to spend, he doesn't even rate a perforation on the program card. His auditors accuse him of lacking an indefinable something, of not having what it takes. What he lacks is the ability to be non-human. His humanity is his Achilles heel. He limps through life bleeding with every step he takes.

Bettina Schwarzschild. The Not-Right
House (Missouri). 1968. p. 1

The method for the stories [*Color of Darkness*] involves an unreal emotional dialectic between friends or among members of a family.

Each confrontation results in a revelation of mutual desperation rather than resolution.

The collection takes its title from the story of a man whose wife has deserted him. He suffers from an inability to remember the color of his wife's eyes, or, indeed, those of his maid, Mrs. Zilke, or his son, Baxter. Existential darkness does not facilitate color discrimination. But more importantly this amnesia characterizes what I believe to be the keynote of Purdy's work in the 50s—the impossibility of a rebirth in America. . . .

Despite the desperate denunciation in the themes of these stories, a promise remains in their method. In order to present his vision, Purdy had to perform some magic with technique. The actions proceed within the crucible of irony. In each of these stories, Purdy grounds the decaying spirits of the characters in an animistic world. His stay in Mexico supplied him with a sense of primitivism he delicately balances with America's cultural decadence.

Donald Pease in The Fifties, edited by Warren
French (Everett/Edwards). 1970. pp. 146–7

Mr. Purdy is and has been a fantasist, despite the creeping realism of some of his short stories. His writing is clearly an outgrowth of the uniquely American strain of comic-nihilistic fantasy which sprang from Nathaniel Hawthorne's guilty Puritan nightmares and bloomed in the 1930's at the hands of Nathanael West. Unfortunately, as satire has gradually been overwhelmed by the absurdity of mid-century life and this dark fantasy has spread and rooted itself in our art, Mr. Purdy's fiction, shocking and revolutionary in the beginning, has come to seem conservative and familiar. . . .

Purdy's polymorphous-perverse sexuality, though it permeates [*I Am Elijah Thrush*] as it does practically everything he has written, pales into ingenuousness next to the meticulous concupiscence of Establishment writing. And in an era in which controversy seems to be the lifeblood of literature, Purdy eschews mention of politics, war and ecology, and handles the issue of racism with such a soft touch that one is scarcely aware of the protagonist's color.

Robert Boyd. Nation. May 15, 1972. p. 636

Imagine a critic whose preferences and prejudices when it comes to modern American fiction have been formed by a regular reading of, say, Saul Bellow, Norman Mailer and John Updike—what might he be expected to say about a novel with the following scenario? The narrator is a young black, Albert Peggs, in love with a golden eagle; he becomes involved with an aging actor, "mime, poet, and painter" called Elijah

Thrush, who is himself in love with his mute great-grandson. He also becomes the memoirist of an heiress, Millicent de Frayne, who stopped growing old in 1913 when she fell in love with Elijah Thrush. All four of these people, plus the bird, are linked together in a number of ways which takes the book far beyond the simply narrative. Albert's account outlines the frightening (and comic) ascendancy of Millicent over all of them, a series of preemptive power plays which culminates in a funereal wedding banquet on board a ship at sea. Albert is last heard taking over, from the doomed Elijah, Elijah's role in his theater.

Our imaginary critic may well be tempted to dismiss it as perverse farce, a weird homoerotic daydream or nightmare, a frivolous and mannered piece of idiosyncratic surrealism, in all cases lacking the sort of pained "relevance" which he feels he can find among his preferred novelists. This, I fear, is how some American critics are going to receive James Purdy's most recent novel [I Am Elijah Thrush], of which the above scenario is a crude outline. Purdy has never, it seems to me, been done justice by many of the leading contemporary critics and one reason, it may be, is that they simply don't know how to read his work properly.

Tony Tanner. *PR*. Fall, 1972. p. 609

Malcolm, James Purdy's first novel, was published in 1959 and has not suffered from want of acclaim. The praise has been richly deserved, for Purdy may be the most skillful black-humorist around. No one, however, has given Purdy credit for the full achievement of *Malcolm*. The novel generally is applauded for its wit, style, and deft handling of the disturbing themes of loneliness and lack of identity in the bizarre nightmare of modern existence. In addition, Purdy's gift for sharp and sweeping satire rakes such targets as marriage, art and artists, sex, status, and adolescence. The last is a tempting critical morsel, for it makes the novel classifiable as a *bildungsroman*. Without question *Malcolm* is a story of a young man confronting adulthood, for initiation is its central theme. The novel has been called "an allegory of growing up." However, Purdy has not written merely another novel of adolescence in a century already overstocked. Instead, he has offered us a sport on that type, using the genre to satirize it, with a wry approach to form as well as content. Viewed this way, the satire of an already cheerless book is deepened, and the blackness of its humor becomes more pervasive, more complete, and more grim.

Charles Stetler. *Critique*. 14, 3, 1973. p. 91

A relationship between a patron and a protégé is basic to the "economy" of James Purdy's microcosm, and as the most pervasive human relationship, it colors everything else in his novels, stories, plays and poems—right up to metaphysics.

Although the patron sometimes pretends to encourage some talent or genius in the protégé, the relationship occurs most frequently in cases hardly distinguishable from the pervasive theme of "corruption of innocents," which runs throughout his works, wherein the protégé is valued for beauty, youth, wit, and unspoiled naïveté, regardless of artistic or creative powers. It blends in closely, on the domestic level, with parental-filial relations (and their "playing-house" imitations), with master-servant situations, and with a very large number of marriages in which, typically, a hopelessly infatuated wife, usually older than her mate, works to support a sexually ambivalent husband with artistic ambitions who is a total failure. This marriage pattern, of course, has mother-son overtones.

Frank Baldanza. AL. Nov., 1974. p. 347

In a Shallow Grave is a modern Book of Revelation, filled with prophesies, visions and demonaic landscapes. . . . Purdy's most recent novels, *The House of the Solitary Maggot* and *I Am Elijah Thrush*, have been cranky, meandering exercises. The books tend to creak. They reflect in a sorry way the beautiful, ribbed dream world of *Malcolm*, Purdy's first novel.

[*In a Shallow Grave*] perhaps will bring to Purdy the wider audience he deserves. Written in a sparse yet rough-edged style, it indicates the dilemmas of Purdy's writing. There have always been briers in his voice, as if he meant to tear at his readers with a kind of harsh music. Purdy is one of the most uncompromising of American novelists. Working in his own dark corner, he has collected his half-fables about a corrosive universe where children search for their fathers and are waylaid by endless charlatans and fools.

The very awkwardness of his lines, that deliberate scratching of the reader's ear, is Purdy's greatest strength. It allows him to mix evil and naïveté without spilling over into melodrama and tedious morality plays. There are no "legitimate" people in Purdy's novels, just fleshy ghosts like Garnet and Potter Daventry [in *In a Shallow Grave*]. Underneath Purdy's brittle language is a sadness that is heartbreaking, the horror of isolated beings who manage to collide for a moment, do a funny dance and go their separate ways.

Jerome Charyn. NYT. Feb. 8, 1976. p. 3

PYNCHON, THOMAS (1936–   )

The world of *V.* is pluralistic, one of unlimited points of view, with reality presumably emergent out of the reconciliation of these diverse perceptions. Thus chancelleries all over the world piece together their picture of an ever-threatening but unknown enemy. And thus both the Stencils—father and son, British Foreign Office agent and amateur historian in search of his past—grope to connect their scraps of information into a coherent design, Stencil *père* on the scene, so to speak, at first hand and Stencil *fils* at second hand from the tantalizing *memento mori* of his father. This patchwork quilt approach to reality is brilliantly dramatized by Pynchon in the eight versions of the narrative action (more accurately the eight points of view imagined by Herbert Stencil) that comprise all we learn of the intrigues of British spies in Egypt on the eve of the Fashoda incident. The irony is that the eyewitnesses are all peripheral to the action. From the casual observation and incidental eavesdropping of a cafe waiter, a hotel factotum, an English confidence man (who is incidentally a blatant parody of [Nabokov's] Humbert Humbert), a train conductor, a garry driver, a burglar, and a beerhall waitress, only a fragmentary conception of what is happening can be constructed. It is as if the Fashoda incident were rendered on seven picture postcards and mailed by foreign correspondents unable to find transportation to the front or wire service to the home office. Nor in the culmination of the action are we helped to any understanding of what the spies were about. Narrated omnisciently in the elliptical manner of stage directions for a melodrama, the situation is left, as [Robert] Sklar has complained, "deliberately shrouded in mystery." But is not that Pynchon's point about what men call history? that it is an omnia gathering of irrelevancies from which sense is manufactured.

> Max F. Schulz. *Black Humor Fiction of the Sixties* (Ohio. Univ. Pr.). 1973. pp. 79–80

If the shape of *V.* is a redundant row of yoyoing V's, the shape of Pynchon's second novel, *The Crying of Lot 49*, is an equally futile circle. The reader begins with the hermetic title and ends with the words, "the crying of lot 49"—"crying" being a term from auctioneering and "lot 49" a particular batch of objects up for sale. The story of Mrs. Oedipa Maas's quest for the meaning of a legacy dwells, even more than *V.*, on mythic figurations of destructive self-closure: Oedipus, Narcissus, Echo. And—almost as with the numerological figures that buttress the religious art of the Middle Ages and the Renaissance—myth in *The Crying of Lot 49* is buttressed by mathematics, not in headily ascending patterns of three or four or golden sections, but by self-limiting patterns of frustrated numerals, repeating or redundant. The end of Oedipa's quest is as empty as the end of Stencil's, and she finally glimpses a universe compressed into an America of no vocabulary but ones and zeroes, something and nothing, arranged in mindless patterns that alternately suggest a centuries-old conspiracy of waste and death or a mindless muddle.

> William Harmon in *The Comic Imagination in American Literature*, edited by Louis D. Rubin, Jr. (Rutgers). 1973. pp. 382–3

Chance meetings in Pynchon's novels are exploited as parodies of realism by being accepted as part of the normal, necessary order of events. A line of action that is entirely arbitrary, that is taken by chance, links perfectly with others that are stumbled upon, and all of them lead somehow to the right place. Yet this right place, whether it be V. or a full disclosure of the Tristero system, is never finally reached. The clues that Oedipa Maas assembles about the Tristero in *The Crying of Lot 49* are all happened upon accidentally, through a Jacobean play, a lavatory wall, a chance meeting with another character in a labyrinthine munitions plant, and so on. The atmosphere of a multitude of possibilities is created, an infinite proliferation of plot lines; yet the one that is followed is the only one, the right one, the way out; and yet again, it brings us no closer to an answer, an identity, a V., a meaningful pattern, than we were to begin with.

> John Vernon. *The Garden and the Map* (Illinois). 1973. p. 65

Anyone who's read Pynchon before hardly needs to be told that *Gravity's Rainbow* is pyrotechnically brilliant in its juxtaposition of the humblest sludge of pop culture, the specialized vocabularies of organic chemistry or rocket technology, and the rarefied heights of abstract speculation. His immense documentation, neither show-off nor suffocating, enables him to move with ease from London during the blitz to Southwest Africa in 1904 to a remote village in Central Asia. And he is blissfully funny. Where his talent has grown in the ten years since *V.* is just where one would have hoped, in the realm of feeling. The openness and suppleness of his polysexual tenderness is as breathtaking as his reach into extremes of anguish, obsession and brutality. *Gravity's Rainbow* is moving in ways I don't remember being moved by *V.*, dazzling as that first novel was.

> Walter Clemons. *Nwk.* March 19, 1973. p. 94

Only three American novels of the last seven or eight years even approach *Gravity's Rainbow* in ambition, chutzpah and achievement: Norman Mailer's *An American Dream*, Pynchon's own *The Crying of Lot 49* and E. L. Doctorow's *The Book of Daniel*. But good as each is in its way, each pales next to this massive, mind-blowing, stomach-turning, monstrously comic new milestone in fiction. *Gravity's Rainbow* combines the encyclopedic scope of *V.*, his first novel, with the intricacy of *The Crying of Lot 49*, his second, yet goes past both of them to grave ribaldry not even they realized. This novel is going to change the shape of fiction, if only because its genius will depress all competitors. . . .

Writing about a world of bizarre irresponsible bastards paranoiacally besieged by systematic cabals, plots, secret cartels within secret conglomerates, Pynchon shows the perpetual paradox of this necessary but inadequate pushing of things to be omens and pushing of omens to be systems. . . . Yet while clearly committed to the Slothrops—the slowly placed inhabitants of paper bureaucracies—he avoids crystallized certainty, refuses to lock himself into any system, perplexes and astonishes us with his satisfyingly unschematic vision of a world far more complex than we have known.

W. T. Lhamon, Jr. *NR*. April 14,
1973. pp. 24, 28

Gravity's Rainbow is a picaresque, apocalyptic, absurdist novel that creates a complex mythology to describe our present predicament. It is supposedly about a brief period in the decline of the West—fall, 1944, through fall, 1945. It is actually about our entire century, from the roots of the First World War through the final calamity, which keeps on threatening right up to press time. Beyond that, it is about the whole modern tendency of man to subordinate himself to the whims of the products of his intelligence, to the self-aggrandizing dictates of machines. It is also about the paranoia this subordination instills in men—a paranoia of which they are absolved as their persecution dreams come true and, ironically, destroy them.

If I have suggested an icily intellectual book by these adumbrations, I'm sorry. *Gravity's Rainbow* attempts to conceal its author's ultimately guiding intellect beneath a long series of marvellous, polyglot sideshows that entertain before they edify.

L. E. Sissman. *NY*. May 19, 1973. p. 138

An embarrassment of riches? Perhaps. But the man can write. The real problem is not Pynchon's talent per se, but rather how that talent is applied. The sameness of tone throughout *Gravity's Rainbow* makes for tedium. By the time the reader is halfway through the book (assuming he gets this far), he feels that he has reached a point of diminishing returns. The always cool, hip voice of the constantly winking creator (Look, Ma, I'm writing, playing games, being clever) becomes less and less attractive. Pynchon's canvas, which at first seemed so vast, now appears limited, closed. The reader senses the somewhat sophomoric sensibility behind the book and seeks relief. There is none. Only more characters and events filtered through that same irritating sensibility. Scenes accumulate, there are often striking set-pieces of writing, but the book lacks tension and fails to build. Although Pynchon traces the progress of paranoia, shows men constructing the systems and machinery that will eventually destroy them, creates a nervous world of total confusion and sudden death, he has no particular point of view about any of these things. He demonstrates and records in minute detail, but he doesn't probe, penetrate or seek to illuminate.

Ronald De Feo. HdR. Winter,
1973–4. pp. 774–5

The essential pattern of life, from dust to order to dust, is echoed in the title image of the novel: gravity's rainbow, the parabolic path that gravity imposes on the V2 rocket. Indeed, Pynchon spends so much time on the biography of the rocket just to point out how apt the parallel is. The rocket, too, starts as a disordered scattering of atoms, from iron in the mountains to alcohol latent in potatoes. Man begins to reduce the entropy of those collected atoms, assembling them in one place, arranging them to take on technological life. "Beyond simple steel erection, the Rocket was an entire system *won*, away from the feminine darkness, held against the entropies of lovable but scatterbrained Mother Nature . . ." (p. 324). The rocket is fired, and carrying out its analogy to life, it burns and rises—"You will come to understand that between the two points, in the five minutes, *it* lives an entire life" (p. 209). Eventually its maximum altitude is reached, where gravity, the manifestation of destiny and the laws of physical process, overcomes the vertical momentum. The rocket must bend to the general flow, and it descends to the earth to disintegrate in a final burst of energy and scattering of atoms. Applied technology has recapitulated fundamental science. Both life and the rocket rise from the rubble, burn bright for a while, and then return to the rubble to be rewoven into life again. The moment of life has been made thermodynamically possible by a continuous process of decay and reconstruction: "But every true god must be both organizer and destroyer" (p. 99).

Alan J. Friedman and Manfred Puetz.
CL. Summer, 1974. pp. 346–7

• RABE, DAVID (1940–   )

It is supposedly a simple matter to write or stage a play depicting the horrors of war. That is not so. People screaming in agony, bodies flung about, wounds inflicted, harsh words yapped, ruthless cruelty on all sides nearly always become commonplace and boring in the usual anti-war play or picture. They are piteous preachments thundered at us in sham stage hyperbole; we do not believe them. This is not the case with *The Basic Training of Pavlo Hummel*. The staging is largely stylized (without artiness), the gunfire is not deafening, no blood spurts out from the injured, but the sense of real men at war is present. We come to know the human abjectness of it all. It is haunting in its personal challenge. . . .

It is the first play provoked by the Vietnamese disaster which has made a real impression on me.

Harold Clurman. *Nation*. June 7, 1971. p. 733

The Basic Training of Pavlo Hummel is the first play to deal success-fully with the Vietnam war and the contemporary U. S. Army. Unlike George Tabori's *Pinkville*, which whipped up a froth of hysteria at the Army as a training ground that turned pink-cheeked American kids into savage Blue Meanies, young playwright David Rabe treats the Army as a microcosm of the ironies and personalities at large in the society itself. His unheroic hero, Pavlo Hummel, is a strong dramatic invention, a kid with a weird charm mixed up with streaks of violence and the endemic quasi-madness of our time. . . . The play cuts beneath politics to display the true horror of humans on both sides driven to bestiality, a situation in which the actual killing is only the most extreme example.

Jack Kroll. *Nwk*. June 14, 1971. p. 70

Although [*The Basic Training of Pavlo Hummel*] tells us very little about Vietnam, it paints an impressively accurate picture of the military life and its pathetic waste of men and boys. The basic-training phase of the action features a jazzy first sergeant . . . who catches the ironic humor of an experienced soldier having fun dehumanizing recruits into reasonably efficient dogs with the conditioned reflexes that give them a chance for survival in a shooting war.

A second irony in the play is that Pavlo does survive the shooting, but eventually loses his life in a brothel. Here Pavlo encounters another soldier with the girl he wants, and instead of waiting his turn viciously attacks and humiliates his rival. The soldier responds by throwing a grenade into the brothel. There is a flaw in all this, because we are not able to connect Pavlo's sudden sadistic behavior with his Army experience. And although the play includes a chorus character, the significance of the action, beyond a vague suggestion that war is a tragedy of meaningless accidents, fails to emerge. On the other hand, it might have required a wrenching of the material to make this important point clearer. And to wrench the material could have poisoned the honesty of this impressively authentic play.

Henry Hewes. SR. July 10, 1971. p. 36

Nothing in *The Basic Training of Pavlo Hummel* prepared me for the dramatic intensity of *Sticks and Bones*. It has been a long time since I sat in an audience so moved and horrified by what went on in front of them. It was a stage trick that put the cap on the audience's distress, a wrist-cutting which, in the intimacy of the small theater, was so much more real than all the blood that flooded the screen in *The Wild Bunch*. It was not a trick that would have worked, however, if the play—below the surface, at least—had not been driving toward that final, inevitable suicide. Nor would it have been so effective—all those lowered eyes, turned heads, involuntary attempts not to look—had the play not been about the peculiarly American habit of refusing to see, to hear, to admit the ugly and the painful.

Gerald Weales. Com. March 10, 1972. p. 15

Sticks and Bones concerns the relationship of a former All-American boy to his family upon his return from Viet Nam. His tour of duty has left him blind and infected from an affair with a "yellow whore." Rehabilitation has already been the subject of post-war dramas from *The Best Years of Our Lives* to *The Men* and beyond. But Rabe's version happens to be about Viet Nam rehabilitation. The father and mother are named Ozzie and Harriet, the kid brother Rick, and the blind son David, of course. He is malevolence personified. As soon as he arrives home, David commences to drive his parents, brother, and priest insane simply by telling the truth about his war experiences. His calm descriptions of American atrocities, his quiet hatred for his family, his patient attempts to torture them form the action of the play.

    Sticks and Bones' most interesting facility is the ease with which it switches styles. It bounces from situation comedy to satire to tragic melodrama just when the audience acclimates itself to a set texture. Ozzie and Harriet initially appear in a typical middle-class Levittown home with wall-to-wall Sherwood shag, knotty pine panelling and lots of plastic and brass things hanging around. They watch TV, take aspirin, mouth Americana truisms, and feed Rick fudge and milk as he bounces in and out of the living room strumming a guitar and screeching: "Hi, Mom! Hi, Dad!" idiotically. But as the play develops, it becomes progressively difficult for the three to hold onto their life-fabric. David exists only to destroy his family's protective values. When he does, the play's tone changes drastically, Ozzie becomes a contemporary Willie Loman, sick, tortured, eloquent in his failure. Harriet is transformed into a frightened, librium-taking neurotic. And Rick becomes vicious.

Rabe's style, although not yet matured, indicates a brilliant future. He can write heightened parody with accuracy. At the same time, he can give his characters monologues of poetic introspection almost Chekhovian in tone. He is a man with the passion to describe the new insanity of our Establishment world in a way which cannot be dismissed. If the play seems bumpy and over-written in spots, there is enough consistently there to justify our enduring the occasional roughness.

Gil Lazier. ETJ. May, 1972. p. 197

When I read that Rabe's The Orphan was an Orestes play set in both past and present and featuring two Clytemnestras, I resolved to expect little; but never, never would I have expected the author of The Basic Training of Pavlo Hummel and Sticks and Bones to contrive such a strained, pretentious, muddled, clumsy and almost completely flavorless piece of claptrap. The idea, if it can be called one, is that Orestes is reincarnated in Charles Manson; that Agamemnon, Aegisthus, Calchas are the forerunners of the present American establishment and its materialism, militarism and mumbo-jumbo. Clytemnestra is America herself, the traitorous mother who becomes identified with pregnant Sharon Tate. Rabe was actually seduced by his producer, Joe Papp, into spelling this out in a program note more clotted in its prose than the play itself. The notion is not only an insult to poor Miss Tate, it may even be unfair to Charles Manson. Aeschylus I won't worry about; to his peripatetic shade, it is merely a stinkweed among the asphodel.

John Simon. NYM. April 30, 1973. p. 98

[Rabe's] first two plays, produced in 1971 and 1972, got much praise and many awards. Now it's 1973. His latest play, The Orphan, was recently produced . . . and the critical consensus was that this writer of exceptional gifts had slipped somewhat. . . . To me, the play was merely infested with the disease that had been evident in the two earlier ones. . . .

His one apparent avenue to effective writing led through antigrandness; his critical reception in general led him to think—or anyway didn't discourage him from thinking—that he is equipped for the grand. Now those who myopically encouraged him can no longer blink at the bankruptcy; after the praise, now come the tsks-tsks. I don't mean that once having praised him they were obliged to go on praising him forever; I mean that *The Orphan* is not much different from or worse than the work they praised; and now they have to know it.

Stanley Kauffmann. *NR.* May 26, 1973. p. 22

Unfortunately, [*The Boom Boom Room*] is not a good play, not a good play at all.

Mr. Rabe's heroine is a Philadelphia go-go girl named Chrissy, who is trying as she says, "to get some goddam order in my stupid life." Chrissy is in some ways a female equivalent of the hero of Mr. Rabe's first play, *The Basic Training of Pavlo Hummel*: confused, inarticulate, not very bright, yearning and groping and stumbling after some kind of decent life she cannot even envision clearly, and has no real chance of attaining. . . .

The trouble is that Mr. Rabe's play never gets anywhere either. It tells us not very much about Chrissy, and it tells it not very clearly, and what it does tell us seems of no very great significance. The play is loose, flaccid, unfocussed, wandering uncertainly in and out of realism and expressionism, comedy and serious drama—not fusing these opposites, not poising them effectively against each other, just wandering.

Julius Novick. *VV.* Nov. 15, 1973. p. 74

The shock of David Rabe's play [*The Boom Boom Room*] is the shock of truth, the most valid dramatic use of that emotion. Rabe's intention couldn't be clearer. By the creation of a repugnant world of anti-human cruelty, ugliness, and degradation, he throws into sharp relief the plight of his heroine, Chrissy, the go-go dancer and onetime hooker who is desperately trying to escape from that world. There is something fierce about the way he throws himself into Chrissy's tortured soul, not only examining but sharing all the doubt and pain and fear, every drop of the anguished self-loathing she feels for herself. The depth of his capacity for compassionate empathy is astonishing. . . .

The remarkable quality about David Rabe is his willingness to confront the alien culture of the Boom Boom Room and the level of society it represents. Not only does he face it head on, and attempt to understand and communicate the dynamics of the people who live in it, but he also finds amidst the wretchedness and ugliness a good deal of character and dignity. Chrissy—remember—is not one of us, but one of Them. Maybe that's the real threat, the fear that if we look hard enough at Them, "the others," we might see beyond the effects of their dehumanization. We might even see the humanity of these people we would prefer to avoid in life.

Marilyn Stasio. *Cue*. Dec. 3, 1973. p. 2

David Rabe wants to be a great playwright. And he wants to put on the stage the viewpoint of that large and unhappy majority, of lower- and lower-middle-class Americans, who are only beginning to discover that they have a voice. Mr. Rabe has in some ways the power to become a great playwright: the moral reversals wouldn't offend so much if they didn't carry so much conviction. *In the Boom Boom Room* is studded with scenes and speeches of great power, truth, and beauty, especially in the second half. A couple of them, like the go-go captain's monologue, almost make it up to the poetry towards which Rabe aspires.

But the good things get sunk in a mire of uncertainty and awkwardness. . . .

There isn't any doubt about Rabe's integrity. But he isn't, as of yet, an independent artist; he hasn't been able to create a play in which he can pull himself out of the situation and look at it with full kinship and full objectivity. It's awful to have to watch, in so public a place as a theatre (as a Public Theatre), a man's struggle with his own worst instincts. Such dramatic power as there is in Rabe's work right now comes from this struggle. But it's more akin to bear-baiting than to what one usually goes to the theatre for, and I dislike the idea of treating a playwright as a bear, even if he misguidedly offers himself for the role. Some day David Rabe will write a complete play, but until then I propose that we leave him, sympathetically, to work out his self-situation in private.

Michael Feingold. *VV*. Dec. 16, 1974. pp. 101–2

This is the first time Mr. Rabe has written a totally straightforward play [*Streamers*]—his earlier work has always been full of somewhat elusive and tricky time changes. Here he is telling a plain tale plainly—and yet very effectively. He has technically set his sights lower, but his image of death as a fall from life is well taken, his characters and dialogue have an air of cinematic familiarity (which nowadays is a fiction almost closer to reality than truth), the play moves to its bloody climax as if chased by the hounds of hell.

He is not above cheap tricks. . . . The drama deliberately sets out to shock—it uses more tomato ketchup than a B feature gangster movie— and quite often its mixture of joshing playfulness and harrowing horror does seem over-contrived. . . . But deep at the back of it lies Mr. Rabe's metaphor of death as an accidental joke, and this in the long run gives what could have been merely a rather bloody barrack-room melodrama the eloquence of resonance.

Clive Barnes. NYTd. Feb. 3, 1976. p. 45

RAHV, PHILIP (1908–1974)

[Rahv] had one of the best minds of his time. Through his writing, his editing of the great magazine, *Partisan Review*, his insistence upon the significance of certain writers of the past and the present, through all of this he had a sharp effect upon the intellectual and cultural scene. Rahv's passion was to judge American culture in the light of the best European tradition. He knew Russian, German, and French well, and of course was saturated in English and American cultural history.

The outstanding theme of Rahv's efforts was, I think, a contempt for provincialism, for the tendency to inflate local and fleeting cultural accomplishments. This slashing away at low levels of taste and at small achievements passing as masterly, permanent monuments was a crusade some more bending souls might have grown weary of. But he was not ashamed of his extensive "negativism" and instead went on right up to the end scolding vanity and unworthy accommodation.

Elizabeth Hardwick. NYR. Jan. 24, 1974. p. 6

A powerful intellect, a massive, overpowering personality and yet shy, curious, susceptible, confiding. All his life [Rahv] was sternly faithful to Marxism, for him both a tool of analysis and a wondrous cosmogony; but he loved Henry James and every kind of rich, shimmery, soft texture in literature and in the stuff of experience. He was a resolute modernist, which made him in these recent days old-fashioned. It was as though he came into being with the steam engine: for him, literature began with Dostoevsky and stopped with Joyce, Proust and Eliot; politics began with Marx and Engels and stopped with Lenin. He was not interested in Shakespeare, the classics, Greek city states; and he despised most contemporary writing and contemporary political groups, being grumblingly out of sorts with fashion. . . .

Mary McCarthy. NYT. Feb. 17, 1974. p. 1

RANSOM, JOHN CROWE (1888–1974)

I scarcely need to remind you that this quiet man, whose life has been so perfectly private that it could bear any public scrutiny, has given us poems which are minor only in that they are not long, but major in their inclusive irony. For no poet of our age, not even his exact contemporary T. S. Eliot, has surpassed [Ransom] in the awareness of the shadowy back room of the human condition, where "invisible evil, deprived and bold" makes its bid for domination. Yet, looked at closely, all the magnificent poems of the Ransom canon are love poems, celebrating love's triumph even in renunciation. The famous "precious objects" are the objects of love, even though they must, like the lovers, vanish into the thin air of human failure and eventually of death.

Allen Tate. SwR. Summer, 1968. p. 376

Ransom's basic impulse is . . . a fury against abstraction, against the predatory and ruthless intellect that would destroy (through its instrument, applied science) or ignore the rich particularity of the world's body; against this he exhibits a protective tenderness for the useless and undefined and helpless: for children, old people, the illogical textural details of poems as against their logical or prose structure: for the preposterously unrealistic Captain Carpenter as against his very efficient opponents. He defends play, enjoyment, contemplation, and the aesthetic experience which is allied to them.

But—and this is a point often ignored or obscured—Ransom is a genuine dualist. One cannot say that he is at bottom a believer in one or the other of the two opposed attitudes. He protests against the abstracting intellect because he believes it to be, as embodied in modern science, a present danger; the danger is that it may win too complete a victory, drying up or denying the pleasures of the innocent sensibility. But Ransom never repudiates logic or science; he would not give a complete victory to emotion, texture, play, innocence, and uselessness even if he could. . . . As his prose makes clear, Ransom himself has always remained a thoroughgoing skeptic: beneath the personal charm and the gentle and courteous manner he has been detached, unbelieving, unillusioned, perhaps inclining rather more to the scientific attitude, or at least increasingly sympathetic toward it. There has been a radical hardheaded skepticism, a kind of bleakness, beneath the "traditional" surface. The irony in Ransom's poetry is profound and unresolved; it is tragic, for its only resolution is in the idea of death.

Monroe K. Spears. Dionysus and the City
(Oxford—N.Y.). 1970. pp. 157–9

It is interesting that Ransom, like many of the poets of this century, believes that myth functions on an unconscious level; his conception of this level of experience, however, is very different from Yeats's, Auden's, Muir's or Aiken's, since for Ransom the significant unconscious communication that myth establishes is essentially religious and dogmatic. Beneath the "commonplace" situation of "Prelude to an Evening" Ransom sees the pattern of the "great Familial Configuration which had been ordained in our creation"; thus, from his point of view, the man returning to his household at evening enacts "a crucial and habit-forming moment in his history," which symbolizes the continuous religious history of mankind.

Lillian Feder. *Ancient Myth in Modern
Poetry* (Princeton). 1971. p. 397

Ransom's view of the world and his poetry . . . come from the conviction that neither science nor abstract philosophy will avail to make sense of the world, and, while some sort of rational humanism might, this is an attitude for which this world has no use. The world is obsessed by what it cannot use and will not use what it can. To this awareness Ransom brings a Calvinism which denies that man's destiny, or for that matter his right, is to dominate the world he finds himself in. Calvinism is not a world-affirming attitude, but Ransom is more than a Calvinist; he is a poet, and if John Calvin keeps him from trying to master or manipulate the world, he does not keep him from knowing it and loving it. This is all man has left. And to the poet, knowledge and love depend finally upon man's sensibilities, his awareness of the points of contact between his senses and the concrete, phenomenological world.

He takes not a despairing but an ironic view of his inability to master, to overcome the world which is his and yet is not his, and in this ironic pose finds a comfortable detachment. This ironic detachment, in turn, enables him to keep both worlds—the desirable and impossible world of the scientist and the abstract philosopher and the inescapable and painful world of John Calvin and the poet—balanced one against the other.

Miller Williams. *The Poetry of John Crowe
Ransom* (Rutgers). 1972. p. 11

● REED, ISHMAEL (1938–   )

Blacks and whites, avant-garde and mass culture, politics, even Reed's alma mater, the University of Buffalo, have their turn [in *The Free-*

Lance Pallbearers]. Features of the Gothic novel superimposed on an already flimsy plot do not help matters much, although the Reverend Eclair Porkchop makes a fine vampire. The attempt to turn Bukka into a revolutionary ten pages from the end, when he accidentally discovers what goes on in the underground vaults of Harry Sam's motel-castle, seems tacked on and insignificant. . . .

In considering the book's stylistic blunders . . . one cannot help but note that the direction of Reed's experiment deserves attention. Perhaps his next book will resemble a sort of third-person Huckleberry Finn, amalgamating many tongues of black and white America. For the moment we have only a disorganized collection of excellent ideas and brilliant but isolated vignettes.

Barbara Joye. Phylon. Winter, 1968. p. 411

Although Ishmael Reed's first novel [*The Free-Lance Pallbearers*] is set in a country where the people are obsessed by excrement, its leader is a cannibalistic pederast, and the police and judicial functions are carried out by idiotic brutes against a general citizenry so repulsively indifferent that it seems to deserve them, the book will make you laugh out loud. The plot is thin to invisible, but Reed's here . . . serves as a weird telescope for a society that is terrifying for its violence and passive hypocrisy, yet somehow hilarious as well. [*The Free-Lance Pallbearers*] succeeds in doing in 155 pages what Norman Mailer's *Why Are We in Vietnam?* swiped valiantly at. If comparisons are to be made, they should be to Burroughs, but this novel is all Mr. Reed's own. Read it.

Sara Blackburn. Nation. Feb. 5, 1968. p. 186

For all the talk of a black aesthetic, few black novelists have broken sharply with the traditional devices of the realistic novel. One writer who departs from such conventions, however, is 31-year-old Ishmael Reed. Reed writes highly visual, surrealistic fantasies—he calls them "movie books"—set in far-out lands of his imagination.

His first novel, *The Free-Lance Pallbearers,* uses an explosive combination of straightforward English prose, exaggerated black dialect, hip jargon, advertising slogans and long, howling, upper-case screams to describe the wanderings of young and innocent Bukka Doopeyduk through a mad, *1984*-style country called Harry Sam. . . .

Reed's second novel, a "Hoo-Doo Western" called *Yellow Back Radio Broke-Down* . . . is written in the same irreverent vein.

Robert A. Gross. Nwk. June 16,
1969. pp. 96–96C

We come to realize that the Kid [in *Yellow Back Radio Broke-Down*] is Lucifer (no surprise in a book of changes) and that Drag is the church—specifically, organized religion in America. . . . The elements of fragmentation, the puzzling shifts in language that Reed uses so brilliantly, the seemingly anarchic construction of the book are, in fact, part of a strictly disciplined whole. And to leave it at the confrontation between the Negro and the plastic white American is not enough. . . . If you wish, read this book as a comic satire, as black and sassy as Reed himself. But remember that the author also has a reputation as a poet and you should be aware that the structure of his book is as rigid as the poetic meter of the title.

Leonore Fleischer. *Book World.*
Aug. 10, 1969. p. 3

Ishmael Reed is a poet. Like LeRoi Jones, he has taken the American language out on a limb and whipped it to within an inch of its life. In so doing he has revitalized the American language with the nitty-gritty idioms of black people's conceptualization of what it means to live in dese new-nited state of merica. As a poet and a novelist, Reed has the imagination of a psychopath who is God, or who is Satan Himself— ghosts, voo-doo, rattlesnakes, weird rites, hoo-doo, superstitions, multiple schizophrenia, beasts, metempsychosis, demons, charms, visions, hallucinations. In fact, the novel is Reed's voo-doo doll. He once said that the novel is the worst literary form God ever visited upon mankind. Reed has risen the novel from a dead doll with pins in it into a living breathing walking talking animal. This is a thing more authentic, more difficult, more dangerous, more human than science can ever achieve. By this I mean Ishmael Reed employs the mumbo-jumbo witch-doctor experimental epistemology of the Afro-American folk heritage in combination with the psychotic semantic categories of the West to achieve a highly original, secular and existential portrait of what is going on, and has gone on, in our daily lives. Reed is not mad, he is supersane; it is America that is mad and, like the other secular existential black writers Reed depicts—no, Reed *explodes*—this madness before our very eyes.

Calvin C. Hernton in *Amistad 1*, edited by
John A. Williams and Charles F. Harris
(Random). 1970. pp. 221–2

[*Mumbo Jumbo*], written with *black* humor, is a satire on the unfinished race between the races in America and throughout history. It is a book of deliberate unruliness and sophisticated incongruity, a dazzling maze of black-and-white history and fantasy, in-jokes and outrages, erudition and superstition. Not only to white readers like myself will the way into and out of this maze be puzzling. For though it's a novel, the author's method is not novelistic. Wholly original, his book is an unholy cross between the craft of fiction and witchcraft.

I don't mean merely that *Mumbo Jumbo* is *about* such mysteries as HooDoo or VooDoo. . . . I mean that it attempts through its deadpan phantasmagoria of a plot, and through the black art of the Magus as storyteller, to achieve the kind of hold on the reader's mind that from ancient times and in primitive contexts has always been associated with the secret Word, the sacred Text.

Alan Friedman. NYT. Aug. 6, 1972. p. 1

This is Reed's own myth, a contemporary black folk tale, created especially for our era. In his own distinctive way, Reed blurs the boundaries between pagan mythology, Biblical and secular history, and fiction. The result is a form embodying something more than the sum of its parts. It's the true spiritual history of the black race, black in its emotional tone as well as its form and point of view. Moreover, it illustrates a critically important quality of the black spirit, its inextinguishability. However important are the forms by which Jes Grew [in *Mumbo Jumbo*] is known and practiced, they are expendable. . . . Jes Grew doesn't die; only its forms can be destroyed. . . . Others who have expressed similar sentiments have sounded sophomoric at best, ill-humored and pugnacious at worst. Reed, however, wins us over by the breadth of his allusions and the seeming inexhaustibility of his imagination.

Jerry H. Bryant. Nation. Sept. 25, 1972. p. 245

Mumbo Jumbo isn't at all concerned with the traditional province of fiction, the registration of individual consciousness. Rather, as in his earlier books . . . Reed opens fictional art to the forms and mythic possibilities of popular culture, pursuing not psychological description but a perspective on history.

He finds his apparatus in our most naïve and childish imaginings. . . .

Reed's satiric imagination, by putting white and black culture together for his own purposes, plays with a hope for something more than a negative and hostile relation between them. But if blacks are to redeem the white soul from its bondage to sterile reason, they must learn uncompromisingly to be themselves. . . .

Reed's is a quick and mocking mind, and I'm not sure how seriously he means his historical myth. But I'm content to read it as I read the "systematic" works of Blake and Yeats, not primarily as analysis but as an act of continuous and powerful invention, a demonstration that the imagination, black or white, when released from conventional forms and the idea of a monolithic history, can be wonderfully entertaining and instructive, moment by moment, about the sorry narrowness of our self-understanding and our expectations about art. Ishmael Reed's elsewhere turns out to be right next door, but his news of it is very new indeed.

Thomas R. Edwards. *NYR*. Oct. 5, 1972. p. 23

Reed's theory of history as a vast paranoid conspiracy of white against nonwhite reminds me of nothing so much as Thomas Pynchon's last novel, *The Crying of Lot 49*, in which the heroine stumbles upon a frightening underground postal system, W.A.S.T.E., that has lasted through the centuries and emigrated from Europe to America. Both Reed and Pynchon bolster their theories with a mass of semifacetious pseudoscholarship. Both create characters that are little more than cartoons. Both use the form of the put-on, the joke, to convey a deadly earnest message: That there are vast and inexplicable forces at work behind modern civilization, which turn us into nothing better than cartoon characters; that history itself has gone out of control. Given all that is irrational in the currents of contemporary history, the crackpot-conspiracy theory of one day becomes the working hypothesis of the next. Why, after all, did Sigmund Freud call America "a big mistake"? Did he know something we don't know? Ishmael Reed's far-out explanation is as good as any.

Andrew Gordon. *SR*. Nov., 1972. p. 77

With [*Conjure*] Reed, the author of three well-regarded experimental novels, has created an exceptional set of black-oriented poems. They represent a conscious production of an exclusively black aesthetic for American Negroes, which Reed calls "Neo-Hoo-Doo." The longer poems . . . are almost academic in structure and content, but the ex-plicator will have to be thoroughly briefed in Afro-American culture and ghetto life styles. . . . Reed is a more disciplined but no less angry poet than Imamu Amiri Baraka (LeRoi Jones) or Don L. Lee. . . .

Robert S. Bravard. *LJ*. Dec. 15,
1972. pp. 3992, 3994

"Patarealism," a term coined by Ishmael Reed, aptly describes the ex-travagant absurdities of his two novels, *The Free-Lance Pallbearers* (1967) and *Yellow Back Radio Broke-Down* (1969). Terror, laughter, and anarchy strike in Reed's imagination, which draws on Black ex-perience—phrases like "crazy dada nigger" occur in his work—yet re-fuses the definitions of any society. Elements of madcap violence, hip argot, tall tale, pornography, and "Hoo-Doo"—Reed's version of Afri-can juju magic—abound in his fiction. As for the novel form itself, a character says: "It can be anything it wants to be, a vaudeville show, the six o'clock news, the mumblings of wild men saddled by demons."

Ihab Hassan. *Contemporary American Literature* (Ungar). 1973. pp. 172–3

Ishmael Reed is a prolific writer who . . . writes in more than one medium. His novels . . . have already consolidated his reputation as one of those black writers who refuse to be categorized according to the relevance of his theme. He asks no favors of any orthodoxy, but lets his imagination make its bid for the creation of new forms. Yet one cannot fail to notice the craft and discipline with which he controls the natural swing and bounce of his verse.

In his latest collection, *Conjure*, Reed offers us a sharp and provocative contrast in style. If [Derek] Walcott's echoes are those of the classical humanist, grave and formal, Reed's tone and rhythm derive from the militant tradition of the black underground. But his is an unusual brand of militancy; it is much concerned with the politics of language. He argues for a clean, free struggle between the liberating anarchism of the black tongue and the frozen esthetic of a conventional White Power. . . . His verse is distinguished by a fine critical intelligence, and his stance before the wide variety of American life is supremely confident. He can evoke with poetic realism the savagery which shaped the pioneering spirit as well as crystallize the fraudulence at the heart of the "civilizing" mission.

George Lamming. *NYT*. May 6, 1973. p. 37

Although Ishmael Reed imports an elaborately constituted mythology from Osirian Egypt and ceaselessly invokes West Indian voodoo ritual to legitimize the African strain in his poetry and fiction, his mode of writing for the most part is essentially newfangled American tall-talk refracted through the hyperbolic declamatory style of William Burroughs. "Neo-Hoo-Doos are detectives of the metaphysical about to make a pinch," Reed writes in his new book of poetry, *Conjure*. "We have issued warrants for a god arrest. If Jeho-vah reveals his real name he will be released on his own recognizance de-horned and put out to pasture." Burroughs' remarkable ability to transform the street idiom of junkies and criminals into a richly metaphorical language, to project a Manichean view of the modern world that imaginatively comprehends its socio-political realities, has had from the start a profound influence on Reed's approach to writing, but the debt is only partial and the difference significant. The "nova conditions" Burroughs describes in *The Soft Machine* and *Nova Express* as the terminal strife of the West read differently on Reed's astral charts. . . . The collapsing star which for

Burroughs signifies the status of Western civilization is for Reed the energy of a new galaxy in the throes of creation.

Neil Schmitz. *MPS*. Autumn, 1973. pp. 218–9

[Reed's] new novel, *The Last Days of Louisiana Red*, might serve as a textbook on irony. In it he blends paradox, hyperbole, understatement and signifyin' so expertly that you can almost hear a droll black voice telling the tale as you read it.

One of Reed's best satiric methods is the interweaving of fantastic verbal absurdities with the familiar absurdities of everyday life. . . .

The primary targets of Reed's wit are the black revolutionary organizations that sprang up in places like Berkeley in the 1960s. He condemns their use of revolutionary violence, which was at times indistinguishable from old-fashioned crime. The posturing, the rhetoric and the exploitation that sometimes characterized actual movements symbolize the forces of foolishness and evil in Reed's hoodoo drama. . . .

Reed appears deeply concerned with the relationship between the sexes, but on this topic his perspective is frighteningly distorted. Throughout *The Last Days of Louisiana Red* there is joking contempt toward women, particularly black women. When he satirizes the women's movement his originality disappears and he falls back on the tired stereotype of feminists as man-hating dykes. The method for subduing these "fierce, rough-looking women" is attack and rape. . . . Reed's views on a difficult problem are antediluvian and for this reader they cloud the entire impact of his work. If he is so insensitive in this area, how can he be so incisive in others? (Can I laugh with a man who seems so hostile toward me?) As a critic I found *The Last Days of Louisiana Red* brilliant. As a black woman I am not nearly so enthusiastic.

Barbara Smith. *NR*. Nov. 23, 1974. pp. 53–4

REXROTH, KENNETH (1905–   )

Kenneth Rexroth has always written poetry in a crystalline, ingratiating style. His poems have an inviting ease and grace, a naturalness that was bound to be welcomed by readers who had grown impatient with the insupportable prolixity of so much modern poetry. But Rexroth's poems have become sadly predictable in recent years. All the saying is in the same key; there is little range or breadth of vision. A genial, meandering voice delicately, if wearily, coasts over the surfaces of things, of thoughts, mildly murmuring in rooms of his dream where he has come to feel too much at home for his own comfort, or for ours. . . . It is a pious poetry, a respectable and dignified poetry of deep sanctity, but alas, a poetry that conspicuously shuts out all trace of the darker being, the rowdy, earthy, dazzling personality that launched the San Francisco literary "renaissance" over a decade ago and continues to electrify his critical works today. One wonders, in vain, why Rexroth seems to have trapped himself early on in a poetics which narrowly restricts itself to a mere corner of his experience.

Laurence Lieberman. Poetry. April, 1969. p. 42

Although there is clearly development in Rexroth's work from its beginnings to the present, it is a qualified development. Early poems are tortured in syntax, heavily laden with the terminology and perspectives of science. Some of these, influenced by "literary cubism"—for example, "Fundamental Disagreement with Two Contemporaries," "Into the Shandy Westerness"—are more thoroughly fragmentary than any discussed here. These characteristics are soon transformed from general style to occasional device; the clearly defined image, the terse philosophical statement become dominant modes. "Leaving L'Atelier-Aix-en-Provence," for example, one of Rexroth's best imagistic poems, comes not from the period when Imagists were dominant, but from "Godel's Proof, New Poems 1965." These changes, however, are not dramatic; what is dominant in one period is usually present, or at least latent, in the others. Themes vary even less. Of course, contemporary events in the world at large, and in the poet's own life, are reflected in his poems; but the camping trips to the mountains, the concern with woods and stars, the sharp contrasts of the city, are present throughout, as is Rexroth's involvement in the human condition and his wish to order experience.

In one area, though, there is important change; Rexroth has never stopped experimenting with rhythms, which not surprisingly are crucial to the success of his poems. Here his work is most vulnerable; here his successes, when they come, are most striking.

Karl Malkoff. SoR. Spring, 1970. p. 578

Rexroth . . . approaches poetry as a total organic process—visionary, communicative, sacramental—in which no aspect is extrinsic: all actuality is part of that process of creation. He is by no means indifferent to prosody and other formal considerations; he is, actually, Classical in his precision. But prosody is subordinate to vision. Poetry turns out to be not an imitation of life but a state of being alive. It is not merely artifice or invention, not primarily a formal, verbal construction, nor an instrument for instruction and pleasure. It is not a means to an end but an end in itself—and not art for art's sake, but being for being's sake. Nor is it simply the expression of ideas and feelings, conscious or unconscious; and it is not regarded by Rexroth as the product of "objective" (biological or social) or "subjective" forces (such as intellect or imagination). Traditional dualisms between life and poetry, poetry and poet, poet and community dissolve in his transcendent view of creative process.

In theory and practice Rexroth is akin to such visionary poets as William Blake, W. B. Yeats, and D. H. Lawrence; like Walt Whitman, the American poet with whom he has the most in common, he is "a kosmos."

Morgan Gibson. Kenneth Rexroth
(Twayne). 1972. pp. 21–2

RICH, ADRIENNE (1929–   )

Adrienne Rich, in her fifth book, *Leaflets*, comes to us so garlanded with honors that one tends to expect each poem to be a masterpiece. This is, of course, unfair. Yet she does manage, in the book as an entirety, to display complete mastery, absolute assurance of movement and tone. I do not find the book great, but I do find it faultless. One fashionable mode at the moment is poetry in free verse with surrealistic jumps between its lines and an ending of deliberate banality, a drop into flatness which constitutes the shock of the poem; another is free verse written with conscious flatness, whose last lines lift in sudden flight into sentimental lyricism, which the preceding lines pull back on like a kitestring. Miss Rich avoids both of these over-used methods.

Mona Van Duyn. Poetry. March, 1970. p. 433

Like other cultivated poets of her generation—like Merwin, Snodgrass and James Wright—Adrienne Rich is haunted into significance as much by what she has changed *from* as by changing at all or by what she is changing to. Recurrence, memory, any presentiment of the old order, of the poem as contraption, is what this poet obsessively, creatively combats. In her sixth book [*The Will to Change*], then, there will be a constant imagery of inconstancy, of breaking free, of fracturing, of shedding and molting. . . .

The governing (or anarchic) emblems in this taut, overturning book are more likely to be drawn from almost anywhere than from poetry, from anything but verse in its decorous accorded sense, the ritual of a departure and return, a refrain which is indeed a refraining as well, a reluctance to violate repetition. Rather the figures will be derived from dreams and dedications, letters, elegies, photographs, movies. . . . The movies . . . are the major representative form here, and the major piece in this book is an extended series of writings called, focally, "Shooting Script"—what Adrienne Rich herself calls a conversation of sounds melting constantly into rhythms, "a cycle whose rhythm begins to change the meanings of words."

Richard Howard. PR. Winter,
1971–2. pp. 484–5

The forcefulness of Diving into the Wreck comes from the wish not to huddle wounded, but to explore the caverns, the scars, the depths of the wreckage. At first these explorations must reactivate all the old wounds, inflame all the scar tissue, awaken all the suppressed anger, and inactivate the old language invented for dealing with the older self. But I find no betrayal of continuity in these later books, only courage in the refusal to write in forms felt to be outgrown. I hope that the curve into more complex expression visible in her earlier books will recur as Rich continues to publish, and that these dispatches from the battlefield will be assimilated into a more complete poetry. Given Rich's precocious and sustained gifts, I see no reason to doubt her future. The title poem that closed The Diamond Cutters says that the poetic supply is endless: after one diamond has been cut, "Africa/ Will yield you more to do." When new books follow, these most recent poems will I think be seen as the transition to a new generosity and a new self-forgetfulness.

Helen Vendler. Parnassus. Fall–
Winter, 1973. p. 33

It is rare that the poet-turned-activist survives as a poet. Adrienne Rich is an exception. In seven decisive steps from her first volume of poems to her most recent, she has increasingly closed the gap between her public and private selves, never criticizing what is outside herself without criticizing what is within. In so doing, she admits that oppression is as much the creation of the oppressed as the oppressor. To be "stern with herself" is thus the axis of her poetic and political commitment, and it is in this way that her poems are moral without being moralistic, sensitive without bleeding sap.

Language is the weapon of her revolution; the proper naming of her pain as woman, poet, activist, and human being in a decadent civilization is her strategy; the revolution of the human spirit is her goal.

Diving into the Wreck, her seventh volume of poems, is revolutionary in ways we ordinarily think revolutionary: it is feminist, anti-war, pro-ecology, anti-order; it rejects a whole tradition of formal poetics. But it is not a simple rendering of revolutionary themes.

Gale Flynn. *HC*. Oct., 1974. pp. 1–2

ROBINSON, EDWIN ARLINGTON (1869–1935)

The quality of Robinson's newness has almost always been a subject for argument. But by the time of his *Man against the Sky* volume, he had fairly outlasted rejection by his elders, who genteelly deprecated his work for its prosiness and inglorious realism. Almost at once the tables were turned, and he found himself classed as obsolete by young men who denounced him as genteel and conventional. With his long look back to Wordsworth and the language and form in which he cast his latter-day Immortality Ode ["The Man against the Sky"], he was identified with the nineteenth-century world whose passing he tried to measure. His juniors were tempted to think that Prufrock's evening "spread out against the sky/Like a patient etherized upon a table" reduced to triteness the old-fashioned sunset which, early and late, was a controlling symbol in the older poet's work. Within five years, Eliot was dismissing Robinson as "negligible," and all the disdainful young men joined in. Readers who were arrested by the highly dramatic language of Eliot's monologues felt themselves merely deterred by Robinson's slow-paced reflectiveness. His grave manner did not call attention to itself in any case, but when minds were tuning to the flashing wit of a brilliant modernism, his subtlety and strength were easy to miss. His being formal was misunderstood by those who were reacting against the politeness of polite letters. His tone of consideration and reconsideration led them rashly to conclude that he was stolid. Formality, thoughtfulness, and reticence concealed his emotional depth—though not from everyone.

J. C. Levenson. *VQR*. Autumn, 1968. pp. 591–2

Robinson's poetic problem . . . was to transform the abstract ideas and sentimental, cliché-ridden metaphors of his day into poetry. In a sense he was trying to restore life to a worn-out language without abandoning that language. He succeeded to the degree to which he could place sufficient distance between his ideas and his own voice through the use of character. When, as in "Captain Craig," the persona voice articulates Robinson's ideas, the success is qualified. When, as in "Flammonde," the idea is embodied in the whole perceptual process of the poem,

Robinson achieves a degree of artfulness superior to that of anyone writing at the turn of the century.

The strategy of "Flammonde" forms the basis of Robinson's most successful character poems. "Richard Cory," "Old King Cole," "Ben Jonson Entertains a Man from Stratford," "Bewick Finzer," "Cliff Klingenhagen," "Aaron Stark"—all are ultimately as mysterious as is "Flammonde." In each case the simple perception of the persona voice falls into an unresolved paradox which leaves the final impression of a spiritual order above man's comprehension, yet controlling his destiny with an unswerving necessity. Although such poems use the language of a materialistic century, Robinson's strategy of character allowed him to make it express his faith in the power of spirit.

Part of Robinson's triumph as a poet is that he could formulate such a strategy given the language with which he had to work. Part of his limitation is that he could never go beyond it. The new poetic language born with Pound and Eliot achieved an integration of image and feeling and an artful distance produced by density of context which remained beyond Robinson's talent.

> William J. Free in *Edwin Arlington Robinson:*
> *Centenary Essays*, edited by Ellsworth
> Barnard (Georgia). 1969. p. 29

Though love acquires a sensual power in *Tristram* which is new in Robinson's work, it does not change in any fundamental way old views toward the basic problems of human existence. We can see in Robinson's Arthurian poems an extension of those in *The Torrent and the Night Before* and in *The Children of the Night*. There, we may recall, man is shackled by the weaknesses of his own nature—by selfishness, indifference, and stupidity, limitations that create a twilight world more akin to death than life. Hope exists in the confidence that the Light will come. How? We don't quite know. Robinson suggests somewhat tentatively that improvement in man's estate rests in God's love and in art. If we turn our eyes to the Arthurian scene, we shall discover that man's vices have become something more malignant than "sin's frail distress." Selfishness is now vulgar self-indulgence; indifference, now treachery and disloyalty; and stupidity, the criminal neglect of urgent responsibilities. What stands as a dyke holding back the flood of destruction is art—Merlin's, indeed, and Arthur's—and love—any form of it, not exclusively God's. Here it is preeminently the nobler passions of an Arthur not twisted by Gawaine's hate or of a white Isolt who attains ultimate understanding on a lonely beach in Brittany. In Robinson's Camelot we have no pure Galahad and no Holy Grail; we are left, when Camelot has vanished in flames, only with the figure of a battered

Lancelot who possesses the hope that in the darkness "the Light" would come and the confidence that "There are worlds enough to follow." . . . Robinson has erected the towers of Camelot on familiar ground, perhaps, even in New England, well within the walking range of men of his own time, and of later times.

> Charles T. Davis in *Edwin Arlington Robinson:*
> *Centenary Essays*, edited by Ellsworth
> Barnard (Georgia). 1969. pp. 102–3

If one were to suggest a contemporary American artist to illustrate the poems of Robinson, it would be David Levine, the brilliant caricaturist of the *New York Review of Books*, the Daumier of the Left. We can imagine Levine dispatching Richard Cory, Aaron Stark, Cliff Klingenhagen, Reuben Bright, and Flammonde, to name only a few characters, with easily rendered, hard-edged lines. He could, because Robinson's characters, especially those of the short poems, display a rigidity that is, in a sense, a parody of authentic identity. They have, to use Wilhelm Reich's phrase, seemingly impenetrable "character armor." In fact, when their "armor" is broken, often in violent and self-destructive ways, as in "Richard Cory" and "Reuben Bright," a first impulse is to laugh. The sudden imposition of the human upon the mechanical, to use Henri Bergson's formula for comedy, provokes a momentary exhilaration. These characters seem always to overthrow their rigid, defensive selves —the selves that are machinelike in their repetition-compulsions. In their efforts, what underlying forces are trying to come into being are not always clear. Little or no dialogue occurs between the contending impulses, and when the self is so divided as to have unconscious materials completely cut off from consciousness, the break-through takes on hysterical qualities.

> H. R. Wolf in *Modern American Poetry*,
> edited by Jerome Mazzaro (McKay).
> 1970. pp. 46–7

ROETHKE, THEODORE (1908–1963)

Roethke came closest of the poets of our time to repossessing the essential ways of knowing and feeling of our major poetic tradition, the tradition defined by Emerson, Whitman, and Dickinson. . . . Roethke was a Transcendental poet, a nature poet, and a poet of the transcendent self conceived both as representative and as defined by its capacity for growth. He was a poet dedicated to a new or "high" kind of "seeing," ultimately to illumination or mystic vision, a realization in experience, not in theory, of what Emerson referred to as the seer "becoming" what he sees. He was a poet who hoped to speak both for and to his time by discovering his own identity—and then creating a new identity capable of moving in a larger circumference by recognizing, accepting, and including within the self more "things," more of "fate," more of the tough resilience of the "not-me."

Hyatt H. Waggoner. American Poets
from the Puritans to the Present
(Houghton). 1968. pp. 564–5

The two chief questions which the collection of Roethke's poems [Collected Poems] poses are (1) whether he digested his obvious borrowings from Eliot, Yeats, Hopkins, Dylan Thomas and Whitman, and (2) whether he ever got beyond the undoubted achievement of the "greenhouse poems" in his 1948 volume The Lost Son. Breaking things down in these poems to their lowest common factors, he speaks with his own voice and with a painful urgency. The poems smell of the earth and crawl with life; plants and little creatures like snails are seen not just closely but as equals. The verse runs its fingers right down into the roots of vegetable and animal existence. But it is a child's vision, which threatens to dissolve each time the poet comes anywhere near to putting it in an adult perspective. . . .

Roethke shared (or got infected with) his father's love of order, and it seems to have been a failure to achieve it in his own right that drove him both to his eclecticism and to the rather confused mysticism which falsifies the focus of so many of his later, more ambitious poems.

Ronald Hayman. Encounter.
Feb., 1969. pp. 74–5

[Roethke's] poetry is often close to nursery rhymes and nonsense verse, and he cultivates his affinity to earlier mad poets: Traherne, Smart, Blake, the mad old wicked Yeats. In this non-human visionary world of childhood fears and adult madness, the Dionysian element is very plain. But the weakness is also plain: the world of normal adult experience is so remote that, both in content and technique, the poetry is limited, tending to obsessive concern with certain experiences and to incoherence on the verge of real obscurity. Roethke apparently realized this, and in his later verse was moving out toward a wider range and clearer organization, as in "Four for Sir John Davies."

Monroe K. Spears. Dionysus and the
City (Oxford—N.Y.). 1970. p. 247

At his death in 1963 Roethke left 277 notebooks in which he had jotted down, for 20 years, fragments of verse, aphorisms, elliptical injunctions to himself, remarks about teaching poetry, reveries and random observations (surprisingly few and mild) about other poets. The notebooks evidently served Roethke as a verbal compost heap. He would on occasion raid it for lines and images and graft them onto his current work.

David Wagoner, the poet who selected and grouped the extracts that compose *Straw for the Fire*, suggests that Roethke didn't use the material because "he was sometimes dealing with material too painful to complete" and "he loved incompleteness, perhaps because it represented a promise that he would never exhaust himself." . . .

More likely, though, the material did not meet Roethke's high artistic standards. For the melancholy fact is that there is very little here that is not more eloquently said in the *Collected Poems* and in *On the Poet and His Craft*.

Herbert Leibowitz. *NYT*. April 9, 1972. p. 4

Nature does not by itself define Roethke's sensibility, both tortured and naïve, so human and animal. He is also a poet of the unconscious, of childhood, leaning to beginnings, clutching for roots; he returns farther back than where life began, to start again; and like many Romantics, he reaches for death. He is a dream poet, wishing his way everywhere; a love singer, sensual and pure; an author of nonsense verse and childhood lyrics. A bare Self—"I'm naked to the bone"—undergoing journeys to the interior, moving outward toward a woman, an animal, a flower, speaks in rhythms of its own. . . .

There are moments when Roethke comes too close to the great authors who influenced his work; when his poetry gives itself to clichés of doxology; or when the focus of his insight, excluding much of the human world, seems too special. These moments are infrequent. More often, he is a poet of the indicative; being, not doing, is his joy. He is the recipient of some aboriginal magic, nature-blessed, master of some hysteria no Word can allay. He is, finally, a true original who may not shape American verse, yet henceforth must occupy a unique place in the soul of poetry.

Ihab Hassan. *Contemporary American Literature* (Ungar). 1973. pp. 98–9

This unity of opposites indicates the way in which Roethke's world is a total alternative to the dualistic structures of classical Western thought, an alternative that is manifest in our most primary, everyday experience. Body and world, subject and object, time and space, fantasy and reality, child and man, all exist in a perfect unity, a unity given previous to any reflection, and a unity that couldn't conceivably be otherwise. But each exists also as perfectly autonomous; each is bounded and liberated by itself; each is a hole, a mouth. The garden, Roethke's world, is the condition of growth; it is open-ended, a mouth, since it leaves itself and fills itself in the becoming motion that is growth. This includes the world of inanimate as well as animate things, since the life of that world is the perfect unity of life and death, of Being and Nonbeing, that infuses every moment of our lives.

John Vernon. *The Garden and the Map* (Illinois). 1973. p. 190

ROTH, PHILIP (1933–   )

Portnoy's complaint presents the schlemiel condition as unbearable; and for all its dialect-humor the punch line seriously implies that the purgation of the narrative ought to be the starting point in the cure. The Jewish joke was conceived as an instrument for turning pain into laughter. *Portnoy's Complaint* reverses the process to expose the full measure of pain lurking beneath the laughter, suggesting that the technique of adjustment may be worse than the situation it was intended to alleviate.

We are back in a new enlightenment, and as the group is thought to have control over its destiny, it must be satirized for failing to execute its proper task. There is no toleration for irony, although irony is the hero's life-style, not to mention the author's, and the willingness to retire with the philosophic shrug, "Oy, civilization and its discontents," is considered a betrayal of joyous potential. The self-hatred of which most unfavorable critics accuse the book grows from the rather self-loving notion that we could be better if only we tried, the tired but persistent thesis of the little engine that could. By this light, the little man who couldn't ceases to be the model of humanity and becomes again the mockery of its failings.

Ruth R. Wisse. *The Schlemiel as Modern Hero* (Chicago). 1971. pp. 120–1

The comedy of *Portnoy's Complaint* is at one level, as Alex complains, that he is "living in the middle of a Jewish joke"; at another, that the various fantasies, including his own, keep colliding with each other. If in *When She Was Good*, Roth's heroine had trouble living the American middle-class morality she had swallowed because others would not let her, in this novel Portnoy has trouble living the immorality he wants to accept—for the same reason. But like most comedy, at bottom there is little that is really funny at all, and in the wake of Alex Portnoy's misadventures are such finally pathetic characters, however amazing in their fictive particularity, as Mary Jane Reed, "The Monkey," whose vulnerable and nearly chaotic humanity shows up the shallow narcissism of her lover most devastatingly of all.

With others I remain unconvinced, nevertheless, despite all its wealth of particularity, its nostalgic and accurate evocation of Jewish lower middle-class life in the thirties and forties, and its other fictional achievements, that *Portnoy's Complaint* is more than a *tour de force*, an inevitable and logical culmination of the fantasy life that *Playboy* magazine has so studiously fostered among us. The danger—it is an altogether real one—is that we accept the comic fantasy and make it our own; or in other words, that we fall into Caliban's dream and envision all the land peopled with little Portnoys. Our reality is deeper and darker than this. Roth hints at it, as I've indicated, but his great gifts of caricature and humor in this novel are overwhelming.

Jay L. Halio. *SoR*. Spring, 1971. pp. 638–9

Roth is not a "natural" novelist at all, the kind who loves to tell stories, chronicle social life, pile on characters, and if in his early fiction he seems willfully bent on scoring "points," in the novels his will exhausts itself from the sheer need to get on with things. He is an exceedingly joyless writer, even when being very funny. The reviewers of his novels, many of them sympathetic, noticed his need to rub our noses in the muck of squalid daily existence, his mania for annotating at punitive length the bickerings of his characters. Good clean hatred that might burn through, naturalistic determinism with a grandeur of design if not detail, the fury of social rebellion—any of these would be more *interesting* than the vindictive bleakness of Roth's novels.

Irving Howe. *Cmty*. Dec., 1972. p. 74

Yet what made Roth stand out—there was now a rut of "Jewish novelists"—was his "toughness," the power of decision and the ability to stand moral isolation that is the subject of his story "Defender of the Faith." There was the refusal of a merely sentimental Jewish solidarity. At a time when the wounds inflicted by Hitler made it almost too easy to express feelings one did not have to account for, but when Jews in America were becoming almost entirely middle-class, Roth emphasized all the bourgeois traits that he found. He cast a cold eye on Jews as a group; he insisted, by the conscious briskness of his style and his full inventory of the exaggerated, injurious, sordid, hysterical, that *he* was free.

Alfred Kazin. *Bright Book of
Life* (Little). 1973. p. 145

Parts of [*My Life as a Man*] are reminiscent of *Portnoy's Complaint*, but what frequently remained undeveloped in that book is more deeply attacked in this one. The stories read as if they were originally written in something approaching hysteria—but then rewritten, and rewritten again. The novel is chaotic in its emotions, but nicely controlled as conscious art, and its more subtle considerations surface when it is read a second time. . . .

Roth's best work, so far, has transformed intense private experience into fiction that speaks for its era, no matter how eccentric the basic metaphor of the works might be. A drop-out from graduate school at the University of Chicago, Roth is continually aware of himself as a writer in a variety of traditions, and he is ironically aware of the distance between life and the kind of art we are taught to admire.

Joyce Carol Oates. *APR*.
May–June, 1974. p. 45

In his new book *My Life as a Man*, which deals with the operatically unhappy marriage of a successful young writer, Roth returns to the quasi-autobiographical mode of *Portnoy's Complaint* and *Goodbye, Columbus*, and the result is good enough to confirm the misdirection of the last three books, [*Our Gang, The Breast, The Great American Novel*], just as *Portnoy's Complaint* revealed what was missing from the three that preceded *it*. It confirms that despite his superb gifts as a mimic, *tummler* and hyperbolist Roth is only good at fantasticating materials from his own life. As a satirist of Nixon or Bill Veeck he is clever but uninspired. (He especially lacks any political savvy.) As a satirist of middle-class Jewish life in Newark or the suburbs he is brilliant and wicked, endowed with a perfect ear and a cold eye, a bit like the early Mary McCarthy. And faced with the traumas of family life and the conflicts of the mental and moral life in *Portnoy's Complaint*, Roth can be not only funny but lyrical—emotion recollected in hysteria—with the poignance of one who is so miserable he can only crack jokes. . . .

At the root of the creative problem is the pervasive ungenerosity that has always marked Roth's work. (His early Jewish critics were misguided; his quarrel was not with Jews but with people.) Even a satirist must love his characters a little, especially if he also loathes them. He must be drawn to them in an animating way, must *need* to give them life. He can't use novels simply to settle old scores. Roth's genius is all for surfaces—the telling descriptive detail, the absurd mannerism, the tics and turns of real speech, the ludicrous flaw of personality—rarely for human depths. He does have an affinity for people at their most frantic, pompous and ridiculous, in part because he admires the

sheer energy of human waste, but also because they confirm his own
sense of superiority.

Morris Dickstein. NYT. June 2, 1974. p. 1

Not all readers will find Roth's comedy of desperation [*My Life as a
Man*] risible, even those who no longer expect it to rest on the kind of
bedrock decency the social humorists of England are used to. This
author's rather heartless solipsism will always tend to undermine first-
person humour, and here, where there is even fundamental doubt as to
the identity of the self in whose name knowledge is claimed, the possibility that one is being browbeaten in laughing more derisively than one
would temperamentally like is stronger than ever. What seems certain is
that Roth is reserving the last laugh in this instance to himself, and that
we might do well to leave him to it, abandoning ourselves in the mean-
time to the rampant Schadenfreude of these pages.

Russell Davies. TLS. Nov. 1, 1974. p. 1217

RUKEYSER, MURIEL (1913–   )

Muriel Rukeyser is a poet of dark music, weighty and high-minded. *The
Speed of Darkness*, the title of her new book, is indicative of the oracular soothsaying quality of much of her writing—for me, a defeating
tendency of her style which often nullifies any attentiveness to detail.
Her mystical vision is so dominant in the mentality of some poems, the
writing becomes inscrutable, as she packs her lines with excessive symbolism or metaphorical density.

    Her firmest art is the linear and straightforward delivery of her
story-telling anecdotal poems, the longer biographical poems, and letter-
poems to friends expressing an open declaration of personal faith. In all
of these genres, her symbolism is balanced by clean, open statement. In
"Endless" and "Poem" . . . personal lyrics irradiating pathos from the
recollection of harrowing life-moments, Miss Rukeyser achieves a naïve
forthrightness—an artlessness—which, as in the most lastingly valuable
personal letters (those of Keats, for example), derives a universal moral
faith from plainspoken events authentically observed and recorded. In
these poems, Miss Rukeyser is most nearly able to make her experience
—her recollected terror and madness—our own. Her absorptively
sympathetic portrait of the German artist, Käthe Kollwitz, one portion
of a continuing sequence of biographical works (*Lives*), is the most
arresting long poem in the new collection. Miss Rukeyser displays wis-

dom as self-critic in choosing to adapt so many recent poems from biographical and historical studies, since the task of accurately restoring a human lifetime in verse compels a precision in the enumeration of items of dailiness that offsets her frequent tendency to drift into cloudy abstraction.

Laurence Lieberman. *Poetry*.
April, 1969. pp. 42–3

Rukeyser's first collection of poems, *Theory of Flight*, won the Yale Prize for Younger Poets in 1935. Since that year, new wars, changing attitudes toward minorities, women, the body and sex, and renewed interest in New England Transcendentalism, as well as the pursuit of a more profound understanding of complex and terrifying human relationships, cause us, in the seventies, to define Rukeyser as a poet far different from the one she has traditionally been assumed to be. The neglect her poetry has suffered has delayed recognition of her work as deeply rooted in the Whitman-Transcendental tradition.

Her belief in the unity of Being, her reliance on primary rather than on literary experience as the source of truth and the resultant emphasis on the self, the body and the senses, as well as the rhythmic forms and patterns that inevitably emerge from such beliefs, tie Rukeyser to her forebears in the nineteenth century. At the same time, through her highly personal contemporary voice, they project her into our era which, with its radical departures from traditional Transcendentalism, is yet a reaffirmation of it, with Rukeyser as one of its important figures.

Virginia R. Terris. *APR*.
May–June, 1974. p. 10

SALINGER, J. D. (1919–   )

Despite his limited production Salinger with his complementary creations of Holden Caulfield and Seymour Glass (both surrounded by siblings) so captivated the fancies of the Americans of this intellectually
and emotionally arid era that the decade of the 50s can justly be called
from more than a literary point of view "The Age of Salinger." The
relationship between the world of Salinger's fiction and the world outside is complex, but it is perhaps best suggested in Holden Caulfield's
despairing cry after he searches for a "place that's nice and peaceful,"
"There isn't any." . . .

[Salinger] sees the material world as absolutely corrupt. . . . One
can save one's self only by limiting one's criticism to one's self and
resisting the temptation for public acclaim. The man whose vision is too
clear to enable him to close his eyes to this world cannot hope to
communicate with it. He can hope to make a spectacular exit that may
keep alive some glimmering memory of the "niceness" we can know
only momentarily.

Warren French in <i>The Fifties</i>, edited by
Warren French (Everett/Edwards).
1970. pp. 12–3, 37–8

Although *The Catcher in the Rye* is a fine novel, the Glass stories are
increasingly slack, tedious, and mendacious affirmations of an illusory
reality. Ultimately [Salinger's] liturgy denies life and love by denying
the earth on which they occur. Frost puts the matter well at the end of
"Birches":

> . . . Earth's the right place for love:
> I don't know where it's likely to go better.

On Salinger's planet, love doesn't go at all.

Richard H. Rupp. *Celebration in Postwar
American Fiction* (Miami). 1970. p. 131

It is easy enough to catalogue Salinger's faults—few important writers
are more vulnerable than he; but the more relevant task would seem to
be a consideration of why he has interested and often obsessed more
readers than any other serious American author since the Second World

War, why he has been, as [Norman] Mailer himself admits, "everybody's favorite."

We might begin by citing Salinger's compassion for the victims and fallen figures of an urban America; his self-conscious, chastening wit; or his remarkable ability to illuminate character through the finest detail. But the deeper, more permanent attraction of Salinger's work must have something to do with his treatment of suicide and survival, his attempt to suggest a mode of survival in this world that is not without meaning and a little dignity. . . .

In Salinger's fiction one feels a persistent idealism despite the profound distrust of all those forms of authority that contribute to conformity of mind and spirit. Indeed the struggle between idealism and authority causes the special tension of Salinger's work; it is a struggle that drives the hero to the point of madness and suicide.

Theodore L. Gross. *The Heroic Ideal
in American Literature* (Free).
1971. pp. 263–4

In a world too plainly made "absurd" by our inability to love it, the Glasses are loved by their relative and creator, J. D. Salinger, on every inexhaustible cherished inch of their lives. His microscopic love for them compels them into our field of vision; we see them through the absoluteness of Salinger's love and grief. And non-Glasses are spiritual trash. . . .

Yet for all this eerie devaluation of everyone outside the Glass family, the whole charm of Salinger's fiction lies in his gift for comedy, his ability to represent society as it is, for telltale gestures and social manners.

Alfred Kazin. *Bright Book of
Life* (Little). 1973. p. 115

A while back one could read Salinger and feel him to be not only an original and gifted writer, a marvelous entertainer, a man free of the slogans and clichés the rest of us fall prey to, or welcome as salvation itself, but also a terribly lonely man. Perhaps he still feels lonely; but he is, I think, not so alone these days. The worst in American life he anticipated and portrayed to us a generation ago. The best side of us— Holden and the Glasses—still survives, and more can be heard reaching for expression in various ways and places, however serious the present-day assaults from various "authorities." I put down *The Catcher in the Rye* and *Franny and Zooey* this year again grateful to their author. I wondered once more how to do justice to his sensibility: his wide and generous responsiveness to religious and philosophical ideas, his capacity to evoke the most poignant of human circumstances vividly and honestly, and with a rare kind of humor, both gentle and teasing.

Robert Coles. *NR*. April 28, 1973. p. 32

SANDBURG, CARL (1878–1967)

Sandburg deserves to be remembered. He is still, probably, the most important of the Midwestern literary pioneers of the age when Chicago was a raucous nest of singing birds, superior by his range and more attractive in his public persona than Dreiser, Vachel Lindsay or Edgar Lee Masters.

Sandburg was consciously a "representative man." . . . He celebrated the glories of Middle America: Chicago was the "city of the Big Shoulders." Some of Sandburg's verse is still remembered, but he was no Whitman; and the standards of poetic achievement have risen since the remote days when Chicago was the American Athens. . . .

His real epic achievement was his immense life of Lincoln, which was not merely long but often penetrating, despite its numerous academic deficiencies.

TLS. Feb. 12, 1971. p. 175

SANTAYANA, GEORGE (1863–1952)

The profession of essentialist critic or literary psychologist suited Santayana in a two-fold way. Aesthetically and poetically it enabled him to find beauty in those high contemplative moments in which, as he says in "A General Confession," he felt life to be "truly vital when routine gives place to intuition, and experience is synthesized and brought before the spirit in its sweep and truth." But these were but momentary transports in the act of thinking. Seldom did they obscure his vision of "unvarnished truths," the most pertinent to him being that the liberal age into which he was born "flowed contentedly towards intellectual dissolution and anarchy." For Santayana was naturally and intellectually alienated from the society in which he lived. Doubtless this alienation makes the modulation in the tone and theory of his criticism. But he does not quarrel as a malcontent and the criticism is not intended to be discordant. It is his capacity to remain aloof from and yet understand—even to identify with—those dominations and powers he knew in Western civilization that characterizes his criticism as the work of a sympathetic literary psychologist.

James Ballowe. DalR. Summer, 1970. p. 159

Santayana's special role in American intellectual life was to be a poet and philosophical materialist in a time and place when that seemed like a contradiction in terms. He was the most cultivated and literate American philosopher of his time but he boldly spurned belief in God, in immortality, or in final causes; he thought that all causal explanation is physical in nature; and he held with David Hume that there are only two kinds of truths, those established by experience and those established by the analysis of intent or meaning. Although he occasionally made exceedingly penetrating forays into technical philosophy, his accomplishments in that area leave much to be desired. Late in his life he became more and more preoccupied with espousing and defending his rather elaborate doctrine of essences, but in my opinion that is not a very important contribution to the history of American philosophy. Santayana would not have been altogether flattered to hear himself likened to Emerson—we have seen that he believed that Emerson was "not primarily a philosopher but a Puritan mystic with a poetic fancy and a gift for observation and epigram"—but it is Emerson who comes to my mind when I try to summarize Santayana's position in American philosophy. If Emerson was the sage of American idealism who had a poetic fancy and a gift for observation and epigram, then Santayana was the similarly endowed sage of American materialism.

Morton White. Science and Sentiment in
America (Oxford—N.Y.). 1972. p. 241

SAROYAN, WILLIAM (1908–   )

For all the present importance to him of Amiel, Mr. Saroyan's mode of writing and cast of mind have always been deeply American, as American as his situation as the son of an Armenian immigrant would allow him to be and would insist on his being. In his contradictory mixture of melancholy and hopefulness, disaffection and chauvinism, anarchic individualism and common populism, fantasmal absurdity and earthy sentimentality, he is of a various company that may from time to time include Whitman, Twain, Sandburg, Anderson, Williams, Cummings, and Henry Miller. His has been an altogether smaller achievement than that of the greatest of those names, but it has been far from negligible, and he deserves more than his present neglect. He has been one of the last interpreters of an earlier, younger America, in his case the Armenian community of Fresno and its surrounding farmlands fifty years ago, its members homesick for the old country, looking for a better life in the new. He has portrayed that world generously, humorously, and of course sentimentally. He has also been incessantly committed, not precisely to his art, but to the act of creativity, to a constructive energy which has been his form of celebrating what he has found to be the good fortune of being alive.

TLS. July 23, 1971. p. 851

I can think of no other American writer—*no* other writer of serious intent —who has remained boyish throughout his entire career. Mark Twain wrote about childhood through child's eyes, but *The Mysterious Stranger* and *Letters from the Earth* come as no surprise from him, while cognate works would be a surprise from Saroyan.

In the long view, it's a sad career. How much he has poured out and how little sticks. What a fresh, unique, welcome voice he had when he started—those early stories, those first carefree plays. In the mid-30s there were phrases from Saroyan ("cookies, raisins in") that were catchwords with me and my friends. The voice is still unique: he has had no memorable disciples or even imitators. But mostly it has kept saying the same things, most of which it had already said better.

Well, if he hasn't really grown he is at least much the same. Some of the places in *Places Where I've Done Time* deliver good quick stabs of feeling. (The most ironic section is one in which Saroyan, the perennial boy, can't communicate with his own children.) The book is sometimes gassy, and sometimes gooey, but it's never fake. Honesty is not enough, particularly when it's youthfully lyric honesty, and when a 40-year career is based on it. But the best thing about Saroyan is that he didn't choose to do it that way, he *had* to do it that way, and sometimes —as sometimes in this book—it's lovely.

Stanley Kauffmann. *NR*. March 25, 1972. p. 22

SARTON, MAY (1912–   )

There are many brief evocations of an actual rural world [in *A Durable Fire*], but it is, every bit of it, so *used* and directed, that what is concrete in it melts and re-freezes as yet another impenetrable abstraction. So, while this kind of poetry appears superficially to work by equivalencies of fact with emotion, nothing in the end has its own real life to begin from: it is all props on which, we are assured, great inner consequences lean. Looking for perceptions of observed nature, all I can find is how they are, one by one, turned immediately to the grasping uses of Human Nature. . . .

May Sarton's poems to her psychiatrist, so obviously intense in gratitude and love, stand as the absolute embodiment of the poet's failure to transform her life into (or should I say, in) poetry: they admit nothing actual—a reticence anyone deserves—but neither do they communicate any convincing reasons for their intensity; mean reality has been replaced by earnest pieties that describe "The Action of Therapy."

Rosellen Brown. Parnassus. Spring–
Summer, 1973. pp. 49–50

A dialogue of undiminished intensity has been carried on in Sarton's work for thirty-seven years. Its greatest daring, the source of its greatest moral energy, has been openness: to experience, pain, the perils of passion, loneliness, and truthtelling. This has inevitably been the dialogue of an isolated human being, a self-dialogue, recognizable certainly to housewives, desperate in loneliness and devoid of the solitude Sarton has created.

Sarton has not avoided the dangers inherent in such an openness and such a dialogue: the appearance of self-indulgence, self-pity. These dangers might as well be mentioned in their harshest form, together with her other sin: a certain laxity of style, a tendency to seize the first metaphor to hand, rather than search out the one, perfect phrase. In the intensity of her exploration, Sarton has not eschewed the assistance of the familiar metaphor, nor always observed the niceties of point of view.

Carolyn G. Heilbrun. Introduction to Mrs.
Stevens Hears the Mermaids Singing by
May Sarton (Norton). 1974. p. xii

May Sarton has designed her *Collected Poems* with a lifelong process in view. Her aim has been to reveal the development of a career and of a person, because the whole of her career is greater than the sum of its stages, despite the brilliance of many individual achievements. She writes of the feminine condition, of art, love, landscape, travel, and the search for a lasting home, and of the inexplicable violence that can wreck even the mildest people. Her tone is often gently didactic. The largeness of her themes makes them worth returning to again and again; her didactic tone helps give her poetry its distinctiveness, for very few poets of this age seem willing to be purposeful about poetry's power to instruct.

Henry Taylor. HC. June, 1974. p. 2

Often [Sarton] give her work (and thus provides us, conveniently with) unusually indicative titles: *Kinds of Love* (1970) or the poetic account of love, aging and her time in psychiatry, *A Durable Fire* (1972). *Journal of a Solitude*, in the same year, advances her conviction that it is not in relationships but in maintaining one's aloneness that a creative woman realizes herself. And *The Small Room* (1961), the book that appealed especially to academic women (I was one then) because it raised (but never tried to solve) the question of how it was possible to be productive, scholarly, creative and yet lead the life women were "destined" for.

As a longtime reader of hers I want to join the celebration because I admire the *nature* of her career—serene-seeming despite "the anguish of my life . . . its rages"; her declared traumas of bisexual love, breakdown, conflict; her increasing productivity (to my mind her book published last summer, *As We Are Now* is one of her finest achievements), everything she has written entirely professional, solid yet sensitive. As a women I feel a closeness to her message, an alliance with her lifelong, solitary control.

Doris Grumbach. NR. June 8, 1974. p. 31

SCHWARTZ, DELMORE (1913–1966)

[Schwartz's] *Selected Poems*, which he edited himself in 1958 and subtitled *Summer Knowledge*, is now re-issued as a paperback. To my mind it contains a great deal of bad poetry; yet never merely bad or merely uninteresting; Schwartz's genius is on every page, twisted, fouled, and set against itself. It is an excruciating record; redeemed (if that is the word) by perfect poems that rise here and there from the tangle, strong, lucid, eloquent, often rather old-fashioned, like wild roses in a bank of weeds. Hence this reprint is useful. But what Schwartz really needs— and let it be soon, before he is forgotten—is a strict selection from all his work in one volume: poems, stories, essays, and some of the wonderful reviews he tossed off so easily to earn a few dollars. If the copyrights can be straightened out (for his relations with his publishers were as chaotic as the rest of his life), this should be undertaken right away by some friendly but tough editor.

Hayden Carruth. Poetry. Sept., 1968. p. 426

It is clear why he was held in such respect, for reading through Delmore Schwartz's essays is like touring the monuments of literary modernism in the company of a wise and entertaining guide. As he ranges over the cultural landscape, he picks out deep generalities and details of language, intellectual background and psychological habit which reveal "the fate of Art and the emotion of the Artist." A lucid explainer of texts and difficult ideas—it comes as no surprise that he was a great teacher—he sets to right what he believes are confusions of method or lapses in sensibility without malice or self-promotion. His polemics indeed might serve as a model of the witty correction of error. He seeks to augment knowledge, not overpower us by glittering acrobatics on the dialectical highwire. The passionate seriousness and unhurried civility of his mind, "his solicitude for all sides of every question," insure a commentary that never falls into triviality or academic solemnity.

"Felix qui potuit rerum cognoscere causas" ("Happy is he who can grasp the causes of things"), the refrain of his early long poem "Genesis," might be taken as the heart of Schwartz's literary creed. As poet, fiction writer, movie reviewer and critic, he is the student of causes, the hidden genesis, "the early morning light." His concern with the way the past exercises its expressive and moral power over a writer's subject matter, style and point of view is mirrored in his poems and short stories where the "family god" and social circle influence his characters' emotional illusions.

Herbert Leibowitz. NYT. Jan. 17, 1971. p. 3

Schwartz's theme has more than a personal dimension. He is sounding a note that goes back 150 years to the first stirrings of romanticism in Europe: the alienation of the artist from middle-class society. This was an especial dogma in the wake of the modernist movement of the 1920s, whose difficult art, addressed to a purified elite, was sometimes built on an attack on modern life in toto, and in the wake of the radicalism of the thirties, which identified the middle class as the special villain of contemporary society. . . .

Where this view of modern life prevails the Jew, especially the secular Jewish intellectual, becomes the quintessential modern man: doubly alienated, from the prevailing national culture and from his own traditional culture, uprooted from the European pale and yet cut off from his own uprooted parents. But the artist who is truly interested in other human beings—and has some concern for his own sanity—soon comes to the limits of alienation as a viable ground for his work. . . .

Delmore Schwartz's best stories move away from this starting-point, toward an empathy for other lives, but they never fully evade these limitations. They are exquisitely wrought but excruciatingly self-conscious. No one would call them expansive. Their main theme remains that of the isolated self and the mysteries of identity that can never be solved but never evaded. For the author himself the final paranoia and anonymity, the trail of broken friendships and brilliant memories, to say nothing of the deterioration of his work, were the final seal of the same failure.

Morris Dickstein. *PR*. No. 1, 1974. pp. 40–1

Delmore had a beautiful lyrical talent, and so long as he continued able to write anything at all, this gift doesn't seem to have left him. It's too early to say what in our period, if anything, will be lasting; but my own judgment, perhaps partial, is that some of his lyrics will survive. . . .

He had great brilliance and potential, I believe, as a critic. His early pieces give very alert and sensitive readings of Hardy, Auden, Tate, and others. He was starting from Eliot as a base, but his young man's mind was swarming with ideas, and he was working toward a position and point of view of his own. But the patience and concentration needed for this were denied him—for a number of reasons, principally perhaps his own mental troubles. . . .

When you add it all up, what have you? Certainly, not something at all negligible. To have written anything, however fragmentary, that lays claim to permanence is a higher achievement than to turn out something fully formed but glittering only for the moment. But just as certainly, a failure—and a failure all the more in relation to the power of the original gifts.

William Barrett. *Cmty*. Sept., 1974. p. 52

SCOTT, WINFIELD TOWNLEY (1900–1968)

Scott had an old-fashioned American sense of independence. He was honest and felt this sometimes as a fault. He had the courage in all these notes [*The Dirty Hand: The Literary Notebooks of Winfield Townley Scott*], so relatively short, easy to read, and fascinating, to entertain justice as a necessity. He writes with a just and fair mind, beyond rancor or pettiness, with modesty and profundity. Reason is his guide, he is in no way frenzied, hortatory, or authoritarian. The judgments of this book shift the emphases of literature as they were felt by his contemporaries and state his own ideas posthumously and well, for our consideration.

The gravity of some of his statements is impressive while the tone of the book is conversational, sane, sometimes witty, always amiable.

He is too intelligent to berate others or to defend himself. He knows that poetry cannot change the world. We are let in on a long private conversation, as it were, he had with himself. Sharing this with him after his death is a moving experience. Some of his pronouncements are aphoristic, some are confessional. All have a kind of finality. They exhibit a triumph of reason.

Richard Eberhart. *Poetry*. Feb., 1970. p. 345

● SELBY, HUBERT (1928–   )

Like most naturalists, Selby depends on the massing of details, but he is more soundly selective than some of his predecessors, and he knows very well how to shape a story. Moreover, though he maintains an air of objectivity, he is capable of compassion. This is hell, he seems to be saying [in *Last Exit to Brooklyn*], and these are people on whom we must have pity. We must resolutely contemplate their squalor, their brutishness, their empty lives, their callousness, and the poverty of their hopes, and we must consider what their existence means to us.

No author that I can think of has presented so impressive and authoritative an account of the life of the people at the bottom of the heap in our so-called affluent society. This is a book that ought to shake us, not because of this word or that, but because a sound craftsman has shown us so much of what we should prefer to ignore.

Granville Hicks. *SR*. Nov. 7, 1964. pp. 23–4

The profound depression *Last Exit to Brooklyn* causes—once one starts seriously to read it—is a measure of an authentic power which carries through and beyond revulsion. . . . There are serious faults in Selby's stories. The degree of violence, the amount of blood and gore and semen, the sheer grotesqueness, sometimes nullifies or engulfs belief. Yet that the author is able to make one believe at all in this sordid, hopeless world is an extraordinary achievement. He does it by a vision of hell so stern that it cannot be chuckled or raged aside, and by a manner of writing which looks tricky but is not—is instead urgent and necessary to that vision. *Last Exit to Brooklyn* is not a book one "recommends"—except perhaps to writers. From them, those who wish to read it, it deserves attention.

Eliot Fremont-Smith. *NYT*. Nov. 8, 1964. p. 67

Above all, Selby is writing about the distortion of love, the rottenness of its substitutes, and the horror and pathos of its perversion. The shock produces total recoil. . . . It's almost as though Selby, who has never read Paul Goodman's utopian proposals, had set out to write a fictional demonstration of their urgency. . . . We must infer what love is through experience beyond *Last Exit to Brooklyn*, or through Selby's compassionate act of having written the book. . . . Selby's people do not know what love is and cannot express it, as Goodman has said, because their society has given them no opportunity to find out. . . . We believe Selby's characters and will never [be] able to forget them. But they are not Everyman. In praising Selby's astonishing power to tear our sensibilities, one must remember that this is part, not all, of the world we would weep for.

Webster Schott. Nation. Dec. 7, 1964. p. 440

I am not persuaded by [*Last Exit to Brooklyn*] that life is hell, though Selby has shown me some of the damned (whom I have seen before a good many times, in recent fiction as well as in life). I do not believe it is necessary for a writer to trap his reader in perverse, revolting emotions in order to make him imagine literarily something of what the characters' experience is like. I dread going to hell, I do not want to be locked in there and abandoned to pain, while I am in those doleful regions I need and pray for help to understand what is happening about and within me. However, if for some reason you want to go uncomprehendingly to hell for a few hours and do not know how to make it on your own, this book provides a reliable way to get there.

George P. Elliott. Cmty. Jan., 1965. p. 86

Hubert Selby Jr.'s *Last Exit to Brooklyn* [is] serious and disquieting . . . in that Mr. Selby, though often loud-mouthed and pretentious, has an educated understanding of the issues at stake. . . .

Mr. Selby neither pities nor condemns. He describes and, by implication, excuses. These people are what they are because, despite money and social benefits, they have no stable background against which to assess their existence and put a value upon it. The traditional framework (religion, family, craft) have all been bulldozed by the industrial and political forces which have brought money and social benefits as a cheap exchange. Since no one knows *who* he is, all he can do is to assert as loudly as possible *that* he is.

Simon Raven. Lon. April, 1966. pp. 113–4

Last Exit to Brooklyn has been attacked as immoral and even pornographic. After a series of trials in England, the book was officially suppressed. *Last Exit to Brooklyn* has also been banned in Italy, and has been the subject of controversy in the United States. The characters in Selby's stories are homosexuals, prostitutes, dope addicts, and hoodlums, and his plots illustrate the degenerate, depraved, and doomed existence they live. Selby's realistic style is as objectionable to many readers as the actions he describes. Nevertheless, Selby is not a salacious or pornographic writer; he belongs to the tradition of the religious-moralist-satirist that includes Swift and Pope and which began with the medieval preachers who denounced lechery and gluttony by presenting repulsive portraits of the sins of the flesh. Selby's description of an unlovely and unloving humanity is expressed in the only language appropriate to both his aesthetic and moral intentions.

Charles D. Peavy. *Critique*. 11, 3, 1969. p. 35

Hubert Selby has a gift for capturing the rage that explodes within every American city. No other American writer has conveyed so brilliantly the fierce, primal competitions of the street, or of the way living can shrink to hating. Selby's first book, *Last Exit to Brooklyn*, was a volatile vision of the seething, raging life of Brooklyn's back alleys, of workers and thieves who brawl in gutters and bars, people for whom life is an endless down. As Selby portrayed it, Brooklyn was not a place so much as it was a nightmare in which manhood could be won only through one man's tormenting another. The relentless pursuit of *machismo* through all the byways of cruelty, the fear of failure that drives men into deeper and deeper vileness are Selby's most gripping preoccupations. For Selby is a clinician of male violence, an explorer of those recesses of consciousness where the question of sexual identity is always in doubt. *The Room* is about the same nexus of sexual chaos and cruelty that gave *Last Exit to Brooklyn* its remarkable force. . . .

Selby is a poet of our decline, a writer who has an unerring instinct for honing our collapse into novels as glittering and as cutting as pure, black, jagged glass.

Josephine Hendin. *SR*. Dec. 11, 1971. p. 37

Selby writes with an obsessive concern for explicit detail, for the precise texture of skin and hair, the exact placement of bodies, particular human odors. . . . We recognize ourselves in the prisoner [in *The Room*]. I think *The Room* assures Selby's place in the first rank of American novelists. His work has the power, the intimacy with suffering and morality, the honesty and moral urgency of Dostoevsky's. . . . *The Room* is a novel profoundly concerned, perhaps too deeply, with America and yet a novel which refuses to sentimentalize the American experiences. *The Room* is a great, moral book.

Dotson Rader. *NYT*. Dec. 12, 1971. p. 5

Selby is Cubby, no longer Duke as he used to be called. He doesn't look at all any more like the thug whose picture is on the back of *Last Exit to Brooklyn*. Instead he resembles an insurance clerk or somebody's father. . . .

Like himself, the people Selby writes about have been in the gutter. His vision comes from the bowels of America. What he believes, he feels. The heart is more important to him than the mind. When asked about other expressions of violence, such as *A Clockwork Orange* or the films of Sam Peckinpah, he replies that he hasn't been to a movie in years and that his violence comes from the gut and is not connected with "social themes or any of that crap."

John S. Friedman. VV. July 14, 1973. p. 30

SEXTON, ANNE (1928–1974)

Love Poems is not sentimental, not trivial, it is simply not believable. The poems have little to do with believable love, having none of love's privacy and therefore too frequently repelling the reader; they have as little to do with believable sexuality as an act of intercourse performed onstage for an audience. Because neither revulsion nor amusement is a fair response to a poet with this much talent, one must, for the sake of the poet and the poems, totally suppress the word "confessional" and substitute the word "fictional." Only then, when the "I" is a character separate from the author, does the woman become as innocent of exhibitionism as Molly Bloom in her soliloquy. One would not, even then, return and return to these poems as one does to other love poems of past and present, because their self-absorption is too great to allow an empathic entrance. . . . However, it is clear, I think, that it is from Miss Sexton's almost incredible feats of "indiscretion" in attitude and image, her grotesque, near-comic concentration on her every emotional and physical pore, and her delineation of femaleness, so fanatical that it makes one wonder, even after many years of being one, what a woman is, that her poems derive their originality and their power, as well as their limitations.

Mona Van Duyn. Poetry.
March, 1970. pp. 431–2

At a reading at the Guggenheim Museum, Anne Sexton—after three books of poems—finished one of her poems and said, "But it is not true." That hall feels cold and artificial. It was a beautiful woman standing there, in a beautiful dress. The expectation and the gossip around one was of confessional poetry. Now this is a curious genre, one taken to promise a new order of secret, and one finds secrets that everyone knows; taken to promise emergent men, emergent women, who may bring to speech the lives of these generations; too, one is often given disposable poems, made without the structural reinforcements, those lattices on which the crystal grows.

However, when Anne Sexton said, "But it is not true," a waver went through the audience. No, I cannot say that, I can speak only for myself. I thought, "It may very well be true." She had cut through the entire nonsense about confessional writing, and returned me to the poem.

The issue in most of Anne Sexton's poems has been survival, piece by piece of the body, step by step of poetic experience, and even more the life entire, sprung from our matrix of parental madness. It is these people, who have come this way, who have most usefulness for us, they are among our veterans, and we need them to look at their lives and at us.

Muriel Rukeyser. Parnassus.
Fall–Winter, 1973. p. 215

Vital as her early volumes were, however, The Death Notebooks goes far beyond them in making luminous art out of the night thoughts that have haunted this poet for so long. The book's epigraph is a line from Hemingway's A Moveable Feast—"Look, you con man, make a living out of your death"—which succinctly summarizes the poet's goal, a goal both shrewdly ironic (at least she can write, and thus make a living out of her obsession) and ambitiously metaphysical (what is there to make a living from except death?). But if irony and shrewdness have always characterized Anne Sexton's work, the largeness of her metaphysical ambition is what is newly notable about The Death Notebooks. The seductions of suicide no longer concern her; the deaths of friends and relatives are secondary. Now, like John Donne, she is lying down in the inescapable coffin that is her own, "trying on," as she tells us, her "black necessary trousseau." In doing this, she has inevitably to define the death that is neither a handful of pills nor somebody else's funeral but, in a sense, a pre-condition of life itself.

Sandra M. Gilbert. Nation.
Sept. 14, 1974. p. 215

SHAPIRO, KARL (1913–   )

In *The Bourgeois Poet* we find still the seeker for "reality" in an age when no one knows any longer what "reality" is ("I am an atheist who says his prayers"). We find a full recognition of the subjectivity of [Shapiro's] early "reporting" poems, with their so much insisted upon "objective" manner ("This is the camera with the built-in lie"). We find insights into the poet's self that strike us as true ("Longing for the Primitive I survive as a Modern, barely"). *The Bourgeois Poet* exhibits Shapiro in his chosen role as the primeval American poet, the "man who begins at the beginning—all over again," the "first white aboriginal." The role demands immense renunciations, which only future development of the poet can justify. But Shapiro ought to be heartened by the examples of Emerson and Dickinson, as he says he is heartened by the example of Whitman.

Hyatt H. Waggoner. *American Poets from the Puritans to the Present* (Houghton). 1968. p. 596

The main thrust of Shapiro's middle career has been the search for a technical means to liberate his passional nature from the overbearing rigor of his intellect. . . . In his poetry, his radicalism took the form of the prose poems of *The Bourgeois Poet*. Whatever the shortcomings of that book, we mustn't forget it is no small triumph to revolt successfully against a guaranteed blue-ribbon instrument for turning out the well-made poem. Merely to have closed the door, unalterably, on his celebrated old style and plunged into total risk of the new is a healthy mechanism for artistic survival. The book's positive force obtains from the impact of Shapiro's middle-aged personality on his youthful learned intelligence, as reflected in the contest between logic and the imagery of hysteria. Though he cannot always break the grip of his intellect, he consistently infuses hallucinatory intensity into the struggle. We witness in this poetry the drama of the critical intelligence, which knows too much for its own health, trying to free itself from insights that threaten to become self-devouring, and so attain a higher graciousness of loving selfhood. This conversion, when successful, is the essence that informs Shapiro's best writing. The freedom he has won for the subject, the image, the language of his poetry in *The Bourgeois Poet* is an astonishing breakthrough out of the fixity of his old constrictive forms. He has unleashed a kind of pure adventurousness of sensibility.

Laurence Lieberman. *Poetry*. April, 1969. p. 46

Few poets in America today have gone through as many transformations of style or as many varieties of subject matter as Karl Shapiro. Beginning as a modern formalist, he later renounced this work as "trash basket" poetry and went on to write free verse paragraphics; recently he returned to traditional songs and sonnets. Among our major poets today, only Robert Lowell has had more success with a similar triple shift from cerebral to visceral to cerebral verse. Just as striking are the varied configurations of Shapiro's major themes. He began as the poet of urban middle-class America, went to topics of war, eventually stressed the Jewishness of his work as its dominant "undercurrent," returned to an assessment of our bourgeois culture, and finally, in his first really happy book, he revelled in the joys of conjugal love.

Not surprisingly, these larger configurations of style and theme have totally obscured another element in his early work—his Southernness. In addition to these major subjects of middle-class urbanism, war, Jewishness, and love, he wrote a dozen or more poems in the 1940's that explicitly concern themselves with aspects of the Southern experience, especially as this experience clusters around the two poles of Jeffersonian social thought and Poesque psychic moods.

Alfred S. Reid. *SHR*. Winter, 1972. p. 35

• SHEED, WILFRID (1930–   )

The easiest comparison is to say that *A Middle Class Education* is something like the early work of Evelyn Waugh. But the early work of Waugh was economically shaped; it never was prolonged or overdone. Here the trouble is one of wasteful size; it is a trouble caused by writing too much about too little. Yet a genuine glitter comes up from this prose repeatedly. There's wit and brilliance, concern and understanding; and these virtues help to compensate for the want of structural control, of firm ordering and economy, and of what Henry James called the "angle of illumination."

Richard Sullivan. *CST*. Jan. 29, 1961. p. 9

Wilfrid Sheed's theme [in *The Hack*] is . . . a breakdown in faith, but he deals with it . . . ferociously, indeed with the savage glee one has come to take for granted in Roman Catholic novelists writing about their co-religionists. The hack of the title is Bert Flax, a writer of inspirational stories and verse for the American Catholic lay press, a professional good man whose inspiration suddenly dries up on Christmas Eve. Much as he flogs himself he cannot bring it back, and he falls into a mental collapse. Flax himself I did not find easy to take seriously; but as a satirical study of life in a New York suburb, with Christmas in full cry, the unpaid bills mounting and last year's toys already broken in the basement, it is often very funny indeed, the reality behind *Satevepost* ads for gracious living and togetherness seen through eyes liverish from jaundice or hangover. There are some splendid glum priests and, to counterbalance them, an equally splendid militantly anti-Catholic American matron, Flax's mother-in-law, ever itching to hand out the birth control pamphlets.

Walter Allen. *NS*. Feb. 22, 1963. p. 281

There is much refreshing [in *Square's Progress*] in Mr. Sheed's approach to the fashionable insinuations always being made about the deadly horrors of suburban living and the supposed enchantments of the alternatives. It is also a welcome surprise to find a writer suggesting that it is more important to be good than sophisticated. But despite many splendid satiric touches and a style which often flashes with brilliance, Mr. Sheed avoids the hazards of his subjects only by a hair's breadth. . . . If Fred Cope had been a little less stupid and Alison a little less mean, one could take them more seriously and believe in their solution more fully. Mr. Sheed's book is provocative, sensible, and often witty. But it is neither visionary nor devastating.

Robert Kiely. *CSM*. Sept. 2, 1965. p. 7

[Mr. Sheed has] an admirably cool comic sense, neither shocked nor much disposed to scold about the pettiness turned up in [*Office Politics*]. He uses his characters observantly but not waspishly to make the point and get on. . . . Wilfrid Sheed has failings of course. For one thing, he has no range outside the middle class and even inside it he sometimes seems to know only magazine writers. . . . Also [he] has a touch of sexual primness . . . and his books sometimes lack body therapy. Sheed knows what he is about though, and if he keeps writing books as witty and shrewd and entertaining as *Office Politics*, nobody will have reason to complain.

Warren Coffey. *BW*. Sept. 11, 1966. p. 4

Instead of being the "exploration of a sensitive man's awakening into integrity" (as we are told on the dust jacket—in fact, as we are told on almost every dust jacket these days), *Office Politics* is more a tempest in a teapot. Except for perhaps George Wren, Sheed's characters are essentially uninteresting. Their struggle for power is real enough—a struggle that can be as compelling in the small office or the small college as it can on Wall Street or in Washington. Yet, as functionaries, as mere pasteboard masks, these characters are pitifully without past or future, exist in a still-well of time, and their struggle is as one dimensional as they are themselves.

The trouble with *Office Politics* is that Sheed is successful in showing modern man divested of hope and expectation. However, when he depicts such men whose lives have given way to ennui, boredom becomes the subject of the novel; and like so many novels about boredom, *Office Politics* becomes a bit of a bore.

Richard Lehan. *WSCL.* Summer,
1967. pp. 445–6

[*The Blacking Factory* and *Pennsylvania Gothic*] deal in different ways with the theme of nostalgia. The nostalgia is of a special kind, and perhaps it is characteristically American. It is provoked not by the memory of any real order which has passed away, but by a sense of blankness in the present, a rootlessness which threatens our survival and which compels us to invent a past, a lost Eden scraped together from whatever Technicolored ephemera our popular culture provides us with. The consequences are a rudimentary form of fascism as long as the lie is not confronted, and the threat of madness when it is. . . .

Sheed has a fine ear for the wry turns of English and American colloquial speech, for the clipped ironies by which we bring our crises down to a more bearable level of intensity. It is largely due to this stylistic gift that both of his central characters are so well realized. Under pressure, Sheed seems to say, we have much in common with the jaunty, wilfully self-assured stand-up comic of vaudeville, stationed on a high empty stage, urging his snappy repartee forward into the darkness.

Daniel M. Murtaugh. *Com.*
Jan. 24, 1969. pp. 532–3

[Max Jamison in *Max Jamison*] was born and raised to examine life critically, and this ceaseless use of the critical intelligence is both his glory and despair. . . . His dilemma is tragically unresolvable (he comes close to madness toward the end) because he really is too good for this world, even though he knows it himself. . . . The decent hero taking arms against a sea of clichés has always been a Sheed speciality, which accounts for his failure to produce a blockbusting novel, since clichés about art and life are the lifeblood of best sellers. But the even larger insight of this new, triumphantly intelligent novel is that criticism is not a mask or a pose, a way for egomaniacs to vent their hostilities or for failed artists to make a buck. It is a deep-dyed view of life, a creatively aggressive attitude to the world rather than the usual mindlessly passive one.

Richard Freedman. Book World.
April 26, 1970. p. 1

Wilfrid Sheed is a writer in transition, but he is not a writer fumbling for a new voice. The distinction is important. Mr. Sheed seems to know precisely where he is going and what he is doing. He has moved from the deliciously brittle satire of the opening chapters of *Office Politics* toward a fiction which, while the dazzle remains, has gained measurably in depth and subtlety. . . .

Max Jamison . . . is Mr. Sheed's best book. It is funny, sad, tough, compassionate; its title character is realized in every nuance of personality; and the writing is splendid.

Jonathan Yardley. NR. May 23, 1970. p. 26

Wilfrid Sheed, a gifted phrase-maker and a thoroughly professional writer who not only knows what he is doing but does it extremely well, has created in Max Jamison, down-at-the-heart critic, playboy, lecturer, celebrity-about-town, and perennial poseur, a character who could be Everyman in these gloomy days. . . .

Jamison is painfully introspective, with few moments of genuine action. . . . There is a certain agony in his search for contentment, or at least some permanent opiate to induce forgetfulness. . . .

This is too dismal a view of a darkly engaging book, which may be read purely as entertainment, or, as I am sure Sheed intended it should, as a sympathetic, occasionally ribald, always engrossing portrait of a tragi-comic man, mired in a profession he no longer respects or truly enjoys, a man doomed to boredom and despair, with only an occasional slight flash of pleasure in prospect to keep him alive until the fall of the final curtain.

Robert Cromie. SR. June 6, 1970. pp. 39–40

Sheed is neither a propagandist nor a commissar. He does not come armed to the event, be it literary or political, with an ideological spear and a theoretical net. Nor does he inflict on the reader (and the event) some stupefying ponderous aesthetic scheme that reads as though it had been translated from the Quechua, which is not of course a written language. Books are not criminals to him, having sinned against history or psychoanalysis or the churches of Christ, Empsom and Roland Barthes. Sheed is a humanist, with all the intelligence and generosity, humor and wonder, the term implies; and nothing human fails to interest him according to its own definition. . . .

Indeed, what's most characteristic about Sheed the humanist is the care with which he chooses his subjects. He probes instead of devouring and understands without destroying. The self is not imposed on every book, person, and event; the self stays behind the style; the book, person, or event commands our awareness. Connections are thus marvelously made, consequences mourned, distinctions celebrated, grace bestowed, without the reader ever sickening of a literary self, an unobstructed *me*, all over him like an inky squid of ego.

John Leonard. Foreword to *The Morning After*
by Wilfrid Sheed (Farrar). 1971. pp. xix–xx

[*The Morning After*] is a book of reviews by a brilliant reviewer who knows all the tricks and openly despises most of them. . . . Even narcissistic authors and corrupt reviewers, who after all usually know or at least nod to their own little failings, must enjoy Sheed's exposures of narcissism and corruption, so long as the names are changed and some of his own blood gets spilled along with theirs, as it certainly does. . . . *The Morning After* as a title makes its own point about reviewing, about what its pleasures consist of and are finally worth, and it's fascinating, if a little sad, to watch so serious and gifted a man daring himself to respect the work he's so good at, pointing at his professional head a gun that, for all you or I or he knows, may be loaded after all. Sheed is probably the best professional reviewer in the business.

Thomas R. Edwards. *NYT*. Oct. 10, 1971. p. 7

By "making it" so thoroughly in America, Sheed may have lost the heritage that would have made him not just a good writer but a great one. I don't know whether his American readers are aware of it, but Sheed's heritage is truly impressive. . . . Sheed is . . . the living representative of four successive generations of men and women of letters, three of them deeply involved with Catholicism. He is probably to some extent trying to escape his heritage—and who could blame him? . . . Perhaps Sheed is reluctant to criticize Americans because in his bones he feels he isn't American. Perhaps his writing would have a little more edge, a little less urbanity, if he lived in England and criticized English life and letters. . . .

Even as things are, Sheed's most telling pieces revolve around the possession, the lack, or the abandonment of roots.

Vivian Mercier. *Nation*. Dec. 20,
1971. pp. 662–3

The detail-work in Sheed's account of the process by which Casey's contrary wills and many minds are formed is only one of [*People Will*

Always Be Kind's] pleasures. The inside dope on the dealings of politicians and on the sordid highs of campaigning gives the reader another pleasure—the kind that has always addicted readers to the novels of major as well as minor old-fashioned craftsmen. The prose, the pace, the humor are pleasures neither old-fashioned nor new-fangled, but simply unique to Sheed's writing. So is a certain quality of moral intelligence, one graced by an unflappable and chastened sanity, a charity precise and unsentimental.

Robert Graves, who has been called a minor poet for over fifty years now, once pointed out that the distinction between major and minor writers tells us less than the distinction between good and bad ones. *People Will Always Be Kind* is a very good novel by a very good novelist.

George Stade. NYT. April 8, 1973. p. 2

Wilfrid Sheed, the son of Catholic writers and publishers Frank Sheed and Maisie Ward, was born in England and came to America at the age of ten. He is today every inch an American novelist, however. He has ranged over a variety of characters and subjects in his books, and it would be pressing a bit to say that all are specifically Catholic. *The Hack* certainly is, though; it details the destruction of a hack writer of conventional pieties for Catholic magazines of the old sort—and the message seems to be that what we don't *mean* can hurt us. But his last novel, published earlier this year, is the most Catholic, the most American, and certainly the most powerful of them all. The title is *People Will Always Be Kind*, and it presents the life of a young United States senator from New York named Brian Casey who is running for President. Casey had polio as a child (as did Sheed, incidentally) and the novel is fundamentally an account of the affect of physical disability on someone of immense ability and ambition. It is, with all this, a fiendishly funny book, one that makes you suspect that a peculiar species of black humor is almost natural to Catholic writers.

Bruce Cook. ALib. Oct., 1973. p. 549

● SHEPARD, SAM (1943–   )

Chicago by Sam Shepard, the best play on both bills [*6 from La Mama*], is a fantasy-comedy about a young man in a bath-tub. . . .

What gives the play its delights is Mr. Shepard's ability to follow fast after the ephemeral half-thought and Kevin O'Connor's ability to speak it, sing it, savor it and hasten over it. The pair of them, aided by Tom O'Horgan's sensitive direction, provide a bright patch of truthful nonsense. . . .

This is a free-flowing salty and touching little rhapsody on a small incident seen through the prism of fantasy.

Stanley Kauffmann. NYTd.
April 13, 1966. p. 36

I immediately liked *Icarus's Mother*; and I still think it is the best of Sam's plays to date—the fullest, densest, most disturbing and provocative. . . . I was struck by the play's smooth, mysterious ascent from cozy reality to high lyricism and symbolism, its debonair plunge into the sharky deeps of resonant meaning. All Sam's plays use the stage to project images: they do not relate to the spectator by reflecting outside reality (they are not psychological or political); rather they relate to reality by operating directly on the spectator's mind and nerves. The imagery is surreal, the method nonrational, the sensibility hunchy. It's always hard to tell what, if anything, Sam's plays are "about"—although they are unmistakably alive.

Michael Smith in Five Plays by Sam Shepard
(Bobbs-Merrill). 1967. p. 26

Red Cross is a cool play—in the sense that it is dense, not brought to the point of intellectual clarity, embedded in a series of metaphors which are all interconnected—and because it is a cool play, it must be treated as such, *not* "hotted up" by filling in the seemingly empty places where not enough is said to make for clear, unitary, conscious meaning. (Two facts are relevant here: (1) Sam can be extraordinarily precise and articulate whenever he feels the necessity of it; (2) He is not a willful obscurantist.) Sam is more interested in *doing* something to audiences than saying something to them, and what he wants to do has no relationship to the purging of emotions through identification or total involvement. It is more like the way changing a room's temperature does something to the people in it.

Jacques Levy in Five Plays by Sam Shepard
(Bobbs-Merrill). 1967. pp. 97–8

Sam Shepard, the author of *La Turista*, is twenty-three years old and even so he is not new to the theater. He is not being "discovered" in this production. His plays have been off-off [Broadway]; in the Café La Mama reportory; he has been at the Cherry Lane and will soon be in print. *La Turista* is his most ambitious play thus far but still it is in the same style and voice as *Chicago* and his other one-act plays. . . . Formless images and meaningless happenings are peculiarly oppressive to the spirit, and the inanities of the experimental theater could make a man commit suicide. Sam Shepard, on the other hand, possesses the most impressive literary talent and dramatic inventiveness. He is voluble, in love with long, passionate, intense monologues (both of the acts end in these spasms of speech) which almost petrify the audience. His play ends with sweating, breathless actors in a state of exhaustion. The characters put on a shawl and begin to declaim like an auctioneer at a slave mart, or a cowboy suit and fall into Texas harangues. They stop in the midst of jokes, for set pieces, some fixed action from childhood, perhaps influenced by the bit in Albee's *Zoo Story*. Despair and humor, each of a peculiarly expressive kind, are the elements out of which the script of the play is made. The effect is very powerful and if it cannot be reduced to one or two themes it is still clearly about us and our lives. The diction, the acting, the direction, the ideas are completely American and it is our despair and humor Shepard gets onto the stage.

> Elizabeth Hardwick in *La Turista* by
> Sam Shepard (Bobbs-Merrill).
> 1968. pp. xii, xiv

If [Jean-Claude] van Itallie makes expressive use of silence as well as noise, Shepard's relentless verbiage and sound effects suggest a recent adolescence submerged in rock, and other racket music—a din appropriate, I suppose, for our urban civilization. We sense with theatrical immediacy that this young man writes out of a milieu of psychedelic coffee-house environments, of outlandish costumes. The author wore one himself. I spotted him immediately, though I had never even seen a picture of him before. . . .

This is a theater of pure experience. It's like taking part in any of the vast number of theatrical activities outside theater walls that are a part of our everyday lives now. What did the killing of Oswald on TV mean—in that moment? This new theater simulates that kind of senseless, "everyday" happening.

> David Madden. *The Poetic Image in Six
> Genres* (Southern Illinois). 1969. p. 208

Except for *Melodrama Play*, the most recent of [Shepard's] published *Five Plays*, which has something approximating a conventional plot, his plays are all constructed in the same fashion. He puts a number of not very well differentiated characters into a situation in which an undefined something seems to be going on and lets them talk, either in long monologues or in exchanges that tend toward single-sentence lines. It is possible to find meaning, in the traditional sense, in his works, to assume that the bookcase chore in *Fourteen Hundred Thousand* is a lifetime task, unwillingly undertaken; that *Icarus's Mother* is about the bomb; that *Melodrama Play* is incidentally concerned with making satirical points about the pop-music industry. Yet the communication of ideas is not Shepard's concern. Of *La Turista* (1967), he told a *New York Times* interviewer (March 5, 1967), "I mean it to be a theatrical event, that's all."

Gerald Weales. *The Jumping-Off Place*
(Macmillan—N.Y.). 1969. pp. 241–2

Sam Shepard, flip, frenetic, anti-ideological, is about as removed from [Ed] Bullins as anyone can be. Trying to describe a Shepard play is like explaining a taste sensation by quoting the relevant parts of a menu. He dispenses verbal and visual images that tell their own story and unravel in their own private world. They are about as accessible as Fort Knox, and one makes the effort only because of a niggling suspicion they are possibly as rich. . . .

Shepard is not so much obscure as he is disjointed. His is a quirky, fey, mildly Saroyanesque turn of mind which trusts its changes of direction as totally as the traveler trusts the instincts of the burro carrying him through the foothills of a foreign countryside. Which is fine for the burro and the traveler.

Charles Marowitz. *NYTts*. April 13, 1969. p. 3

At this writing, Sam Shepard has published eight plays, finished a major work, *Operation Sidewinder*, which must be one of the best unproduced plays in the country, and scripted a new Antonioni film, *Zabriskie Point*. For quantity alone, Shepard's achievements are unusual for an Off-Off-Broadway writer who is also a twenty-six-year-old rock drummer. But more importantly, the consistency and energy of Shepard's work are beginning to give off the honeyed smells of a solid, if still minor, resurrection of values in contemporary American theatre.

Shepard's essential contribution—and I am dealing only with his eight published plays—has been to reclaim for the imagination certain territories lost in a variety of recent cultural floodings. He has brought the word back into a theatre where, since the canonization of Artaud, the word and all that it implies—literacy, literature, imaginative connection—has been silted up with non-verbal, sensory overloads. Total Theatre, Living Theatre, Participatory Theatre, Body Theatre, Orgy Theatre, Assault Theatre, Ritual Theatre, Myth Theatre, Ridiculous Theatre, Game Theatre, Light Theatre—this is the theatrical extension of the cultural milieu in which Shepard has been working out his ideas.

But I believe his plays, taken as thought in a dramatic mode, have acquired a rather different, a critical and ironic, purchase on the central subject of recent theatre and drama, including Shepard's—the value of performance. I mean here performance as the shared style of a generation, the theatricalization of everyday life.

Ren Frutkin. *Yale/Theatre.*
Summer, 1969. p. 22

When Lincoln Center's Drama Repertory Theater set out to offer a season that would examine American life during four eras, it might safely have attempted nothing but revivals. However, its director, Jules Irving, chose instead to include one new play. Called *Operation Sidewinder*, it was written by twenty-six-year-old Café La Mama playwright Sam Shepard and is both fantastic and relevant to today's world. . . .

The play emerges as a memorable and imaginative scenario. We are charmed from the beginning by the Holy Modal Rounders and the "rockabilly" songs they sing between scenes. We are delighted by the blunt candor of the writing, and the playwright's lack of inhibition in treating charged subjects with an irreverent realism. . . .

All in all, this new production established Sam Shepard as an important and frequently compelling new playwright, and *Operation Sidewinder* as a remarkably contemporary work.

Henry Hewes. *SR.* March 28, 1970. p. 24

Despite my worst instincts I cannot prevent myself from mildly loving the plays of (as he is postulated on the pop-art cartoon cover of his all illustrated, all action, if-get-bored-with-the-play-grab-the-cartoon program) Sam! ack! SHEPARD! He is so sweetly unserious about his play [*The Unseen Hand*], and so desperately serious about what he is saying. . . .

Mr. Shepard takes an apocalyptic view of our civilization, and yet, disconcertingly, instead of moralizing at us, he tells us anecdotal jokes, shaggy dog stories, shaggily and doggedly stretch-stretching out to an infinity they cannot possibly quite reach. . . .

He makes jokes—echoes of old movie comedies, disconcerting jokes of realism to hang onto like rafts in a surrealistic sea. He mocks dramatics—to him nothing would be funnier than a fate worse than death. And he needs discipline the way a hemophiliac needs blood. Yet you cannot be uninterested. Or at least you cannot be uninterested if you are at all interested in the American theater.

Clive Barnes. *NYTd.* April 2, 1970. p. 43

Sam Shepard is a lean and handsome man with a lot of luck. He plays a fast, good, loud set of drums and he writes plays that interest me very much. A part of luck is energy and a part is genius and part is quickness. It's a pleasure to talk to Sam because he's direct and he smiles and he can look you right in the eye. When a man is lucky he sends out a loop of feeling or experience from his meat-intellect—it isn't a passive thing —it is a physical swirl right from the body and it returns with new perceptions, insights, and inspiration. . . .

Shepard's plays have a spine that is the thrust of his perceptions. The vertebrae are not obvious because the energy of the perceptions creates a field or an aura surrounding them. We have fields of musculature around our spines, and then electric charge around the musculature —so have these plays. . . .

The plays are virile and crack like a whip and glitter like light in a snake's eye—they are also feral and viable, with part of themselves mysterious and still clinging to blackness while the actors move and sing in the light.

Michael McClure in Mad Dog Blues, and
Other Plays by Sam Shepard (Winter
House). 1972. pp. 1, 3

Sam Shepard is a voice from the "underground," a poet's voice. His plays are mythic. They speak of the contemporary world and subliminally convey a social "message." They possess no specific ideology, they proclaim no prophecy except the ultimate doom of the present state of civilization. They express a yearning for restoration through the ancient virtues of kindness and human brotherhood, unity of flesh and spirit. Because he employs no philosophic identification tags, what he tells us must of necessity remain somewhat vague or ambiguous.

The Tooth of Crime . . . is a characteristic Shepard play and possibly his best. . . . To understand it all prosaically a glossary would have to be supplied. But even as it stands, with much which goes past earshot and quick comprehension, it rings out triumphantly. A good part of the play's merit is in its speech, with its ever changing modalities echoing different jazz or rock styles, crooners, and shouters.

Harold Clurman. Nation.
March 26, 1973. p. 411

The Tooth of Crime builds from an identity between the languages of rock music, crime, and big business. A "hit" in one world is the same/ different from a "hit" in another; a "big killing" is/isn't murder; a "contract" is a contract is a contract. Shepard is a master of the language of the world he has created. In addition to the languages of rock music, street gangs, the Mafia, and the image-makers, Shepard assembles a language spoken by Crow, the "gypsy killer," the young punk moving in on the turf of the established stars. The meeting between Crow and the old man, Hoss, is a conflict of idioms. At one point Hoss pleads, "Hey, can't you back the language up, man, I'm too old to follow the flash." The song-duel between Hoss and Crow, in fact, has many prototypes—from the once popular "Battle of the Bands" to the ritual combats of certain Eskimo peoples. . . .

Working on the play raises the issues of languages—of the concrete essence of the word, of how words are emptied of meaning and filled with new significances. The more we work the more we find that Shepard's words are bound to music, specifically rock music.

Richard Schechner. *Performance*.
March–April, 1973. pp. 61–2

Partly observed, partly absorbed, the characters of [*The Unseen Hand*] are a weird blending of authentic types and media constructs, as seen in McDonald's hamburger joints, bowling alleys, high-school stadiums, or in sci-fic movies, horror films and westerns. Taken together, they mingle past, present, and future into a pastiche of legend and actuality which describes prole America more effectively than the most fastidious documentary. . . .

As for Shepard, he continues to confront American popular culture with a kind of manic exuberance—not exalting its every wart and pimple, like Andy Warhol, but nevertheless considerably turned on, like many of his generation, even by its more brutalized expressions.

Robert Brustein. *NR*. April 21, 1973. p. 23

SIMPSON, LOUIS (1923–   )

The poems in *Adventures of the Letter I* are less cryptic than [Robert] Creeley's and less challenging. But their unflagging charm derives honestly from the poet's own view of his condition. Mr. Simpson seems embarrassed by his blessings. In a world full of naked pain and cruelty, he is almost ashamed to be sane, competent, free. He is also embarrassed by his fellow-countrymen, saddened by the false finale of the American idyll. Implicit in his irony and humour are many of the judgments passed by [Robert] Duncan. But his understatements linger in one's ear; his elegies for an overripe civilization lure and surprise one with their delicate changes of tone, their witty plaintiveness. Surely Mr. Simpson's road would be a good one for more poets to travel.

TLS. July 23, 1971. p. 855

The title of Louis Simpson's volume [*Adventures of the Letter I*] might well serve as a collective title for a great deal of recent American writing. Increasingly, the place and function of the writer, the questions of who he is and what he is supposed to be doing, have become the central themes of American poetry and fiction.

Yet it would be a mistake to place Simpson alongside Mailer or even Lowell, for despite its unpromising title his collection of poems forms a reticent and almost Horatian body of work. The poet is in retreat, defining his own position by reference to his forebears (both Russian and American), his favourite writers, and the contemporary political crises of America. The poet's ego acts as focus, but is not paraded with ostentation. . . . There does seem a genuine distrust of ideas, and in consequence an often myopic vision which presents the minutiae of life in a way that brings many of the poems close to Imagism, leaving them strangely purposeless and incoherent. It is as if Simpson had consciously decided to be a minor poet, and had set out to fumble a few of the big themes (the War, mental illness, Nazism, the moon landings) to prove it.

But the honesty of the poems, and Simpson's enormous technical skill, carry us through, for the most part. And the book does add up to a fairly clear, even sympathetic picture of how the world looks to one man with no particular commitments except to poetry and common sense. One suspects, in fact, that this restrained, humorous book may be read when the latest crew of Great American Writers have followed one another into obscurity.

Grevel Lindop. *CQ*. Winter, 1972. pp. 379–80

These are mostly rather dreamlike pieces [in *Adventures of the Letter I*], often evocative of an experience never quite experienced, as of the Ukraine, where the Jamaica-born poet's mother came from. Because, perhaps, of the subject matter, or for whatever reason, but not, I hope and believe, just to be fashionable, Simpson has here abandoned the precisely articulated stanzaic poems through which he made his reputation. Rhyme is virtually absent, the style is more free and impressionistic, the ear is sure and good. It is difficult to do justice to this collection by quoting. Not only are the poems elusive; many of the shorter ones, with a general drift toward irony, are so carefully understated that they come out sounding trivial. But several of the longer pieces show that quality so rare in our time, a talent for narrative in poetry.

Richmond Lattimore. *HdR*.
Autumn, 1972. p. 478

• SINGER, ISAAC BASHEVIS (1904–   )

As sheer story-telling this sprawling, heaving, churning, lustful (and excellently translated) narrative [*The Family Moskat*] is very effective. In spite of its great length, panoramic sweep, multiplicity of interwoven plots, and bewildering variety of bizarre characters, locales, and situations, the novel moves at a fairly brisk pace, sustaining the reader's interest from the first page to the last.

Starting with Reb Meshulam, the octogenarian creator of the prodigious Moskat fortune, Mr. Singer branches out into a detailed account of the vicissitudes in the lives of the patriarch's many children, grandchildren, stepchildren, inlaws, servants, relatives, friends, friends of friends, acquaintances of relatives, children of grandchildren, and so on ad infinitum. The period covered is the momentous half century prior to World War II, and the dominant motif is the disintegration during that time of Jewish life and traditional values under the impact of a belated modernity and the pressure of a savagely intensified Polish anti-semitism.

Joshua Kunitz. *NYHT*. Nov. 19, 1950. p. 24

To the familiar machinery of Yiddish literature—the small self-contained isolated East European town with its stock of "characters," its family situations, its rituals, its appearance, even its cooking—add a story-teller's imagination too artistic to settle for the reader's response "yeh, yeh, that's how it really was," add a sensibility too mature to plump for official piety, too tough for sentimentality, too aware always to keep a straight face, too wise and compassionate to throw a stone, too con-scious of mystery and the doubleness of things to strike any factional pose and you have Isaac Bashevis Singer's *Gimpel the Fool, and Other Sto-ries*. Frampol, the little Polish town of some of these tales, is not just a repository of reminiscences but a place, like Joyce's Dublin, Hardy's Wessex, Faulkner's Mississippi, where as Gimpel himself says, "every-thing is possible," a theatre where the humanly significant takes place, where dream is confounded with reality, where the seemingly beneficent

Gentleman from Cracow may turn out to be "none other than Ketev Mrir, Chief of the Devils."

Jack Ludwig. *Midstream.* Spring, 1958. p. 90

When I first read "Gimpel the Fool" (in the quick and pungent English of Saul Bellow) I felt not only that I was reading an extraordinarily beautiful and witty story, but that I was moving through as many historical levels as an archaeologist at work. This is an experience one often gets from the best Jewish writers. The most "advanced" and sophisticated Jewish writers of our time—Babel, Kafka, Bellow—have assimilated, even conquered, the whole tradition of modern literature while reminding us of the unmistakable historic core of the Jewish experience. Equally, a contemporary Yiddish writer like Isaac Bashevis Singer uses all the old Jewish capital of folklore, popular speech and legendry, yet from within this tradition itself is able to duplicate a good deal of the conscious absurdity, the sauciness, the abandon of modern art—without for a moment losing his obvious personal commitment to the immemorial Jewish vision of the world.

Perhaps it is this ability to incarnate all the different periods that Jews have lived through that makes such writers indefinably fascinating to me. They wear whole epochs on their backs; they alone record widely separated centuries in dialogue with each other. Yet all these different periods of history, these many *histories*, represent, if not a single point of view, a common historic character. It is the irony with which ancient dogmas are recorded, the imaginative sympathy with which they are translated and transmuted into contemporary terms, that makes the balance that is art.

Alfred Kazin. *Contemporaries*
(Little). 1962. p. 283

Of the four novels of Isaac Bashevis Singer which have so far been translated from Yiddish, only one, an early work, *The Family Moskat*, has the superficial complexity and structure of the contemporary European novel. Singer's other long works, including his newly published novel, *The Slave*, are more skillful fictions which demonstrate a narrative craftsmanship unique to the contemporary literary scene, but they carefully avoid contemporary subject matter, locating themselves in the earlier literary traditions of the moral fable, the parable, the simple tale told naturalistically but having elements of fantasy and the supernatural.

Singer can begin a story by having a devil speak in the first person, or he can proceed to the allegorical, as in *Satan in Goray*, introducing elements of the natural world along the way as frightening commonplaces. In either case, the burden of disproof rests squarely with the reader since both the supernatural and the natural are always vividly realized in fictional terms. By seeming to remove us from the contemporary, Singer uses his disciplined prose to pose various questions concerning God and men while, at the same time, avoiding two of the most obnoxious elements of much Yiddish literature—a heavy-handed "social consciousness" and a bitter-sweet nostalgia.

Richard M. Elman. Com. July 6, 1962. p. 38

In <i>Satan in Goray</i> and <i>The Magician of Lublin</i> . . . a question which is implicit in the other works becomes more explicitly central: what happens when there is a crisis of faith, when faith is threatened? In these two books, as in his others, Singer establishes as a framework what might be called the standard Jewish faith. Primarily this includes belief in the Jewish God, personal, omnipotent, who imposes after death rewards and punishments according to man's virtues and sins. The way to serve God is through <i>halacha</i>, the code of law which is essentially a code of behavior, controlling man's communal and private actions, his objective relations to society, to family, to God.

This framework serves as a standard which is taken for granted in the Jewish communities Singer's characters live in. The novels neither support nor approve it, but use it rather as a background before which the crises of faith operate, and in terms of which they can be understood. In <i>The Magician of Lublin</i> the opponent of faith is partly the Spinozist view which plays so important a part in <i>The Family Moskat</i> and which holds that there is a Creator but that He is distant and unconcerned with the individual and that after death there is nothing. But faith is more basically opposed in this book by the demands of freedom. In <i>Satan in Goray</i> the standard Jewish faith is directly opposed by another, more absolutist and less human, kind of faith.

J. S. Wolkenfeld. Criticism. Fall, 1963. p. 350

Singer is too ruthlessly single-minded a writer to content himself with mere slices of representation or displays of the bizarre. His grotesquerie must be taken seriously, perhaps as a recoil from his perception of how ugly—how gratuitously ugly—human life can be. He is a writer completely absorbed by the demands of his vision, a vision gnomic and compulsive but with moments of high exaltation; so that while reading his stories one feels as though one were overhearing bits and snatches of a monologue, the impact of which is both notable and disturbing, but the meaning withheld.

Now these are precisely the qualities that the sophisticated reader, trained to docility before the exactions of "modernism," has come to applaud. Singer's stories work, or prey, upon the nerves. They leave one unsettled and anxious, the way a rationalist might feel if, walking at night in the woods, he suddenly found himself afraid of bats. Unlike most Yiddish fiction, Singer's stories neither round out the cycle of their intentions nor posit a coherent and ordered universe. They can be seen as paradigms of the arbitrariness, the grating injustice, at the heart of life. They offer instances of pointless suffering, dead-end exhaustion, inexplicable grace.

Irving Howe in *On Contemporary Literature*,
edited by Richard Kostelanetz
(Avon). 1964. p. 580

Singer never loses sight of the fact that his forte is the imaginative transmutation of reality, and if this is a limitation it is one only in Goethe's sense when he said that it is "only by conscious self-limitation that mastery reveals itself."

It is something of the same sort that Fitzgerald may have had in mind when in *The Great Gatsby* he says, "life is much more successful looked at from a single window after all," and coins the paradox that the "well-rounded man" is the most limited of all specialists. A good writer must find the vein of ore which is uniquely his own and mine it conscientiously. Singer has long ago found his vein.

If Singer does not succumb to the temptations of realism, neither is he lured into the vagaries of doctrinaire or fashionable surrealism. Instead, he has made himself at home in an imaginative construct between earth and heaven. His sensitivity, lack of coarseness, shy and elusive charm may well militate against an overwhelming triumph in this country with a large popular audience. But he has made a secure and comfortable place for himself in literature.

Milton Hindus in *Jewish Heritage
Reader*, edited by Morris Adler
(Taplinger). 1965. p. 252

What is immediately striking about the stories and novels of Isaac Bashevis Singer is the contrast between the formidable barriers to understanding which appear to surround his work and the simplicity and directness of his narrative style. This contrast is of much more than purely literary or formalistic interest: a close look at it can, I think, tell us something not only about the nature of his own achievement, but also about problems which are common to all writers of fiction in a time as culturally confused as our own. His work is instructive, among other reasons, because he has had to face these problems in their most extreme form.

The barriers to understanding referred to above are, in a sense, all the same, all one; but they can be approached or described in different ways. The first is simply the fact that so many of Singer's readers can know his work only in translation—the present writer being one of these.... The modes of Yiddish must be more alien to English than those of French or Russian, for example, in exactly the same degree as the society which produced it was so vastly different from any other Europe has known.

That society has ceased to exist: that is the second great barrier to understanding which comes between us and collections of stories like *Gimpel the Fool* or novels like *The Magician of Lublin*. We cannot think of the society existing in a new guise after having undergone a revolutionary transformation, as one is able still to see some of the lineaments of 19th-century England in the England of today. There is no place we can visit, or imagine ourselves visiting, where we can see Singer's people leading anything like the life they lead in his work, or anything organically connected with it. The mass of Jews have abandoned that way of life; those colonies of devoutly Orthodox Jews who still survive do so in corners of cities totally unlike the small towns and villages of 19th-century Poland in which so much of Singer's fiction is set. Everything Singer writes of Europe is a historical reconstruction, having the effect of something willed into existence, either as memorial or parable; it is never a place or a populace we can know for ourselves.

Dan Jacobson. *Cmty.* Feb., 1965. p. 48

If Sholom Aleichem is the Yiddish Mark Twain, Isaac Bashevis Singer is the Yiddish Hawthorne.... Singer's style, in the tradition of Hawthorne and Melville, is often rhetorical and flamboyant, but there is not an ounce of fat on his prose. His characters sometimes bandy proverbs wittily, in the fashion of West Africans, and similarly he is sometimes folksy and proverbial. Singer's most characteristic style is one of sophisticated ironic juxtaposition....

Singer seems almost the only writer in America who believes in the real existence of Satan.

Stanley Edgar Hyman. *Standards*
(Horizon). 1966. pp. 83–4

For some time now Isaac Bashevis Singer has played a curious role in Yiddish and American letters alike. For a decade after the end of the Second World War he figured as one of the last vital exponents of Yiddish fiction, writing of a world that no longer existed for a public that was rapidly diminishing. Then, with the publication of *Satan in Goray* in an English translation in 1955, a larger public began to take note of his work. The bulk of his writings have since become accessible in English. By now the quarterlies print his work, the weeklies praise him, and the critics are beginning to speak of him as one of the important *American* writers of the age. They find him a master story-teller whose fiction, with its animated evocation of strange, demon-ridden worlds, is not merely exotic, but the vehicle for a comprehensive vision which would seem to express something vital to the spirit of the age. There is hardness in it, and bleakness, and a sense of the problems of finding order in a world of violence and chaos.

Yet even as American critics praise him, his original public is turning its back on him. Yiddish readers used to regard him as a fine stylist who had redeemed a dimension of the ancestral world from oblivion. But now these virtues fall into the background and the Yiddish public is beginning to question both his integrity and the validity of his picture of that world. His rogues are no longer seen as imaginative creations, to be enjoyed as that, but as a reflection on the virtue of our grandmothers or the virility of our grandfathers.

Baruch Hochman. Midstream.
March, 1967. p. 66

[Singer] approaches the world from afar—from the recesses of the past and from beyond the grave. His supernatural world seems insulated from modern apparatuses of analysis; his characters are not buttressed by detailed motivations nor are his devils tamed with psychological plausibility. His entire approach and journey are so circuitous and incredible as to be initially unthreatening. But then the artistic sorcery takes hold and the contraries begin to grip. The distant and exotic rapidly become the near and the familiar; Satan appears to know us as well as a psychiatrist knows his patients; the personality begins to recover its hidden shadow or secret sharer; above all, the invitation of inhibited art is taken up by the reader, and the minimum, incomplete vision is fleshed to fullness through response. By building into the structure of his art the Jewish version of the prodigal son, Singer has encouraged his readers—Jewish and not—to undertake a similar journey of historical and biblical transmigration. In the process, the prodigal, like Singer, discovers that his future is his past. Through his vision of the eternal past, Singer also has become typical of the modern writer to whom the longest way round is the shortest way home. Through his aesthetics of the eternal past, Singer is representative of the Jewish writer to whom the oblique and the sensational are the most powerful avenues to the center and to the true.

Irving Buchen. Isaac Bashevis Singer
and the Eternal Past (New York
Univ. Pr.). 1968. pp. 215–6

Because [Singer] is imbued with Old-World Jewish habits of thought more thoroughly than his American counterparts, while continuing undeniably also to be a New-World Jew, the radical sophistication of his creative imagination lends itself uniquely to the attempt to isolate the sources, and to define the achievement of contemporary Jewish-American fiction.

Singer's is a twentieth-century sensibility attempting an imaginative re-creation of the social and religious milieu of Polish Jewry of the previous three centuries. The unique—and now vanished—circumstances of this society confront Singer's historical consciousness with special irrefrangibility. Tolstoy could revert in *War and Peace* to the time of the Napoleonic invasions without risking intellectual dislocation, for his society still assented essentially to the assumptions of his grandfather. But tension of a profound philosophical order, however, affects the moral pattern of Singer's stories as a result of the radically different *Zeitgeists* of the author and his dramatis personae. One of the central paradoxes of Singer's fictional world is that even as he pays loving tribute to the value system of a back-country Jewry, dirty, ignorant, but firm in a simplistic faith in what Dr. Yaretzky in "The Shadow of a Crib" calls "a seeing universe, rather than a blind one," Singer questions such a world picture with the narrative structures he composes for them. His rabbis and pious matrons may think and act in unquestioning accord with a Jewish cosmic vision but their lives present the absurd pattern familiar to the modern sensibility. It is not without significance that in at least three of Singer's novels the historical setting is that of a catastrophe wrought upon the Jews by external circumstances, and that his protagonists are caught between rival claims of the Jewish and non-Jewish worlds. As in a Greek tragedy impersonal fate and individual responsibility merge ambiguously in his stories.

Max F. Schulz. SHR. Winter, 1968. pp. 60–1

Singer has lived in America long enough to leave one intrigued at the ways he differs from other Jewish-American novelists who have retained their imaginative access to the immigrant experience. Principally, instead of portraying man as a social animal, drowning in essential private relationships and hang-ups, he has kept the old Central European sense of man as the pitifully minor participant in a process governed by irresistible historic, religious, economic and political forces—against which he'll be doing well just to keep his head above water.

It is not that on Singer's stage Man is absurd, commitment futile, the Universe mindlessly malevolent, and God would rather not get involved. But while the shlemiehl-heroes of many first-rate Jewish-American novels leave you with a suspicion that all their problems would vanish if ever they could latch on to a good analyst or a good lay, you know that if a Singer hero ever found himself with nothing worse than a soured marriage or a crazy parent, he would be so far ahead of the game there would be no novel worth writing. The hero of a Singer novel comes ready-equipped not only with several millennia of his own history, and all its voracious emotional and ritual demands, but also with scars left by more than a thousand years of the crimes and follies of Christian Europe.

Shimon Wincelberg. NL. Feb. 26, 1968. p. 26

Isaac Bashevis Singer is a plague and a pleasure to most serious readers and critics of fiction. He is a pleasure because he writes with all the felicity of a 19th-century master—and a plague because no one knows where to place him. He is, on the one hand a Yiddish writer—an exponent of a dying language (though he recently said in an interview: "Listen, young man, between dying and dead is a lot of difference"). On the other hand he is full of such modern nuances as irony, the macabre and symbolism. On the one hand he is a chronicler of a certain very special time and place: Polish Jewry and the *shtetl* life in the middle-to-late 19th century (with the exception of *The Slave* which takes place much earlier, during the scourge of Chmielnicki). And on the other hand he is a writer of universals: love, eroticism, passion, God. What to make of him?

Singer is easy to handle if you take his devils, his dybbuks, his saints, his elves as metaphors; mere material designed to illuminate larger symbolic matters. But, I maintain, no one will truly understand the special nature of Singer's genius until they realize he is separated from us by more than the gulf of tradition dividing the old Polish Jew and the modern secular reader. The truth is Singer believes in God, in dybbuks, in magic, in a life after death.

"Let metaphor be God now Gods are metaphors," W. H. Gass has written. But what if God is *not* a metaphor? In one sense it is Singer's eroticism that has misled us. Only in this parochial age and this Protestant country could eroticism and religion appear to cancel each other out. In Singer—as in Judaism—God is as real as a woman's body. And if God and love-sex go hand in hand, cannot the devil and a wild, distorted eroticism also coexist?

Daniel Stern. Nation. Dec. 9. 1968. p. 632

Isaac B. Singer in *The Magician of Lublin* is a conjurer who turns his magic to the creation of a vision of a forty-year-old man's crisis of conscience. In this novel—very probably his best—the reader who escapes the power of the storytelling for a moment in order to reflect can discern three separate patterns of meaning. There is first the tale of a man who rejects his past life and turns to penitence. Here, in the literal world of the novel, Singer accomplishes both the vivid realization of an individual character's struggles and the representation of recurrent (perhaps mythic and archetypal) human experiences. Then, around the uncomplicated certainties of literal plot or archetypal situation Singer weaves an examination of the uncertainties of ethical behavior, and here he constructs a moral world that is insolubly ambivalent. And finally, using all the concreteness of his detailed and almost tangible fictional world, Singer turns to metaphysical themes. Thus at the last he forces the reader to revise his understanding both of literal fact and moral choice in the novel, for he suggests that "facts" have only the meaning they are assigned by human beings, that man may be a "magician" indeed.

Cyrena N. Pondrom in *The Achievement of
Isaac Bashevis Singer*, edited by Marcia
Allentuck (Southern Illinois). 1969. p. 93

In Singer, destiny and freedom are interrelated, not distinct. We are faced, then, by a contradiction between what is true to life and what we assume to be the truth of art. In art, we are almost immediately suspicious of any resolution leading to human satisfaction or fulfillment, while we expect life to yield to individual will, to be structured on layers of order. Paradoxically, we ask our fictional protagonists not to surrender that quality of moral choice which differentiates man from animals, and yet we lock them into a system where they must suffer without complaint, or else complain without hope of escape.

Singer questions these assumptions. Arguing for traditional values, he poses disturbing questions *because* he runs counter to so much of current—and unavoidable—pessimism. He appears to feel for things with different nerve endings; that he writes in Yiddish is simply the verbal indication of the other world which engages him. Yet the more we learn about human nature, the more that sociologists, psychiatrists, even statisticians, tell us, the clearer it is that most people are closer to Singer's mode than to the one presented by our other major European writers. Put another way, Singer is their consciousness, only to surface sporadically.

Frederick R. Karl in *The Achievement of Isaac
Bashevis Singer*, edited by Marcia Allentuck
(Southern Illinois). 1969. pp. 122–3

To the extent that Singer's fables are almost invariably constructed so as to resonate with both pathological and supernatural overtones he resembles Thomas Mann. Like Mann, Singer expresses a thoroughgoing dualism tending to bring into polarized relationships characters and events which begin by being at first indistinctly balanced between stability and instability, disease and health, good and evil. Like Mann, whom he has translated into Yiddish, Singer sees human types as the expression of incalculably complex but distinct historical traditions. And, like Mann, Singer is the master of the ironic suspension of judgment.

More than once in both Mann and Singer, however, such ironic suspension seems decadent and smacks of diabolism. The fact that good and evil cannot be known except by their consequences encourages an ambiguity that is artistically suggestive but morally questionable.

Michael Fixler in Critical Views of Isaac
Bashevis Singer, edited by Irving Malin
(New York Univ. Pr.). 1969. p. 73

Ironically, Yiddish critics do not rate Singer as high as do the English speaking. American readers find appealing his offbeat themes and rejection of social philosophies—in short, his existential stance; Yiddish readers, however, often view him with an uneasiness akin to suspicion. Several Yiddish critics have attacked his tales of "horror and eroticism," his "distasteful blend of superstition and shoddy mysticism," and his "pandering" to non-Jewish tastes. What merit these criticisms may have is vitiated by the obvious resentment accompanying them—a resentment that develops in some literary corners whenever a writer wins recognition beyond the Yiddish pale. Sholem Asch proved a similar target.

Yet Singer does have a perverse, if not morbid, taste for violence, blood, and animal slaughter, not to mention rape, demons, and the grave—all gothic horror story elements. He relishes those medieval superstitions and fears that clung to *shtetl* life into the twentieth century. His devils, demons, and imps may represent a partial deference to the strong contemporary taste for "black humor" in its myriad forms. But primarily his demonology enables Singer to expose the demons driving us all. His devils and imps symbolize those erratic, wayward, and diabolic impulses that detour men from their fathers' piety and morality. Singer's popularity is the more understandable at a time when such practitioners of the gothic and macabre as William Faulkner, Flannery O'Connor, Tennessee Williams, and Edward Albee have won strong acceptance.

Ben Siegel. Isaac Bashevis Singer
(Minnesota). 1969. p. 10

Of the critical approaches to I. B. Singer's fiction, the most usual, as one would assume, has been evaluation of his relationship to the mainstream of Yiddish literature. However, an examination of his short stories yields a striking thematic concern, unexpectedly placing Singer squarely in the broader stream of twentieth century literature. While he sensitively recreates a time and place in modern history dead and all but forgotten, and while his stories superficially reflect a preoccupation with Jewish folklore, Singer repetitively and compellingly focuses on the individual's struggle to find a viable faith in an age possessed by this very problem. Thus, the stories, despite their setting in the nineteenth century Eastern European Jewish ghetto and their deceptive mask of simple folk tales, portray and explore this predominant problem of modern man with all its accompanying apprehension and tension. Specifically, Singer predicates his fiction on the idea that the presence or absence of human faith in God is an eternal, omnipresent dilemma which the individual must resolve for himself, and he consistently shows that man's fate after death, to be in Heaven or Hell, is directly correlated with his degree of faith in God. Accordingly, Singer's stories run from unshakeable belief in God to inflexible trust in the Devil.

Linda G. Zatlin. *Critique*. 11, 2, 1969. p. 40

If only [Singer] were left writing in Yiddish it would still be an important literary language. He is certainly one of the most remarkable American authors who has ever lived, as he is one of the most intensely Yiddish. Is Yiddish writing sinewy, grotesque, haunted, bitterly comic, deeply compassionate? Singer is close to being the most sinewy, grotesque, haunted, bitterly comic, deeply and desperately compassionate of all. Is most of it at its best deeply rooted in the ecstatic brotherhood and fantastic folk culture of Hassidism? Singer is a very Zaddik; if he just believed in the efficacy of the Kabbalistic word, I am sure he could make Golems. His stories are Golems enough, they have an amazing life of their own for works of man.

Kenneth Rexroth. *With Eye and Ear*
(Herder and Herder). 1970. pp. 192–3

It would be hard to decide how interested or disinterested Singer really is. Sometimes he seems to float above the crowded scene. He has a grave, tragic, and pitying sense, but he also thinks highly of cunning and the bizarre. Yet there is a firm aspect to this: the strong Jewish sense of history which is even, at times, worshipped. A storyteller like Singer is really keeping the archives of the race lively on the tongue. And because of the ghastly destruction of the Jews, their language and culture in Poland, he has felt a passion for rescuing and playing with what he can. It is chilling to know that he is describing ghosts who cannot even haunt because their habitat has been wiped out.

V. S. Pritchett. *NYR*. May 7, 1970. p. 10

If I. B. Singer had written only "Gimpel the Fool" it would have been enough. But his singular power as a cabalistic writer determined to describe the world of Jewish Gothic continues to grow and gather energy. In his middle 60s now, Singer seems to go from strength to strength as though increasing age had become the generative force. This newest book [*A Friend of Kafka*] is by far the best thing we have from him. Singer's short stories are far superior to his novels, as is not entirely surprising in view of the fact that the paradigms for traditional Jewish writing, a "wisdom literature," have always been the proverb, the parable and the folk tale.

Dan Isaac. *Nation*. Nov. 2, 1970. p. 438

Singer is a religious writer. He is interested primarily in the nature of faith, especially when it is tested by holocaust or crisis. How far should one accept the family, the community and the universe? What is the limit of rebellion? Should Jews be "modern" (that is, create new law) or old-fashioned? Such difficult questions appear not only in the comprehensive, open novels but in the closed novels and short stories as well. There is, after all, a unified—shall we call it obsessive?—vision behind *The Family Moskat* and "Cockadoodledoo."

I have suggested that at times Singer is so eager to devote his energy to questions of faith that he turns to stereotyped characters—the rebellious Yash or Ezriel; the devout Calman or Schmul-Leibele—and that we feel they are rather easily understood. They are then lifeless and programmatic. There is no doubt that Singer is more comfortable with tense, ambivalent heroes than with humble ones. I am especially impressed, to name only a few, by Yoineh Meir of "The Slaughterer," the narrator of *In My Father's Court*, and Dr. Kalisher of "The Séance."

Irving Malin. *Isaac Bashevis Singer*
(Ungar). 1972. p. 106

Isaac Bashevis Singer manages to make do with a short list of questions that he relentlessly poses to his wide world of fictional people: Is there a God? Does He rule, or has He abdicated? Is He malign? In the absence of God, what principle moves us? To what end? A few questions, so fundamental that they intimidate most writers, and with good reason: No matter is more likely to disappear in a heat-mist of misbegotten metaphysics than the Big Question—yawn—of what it all means.

Singer, by ruthlessly suppressing rhetorical ornaments, by holding to the principle that a fictional character's given boundaries cannot be violated, brings off grand fables. His two previous novels, *The Manor* and *The Estate*, were family and national epics, panoramas of Jewish life in nineteenth-century Poland. His new novel [*Enemies*] extends Singer's range by limiting his means. It is spare, barren, and strait.

Geoffrey Wolff. SR. July 22, 1972. p. 54

Isaac Bashevis Singer is a master story teller, a Yiddish Poe, impish narrator of things supernatural. His concerns are essentially religious; in large measure Jewish mysticism and folklore structure his vision and determine his style. However, his appeal transcends the parochial, for as his characters incessantly search out their elusive God, Singer evokes a universe akin to those of secular absurdists, a place where man appears alienated from any source of meaning and where the phenomenal world forever disintegrates about him. But while the vision of the absurdist is a recognition of nothingness and a justification for despair, Singer's is a more paradoxical sighting. He celebrates the impenetrable mysteries of creation, but, because those mysteries may conceal, not the splendor of Jehovah, but the face of evil, the celebration forever gives way to an apparition of eternal torment in worlds as yet unknown. Singer's doubt concerning the nature of eternity produces fiction which maintains an uneasy coalescence of dread and consolation. That same doubt prevents his tales from becoming moral allegories or exempla, for rarely is Singer so arrogant as to proffer an answer to the dilemma of human existence. Yet doubt never precludes the possibility that answers do exist, so always, Job-like, he gropes towards illumination.

Grace Farrell Lee. HC. Dec., 1973. pp. 1–2

SNODGRASS, W. D. (1926–   )

After Experience, a remarkable book, is true to . . . the sense of a poetic fate which is at the same time a poetic vocation. . . . The book is full of care for the things by which life is preserved, if it is preserved; as two lovers try to send a kite aloft, "to keep in touch with the thing." And many poems imply a life, long ago, far away, which man and wife lived and shared. Now the objects of that life are gone, but mortally active, too, as reminders, mementos.

The Orphic poet turns grief into song by turning life into ritual, then into play; as a father plays with his lost child. Mr. Snodgrass tells himself, as if to justify the cost, that something like this has been going on, in art and thought, for a century: the destruction of matter for the energy released by the destruction. . . . Mr. Snodgrass's new poems may be received in this setting, attempts to read the fracture of his personal life as an act of destruction, a necessary act if new energy is to be released.

Denis Donoghue. *NYR*. April 25, 1968. p. 18

Snodgrass began his career during the doldrums of the fifties when it seemed that every other poet was sitting in a confessional box or lying on his analyst's couch, composing some wry or decorous plaint about the latest domestic row. And while the talent was more brusque, *Heart's Needle* had all the marks of fashion: clever craftsmanship, witty rhymes, careful irony, the cultivation of private sentiment. What is news about *After Experience* is that without sacrificing what Henry James called the "felicity of scale" Snodgrass gives promise of shaking free of the academic (and those well-made quatrains) and regraduating his lute.

Herbert Leibowitz. *HdR*. Autumn, 1968. p. 563

In general, *Heart's Needle* is a poetry of experience, of present tense and present tension; *After Experience* (1968), as its ambiguous title implies, is at once a poetry of the poet's meditation on past happenings and a poetry of his determination to experience new ways of seeing, acting, and feeling. By the time of its appearance—though some of the poems date back to when Snodgrass was composing *Heart's Needle*—the poet has survived certain experiences and is out, after these, looking for others that will continue to make him feel alive. Snodgrass tells us again and again that one can exist only by living the passionate life, by freeing the soul, though this action itself will inevitably bring grief to those we love the most. . . .

Many of the lyrics in *Heart's Needle* are lasting achievements, but the title sequence of ten poems, one for each season over a period of two and a half years, is one that makes Snodgrass' volume as important as, perhaps, only a half dozen others during this century of American verse. The poet-father's voice here is unique: urgent but controlled, muted but passionate, unassuming but instructive. Snodgrass manages a poetry that moves from his own psychological problems to suggest what it feels like to be a man and to live in the mid-century world.

William Heyen in *Modern American Poetry*, edited by Jerome Mazzaro (McKay). 1970. pp. 352–3, 355

[Snodgrass's] verse is witty, candid, and self-ironic. His world is essentially the secular world apprehended through autobiography and all its peculiar embarrassments. His first book, *Heart's Needle* (1959), is also one of the first to adopt the stance of self-exposure among poets trained in verbal *politesse*. Though Snodgrass favors regular verse forms, his language is direct, homey in the nuances of American speech, and striking in its sudden personal twists. A student of Lowell and also an admirer of Jarrell, Snodgrass exemplifies the post-formalist as well as the Post-Romantic trend toward individual expression, neither academic nor Beat. Speaking of his love, his divorce, or his own daughter, he manages also to make echoes of the Korean War part of his voice. Impish in humor, complex in his sincerity, still somehow cool, he seeks in his first book to know his "name." "Poets of our generation," he admits, "have such extensive resources for disguising ourselves from ourselves." Disguise, confession, and self-division—these are the curse and cure of Snodgrass, the burden he seeks to depose in *After Experience* (1968). Reaching for some form of reconciliation richer than psychoanalysis can ever afford the indigent ego, he expresses a Self reborn in poems of "blunt beauty," controlled in their new-found release. His talent, however, remains special, his essential contribution to poetry still moot.

Ihab Hassan. *Contemporary American Literature* (Ungar). 1973. pp. 128–9

● SNYDER, GARY (1930–   )

In Snyder's first book (*Rip Rap*), he has a poem on the metamorphosis from rural poverty to suburban accretion, closing wryly with the observation that only he, of all the members of his family, had remained poor. But he had not multiplied his wants. . . .

[*Myths and Texts*] remains free of unimportant desires. The substance of the book is an amalgamation of Indians, the Orient, and the vision of an ecological balance witnessed in youth and now destroyed. It's easy and in some quarters smart to smirk at people who take up Buddhism and have a sense of identity with men at work. This can't be done with Snyder: it's all so natural, both the knowledge and the work. He's made a discipline from Buddhism, Amer-Indian myth, and the immediacy of work in an unspoiled natural setting. The work is itself a reward, but it also destroys the very element from which it takes its sustenance. . . . The elegy of involvement: to have witnessed, it was necessary to be one of the destroyers. His sense of involvement keeps him from invective. This world is part of his total fabric, and he cannot falsely externalize it. He cannot point with awe to the objects of his experience, because they have become attached to him through touch and action. It is not even necessary for him to lament this world which, through his poetry, he has preserved. He moves fluently through this world as a local spirit taking the forms of Coyote and Han Shan and a ghostly logger. In these poems, action and contemplation become identical states of being, and both states of secular grace. From this fusion wisdom emerges, and it is not useless but timed to the event. The result is a terrible sanity, a literal clairvoyance, an innate decorum.

Thomas Parkinson. *PrS*. Winter,
1960–61. pp. 383–4

A Range of Poems . . . is a remarkably solid book, strong and sharp, all of a piece. . . . Mr. Snyder is a poet whose style has been, from the first, assured and unassailable in its commitment to the exact image, the lean phrase, the faithful but detached record of things seen. The increasing terseness of diction and tension of rhythm evident in the later sections are simply refinements of a control already impressive in *Rip Rap*. . . .

I read him as profoundly anti-Christian, in the sense that he needs no personal redemption, no consolation for being human; he is quite happy to be a curious and very much alive particle of the world.

Lisel Mueller. *Poetry*. Jan., 1968. pp. 254–5

Snyder's [*The Back Country*] is plain, spare, approaching the condition of pure verbal notation. Photography, not music, is his ideal medium, or perhaps he is seeking the English equivalent of the Chinese ideogram. . . . It is no wonder that a poet so strongly visual should turn to Japan and China for his inspiration. . . . This is a strange volume, filled with mountains, woods, pine needles, smoke, and snow. Mr. Snyder's best poems are hieroglyphic in the true sense, summoning glimpses of dark gods, of Artemis, of Hell. His weakest poems are merely echoes of the outworn imagist tradition of Williams and Pound. . . . Along with Allen Ginsberg and Jack Kerouac, [Snyder] was one of the original San Francisco "beat" poets. He figures as the hero of Kerouac's *The Dharma Bums*.

Victor Howes. *CSM*. May 29, 1968. p. 11

Snyder is content to describe the great outdoors and sentimental moments; his poems are snapshots taken on the road, bits of quaint information. . . . There is a fallacy in his idea of poetry—I think going back to W. C. Williams—that the poet is a holy man who has only to point to an object; the initiate will perceive its significance. What actually results, however, is a lack of tension, an absence of drama. This may be the peace of the Orient, but I doubt it. I think it just monotony.

Louis Simpson. *Harper*. August, 1968. p. 76

The best book of American poetry so far this year is Gary Snyder's *The Back Country*. Some older German poets used to hope they could use common words like "rock" and "kettle" so crisply, freshly, that they would become the things, and one would see the objects as if for the first time. Snyder can do it. His is no mere Descriptive Poetry, but an acute visual *and* tactile sense reacting on an extraordinary verbal gift. The nouns sparkle, the verbs shimmer, and they clack together like pebbles; the Far West mountain poems are as good as a hike. He is the first writer since Gertrude Stein to make *lists* which are poetry. And to show you how good his verbs are, he can make actions as exciting as things— no one living writes better poems about work.

Gerald Burns. SWR. Autumn, 1968. p. 446

Gary Snyder has a much wider range [than Robert Creeley] because he is more fruitfully open to the world outside, but he also falls easily into mannerisms and he is bad at structuring his verse. The shorter poems are the more successful ones.

Most of his verse has the ripe tang of impromptu living about it and if it seems to be *about* something in a way that Creeley's doesn't, it is partly that he has neither lived in order to write nor written in order to live but lived first and written second. He has been a merchant seaman, a wood-cutter, and a student in a Buddhist monastery. He doesn't believe in isolation for the artist. . . . He has also said that the rhythms of his poems follow the rhythms of the physical work he is doing and the life he is leading at the time. This is true, and the poems take their subjects very directly from immediate experience. . . .

Snyder has obviously been influenced by the style and rhythms of Japanese verse, particularly those of the haiku, and it is interesting to see, in the seven or so years that *The Back Country* covers, how he succeeds better and better at assimilating the influence. Some of the earlier poems handle English almost as if it were a foreign language, getting a long way from natural speech rhythms and hammering phrases into a concentrated powder, as if to make a soup cube. But in "Looking at Pictures to be Put Away," the Japanese influence is barely discernible, though clearly he would never have arrived at this kind of distillation but for the earlier experiments. . . . He tends to write in terms of unrelated instants of experience, in present participles and past participles, letting the noun-pictures proliferate and cutting down on verbs which might commit him to deeper participation, or even to a clear statement of attitude. But many of the later poems show his capacities for directness, comedy, abuse and dramatisation. And these surprise us because we've seen so little of them. He has a galloping talent but he hasn't always given it enough rein.

Ronald Hayman. Encounter.
Feb., 1969. pp. 78–9

[*The Back Country*] puts the earlier works into a unified perspective, and in a sense sums up Snyder's experience as a man living in and reacting to the Western ethos. It constitutes a pilgrimage away from an industrial-suburban civilization, reaching steadily deeper, psychically, toward a human universe involving once again an astonishing physical reality. The pilgrimage is from the West to the Orient, from the city to the American wilderness. Both facets of this pilgrimage complement the other. From the East the poet draws the contemplative, historic-minded inwardness and the sparse, imagistic poetic diction, closely resembling the method of the popular haiku form. He draws from the American wilderness his sense of the salvation possible within our cultural framework, stressing the old myths and realities of our physical heritage, our physical environment.

Edward Zahniser. *LW*. Spring, 1969. p. 35

One senses how domineering the regime of experts has become when one recognizes the lengths to which contemporary radicalism must go in seeking to outflank its values and metaphysical assumptions. An eloquent example of such an effort is Gary Snyder's *Earth House Hold* which seeks to recall the ecological intelligence to be found in poetic and primitive life styles. For Snyder, who learned his social theory from Zen masters and redwood trees, our salvation depends upon recapturing the spirit of "the ancient shamanistic-yogic-socioeconomic view." . . .

The audience for Snyder's rhapsodic appeal is small, largely the young and the dropped out who cling on and make do, chanting mantras at the social margins. . . . Unhappily, visionaries like Snyder are regarded as the heretics in residence of our pluralistic technocracy and their words make light weight in the scales of power.

Theodore Roszak. *Nation*. Sept. 1, 1969. p. 182

Snyder is the principal controversialist of the counter culture because he simply refuses controversy altogether. He acts on the assumption that the old world is totally, irrevocably, stone dead. He confronts it simply by being there. Why does he stay around? The bodhisattva's vow is, "I will not enter Nirvana until I can take all sentient creatures with me." But the bodhisattva doesn't consciously make a vow. He is a bodhisattva out of transcendental indifference. As far as he is concerned he is just plain old Smoky the Bear.

The dead society was urban, its culture the pleasure of a clerkly caste. Allen Ginsberg cries, "Woe, woe to the bloody city of Jerusalem!" Snyder, like Benedict of Nursia, or the yamabushi of Japan, goes to the wilderness. His values are those of the wilderness, of the lynx on the branch, the deer in the meadow. The confrontation is total. There are no bears amongst the roses, only a critic who supposes things false and wrong. . . .

I do not believe that there is a single individual who has more influence on the youth who leave the dead society for the counter culture than Gary Snyder. He makes explicit what the musicians play and sing.

Kenneth Rexroth. With Eye and Ear (Herder and Herder). 1970. pp. 214, 217

As a cultural figure, [Snyder's] durability is evidenced by his fame having outlasted all three of the major movements in the American West since World War II—the Beat Generation, the Zen interest of the 50's, and the Hippies of the 60's. The strong points of these currents—creative alienation from robotlife, purified mind, and gentle community, respectively—had been present in Snyder's work from the start, and his steady focus on wilderness clarity helped him avoid the well-publicized pitfalls along the way. Thus he has always seemed ahead of the times, which is essential for a popular American bard-seer. Another, more fundamental requirement for such a figure is that his work, thought, and life be of a piece; as I hope I have shown, it is almost inevitable that this be true of the ecological vision. In our accelerating re-examination of civilization in the light of enduring perceptions and longings, it is not too much to suggest that Gary Snyder's insights can be extremely valuable.

Thomas J. Lyon. KanQ. Spring, 1970. pp. 123–4

Like Lawrence and Williams before him, to cite only two of the pioneer modern writers with whom he stands, Snyder would redress our culture by restoring the vital and the feminine, by voyaging historically and psychically to Pagany, and by charting for us new contours of feeling.

We should not expect him by himself to work this great change. This is the mistake of those who confuse poetry with politics, critics like Peter Levi, who says that we need Snyder's poetry but adds that "his medicine is not going to cure anything. . . ." His work is political because it bears witness; on this account one respects the ways it combines autobiography and utopia. We should accept his optimism—can an ecological conscience be created in time to save a devastated universe? —as a condition of the work, as an act of faith founded on profound basic trust. It is not the register of social naïveté. The distance from lookout to ashram is long and difficult; it is not easy for us to enter the back country nor find the archaic springs. We cannot expect literature to cure us, only to hearten us by showing us new and true possibilities and how much may be achieved in life and art by conscious endeavor. Snyder's work, already a substantial achievement, does this. And it may be especially heartening to us because in it an American poet has finally turned to the Orient and shown how much of America might yet be discovered in a passage to India.

Sherman Paul. *IowaR*. Fall, 1970. pp. 84–5

If Allen Ginsberg was the Beat Generation's Walt Whitman, then Gary Snyder was its Henry David Thoreau. Or to put it even more emphatically, Snyder is the present generation's Thoreau, for far from diminishing, his popular influence has increased over the past ten years. . . .

Gary Snyder has become a sort of prophet of the essential in human life, and in his own way a great liberator, too. His concern with ecology and the physical environment of America . . . is not just fashionably recent. It is and has been as fundamental to his own thought as it was to Thoreau's a hundred years before. And he, unlike Thoreau, was born to the pioneer life. . . .

He was on hand to greet Allen Ginsberg when Ginsberg arrived in India and to show him around the country. And that, symbolically, was what Gary Snyder did for many of the Beats and for many times more of the generation that followed them: he introduced them to the East. . . .

Anyone who supposes Gary Snyder's Oriental proclivity separated him from the American literary mainstream in general, or from Henry David Thoreau in particular, simply has no appreciation of the widespread early influence of eastern philosophy and religion on our literature. . . .

A man of remarkable intellect and flexibility, [Snyder] seems less interested in hammering out a synthesis drawn from the best of East and West, than he does simply in containing both within himself.

Bruce Cook. *The Beat Generation*
(Scribner). 1971. pp. 28–30

His theme is not, really, "wild nature"; man and nature are one . . . and to speak of one without the other is meaningless. He asks, What should you know to be a poet? and answers "all you can about animals as persons."

The breadth of world-view corresponds to a breadth of terms of reference, sometimes similar to lists but always interesting, highly articulated, and immediately felt, falling naturally into structure. . . .

The relatedness of all things is a cliché in Western civilization, where it is known as the Chain of Being, but it is reinvigorated with an Eastern admixture in Snyder's poetry. And Gary Snyder gives the curious impression of being always outdoors—or creates the illusion that, even when he is indoors, he never stops being also outdoors. . . .

The poems refer directly outward, to the world; in this sense traditional "craftsmanship" and hypotaxis are lacking, intentionally so, in favor of another craftsmanship which is rarely taught. It is the fidelity to a sense of the world which makes this poetry so valuable. It is profoundly unsolipsistic. The separations which we often allow to creep into our lives (inner world/outer world; rational/irrational; subjective/objective; ego/id) are absent. Gary Snyder's poems are marvellously undefensive, generous, and contain much joy.

John R. Carpenter. *Poetry*.
June, 1972. pp. 168–9

Like the early Romantics, [Snyder] believes that the subjects and language of poetry should be rooted in the common life, which he has known intimately. . . .

Like Thomas Merton, Snyder recognizes the late nineteenth-century ghost dances of the American Indians as an effort to recapture a lost communal culture. He is, however, more optimistic and revolutionary than Merton in his hope that modern society may be able to reach back to its primitive roots through changes in social organization directed toward the ideal of a tribal or communal family of man. . . .

In his veneration of nature, his Eastern mysticism, and his revolutionary hopes, Gary Snyder is very much in the current of the times. Whether or not his revolutionary goals are capable of realization (a point on which Snyder is more optimistic than most poets of his generation), his work is a valuable leaven to the process of continuing change in poetic and social forms.

Walter Sutton. *American Free Verse*
(New Directions). 1973. pp. 188–90

● STAFFORD, WILLIAM (1914–   )

There are poets who pour out rivers of ink, all on good poems. William Stafford is one of these. He has been called America's most prolific poet, and I have no doubt that he is. He turns out so much verse not because he is glib and empty, but because he is a real poet, a born poet, and communicating in lines and images is not only the best way for him to get things said; it is the easiest. His natural mode of speech is a gentle, mystical, half-mocking and highly personal daydreaming about the landscape of the western United States. Everything in this world is available to Mr. Stafford's way of writing, and I for one am very glad it is. The things he chooses to write about—I almost said "talk"—seem in the beginning more or less arbitrary, but in the end never so. They are caught up so genuinely and intimately in his characteristic way of look-ing, feeling, and expressing that they emerge as fresh, glowing creations; they *all* do, and that is the surprising and lovely fact about them. [1961]

James Dickey. Babel to Byzantium
(Grosset). 1971. pp. 139–40

Stafford's subject-matter is usually important in itself. (The theory that subject-matter is nothing, the treatment everything, was invented to comfort little minds.) Also, he deals with his subject directly; that is to say, he has a personal voice. Contrary to what many poets believe nowadays, it is not necessary to spill your guts on the table in order to be "personal," nor to relate the details of your aunt's insanity. What is necessary is originality of imagination and at least a few ideas of your own. Another point in favor of Stafford is that he actually writes about the country he is living in; all sorts of ordinary places, people and animals appear in his poems, and not as subjects of satire, but with the full weight of their own existence. As we read Stafford we are aware of how much has been omitted from modern American poetry only be-cause it is not literary, or because it springs from the life of ordinary, rather than "alienated" people. An observer from another country would be struck by the absence from American poetry of the American landscape; he would find, also, that the language of our poetry is not the language of our real thoughts; and he might wonder at the psychic disorder this indicates. As for history—it seems we are trying to forget it. But Stafford is one of the few poets who are able to use the landscape and to feel the mystery and imagination in American life. . . . He is a poet of the people, in the deepest and most meaningful sense. And a poet of Nature—in a time when poets claim our attention because they are unnatural, pitiable, demoralized. His poems are strong and true; rightly understood, they will enrich our lives.

Louis Simpson. HdR. Autumn, 1961. p. 462

Luckily for Mr. Stafford and for us, *West of Your City* is an exception-ally fine first volume. Readers of his widely published work are not surprised. Many agree with Louis Simpson that there is really not so great a distance between the work of William Stafford and the products of the new "establishment" as fashionable critical response and major literary awards would suggest.

Perhaps because Mr. Stafford writes a great deal without pushing or pulling too hard he almost always writes well. His idiom is decep-tively casual. . . . Even at his best, Mr. Stafford gives me the impression that he is practicing all the time—that he simply needs to throw fewer efforts away each year because he is one of the few people alive who see life from the point of view of a poet.

Whatever their limitations, poets don't happen every year. I have read few first volumes of the order of *West of Your City* since the appearance in 1955 of John Woods' *The Deaths at Paragon, Indiana*. Our nationally acknowledged "younger poets," academic and beat, exhibit a virtuosity of controlled expression or no control at all. Essentially either of these fashionable modes is primarily concerned with the expression of thematic abstractions. For Mr. Stafford, social, religious, and philosophical meanings hover around the poem. They are the radiations only. The westerly direction is not for him an outdated answer to the contemporary predicament. It offers no honey in the horn. But it is the spiritual focus which gives this volume unity and which makes William Stafford a poet of integrity. His intention is consistently to find the formal voice of his immediate experience.

Robert Huff. *PrS*. Spring, 1962. pp. 82–3

[Stafford] is a poet of Existential loneliness and Western space. He seems to write out of an autobiographical impulse, a need to describe and understand his personal experience of the mountains and forests of the Far West. He was born in Kansas, was educated in Iowa, and teaches in Oregon. His memories range widely over these territories and fill his books with images of tornadoes, prairie towns, deserts, mountain-climbing, etc. The technique is not dazzling—there are no verbal fireworks—but Stafford describes the objects of his world carefully and exactly: he has the power to see, the patience to wait for his insights and the ability to construct strong structures of sound and meaning. He is a sort of Western Robert Frost, forever amazed by the spaces of America, inner and outer.

Stephen Stepanchev. *American Poetry since 1945* (Harper). 1965. p. 201

Many of Stafford's best poems are full of nostalgia, some of praise, but they are not of public praise or high rhetoric. They turn the mirror back upon the speaker. Often they are dramas where the point is to recapture something or to face its disappearance, its loss, and yet to gain by having been there. Self-consciously the poems make an odyssey. The speaker is moving back over time to some lost place.

Hazard Adams. *Poetry*. April, 1967. pp. 42–3

William Stafford's grip is always loose, his touch light—almost feathery. Often, a very good poem slips through his fingers, slides away from him, in the closing lines; and this is the risk he takes by his unwillingness to tighten his hold to protect his interests. If the reader feels let down, disappointed, he also senses the poet is content to have lost the poem to save the quiet tenderness of the human voice weaving through it. If we read on, we learn that a few poems end with a magic and bewitching mysticism that is a perfect arrival, a blossoming and fulfillment of the poet's voice, one of the strangest in our literature.

Laurence Lieberman. *YR*. Winter, 1968. p. 262

One of the most restrained poets writing now, William Stafford deals with landscapes—Montana, Kansas, Oregon—and installs therein quiet murmurations of conscience that dominate even his most vivid characters. . . . Bony, unostentatious, and even-tempered . . . [his] poems haunt like overheard confessions; yet it is in silences that they seem to form themselves. . . . [Stafford's] unforced worldliness is full of reverie; he is very much at home in this world, as in his poems, and I for one find them easy to feel at home in. What a hospitable celebrant he is.

Paul West. *Book World*. May 31, 1970. p. 6

[Stafford's] poems are frequently sharp, cold, clear, epiphanies of a past recaptured, rescued, as it were, from time. In the amber of poem after poem, he preserves the memory of a western past that is part of American history. . . . If you have been wondering where the articulate, readable poems have gone in the last third of the twentieth century, you might start with Stafford.

Victor Howes. *CSM*. Sept. 28, 1970. p. 9

STEIN, GERTRUDE (1874–1946)

Regarding the famous aria [in *Four Saints in Three Acts*] "Pigeons on the grass alas," in [Richard] Bridgman's view "anti-supernatural," he is quite wrong, for this is one of the few moments in the opera that Gertrude really explained to me. It is St. Ignatius's vision of the Holy Ghost and it represents a true vision. It begins with "ordinary pigeons" which are "on the grass alas," not doves against the sky as they maybe could be wished to be. But it goes on to a "magpie in the sky on the sky," exactly as one sees these birds in Spain, hanging there trembling, exactly as in many a primitive Spanish painting too, where the magpie, flat and seeming almost to vibrate, does represent the Holy Ghost. And the succeeding declaration, "Let Lucy Lily Lily Lucy Lucy," may indeed, as Bridgman suggests, be "an authorial statement stimulated by the religious context"; but when I treated it as a proof of true vision, as a heavenly chorus heard chanting in some heavenly lingo, Gertrude was ever so pleased.

Virgil Thomson. *NYR*. April 8, 1971. p. 6

[Stein's] is a vision, paradoxically, of the "literally true." The phrase is used as the title for one of her works, and it might be the title of all of them. It compares with the vision of certain mystics who lived with the compelling sense of total illumination, with all the parts of everything seen plainly, in unbroken and simple and easily perceived harmonies, the highest and the lowest together. Stein's vision had that clarity, that intensity, and that ease. She saw the reality of relations—at first, relations of people, then of objects in space, and then of events in time—with as much force and clarity as though they were tangible. The substance of what she saw—or to put it more accurately, the summary of it—was more or less profound or trivial or remarkable as different occasions for observation can be for anyone. But the tangibility of relations, for her, did not blur. There was nothing for her to say *about* them but that they were there; they were so, literally and tangibly true.

Leon Katz. Introduction to *Fernhurst, Q.E.D.,*
and Other Early Writings by Gertrude Stein
(Liveright). 1971. pp. xxxii–xxxiii

What, finally, is our view of Gertrude Stein? A dominating figure, a *femme intrigante*, and a problematic writer. The importance of her language experiments to poets and writers is indisputable. . . .

This pioneering destruction of associative emotion bears its finest fruit in the enigmatic plays and droll librettos, which have the charm of a friendly sphinx. . . . But in the novels, and most notably in *The Making of Americans*, which she stubbornly insisted was her masterpiece, her zeal for classification and repetition asks language to bear too heavy a burden. Unlike Joyce and Proust, the only novelists she'd admit as her equal, her solipsism does not take us into "the secret grottoes of the self" ([William Carlos] Williams's phrase). Compared to Joyce's Dublin and Proust's Paris, her universe is a defoliated landscape.

Herbert Leibowitz. *NYT*. Feb. 3, 1974. p. 2

[Stein] had an extravagant affection not only for words and grammar but for the world at large and almost anything that turned up in it. It was part of her strong personal attraction, that complete attention and welcome to anything in front of her. Combined with her courage and liking for a fight and a determination not to be bored, it made her life a full one, with endless adventures, large and small, and not a few mistakes. But as she said, foolish mistakes are not a bore. Perhaps that life, which she led so actively, is after all her greatest and most interesting creation, though she did not like to think so.

When her work turns out beautiful, the beauty can no doubt have a "solemnity" as she calls it, but as often as not it has an elation, even a gaiety, which comes from the same passion for the world that went into her life.

Donald Sutherland. NYR. May 30, 1974. p. 29

STEVENS, WALLACE (1879–1955)

I am not suggesting that Stevens' poems exist as poems because he dabbled, tongue in cheek, with philosophical ideas. He does often toy, but that is a manner of expression, a method, and not the heart of expression itself. And he does start with philosophical ideas, but that is his donnée, the discursive matter he uses as the vehicle for the expression of his lyric impulses. For Stevens was not the kind of poet who could directly pour out his emotions; he needed doctrinal counters to which he could anchor the fundamental anguish and hopes of the self that could not be satisfied by its own theory of poetry. . . .

The philosophical perspective is often the poem's perspective; irony is the poet's dominant tonality. But the two together do not add up to the poem, to the "gaiety of language" which is a linguistic rendering of the turmoil within the poetic mind that contemplates its own uncertain place in a century in which it has said "no" to the aesthetics and philosophy of romanticism. . . .

When Stevens was writing well, when he was able to get into his poems all the poetry of his subject as well as the bare doctrinal bones of that subject, his work issues not in statement but in uneasiness of tone and the ambiguity of attitude of a man who had deeply irresolvable feelings about himself, the imagination, and the world he had to live in. And, I might add, his poems truly become poems as they are vitalized by his skepticism and irony.

Frank Lentricchia. The Gaiety of Language
(California). 1968. pp. 149–50

Though Wallace Stevens' idiosyncratic vocabulary and imagery have been blamed and praised ever since his first poems appeared in print, his equally odd syntax has been less noticed. It shares nevertheless in his act of the mind, and differentiates him noticeably from other poets, whether the Romantic poets whose dependent heir he is, or his contemporaries in

England and America. Abstractly considered, Stevens' "themes" are familiar, not to say banal, ones, but his poetry reproduces them in a new form, chiefly in an elaborately mannered movement of thought, which changes very little in the course of the *Collected Poems*. It is, needless to say, expressive of several moods, but three large manners can be distinguished, all of them present in Stevens' long poems. The first, in an ecstatic idiom, proclaims, sometimes defiantly, the pure good of being, the worth of vigorous life, the earthy marriages, the secular joys of ploughing on Sunday. The second, despairingly and in tones of apathy, anatomizes a stale and withered life. The third and most characteristic form is a tentative, diffident, and reluctant search for a middle route between ecstasy and apathy, a sensible ecstasy of pauvred color, to use Stevens' own phrase.

> Helen Vendler. *On Extended Wings:*
> *Wallace Stevens' Longer Poems*
> (Harvard). 1969. p. 13

Stevens's later poems both affirm and realize the belief that to the extent that we as men participate in genuine poetry of exploration and discovery, to the extent that we overcome the limits of time and space and sensations and organisms, we rise to a oneness with the supreme fiction of creativity and knowledge. Then, and only then, may we say, "God and the imagination are one. . . ." Then and only then can we sense the joy of the line "How high that highest candle lights the dark." One surmounts his life as a finite ego, as an object in space and time, only at rare, unpredictable moments. But then at least his life is truly poetic and he is at one with the poetic act of making. Poetry based upon such an awareness cannot be described as egocentric.

> Merle E. Brown. *Wallace Stevens: The Poem*
> *as Act* (Wayne State). 1970. p. 34

The affinities between Stevens and the symbolists are so large and pervasive that it is altogether understandable why some have considered him a symbolist poet. Clearly, the convergences of Stevens and the symbolists in their poetic theories are very great. Stevens declares in his "Adagia," "The poet is the priest of the invisible." Baudelaire would not have put it differently. On the other hand, just as there are important differences in poetic art between all of the principal French symbolist poets, so are there striking differences between them and Stevens. The isolated juxtaposition of the poetics and poetry of Baudelaire, Mallarmé, of Valéry with that of Stevens is not nearly as revealing as the examination of Stevens' mind and art against the background of the whole symbolist tradition. His embodiment of that tradition heightens rather than diminishes his originality. In our consideration of Stevens against the background of French symbolism, we must not lose sight of the fact that he was an intensely American poet.

Haskell M. Block in *The Shaken Realist*, edited
by Melvin J. Friedman and John B. Vickery
(Louisiana State). 1970. pp. 212-3

I think the most immediate phrase is that which [Stevens] quotes from his poem called "Asides on the Oboe"—"Thou art not August, unless I make thee so." For at the root of this, as we see at once, is the typically Stevensian notion that nature—the seasons, summer, August—is not real without human intervention, without the poetic power of giving to nature names and significant associations. But having said that, one must go on and make it absolutely clear that Stevens never ceased to be aware of nature's other reality—the brute, alien reality which is essentially inimical or at least indifferent to man. I know of no other poet who in his work was so constantly alive to what I would characterize as poetry's supreme task—to delineate the life of man in relation to nature unconsoled by any supernatural idea. So that if "poetry" can be said to be the subject matter of all Stevens's poems, that subject matter is in fact all that makes a mysterious nature meaningful—or unmeaningful—to humankind.

Roy Fuller. *Owls and Artificers*
(Deutsch). 1971. p. 72

[Stevens'] language of the abstract was not discovered late in life but was an essential counterpart to the more celebrated sights and sounds of *Harmonium*. Stevens was always both an ascetic and a hedonist.

The modern distrust of abstract ideas in poetry has caused a number of critics (Randall Jarrell, for example) to feel that Stevens' poems become less effective as his intellect becomes dominant, but I tend to agree with I. A. Richards that "too much importance has always been attached to the sensory qualities of images." Many of Stevens' abstractions, such as "nothingness," are charged with emotion and truly grounded in the particulars of the world, and a late poem like "The Course of a Particular" is filled with images, and articulates an emotional problem that possibly could not be dealt with using images of an acutely sensory nature. Rather than moving away from emotions, the poems may enlarge the range and quality of emotions, as well as our means of expressing them.

Edward Kessler. *Images of Wallace
Stevens* (Rutgers). 1972. p. 7

This tendency of American Romanticism to identify self-fulfillment with artistic creation and to make the heroic journey the drama of the creative self reaches a culmination in the work of Wallace Stevens. Although Stevens engaged in a good deal of thought about the nature of the hero and heroism, in the poems themselves heroic figures are notably sparse. In the longer poems only Crispin stands forth as a sustained protagonist, and "The Comedian as the Letter C" is more a mockery of Crispin's heroic pretentions than a statement of the possibilities of true heroism. But, like Walt Whitman, Stevens is a poet who is best read at large, and behind the whole canon of his work stands the man himself, a genuinely heroic figure, whose quest is manifest in the very work that reflects and records its results.

> Todd M. Lieber. *Endless Experiments*
> (Ohio State). 1973. p. 243

The style of the middle and later periods is a subtle modification of the early manner. The change becomes apparent when a poem or a passage from *Harmonium* is compared to a passage of similar import from one of the later books. Although the later poems retain much of "the gaiety of language" and "the quirks of imagery" of the poems of his first book, the change of style for a reader fresh from *Harmonium* is apparent in both rhetoric and feeling. The later style has an air of explicit theorizing, even though theory is tentative and undeveloped. Undoubtedly the element of thought is brought more to the fore, and the tone is somewhat deepened, perhaps because it is the tone of a man intent on his illusions, aware that no matter where he looks he is looking inward, and yet considering how far outward the mind seems to reach, "outsensing distances."

> Frank Doggett. *PMLA*. Jan., 1973. p. 124

STICKNEY, TRUMBULL (1874–1904)

Joseph Trumbull Stickney came from an expatriate New England family. Born in Geneva, he grew up, like someone in a Henry James story, in London, Italy and Switzerland. He studied classics (and perhaps became romantically involved with an older woman) at Harvard (graduating six years before Wallace Stevens) and returned to France to study at the Sorbonne, where in 1903 he took the first D. ès L., in Greek, ever awarded an American. The final year of his life was spent teaching Greek at Harvard and in suffering the physical pain of a brain tumor, from which he died the following spring. His Harvard was that of Santayana; his émigré Europe that of his friends Henry Adams and Bernard Berenson. His poems, all sonnets and strophic lyrics full of a romantic Hellenism and a formal sense sometimes stronger than their rhetoric, needed half-apologizing-for under the strictures of modernism. With the current rediscovery of American romantic-verse tradition, his work appears more central than ever. . . . The interest is not in style, but in the grasp of the visionary moment.

John Hollander. NYT. July 16, 1972. p. 5

[Stickney] intended to be no meek sacrifice on the altars of Art and Learning, but managed to deal straightforwardly and memorably with his dilemma in about a dozen poems that show him to be at least as "black" a poet as Robinson and Frost. . . .

Stickney's powers of expression are so fine, so robust and versatile, that one feels immediate pleasure in his technique. Such long landscape poems as "Lakeward," "In Ampezzo," and "At Sainte-Marguerite" are charming virtuoso performances. His dramatic pieces on the Emperor Julian and Cellini are far from negligible. Much of [*The Poems of Trumbull Stickney*] is as disembodiedly vigorous, or energetically angelic, as one could well imagine—wonderful in its way. It seems an American talent of any age, this use of the most elegantly particularized language to create an agreeable roseate haze of ineffable unmeaning— the tenuous and diffident made as tangible as roast beef. Whitman could achieve the same effect by rhapsodizing ten pages of an almanac. Stickney's excuse for this kind of thing is the presence of large quantities of original or reworked juvenilia. Only during his last few years did he write the poems that easily dominate the rest.

R. W. Flint. Parnassus. Fall–
Winter, 1973. pp. 37–8

STYRON, WILLIAM (1925–　　　)

Like the famed *deus ex machina* of Greek mythology, Nat Turner was thrust upon the national consciousness to remind white Americans that, historically, all black revolutionaries have had Achilles heels. What they desire in actuality is not the master's life, but his daughter, and they are so confused about their relationship vis-à-vis white society that any determined assault upon white America, if it comes at all, is many years distant. Therefore these modern-day Nat Turners pose no real threat, for not only are they half-men, but they are sexually disturbed as well, seeking to wage war not in the streets or behind the barricades, but in the bedrooms of white women.

Nat Turner in the hands of Richard Wright, LeRoi Jones or John Williams would have been altogether different. And those who condemn Styron for his portrait, who demand that he portray Nat Turner with any semblance of reality, demand the impossible. To demand a realistic portrayal of blacks by whites is to demand the impossible, for whites are neither mentally nor culturally equipped for the task.

Addison Gayle, Jr., in *Amistad 1*, edited by
John A. Williams and Charles F. Harris
(Random). 1970. pp. 21–2

Perhaps a reader acquainted with Styron's other work could expect, on picking up *The Confessions of Nat Turner*, an enthusiastic celebration of a social revolutionary. If that which I have said so far is true, Styron's narrators seem increasingly fascinated by the need for revolution, the throwing off of oppression. But it turns out that this novel, which would potentially be the most affirmative toward revolutionary acts, casts the social significance of the historical event in an internal and psychological mold. To the degree that Nat is more concerned with the private reasons for his actions and with his doubts and frustrations arising from them than in the basis for the act in the situation within which he and other blacks live, the work withdraws from the affirmative attitude toward revolution which Styron's narrators seem increasingly to have expressed. . . . I would suggest that Styron is moving, with this work, toward a more mythic vision of revolution. What is noteworthy is not the interest in the psychological aspect but in the rather stylized juxtaposition of mythic elements: male and female, sky and earth, land and water.

Wesley A. Kort. *Shriven Selves*
(Fortress). 1972. pp. 133–4

A Virginian by birth, William Styron begins his literary career writing in the Southern manner; soon thereafter, he shows an independent sensibility. His work, brilliant in parts, shifting from rhetoric to sudden poetry, dramatically rich, seeks between violence and ambiguity some definition of personal integrity. The search often fails because Styron seems to lack a felt attitude toward life, a distinctive power of evaluation.

The influence of Faulkner and Fitzgerald appears in Styron's first novel, *Lie Down in Darkness* (1951). Yet the book also harks back to the baroque tradition of John Donne and Sir Thomas Browne; invokes Freud; and still remains Styron's most vivid, most personal, expression.

The novel presents a Southern family locked in a domestic tragedy; love wears the face of guilt or incest, and the search for childhood innocence leads only to self-destruction. Through Peyton, doomed, lovely daughter of the Loftis family, the author makes his symbolic statement on the decay of the South—manners with few morals, dissolving community, fake religiosity—and on the larger trials of the modern world.

Ihab Hassan. *Contemporary American Literature* (Ungar). 1973. pp. 54–5

TATE, ALLEN (1899–   )

While Tate is not often considered among the major American poets of our century, his best poetry represents a high order of accomplishment. In its variety of styles, Tate's work mingles Latin poetry, Dante, the metaphysicals, Poe, and the symbolists—to name only some of the more obvious formative elements. Much of Tate's art is perhaps unduly cerebral; his poetry may not always adequately combine intellect and emotion, and it may occasionally seem unduly parochial in its expression of the burden of southern history. Yet, at its best, Tate's poetry can be profoundly moving, particularly in those poems which fuse the poet's act of historical location, through the invocation of an ancestral past, with themes and circumstances common to all men regardless of their historical and geographical affiliations.

Haskell M. Block in *The Shaken Realist*, edited
by Melvin J. Friedman and John B. Vickery
(Louisiana State). 1970. p. 193

In Tate's verse, even more obviously than in Eliot's, there are powerful forces of order to create a fruitful tension against the forces of disorder. Thus most of Tate's poems are in regular and traditional meters: sonnets, blank verse, quatrains, and various intricate stanza forms strictly followed; epodes, odes modeled on "Lycidas" and on Drayton's "Ode to the Virginian Voyagers." There is no shying away from the conventional iambic pentameter, though much of Tate's best work is done in trimeter (e.g. "Seasons of the Soul") or tetrameter—his use of both these latter forms clearly owing much to Yeats's example. The long poem on which he has been at work for the past two decades, and of which three parts have been published so far, is in terza rima, the strictest and most demanding of all forms in English.

Against this ordered formal background there plays the audacious and elliptical language of the poems, passionate, violent, sometimes obscure.

Monroe K. Spears. *Dionysus and the
City* (Oxford—N.Y.). 1970. p. 173

When there has been a mob, Mr. Tate hasn't been leading it with a loud mouth; when there has been a lynching among poets or other writers, Mr. Tate hasn't been there to give a flick of contempt to the horny toes.

He is a Southern Gentleman of Letters. Yet should one be on any side but one's own? And what is one to say of the writer of a party (a party not being a mob), when one finds it difficult not to be inattentive to his writing? When one finds his writing too removed, with no main root in a layer of sensation?

One reads through Mr. Tate's essays forty years' length of criticism [*Essays of Four Decades*] and one is seldom, or never, outraged. His sentences are never tumultuous: and they are seldom stretched to an effective tightness. Are we missing much, when our attention falters?

TLS. March 19, 1971. p. 320

Like William Butler Yeats, Tate finds in history, not only the ground for his discourse, but the central excitement of his poetry. With the possible exception of Yeats, no poet of our time has possessed a more penetrating discernment of the predicament of modern man with reference to nature and history. In the old Christian synthesis, nature and history were related in a special way. With the break-up of that synthesis, man finds himself caught between a meaningless cycle on the one hand, and on the other, the more extravagant notions of progress—between a nature that is oblivious of man and a man-made "unnatural" Utopia.

In Tate's poetry nature comes in for a great deal of attention— "The Seasons of the Soul" is a typical instance—but Tate rarely exhibits nature for its own sake and never as a kind of innocently pastoral backdrop for man's activities. Since man, who had once thought his journey had a destination, the return to the meaningless round of the seasons is not comforting but terrifying.

Because of his preoccupation with history and human society, one does not often think of Tate as a nature poet, and yet in no poet of our time does the detail of nature make itself felt with more poignance and dramatic power.

Cleanth Brooks. *MQR*. Fall, 1971. p. 227

The initial impression which any selection of Tate's poems enforces is one of formal rigor, especially striking in an age in which poets have thought of traditional form as a thing either to be avoided or rendered with the lowest possible visibility. Tate's formal structures are insistently visible: the *terza rima* of "The Swimmers," the suspended quatrains of "The Traveller," the extraordinary ten-line trimeter stanzas of "Seasons of the Soul." Form is a compelling ritual to which the reader must submit in order to approach this poet's meaning. One never sees in Tate the effortless dexterity of an Auden; stress is always present between style and substance, as though the formal structures were dykes holding back high seas. The conscious constriction of these poems, their sense of being about to burst at the seams, reflects their main burden: the plight of modern man, exiled from the stability of tradition and holding chaos in check with forms which every day are witness to their own fragility.

Robert B. Shaw. Poetry. Jan., 1972. p. 222

TAYLOR, PETER (1917–   )

All of Peter Taylor's stories in *Miss Leonora When Last Seen, and Fifteen Other Stories* have appeared in magazines, and ten were re-printed earlier in collections now out of print. The present collection may then be taken to represent the flower of Taylor's art, for with few exceptions . . . they show a masterful achievement. The title story, and one of the best, treats a major, recurrent theme: the passing of an old order before the onslaught of the new, and the way that people—especially older people, like Miss Leonora—deal with this change. . . . An adaptation is made—Taylor's characters are remarkably adaptable in this way—but this is, after all, the surest sign of their defeat. And what is lost is something quite irretrievable, as these old people know and perhaps more than anyone else correctly value. But they do not whine about it: of their store of human dignity and courage they retain this much to the last, as do the best of Faulkner's characters—the other Southern writer with whom Taylor, despite important differences, is best compared.

Jay L. Halio. SoR. Winter, 1968. pp. 242–3

The world has passed Taylor by. The small towns and cities in the hinterland between the Atlantic and the Mississippi that are his métier have now been spoken for by Spiro Agnew and his boss; the comfortable, stable, and unhappy people he writes about seem almost never to have lived; the style that never calls attention to itself could seem impressive mostly to those surfeited with Faulkner and Warren. But he still is with us, beautifully unchanged; it would be hard to put these stories [in the *Collected Stories*], written over a thirty-year period, in chronological order. His characters are now more absorbed in the past than they used to be . . . but the world is, throughout, small college campuses and roadhouses and front porches and country clubs. What animates a Taylor story is such a slight event, such a small quirk of self, that the landscape must be solid and easily seen for the key, minute point not to be lost. But this very stability of setting, not just of landscape but of social structure and attitude, finally has the effect of rendering the event very close to irrelevant. This is of course not what Taylor wanted, and it would be nice to think that his imperviousness to change is the mark of

one in tune with more eternal verities. But no—in small doses Taylor is
good, but even then he never escapes seeming precious.

Roger Sale. HdR. Winter, 1969–70. p. 710

[His] stories center on character and for this reason Taylor has been
called the "American Chekhov." Actually, Taylor is, if anything, even
more delicate in the way he proceeds by indirection and by irony to
reveal the most heartrending apprehensions about humanity. His razor is
so keen that the deepest cuts may go unnoticed; one can imagine a
grandmother gently smiling over a story which would terrify her grand-
daughter. And here is the greatness of these stories. They offer something to every reader without descending to a mediocre level of
technique or interest. The reader must win his own reward.

VQR. Winter, 1971. p. xiv

Superficially, Peter Taylor's short stories may seem radically different
from Flannery O'Connor's. They are unusually quiet tales of domestic
life, the confrontations of common bourgeois Americans of the mid-
South with common elements of fate, carefully documented with social
observations and oddities of a kind sometimes found in sentimental
fiction. But here and there the grotesque shows through: Taylor's restraint sometimes gives way to his sense of tragedy and disorder; the
comic and the violent rush together, to give us unforgettable stories.
This handsome book, <i>The Collected Short Stories of Peter Taylor</i>, is one
of the major books of our literature.

   Taylor's stories are like dreams: events are brought sharply into
focus, magically and dramatically limited, a sequence of sensations and
speech passes as if in no important relationship to the rest of the world.
And then a mysterious "point" is reached, a point of surrender or relaxation, and the story is complete, completed. Taylor has always been
admired by critics to whom the craft of art is extremely important. But
he writes stories that are far more than neatly crafted; they are both
hallucinatory and articulate, the violence of Taylor's vision being brack-
eted by, even tamed by, the intelligent and gracious voice of his typical
narrators.

Joyce Carol Oates. SoR. Winter, 1971. p. 299

● TOOMER, JEAN (1894–1967)

Reading [<i>Cane</i>], I had the vision of a land, heretofore sunk in the mists
of muteness, suddenly rising up into the eminence of song. Innumerable

UPDIKE, JOHN (1932–)

Not surprisingly there is a good deal of post-coital sadness in this novel [*Couples*]. Updike busies himself with tidying up things or working out his burning of the Tarbox church and the breakup of the couples' society, but there is more feeling to dispose of than can be managed through attention to plot or symbol. For all his attention toward the anyman-hero, Updike has no final right way to feel or think about him, nor is there any suggestion of an alternative life to the ones lived in the novel. Piet and Foxy divorce and marry; we are told, in a *Tender Is the Night* ending, that the Hanemas now live in Lexington, an American town evidently not far from Hornell, N.Y. and Dr. Diver. As I see it there are no consequences to be drawn, lessons to be reaped from these adventures, except that life is very strange and people don't seem satisfied with what they have. With the exception of Saul Bellow, no American novelist says this as strongly as Updike, and adding Mailer to the company we have our three major novelists. Fiction is still human.

William H. Pritchard. *HdR*.
Summer, 1968. p. 376

Updike's *Rabbit* novels—*Rabbit, Run* (1960) and its sequel *Rabbit Redux* (just published)—are his best books. The thesis novels failed because his will and intelligence took the place of emotional force. The autobiographical family novels were full of emotional force yet in the effort to keep it under esthetic control *The Centaur* sometimes became a shade too big and *Of the Farm* a shade too small. But in the *Rabbit* novels the use of the present tense and the choice of a character who stands at one remove from Updike's personal experience shield him from the overpowering rushes of feeling that result in ornate prose, willful intricacies or problems of scale in his other novels.

Richard Locke. *NYT*. Nov. 14, 1971. p. 20

The convincing rebirths in Updike's fiction occur not by changing jobs but by being changed within one's offices. Meaningful changes occur when a person is able to accept the death to his self-interest and the awakening of new life effected in him by the law and grace of vocation. . . .

Many of Updike's characters . . . are called on to spend themselves in offices and jobs which they are tempted to resist. These people struggle between the alternatives of, on the one hand, accepting their places in life with consequent humiliation and even death, and, on the other, rejecting their positions and striving to secure, by their own spiritual effort or fantasy, some sense of escape or salvation. Only some of his characters . . . can accept the dying that comes with their positions in life. But more subtly, several of the young parents in Updike's stories are people who are dying to their own interests and resurrected to new joys. . . .

What Updike seems to take from Luther, then, is a sacramental understanding of work. Work is deadening; work has no direct relation to the religion of grace. But in, through, and under work a man can receive the presence of God first in judgment but then also in grace.

Wesley A. Kort. Shriven Selves
(Fortress). 1972. pp. 80, 83–4

Although it is a comic book, *Bech* is not a very hopeful book. Serious or tragic literature is invariably more hopeful than comic. It is partly Updike's wry estimate of himself and as such may contain a subtle defense of the persistently serious mode of most of his work. Bech is safe, but he is also unproductive artistically; his comic vision may be unable to coexist with the structured, representative, symbolic, coherent, and sincere vision necessary to produce a work of art. . . . Ultimately it is impossible for Bech to think big; he can only think small. It is to the compromised world of *Couples* and *Rabbit Redux* that Updike must return, for it is only within their complicated dialectic of serious and comic that his life-givers have a meaningful role and a plausible identity; and it is only within their intricate logic that his artistic impulse can be both circumspect and viable.

Joyce B. Markle. Fighters and Lovers: Theme
in the Novels of John Updike (New York
Univ. Pr.). 1973. pp. 189–90

If Updike's play [*Buchanan Dying*] held one's attention, its unhistorical features would matter less. But the story must bewilder any reader unacquainted with the details of [President James] Buchanan's life. The scene is the dying man's bedroom. As his now disorderly mind produces events or illusions, they are acted out. Real people come to see him, interrupt the reveries, and are absorbed into them. The sequence of episodes is not chronological but dreamlike.

For this poetic blending of internal idea and external reality there are precedents in Updike's novels, where he often dwells on the ghostliness of his people. The structure of the novels is rarely a line of probable actions, each producing the next. The arrangement of the incidents is more often arbitrary, associative, poetic. The motives and affections of the characters change unpredictably. Even scenes of high drama, like the burning of the church in *Couples*, are undercut by Updike's taste for parody and ventriloquism. The expanding use of recent public events in *Couples, Bech*, and *Rabbit Redux* might have prepared us for the poetic use of history in *Buchanan Dying*.

Irvin Ehrenpreis. NYR. Aug. 8, 1974. p. 8

Short, amusing, confessional, *A Month of Sundays* consists of diary entries composed by the Reverend Tom Marshfield during an enforced retreat to a desert rest home maintained by his denomination for shepherds who flip. . . .

Novels by John Updike are luxury products, as a thousand reviewers have noted: The exterior trim is burnished, the inside hides are matched, the doors thunk gorgeously behind one, and few travelers feel the road. Unremittingly observant, the creator catches even tiny differences between toilets—flushing action at home and away. His eye for the "speaking" incongruity—chewing-gum wrappers crumpled on the floor of the choir—is acute. As for his way with a metaphor: It resembles that of a compactor with kitchen rubbish. In a trice the miscellaneous welter and muck of social existence is packaged in impeccably symmetrical phrases. . . . Nor is such detail mere decoration. Everywhere on the contemporary scene the faithless lead the faithless; the quality of this general experience for leaders and followers alike—the breathless hypocrisy of it, the ceaseless veerings toward, then away from, truth— has an edge of significance; probing clerical insides is a way of showing forth the significance.

But there is a problem, namely, that this author, who knows everything about the age and its tenants, lacks a principle on which to build resistance. He nowhere glorifies corruption or weakness, but nowhere, either, does he discover resources of pride or clarities of discrimination of the kind that unhorse urbanity and shrugging compliance. Church and theology are open doors to his gift, but religion is closed; his "word" charms but does not instruct.

Benjamin DeMott. SR. March 8, 1975. pp. 20–1

John Updike is best known for his twin themes of adultery and aging ex-athletes. But this prolific chronicler of American anxiety has also enjoyed setting human affairs in a subtle religious perspective. Updike's description of Harry Angstrom's soaring golf drive in *Rabbit, Run* was an ecstatic explanation of human union with God. In "The Deacon," published in *Museums and Women*, he played masterfully on the two meanings of "church," using the edifice as a metaphor for the ecclesia.

Now with *A Month of Sundays*, Updike's neo-orthodox Christianity comes full-blown out of his literary closet. . . .

Though not every one of Updike's carefully-turned phrases scores a poetic coup, *A Month of Sundays* is a theological tour de force and a pleasurable, enriching book. As a compendium of Protestant faith, this work fits the Biblical definition; it is Updike's substance of things hoped for, his evidence of things unseen.

Daniel Morrissey. *Com.*
June 6, 1975. pp. 187–8

VAN DOREN, MARK (1894–1972)

Mark Van Doren, whose gift for the quiet conventional lyric has surely been under-praised so far, has reduced his collected poetry by nearly ninety per cent to give us *100 Poems*, a delightful book. And inexpensive, which is no small virtue either. In general I have no quarrel with his selection, though a few poems that I had remembered are lacking. Like most poets who write a lot, Van Doren scores a low percentage of direct hits; but this is neither surprising nor regrettable. He has several dozen poems that are among the best of their kind produced in this century, poems like "High August," "Only for Me," "Civil War," "Time Was when Death," "And So It Was," and some of those about birds and animals. Younger poets, conscious of the mind-breaking formal problems of their own work, may find Van Doren's poems too easy to read; yet other readers, just as sensitive but not professionally engaged, attend them with pleasure; which means, I think, that formally speaking the poems are not only satisfactory but transcendently satisfactory. And most of the best of them are in this little book.

Hayden Carruth. Poetry. Sept., 1968. pp. 424–5

Every new poem was, for Mark Van Doren, the "first poem." [Richard] Howard notes that Van Doren is in that central position that causes difficulty in our modernist insistence on "placing" poets. Having never been in fashion, Mark Van Doren will never, as another astute critic has observed, go out of fashion. Called the one poet "most representative of his country and his times" by Howard Baker, Van Doren was totally devoid of any French influence, unusual for a 20th-century poet. His later poems suggest a country intelligence almost exclusively; there is just one poem in *Good Morning* with an urban theme, "Rain Beautifies the City."

The fact that Mark Van Doren was there "with words when the heartbeat happened" is a matter of importance to the continuity of English-American tradition in poetry, a long line from Dryden through Frost.

William F. Claire. NR. Nov. 3, 1973. p. 30

VIERECK, PETER (1916–   )

Viereck's work has three qualities essential to that of any good poet. He has an individual, sustaining style. He has poetic convictions, flexible in approach but durable in essence. He has an affinity for themes of inherent scope and power. But in addition to these, he has something extremely rare in a mechanical and insulated age, something largely absent from contemporary poetry. To call it a cosmic sense sounds portentous. Yet this is what it is. Roethke had it, Tomlinson, and D. H. Lawrence. It is one poetic quality which is purely a gift, and there is absolutely nothing which can be done to simulate its possession.

Josephine Jacobsen. *MR*. Summer, 1968. p. 591

The career in poetry of Peter Viereck, perhaps more than that of any other writer of our time, can be viewed as an experiment in the symbiosis of poetry and politics. . . . His best satires are memorable events in the history of ideas, without loss of art.

Viereck's earliest poetry served him as an extension of political consciousness into a medium in which paramount ideas of our era could be abstracted from their worrisome contexts in international affairs and viewed freshly and intrinsically through the symbolic machinery of art. Poetry later became for Viereck a mind-style for escaping the risks of socio-political consciousness in playful, if ingenious, literary word-puzzles. But in his most recent work, in going still further beyond literal reality, Viereck returns to full human force and wholeness.

Laurence Lieberman. *Poetry*.
Aug., 1968. p. 342

• VONNEGUT, KURT, JR. (1922–   )

Cat's Cradle is an irreverent and often highly entertaining fantasy concerning the playful irresponsibility of nuclear scientists. Like the best of contemporary satire, it is work of a far more engaging and meaningful order than the melodramatic tripe which most critics seem to consider serious.

Terry Southern. *NYT*. June 2, 1963. p. 20

I am happy to announce that I am likely to become Mr., or Herr, Vonnegut's first convert in these Western isles. . . .

What remains really impressive [in *Cat's Cradle*] is the ingenuity and imagination used to make Bokononism convincing. Its founder's maxims and poems are quoted every two or three pages with startling effect. Bokonon, for instance, rejects the New Testament message "Render unto Caesar the things which are Caesar's" as any Manichaean must. He substitutes "Pay no attention to Caesar. Caesar doesn't have the slightest idea what is really going on." Like many another great thinker, Bokonon finds his inspiration in the most banal sources. Vonnegut admits to scoffing at first at the phrase "dynamic tension" in the Books of Bokonon, recognising this as the slogan of the postal body-builder, Charles Atlas. Atlas's theory was that bodily strength could be acquired without any equipment by pitting one set of muscles against the other. Bokonon adapts this to society—strong society can be built by pitting good and evil against each other and keeping the tension between the two high at all times. Historically it is difficult to deny the accuracy of this observation. By the end of *Cat's Cradle*, it is hard to remember that Bokonon is a fictional character—religions have been built around far less improbable creators before.

Alan Brien. Spec. Aug. 2, 1963. pp. 158–9

A joy to behold is Vonnegut's *Player Piano*, years ahead of its time in 1952, reissued in handsome hardback just as the times catch up. Blackly humorous, extraordinarily well-written, bitter, funny and sharp, this major first novel by a clique-making major writer will not now be forgotten.

Theodore Sturgeon. National Review.
May 17, 1966. p. 478

Kurt Vonnegut's world ends not with a bang, not with a whimper, but with a wink, a shrug and a boop-boop-de-doop. His writing is uneven, his characters flat. . . . What he has he has in glorious abundance: a sense of how bizarre daily life is, a comic gift that uses reality itself as its focus, and now-you-see-it-now-you-don't he'll turn it inside out for laughs, and often, gasps. He is sometimes profound; he has a first-rate mind and an imagination that is staggering. His terrain is near the junction of George Orwell and Lewis Carroll.

Joanne Greenberg. Denver Quarterly.
Summer, 1966. pp. 119–20

Although the machines of *Player Piano* suggest a bogus sense of order, the world of Vonnegut—a world without meaning—is one of disorder, ranging from the untidy to the chaotic. His books are not only about that world; they reflect it. From *Player Piano* to *God Bless You, Mr. Rosewater*, his novels display an increasing fragmentation. He jumps from person to person, from place to place, time to time, often coming to rest for no more than a paragraph or a page. Conventional plot, which is necessary to *Player Piano*, has practically disappeared in *God Bless You, Mr. Rosewater*. Except for the lost and loveless central figures, usually the narrators, around whom the comic distress forms, the characters are mostly cartoon sketches, seen briefly but vividly, designed to make a simple satiric point.

The chapters, particularly in the later novels, are not necessarily units of action, and the brief scenes that are units are often divided for no reason. In *God Bless You, Mr. Rosewater*, every few paragraphs, often in the middle of a conversation, the page of type is broken by a decorative *R*, as though to remind us of the unlikelihood of a beginning or an end.

In *Cat's Cradle*, the same kind of arbitrary division is given a name and a number, so that there are 127 "chapters" in 191 pages in the paperback edition. It is as though the author were providing handholds for the weak to pull themselves from thought to thought, only to have the handholds turn into fences and the narrative into an obstacle course.

Gerald Weales. *Reporter.*
Dec. 1, 1966. pp. 54–5

Vonnegut's prose has the same virtues as his characterization and plotting. It is deceptively simple, suggestive of the ordinary, but capable of startling and illuminating twists and turns. He uses the rhetorical potential of the short sentence and short paragraph better than anyone now writing, often getting a rich comic or dramatic effect by isolating a single sentence in a separate paragraph or excerpting a phrase from context for a bizarre chapter-heading. The apparent simplicity and ordinariness of his writing mask its efficient power, so that we are often startled when Vonnegut pounces on a tired platitude or cliché like a benevolent mongoose and shakes new life into it.

Robert Scholes. *The Fabulators*
(Oxford—N.Y.). 1967. p. 51

Ilium, Titan, Tralfamadore, Nazi Germany, San Lorenzo, Rosewater County, Dresden at the time of the devastating Allied air-raid—these are some of the settings for Vonnegut's six novels to date, and the juxtaposition of the actual and the imaginary in that list gives a clue as to one of his main preoccupations. What is the relation between the facts we encounter and the fictions we invent? Given the terrible historical actuality of the Second World War, what are we to make of the ambiguous role of fantasy in men's lives? And how does all this affect the writer, who longs to communicate and does so by telling lies? It is a growing awareness of the seriousness of Vonnegut's inquiries which has made people realise that he is not simply the science fiction writer he first appeared to be.

His first novel, *Player Piano* (1952), was, to be sure, a fairly orthodox futuristic satire on the dire effects on human individuality of the fully mechanised society which technology could make possible. A piano player is a man consciously using a machine to produce aesthetically pleasing patterns of his own making. A player-piano is a machine which has been programmed to produce music on its own, thus making the human presence redundant. This undesirable inversion of the relationship between man and machine, suggested by the title, is at the heart of the novel.

Tony Tanner. CQ. Winter, 1969. p. 297

A Vonnegut book is not cute or precious. It is literally awful, for Vonnegut is one of the few writers able to lift the lid of the garbage can, and dispassionately examine the contents. . . .

The ultimate difficulty with Vonnegut is precisely this: that he refuses to say who is wrong. The simplest way . . . is to say that everybody is wrong but the author. Any number of writers have done it, with good success. But Vonnegut refuses. He ascribes no blame, sets no penalties. His commentary on the assassination of Robert Kennedy and Martin Luther King is the same as his comment on all other deaths: "So it goes," he says, and nothing more.

One senses that underneath it all, Vonnegut is a nice man, who doesn't really like to say this, but . . . his description of one character might stand for all mankind in his view: "She had been given the opportunity to participate in civilization, and she had muffed it." And of himself, a comment by another character, the author-Nazi-propagandist-pornographer-American spy Howard W. Campbell, Jr. "I speak gibberish to the civilized world, and it replies in kind."

So it goes.

J. Michael Crichton. NR. April 26, 1969. p. 35

[Kurt Vonnegut] has been a writer's writer, serious, technically accomplished, uninterested in accommodating himself to the book trade or the great thundering herd. He has not had, accordingly, one "big book," though he is a better writer—more intelligent, more disciplined—than some people who have, Joseph Heller, for example, or Terry Southern. Mr. Vonnegut is what used to be called a banjo hitter. He has kept rapping out sharp singles while the sluggers lunged and panted and wrote army novels and drove home the Cadillacs. But there have been some signs latterly of a boom in Vonnegut stock, with his *Mother Night* particularly and *Cat's Cradle* being taken up a good deal by young people in the colleges. What appeals to them, I suspect, is the combination of Mr. Vonnegut's gentleness and his stylish sense of the ridiculous in these our times. He may be a growth issue.

Warren Coffey. *Com.* June 6, 1969. pp. 347–8

Vonnegut's art forces us to reimagine horror, a neat trick. . . .

For all of this, *Slaughterhouse-Five* is a very funny novel, as funny as *The Day of the Locust*, which uses humor as still another means of enlightenment. The possibilities of humor come from Vonnegut's double attitude: horror at the way things happen and acceptance that we can do little to change the way things happen. . . .

Because his art does much that others' have been unable to do, it sometimes does less. Characterizations are reduced in complexity, caught in Vonnegut's design, like bugs in amber. Similarly, climaxes are distributed throughout the novel, not set strategically for a final culmination of thematic currents. But these are far from faults, merely other ways to make his points: that all times converge in each climactic moment and each character is lost in cosmic space.

Shaun O'Connell. *AS.* Autumn, 1969. pp. 720–1

Kurt Vonnegut, Jr., is a much more obvious moralist than Barth. His novels have something of Swift in them—not merely in the canny pokes he takes at human weakness and the *status quo*, but a kind of fantasy that allows him, as it allowed Swift, to isolate the objects of his attack and praise. What Vonnegut praises, as we might expect in setting him against the background of the "open decision," is the human being—at least the human being as Vonnegut defines the phrase. The human being is most human—and most praiseworthy—when he lives wholeheartedly in his natural condition, working in the open, doing joyfully and spontaneously for his own support, loving other life, and being loved. Human worth—and hence significance—resides in the *being* of the human. The self is its own reason for being; its being is its own guarantee of its value. The more conscious one is of his being, the more individual he is and the firmer is his guarantee.

Jerry H. Bryant. *The Open Decision: The Contemporary American Novel and Its Intellectual Background* (Free). 1970. p. 303

Happy Birthday, Wanda June . . . with which the novelist Kurt Vonnegut, Jr. makes his debut as a playwright, is an attempt at a satire on the return of Odysseus. Mr. Vonnegut's Odysseus is a paunchy, bearded fellow named Ryan who has been missing for eight years, held captive by Indians in South America. He is a bully and a braggart who calls his young wife "Daughter," boasts of his heroism during the Spanish Civil War and the Second World War, and at the end goes offstage with a loaded rifle to shoot himself. In short, he is a caricature of Hemingway, drawn in pure venom. A dreadful, cheap idea, and certainly unworthy of the clever Mr. Vonnegut's considerable talent—talent for comedy, that is, which, while slighter than Hemingway's, for example, often pays off. No talent for abstract thought is discernible on the stage of the [Theatre] de Lys. Although I'd just as soon simply laugh at anyone as funny as Mr. Vonnegut and let it go at that, he demands to be taken seriously, and when he starts moralizing he becomes obvious and silly, almost sinking his play. Not quite, though; there are plenty of good, quirky jokes and funny scenes and there are enough good performances to save it.

Edith Oliver. NY. Oct. 17, 1970. p. 143

Among contemporary writers, Kurt Vonnegut stands out as a gruff sentimentalist with a soft spot in his heart for science fiction. . . . Vonnegut . . . often wavers between the future and the past, the story in its slickest form and the vision of things to come, the bombings of Dresden and the destroying of the planet Tralfamadore. Furthermore, some of his science fiction—*Player Piano, Welcome to the Monkey House*—is in the old form of dystopia: an extension of the absurd or destructive tendencies of the present, a scientized homily, satire, or warning. This is understandable; Vonnegut is really a simple moralist, haunted by the reality of death. (The refrain, "So it goes," follows each mortal event in *Slaughterhouse-Five*, like water drops in Chinese torture.) Typically, his own moral confession sounds a bit cute: "And I realize now that the two main themes of my novels were stated by my siblings: 'Here I am cleaning shit off practically everything' and 'No pain.' "

Time warps, spaceships, and galactic materializations aside, Vonnegut, an earthling like all of us, can not push his vision past the ironic barrier of the mind. He bestows on his ideal creatures, the Tralfamadorians, the supreme privilege of blowing up the universe. They blow it up, of all things, experimenting with a new fuel for their flying saucers. So much, then, for Universal Time and Space, where vision and extinction finally become one.

Ihab Hassan in Liberations, edited by Ihab
Hassan (Wesleyan). 1971. pp. 193–4

The main concern of Vonnegut's novels is the illusions men live by. These illusions fall into two categories. On the one hand, Vonnegut treats those illusions that make human existence more miserable than it need be. The significance man attaches to such artificial distinctions as race, nationality, even national dogma, forces him to overlook the common humanity that links all men. . . . Like the illusions caused by nationalism and racial prejudice, what might be called the Great-American-Success-Illusion also fosters invidious distinctions. . . .

The second kind of illusion Vonnegut examines lies beyond protest. Whereas the first contributes to human despair and should be discarded, the second helps prevent despair and seems essential to human contentment. This is the illusion of a purposeful universe. Those who embrace it believe the world contains plan, meaning and a moral order, and that in the end all things work for the best. . . . Vonnegut's belief in a purposeless universe constitutes his main theme. . . . Protest . . . implies hope for reform. Like most novelists of the absurd, however, Vonnegut entertains little hope for either social or individual reform. Comic absurdity informs all things, including man and his institutions. . . . In the face of such all-encompassing absurdity, what is the proper response for man? Vonnegut offers at least three possible answers to this question. Man may practice uncritical love, hoping through kindness and charity to lend some meaning to an otherwise meaningless human condition. Or he can manufacture new illusions to supplant the old—comforting lies that will shelter him from the icy winds of an absurd universe. Finally, he can simply accept the absurdity of his condition, neither affirming nor denying it and never asking the most meaningless of questions, Why?

Charles B. Harris. *Contemporary American*
Novelists of the Absurd (College and
University). 1971. pp. 54, 56, 60–1, 64, 66–7

Vonnegut is always at home with characters who are not with it in our kind of world, people whose total helplessness and inability to explain *anything* have indeed made them unworldly, extraterrestrial, open to mischief from outer space. Vonnegut's use of space fiction is always too droll for my taste, a boy's fantasy of more rational creatures than ourselves. . . .

Vonnegut is at his best not in *Slaughterhouse-Five* but in such satires of the American scene as *God Bless You, Mr. Rosewater*. In these his authentic bitterness at the souring of so many American hopes takes on the wildly comic quality natural to him. In *Slaughterhouse-Five* he seems, all too understandably, subdued by his material and plays it dumb. The book is short, loose, and somehow helpless. But Vonnegut's total horror of war has endeared him to the young, who find it hard to believe that even World War II had a purpose, and who see themselves as belonging to the universe at large rather than to the country that sends them to fight in Asia. Vonnegut's fixed social idea, especially in *Slaughterhouse-Five*, is a human vulnerability too innocent in the face of war to offer any political explanation or protest.

Alfred Kazin. *SR.* Feb. 6, 1971. p. 15

Like any writer who pleases a large audience, Vonnegut has his virtues: gimmicks that work, bright observations, some good jokes. But, as Gertrude Stein noted, remarks aren't literature; and they certainly don't produce major reputations. Vonnegut appeals because he has wed the styles of modern skepticism and later "cool" to a mitigating earnestness. That he is beloved by youngsters isn't difficult to understand. His own spiritual age is late adolescence: the time when a flip manner often disguises priggishness, when skepticism is just a hedge against vulnerability, when prejudice disdains the search for proof and inexperience limits one's power to imagine, when confidence in one's special distinction reveals itself in the very fervor with which it is denied and the herding instinct asserts a need for independence. That Vonnegut is beloved by critics (and presumably adult readers) is more disconcerting. For them, he provides an easy bridge from an age of skepticism and baffled hope to one of faith in any nostrum that bears the certifications of novelty and youth. Moreover, he provides this bridge without requiring his adult readers to change the style—the trappings of modernism— as well as the content of their belief. Vonnegut lets us have things both ways. He is important not in his effect but as a symptom. He can tell us nothing worth knowing except what his rise itself indicates: ours is an age in which adolescent ridicule can become a mode of upward mobility.

Charles Thomas Samuels. *NR.*
June 12, 1971. p. 32

Kurt Vonnegut, Jr., through six novels and more than fifty stories, has crafted for his readers an exceedingly mad world. Grouped perhaps rashly with the Black Humorists, Vonnegut holds his own, matching Yossarians with Howard Campbells, Guy Grands with Eliot Rosewaters, and Sebastian Dangerfields with Malachi Constants. But unlike Joseph Heller, Vonnegut is prolific, tracing his vision through many different human contexts. He surpasses Terry Southern by striking all limits from human absurdity: destruction by nuclear fission is for Vonnegut the most passé of apocalypses. Moreover, he teases us with a Mod Yoknapatawpha County; "Frank Wirtanen" and "Bernard B. O'Hare" (originally characters in his third novel, *Mother Night*) and others appear again and again, always (as befits the modern county) in a maddening metamorphosis of roles. Favorite cities such as "Rosewater, Indiana" and "Ilium, New York" are storehouses for the paraphernalia of middle class life which so delight Vonnegut, whose region is one of cultural value rather than geographical place. But unlike Southern and Bruce Jay Friedman, who mock such culture in the socio-satiric mode of Evelyn Waugh (Southern scripted *The Loved One* for the movies), Vonnegut uses his roots more like John Barth uses Maryland: interest lies beneath the surface and the surface itself is constantly changing. Vonnegut, in short, demands independent investigation. One finds at the end of Vonnegut's vision a "fine madness" indeed, but a madness at the same time more clinical and more comic than found elsewhere.

Jerome Klinkowitz. Critique.
12, 3, 1971. pp. 38–9

In attempting to account for Kurt Vonnegut's sudden and immense popularity with readers, especially college students, one is eventually forced to conclude that his brilliant technique has been largely responsible, this same technique which was dismissed as "flashy" by his early critics. Flashy it is, but no more so than Mark Twain's or Hart Crane's, two among the many writers who have suffered from modernity, and although no claim is made for Vonnegut being of comparable stature, the similarities in their treatment by the more conservative critics are too evident to overlook. Perhaps even more than the fantastic and science-fictional subjects of his novels, the apparent slickness with which he has written them has militated against early critical success, and, ironically, has produced his popular victory, which in turn caused critics to overpraise his most poorly written novel.

David H. Goldsmith. Kurt Vonnegut: Fantasist
of Fire and Ice (Bowling Green). 1972. p. 30

No novelist in the sixties is more aware of the necessity of exorcising our dreams of death than Kurt Vonnegut, Jr., and no novelist is more avid in his use of the fable form as an exorcising comfort and a loving gentle prod. The dark, tough, apocalyptic quality of Vonnegut's vision results from his hard-minded recognition that we do commit sins against ourselves which need to be exorcised. . . .

The final dark implication, which Vonnegut shares with a great many other writers, is that we too are headed for cataclysm unless we find something to live by. Vonnegut does offer two possibilities—we can learn to love each other, or we can each create our own illusion, some mythology which will help us to learn to live together. Neither possibility makes life meaningful, but both do offer a way to stay alive, and maybe even have some fun.

The particular power of Vonnegut's work—especially in the four books which develop his distinctive voice, all published in the sixties—is in the deceptively simple way he deals with the extraordinary nature of contemporary fact. Vonnegut is a master of getting inside a cliché and tilting it enough off center to reveal both the horror and the mystery that lies beneath the surface of the most placidly dull and ordinary human response.

> Raymond M. Olderman. *Beyond the Wasteland*
> (Yale). 1972. pp. 189, 191

Vonnegut is the sort of writer whom you either like a lot or dislike a lot; if you like one of his books, you are likely to enjoy the others. If you read one or two and don't like them, you might as well stop and accept the fact he's not for you. But even if you like them all, you have favorites. One of my favorites turned out to be *The Sirens of Titan*, and that surprised me, because it was supposed to be the most "science-fiction" type of all his books, and I don't like science fiction. By that I mean I don't like books that have green monsters with five arms, and lost tribes that are ruled by electronic lizards.

But Vonnegut's "science fiction" wasn't like that at all. It was about people, doing things that people might do if things had just turned out a little differently; or maybe if we *knew* more of what was really going on.

> Dan Wakefield in *The Vonnegut Statement*,
> edited by Jerome Klinkowitz and John
> Somer (Delacorte). 1973. p. 62

Vonnegut had latched on to a truly original American idiom, as American as TV or napalm or napalm-abhorrers, as fragmented and discontinuous as contemporary experience. A consideration of Vonnegut's idiom, I would say, should take into account everything from his great ear, his sense of the way Americans talk, his sense of timing (as active and keen as Paul McCartney's—a compliment one does not bestow lightly), to his formal idiosyncrasies, beginning with *Mother Night* in 1961: the short chapter form; the sharp image; the short, quick scene; the fragmented time sequence; the speed of narration generated by these formal characteristics. If one were to play Marshall McLuhan here, one might point out that Vonnegut's fiction is a clever formal approximation of, or at least shares many elements of, watching television. This might offer another explanation for Vonnegut's appeal to the TV generation, those who have *always* had television, not to mention those of us, more

or less aged, who, according to McLuhan, have also had our sense ratios
hopelessly rearranged by it.

Joe David Bellamy in *The Vonnegut Statement*,
edited by Jerome Klinkowitz and John
Somer (Delacorte). 1973. pp. 81–2

With the invention of his schizophrenic manner, Kurt Vonnegut, Jr.,
created the technical perspective that he needed to exorcise the distract-
ing and consuming cloud of Dresden, to resolve the aesthetic problems
he discovered in *The Sirens of Titan*, and to re-invent himself and his
universe in his "lousy little book" that sings like the crystal goblet of the
schizophrenic planet Mercury. . . . Because his moral confrontation with
Dresden was steady and persistent through his career, the affirmation of
life, vibrating in this climactic novel [*Slaughterhouse-Five*] is based not
on self-deception but upon the greatness of the human spirit confronted
by great adversity. More important, though, the integrity of this affirmation signals the aesthetic strength and freedom of Vonnegut's vision, a
vision that captures the essential spiritual dilemma of contemporary
man and represents an enduring contribution to his literary heritage and
to man's quest for "wonderful *new* lies."

John Somer in *The Vonnegut Statement*,
edited by Jerome Klinkowitz and John
Somer. (Delacorte). 1973. pp. 252–3

Kurt Vonnegut's *Breakfast of Champions* is more provocative as a straw
in the wind than a work of literature. It has almost no narrative interest,
almost no "solidity of specification," almost no moral complication, and
almost none of the inside-dopesterism characteristic of books that sell
very well; yet it has sold not merely well but best. What it does have is
play, wit, structural unpredictability, some ingenious mimicry of American speech, and an absurdist vision continuous with Vonnegut's previous work, though here with a different tonal range. It seems to me
possible that our literary sociology is changing in some ways that are not
yet clear and that Vonnegut's rather unpretentious book, so astonish-
ingly different from any previous bestseller, may mark the beginning of a
different and wider public for new, unconventional fiction. . . .

Vonnegut's book is structured around the life and times of a Mid-
land City Pontiac dealer named Dwayne Hoover, whose wife has
committed suicide by drinking Drano, whose son is a homosexual cocktail pianist, who is himself mad throughout the book and berserk at
its end. But the life of the book does not reside in the continuity of its
central figures. The life of the book resides in its "bits," its gags, its
lines, its long succession of comic-apocalyptic events, even its drawings.

So it is that it seems pointless to criticize the book for being self-indulgent and messy; of course it is. It does not, however, seem pointless to criticize the book for its triviality. For, touching again and again on the curious and desperate backwaters of American culture, the book nevertheless dissipates much of its force with schoolboy bathroom jokes, penis measurements, and a good portion of foolishness that seems neither buoyant enough nor clever enough to justify its existence.

Philip Stevick. *PR*. No. 2, 1974. pp. 302, 304

• WAKOSKI, DIANE (1937–   )

Still in her 20's, Diane Wakoski has already gained recognition as a poet of genuine talent. A Southern Californian with a Berkeley B.A., she now lives in New York, where she teaches in a junior-high school. . . . [Her work] is youthful, spacious, sunny, exuberant, excited, and though filled with teaching, it is free from pedantry. Among the many virtues of her poetry, the rarest and most wonderful is its ease, its grace, its natural-ness. This is not to say that her poetry is "easy." Indeed, her surrealistic symbols are often extremely demanding, but her poems never demand exertions from the reader whom they do not repay with immediate and abiding joy.

Robert Regan. LJ. March 1, 1966. p. 1231

In her *George Washington Poems* [Diane Wakoski] has revived the figure of the Father of Our Country as a genuine living fictional per-sonage, but in totally unexpected ways—at least to me. He becomes neither the historical figure, nor a mythological one; but instead a changeable person, variably George, the General, Mr. President, a father figure, an enlightened aristocrat, and ultimately a projection of the poet herself, slipping back and forth in time, with whom she converses, or to whom she declaims, in the cheerfullest terms imaginable, about her own life, her actual father and husband, her sense of relationship to her country, and many other themes. The ramifications are endless. Her body becomes a map, for instance; her personal being, the history of the nation. If Miss Wakoski's scheme has a flaw, it is the playfulness that pervades it, but perhaps this is essential, perhaps the scheme would collapse without it.

Readers who insist that poetry cannot be poetry which does not rise from and return to a sense of conviction, will be dissatisfied with *The George Washington Poems*, as will those who prefer a stronger, more complex language than the post-Beat idiom used by Miss Wakoski (as I generally do myself). But poetry or not, this book delights me. It is exactly the sort of book I should like to find, but never do, at my bedside when I go visiting in somebody else's house.

Hayden Carruth. HdR. Summer, 1968. p. 408

I have been following Miss Wakoski's career for several years, listening to her read in public and brooding over her poems in books and periodi-cals. I have been consistently impressed by her ability to convey the emotions of terror and desire, the experience of a vulnerable spirit in an environment of overwhelming verticals and horizontals. Bright, arresting images and perceptions leap from the pages of her poems, some of them whimsical and naïve, others profound and breathtakingly original. Yet, though her flights are imaginative, she permits a great deal of reality to enter her poems, often transmogrified, to be sure—as it inevitably would be under pressure of strong feelings of anger, alienation, or frustrated love.

It is the feeling of love that is particularly interesting. The speaker of her poems is forever reaching out for love and withdrawing in pain, as though she has touched atomic waste. In fact, many of the poems are addressed, rather reproachfully, to an unnamed male figure who is both lover and betrayer. This figure is sometimes a father and sometimes a husband and, occasionally, George Washington, who serves as a sort of paragon of virtue, a great generative and controlling force, in Miss Wakoski's private mythology.

Stephen Stepanchev. NL. Dec. 2, 1968. p. 18

Diane Wakoski's new book, *Inside the Blood Factory,* presents at first reading a bewildering array of talent. She can work in many different forms: prose paragraphs, the short, tight lines of Williams or H.D., the free surrealistic movement, the loping Whitmanesque line. In one poem, "Sestina for the Home Gardener," she creates a witty variation on that ancient form, maintaining the precision of the mode, while lengthening the lines and pouring out the images in a profusion that threatens to break the pattern, but never quite does so. At the same time the volume shows a similar range of themes and materials: an elegy to the dead, a memorial of a father in the Navy, images of ancient Egypt, George Washington, Beethoven, a sequence to a man who drives a "silver Ferrari," a sequence based upon the Tarot deck, or a poem about a scene where a mother slices oranges for her invalid son.

This list of subjects may suggest a little of the range of Miss Wakoski's vision, which touches with a generous affection the things of life and finds a home for them within the self. . . . All this variety of movement, whether in rhythm or in image, builds up to the total impact of a powerful poetic mind, continuously absorbing and recreating the current of experience, pooling it in sections that hold together by her deliberate technique of repetition. . . . Out of it all comes some of the most striking poetry produced in New York City during the past decade.

Louis L. Martz. YR. Summer, 1969. pp. 603–5

The dominant theme in this latest volume of poems [*The Motorcycle Betrayal Poems*], in case you haven't guessed, is *betrayal*. It's in the title, in the dedication, and in most of the poems. "The only man who's never/betrayed me/is my accountant," she says, which tempts us to conclude, syllogistically, that he is, therefore, no man. The assumption throughout her work is that men are by nature as prone to betrayal as mortality. Just as she can not resist mentioning it in a poem, we find it hard to resist mentioning that her father left when she was two. But psychiatry and poetry are antipathetic; it's unnecessary to violate her psyche. In spite of the fact that she insists that her life is laid bare in her poems, we should force ourselves to act as though there is a gap between life and art, between Diane Wakoski the private person and Diane Wakoski the public artist. Let her deny it; it's still true. It is always true—of every writer. So any comments we make here must really be about the voice in the poems, not the author's personal voice. Everybody acts a little funny in front of a camera. . . .

That Diane Wakoski has talent few people can deny. Sometimes that talent produces a startling image, a great passage, or even a near-great poem. But at other times that talent is ruined by speed, ambition, and self-pity.

Robert DeMaria. MedR. Spring, 1972. p. 55

[Wakoski] cultivates the longer poem; although there are short poems in [*Greed*], she often requires considerable length to say what she wants to say . . . yet she says it, and that is what counts. The reader has the feeling of a strong, centrifugal force, rarely centripetal. . . .

Her facility is particularly apt for describing *desires*, pleasure, and wishful thinking. When she writes about pain she is less convincing; there is much violence in her book—blood, bruises, scars. . . .

Her desires are open, liberal, attractive, and spendthrift; she has a marvelous desire to encompass everything.

John R. Carpenter. Poetry.
June, 1972. pp. 165–6

Diane Wakoski knows how to make words into poems. Her precise and straightforward style organizes not-quite-reality, and pushes it into the right contact. At all times in these two books [*The Motorcycle Betrayal Poems* and *Smudging*] Wakoski is in control, she is the craftsman. Although her poems are not traditional structures, she builds them solidly with words which feel chosen, with repetition of images throughout a poem . . . and with exact observation. . . .

These two books are remarkable because Diane Wakoski has successfully balanced the life of emotion against the life of intelligent reflection, through the medium of poetry. The poems sound true in your heart, true in your mind, and true in your ear.

Debra Hulbert. PrS. Spring, 1973. pp. 81–3

Diane Wakoski has been unreadable for five years. Our good writers are liable to terrible slumps, though none has beaten Wordsworth's record. Personalists are always by definition in danger of substituting liking for principle. In *Greed, Parts 8, 9, 11* she's pulling out of it. As it was you had to tell students what books of hers not to read (everything after *Inside the Blood Factory*). The words are still too conceptual, moving at speech's rate without its weight, but that rate and the lumber-pile of line *become* weight (again) in this. You have to read her with love, though, to see it. She's *over* writing to audience expectations (or to a mythic self-image, as in the hideous Breadloaf lecture), by the brave device of parts 8 and 9, and begins to be clear what metaphor, for instance, won't do. She's never (or only once) *merely* cute. *Greed* 11 really begins to be a way to write lines that are sense-units but not for that reason stupid. The book is anchored on her but no longer exploits her. She may write bad things again, but after this won't print them. Bet.

Gerald Burns. SWR. Summer, 1973. p. 280

WARREN, ROBERT PENN (1905–   )

Robert Penn Warren is a poet perhaps excessively conscious of the great themes of poetry: death as waiting horror; time—or rather the memory of events in time—as a source of disillusion giving special urgency to the task of abstracting moments of meaning from the meaningless flux; nature as background and scene of the human drama, and as alternately a threat to or escape from moral dilemmas; love as a dangerous ideal and yet, with luck, a blessed reality. I say too conscious because we are often made uncomfortable by the attitude Warren takes toward his people and the circumstances of their fate. He knows—or seems to know—their meanings too well. Adept as he is in the uses of irony, he seldom falls into the obvious traps of sentimentality, but he also rarely surprises us into new and unexpected insights about the moral meaning of experience. Once we become familiar with his scheme of things, we become conscious of prearranged conclusions. Warren is better at keeping his characters in suspense—usually confused or wrongheaded, they are always learning through suffering—than his readers. There is, of course, nothing wrong in the attempt to moralize experience; but the experience should seem large and unruly enough to resist encapsulation. Warren's "rage for order" is sometimes in excess of the felt life to be ordered.

John Rees Moore. SoR. Spring, 1968. pp. 320–1

It has now been fifteen years since Robert Penn Warren returned to lyric poetry in the writings of his volume *Promises: Poems 1954–1956*. His new volume, *Incarnations*, fulfills those promises. Warren has moved now into subtle and firm command of his own idiom, with an effect well-described by his chosen title. These poems incarnate, by movement of spoken words, by images of fruit and sea and city, a sense of spirit flowing through all existence, or as he puts it in one poem, a sense of "the furious energies of nature." These are sequences with many settings: first, a Mediterranean island off the coast of France; next, the dismal setting of a Southern prison; then, in New York City, the scene of a pedestrian accident near old Penn Station; and lastly, a few poems set in the mysterious "Enclaves" of memory. What is most remarkable about these poems is their quiet deftness in weaving together a universe of sights and sounds within the mind of this sensitive speaker.

Louis L. Martz. *YR*. Summer, 1969. p. 596

[Warren] has long been known as a founding father of the New Criticism and an upholder of the impersonality of art, and yet, reading the *Selected Poems*, one sees him as an intensely personal writer of an almost Wordsworthian kind, constantly reverting to the experiences, scenes and legends of his boyhood. Certainly, in his most recent work, one has a sense of being given successive insights into the unfolding of a poet's mind rather than of being shown a series of icons. At times in his career Warren's attempted combination of native allegiance and Eliotesque literary sophistication rather noticeably failed him, as in his long poem, "The Ballad of Billie Potts," where the folk-rock vigor of the central narrative is hardly matched by the lugubrious imitations of late Eliot in the interpolated reflective passages. . . . In contrast, his most recent work has remarkable ease and a striking intensity of language, both of them, it seems, the fruit of many years of application to the craft of poetry.

Bernard Bergonzi. *SoR*. Winter, 1970. p. 209

The "vision" of Robert Penn Warren's *Audubon* is of two kinds: one invokes that pictorial sense which allowed Audubon to observe and record the birds of America; the other, that sense of the dream which prompted his grand project in the wilderness. This doubleness, along with his uncertainty as to his origins and identity, gives a peculiarly American definition to the Audubon of Warren's poem. His fascination in the wilderness and his business enterprises in Europe; his immersion in the texture of natural things and the abstraction necessary to his great and public design; the precision of his rifle, which was the necessarily brutal instrument for getting the "material" for the precision of his art—

this play of contradictory forces makes him seem a type of the American artist. Indeed, some of this same doubleness characterizes Warren's poetry: on the one hand, he sees events as part of a great fabric of gothic American history, as in *Brother to Dragons*, while on the other he offers modest and precise renderings of things seen and felt, near yet hard to explain, as in "The Day Dr. Knox Did It." There is in his work an impulse toward final and epic conception, combined with the instinct for exact perception in the tentative forms of lyric and conversation. And it is perhaps for this reason that the figure of Audubon appeals to him: as an example of how vision and fact can be brought together. The achieved balance works to make this Robert Penn Warren's finest poem.

Norman Martien. PR. No. 1, 1971. p. 122

For me, reading a new book by Robert Penn Warren ([*Meet Me in the Green Glen*] is his ninth novel) is like encountering once again a stout-hearted father-figure as dependable (which is not to say predictable) as the day is long. I know ahead of time that the book—whether novel, poems, stories or essays—will be authentic, gritty with felt life. Approaching a new novel, I know, or think I know, it will have some of the virtues of the conventional popular novel—recognizable and accessible plot and shape, for instance. The setting will be rural, the action tangled and bloody, the characters country people. The tone of the prose used to dramatize their lives might be in turn lyrical, elegiac, satirical. In that prose, that narrative, will float certain obsessive images, certain brooding abstractions which will, in the fullness of time, meld, pay off, sweep the table.

James Boatwright. NYT. Nov. 7, 1971. p. 6

WELTY, EUDORA (1909–   )

In *Losing Battles* the traditional drama of Agrarian *versus* Industrial—appearing obliquely and yet in a completely significant way—takes on a complexity demanding an explication hardly even to be begun in a summary comment. In this story—which may well be Miss Welty's greatest achievement and one that assures her, if any further assurance is needed, of her place among the great American story tellers of this century—we are again in the domain of a fictional county. It is Boone County in the northeast hill country of Mississippi. . . .

[The conflict] sounds a little like Thomas Hardy, and it is to some extent. What finally comes from the clash between Miss Julia and the family tribe of the Banner community, however, is the result of Miss Welty's genius for seeing life not so much in the manner of Hardy as in that of her favorite novelist, Jane Austen. She transforms the drama of the dispossession of the country people in America into a highly ironic comedy of universal human motives.

Lewis P. Simpson. SoR. Summer,
1970. pp. xxii–xxiii

It is not craftsmanship which has been the most important factor in determining [Eudora Welty's] new place in American letters. One suspects that critics have finally begun to realize that, far from being narrow in scope, her work is prodigious in its diversity and reveals a mind and sensibility capable of almost anything. There is no typical Eudora Welty story in the sense that there is a typical Ernest Hemingway story. She may have stolen from herself on occasion, but she has never precisely re-created an earlier work, and most of her stories are unique in the way that true literature always is. There is nothing like "The Wide Net" anywhere else in fiction, and at least a dozen of her stories stand alone in the same way.

On the other hand, quite apart from these earlier works, *Losing Battles* is itself a novel on which to build a literary reputation. Like *Delta Wedding*, to which it bears some superficial resemblance, it is essentially a story about the family and its larger manifestation, the community. But *Losing Battles* has social, historical, and philosophical dimensions which are not to be found in the earlier work, and it is these dimensions which have undoubtedly convinced some of the more sociologically-minded critics that Miss Welty deserves a place in the first rank of contemporary novelists.

Thomas H. Landess. SwR.
Autumn, 1971. pp. 626–7

Eudora Welty's novel, *The Optimist's Daughter*, which first appeared in *The New Yorker* of March 15, 1969, is a miracle of compression, the kind of book, small in scope but profound in its implications, that rewards a lifetime of work. Its style is at the service of a story that follows its nose with the instincts of a good hunting dog never losing the scent of its quarry. And its story has all those qualities peculiar to the finest short novels: a theme that vibrates with overtones, suspense and classical inevitability.

Known as a "Southern regionalist," Miss Welty is too good for pigeon-holing labels. Though she has stayed close to home, two interlocking notions have been demonstrated in her fiction: how easily the ordinary turns into legend, and how firmly the exotic is grounded in the banal. They are subjects only partly dependent on locale. In *The Optimist's Daughter*, we are in the South once more, but a South where real distinctions are made between Texas and Mississippi, and Mississippi and West Virginia. And if place has been Miss Welty's touchstone, the pun implicit in the word "place" comes alive in her new novel; its colloquial meaning—caste, class, position—is as important as its geographical one.

Howard Moss. NYT. May 21, 1972. p. 1

Innocence enmeshed by schemers, gullibility abused, a harmless, hopeless simplicity too grand for deceitful living has been a theme in Eudora Welty's fiction since *The Robber Bridegroom*, 1942. . . . But in Miss Welty's new novel [*The Optimist's Daughter*] this very innocence ceases to be comic or charming and becomes lethal, a crucial failure to do business with the world, a special vulnerability, not a peculiar state of grace; not innocence at all, finally, but a form of guilt, the weakness both of individual men and a whole Southern style. . . . The book is so powerful . . . stern, and funny in a way that has nothing to do with Miss Welty's earlier comic writing. Or rather, that has all too much to do with it, since it is concerned with taking it back. The engaging and irresponsible Uncle Daniel, say, of *The Ponder Heart*, has become . . . the helpless judge of *The Optimist's Daughter*, dignified but too delicate, not half as fit for life as he thought.

Michael Wood. NYR. June 29, 1972. p. 9

The Optimist's Daughter is an unlikely triumph, combining Chekhovian understatement with Faulknerian verve, displaying the author's powers at their best. She has lost nothing over the years: her unerring ear, the comic vitality of her characters, the authenticity of furniture and flowers and small-town mores remain compelling. And the profundity of her moral imagination has deepened. Little of obvious significance happens in this book. An old man dies, his daughter grieves, his young second wife feels an injustice has been done her (on her birthday!). There is a southern funeral, unexpectedly invaded by the wife's implausible relatives. The daughter, Laurel, returns to Chicago, where she works. She thinks about her own long-dead husband, and about what her marriage meant. What makes such events important is the penetration with which the characters are judged and the intensity with which they are loved.

Patricia Meyer Spacks. HdR.
Autumn, 1972. p. 509

WEST, NATHANAEL (1906–1940)

West's satire reached to every aspect of society. Perhaps he may be most accurately called, in Kenneth Burke's phrase, "a universal satirist" who, unlike the "satiric propagandist," refuses to make a "clear alignment of friends and foes" and condemns both. West adamantly opposed society's excesses and confusions, its muddy and absurd antics, its compromises and corruptions. But behind his irony lay a sense of the possibilities for good of man and society. This was a faith which his experience could neither support nor entirely destroy. He was as passionate about his hopes in private as he was vehement in depicting his horrors in his fiction. . . . Pope justified his satire of fools in *The Dunciad* by explaining that they became dunces by neglecting their "lawful callings." West, similarly, does not satirize men themselves, only the masks men wear and the illusions they cherish: these are their unlawful callings. Though he lived in and wrote of a world riddled with delusion, he seems to have believed with Freud that the future of illusion could be its disappearance. His satire was designed to return man to himself, to his "lawful callings."

Jay Martin. *Nathanael West: The Art of His Life* (Farrar). 1970. p. 320

The world of West, we must never forget for a moment, that "peculiar half-world," as he called it himself, escaped all the clichés of politics, even of the left-wing orthodoxy to which he himself subscribed. Apocalyptics was his special province; and for the sake of a vision of the End of Things, he was willing to sacrifice what his Communist mentors had taught him was a true picture of society. Once out of his books, he felt obliged to apologize for his vision (writing to Jack Conroy, for instance, "If I put into *The Day of the Locust* any of the sincere, honest people who work here and are making such a great, progressive fight . . . [he is talking about Hollywood] the whole fabric of the peculiar half-world which I attempted to create would be badly torn by them"); but once inside them, he remained utterly faithful to that vision, however alien it might be to the Stalinist's theoretical America.

Leslie Fiedler. *Collected Essays*, vol. 2 (Stein and Day). 1971. p. 240

The special, ugly-poetic flavor of West's fiction—the sense of "flowers that smelled of feet"—sprang from a contradiction in his response toward emotion in others. On the one hand, West was repelled by the "secondhand" dreams and feelings of the mass of Americans. On the other, he had—as a result of managing two hotels during the Depression —an acute and aching knowledge of their undeniable suffering. Steaming open letters in the hotels and later cultivating Hollywood grotesques, West was a voyeur of suffering and, guiltily, he knew he had nothing to offer the bored and cheated, except a compassion that they did not want and could not use. His brief books, volleys of scorn and pain, are acts of a generous despair. And yet, so little hopeful was West, so cynical was his generosity, that he ungenerously earned a living by tossing off cheap film scripts in Hollywood—betraying in one medium those whom he pitied in another.

All told, it is false to speak of West—as Jay Martin does—as a moralist in the great tradition of those who have had, in Yeats's words, dreams "of an impossibly noble life."

Calvin Bedient. PR. No. 3, 1971. p. 349

After Hemingway, the "unmistakable" as the point of style, his special clarity and grace, was to become a faint memory in the violently flashing images with which Nathanael West rendered the atomized emotions of *Miss Lonelyhearts* and the surrealistically overpainted Hollywood of *The Day of the Locust*. West was as prophetic of a new consciousness in fiction as Hemingway had been in his day; his instinct about the ever-growing disturbance around him was to survive him (he was killed speeding to Scott Fitzgerald's funeral in 1940), although even his best writing was impatient, unsteady, and composed by violently oscillating passages, like action painting twenty years later.

Alfred Kazin. Bright Book of
Life (Little). 1973. pp. 17–8

WHARTON, EDITH (1862–1937)

Mrs. Wharton seems to be saying that, from a spiritual perspective, society, considered as the supreme lawgiver, is an illusion or a downright fiction. It is an arena of distraction, a kind of Vanity Fair. What *The House of Mirth* asserts is that no life possesses spiritual vitality until it is motivated by belief in its own significance. Obviously, the enigmatic and revelatory word that Lily does not achieve until the end of her life is "faith." Only with it can a successful quest be pursued against all the equivocating counter-claims and inducements of society, against the ostensible absurdity of life itself. . . .

Faith, as Edith Wharton defines it, is no generalized and temperamental optimism; it is, instead, an almost mystical assurance that only moral action can save the ever-threatened continuity of human existence. Beset by dangers inherent in social arrangements, man clings to survival by the thread of his moral instincts; he is, at his best, motivated by what Mrs. Wharton calls, in *Sanctuary*, "this passion of charity for the race." In other words, goodness is useful, and men and women must, under pain of extinction, bequeath it to their children.

James W. Gargano. *AL*.
March, 1972. pp. 140–1

In her best, most representative works, Mrs. Wharton continually returned to the idea of tradition and the need of viable modes of cultural transmission as important factors affecting the character of man's social history. She continually argued the necessity of the individual's commitment to the cultural tradition; the danger of alienation from it; the catastrophe which ensues when social upheavals like revolution, anarchy, and war destroy the slowly and delicately spun web of that tradition; and the necessity of imaginatively preserving—if necessary even reconstructing—the precious values of the past. Her artistic treatment of the theme of tradition usually involved two methods. The first was to dramatize the importance for men of the web of culture, manners, and mores which enclose them and to warn of the disaster in store for those who become culturally deracinated or alienated and for those who destroy the delicate web in a radical obsession to reform it. And the other method, evident in the final years of her life, was an impulse to reconstruct—archeologically, as it were—the social world of her youth: the traditions which vitalized the culture of Old New York in the period from about 1840 to 1880. She hoped to revive the memory of a set of slowly evolved cultural values suddenly wiped out by a succession of destructive changes in American life beginning in the 1880's—including the rise of the industrial plutocracy ("the lords of Pittsburgh," as she called them); massive immigration which totally altered the ethnic character of New York City; the first World War, the depression, and the New Deal; and the nationalistic hatreds, at the close of her life in 1937, building toward the Second World War.

James W. Tuttleton. *YR*.
Summer, 1972. pp. 564–5

The value of [Wharton's] work may have little to do with its hidden origins; but creative work, as a writer, gardener, and interior decorator, was clearly what rescued her. Without that she would have succumbed to the panics of her childhood, the breakdowns of her early married years, and the neurotic depressions and exhaustions of maturity. A woman of incredible energy and vitality, she kept her balance with the help of a relentless social round, but it was literary accomplishment that supplied the gyroscope of her selfhood.

From the abundance of her bleak frustrations Wharton wrung a view of human possibility that must touch any perceptive reader. She may seem to deal with the evolution of manners and the woes of marriage. But she really employs these materials to illustrate deep and persuasive moral insights. A story like "Bunner Sisters," a novella like *Ethan Frome* or *Summer*, achieves its immense power by the victory of her imagination over the apparent straitness of her background. In these amazing works she deals with the most impoverished of American lives, always implying that in the lowest as in the highest strata of society the chance of sinking yet farther or of aspiring yet higher remains present. No class is exempt from the dangers of pride or the chastening rod of humiliation.

Irvin Ehrenpreis. NYR. Nov. 13, 1975. p. 6

WHEELWRIGHT, JOHN BROOKS (1897–1940)

John Wheelwright, descended in all branches of his family tree from Boston Brahmins, and certainly in the thick of things, literary and political, in his day, was nonetheless, perhaps because of the sheer force of his personality, a singularly independent poet. He was more open to international influences and more engaged than most of his contemporaries. He was a Trotskyite, an Anglo-Catholic, and a most perceptive critic of architecture, and as poet, revolutionary, architect, and Catholic he was a totally committed activist. He was also one of the last of his kind in America, a great aristocratic eccentric.

His poetry is full of hidden references and echoes. It does not need notes, but if anyone chose to annotate it, it would require far more apparatus per line than Eliot's or Pound's, but unlike theirs, this is not at all apparent. He was one of the best-read persons in every imaginable field that I have ever met, capable of carrying on a conversation about the snails of South America, the theoretical foundations of Russian anarchism, and the medieval English Rite of Sarum simultaneously. He was struck down late at night by a drunken driver on the bridge over the

Charles River which his father had built, and died at the age of forty-three. His early death was an immeasurable loss to American poetry.

Kenneth Rexroth. American Poetry
in the Twentieth Century (Herder
and Herder). 1971. pp. 116–7

In John Wheelwright we confront both a poet and a place, indissolubly mixed in every mode and mood—the old Yankee element at an especially grim moment. We hear the hanging judge and smile at the Hasty Pudding clown. We are whisked to the far Asiatic reaches of New England spirituality where rococo costume drama oddly consorts—as it does in the Bible—with the roaring beasts and lurid colors of the Apocalypse, the "Apocalypse of Wheels."

R. W. Flint. Parnassus. Fall–
Winter, 1973. p. 47

WILBUR, RICHARD (1921–   )

Wilbur does not suppose, as Poe does, that the intellect and the moral sense are inimical to the apprehension of beauty. Quite the contrary. In Wilbur's poetry beauty is realized only upon the exercise of man's intellectual and moral faculties. This condition has much to do with Wilbur's style and tone. The poems have, characteristically, a moral design, and this design is, if anything, emphasized rather than merely insinuated. Similarly, the poems are deliberate meditations. They rely heavily on argument and debate and they use much intellectual irony, paradox, and ambiguity. These techniques are not employed in slavish imitation of what was, in Wilbur's formative years, a fashion in poetry. They reflect, rather, the value he places on the life of the mind.

In general, Wilbur's poems envision two kinds of change, disintegrative and metamorphic. Wilbur suggests that a genuine reverence for life can be attained if one has the capacity to see beyond disintegrative change, into the metamorphic and regenerative life of the universe. Metamorphic change is not without its own tragic consequences, but the tragedy is always redeemed by the fulness of being which metamorphosis effects. Insight into this redemptive process is possible only when both the intellect and the moral sense are intact. Wilbur's poetry is therefore much concerned with a certain quality of vision, a certain way of seeing into things. The presence of this vision is registered by perception of what he calls the beautiful changes.

John P. Farrell. WSCL. Winter, 1967. p. 76

The title of Wilbur's second book was *Ceremony*, and that word still expresses, I think, much of his most central approach to the poem. To Wilbur . . . it seems to me that form is a means of understanding, the shape of the poem one of the most serious comments on the meaning of the poem. And it seems also that form functions as a kind of charm: ceremony is the way in which the tissue of events is not only understood, but made moral and substantial. . . .

An intelligent affection, and an intelligent remorse; a sense of event in a long and various context: these are the qualities that seem most central here. They will not allow a poetry of extremes: the howl of absolute emotion or the arid geometries of absolute intellection. Aware both of people and their contexts, they celebrate that difficult thing: the simultaneous tenuousness and necessity of civilization.

William Dickey. HdR. Summer, 1969. p. 364

Although he is recognized as a major American poet, Wilbur is not prolific. *Walking to Sleep* comes eight years after *Advice to a Prophet* (1961) and consists of only twenty-four poems and eleven translations. Wilbur admirers, however, will be gratified by the usual Wilbur virtues and, perhaps, by suggestions of some new directions.

Elegance, wit, a quiet yet sensuous tone, and careful craftsmanship are as evident as ever. Wilbur's characteristic concern with form is also evident. Eighteen of his twenty-four poems rhyme and many of his earlier forms recur. . . . Previously the major criticism of Wilbur has been that his poetry, while superb technically, has been too restrained, too indirect; he has, his critics argue, too fully accepted Eliot's doctrine of the extinction of personality. These critics may find *Walking to Sleep* mildly encouraging in that Wilbur does present several first person poems in which the first person is clearly Wilbur himself. . . .

Walking to Sleep also offers more of Wilbur's nature poetry, a poetry which seems a dynamic life force in the universe and perceives analogues between the operation of this life force in nature and in man.

Paul Cummins. CP. Spring, 1970. pp. 72–5

The truth is that Mr. Wilbur has never allowed his gifts the freedom they deserve. He has shortened the leash whenever the creatures ran too near the onlooker. An instinct for simile, unobtrusive though precise, is applied to a boy feeding himself as he reads: "The left hand, like a mother-bird in flight/Brings him a sandwich." It also reaches the sound of tanks approaching a city in wartime, "like the clearing of a monstrous throat." But neither image snaps at the reader. Mr. Wilbur's tact would not let it. Just as accurately and expressively, he represents the leaves of thyme as "a green countlessness" and the heavenly constellations as "grand, kept appointments of the air." But his brilliant descriptive powers are never stretched so far as to indulge the poet at the risk of tiring the reader. Perhaps they might be. Mr. Wilbur's humour (two attempts at satire fail) irradiates his wit and word play. In "Seed Leaves," a poem that Herrick could not improve, it gives the most benign humanity to the birth of a plant. But sometimes wit should run wild. These hints are not meant to say that the poet should transform himself into another person. Rather they mean he should be more himself. He should let his audience find him, whoever he decides to be.

TLS. May 21, 1971. p. 580

Those privileged to see the Phoenix Theatre production of *The School for Wives* in Richard Wilbur's translation know how beautifully it played and how merrily it was received by the audience. How does it read? I wondered *that* when I saw it. Now I know. It reads beautifully too, and is a total delight. Wilbur has *re-created* the French original with all the wit, polish, grace, pace, and clarity of a master translator. In the natural contexts of the play, nature wins out. The *young* lady gets the *young* man, and that lunatic ass of an Arnolphe is spared what would have been a disastrous marriage—all in the salutary confines of rhymed couplets. It is like eating one's cake and having it too. Ultimately, *The School for Wives* is an artistic triumph both for Molière and for Wilbur.

George Meredith complained in his essay *The Idea of Comedy*: "Translating Molière is like humming an air one has heard performed by an accomplished violinist of the pure tone without flourish." Richard Wilbur has changed all that, permanently.

Philip Murray. *Poetry.* July, 1972. p. 231

WILDER, THORNTON (1897–1975)

Is it [Wilder's] fault he has had the dramatic sense to anticipate his audience's objections? The answer is that more than in any other art first-rate drama demands first-rate audiences. Perhaps Wilder has been overly conscious of his role as mediator between highbrow sensibility and middlebrow taste, perhaps he has too strenuously adapted his intellectual proclivities to the demand of the bourgeois theatre's "group mind." . . . The greatest of modern dramatists enlarged audience taste precisely by not conceding to it. But Wilder in play after play feels compelled to underline the obvious or provide a graspable theme "nugget." . . .

Wilder's almost maddening tendency to aphorize contradicts his avowed aim, articulated in the Introduction to *Three Plays*, to disturb middleclass complacency: the theatre he rejected was "not only inadequate, it was evasive . . . it aimed to be soothing." He is enmeshed rather in the snares of what Dwight MacDonald has termed "midcult," the submerging of complexities in the tepid ooze of a cozy universality and folksiness. . . . One notes these tendencies with regret, for Wilder's dramatic instinct and theatrical inventiveness are undeniable. Most of his plays, particularly *The Skin of Our Teeth*, hold the stage despite their defects. One keeps wishing that he hadn't played it so safe and that along with Joyce's ideas he had been more influenced by the Irishman's artistic intransigence.

Gerald Rabkin in *The Forties*,
edited by Warren French
(Everett/Edwards). 1969. p. 120

Between the affirmation of earthly life and the difficulty or impossibility of ever fully understanding it there is a wide gap that perhaps reaches its extreme in the "Alcestiad." Alcestis wishes to serve her god in order to live in "reality"—she wishes to merge with the divine. She disavows earthly life, but later, through great happiness and intense suffering, the god whom she wishes to serve shows her that even love is not the meaning of life. Thus she spans the widest arc of all the Wilder figures.

In all these works of Wilder, the religious question How does one live? is never formulated as a theory. If there is something absolute by which human beings can orient their lives, it is neither the state nor society nor the rationale of technology. All these authorities have their limits beyond which questions such as the relation of the individual to the universal become crucial.

We cannot ignore the theme of the future. Thornton Wilder's work, in an immaterial sense, contains the man of the twentieth century who, in the maelstrom of toppling orders, has frighteningly lost his orientation. Faced with the question of how to live, what is left for him but to trust, like Caesar, the promise that grows out of the unknowable?

Hermann Stresau. *Thornton Wilder*
(Ungar). 1971. p. 103

This wonderfully entertaining novel [*Theophilus North*] is really several novels. . . . The writing, most of it in dialogue, is supple, civilized, radiant with wisdom. It is an irresistible book.

Its sunny disposition at the close of a long and distinguished career can only be matched, of late, by Thomas Mann's *Felix Krull*. There is the same delight in deception in both. . . . Granville Hicks has suggested that Theophilus is really Christ. This seems to me a vulgarization stem-ming from that kind of symbol-hunting criticism in which everything is invariably what it was *not* for the author. Wilder is simply not writing this kind of fiction. Theophilus is what he is, a very real person mounted on a bicycle in a real city, both a sinner and a saint of sorts. The whole point of one section at the end, in which he is taken as some sort of faith-healer, is to show that only God can perform miracles, not man. In any event, to be able to write a book as genial as this, and one as wholly unassuming, at close on eighty years of age is itself a testimony to the human race. I was extremely sorry to put it down.

Geoffrey Wagner. *National Review*.
Dec. 7, 1973. p. 1368

In a sense, [*Theophilus North*] puts the reader in touch with two grand old men, Wilder himself and Theophilus, who tells the story of his 30th summer from the vantage point of his old age. It is a lively story, a series of picaresque incidents now tender, now hilarious, now satiric, always absorbing. But it is also a comment from a seasoned writer on the relationship between life and literature. . . .

Both Theophilus and Wilder bring to mind a third old man, Prospero. We *are* such stuff as dreams are made on, they all remind us; and perhaps nothing is more real than the "insubstantial pageant" that a gifted memory and imagination can create through the ordered beauty of language. The reminder is timely.

Elizabeth M. Woods. *Am.*
Dec. 15, 1973. p. 472

WILLIAMS, TENNESSEE (1914–   )

Often clearly aspiring to the conditions of poetry, Williams creates for himself an advantage which is not always available to other dramatists who start from the realistic or naturalistic base: like Synge and O'Casey, he puts his words into the mouths of an essentially imaginative people who speak in the rhythms and colorful imagery of a region favorable to poetry.

Even more to the point . . . by staging his dramas in a realm just so much apart from "average" American life as the deep South and by having his characters speak in the distinctive language of that realm apart, Williams succeeds in distancing his plays from the purely realistic mode to a degree sufficient to justify and disguise a certain characteristic exaggeration and distortion of reality which permeates his entire canon. Under the speech of most of his characters there runs the faint but unmistakable thorough bass of grotesque folk comedy. The tone provided by this suggestion of the comic folk tale varies according to Williams's intention, and, accordingly, the success of its effect depends upon the amount of distance he would have us put between the characters and ourselves.

Leland Starnes. MD. Feb., 1970. p. 357

Perhaps Williams' quest in his journey of violence is to destroy the myth of art because it demonstrates yet another spiritual aspiration of man. If this is his goal, bred out of the extreme disillusionment of his romanticism, he has succeeded but too well in his last plays. For it is increasingly apparent upon a closer inspection of these plays that the host of idealist-heroes who are bent upon satisfying their sexual urges through the dramatist's superimposed veil of sexual-spiritual sublimation are in reality, *poseurs*. The world of these plays is one in which the pretense to spiritual need is arbitrarily welded to physical cravings. Punishment is subsequently meted out through violence. Thus the irreconcilable fact always emerges: spirituality and moral truth are given the lie; they are sheer deceits, unattainable because men and life are irredeemably corrupt and without purpose. . . .

It is not a violence that grows from within the life condition of the plays, but a violence superimposed upon the characters by the playwright as a means of punishment.

James Hashim. Players. Feb.–
March, 1970. p. 127

Williams gave Southern grotesques dignity on the Broadway stage. Even the farcical *Rose Tattoo* is peopled with giants by comparison with [Caldwell's] *Tobacco Road*. Though shocking sexuality rather than human warmth may account for his Broadway success, Williams has managed to combine shocking sexuality with human warmth, sometimes in the same play. . . . Like O'Neill and Miller, Williams wrote few organically flawless dramas. He does not often hammer like O'Neill, he does not often preach like Miller, but he too often indulges in gratuitous violence and irrelevant symbol. At his best, however—*The Glass Menagerie, A Streetcar Named Desire*, first version of *Cat on a Hot Tin Roof, The Night of the Iguana*, and even *Camino Real*—Williams expands American stage dialogue in vocabulary, image, rhythm, and range.

Ruby Cohn. Dialogue in American
Drama (Indiana). 1971. p. 129

Though Tennessee Williams' *Out cry* is a two-character play it is essentially a soliloquy. . . . The two characters are brother and sister: each is part of the other and both are one person—the author.

The theme is fear. A moral impasse is at its root. It is nearly impossible to go on living when one feels oneself cut off from the surrounding world. Retreating into oneself from dread produces an isolation wherein there is no sound connection with either the self or other selves. This induces something akin to incest or schizophrenia; insanity is close by. . . .

I have too much respect for Williams to say that this has become his permanent state of mind. Even in *Out cry* there is much of his theatrical ingenuity and power of statement—it is by no means as unintelligible as some assert—but it is too limited in its symbolic imagery and construction (its import is sentimentally existential) to hold us for two hours. It was probably indispensable for Williams to write this confessional piece; until he had done so he might have found it unthinkable to proceed further in his career. But now that he has written it and seen it produced, we can only hope that he will turn his gaze outward again. No matter how far he ranges, his presence will still be palpable.

Harold Clurman. Nation.
March 19, 1973. p. 380

In *A Streetcar Named Desire* Williams found images and rhythms that are still part of the way we think and feel and move. Stanley Kowalski and Blanche Du Bois belong in the general company of Hemingway's Jake Barnes and Brett Ashley or Fitzgerald's Gatsby and Daisy as archetypal figures, as real as our dreams, nightmares and desires—in other words, realer than most of us. In this play as in no other, Williams was able to do his particular thing, to take the fragments of his divided self and turn them into the dramatis personae of an ideal conflict. . . .

In Williams a profound puritanism warred with a fierce sensuality, the feminine warred with the masculine, poetic idealism warred with what Yeats called "the foul rag-and-bone shop of the heart." In Blanche and Stanley he found the perfect objective correlatives for these opposites and he created one of the few authentic protagonist-antagonist relationships in contemporary theater. . . .

Jack Kroll. Nwk. May 7, 1973. pp. 109–10

A romantic, a solitary fantasist of desire, [Williams] can combine poetic delicacy with primal violence, capture the frailty of man's spirit and his voracity. Enacting the explosive drama of the subconscious, Williams also exposes a civilization in which deviants or outsiders, the "fugitive kind" always perish. These, however, are as often victims of their own guilt or illusion as they are prey to the world's brutality.

His vision owes something to the Southern gothic tradition, from Poe to Faulkner, and owes even more to the erotic mysteries of D. H. Lawrence, whom Williams admires. His dramatic sensationalism—his ready use of nymphomania, homosexuality, rape, castration, murder, cannibalism—which may account for his popular success, should also be seen as a projection of an imagination haunted by death. At the same time, Williams fastens on sexuality as a metaphor of life. The perversion of desire reflects the identity of his characters; its absence defines the terrors of their isolation. His ultimately religious apprehension of love prompts him to portray redemptive figures in the composite image of Christ, Orpheus, and Dionysus, who embody sacrifice, poetry and nature in their mutilated flesh. Savage and sometimes even malignant, the dark gods promise man no pabulum, no happiness.

Ihab Hassan. Contemporary American Literature (Ungar). 1973. pp. 141–2

WILLIAMS, WILLIAM CARLOS (1883–1963)

It does not particularly matter how we approach [Williams's] poems; provided we approach them. It is good to meet them with a sense of their historical pressure, the sense of the weight of feeling behind them. Some readers are first attracted by Williams's personality, the impression of being at ease, informal, taking high risks: there are no Sabbaths in his week. Others simply listen to the words as they come. The "propriety of cadence" which Charles Tomlinson admired in Williams is a constant delight. Reading him is like going through a diary, skipping here and there when the voltage of the writing is low, but marking the passages which are wonderfully charged with feeling.

Denis Donoghue. The Ordinary Universe (Macmillan—N.Y.). 1968. p. 188

Williams is the greatest prosodist of his generation because he is the greatest poet. Perhaps he really did believe in prehensile feet, and worked entirely by ear, but it's extremely doubtful. A lifetime spent as a doctor, especially a pediatrician handling troubled mothers, had taught him a certain canniness and subterfuge in dealing with the will to delusion. Whitman's ceremonial chant, Sandburg's folk speech, Ezra Pound's echoes of the Latin hexameter and elegiac distich, H.D.'s strophic imitations of the choruses of Euripides, Goethe, Hölderin, Matthew Arnold, the sprung rhythms of Gerard Manley Hopkins and Robert Bridges, the *vers libre* of Vielé-Griffin and the different free verse of the generation after Apollinaire, all these explorations are pulled together and synthesized by Williams.

Kenneth Rexroth. *American Poetry in the Twentieth Century* (Herder and Herder). 1971. p. 80

Not free, like Pound and Eliot, to study and by temperament restless, Williams naturally turned against "literature" and sought a way counter to theirs with the bare hands and the naked mind, sought heroically to make a virtue of his necessity, out of the here and now, the local and the immense moment. Harried by his doctoring ("He saw by his own account a million and a half patients and delivered 2,000 babies.") and by his doubts and despair, he found his therapy in writing. . . .

Embattled and embittered before Eliot's victory, Williams knew a deep need to justify himself and to deny others, contradictorily enough in the name of openness and all-inclusiveness. Yet such an attitude is, when enunciated into a rigid principle, regrettable and even destructive. The belief in the new and in change, put as dogmatically as Williams puts it here [in *Imaginations*] and his followers after him, if we agree with them, might make us wonder why we should read *this* work; some of it is now 50 years old or from a time and place certainly no longer immediately our own.

Theodore Weiss. *Encounter*. Dec., 1971. p. 73

There is a critical undertow pulling against Williams. He has not yet been given his seat in the same pantheon with Yeats and Eliot, Pound and Stevens. And if this current of opinion has shown signs of radically shifting in the very recent past among critics and scholars (working poets have known better), there are still those who see Williams as an interesting metrical experimenter and even an increasingly popular poet, but certainly not truly a major figure to contend with. But they are wrong. The truth is that Williams is major; not only does he have the quantity—nearly fifty books and some six hundred magazine publications and book introductions—but he is, with Pound and Yeats, one of a handful of real innovators in prosody, and perhaps the supreme master of the oblique design (meriting comparison with Joyce and Cézanne in this) in modern poetry.

Paul Mariani. *MR*. Autumn, 1972. p. 663

Despite moments of success, the prevailing mood of *Paterson* is one of defeat and failure, through which the hero doggedly continues his search, examining all things, endlessly attempting to achieve marriage, always rebounding from defeat to seek out the beautiful thing. The hero's determination is, of course, a major attribute of his intensity; and it is again useful to compare the heroic vision of *In the American Grain*, for most of the heroes discussed favorably there are admired largely for their endurance and perseverance in the face of failure and adversity.

Todd M. Lieber. *Endless Experiments*
(Ohio State). 1973. p. 214

Williams's insistent point, "No ideas but in things" may be thought of as pure Platonism or the medical doctor's *sine qua non* or the good poet's unintimidatable perception or all three. Plato, Williams learned as a boy, says our love rises upward from the things we know to things of abstract perfection. The medical doctor bases his diagnosis, even more his prognosis, upon embodied evidence. A poet like Williams sees, for an example, some pointed trees. He observes them with Platonic love, a clinical eye, and Dionysian rapture, regarding at the same time and in a similar way the very process of observation, his emotions, his words, and the lines and sounds the words make. He may also be imagining the feelings of the trees and of the objects near them. From these multiplex relationships mysteriously comes a poem, a new form, a *made* thing. It can be filled with ideas, but the ideas come after the feelings and words, caught among the lines or hovering like a hummingbird above blossoms.

Emily Mitchell Wallace in *William Carlos
Williams*, edited by Charles Angoff
(Fairleigh Dickinson). 1974. pp. 28–9

WILSON, EDMUND (1895–1972)

The manner of Wilson's casual book reviewing in the forties and fifties was, if anything, more assured than ever. It remained one of the pleasures of his critical style that he had nothing at all of the pontifical solemnness then flourishing in the Eliot-infected literary quarterlies. Yet if any American reviewer seemed to speak *ex cathedra*, it was he. The price of this authority, however, was for the first time a certain remoteness from current developments. He continued to write on new books and authors as well as established names. But his work was less and less an inclusive record of the literary temper and achievement of the present moment. (The new era, it must be said, was a less distinguished one than the twenties and much less in need of critical translation.) . . .

In [his] most recent phase we still find Edmund Wilson, as in

1919 and 1932, affirming his disaffection from modern society as he regularly encounters it and as he understands its historical formation. He has done this in so many words and also, increasingly, through choice of subject. His last large-scale undertaking, *Patriotic Gore: Studies in the Literature of the American Civil War* (1962), is an examination of that time in earlier history when the American nation came closest to dissolution and of the effects of this ordeal on battle-shocked survivors; one may feel that nothing has yet been written of greater relevance to the civil-rights ordeal of the 1960's, and hardly anything that is more despairing in its implications.

Warner Berthoff. Edmund Wilson
(Minnesota). 1968. pp. 12–3

Although it has not always loomed as one of the major themes of his work, there is a deep and abiding strain of family piety in the writings of Edmund Wilson. It makes itself felt with particular force in those autobiographical evocations of the world of his youth—the world of his parents and his teachers—which recur throughout his books and constitute some of his very best writing. It gives to his sense of history, especially American history, both its special tone of elegiac regret and its sharp feeling of personal involvement. It forms, moreover, the essential background to the recital of exasperations and distaste which has come in recent years to dominate Wilson's accounts of his forays into contemporary life.

Whatever judgment posterity may render on his achievements as a literary critic and historian—I myself happily concur in the current view that he is our greatest living man of letters—Edmund Wilson will always have a place in our literature as a chronicler and memorialist of American life. Without making a romance out of what was, in fact, a painful family history, without falsifying the often grim fate of his own contemporaries, he has somehow made of his deepest filial attachments and his gift for friendship a vivid instrument for understanding the historical current of his own time.

Hilton Kramer. NYT. Aug. 29, 1971. p. 1

During the 1920s Edmund Wilson created for himself a special position in the republic or anarchy of American letters: he became the Sainte-Beuve of a new literature. From his editorial desk first at *Vanity Fair*—where he shared it with John Peale Bishop, a gifted friend from Princeton—then after 1926 at *The New Republic*, he scanned the horizon for new talents and wrote perceptive comments on each of them. Sometimes his comments were the first, as in the case of Hemingway. He took a special interest at the time in writers of his own generation, the ones that served briefly in the Great War, and he did a great deal to shape the public images of Fitzgerald, Dos Passos, Wilder, Cummings and the *Fugitive* group.

Writers listened to Wilson as they did not often listen to other critics, and many of them tried to meet his difficult standards. At Princeton (class of '16) Dean Gauss had inspired him with the ambition to create "something in which," as he says in his tribute to Gauss, "every word, every cadence, every detail, should perform a definite function in producing an intense effect." The effect was what he hoped to find in new writers, and he scolded them, if in reasonable terms, when they fell short of producing it.

Malcolm Cowley. NR. July 1, 1972. p. 25

WINTERS, YVOR (1900–1968)

Mr. Winters is concerned . . . with life on the brink of darkness, where fear and terror come unsolicited and the available forms of order, to be good enough for the need, must be, in their own way, implacable. The forms of order which persuade, delight, and beguile are not enough; they are no good, it seems, when darkness insists. If much of Mr. Winters's work is dour and sullen, the reason is that this is the only kind of order he is prepared to invoke, darkness being what it is. It is hardly necessary to say that in his critical work the hated darkness takes the form of error, the stupidity of powerful men, the conspiracy against intelligence.

Denis Donoghue. NYR. Feb. 29, 1968. p. 22

The state of poetry, as it seems to me, is in dire need of a truly conservative critic who would have authority: conservative but not reactionary, hard but not rigid, traditional but not hidebound. Such a critic might do something at least to query the current fashions, something to suggest that neither frenzied notations of one's symptoms to and from the psychiatrist's office nor pseudo-Oriental bardic rhapsodies constitute the whole art of poetry. Winters had the gifts to be such a critic. But somehow, he was shunted, or shunted himself, into a siding. His gifts remained, and so did his utter devotion to literature and poetry; but more and more they operated in an ever-narrowing circle of rejection and prejudice. His authority diminished proportionately: to his loss, no doubt, but also to poetry's.

Patrick Cruttwell. HdR. Summer, 1968. p. 416

Winters' post-Symbolist poems are the most characteristic and important of his mature work. They belie the common view of Winters as primarily a poet of abstractions; and if he is didactic and moralistic, these qualities inhere in poems displaying a surface texture of intense sensuousness. In discussing these poems I have concentrated on their abstract significance, in order to show something of the way his method works. This sort of analysis is one-sided, and it makes the poems sound mechanical. The poems I have discussed are extraordinarily perceptive in respect to the external world they describe and in respect to language; the precise yet evocative language is, in his own phrase, a form of discovery. The lines are living lines.

Winters is, I think, a major poet, a poet of no less stature than Williams, Pound, Eliot, Crane, or Frost. If this is true, then the low state of his reputation may seem to require some explanation. One problem is that to many readers his poems have seemed old-fashioned, having nothing to say to them, not "modern." His restrained tone, his emphasis on rationality and control of the emotions, his sometimes explicit moralism, are partly the basis of this feeling, along with the regularity of his metrical and stanzaic forms. . . . There is also a tendency to regard his poems as versified footnotes to his criticism, which has attacked virtually every well-known literary figure since the eighteenth century and earned Winters the reputation of a crank. Winters' best post-Symbolist poems, though their paraphrasable content is consistent with his critical essays, are less assertive and dogmatic. His ideas, in the adventure with form that produces poetry, are complicated and qualified; but critics have used his more immediately accessible poems in the abstract style to attack his "banality and oversimplification."

Howard Kaye. SoR. Winter, 1971. pp. 193–5

I think it is time for the dismissals [of Winters] to cease. I speak as one who rejects a number of Winters's judgments and will continue to do so. About his importance in forming the taste of the age, and his true sensibility for poetry, and his grandeur as a writer of prose, it would be merely dishonest to give credit in a qualified way. He is a central figure in the history of modern poetry, and a critic to return to for the reviving charge of disagreement or assent: one of the very few teachers of any kind from whom it is always possible to learn.

Approximately two-thirds of the present collection [*Uncollected Essays and Reviews*] is a verse chronicle. Much of it appeared in *Poetry* magazine directly after the reign of Ezra Pound and had, one may assume, a small but most attentive audience. Some of the discoveries are William Carlos Williams, Hart Crane, Theodore Roethke and J. V. Cunningham. The animadversions include Jeffers, Aiken, Zukofsky,

Jarrell, Berryman and a myriad of worthies heard from neither before nor since. As a record of individual good taste vigorously defended, it has only Jarrell's *Poetry and the Age* for a peer.

David Bromwich. *NYT*. May 19, 1974. p. 36

WRIGHT, JAMES (1927–   )

Irresistibly drawn to the souls of beings who have wasted their lives—or who have been devastated *by* life—Wright's soul becomes, at last, hopelessly and lovingly entangled with theirs. He has the largeness of heart of the great empathizers, and worse, a mind suicidally honest, a mind hellishly bent on stripping away all self-protective devices. His best poems enact the drama of a mind struggling, usually with punishing success, to resist the temptation to take solace from its own compassionating ardor. The pain he feels for another never becomes a disguised way of cheering himself up. It is a tougher thing. The poems in this book [*Shall We Gather at the River*] are nearly identical to those of Wright's last book in form, but they have advanced to an altogether new spiritual magnitude. Perhaps the most serious obstacle to the new life of spirit is brevity of form. I feel that this tendency has become a handicap which impedes a full blossoming into the massive raw-boned jaggedness of form which, as in the superb "Minneapolis Poem," can provide the structural leverage needed to render the fuller sense of life newly available, but somehow left unbodied, in many of the short poems. The best work in this volume demonstrates clearly that Wright has the skill and fortitude needed to rid his art of the leaning to premature closure that often stifles his ablest, most incandescent, vision.

Laurence Lieberman. *Poetry*. April, 1969. p. 41

I have dwelt on James Wright's linguistic boldness; but he is equally unusual for his human intensity and scope. His themes are almost obsessively constant, from his earliest work: his is a "profound poetry of the poor and of the dead," to quote Stevens; a strength of misery in love, and an equally strong desire to transcend the bodily self into a delicacy intuited from animals, stones, dreams. James Wright is a mythopoeic poet, the sole owner and proprietor of names and, especially, places: the Northern Great Plains where he thinks of "the sea, that once solved the whole loneliness/Of the Midwest"; and his native southeastern Ohio, with its towns named for super-corporations, its fated, exhausted Eastern Europeans, its river which is at once sacred place and "Tar and chemical strangled tomb." As one reads through the book, Wright's places come to seem, like Winesburg or Yoknapatawpha, less the accidents of one life than the necessary epiphanies of the whole American experience. For all these reasons, he remains, for me, with the exception of Gary Snyder, the most interesting, and still promising, of his contemporaries.

Alan Williamson. Poetry. Feb., 1972. p. 298

Wright's poems are deeply personal. In his politically oriented works he lacks the sense of objective event we find in a Lowell; his poem is dependent on a private relationship to history and—even in his latest poems—to the poem as process for the speaker and reader. In this sense he is like Pound, though Wright's ordering is tonal, not structural. Whether this personalism is a limitation to his vision later poems will show. For the present, Collected Poems reminds us that one of our major poets is still growing.

Peter Cooley. CP. Spring, 1972. p. 79

James Wright started out in the fifties with a great bolt of visionary silk, which he cut, in the fashion of the day, to symmetrical patterns. His poems won prizes, but were so hard to believe, so safely and slickly "art," that they seemed only a vast closet of ceremonial robes to be taken out, worn as one bowed before the formal dignity of poetry, and returned, spotless.

It was toward the end of Saint Judas, his second volume, that, with a slam, Wright walked out on high art. His voice suddenly sharpened. . . . In The Branch Will Not Break (1963), his best volume, and Shall We Gather at the River (1968), his poems became so wincingly resentful and chagrined that their wires seemed disengaged. Wright lost the heart for wholeness. . . .

Wright's unusual tenderness for animal and beaten human life, his suffering over the inability to wing upward, to embrace creation ("what are you going to do?"), makes his a moving, enlarging sensibility, but his relation to the poetic medium has always been misjudged. If his early poems carried a formal will like a knife between the teeth, the recent work is either too bitter or too painfully happy for its own self-possession: all wound.

Calvin Bedient. NYT. Aug. 11, 1974. p. 6

WRIGHT, RICHARD (1908–1960)

Perhaps it is Bigger's Satanic election of violence, rather than his continued undying hatred of whites, that so terrifies Max at the close of the novel [*Native Son*]. Max senses that as a Communist he too has dispensed with the old social order—but the metaphysical vacuum that has been created does not necessarily lead men like Bigger to communism; it may just as easily lead to the most murderous kind of nihilism. Max's horror was to become Wright's own dilemma two years after the publication of *Native Son*, when he himself left the Party. He could no longer accept the assumptions of communism, yet the prospects of a new world of positive meaning and value seemed very distant indeed. It is, then, in the roles of a Negro nationalist revolutionary and a metaphysical rebel that Wright most successfully portrays Bigger. And it is from these aspects of Bigger's character rather than from any Marxist interpretation that Wright's sociology really emerges.

Edward Margolies. *Native Sons*
(Lippincott). 1968. p. 83

Wright was a man of great passion but of few ideas; throughout his life he responded intellectually to current movements—to whatever was culturally *de rigueur*—and just as he had begun his career by subscribing to communism and by creating fiction similar to that of Theodore Dreiser—the influence of *The American Tragedy* on *Native Son* is too obvious to pursue—he was soon greatly affected by the existentialist movement that was developing in Europe in the 1940's.... As an outsider—religiously, politically, artistically, and racially—to America, Wright embraced existentialist thought and used it as the philosophical framework of his next novel, *The Outsider* (1953), in which he creates an ambiguous man, Cross Damon, who attempts to achieve noble ends through brutal deeds, who is a cross between Christ and the Devil, and who seeks, at all costs, absolute personal freedom. Although Cross Damon is responsible for four deaths, the deaths have been the consequence of his rebellion against a hostile society, and he dies in innocence, his purpose accomplished....

Without the ideological support of communism and existentialism, Wright's work lost its pseudo-intellectualism, the possibility for any kind of idealism, and became what it really always was—a raging indictment of America. His last three works of fiction are nightmare visions of his rejected country.

Theodore L. Gross. *The Heroic Ideal
in American Literature* (Free).
1971. pp. 155–6

Wright's humanism . . . constitutes one of the most cogent reasons to consider him a prophetic writer. Instead of hailing him as a pioneer of Black Power, it would perhaps be better to regard him as precursor of what Black Power could lead to, and as an accurate, observant and involved critic of his times. . . . Wright claimed this right to coexistence for each one of us when he claimed the black American's right to express himself without a label, without being limited to a role as representative of a race, nation, class or religion. For the sake of all Americans, he wanted, as an American, to be allowed to criticize America. He dared, as a Black, to criticize the nascent state of Ghana; he made it his duty, as a Westerner, to denounce the West. After having asserted, in both his fiction and his political writing, the individual's right to survive against any system, Wright attempted to act as a critical conscience of our world. If he was never wholly successful, the partial replies to his questions and his incompleted projects still represent a greater gain for mankind than a more perfect success as a traditional writer would have brought. For this reason, Wright must not be judged on his writing alone; his career as a militant intellectual must also be put on the scale. He can then be evaluated as one of Ralph Waldo Emerson's living pillars of an era, a "representative man."

Michel Fabre. *The Unfinished Quest of
Richard Wright* (Morrow). 1973. p. xx

Wright's harsh experiences with cruelty—dreamlike in quality, unreal and ambiguous—had made his life seem nightmarish. The infusion of this perception of reality into his writing gave his work its strength and its goals. Both strength and weaknesses came from an intense desire to detail and underscore the hell—the shadow world—a black man had to endure. At times he gave in to the temptation to editorialize, to polemicize, to arrest his narrative with abstract psychological or sociological comment; at other times he was able to combine a poetic lyricism with the harsh, brilliantly evocative prose of cruelty that made black readers say he was honest and accurate. That same prose made some white readers say Wright exaggerated; it was prose from which no white reader could receive cathartic release.

David Bakish. *Richard Wright*
(Ungar). 1973. pp. 98–9

The relation of Bigger Thomas [in *Native Son*] to America is complex, but any understanding of it must begin with the assumption that he is a native son, a true American. Wright transforms the bad nigger stereotype into a vital character by treating the basic stereotype as an inherently American character. Like Captain Ahab, Huck Finn, or Jay Gatsby, Bigger Thomas is an American individualist seeking to create himself and his world in defiance of all. Wright exploits actions conventionally assumed to demonstrate the innate evil or bestiality of the bad nigger to express Bigger's desire for self-realization.

Like most American novelists, Wright sees the individual as the creative force in human life, and he presents Bigger Thomas as a creative individual. That does not mean, however, that he sanctions Bigger's career. On the contrary, Bigger functions as a vivid metaphor for the failure of American life. *Native Son* is a criticism of America, but it is not "social" criticism; it attacks poverty and slums and rats, of course, but its fundamental concern lies with the quality of human relations fostered by our culture.

Richard E. Baldwin. *MR*.
Spring, 1973. pp. 378–9

The big question of Book III [of *Native Son*] is whether Bigger will find himself. It is not answered until the very end of the novel, the farewell scene with Max. "At the end," says [Irving] Howe, "Bigger remains at the mercy of his hatred and fear." It is hard to make men hear who will not listen. Seven times in the last page and a half of the novel Bigger cries out to Max, "I'm all right," the last time adding, "For real, I am." The repeated assurance "I'm all right" obviously means that Bigger is not at the mercy of fear, that he is sure that he will not, as he had dreaded, have to be dragged to the electric chair, kicking and screaming, filled with animal terror because he had not been able to find human dignity. He has found what he had sought, an understanding of himself that "could lift him up and make him live so intensely that the dread of being black and unequal would be forgotten; that even death would not matter, that it would be a victory." The meaning for his life, which Max had thought to gain him the opportunity to build during life imprisonment, he had grasped from his recent experience under the duress of death.

Paul N. Siegel. *PMLA*. May, 1974. p. 521

WYLIE, ELINOR (1885–1928)

[Wylie] is not, after all, inconsistent in her attitude toward the disparity between the desires or aspirations of the individual and the satisfactions and fulfillments that earthly existence offers him; in her deeply romantic view, the world is an inadequate environment for the individual self. The "self" desires rarity, variety, fineness, beauty, delicacy; the world offers commonness, sameness, coarseness, ugliness, and grossness. Under the ordinary conditions of human life, exquisite esthetic distinctions are an impertinence and fine moral distinctions are futile.

Elinor Wylie's poetry at its best recognizes a dimension of the human spirit least accommodated in existence; her art affirms the validity of the desire for quality in human life—fineness, rarity, delicacy, beauty, and variety.

Thomas Alexander Gray. Elinor Wylie (Twayne). 1969. p. 156

• YURICK, SOL (1925–   )

The steady soldier [in *The Warriors*], the dreamer sick with intimations of cowardice, the violent giant, half shield, half menace; the young recruit, to be blooded and sheltered—these are living anachronisms: bronze-age infantry tossed by some grotesque time trick into a twentieth century metropolis. Their native land is a half dozen square blocks, their known world fifty or so square miles, the race to which they belong a few thousand boys and girls who live the gang life. They are ignorant, superstitious, lecherous, cruel and treacherous—by society's standards. Yurick has set up the prisms that allow one to judge them by their own. It is only fair, and carries the bonus of a story that blazes through the hot city night.

Robert Hatch. Nation. Nov. 22, 1965. p. 395

What we have in *Fertig* is not a sort of study in the psychology of murder in the manner of, say, Simenon, nor much less is it an impassioned and protracted dialogue between the criminal and his hunted after *Crime and Punishment.* . . .

This novel is quite different. Sol Yurick has invited us to consider the big, front-page murder as an elaborate public ritual, a sort of sacred drama which is played out to provide society with entertainment and emotional catharsis. This seems quite genuine. I found Yurick's insight —which in these terms at least is quite fresh—to be simply and unarguably true.

Bruce Cook. Com. Oct. 14, 1966. p. 60

The early parts of [*The Bag*] contain some of the most powerful descriptions of where it's really at—in welfare centers and on the streets— that I've come across in recent literature. . . .

This is a work of great energy and passion, an accurate depiction of the sociology of the contemporary despair, that suffers from its reductionism of all to one particularity, one obsession, one ideology, and one issue. It's a potpourri of failures posing as a novel of ideas. Its faults are the faults of one who has blown his mind over his own enthusiasms. But that is preferable by far, to those tiny dry exercises in symbolic form from which the novel's protagonist is in such flight that he can only end up with the mob at the bottom.

Richard M. Elman. NYT. May 19, 1968. p. 38

The fastidious may quibble over Yurick's rawness. The Despair Incorporated Boys may long for the concrete gardens of the French anti-novels. The Mainliners-on-the-Absurd may opt for the aspirin of Black Humor. But Sol Yurick is no such cop-out. With rare responsibility he has brilliantly conceived and powerfully executed a portrait of the sight, sound, smell and taste of Urban Now, beneath the plastic; and he has renewed the novel as a social transaction. Either we respond, or the credit card will be our guillotine.

John Leonard. *Life*. May 24, 1968. p. 8

A work of fiction has appeared that augurs the shape of the new novel about the Negro. Sol Yurick is a white, Jewish, possibly lapsed bourgeois writer, whose talent and beauty of compassion are magnificent. In *The Bag*, his third novel, he writes about many people all caught up in the blackness of New York City and its sick welfare system. Only some of his characters are Negro, but the ambience of the Negro *scene* colors every page and is indivisibly tied to Yurick's conception of New York. No longer is the violence abortive or repressed; it is *there*, and it seems the only way out, a cleansing away by blood bath. In this use of the riot scene, Yurick's novel seems like so many African novels of the past decade. The moderates, the ones willing to see both sides of a neighborhood, are crushed, while the extremes—corrupted and expedient—survive to fight their coming battles.

Martin Tucker. *Nation*. July 8, 1968. p. 28

For his third novel, Sol Yurick, who launched himself well with *The Warriors* and *Fertig*, has taken what may well be all of New York City and sliced it like a many-layered cake to expose every level. The only thing small about *The Bag* is the title. . . .

Black nationalists, hippies, the greedy and the grimy surge through the Yurick panorama grasping for millions or just their semi-monthly relief check. Because the novel is a kaleidoscope of *now* it is as difficult to synopsize as to describe inch by inch a painting by Pollock.

The Bag is at its best in the action scenes; in the introspective passages a character mentally turned on is sometimes a character turned too loose, forcing the reader to hang on and plod through pages of mental rambling where often the words seem more important to the author than the thoughts they combine to form. . . .

But nitpicking aside—and I admit that I am—*The Bag* is a novel of merit. It dares to move in close to where the action is.

Haskel Frankel. *SR*. July 20, 1968. p. 26

Imagine, if you can, a superb writing team composed of Hugh Selby, Jr. for violence and slum realism, Terry Southern for *Magic Christian*-vintage nasty humor, the *Armies of the Night* Mailer for impressionistic comment on the New Left, Tom Wolfe, when he was new and we loved him, for frenetic, driving style, and I-don't-know-who for political sensibility. Then give the result to Mark Rudd for copy-editing. Or, substitute your own modern culture heroes, if you want, just so long as they are smart, aggressive, and mean. If you are really lucky, the upshot of the team effort will be something as good as Sol Yurick's *The Bag*.

Thomas Miller. Com. Oct. 4, 1968. p. 30

There's a brief vignette of Sol Yurick's contemporary Mailer in *The Bag*. Unlike Mailer, Yurick has no boy-wonder reputation to build on: his three novels all date from the later 1960s. And in life he's remained a shy figure untouched by power, uncompromisingly to the left of all respectable politics. But power, its interlocking constellations, conspiracies and charismatic leaders, is what preoccupies him, with its obverse a passionate concern for the individuals at the base of the power pyramid.

The Warriors dealt with the private power structure of the juvenile gangs, *Fertig* with politicians manipulating a murder trial to their own advantage. Broader and longer, *The Bag*, in the same Manhattan setting and with some of the earlier characters, is sprawling, uneven and brilliant. Its ethos is that of countless interminable late-night conversations, particularly with the militant young. It mirrors, better than any other fiction that I know, the mounting frenzy for radical change in a New York as revolutionary, as schismatic, as stifled as 19th-century St. Petersburg.

Clive Jordan. NS. Jan. 9, 1970. p. 55

Because Yurick's material is so solid, even excursions into the fanciful and the "surreal" seem, in his hands, somehow realistic. . . .

As if he had become impatient with the limitations of realism, he attempts several abstract, rather musical and formless stories [in *Someone Just Like You*] in which many people participate in rituals meant to free them from individuality, self-consciously celebrating births and deaths. . . . If these stories seem to me less successful [than the realistic ones], it is not because there is anything wrong with Yurick's experimental vision, but only because he has not yet found an artistically or dramatically compelling structure for this vision; and I admit to being prejudiced in favor of the kind of writing he can do so well, with his formidable knowledge of reality, his ability to synthesize facts into esthetic experiences. Any modestly gifted writer can venture into "surrealism." Few indeed can handle the densities and outrageous paradoxes of "real" life. The straightforward sections of *The Bag* and *Fertig* and the un-fantasized horrors of [*Someone Just Like You*'s] realistic stories, have a power to move us, urgently and deeply, that cannot be matched by any of the author's superficially sophisticated contemporaries. And one might argue, ultimately, that ordinary life in our great modern cities is already fantastic enough.

Joyce Carol Oates. NYT. Sept. 3, 1972. p. 7

● ZUKOFSKY, LOUIS (1904–   )

Of all the birthday presents of the quatercentenary [of Shakespeare], none has come close to the poet Louis Zukofsky's offering, a discursive book of 470 pages called *Bottom: On Shakespeare*, boxed with a second volume by his wife, the composer Celia Zukofsky, a musical setting for *Pericles*.

The body of Zukofsky's book is a cycle of essays, or "an alphabet of subjects," from A to Z. The momentum that carries the reader fascinated through this poet's notebook of perceptions is generated in the introduction, 90 pages ostensibly about eyes ("let the audience look to their eyes," cries Bottom). What emerges is a kind of dance of imagery and words which Zukofsky, with pure delight, has set in motion. It is Shakespeare's peace of mind that intrigues him, the balance of the poet's argument within itself. An elaborately cultivated imagination has limits and contours—one begins to wonder if Shakespeare's have ever been found—but there are interior harmonies that act like music in their repetitions and contrasts and which visually are inexhaustible of interest. Zukofsky reports from a lifetime's study of these harmonies, and before we are well into the book we meet a Shakespeare classrooms and theatres have never heard of. . . .

For Zukofsky Shakespeare is an elaborate argument that flows, a voice all its own, in and out of characters, from play to play. It is an argument about love, about understanding, about truth. "It argues with no one," he says, "only in itself." With the humblest touchstone—Bottom's wildly innocent fantasia on Shakespeare's great theme that love is to reason as eyes are to mind—here is the greatest meditation, certainly the most intricately lucid and beautiful, ever built around the thousand forms of a single thought.

Guy Davenport. *National Review*.
Oct. 6, 1964. pp. 874–6

All: The Collected Short Poems, 1923–1958, by Louis Zukofsky, traces the development of a writer who has taken the examples and injunctions of Ezra Pound and William Carlos Williams more seriously and devotedly than perhaps any other contemporary poet, and who has become something of a tradition all by himself. His has been an underground reputation, until recently; but his admirers and devotees have been absolute in their respect for him, from the days of *An "Objec-*

tivists" Anthology published thirty-five years ago. Like Pound and Williams, he has been concerned to discover what is really viable for *him* in all poetry, and so viable for his own work; but he has also encouraged, if unwillingly, a kind of dogmatic eclecticism that has done some of his disciples more harm than good, and that has put an enormous burden on some of his own engaging, brief, and unpretentious pieces, which make *All* the book that it is. More often than not, however, Zukofsky imposes on the reader a burden of seriousness (in Auden's sense of the word) that is difficult to justify. . . . He implies that his reader must be willing to go the whole way with him, even holding in his mind the private knowledge to which he sometimes alludes in his notes. To put it another way, his poetry sometimes seems to have been composed to illustrate a preconceived theory; its limitations are those of the pioneer—say, Schoenberg. Impressive as his work sometimes is, one is seldom sure that one has "got" it as Zukofsky intends one to get it.

Samuel French Morse. *CL.*
Winter, 1968. pp. 116–7

Louis Zukofsky's book [*All: The Collected Short Poems, 1956–1964*] is a companion volume to his *All: The Collected Short Poems, 1923–1958*. There is some overlap because the earlier volume did not include some poems which now find a place in the second book. Zukofsky is an American who has been writing for forty-five years. There are so many American poets now on the scene that it is difficult for many English readers to decide for themselves which are important and which are less so. Zukofsky is important. He represents, for all his modernistic technical experiments, the middle way of American poetry during the past thirty or so years. His poetic godfather is William Carlos Williams, but his vision is entirely his own. He is really an impressionist who is able to capture an atmosphere or seal an idea within remarkably small compass. He possesses a sensitive eye and an individual way of communicating thoughts and feelings. Nothing seems to escape him. He is as much at home with natural phenomena as with everything else in the contemporary American scene, though he does not dwell for long on fashionable politics. In his way he is a satirist not unlike our own Stevie Smith. But although his bite is sharp, he does not leave behind lasting wounds. He may, perhaps, have written too much about the same things and in the same way, but he is a satisfying writer whose poems on the page give as much pleasure to the eye as they do to the ear.

Leonard Clark. *PoetryR.* Summer, 1968. p. 109

A lifetime's work, as ambitious as *Paterson* or the *Cantos*, Mr. Zukofsky's long poem [*"A" 1–12*] cannot be criticized here but merely hailed with the respect it deserves. The constructive idea is a free, expansive form which can bring in the most remote and intellectual ideas, if they are creative ideas, and the most personal anecdotes of a lifetime: prose, documents, antipoetic detail can also be fitted in somehow.

Robert Creeley, in his useful introduction, speaks of this mode as the poem as autobiography. . . . One should merely note that this new form is not free form: in *Paterson*, in the *Cantos*, and here, there are three fairly rigorous technical rules of abruptness, disjunction and elimination of prosy explanatory context (so that each of these poems sends the reader out on a research job about the life and reading of the poet). Such poems are also open-ended in two senses; there is no formal reason for their not being added to indefinitely, so long as the poet remains alive and interested. More subtly, they are open-ended at the beginning as well as the end: *Paterson* and the *Cantos* make fullest sense if read as expansive continuations of what the author was doing in his earlier, shorter poems. . . .

Yet it would be wrong to think of Pound, Williams or Zukofsky as simply packing a number of perfect small imagist poems in a kind of loose conglomerate of assertion and anecdote. A certain sense of trembling and dangerous continuity, like soft stuff catching on to the next rock and becoming a thread or a nerve, makes the reading of such long poems, in this new style, peculiarly exciting, the reader himself becoming the constructor. Zukofsky's own essays [*Prepositions*] will be an indispensable text for whoever does undertake the really hard thinking that will be necessary to see how imagism, a cult partly of the very short, the very depersonalized or objective poem, could result in the end in extremely long, personal and subjective poems of a quite new kind.

G. S. Fraser. PR. Summer, 1968. pp. 471, 473

Short of silence, no one could be less loquacious than Louis Zukofsky. *Ferdinand*, a long short story completed in 1942 (why not published in England before?), is a masterpiece of brevity and precision. Each word, every image, seem perfectly selected and exactly placed. The whole, a history of a young man abandoned by his parents and brought up by an aunt and uncle, gives the impression of a much longer work. Deprived of parental affection, Ferdinand becomes "practical in risking little . . . he took care of his own constraints, emphasizing his emptiness and affecting to be quiet." Yet, for all his quietness, he is haunted by yearnings and fears. He grows, takes a job; war breaks out, and on a car trip through America he faces and dreams through "a latent fear that some day would find him in a collision."

On the surface this is a simple story, which reminded me of Nabokov. With the same cunning he veils complexity in simplicity. He has the same powers of obsessive observation, similar imagery and cadences, and a love for words that never gets out of hand. Perfection of form and expression does not—as can happen—preclude humanity. Ferdinand is a complete and moving character, as are the aunt and uncle. Zukofsky is best known as a poet. I wish he would write a novel.

Janice Elliott. NS. Nov. 29, 1968. p. 762

It Was . . . deals with a writer's long effort, conscious and unconscious, to write a perfect simple sentence that will put the only possible words in the only possible order; suddenly the sentence comes to him, and Zukofsky ends the story with it. Since the story is only four pages long, it should have been and doubtless was intended to be a little miracle of enclosure, a work of art whose subject is itself; but Zukofsky's prose, though better here than in *Ferdinand*, is far from miraculous: his narrator's sentence, for example, in the absence of its imaginary context is not impressive. And even so, this story comes through as most of Zukofsky's poetry comes through, largely on the strength of its good intentions.

J. Mitchell Morse. HdR.
Summer, 1969. pp. 319–20

Little is not a difficult book—or, rather, only as difficult as the reader will force it to be. It is an autobiographical novel, or poem, but whatever it is, it is a pleasure to read because of its story and because of Zukofsky's range of language and wit. The three main characters (Dala, Verchadet, and Little) are Zukofsky, his wife, and his son Paul. Little, as was Paul, is a violin prodigy, and *Little*, in which Zukofsky's main source of imagery, as in his poetry, is music, portrays the artist from childhood to young manhood. . . .

Even on a surface level, *Little*'s plot is intriguing, its details consistently enjoyable. Its puns, puzzles, and word games are genuinely funny and, since they usually occur within the minds and during the conversations of characters of heightened consciousness and sophistication, they do not seem artificially imposed. Because Dala, Little, and Verchadet are so ultra-intelligent I sometimes find myself lamenting my own dullness as I feel points and jokes going over my head—what, for example, does the "for careenagers" of the title mean?—but I always enjoy the book's sounds and its rhythms, and am anxious to proceed.

William Heyen. SR. Dec. 5, 1970. p. 31

Admired by Charles Olson, Robert Duncan, Robert Creeley, and a generation of avant-garde writers who esteem Ezra Pound and William Carlos Williams, Louis Zukofsky remains an enigmatic and generally misunderstood figure. Even the members of the so-called Objectivist group that gathered around him in the thirties often found his work impenetrable and today the situation has been compounded by the appearance of his five-hundred page "metaphysics of cognition," *Bottom: On Shakespeare*, and his still unfinished masterpiece, *"A,"* a quasi-autobiographical poem written over a lifetime. Just as the theories he presented as guest editor of the Objectivist issue of *Poetry* in 1931 were met with silence or confusion, so he has rarely been discussed outside the little magazines. But Zukofsky is more than a coterie poet or a man who owes his place in literary history chiefly to his association with Ezra Pound. To the contrary, he is, for all his eccentricity, both a germinal part of the whole nominalist trend of twentieth-century poetry and a craftsman of extreme subtlety.

L. S. Dembo. *AL*. March, 1972. p. 74

Just as the *Catullus* is, in large part, a denial of the referential value of language and an assertion, instead, that "aurality is meaning," the *Autobiography* belies conventional expectation by being not a reference book about the poet's life (Zukofsky is, in a sense, our only anti-confessional poet), but by being a blue print for the musical production of some of his poems (what a poet's life is, after all, *about*). Except for occasional short statements about his "life" (concessions to the genre), the *Autobiography* consists of twenty-two musical forms which, Zukofsky writes, were "final intentions of the words." The work must be performed, heard, to be understood. Beyond the pleasure of its *meaning*, beyond, too, the pure charm of the work's conception, the *Autobiography* is instance of that stage in the writer's formal dynamic in which words, no longer reaching toward music's measure, have, through projection of their own implications, been assimilated into it. The measure of Zukofsky's life is in that union.

Whether the current accessibility of Zukofsky's work will provide him with the critical recognition he deserves (he has been publishing, without great notice, since 1921), his "vogue" is at any rate a suggestion that American poetry may be seeking what it never really has had—a workable classicism of its own. What *"A"* offers to that possibility is a circumstance in which technique mediates between the large American voice, on the one hand, with its "statements," its social concern, and the intimate lyric voice, on the other, with its privacy, its feelings. Zukofsky's classicism is not aestheticism, not art compromising reality, but art dealing from "the structure of its own house." It is all very much like music.

Thomas A. Duddy. *MPS*. 3, 6, 1973. pp. 255–6

BIBLIOGRAPHIES

The bibliographies list the major books and plays of the authors included in this work; the dates are of first publication or, in the case of plays, usually of first production. Pamphlets, one-act plays, juveniles, contributions to multi-authored collections, and other minor publications are included only selectively. Stories and articles in periodicals are not included.

The bibliographies of all authors in the three-volume Fourth Edition have been updated through January, 1976. Those authors whose criticism has not been updated are marked with *. Any author from the fourth edition not listed in these bibliographies has had no new publication since 1968.

The bibliographies of the authors added in this supplement (preceded by a bullet) are complete through January, 1976, with the exceptions noted above.

GENRE ABBREVIATIONS

a	autobiography	n	novel
b	biography	p	poetry
c	criticism	pd	poetic drama
d	drama	r	reminiscence
e	essay	rd	radio drama
h	history	s	short stories
j	journalism	sk	sketches
m	memoir	t	travel or topography
misc	miscellany	tr	translation

JAMES AGEE
1909–1955

The Collected Short Prose of James Agee, 1969

CONRAD AIKEN
1889–1973

Collected Poems: 1916–1970, 1970; The Clerk's Journal, 1971 [1911] (p); Collected Criticism (orig. A Reviewer's ABC), 1971

EDWARD ALBEE
1928–

All Over, 1971 (d); Seascape, 1975 (d)

NELSON ALGREN
1909–

The Last Carousel, 1973 (s)

• A. R. AMMONS
1926–

Ommateum; with Doxology, 1955 (p); Expression of Sea Level, 1964 (p); Tape for the Turn of the Year, 1965 (p); Corson's Inlet, 1965 (p); Northfield Poems, 1966; Selected Poems, 1968; Uplands, 1970 (p); Briefings, 1971 (p); Collected Poems: 1951–1971, 1972; Sphere: The Form of a Motion, 1974 (p); Diversifications, 1975 (p)

ROBERT ANDERSON*
1917–

Solitaire/Double Solitaire, 1971 (d); After, 1973 (n)

SHERWOOD ANDERSON
1896–1941

Sherwood Anderson's Memoirs (rev. ed.), 1969; The Buck Fever Papers, 1971 (e); Sherwood Anderson/Gertrude Stein, 1973 (letters,e)

• JOHN ASHBERY
1927–

Turandot, and Other Poems, 1953; Some Trees, 1956 (p); The Poems, 1960; The Heroes, 1960 (d); The Compromise, 1960 (d); The Tennis Court Oath, 1962 (p); Rivers and Mountains, 1966 (p); (with James Schuyler) A Nest of Ninnies, 1969 (n); Fragment, 1969 (p); The Double Dream of Spring, 1970 (p); Three Poems, 1972; Self-Portrait in a Convex Mirror, 1975 (p)

LOUIS AUCHINCLOSS
1917–

Motiveless Malignity, 1969 (e); Second Chance, 1970 (s); Edith Wharton: A Woman in Her Time, 1971 (b); Henry Adams, 1971 (c); I Come as a Thief, 1972 (n); Richelieu, 1972 (b); The Partners, 1974 (n); A Writer's Capital, 1974 (a)

W. H. AUDEN
1907–1973

Collected Longer Poems, 1969; Collected Shorter Poems, 1969; Secondary Worlds, 1969 (e); City without Walls, 1970 (p); A Certain World: A Commonplace Book, 1970 (misc); (with Paul B. Taylor) The Elder Edda, 1970 (tr); Academic Graffiti, 1971 (p); Epistle to a Godson, 1972 (p); Forewords & Afterwords, 1973 (e); Thank You, Fog: Last Poems, 1974 (p); (with Leif Sjoberg) Evening Land (by Per Lagerkvist), 1975 (tr)

GEORGE AXELROD*
1922–

Where Am I Now—When I Need Me?, 1971 (n)

JAMES BALDWIN
1924–

(with Margaret Mead) A Rap on Race, 1971 (conversations); No Name in the

Street, 1972 (e); (with Nikki Giovanni) *A Dialogue*, 1973 (conversations); *If Beale Street Could Talk*, 1974 (n)

DJUNA BARNES
1892–

Ladies Almanack, [1928] 1972 (n)

PHILIP BARRY*
1896–1949

States of Grace: 8 Plays by Philip Barry, 1975

JOHN BARTH
1930–

Chimera, 1972 (n)

• DONALD BARTHELME
1931–

Come Back, Dr. Caligari, 1964 (s); *Snow White*, 1967 (n); *Unspeakable Practices, Unnatural Acts*, 1968 (s); *City Life*, 1970 (s); *The Slightly Irregular Fire Engine*, 1971 (juvenile); *Sadness*, 1972 (s); *Guilty Pleasures*, 1974 (s); *The Dead Father*, 1975 (n)

S. N. BEHRMAN*
1893–1973

People in a Diary, 1972 (m)

SAUL BELLOW
1915–

Mr. Sammler's Planet, 1970 (n); *Humboldt's Gift*, 1975 (n)

• THOMAS BERGER
1924–

Crazy in Berlin, 1958 (n); *Reinhart in Love*, 1962 (n); *Little Big Man*, 1964 (n); *Killing Time*, 1967 (n); *Vital Parts*, 1970 (n); *Regiment of Women*, 1973 (n); *Sneaky People*, 1975 (n)

JOHN BERRYMAN
1914–1972

Homage to Mistress Bradstreet, and Other Poems, 1968; *The Dream Songs*, 1969 (p); *Love & Fame*, 1970 (p); *Delusions, Etc.*, 1972 (p); *Recovery*, 1973 (n)

AMBROSE BIERCE
1842–1914?

Collected Writings, 1946; *The Enlarged Devil's Dictionary*, 1967; *The Ambrose Bierce Satanic Reader*, 1968 (j); *Complete Short Stories*, 1970

ELIZABETH BISHOP
1911–

The Complete Poems, 1969

• ROBERT BLY
1926–

Silence in the Snowy Fields, 1962 (p); *The Sea and the Honeycomb*, 1966 (p); *The Light around the Body*, 1967 (p); *The Teeth-Mother Naked at Last*, 1970 (p); *Sleepers Joining Hands*, 1972 (p); *Jumping Out of Bed*, 1973 (p); *Friends, You Drank Some Darkness*, 1975 (tr)

LOUISE BOGAN
1897–1970

A Poet's Alphabet, 1970 (c); *What the Woman Lived*, 1973 (letters)

VANCE BOURJAILY*
1922–

Brill among the Ruins, 1970 (n)

PAUL BOWLES
1910–

The Thicket of Spring, 1971 (p); *Without Stopping*, 1972 (a)

KAY BOYLE*
1903–

Testament for My Students, 1970 (p); The Long Walk at San Francisco State, 1971 (e); The Underground Woman, 1975 (n)

• RICHARD BRAUTIGAN
1935–

A Confederate General from Big Sur, 1964 (n); The Pill versus the Springhill Mine Disaster, 1969 (p); In Watermelon Sugar, 1969 (n); Trout Fishing in America, 1970 (n); Rommel Drives on Deep into Egypt, 1970 (p); The Abortion, 1971 (n); Revenge of the Lawn, 1971 (s); The Hawkline Monster, 1974 (n); Willard and His Bowling Trophies, 1975 (n)

CLEANTH BROOKS*
1906–

A Shaping Joy, 1972 (c)

GWENDOLYN BROOKS
1917–

Riot, 1970 (p); Family Pictures, 1971 (p); The World of Gwendolyn Brooks, 1971 (collected works); Jump Bad, 1971 (p); Report from Part I, 1973 (a); Beckonings, 1975 (p)

VAN WYCK BROOKS*
1886–1963

The Van Wyck Brooks–Lewis Mumford Letters, 1970

PEARL S. BUCK*
1892–1973

Pearl S. Buck: A Biography (by Theodore F. Harris), 1969 (taped conversations); The Good Deed, 1969 (s); The Three Daughters of Madame Liang, 1969 (n); The Kennedy Women, 1970 (b); China as I See It, 1970 (e); Man-

dala, 1970 (n); The Story Bible, 1971; Pearl S. Buck: A Biography, vol. 2 (by Theodore F. Harris), 1971 (letters); Pearl Buck's America Travelogue, 1972; Oriental Cookbook, 1972; Once upon a Christmas, 1972 (misc); China Past and Present, 1972 (e); All Under Heaven, 1973 (n); The Rainbow, 1974 (n); East and West, 1975 (s)

FREDERICK BUECHNER
1926–

The Hungering Dark, 1969 (e); The Entrance to Porlock, 1970 (n); The Alphabet of Grace, 1970 (e); Lion Country, 1971 (n); Open Heart, 1972 (n); Love Feast, 1974 (n)

• CHARLES BUKOWSKI
1920–

Flower, Fist and Bestial Wail, 1961 (p); Longshot Pomes for Broke Players, 1962 (p); Run with the Hunted, 1962 (p); It Catches My Heart in Its Hands, 1963 (p); Cold Dogs in the Courtyard, 1965 (p); Crucifix in a Death-Hand, 1965 (p); Confessions of a Man Insane Enough to Live with Beasts, 1965 (misc); All the Assholes in the World and Mine, 1966 (m); Poems Written before Jumping Out of an 8 Story Window, 1968 (p); At Terror Street and Agony Way, 1968 (p); Notes of a Dirty Old Man, 1969 (misc); The Days Run Away Like Wild Horses over the Hills, 1970 (p); Erections, Ejaculations, Exhibitions and General Tales of Ordinary Madness, 1972 (s); Mockingbird Wish Me Luck, 1972 (p); Fire Station, 1973 (p); South of No North, 1973 (p); Burning in Water, Drowning in Flame, 1974 (p); Post Office, 1974 (p); Life and Death in the Charity Ward, 1974 (p); Factotum, 1975 (n)

• ED BULLINS
1936–

Goin' a Buffalo, 1968 (d); A Son, Come Home, 1968 (d); The Electronic Nigger,

1968 (d); *Clara's Old Man*, 1968 (d); *In the Wine Time*, 1968 (d); *Five Plays*, 1968; *The Duplex*, 1970 (d); *The Pig Pen*, 1970 (d); *The Hungered One*, 1971 (s); *In New England Winter*, 1971 (d); *The Fabulous Miss Marie*, 1971 (d); *Four Dynamite Plays*, 1972; *The Theme Is Blackness*, 1972 (d); *The Reluctant Rapist*, 1973 (n); *House Party*, 1973 (d)

WILLIAM BURROUGHS
1914–

The Job, 1970 (interviews, with Daniel Odier); *The Wild Boys: A Book of the Dead*, 1971 (n); *Exterminator!*, 1973 (misc); *The Last Words of Dutch Schultz*, 1975 (n)

ABRAHAM CAHAN*
1860–1951

The Education of Abraham Cahan, 1969 (a) [new translation of *Bletter von Mein Leben*]

JAMES M. CAIN*
1892–

Cain X 3, (*The Postman Always Rings Twice, Mildred Pierce, Double Indemnity*), 1969 (3n); *Rainbow's End*, 1975 (n)

ERSKINE CALDWELL
1903–

The Weather Shelter, 1969 (n); *The Earnshaw Neighborhood*, 1971 (n); *Annette*, 1973 (n)

• HORTENSE CALISHER
1911–

In the Absence of Angels, 1951 (s); *False Entry*, 1961 (n); *Tale for the Mirror*, 1962 (s); *Textures of Life*, 1963 (n); *Extreme Magic*, 1964 (s); *Journal from Ellipsia*, 1965 (n); *The*

Railroad Police, and The Last Trolley Ride, 1966 (s); *The New Yorkers*, 1969 (n); *Queenie*, 1971 (n); *Herself*, 1972 (a); *Standard Dreaming*, 1972 (n); *Eagle Eye*, 1973 (n); *The Collected Stories*, 1975

TRUMAN CAPOTE
1924–

The Dogs Bark, 1973 (j)

WILLA CATHER
1876–1947

The Kingdom of Art, 1967 (c); *The World and the Parish* (ed. William M. Curtin), 1971 (e); *Uncle Valentine, and Other Stories* (ed. Bernice Slote), 1973

RAYMOND CHANDLER
1888–1959

The Midnight Raymond Chandler, 1971 (misc)

JOHN CHEEVER
1912–

Bullet Park, 1969 (n); *The World of Apples*, 1973 (s)

KATE CHOPIN
1851–1904

The Complete Works, 1969

JOHN CIARDI*
1916–

The Paradiso, 1970 (tr); *Lives of X*, 1971 (p)

RICHARD CONDON
1915–

Mile High, 1969 (n); *The Vertical Smile*, 1971 (n); *Arigato*, 1972 (n); (with Wendy Bennett) *The Mexican Stove*, 1973 (t and cookbook); *And*

CONDON *(Cont.)*
Then We Moved to Rossenarra, 1973
(t); *Winter Kills*, 1974 (n); *The Star
Spangled Crunch*, 1974 (t); *Money Is
Love*, 1975 (n)

• EVAN S. CONNELL, JR.
1924–

The Anatomy Lesson, and Other Stories,
1957 (s); *Mrs. Bridge*, 1959 (n); *The
Patriot*, 1961 (n); *Notes from a Bottle
Found on the Beach at Carmel*, 1963
(p); *At the Crossroads*, 1965 (s); *Diary
of a Rapist*, 1966 (n); *Mr. Bridge*, 1969
(n); *Points for a Compass Rose*, 1973
(p); *The Connoisseur*, 1974 (n)

• ROBERT COOVER
1932–

The Origin of the Brunists, 1966 (n);
*The Universal Baseball Association,
Inc., J. Henry Waugh, Prop.*, 1968 (n);
Pricksongs and Descants, 1969 (s); *A
Theological Position*, 1972 (d)

MALCOLM COWLEY
1898–

A Many-Windowed House, 1970 (c);
A Second Flowering, 1973 (r)

HART CRANE
1899–1932

Robber Rocks, 1969 (letters); *Letters
of Hart Crane and His Family*, 1974

ROBERT· CREELEY
1926–

Mazatlan: Sea, 1969 (p); *Pieces*, 1969
(p); *The Charm: Early and Uncollected
Poems*, 1970; *A Quick Graph: Collected
Notes and Essays*, 1970; *As Now It
Would Be Snow*, 1971 (p); *St. Martin's*,
1971 (p); *A Day Book*, 1972 (p);
Listen, 1972 (d); *Contexts of Poetry*,
1973 (interviews)

E. E. CUMMINGS
1894–1962

Selected Letters, 1969; *Complete Poems:
1913–1962*, 1972

EDWARD DAHLBERG
1900–

The Confessions of Edward Dahlberg,
1971 (m); *The Sorrows of Priapus* (rev.
ed.), 1972 (e); *The Gold of Ophir*,
1972 (e,anthology)

BERNARD DeVOTO
1897–1955

The Letters of Bernard DeVoto, 1975

PETER DE VRIES
1910–

Mrs. Wallop, 1970 (n); *Into Your Tent
I'll Creep*, 1971 (n); *Without a Stitch in
Time*, 1972 (s, sk); *Forever Panting*,
1973 (n); *The Glory of the Hummingbird*, 1974 (n)

JAMES DICKEY
1923–

*The Eye Beaters: Blood, Victory, Mad-
ness, Buckhead and Mercy*, (1970 (p);
Deliverance, 1970 (n); *Self-Interviews*
(recorded and ed. Barbara and James
Reiss), 1970; *Sorties: Journals and New
Essays*, 1971; *Jericho*, 1975 (t)

EMILY DICKINSON
1830–1886

Selected Letters, 1971

• JOAN DIDION
1934–

Run River, 1963 (n); *Slouching towards
Bethlehem*, 1968 (e); *Play It as It Lays*,
1970 (n)

● **E. L. DOCTOROW**
1931–

Welcome to Hard Times, 1960 (n); *Big as Life*, 1966 (n); *The Book of Daniel*, 1971 (n); *Ragtime*, 1975 (n)

J. P. DONLEAVY*
1926–

The Onion Eaters, 1971 (n); *The Plays of J. P. Donleavy*, 1972; *A Fairy Tale of New York*, 1973 (n); *The Unexpurgated Code: A Complete Manual of Survival and Manners*, 1975

HILDA DOOLITTLE
1886–1961

Hermetic Definitions, 1972 (p); *Trilogy*, 1973 (p)

JOHN DOS PASSOS
1896–1970

The Portugal Story: Three Centuries of Exploration and Discovery, 1970 (h); *Easter Island: Island of Enigma*, 1971 (t); *The Fourteenth Chronicle*, 1973 (letters and diaries); *Century's Ebb*, 1975 (n)

● **ROSALYN DREXLER**
1926–

I Am the Beautiful Stranger, 1965 (n); *The Line of Least Existence*, 1967 (d); *One or Another*, 1970 (n); *To Smithereens*, 1972 (n); *The Cosmopolitan Girl*, 1975 (n)

ALAN DUGAN
1923–

Collected Poems, 1969; *Poems 4*, 1974

ROBERT DUNCAN
1919–

Program Notes and Reminiscences, 1970 (r); *Derivations: Selected Poems*, 1950–1956, 1970; *The First Decade: Selected Poems, 1940–1950*, 1970; *Passages 31–35*, 1970 (p)

● **WILLIAM EASTLAKE**
1917–

Go in Beauty, 1956 (n); *The Bronc People*, 1958 (n); *Portrait of an Artist with Twenty-six Horses*, 1963 (n); *Castle Keep*, 1965 (n); *The Bamboo Bed*, 1969 (n); *A Child's Garden of Verses for the Revolution*, 1971 (misc); *Dancers in the Scalp House*, 1975 (n)

RICHARD EBERHART
1904–

Fields of Grace, 1972 (p)

WALTER EDMONDS*
1903–

Bert Breen's Barn, 1975 (juvenile)

T. S. ELIOT
1888–1965

The Complete Poems and Plays, 1969; *The Waste Land: A Facsimile and Transcript of the Original Drafts Including the Annotations of Ezra Pound*, 1971 (p); *Selected Prose*, 1975

GEORGE P. ELLIOTT
1918–

From the Berkeley Hills, 1969 (p); *Conversions: Literature and the Modernist Deviation*, 1971 (c); *Muriel*, 1972 (n)

JAMES T. FARRELL*
1907–

Childhood Is Not Forever, 1970 (s); *The Invisible Swords*, 1971 (n); *Judith*, 1973 (s)

HOWARD FAST*
1914–

Samantha [E. V. Cunningham, pseud.], 1967 (n); *Cynthia* [E. V. Cunningham, pseud.], 1968 (n); *The Assassin Who Gave Up His Gun* [E. V. Cunningham, pseud.], 1969 (n); *The General Zapped an Angel*, 1970 (s); *The Crossing*, 1971 (h); *The Hessian*, 1972 (n); *Millie* [E. V. Cunningham, pseud.], 1973 (n)

WILLIAM FAULKNER
1897–1962

Flags in the Dust, 1973 (n)

LAWRENCE FERLINGHETTI*
1919–

The Secret Meaning of Things, 1969 (p); *Tyrannus Nix*, 1969 (p); *Three by Ferlinghetti*, 1970 (d); *The Mexican Night*, 1970 (t); *Back Roads to Far Places*, 1971 (p); *Open Eye, Open Heart*, 1973 (p)

LESLIE FIEDLER
1917–

Being Busted, 1970 (m); *Collected Essays*, Vols. I and II, 1971; *The Stranger in Shakespeare*, 1972 (c); *The Messengers Will Come No More*, 1974 (n)

F. SCOTT FITZGERALD
1896–1940

F. Scott Fitzgerald in His Own Time, 1971 (misc); *Dear Scott/Dear Max: The Fitzgerald–Perkins Correspondence*, 1971; *As Ever, Scott Fitz—: Letters between F. Scott Fitzgerald and His Literary Agent, Harold Ober, 1919–1940*, 1972; *The Basil and Josephine Stories*, 1973; (with Zelda Fitzgerald) *Bits of Paradise*, 1974 (s)

ROBERT FITZGERALD*
1910–

Spring Shade, 1971 (p,tr); *The Iliad*, 1974 (tr)

WALLACE FOWLIE*
1908–

The French Critic, 1968 (c); *Stendhal*, 1969 (c); *Lautréamont*, 1973 (c); *French Literature: Its History and Meaning*, 1973 (c); *Letters of Henry Miller and Wallace Fowlie*, 1975

WALDO FRANK*
1889–1967

The Memoirs of Waldo Frank, 1973

HAROLD FREDERIC
1856–1898

Stories of York State, 1966

BRUCE JAY FRIEDMAN
1930–

Steambath, 1970 (d); *The Dick*, 1970 (n); *About Harry Towns*, 1974 (n)

ROBERT FROST
1874–1963

The Poetry of Robert Frost, 1969; *A Time to Talk: Conversations and Indiscretions* (recorded by Robert Francis Frost), 1969; *Family Letters of Robert and Elinor Frost*, 1972; *Robert Frost on Writing*, 1973 (e)

DANIEL FUCHS
1909–

West of the Rockies, 1971 (n)

• R. BUCKMINSTER FULLER
1895–

The Time Lock, 1928 (e); *Nine Chains to the Moon*, 1938 (e); *Education Au-*

tomation, 1962 (e); *Untitled Epic Poems on the History of Industrialization*, 1962 (p); *Ideas and Integrities*, 1963 (e); *No More Secondhand God, and Other Writings*, 1963 (p); *Operating Manual for Spaceship Earth*, 1969 (e); *Utopia or Oblivion*, 1969 (e); *The Buckminster Fuller Reader*, 1970; *Intuition*, 1972 (p); *Synergetics*, 1975 (e)

● **WILLIAM GADDIS**
1922–

The Recognitions, 1955 (n); *JR*, 1975 (n)

● **JOHN GARDNER**
1933–

The Resurrection, 1966 (n); *The Wreckage of Agathon*, 1970 (n); *Grendel*, 1971 (n); *The Sunlight Dialogues*, 1972 (n); *Jason and Medeia*, 1973 (p); *Nickel Mountain*, 1973 (n); *The King's Indian: Stories and Tales*, 1974

JEAN GARRIGUE
1914–1972

Chartres and Prose Poems, 1971 (e,p); *Studies for an Actress, and Other Poems*, 1973

● **WILLIAM H. GASS**
1924–

Omensetter's Luck, 1966 (n); *In the Heart of the Heart of the Country*, 1968 (s); *Fiction and the Figures of Life*, 1971 (c); *Willie Masters' Lonesome Wife*, 1972 (n)

JACK GELBER*
1932–

Sleep, 1972 (d); *Barbary Shore*, 1973 (d)

WILLIAM GIBSON*
1914–

A Season in Heaven, 1974 (m)

ALLEN GINSBERG
1926–

Airplane Dreams, 1969 (p); *Indian Journals*, 1970 (p,e); *Kaddish*, 1972 (d); *The Fall of America*, 1973 (p); *Allen Verbatim*, 1974 (e); *The Visions of the Great Rememberer*, 1974 (r)

HERBERT GOLD*
1924–

The Great American Jackpot, 1970 (n); *The Magic Will*, 1971 (s,e); *My Last Two Thousand Years*, 1972 (a); *Swiftie the Magician*, 1974 (n)

● **PAUL GOODMAN**
1911–1972

The Grand Piano, 1942 (n); *Stop-Light: Noh*, 1945 (pd); *The Facts of Life*, 1945 (s,d); *State of Nature*, 1946 (n); *Kafka's Prayer*, 1947 (c); (with Percival Goodman) *Communitas*, 1947 (e); *The Break-up of Our Camp*, 1949 (s); *The Structure of Literature*, 1954 (e); *The Empire City*, 1959 (n); *Our Visit to Niagara*, 1960 (s); *Growing Up Absurd*, 1960 (e); *Drawing the Line*, 1962 (e); *Utopian Essays and Practical Proposals*, 1962 (e); *The Community of Scholars*, 1962 (e); *The Lordly Hudson, and Other Poems*, 1962; *Making Do*, 1963 (n); *The Society I Live in Is Mine*, 1963 (e); *Compulsory Mis-Education*, 1964 (e); *People or Personnel*, 1965 (e); *Three Plays*, 1965; *Five Years*, 1966 (m); *Hawkweed*, 1967 (p); *Like a Conquered Province*, 1967 (e); *Adam and His Works*, 1968 (s); *North Percy*, 1970 (p); *New Reformation*, 1970 (e); *Tragedy and Comedy*, 1970 (d); *Homespun of Oatmeal Gray*, 1970 (p);

GOODMAN *(Cont.)*
Speaking and Language, 1972 (e); *Little Prayers and Finite Experience*, 1972 (misc); *Collected Poems*, 1974

● **CAROLINE GORDON**
1895–

Penhally, 1931 (n); *Aleck Maury, Sportsman*, 1934 (n); *None Shall Look Back*, 1937 (n); *The Garden of Adonis*, 1937 (n); *Green Centuries*, 1941 (n); *The Women on the Porch*, 1944 (n); *The Forest of the South*, 1945 (s); *The Strange Children*, 1951 (n); *The Malefactors*, 1956 (n); *How to Read a Novel*, 1957 (c); *A Good Soldier: A Key to the Novels of Ford Madox Ford*, 1963 (c); *Old Red, and Other Stories*, 1963; *The Glory of Hera*, 1972 (n)

WILLIAM GOYEN*
1918–

A Book of Jesus, 1973 (e); *Selected Writings*, 1974; *Come, the Restorer*, 1974 (n); *The Collected Stories*, 1975

SHIRLEY ANN GRAU*
1929–

The Condor Passes, 1971 (n); *The Wind Shifting West*, 1973 (s)

PAUL GREEN*
1894–

Cross and Sword, 1966 (d); *Home to My Valley*, 1970 (misc)

HORACE GREGORY*
1898–

The House on Jefferson Street, 1971 (a); *Spirit of Time and Place*, 1973 (e)

A. B. GUTHRIE*
1901–

Arfive, 1971 (n); *Wild Pitch*, 1973 (n); *The Last Valley*, 1975 (n)

DASHIELL HAMMETT
1894–1961

The Continental Op, 1974 (s)

● **LORRAINE HANSBERRY**
1930–1965

A Raisin in the Sun, 1959 (d); *The Movement: Documentary of a Struggle for Equality*, 1964 (e); *The Sign in Sidney Brustein's Window*, 1965 (d); *To Be Young, Gifted and Black*, 1969 (d); *Les Blancs*, 1970 (d); *Les Blancs, and the Last Plays of Lorraine Hansberry*, 1972

JOHN HAWKES
1925–

Lunar Landscapes, 1969 (s); *The Blood Oranges*, 1971 (n); *Death, Sleep & the Traveler*, 1974 (n)

JOSEPH HELLER
1923–

Something Happened, 1974 (n)

LILLIAN HELLMAN
1905–

An Unfinished Woman, 1969 (m); *The Collected Plays*, 1972; *Pentimento*, 1973 (m)

ERNEST HEMINGWAY
1899–1961

The Fifth Column, and Four Stories of the Spanish Civil War, 1969 (d,s); *Islands in the Stream*, 1970 (n); *The Nick Adams Stories*, 1972

JOHN HERSEY*
1914–

Letter to the Alumni, 1970 (e); *The Conspiracy*, 1972 (n); *My Petition for More Space*, 1974 (n)

CHESTER HIMES
1909–

The Crazy Kill, 1960 (n); *The Big Gold Dream*, 1960 (n); *A Rage in Harlem* (paperback reissue of *For Love of Imabelle*), 1964; *The Real Cool Killers*, 1966 (n); *Blind Man with a Pistol*, 1969 (n); *The Quality of Hurt*, 1972 (a); *Black on Black*, 1973 (s,e)

• ISRAEL HOROVITZ
1939–

Line, 1967 (d); *It's Called the Sugar Plum*, 1967 (d); *The Indian Wants the Bronx*, 1968 (d); *Rats*, 1968 (d); *First Season*, 1968 (d); *Chiaroscura*, 1969 (d); *The Honest-to-God Schnozzola*, 1969 (d); *Leader*, 1969 (d); *Acrobats*, 1971 (d); *Cappella*, 1973 (n); *Dr. Hero*, 1973 (d); *Alfred the Great*, 1974 (d); *The Primary English Class*, 1976 (d)

• RICHARD HOWARD
1929–

Quantities, 1962 (p); *The Damages*, 1967 (p); *Alone with America*, 1969 (c); *Untitled Subjects*, 1969 (p); *Findings*, 1971 (p); *Two-Part Inventions*, 1974 (p)

IRVING HOWE*
1920–

Decline of the New, 1970 (e); (ed.) *Beyond the New Left*, 1970 (anthology); (ed., with Eliezer Greenberg) *Voices from the Yiddish: Essays, Memoirs, Diaries*, 1972 (anthology); (with Carl Gershman) *Israel, the Arabs and the Middle East*, 1972 (e); (ed.) *The World of the Blue-Collar Worker*, 1972 (anthology); (ed.) *A Treasury of Yiddish Poetry*, 1972 (anthology); *The Critical Point*, 1973 (e); *World of Our Fathers*, 1976 (h)

LANGSTON HUGHES
1902–1967

The Panther and the Lash, 1967 (p); *Good Morning Revolution*, 1973 (misc)

WILLIAM INGE*
1913–1973

Good Luck, Miss Wyckoff, 1970 (n); *My Son Is a Splendid Driver*, 1971 (n)

HENRY JAMES
1843–1916

The Speech and Manners of American Women, 1973 (e); *The Letters of Henry James*, vol. 1, 1974; vol. 2, 1975

RANDALL JARRELL
1914–1965

The Complete Poems, 1969; *The Third Book of Criticism*, 1969; *Jerome: The Biography of a Poem*, 1971 (c); *Faust, Part I*, 1972 (tr)

• JAMES WELDON JOHNSON
1871–1938

The Autobiography of an Ex-Colored Man, 1912 [repr. 1927 with spelling "Ex-Coloured"] (n); *Fifty Years, and Other Poems*, 1917; (with Horace Kallen) *Africa in the World Democracy*, 1919 (e); *God's Trombones*, 1927 (p); *Black Manhattan*, 1930 (e); *St. Peter Relates an Incident: Selected Poems*, 1930 (private), 1935 (trade); *Along This Way*, 1933 (a); *Negro Americans, What Now?*, 1934 (e)

JAMES JONES
1921–

The Merry Month of May, 1971 (n); *A Touch of Danger*, 1973 (n); *World War II*, 1975 (h)

LeROI JONES (AMIRI BARAKA)
1934–

Four Black Revolutionary Plays, 1969; Black Magic Poetry, 1969; Slave Ship, 1969 (d); (with Fundi [Billy Abernathy]) In Our Terribleness: Some Elements and Meaning in Black Style, 1970 (misc); Jello, 1970 (p); Raise Race Rays Raze: Essays Since 1965, 1971; Mad Heart and a Black Mass, 1972 (d); A Recent Killing, 1973 (d); Sidnee Poet Heroical, 1975 (d)

MacKINLAY KANTOR*
1904–

(with Tim Kantor) Hamilton County, 1970 (t); I Love You, Irene, 1972 (m); The Children Sing, 1973 (n); Valley Forge, 1975 (n)

JACK KEROUAC
1922–1969

Visions of Cody, 1973 (n) [uncut version of 1960 publication]

• KEN KESEY
1935–

One Flew Over the Cuckoo's Nest, 1962 (n); Sometimes a Great Notion, 1964 (n); Kesey's Garage Sale, 1972 (misc)

• GALWAY KINNELL
1927–

What a Kingdom It Was, 1960 (p); Flower Herding on Mount Monadnock, 1964 (p); Black Light, 1966 (n); Body Rags, 1968 (p); The Book of Nightmares, 1971 (p); The Avenue Bearing the Initial of Christ into the New World: Poems, 1946–1964, 1974

• JERZY KOSINSKI
1933–

(as Joseph Novak) The Future Is Ours, Comrade, 1960 (e); (as Joseph Novak) No Third Path, 1962 (e); The Painted Bird, 1965 (n); Steps, 1968 (n); Being There, 1971 (n); The Devil Tree, 1973 (n); Cockpit, 1975 (n)

STANLEY KUNITZ
1905–

The Testing-Tree, 1971 (p); (with Max Hayward) Poems of Akhmatova, 1973 (tr); A Kind of Order, A Kind of Folly, 1975 (e)

RICHMOND LATTIMORE
1906–

Poems from Three Decades, 1972; Iphigeneia in Tauris, 1973 (tr)

DENISE LEVERTOV
1923–

Selected Poems (by Guillevic), 1969 (tr); Summer Poems, 1969; Relearning the Alphabet, 1970 (p); To Stay Alive, 1971 (p); Footprints, 1972 (p); The Poet in the World, 1973 (e); The Freeing of the Dust, 1975 (p)

MEYER LEVIN*
1905–

The Settlers, 1972 (n); The Obsession, 1974 (m); The Spell of Time, 1974 (n)

ROBERT LOWELL
1917–

(with Jacques Barzun) Phaedra and Figaro), 1961 (tr); Notebook 1967–68, 1969 (p); Prometheus Bound, 1969 (d); Notebook, 1970 (p); The Dolphin, 1973 (p); History, 1973 (p); For Lizzie and Harriet, 1973 (p)

MARY McCARTHY
1912–

The Writing on the Wall, and Other Literary Essays, 1970; Birds of America,

1971 (n); *Medina*, 1972 (j); *The Seventeenth Degree*, 1974 (j); *The Mask of State*, 1974 (j)

CARSON McCULLERS
1917–1967

The Mortgaged Heart: The Previously Uncollected Writings of Carson Mc-Cullers, 1971 (misc)

DWIGHT MACDONALD*
1906–

Dwight Macdonald on Movies, 1969 (c); *Politics Past* (new ed. of *Memoirs of a Revolutionist*), 1969

ROSS MACDONALD
(KENNETH MILLAR)
1915–

The Goodbye Look, 1969 (n); *Archer at Large* (*The Galton Case, The Chill, Black Money*), 1970 (3n); *The Underground Man*, 1971 (n); *Sleeping Beauty*, 1973 (n); *On Crime Writing*, 1973 (e)

PHYLLIS McGINLEY*
1905–

Saint-Watching, 1969 (e)

● THOMAS McGUANE
1940–

The Sporting Club, 1969 (n); *The Bushwacked Piano*, 1971 (n); *Ninety-two in the Shade*, 1973 (n)

ARCHIBALD MacLEISH
1892–

Scratch, 1971 (d); *The Human Season: Selected Poems 1926–1972*, 1972; *The Great American Fourth of July Parade*, 1975 (pd)

NORMAN MAILER
1923–

Of a Fire on the Moon, 1970 (j); *The Prisoner of Sex*, 1971 (e); *Maidstone: A Mystery*, 1971 (scenario, e); *Existential Errands*, 1972 (misc); *St. George and the Godfather*, 1972 (j); *Marilyn: A Biography*, 1973; *The Faith of Graffiti*, 1974 (e); *The Fight*, 1975 (j)

BERNARD MALAMUD
1914–

Pictures of Fidelman, 1969 (s); *The Tenants*, 1971 (n); *Rembrandt's Hat*, 1973 (s)

ALBERT MALTZ*
1908–

Afternoon in the Jungle, 1971 (s)

H. L. MENCKEN
1880–1950

A Gang of Pecksniffs, 1975 (j)

● WILLIAM MEREDITH
1919–

Love Letter from an Impossible Land, 1944 (p); *Ships and Other Figures*, 1948 (p); *The Open Sea*, 1958 (p); *The Wreck of the Thresher*, 1964 (p); *Earth Walk: New and Selected Poems*, 1970; *Hazard, the Painter*, 1975 (p)

JAMES MERRILL
1926–

The Fire Screen, 1969 (p); *The Country of a Thousand Years of Peace, and Other Poems* (new and enlarged ed.), 1970; *Braving the Elements*, 1972 (p); *The Yellow Pages*, 1974 (p)

THOMAS MERTON*
1915–1968

The Geography of Lograire, 1969 (p); *My Argument with the Gestapo*, 1969 (n); *Contemplative Prayer*, 1970; (with text by John Howard Griffin) *A Hidden Wholeness*, 1970 (photographs); *Contemplation in a World of Action*, 1971 (e)

W. S. MERWIN
1927–

Transparence of the World (poems by Jean Follain), 1969 (tr); *Animae*, 1969 (p); *Song of Roland*, 1970 (tr); *The Miner's Pale Children: A Book of Prose*, 1970; *The Carrier of Ladders*, 1970 (p); *Love Poems* (by Pablo Neruda), 1972 (tr); *Writings to an Unfinished Accompaniment*, 1973 (p); *Asian Figures*, 1973 (tr)

JAMES A. MICHENER*
1907–

The Quality of Life, 1970 (e); (with drawings by Jack Levine) *Facing East*, 1970 (art book); *Kent State: What Happened and Why*, 1971 (j); *The Drifters*, 1971 (n); *A Michener Miscellany*, 1973; *Centennial*, 1974 (n)

JOSEPHINE MILES*
1911–

Poetry and Change, 1974 (c); *To All Appearances*, 1975 (p)

ARTHUR MILLER
1915–

(with Inge Morath) *In Russia*, 1969 (t); *The Creation of the World and Other Business*, 1972 (d)

HENRY MILLER
1891–

My Life and Times, 1971 (m); *Henry Miller in Conversation with George Belmont*, 1972; *Insomnia*, 1974 (m); *Letters of Henry Miller and Wallace Fowlie*, 1975; *The Nightmare Notebook*, 1975 (journal); *Henry Miller's Book of Friends*, 1976 (r)

WRIGHT MORRIS
1910–

A Bill of Rites, A Bill of Wrongs, A Bill of Goods, 1968 (e); *A Reader*, 1970 (misc); *Green Grass, Blue Sky, White House*, 1970 (s); *Fire Sermon*, 1971 (n); *War Games*, 1971 (n); *Love Affair—A Venetian Journal*, 1972; *The Inhabitants*, 1972 (e); *A Life*, 1973 (n); *Here Is Einbaum*, 1973 (s)

LEWIS MUMFORD
1895–

The Van Wyck Brooks–Lewis Mumford Letters, 1970; *The Myth of the Machine: The Pentagon of Power*, vol. II, 1970 (e); *The Letters of Lewis Mumford and Frederick J. Osborn: A Trans-Atlantic Dialogue, 1938–1970*, 1972; *Interpretations and Forecasts: 1922–1972*, 1973 (e); *Findings and Keepings*, 1975 (misc)

VLADIMIR NABOKOV
1899–

Ada; or, Ardor, 1969 (n); *Mary*, 1970 (n, tr. by Michael Glenny); *Poems and Problems*, 1971 (p); *Glory*, 1971 (n); *Transparent Things*, 1972 (n); *A Russian Beauty*, 1973 (s, tr. by Dmitri Nabokov); *Strong Opinions*, 1973 (misc); *Look at the Harlequins!*, 1974 (n); *Tyrants Destroyed*, 1975 (s)

OGDEN NASH*
1902–1971

Bed Riddance, 1970 (p); The Old Dog Barks Backward, 1972 (p); I Wouldn't Have Missed It, 1975 (p and drawings)

HOWARD NEMEROV
1920–

Reflexions on Poetry & Poetics, 1972 (c); Gnomes & Occasions, 1973 (p); The Western Approaches, 1975 (p)

REINHOLD NIEBUHR*
1892–1971

Justice and Mercy, 1974 (e)

ANAIS NIN
1903–

The Novel of the Future, 1968 (e); Diary, vol. III, 1969; Diary, vol. IV, 1971; Anais Nin Reader, 1973

FRANK NORRIS*
1870–1902

A Novelist in the Making: A Collection of Student Themes and the Novels "Blix" and "Vandover and the Brute," 1970

• JOYCE CAROL OATES
1938–

By the North Gate, 1963 (s); With Shuddering Fall, 1964 (n); Sweet Enemy, 1965 (d); Upon the Sweeping Flood, 1966 (s); A Garden of Earthly Delights, 1967 (n); Expensive People, 1968 (n); Anonymous Sins, & Other Poems, 1969; them, 1969 (n); Sunday Dinner, 1970 (d); The Wheel of Love, 1970 (s); Love and Its Derangements, 1970 (p); Ontological Proof of

My Existence, 1972 (d); The Edge of Impossibility, 1972 (c); Marriages and Infidelities, 1972 (s); Wonderland, 1973 (n); Angel Fire, 1973 (p); The Hostile Sun: The Poetry of D. H. Lawrence, 1973 (c); Do With Me What You Will, 1973 (n); New Heaven, New Earth, 1974 (c); The Hungry Ghosts, 1974 (s); Where Are You Going, Where Have You Been?: Stories of Young America, 1974; The Goddess, and Other Women, 1974 (s); Miracle Play, 1974 (d); The Poisoned Kiss, 1975 (s); The Seduction, and Other Stories, 1975; The Assassins, 1975 (n); The Fabulous Beasts, 1975 (p)

EDWIN O'CONNOR*
1918–1968

The Best and the Last of Edwin O'Connor, 1970 (misc)

FLANNERY O'CONNOR
1925–1964

Mystery and Manner, 1969 (h,c); The Complete Stories of Flannery O'Connor, 1971

• FRANK O'HARA
1926–1966

Try! Try!, 1950 (d); Change Your Bedding, 1951 (d); A City Winter, and Other Poems, 1952; Meditations in an Emergency, 1957 (p); Jackson Pollack, 1959 (e); Odes, 1960 (p); The New Spanish Painting and Sculpture, 1960 (e); Second Avenue, 1960 (p); Awake in Spain, 1960 (d); Lunch Poems, 1964; The General Returns from One Place to Another, 1964 (d); Robert Motherwell, 1965 (e); Love Poems, 1965; Nakian, 1966 (e); In Memory of My Feelings, 1967 (p); Collected Poems, 1971; Selected Poems, 1974; Art Chronicles 1954–1966, 1975; Standing Still and Walking in New York, 1975 (p)

JOHN O'HARA
1905–1970

The O'Hara Generation, 1969 (s); Lovey Childs, 1969 (n); The Ewings, 1972 (n); The Time Element, & Other Stories, 1972

• CHARLES OLSON
1910–1970

Call Me Ishmael, 1947 (c); Mayan Letters, 1953 (e); Projective Verse vs. the Non-Projective, 1959 (c); The Maximus Poems, 1960; The Distances, 1960 (p); A Bibliography on America for Ed Dorn, 1964 (bibliography); Proprioception, 1965 (e); Selected Writings, 1966 (misc); Human Universe, and Other Essays, 1968; Maximus Poems IV, V, VI, 1969; Letters for Origin, 1970 (e); Archaeologist of Morning, 1971 (p); Poetry and Truth, 1971 (misc); Additional Prose, 1974 (e); The Post Office, 1974 (s); Charles Olson and Ezra Pound: An Encounter at St. Elizabeths, 1975 (r); The Maximus Poems, vol. 3 ,1975

• CYNTHIA OZICK
1928–

Trust, 1966 (n); The Pagan Rabbi, and Other Stories, 1971; Bloodshed, and Three Novellas, 1976 (s)

DOROTHY PARKER*
1893–1967

Constant Reader, 1970 (e)

KENNETH PATCHEN*
1911–1972

Sleepers Awake, 1969 (p); Aflame and Afun of Walking Faces, 1970 (fables); Wonderings, 1971 (p); There's Love All Day, 1971 (p)

WALKER PERCY
1916–

Love in the Ruins, 1971 (n); The Message in the Bottle, 1975 (e)

• SYLVIA PLATH
1932–1963

The Colossus, and Other Poems, 1957 (Br. ed.), 1962 (Amer. ed.); The Bell Jar, 1963 (Br. ed.), 1971 (Amer. ed.) (n); Ariel, 1965 (Br. ed.), 1966 (Amer. ed.) (p); Crossing the Water, 1971 (p); Winter Trees, 1971 (Br. ed.), 1972 (Amer. ed.) (p); Letters Home: Correspondence 1950–1963, 1975

KATHERINE ANNE PORTER
1894–

The Collected Essays and Occasional Writings of Katherine Anne Porter, 1970 (misc)

EZRA POUND
1885–1972

Drafts and Fragments of Cantos CX–CXVII, 1969 (p); Confucius, 1969 (tr); Gaudier-Brzeska (enlarged ed.), 1970 (b); Selected Cantos, 1970 (p); The Cantos [1–117], 1970 (p); The Waste Land (by T. S. Eliot), 1971 (annotations); Selected Prose 1909–1965, 1973

J. F. POWERS*
1917–

Look How the Fish Live, 1975 (s)

• JAMES PURDY
1923–

63: Dream Palace, 1956 (s); Color of Darkness, 1957 (s); Malcolm, 1959 (n);

The Nephew, 1960 (n); *Children Is All*, 1962 (s); *Cabot Wright Begins*, 1964 (n); *Eustace Chisholm and the Works*, 1967 (n); *Jeremy's Version*, 1970 (n); *I Am Elijah Thrush*, 1972 (n); *The House of the Solitary Maggot*, 1974 (n); *In a Shallow Grave*, 1976 (n)

THOMAS PYNCHON
1936–

Gravity's Rainbow, 1973 (n)

• DAVID RABE
1940–

Sticks and Bones, 1969 (d); *The Basic Training of Pavlo Hummel*, 1971 (d); *The Orphan*, 1973 (d); *The Boom Boom Room*, 1973 (d); *In the Boom Boom Room* (rev. ed.), 1974 (d); *Streamers*, 1976 (d)

PHILIP RAHV
1908–1974

Literature and the Sixth Sense, 1969 (c)

JOHN CROWE RANSOM
1888–1974

Selected Poems (rev. and enlarged), 1969; *The Poetic Sense*, 1971 (e); *Beating the Bushes*, 1972 (e)

• ISHMAEL REED
1938–

The Free-Lance Pallbearers, 1967 (n); *Yellow Back Radio Broke-Down*, 1969 (n); *Mumbo Jumbo*, 1972 (n); *Conjure*, 1972 (p); *Chattanooga*, 1973 (p); *The Last Days of Louisana Red*, 1974 (n)

KENNETH REXROTH
1905–

Classics Revisited, 1968 (c); *Selected Poems* by Pierre Reverdy, 1969 (tr);

The Alternative Society, 1970 (e); *With Eye and Ear*, 1970 (e); *Love and the Turning Year*, 1970 (tr); *American Poetry in the Twentieth Century*, 1971 (c); (with Ling Chung) *The Orchid Boat* (tr); *The Elastic Retort*, 1973 (e); *New Poems*, 1974; *Communalism*, 1974 (h)

ADRIENNE RICH
1929–

Leaflets, 1969 (p); *The Will to Change*, 1971 (p); *Reflections* (by Mark Insingel), 1972 (tr); *Diving into the Wreck*, 1973 (p); *Poems*, 1975

THEODORE ROETHKE
1908–1963

Straw for the Fire, 1972 (selections from notebooks)

OLE RÖLVAAG*
1876–1931

The Third Life of Per Smevik, 1971 (n)

PHILIP ROTH
1933–

Portnoy's Complaint, 1969 (n); *Our Gang*, 1971 (n); *The Breast*, 1972 (n); *The Great American Novel*, 1972 (n); *My Life as a Man*, 1974 (n); *Reading Myself and Others*, 1975 (c)

MURIEL RUKEYSER
1913–

The Traces of Thomas Hariot, 1971 (b); *Breaking Open*, 1973 (p)

CARL SANDBURG
1878–1967

The Complete Poems (rev. and expanded), 1970; *The Sandburg Treasury*, 1970 (misc)

WILLIAM SAROYAN
1908–

Letters from 74 Rue Tailbout, 1969; *Making Money, and 19 Other Very Short Plays*, 1970; *Days of Life and Death and Escape to the Moon*, 1970 (e); *Places Where I've Done Time*, 1970 (m); *The Rebirth Celebration of the Human Race at Artie Zabada's Off-Broadway Theatre*, 1975 (d)

MAY SARTON
1912–

The Poet and the Donkey, 1969 (n); *Kinds of Love*, 1970 (n); *A Grain of Mustard Seed*, 1971 (p); *A Durable Fire: New Poems*, 1972; *Journal of a Solitude*, 1973 (m); *As We Are Now*, 1973 (n); *Collected Poems*, 1974; *Punch's Secret*, 1974 (juvenile); *Crucial Conversations*, 1975 (n)

MURRAY SCHISGAL*
1926–

The Chinese, 1970 (d); *Dr. Fish*, 1970 (d); *An American Millionaire*, 1973 (d); *All Over Town*, 1974 (d)

BUDD SCHULBERG*
1914–

Sanctuary V, 1970 (n); *Loser and Still Champion: Muhammad Ali*, 1972 (b); *The Four Seasons of Success*, 1972 (m); *Swan Watch*, 1975 (r)

DELMORE SCHWARTZ
1913–1966

Selected Essays, 1970

WINFIELD TOWNLEY SCOTT
1910–1968

The Dirty Hand: The Literary Notebooks of Winfield Townley Scott, 1969; *Alpha Omega*, 1971 (misc)

• HUBERT SELBY
1928–

Last Exit to Brooklyn, 1964 (n); *The Room*, 1971 (n)

ANNE SEXTON
1928–1974

Love Poems, 1969; *Mercy Street*, 1969 (pd); *Transformations*, 1971 (p); *The Book of Folly*, 1972 (p); *The Death Notebooks*, 1973 (p); *The Awful Rowing toward God*, 1975 (p)

KARL SHAPIRO
1913–

White-Haired Lover, 1968 (p); *Edsel*, 1971 (n); *The Poetry Wreck*, 1975 (c)

IRWIN SHAW*
1913–

Rich Man, Poor Man, 1970 (n); *God Was Here, But He Left Early*, 1973 (s); *Evening in Byzantium*, 1973 (n); *Nightwork*, 1975 (n)

• WILFRID SHEED
1930–

A Middle Class Education, 1960 (n); *The Hack*, 1963 (n); *Square's Progress*, 1965 (n); *Office Politics*, 1966 (n); *The Blacking Factory, and Pennsylvania Gothic*, 1968 (n); *Max Jamison*, 1970 (n); *The Morning After*, 1971 (e); *People Will Always Be Kind*, 1973 (n); *Three Mobs: Labor, Church and Mafia*, 1974 (e); *Muhammad Ali*, 1975 (b)

• SAM SHEPARD
1943–

The Rock Garden, 1964 (d); *Up to Thursday*, 1965 (d); *Chicago*, 1966 (d); *Red Cross*, 1966 (d); *Icarus's Mother*, 1966 (d); *La Turista*, 1967 (d); *Cow-*

boys #2, 1967 (d); *Five Plays*, 1967; *Forensic and the Navigators*, 1968 (d); *Operation Sidewinder*, 1970 (d); *The Unseen Hand*, 1970 (d); *The Mad Dog Blues*, 1971 (d); *Cowboy Mouth*, 1971 (d); *Mad Dog Blues, and Other Plays*, 1972; *The Unseen Hand, and Other Plays*, 1972; *The Tooth of Crime*, 1973 (d); *Hawk Moon: A Book of Short Stories, Poems and Monologues*, 1973; *The Tooth of Crime, and Geography of a Horse Dreamer*, 1974 (d)

NEIL SIMON*
1927–

The Last of the Red Hot Lovers, 1969 (d); *The Out of Towners*, 1970 (screenplay); *The Gingerbread Lady*, 1970 (d); *The Prisoner of Second Avenue*, 1971 (d); *The Comedy of Neil Simon* (6 plays and the musical *Promises, Promises*), 1971; *The Sunshine Boys*, 1972 (d); *The Good Doctor*, 1973 (d); *God's Favorite*, 1974 (d)

LOUIS SIMPSON
1923–

Adventures of the Letter I, 1972 (p); *North of Jamaica*, 1972 (a); *Three on the Tower*, 1975 (c)

• ISAAC BASHEVIS SINGER
1904–

The Family Moskat, 1950 (n); *Satan in Goray*, 1955 (n); *Gimpel the Fool, and Other Stories*, 1957; *The Magician of Lublin*, 1960 (n); *The Spinoza of Market Street*, 1961 (s); *The Slave*, 1962 (n); *Short Friday, and Other Stories*, 1964; *In My Father's Court*, 1966 (m); *Selected Short Stories*, 1966; *Zlateh the Goat, and Other Stories*, 1966 (juvenile); *The Fearsome Inn*, 1967 (juvenile); *The Manor*, 1967 (n); *Mazel and Shlimazel*, 1968 (juvenile); *The Séance, and Other Stories*, 1968; *The Estate*,

1969 (n); *Day of Pleasure*, 1969 (juvenile); *Elijah the Slave*, 1970 (juvenile); *A Friend of Kafka, and Other Stories*, 1970; *Joseph and Koza*, 1970 (n); *An Isaac Bashevis Singer Reader*, 1971; *Alone in the Wild Forest*, 1971 (juvenile); *The Topsy Turvy Emperor of China*, 1971 (juvenile); *Enemies*, 1972 (n); *Hassidim*, 1972 (e); *The Wicked City*, 1972 (juvenile); *A Crown of Feathers*, 1973 (s); *Why Noah Chose the Dove*, 1974 (juvenile); *Passions*, 1975 (s)

All publication dates refer to English translations; the original Yiddish books in some instances appeared many years earlier.

W. D. SNODGRASS
1926–

In Radical Pursuit, 1975 (c)

• GARY SNYDER
1930–

Rip Rap, 1959 (p); *Myths and Texts*, 1960 (p); *Rip Rap and Cold Mountain Poems*, 1965 (p); *A Range of Poems*, 1967; *The Back Country*, 1968 (p); *Earth House Hold*, 1969 (p); *Regarding Wave*, 1970 (p); *Six Sections from Mountains and Rivers without End Plus One*, 1970 (p); *Turtle Island*, 1974 (p,e)

SUSAN SONTAG*
1933–

Styles of Radical Will, 1969 (e); *Duet for Cannibals*, 1970 (screenplay); *Brother Carl*, 1974 (screenplay)

JEAN STAFFORD*
1915–

The Collected Stories of Jean Stafford, 1969

• WILLIAM STAFFORD
1914–

West of Your City, 1960 (p); *Traveling through the Dark*, 1962 (p); *The Rescued Year*, 1966 (p); *Friends to This Ground*, 1967 (c); *Allegiances*, 1970 (p); (with Robert H. Ross) *Poems and Perspective*, 1971 (c); *Someday, Maybe*, 1973 (p)

WALLACE STEGNER*
1909–

The Sound of Mountain Water, 1969 (misc); *Joe Hill* (orig. *The Preacher and the Slave*), 1970 (n); *Angle of Repose*, 1971 (n); *The Uneasy Chair*, 1973 (b)

GERTRUDE STEIN
1874–1946

Gertrude Stein on Picasso, 1970; *Fernhurst, Q.E.D., and Other Early Writings*, 1971; *A Primer for the Gradual Understanding of Gertrude Stein*, 1971 (anthology, much of it previously uncollected or unavailable); *Sherwood Anderson/Gertrude Stein*, 1973 (letters, e)

JOHN STEINBECK*
1902–1968

Journal of a Novel, 1969 (letters); *John Steinbeck: A Life in Letters*, 1975

WALLACE STEVENS
1879–1955

The Palm at the End of the Mind, 1971 (p)

TRUMBULL STICKNEY
1874–1904

The Poems of Trumbull Stickney, 1972

WILLIAM STYRON
1925–

In the Clap Shack, 1973 (d)

HARVEY SWADOS*
1920–1972

Standing Fast, 1970 (n); *Standing Up for the People*, 1972 (b-juvenile); *Celebration*, 1975 (n)

ALLEN TATE
1899–

The Swimmers, 1971 (p); *Memoirs and Opinions: 1926–1974*, 1975 (m,c)

PETER TAYLOR
1917–

The Collected Stories, 1969; *Presences: Seven Dramatic Pieces*, 1973

• JEAN TOOMER
1894–1967

Cane, 1923 (n); (with others) *Problems of Civilization*, 1929 (e); *Essentials: Definitions and Aphorisms*, 1931 (misc); *The Flavor of Man*, 1949 (e); *The Wayward and the Seeking: A Miscellany of Writings*, 1974

LIONEL TRILLING*
1905–1975

Sincerity and Authenticity, 1972 (e); *Mind in the Modern World*, 1973 (e)

MARK TWAIN
1835–1910

Mark Twain's Notebooks and Journals, vols. 1 and 2, 1975

JOHN UPDIKE
1932–

Midpoint, 1970 (p); Bech: A Book, 1970 (n); Rabbit Redux, 1971 (n); Museums and Woman, 1972 (s); Buchanan Dying, 1974 (d); A Month of Sundays, 1975 (n); Picked-up Pieces, 1975 (misc)

MARK VAN DOREN
1894–1972

That Shining Place, 1969 (p); Carl Sandburg, 1969 (c); (with Maurice Samuels) In the Beginning, Love, 1973 (conversations); Good Morning, 1973 (p); (with Maurice Samuels) The Book of Praise, 1975 (conversations)

PETER VIERECK
1916–

Soviet Policy Making, 1967 (e)

• KURT VONNEGUT, JR.
1922–

Player Piano, 1952 (n); The Sirens of Titan, 1959 (n); Mother Night, 1961 (n); Canary in a Cat House, 1961 (s); Cat's Cradle, 1963 (n); God Bless You, Mr. Rosewater, 1965 (n); Welcome to the Monkey House, 1968 (s); Slaughterhouse-Five, 1969 (n); Happy Birthday, Wanda June, 1971 (d); Between Time and Timbuktu, 1972 (d); Breakfast of Champions, 1973 (n); Wampeters, Foma, & Granfallons, 1974 (e)

• DIANE WAKOSKI
1937–

Coins and Coffins, 1962 (p); Discrepancies and Apparitions, 1966 (p); The George Washington Poems, 1967; Greed, Parts 1 and 2, 1968 (p); Inside the Blood Factory, 1968 (p); Greed, Parts 3 and 4, 1969 (p); The Magellanic Clouds, 1970 (p); The Motorcycle Betrayal Poems, 1971; Greed, Parts 5–7, 1971 (p); Smudging, 1972 (p); Greed, Parts 8, 9, 11, 1973 (p); Dancing on the Grave of a Son of a Bitch, 1973 (p); Trilogy, 1974 (p); Virtuoso Literature for Two and Four Hands, 1975 (p)

ROBERT PENN WARREN
1905–

Incarnations, 1968 (p); Audubon: A Vision, 1969 (p); Homage to Theodore Dreiser on the Centennial of His Birth, August 27, 1871–December 28, 1945, 1971 (c); John Greenleaf Whittier's Poetry, 1971 (c); Meet Me in the Green Glen, 1971 (n); Or Else, 1973 (p); Democracy and Poetry, 1975 (e)

EUDORA WELTY
1909–

Losing Battles, 1970 (n); One Time, One Place—A Mississippi Album, 1971 (notes to photographs); The Optimist's Daughter, 1972 (n)

JOHN HALL WHEELOCK*
1886–

By Daylight and in Dream: New and Collected Poems, 1904–1970, 1970; In Love and Song, 1971 (p-juvenile)

JOHN BROOKS WHEELWRIGHT
1897–1940

Collected Poems, 1972

E. B. WHITE*
1899–

The Trumpet of the Swan, 1970 (juvenile)

REED WHITTEMORE*
1919–

Fifty Poems Fifty, 1970; *William Carlos Williams: Poet from New Jersey*, 1975 (b)

RICHARD WILBUR
1921–

Walking to Sleep, 1969 (p); *School for Wives*, 1971 (tr); *Opposites*, 1973 (p-juvenile)

THORNTON WILDER
1897–1975

Theophilus North, 1973 (n)

TENNESSEE WILLIAMS
1914–

Dragon Country, 1970 (d); *Small Craft Warnings*, 1972 (d); *Out cry*, 1973 (d); *Eight Mortal Ladies Possessed*, 1974 (s); *Moise and the World of Reason*, 1975 (n); *The Red Devil Battery Sign*, 1975 (d); *Memoirs*, 1975

WILLIAM CARLOS WILLIAMS
1883–1963

Imaginations (*Kora in Hell, Spring and All, A Novelette, The Great American Novel*, and other prose), 1970; *Embodiment of Knowledge*, 1974 (misc)

EDMUND WILSON
1895–1972

The Fruits of the MLA, 1968 (e); *The Duke of Palermo, and Other Plays*, 1969; *The Dead Sea Scrolls, 1947–1969*, 1969 (e); *Upstate: Records and Recollections of Northern New York*, 1971; *The Devils and Canon Barham*, 1973 (e); *The Twenties*, 1975 (diaries)

YVOR WINTERS
1900–1968

Uncollected Essays and Reviews, 1973 (c)

THOMAS WOLFE*
1900–1938

Notebooks, 1970; *The Mountains*, 1970 (d)

HERMAN WOUK*
1915–

The Winds of War, 1971 (n)

JAMES WRIGHT
1927–

Collected Poems, 1971; *Wandering: Notes and Sketches by Herman Hesse*, 1972 (tr); *Two Citizens*, 1973 (p)

• SOL YURICK
1925–

The Warriors, 1965 (n); *Fertig*, 1966 (n); *The Bag*, 1968 (n); *Someone Just Like You*, 1972 (s); *An Island Death*, 1975 (n)

• LOUIS ZUKOFSKY
1904–

Some Time, 1956 (p); *"A" 1–2*, 1959, 1966 (p); *Arise, Arise*, in *Kulchur*, 2, 6, 1962, in book form, 1973 (d); *Bottom: On Shakespeare*, 1963 (c); *All: The Collected Short Poems, 1923–1958*, 1965; *All: The Collected Short Poems, 1956–1964*, 1966; *Prepositions: Collected Critical Essays*, 1967 (c); *Ferdinand, and It Was*, 1968 (2n); *"A" 13–21*, 1969 (p); (with Celia Zukofsky) *Catullus*, 1969 (tr); *Autobiography*, 1970 (a); *Little: For Careenagers*, 1970 (n); *All: The Collected Short Poems 1923–1964*, 1971 (p); *A-24*, 1972 (p); *"A" 22 & 23*, 1975 (p)

COPYRIGHT ACKNOWLEDGMENTS

1962, 1963, 1964, 1965, 1966, 1967, 1968 by James Dickey (Ashbery, Kinnell, Meredith, Olson, Stafford); *Nathanael West: The Art of His Life* by Jay Martin. Copyright © 1970 by Jay Martin; *Doings and Undoings* by Norman Podhoretz. Copyright © 1953, 1954, 1955, 1956, 1957, 1958, 1959, 1962, 1963, 1964 by Norman Podhoretz (Goodman); *The Life of Emily Dickinson* by Richard B. Sewall. Copyright © 1974 by Richard B. Sewall; Wilfrid Sheed's text and John Leonard's Foreword from *The Morning After* by Wilfrid Sheed. Copyright © 1963, 1965, 1966, 1967, 1968, 1969, 1970, 1971 by Wilfrid Sheed and Foreword copyright © 1971 by Farrar, Straus and Giroux, Inc. (Coover). Reprinted with the permission of Farrar, Straus & Giroux, Inc.

SUZANNE C. FERGUSON. From article on Barnes in *The Southern Review.*

FONTANA PAPERBACKS. From Richard Poirier, *Mailer.*

ESTATE OF FORD MADOX FORD. From article on Gordon in *The Bookman.*

FORTRESS PRESS. From Wesley A. Kort, *Shriven Selves* (De Vries, Malamud, Styron, Updike).

RICHARD FOSTER. From essay on Fitzgerald in *Sense and Sensibility in Twentieth-Century Writing*, Brom Weber, ed.

G. S. FRASER. From articles on Howard, on Zukofsky in *Partisan Review.*

ADDISON GAYLE, JR. From essay on Faulkner, Styron in *Amistad 1.*

HENRY GIFFORD. From essay in *Marianne Moore*, Charles Tomlinson, ed.

RICHARD GILMAN. From Introduction to Rosalyn Drexler, *The Line of Least Resistance.*

KENNETH GRAHAM. From article on Berger in *The Listener.*

GRANADA PUBLISHING LTD. From C. W. E. Bigsby, *Confrontation and Commitment* (Hansberry).

GREENWOOD PRESS. From Margaret Perry, *A Bio-Bibliography of Countee P. Cullen.*

JAY L. HALIO. From articles on Hawkes, on Roth, on Taylor in *The Southern Review.*

BARBARA HARDY. From essay on Plath in *The Survival of Poetry*, Martin Dodsworth, ed.

HARPER & ROW. From Robert Lowell's Foreword to *Ariel* by Sylvia Plath. Copyright © 1966 by Ted Hughes; *American Poetry since 1945* by Stephen Stepanchev. Copyright © 1965 by Stephen Stepanchev (Ashbery, Bly, Olson, Stafford); *Mortal Consequences* by Julian Symons. Copyright © 1972 by Julian Symons (Chandler, Hammett, Macdonald); *City of Words: American Fiction 1950–1970* by Tony Tanner. Copyright © 1971 by Tony Tanner (Barth, Burroughs).

HARVARD UNIVERSITY. Department of English and American Literature and Language. From essays by Roger Rosenblatt on Hughes in *Veins of Humor*, Harry Levin, ed.; Gordon O. Taylor on Adams; Philip M. Weinstein on H. James in *The Interpretation of Narrative*, Morton W. Bloomfield, ed.

in Vol. XXII No. 1 (Spring, 1969). Copyright © 1969 by The Hudson Review, Inc.; Anthony Hecht on *Poems 3* by Dugan, on *The Blue Swallows* by Nemerov in Vol. XXI No. 1 (Spring, 1968). Copyright © 1968 by The Hudson Review, Inc.; Richmond Lattimore on *Adventure of the Letter I* by Simpson in Vol. XXV No. 3 (Autumn, 1972). Copyright © 1972 by The Hudson Review, Inc.; Herbert Leibowitz on *New and Selected Poems* by Garrigue in Vol. XXI No. 3 (Autumn, 1968). Copyright © 1968 by The Hudson Review, Inc.; Herbert Leibowitz on *Planet News* by Ginsberg in Vol. XXII No. 3 (Autumn, 1969). Copyright © 1969 by The Hudson Review, Inc.; Herbert Leibowitz on *After Experience* by Snodgrass in Vol. XXI No. 3 (Autumn, 1968). Copyright © 1968 by The Hudson Review, Inc.; J. Mitchell Morse on Zukofsky in Vol. XXII No. 2 (Summer, 1969). Copyright © 1969 by The Hudson Review, Inc.; Neal J. Osborn, "Toward the Quintessential Burke" in Vol. XXI No. 2 (Summer, 1968). Copyright © 1968 by The Hudson Review, Inc.; William H. Pritchard on Jarrell, on *The Writing on the Wall* by Mary McCarthy in Vol. XXIII No. 2 (Summer, 1970). Copyright © 1970 by The Hudson Review, Inc.; William H. Pritchard on *The Fall of America* by Ginsberg in Vol. XXVI No. 3 (Autumn, 1973). Copyright © 1973 by The Hudson Review, Inc.; William H. Pritchard on Updike in Vol. XXI No. 2 (Summer, 1968). Copyright © 1968 by The Hudson Review, Inc.; Roger Sale on *The Collected Stories of Peter Taylor* in Vol. XXII No. 4 (Winter, 1969–70). Copyright © 1970 by The Hudson Review, Inc.; John Simon on *A Moon for the Misbegotten* by O'Neill in Vol. XXVII No. 2 (Summer, 1974). Copyright © 1974 by The Hudson Review, Inc.; Louis Simpson on Stafford in Vol. XIV No. 3 (Autumn, 1961). Copyright © 1961 by The Hudson Review, Inc.; Patricia Meyer Spacks on Welty in Vol. XXV No. 3 (Autumn, 1972). Copyright © 1972 by The Hudson Review, Inc.; Gerald Weales on *Fire Sermon* by Morris in Vol. XXIV No. 4 (Winter, 1971–72). Copyright © 1972 by The Hudson Review, Inc. All selections reprinted by permission from *The Hudson Review*.

INDIANA UNIVERSITY PRESS. From essays by Anne Sexton, Ted Hughes in *The Art of Sylvia Plath*, Charles Newman, ed.; Ruby Cohn, *Dialogue in American Drama* (Albee, A. Miller, T. Williams).

INTERNATIONAL CREATIVE MANAGEMENT. From John Leonard's Foreword to Wilfrid Sheed, *The Morning After*; Wilfrid Sheed, *The Morning After* (Coover); articles by Earl Shorris on Algren, on Barthelme, on Gass in *Harper's Magazine*. Reprinted by permission of International Creative Management and Earl Shorris. First printed in *Harper's Magazine*. Copyright © 1972–73 by *Harper's Magazine*.

LEE A. JACOBUS. From essay on L. Jones in *Modern Black Poets*, Donald B. Gibson, ed.

FREDRIC JAMESON. From article on Chandler in *The Southern Review*.

THE JOHNS HOPKINS UNIVERSITY PRESS. From article by Vivienne Koch on Gordon in *Southern Renascence*, Lewis D. Rubin, Jr., and Robert D. Jacobs, eds.; Mark Van Doren's Foreword to *The Selected Letters of Robinson Jeffers*, Ann N. Ridgeway, ed.

D. A. N. JONES. From article on Bullins in *The Listener*.

JOURNAL OF MODERN LITERATURE. From article by A. Poulin, Jr., on Howard.

DAVID KALSTONE. From article on Bishop in *Partisan Review*.

OHIO STATE UNIVERSITY PRESS. From Todd M. Lieber's *Endless Experiments: Essays on the Heroic Experience in American Romanticism* (Stevens, W. C. Williams).

THE OPEN COURT PUBLISHING COMPANY. From Roy Fuller, *Owls and Artificers* (Moore, Stevens).

OPPORTUNITY. From article by Gorham B. Munson on Toomer. Reprinted with permission of the National Urban League.

ALICIA OSTRIKER. From article on Dugan in *Partisan Review*.

PETER OWEN. From Carolyn G. Heilbrun's Introduction to May Sarton, *Mrs. Stevens Hears the Mermaids Singing*.

OXFORD UNIVERSITY PRESS. From *Harlem Renaissance* by Nathan Irvin Huggins. Copyright © 1971 by Oxford University Press, Inc. (Cullen, Hughes, O'Neill); *Richard Eberhart: The Progress of an American Poet* by Joel Roache. Copyright © 1971 by Joel Roache; *The Fabulators* by Robert Scholes. Copyright © 1967 by Robert Scholes (Vonnegut); *Dionysus and the City: Modernism in Twentieth-Century Poetry* by Monroe K. Spears. Copyright © 1970 by Monroe K. Spears (Berryman, Dickey, Ransom, Roethke, Tate); *Science and Sentiment in America: Philosophical Thought from Jonathan Edwards to John Dewey* by Morton White. Copyright © 1972 by Morton White (W. James, Santayana). Reprinted by permission of Oxford University Press, Inc.

CYNTHIA OZICK. From article on Calisher in *Midstream*.

PARNASSUS. From articles by Rosellen Brown on Sarton; Donald Davie on Lowell; R. W. Flint on Stickney, on Wheelwright; Diane Middlebrook on Ginsberg; Ralph J. Mills, Jr. on Eberhart, on Levertov, on MacLeish; Eric Mottram on Levertov; M. L. Rosenthal on Creeley; Muriel Rukeyser on Sexton; Richard Saez on Merrill; Robert Stock on Nemerov; Helen Vendler on Rich; Larry Vonalt on Berryman; Robert Weisberg on Lattimore; Thomas R. Whitaker on Aiken.

PARTISAN REVIEW. From Calvin Bedient, "Blind Mouths." Copyright © 1972 by Partisan Review (Oates); Calvin Bedient, "In Dreams Begin." Copyright © 1971 by Partisan Review (West); John Malcolm Brinnin, "Plath, Jarrell, Kinnell, Smith." Copyright © 1967 by Partisan Review (Plath); Peter Brooks, "The Melodramatic Imagination." Copyright © 1972 by Partisan Review (H. James); Elizabeth Dalton, "Ada or Nana." Copyright © 1970 by Partisan Review (Nabokov); Martin Duberman, "Theater 69." Copyright © 1969 by Partisan Review (Bullins, Hansberry); Thomas R. Edwards, "The Indian Wants the Bronx." Copyright © 1968 by Partisan Review (Fiedler); G. S. Fraser, "The Magicians." Copyright © 1971 by Partisan Review (Howard); G. S. Fraser, "A Pride of Poets." Copyright © 1968 by Partisan Review (Zukofsky); Alan Helms, "Growing Up Together." Copyright © 1972 by Partisan Review (Ashbery); Maureen Howard, "Other Voices." Copyright © 1968 by Partisan Review (Bowles); Richard Howard, "Changes." Copyright © 1971 by Partisan Review (Rich); David Kalstone, "All Eye." Copyright © 1970 by Partisan Review (Bishop); Kenneth Koch, "Poetry Chronicles." Copyright © 1961 by Partisan Review (F. O'Hara); Norman Martien, "I Hear America Singing." Copyright © 1971 by Partisan Review (Warren); Alicia Ostriker, "Of Being Numerous." Copyright © 1972 by Partisan Review (Dugan); Jane Richmond, "To the End of the Night." Copyright © 1972 by Partisan Review (McGuane); Philip Stevick, "Voice and Vision." Copyright ©

RAINES & RAINES. From James Dickey, *Babel to Byzantium*. Copyright © 1956, 1957, 1958, 1959, 1960, 1961, 1962, 1963, 1964, 1965, 1966, 1967, 1968 by James Dickey (Ashbery, Kinnell, Meredith, Olson, Stafford).

RANDOM HOUSE, INC. From A. Alvarez, "Prologue: Sylvia Plath" in *The Savage God: A Study in Suicide*; *The Unwritten War* by Daniel Aaron. Copyright © 1973 by Daniel Aaron. Reprinted by permission of Alfred A. Knopf, Inc. (Bierce, Faulkner, Frederic, Howells, Twain); *The Confusion of Realms* by Richard Gilman. Copyright © 1963, 1966, 1967, 1968, 1969 by Richard Gilman. Reprinted by permission of Random House, Inc.; Steven Marcus's Introduction (Copyright © 1974 by Steven Marcus) to *The Continental Op* by Dashiell Hammett. By permission of Random House, Inc.; Carl Van Vechten's Introduction (Copyright © 1927 and renewed 1955 by Carl Van Vechten) to James Weldon Johnson, *The Autobiography of an Ex-Coloured Man*. Reprinted by permission of Alfred A. Knopf, Inc.; John A. Williams's essay on Himes in *Amistad 1*, John A. Williams and Charles F. Garris, eds.

RENASCENCE. From article by Meta Lale and John Williams on Kosinski.

KENNETH REXROTH. From article on Goodman in *American Poetry Review*.

ADRIENNE RICH. From article on Goodman in *American Poetry Review*; essay in *Randall Jarrell, 1914–1965*, Robert Lowell, Peter Taylor, and Robert Penn Warren, eds.

JESS RITTER. From essay on Heller in *Critical Essays on Catch-22*, James Nagel, ed.

JAMES E. ROCKS. From "The Mind and Art of Caroline Gordon" in *The Mississippi Quarterly*.

DEBORAH ROGERS LTD. From articles by Anthony Burgess on Calisher, on Eastlake in *The Listener*.

ROGER ROSENBLATT. From essay on Hughes in *Veins of Humor*, Harry Levin, ed.

ROUTLEDGE AND KEGAN PAUL. From D. E. S. Maxwell, *Poets of the Thirties* (Auden).

LOUIS D. RUBIN, JR. From essays by James M. Cox on Twain, William Harmon on Pynchon, C. Hugh Holman on Lardner, Robert D. Jacobs on Faulkner, Jay Martin on Bierce, Louis D. Rubin, Jr., on Mencken in *The Comic Imagination in American Literature*, Louis D. Rubin, Jr., ed.

MILTON RUGOFF. From article on Gaddis in *New York Herald Tribune Book Section*.

RUTGERS UNIVERSITY PRESS. From George W. Bahlke, *The Later Auden: From "New Year Letter" to "About the House."* Copyright © 1970 by Rutgers University Press; Miller Williams, *The Poetry of John Crowe Ransom*. Copyright © 1972 by Miller Williams. Reprinted by permission of the author and Rutgers University Press.

SALMAGUNDI. From articles by Harold Bloom on Ashbery; Robert Boyers on Dugan; Henry Pachter on Goodman; Hyatt H. Waggoner on Ammons.

ERNEST SANDEEN. From article on Blackmur in *Poetry*.

Private Eye: The Novels of Dashiell Hammett"; Herbert Ruhm, "Raymond Chandler: From Bloomsbury to the Jungle—and Beyond," in *Tough Guy Writers of the Thirties*, David Madden, ed. Copyright © 1968 by Southern Illinois University Press; Gerald Weales, "No Face and No Exit: The Fiction of James Purdy and J. P. Donleavy," in *Contemporary American Novelists*, Harry T. Moore, ed. Copyright © 1964 by Southern Illinois University Press; *The Confessional Poets* by Robert Phillips. Copyright © 1973 by Southern Illinois University Press (Plath); *In A Minor Chord* by Darwin T. Turner. Copyright © 1971 by Southern Illinois University Press (Cullen, Toomer). Reprinted by permission of Southern Illinois University Press.

SOUTHWEST REVIEW. From articles by Gerald Burns on Snyder, on Wakoski.

BARRY SPACKS. From article on Dugan's *Poems* in *Poetry*.

PATRICIA MEYER SPACKS. From essay "Free Women" in *The Hudson Review* (Hellman).

THE SPECTATOR. From articles by Peter Ackroyd on McGuane; Alan Brien on Vonnegut; John Wain on Plath; Auberon Waugh on Brautigan, on Gardner.

SPIRIT. From articles by Sally Andersen on Oates; Lynda B. Salamon on Plath.

KATHLEEN SPIVACK. From article on Levertov in *Poetry*.

THE SPRINGFIELD UNION AND SPRINGFIELD REPUBLICAN. From article by Richard McLaughlin on Purdy.

ST. MARTIN'S PRESS, INCORPORATED. From George Garrett's essays on Connell, on Olson in *American Poetry*, John Russell Brown, Irvin Ehrenpreis, Bernard Harris, eds. By permission of St. Martin's Press, Inc. and Macmillan Co., Ltd.

WILLIAM STAFFORD. From articles on Brooks, on Olson in *Poetry*.

MARILYN STASIO. From article on Rabe in *Cue*.

STEIN AND DAY. From Leslie A. Fiedler, *The Return of the Vanishing American*. Copyright © 1968 by Leslie Fiedler (Berger, Kesey); *The Collected Essays of Leslie Fiedler*. Copyright © 1971 by Leslie Fielder (Ginsberg, West). Reprinted by permission of Stein and Day Publishers.

GEORGE STEINER. From article on Plath in *The Reporter*.

PHILIP STEVICK. From articles on Burroughs, on Kosinski, on Vonnegut in *Partisan Review*.

DABNEY STUART. From article on Bukowski in *Poetry*.

STUDIES IN THE LITERARY IMAGINATION. From article by Pamela Shelden on H. James.

STUDIES IN THE NOVEL. From article by John M. Reilly on Toomer.

WALTER SUTTON. From essay on Pound in *Sense and Sensibility*, Brom Weber, ed.

SWETS PUBLISHING SERVICE. From article by G. A. M. Janssens on Bly in *English Studies*.

INDEX TO CRITICS

Names of critics are cited on the pages given